Introduction to Human Communication

Introduction to Human Communication

PERCEPTION, MEANING, AND IDENTITY

Susan R. Beauchamp
Bryant University

Stanley J. Baran
Bryant University

New York   Oxford
OXFORD UNIVERSITY PRESS

Oxford University Press is a department of the University of Oxford.
It furthers the University's objective of excellence in research,
scholarship, and education by publishing worldwide.

Oxford   New York
Auckland   Cape Town   Dar es Salaam   Hong Kong   Karachi
Kuala Lumpur   Madrid   Melbourne   Mexico City   Nairobi
New Delhi   Shanghai   Taipei   Toronto

With offices in
Argentina   Austria   Brazil   Chile   Czech Republic   France   Greece
Guatemala   Hungary   Italy   Japan   Poland   Portugal   Singapore
South Korea   Switzerland   Thailand   Turkey   Ukraine   Vietnam

For titles covered by Section 112 of the US Higher Education
Opportunity Act, please visit www.oup.com/us/he for the
latest information about pricing and alternate formats.

Published by Oxford University Press
198 Madison Avenue, New York, NY 10016
http://www.oup.com

Library of Congress Cataloging-in-Publication Data
Beauchamp, Susan R., author.
Introduction to human communication : perception, meaning,
and identity / Susan R. Beauchamp, Bryant University;
Stanley J. Baran, Bryant University.
     pages cm
  ISBN 978-0-19-026961-6
  1. Communication. 2. Interpersonal communication.
  I. Baran, Stanley J., author. II. Title.
  P90.B3385 2017
  153.6—dc23

                                   2015028104

Printing number: 9 8 7 6 5 4 3 2

Printed in Canada
on acid-free paper

Mom, every chapter of this book is, in so many ways, influenced by your unwavering dedication to family. We love you beyond measure.

Brief Contents

Contents

CHAPTER 3   Verbal Communication   49

CHAPTER 4 Nonverbal Communication 71

PART 2 COMMUNICATION CONTEXTS

CHAPTER 7   Communicating in Small Groups   143

CHAPTER 8   Organizational Communication   165

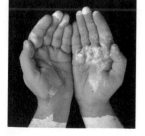

CHAPTER 9   Intercultural Communication   187

CHAPTER 10   Mass Communication   209

CHAPTER 11   Media Literacy   235

CHAPTER 12 **Social Media and Communication
Technologies   259**

Preface

One of the great advantages of teaching Introduction to Communication is that it allows instructors and their students to talk about everything because every aspect of life—personal, social, political, cultural, relational, familial—involves communication. But the nature of the course also presents some challenges:

1. What gets covered and what gets left out? In other words, how does the class cover all the important material in one semester?

2. Given everything the course is designed to cover, how does the material connect with students' everyday lives? Where is the balance between the theoretical and what's relevant to students?

3. What's the best way to ensure that the course's learning objectives are met?

We have carefully designed this text in answer to these questions, drawing on scores of surveys and reviews, along with our collective 60 years of university teaching experience. *Introduction to Communication: Perception, Meaning, and Identity* offers a comprehensive, readable, and balanced survey of the discipline. Using vivid and contemporary examples, we cover the basics of communication theory and research and provide tools to help students become more competent, confident, and ethical communicators. We show students the relevance of communication in their daily lives so that they can apply their newfound knowledge of the communication process in a variety of contexts.

The Philosophy of This Text

Communication is about mutual, transactional *meaning making*, working with others to craft common understanding. It is also about how we *perceive* our world and how we create our *identity*; we know ourselves and our world through interaction with others. Helping students gain more effective control over perception, meaning making, and identity is the story of this book.

How do we begin to understand this complex world and our place in it? *Through communication*. The value of this course is in showing students how to think critically about themselves and the worlds they inhabit, negotiate, create, and recreate—face-to-face and in front of screens—*through communication*. We do this, in

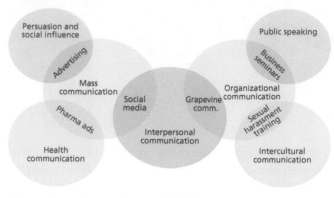

Intersections of Communication Subfields

part, by emphasizing the interdisciplinary and overlapping nature of communication studies, encouraging students to make more connections, to expand the breadth and depth of their knowledge, and to apply that knowledge in their lives.

Pedagogical Features

The pedagogical features we developed for this text reflect our philosophy and emphasize applications, asking students to challenge assumptions about themselves and their world.

- **Ethical Communication** boxes present ethical dilemmas that communicators face, on topics such as lying (Chapter 3), whistleblowing (Chapter 8), and advertising to children (Chapter 11). These features prompt students to examine complex situations and weigh their own choices.

- **Personally Responsible Communication** boxes remind students that they are what they communicate, asking them to consider their responsibility in personal communication situations. Topics include speaking inclusively (Chapter 3), practicing active listening (Chapter 5), and self-diagnosing Internet addiction (Chapter 12).

- **Socially Responsible Communication** boxes ask students to consider how much responsibility they have to the larger culture, encouraging more thoughtful communication. Topics include stereotyping (Chapter 9), media conduct (Chapter 10), and the Speak Up program for patient safety (Chapter 14).

- **Communication in the Workplace** boxes present direct, hands-on advice for career success. Topics include dealing with on-the-job conflict (Chapter 6), tips for successful teamwork (Chapter 7), and the dos and don'ts of workplace persuasion (Chapter 13).

- **Thumbnail Theory** features appear in the margins to summarize the core theories presented in the text. Our aim is to make theory accessible and highlight why it matters in real life.

In addition, several other features help students get the most from the book:

- Learning Objectives at the beginning of each chapter
- A Review of Learning Objectives at the end of each chapter, highlighting key points
- Λ Running Glossary and a list of Key Terms
- Questions for Review
- Questions for Discussion.

Organization

In designing a survey text that is comprehensive yet concise, we had to make some difficult decisions about what to include. We worked to offer the broadest, most contemporary overview of the discipline available, one tied to students' everyday realities and their career aspirations, regardless of major.

The text is organized into 15 chapters (to fit the typical semester) and divided into two parts, *Foundations of Communication* and *Communication Contexts*, offering balanced coverage of the entire field of communication. Part I includes a chapter on communication research and inquiry (Chapter 2) and covers verbal communication (Chapter 3), nonverbal communication (Chapter 4), and listening (Chapter 5). Part II builds on this foundation to examine communication in a wide variety of contexts. These chapters include relational and conflict communication (Chapter 6), communicating in small groups (Chapter 7), organizational communication (Chapter 8), and intercultural communication (Chapter 9), as well as mass communication (Chapter 10), media literacy (Chapter 11), social media and communication technologies (Chapter 12), persuasion and social influence (Chapter 13), and health communication (Chapter 14). An optional crash-course on public speaking (Chapter 15) gives students the basic skills and confidence to communicate publicly.

Ancillary Package

A comprehensive set of ancillary materials for instructors and students accompanies *Introduction to Human Communication*.

Online Learning

- **Dashboard** delivers high-quality content, tools, and assessments to track student progress in an intuitive, Web-based learning environment.
  - Dashboard gives instructors the ability to manage digital content from *Introduction to Human Communication* and its supplements in order to create assignments, administer tests, and track student progress. Assessments are designed to accompany this text and are

automatically graded so that instructors can check students' progress as they complete their assignments. The color-coded gradebook illustrates at a glance where students are succeeding and where they can improve.

- With Dashboard, students have access to a variety of interactive study tools designed to enhance their learning experience, including videos and exercises, critical thinking activities and questions, and multiple-choice pre- and post-tests to accompany each chapter.

- Dashboard is engineered to be simple, informative, and mobile. All Dashboard content is engineered to work on mobile devices, including iOS platforms.

- **Course cartridges** for a variety of Learning Management Systems, including Blackboard Learn, Canvas, Moodle, D2L, and Angel, allow instructors to create their own course websites, integrating student and instructor resources available on the Ancillary Resource Center and Companion Website. Contact your Oxford University Press representative for access or for more information about these supplements or customized options.

For Instructors

- **Ancillary Resource Center (ARC) at www.oup-arc.com.** This convenient, instructor-focused website provides access to all of the up-to-date teaching resources for this text—at any time—while guaranteeing the security of grade-significant resources. In addition, it allows OUP to keep instructors informed when new content becomes available. The following items are available on the ARC:

  - The **Instructor's Manual** includes syllabus preparation tools, a sample syllabus, chapter-based assignment ideas, and suggestions for audiovisual materials.

  - The comprehensive **Computerized Test Bank** offers over 900 exam questions in multiple-choice, short-answer, and essay formats, with each item classified according to Bloom's taxonomy and tagged to page and section references in the text.

  - **PowerPoint-based lecture slides** highlight key concepts, terms, and examples, and incorporate images from each chapter. With streamlined text, a focus on visual support, and lecture tips in the notes section, these presentations are ready to use and fully editable to make preparing for class faster and easier than ever.

  - *Now Playing*, **Instructor's Edition**, includes an introduction on how to incorporate film and television clips in class, as well as even more film examples, viewing guides and assignments, a complete set of sample responses to the discussion questions in the student edition, a full list of references, and an index by subject for ease of use. *Now Playing* also has an accompanying companion website at

www.oup.com/us/nowplaying, which features descriptions of films from previous editions and selected film clips.

- **Two optional chapters for download: Public Speaking: Research, Writing, and Delivery; and Persuasive, Informative, and Other Types of Speaking.**
- A downloadable **guide to Interviewing**.

For Students

- *Now Playing* (print), available free in a package with a new copy of the book, looks at contemporary films and television shows through the lens of communication principles. Updated yearly, it illustrates how communication concepts play out in a variety of situations, using mass media that are interactive, familiar, and easily accessible to students.
- The **Companion Website** at **www.oup.com/us/beauchamp** offers a wealth of study and review resources, including learning objectives, summaries, chapter quizzes, flashcards, activities, and links to a variety of media-related websites.

Acknowledgments

We were fortunate to have had the assistance of many people in the writing of this book. Most important, we have drawn on the research and thinking of a century's worth of communication thinkers and researchers, not to mention their colleagues in the other social sciences and humanities. Their research and writing have inspired and guided the field's contemporary thinking. It's an exciting time to study communication, and the work that has come before has made this book—and the discipline itself—possible.

We relied, too, on the sharp eye and teaching experience of our reviewers, who improved and enriched our work. In particular, we thank the following reviewers commissioned by Oxford University Press:

Jerry L. Allen
University of New Haven

Carla Harrell
Old Dominion University

Andrew F. Herrmann
East Tennessee State University

Karen Isaacs
University of New Haven

Dan Kozlowski
Saint Louis University

Jennifer A. Marshall
California State University, Northridge

Kelly Odenweller
West Virginia University

William Price
Georgia Perimeter College

Greg Rickert
Bluegrass Community & Technical College

Jill Schiefelbein
Arizona State University

Bruce Wickelgren
Suffolk University

Thanks also to the team at Oxford University Press. Their professionalism, encouragement, and advice sustained us. This is an organization that trusts its authors. For that we are especially grateful.

Our colleagues, students, friends, and extended family deserve our appreciation as well. Not only did they let us bore them with our tales of writing woe, but a few appear in photos in these pages. Finally, we are grateful to one colleague in particular. Dr. Wendy Samter was our Chair and is now our Dean. Several years ago, she gave us the task of evaluating all the Introduction to Communication texts available for adoption. We took that job to heart, and although not completely dissatisfied with the available options, we did discover that these books lacked sufficient attention to (1) the discipline as a social science and (2) newer mediated forms of communication. As such, Wendy initiated the journey that produced this book and encouraged and supported us at every step along the way.

We must also thank our immediate families. Our children, Jordan and Matt, were the inspiration for many of our examples. Jordan is a recent graduate who majored in Communication and is now in the midst of a burgeoning career, and Matt is still in school and preparing to make his mark. They are great kids; we are exceedingly proud of them.

We thank you for taking the time to read our thoughts on the course and how we believe it should be taught. And we commend you for committing yourself to this important and exciting discipline.

SRB & SJB

Introduction to
Human Communication

1

The Communication Process

Perception, Meaning, and Identity

This is the job you want, no question. It's one anyone would want—working at a hospital in a great up-and-coming community, having significant responsibilities, getting paid a real salary.

You've done your research. You know that employers consider good communication skills the most important factor not only in job performance, but in career advancement (Sternberg, 2013). Another piece of research you discovered showed that communication competencies were the most-often mentioned keys to success in management (Whetton and Cameron, 2005).

So you now know how to build your case. You go over your notes one last time. This is what the interviewers will hear from you: "I will have to interact with all kinds of staff and clients, and I bring solid verbal and nonverbal communication skills to the job. On teams where there are inevitable tensions, my conflict and group communication studies will be an asset. I know, too, that I will be working with people from many different backgrounds, and my intercultural communication coursework has prepared me well. Just as important, I have classroom experience in health communication, especially in using the media to promote healthy behaviors. In fact, in this position I can combine my media literacy with my interpersonal communication and persuasion skills."

You're ready. With this background, how could you fail?

The skills and strengths mentioned in this anecdote represent different chapters in this book. Of course the vignette is fictional, but the research it mentions is real. Communication is indispensable not only to professional success but to success as a person. Good communication skills can make you a better friend, parent, colleague, and citizen. Competent communication and media literacy can make interacting with people more satisfying, consuming media more fun, and experiencing life more meaningful.

Learning Objectives

1.1   Illustrate how models of communication evolved from linear to transactional.

1.2   Demonstrate how communication is an ongoing and dynamic process of creating meaning.

1.3   Contrast the transmissional, constitutive, and ritual views of communication.

1.4   Explain the power of culture as the backdrop for creating meaning.

1.5   Describe the relationships between perception, communication, and identity.

1.6   Explain when and how communication grants power.

The Process of Creating Meaning

communication The process of mutual creation of meaning.

We communicate to create, recreate, and understand our realities. Communication allows us to control our environments. It is how we know ourselves and how we let others know us. **Communication**, the process of mutual creation of meaning, is breathtakingly simple and often maddeningly complex. As cognitive scientist Benjamin Bergen explains,

Communicating—mutually creating meaning—is part of what makes us human.

Constantly, tirelessly, automatically, we make meaning. What's perhaps most remarkable about it is that we hardly notice we're doing anything at all. There are deep, rapid, complex operations afoot under the surface of the skull, and yet all we experience is seamless understanding. Meaning is not only constant; it's also critical. With language, we can communicate what we think and who we are. Without language, we would be isolated. We would have no fiction, no history, and no science. To understand how meaning works, then, is to understand part of what it is to be human. And not just human, but uniquely human. (2012)

The Evolution of Communication Models

In the first half of the last century, the field of communication studies was newly established. Scholars saw communication as a process that followed a **linear model**; that is, messages travel in a more or less straight line from a *source*, through a *medium*, to a *receiver*. The most famous expression of this idea is political scientist Harold Lasswell's (1948):

Who? Says *What?* Through *which* channel? *To whom?* With *what effect?*

The **source** has a goal in mind, creates a message, and selects a means (or **medium**) to deliver it; the **receiver** receives it and does or does not do what the source wants. Think of public relations and health professionals using online public service announcements to convince teens to avoid binge drinking. If the message does not have the desired effect, the source should modify the message or change the medium. In its simplest form, the linear model of communication looks like this:

Source ⟶ Message ⟶ Receiver

FIGURE 1.1 Simplified Linear Model of Communication

But maybe the message did not have the desired effect because of *noise* somewhere along the line. **Noise** is anything that interferes with the process of communication, and it exists in a variety of forms:

- *Physical noise*—something outside the communication effort itself; your roommate plays a loud video game while you're trying to talk on the phone.
- *Semantic noise*—a problem in the construction of the message; your professor uses completely unfamiliar technical jargon.
- *Psychological noise*—predispositions, biases, or prejudices that shape how you construct and interpret messages; consider what different politicians mean when they talk about "freedom" and what voters of different political leanings take away when they hear that word.
- *Physiological noise*—sometimes you are simply not operating at full communication capacity because you are tired or hungry or sick.

How do sources know if their communication efforts are successful? They look for **feedback**, a response to their message. Now the linear model is a little less linear and it looks like this:

Source ⟶ Message ⟶ Receiver

Feedback

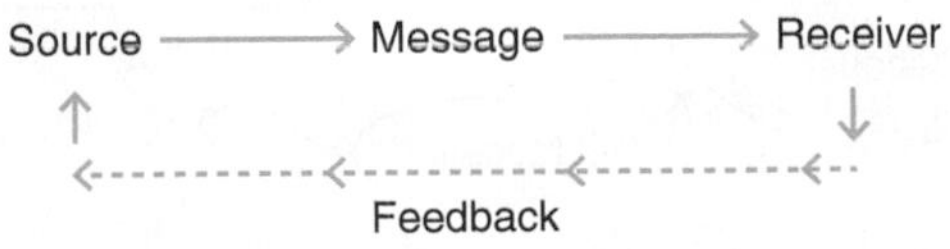

FIGURE 1.2 The Linear Model of Communication, Including Feedback

---

linear model A representation of communication as a linear process, with messages traveling from a source, through a medium, to a receiver.

source In a linear communication model, the originator of a message.

medium In a linear communication model, the carrier of a message.

receiver In a linear communication model, the recipient of a message.

noise Anything that interferes with the process of communication.

feedback Response to a message.

source-dominated model A representation of communication efforts as primarily within a source's control.

This, however, is still a **source-dominated model** of communication; that is, it still views the success of the communication effort as primarily within the source's control. But isn't feedback a message? Hasn't the receiver now become the source, sending a message back to the original source, who is now the receiver?

The limits of the source-dominated view of communication become obvious as soon as we understand communication as a *reciprocal, ongoing process*, with all parties engaged in creating shared meaning. Communication researcher Wilbur Schramm (1954) used this idea, originally offered by psychologist Charles E. Osgood, to create a more accurate model of communication, one having no source, no receiver, and no feedback. Stressing communication as *interaction*, it represents the participants in the communication process as *interpreters*, working together to create meaning by encoding and decoding messages. **Encoding** is transforming a message into an understandable sign and symbol system—for example, speaking in English or shooting a video using familiar visual storytelling conventions. **Decoding** is interpreting those signs and symbols—for example, listening to the speaker or watching the video and drawing meaning from them. Figure 1.3 shows this model of communication.

encoding Transforming a message into an understandable sign and symbol system.

decoding Interpreting signs and symbols.

Schramm made another important point: all that encoding and decoding takes place against the backdrop of communicators' fields of experience. That means that

- *Communicators create and interpret messages in terms of what they already know and have experienced.* "Communication involves the total personality," wrote communication theorist Dean Barnlund. Encoding and decoding can never be separated because "meanings [are] generated by the whole organism" (1962, p. 199). For example, when you live at home, you and your parents no doubt have somewhat different ideas of what "cleaning your room" means.

- *There can be no communication unless interpreters share a common set of experiences.* Vielleicht sprichst Du Deutsch? Unless you speak German, that message has no meaning. If German is not part of your experience, you and a German speaker cannot communicate very well. Messages are sent; meaning is *made*.

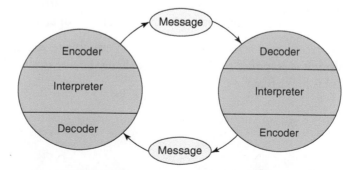

FIGURE 1.3 Osgood and Schramm's Model of Communication

You and a friend might have different ideas about the meaning of "dog."

- No two communicators share exactly the same set of experiences, so there is always some negotiation of meaning. You and your friend both have experienced "dog," but that small, fluffy, squeaking thing he brings with him everywhere he goes is not what you mean by "dog."

Communication, then, is the process of mutual creation of meaning. It is *social*—it involves people in interaction; it is a *process*—its parts operate interdependently and continuously; and it is *dynamic*—it is always changing. This last characteristic defines modern notions of communication as **transactional**—*communication changes the communicators*. Each new message, decoded into meaning by an interpreter, changes that interpreter. He or she is no longer the same person, simply by virtue of having added new meanings to his or her set of experiences. In fact, the transactional view assumes that communication has not occurred unless change occurs in the participants (Pearce, Figgins, and Golen, 1984). In a sense, then, communicators enter into a deal, a transaction: the more they work at their negotiation of meaning to better align their fields of experience, the better they can make meaning (in other words, the better they can communicate). Figure 1.4 illustrates the transactional model.

transactional model A representation of the elements of communication as interdependent and the process of communication as ongoing and dynamic.

Transmissional, Constitutive, and Ritual Views of Communication

The linear model of communication falls under the **transmissional view**, which sees communication as the process of sending and receiving—transmitting or transferring—information from one person to another. By contrast, the transactional model falls under the **constitutive view**, which sees communication as creating (constituting) something that did not exist before.

In this second view, communication does not simply represent some objective world that preceded it; it produces and then reproduces a new reality—shared meaning—and as a result, new experiences for the communicators, who are now themselves changed (Craig, 1999). For example, say a classmate invites you to her home for Thanksgiving break. She may say, "I know you live

transmissional view The perspective that communication is the process of sending and receiving information from one communicator to another.

constitutive view The perspective that communication creates something that did not previously exist.

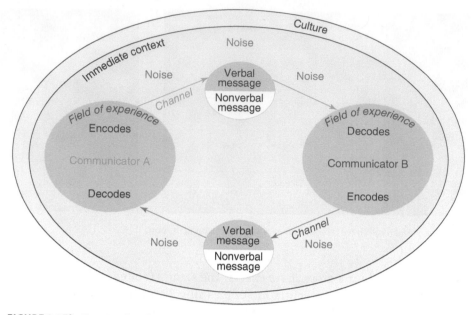

FIGURE 1.4 The Transactional Model

pretty far away, so how would you like to come home with me for the holiday?" The transmitted message is clear: "Do you want to come to my house for Thanksgiving, yes or no?" But what new "thing" has been constituted (produced) by those few words? In you, a new reality—a new understanding of what kind of person she is and the knowledge that, possibly, she wants to be your friend. When you say "Yes," she realizes that you welcome her friendship. Together, you have constituted a new understanding of the nature of your relationship. More important, you have made a new friend.

To emphasize the extraordinary impact of this mutual creation of meaning, sociologist and communication scholar James Carey offered a third view of how communication works. For Carey (1989), the **ritual view** links communication to

> "sharing," "participation," "association," "fellowship," and "the possession of a common faith." It has the same root as the words "commonness," "communion," "community" . . . A ritual view of communication is directed not toward the extension of messages in space but toward the maintenance of society in time; not the act of imparting information but the representation of shared beliefs. (pp. 18–19)

In other words, communication constitutes culture.

Revisit the example of the Thanksgiving invitation. We've seen that the simple message transmitted from your classmate to you was, "Want to come to my house, yes or no?" But the invitation was special because it was for Thanksgiving. The holiday is imbued with all kinds of rituals that bind families in meaning: who gets invited, where people sit, who is relegated to the kids' table, what is on the menu, who falls asleep on the sofa. Thanksgiving is also part of a larger ritual that binds together the millions of people who celebrate it, from the 30-pound turkey to the big parades and even bigger football

ritual view The perspective that communication is directed not toward the extension of messages in space but toward the maintenance of society in time and the representation of shared beliefs.

It wouldn't take a visitor long to identify your family's Thanksgiving rituals, such as your Uncle Carl falling asleep on the sofa. These specific rituals are part of the broader holiday tradition.

games. One set of rituals helps define a family's culture; another set helps define American culture. Both are representations of shared beliefs. You will quickly learn how to act at your new friend's Thanksgiving celebration in accordance with her family's traditions, which are within the context of the national tradition.

The Power of Culture

No two people ever share precisely the same culture. Your culture is defined not only by your country but also by your gender, for example, and your specific set of geographic and ethnic experiences. Think of the words you use. Depending on where you live, you may enjoy an occasional *sub sandwich* or maybe a *grinder* or possibly a *hoagie*, perhaps a *po' boy, hero, torpedo,* or *zeppelin*. And again, depending on where you call home, you may sell your excess stuff at a *garage sale* (Midwestern United States and the West Coast), a *yard sale* (most of the East Coast and the Mountain States), or a *tag sale* (Western Massachusetts and Connecticut). You may or may not be a part of campus Greek life. If you are a baseball fan, you may be part of Red Sox Nation; if you are a football fan, you may well be a Cheese Head (a Green Bay Packers fan), dwell in the Dog Pound (a Cleveland Browns fans), or hang out with the Hogs (Washington Redskins fans). Or you may be troubled by the fact that a sports franchise in our nation's capital uses a racial slur as its nickname (Enten, 2014).

When we communicate with others, we find what is common to our experiences—language is an obvious example—and then we mutually negotiate new meanings, creating even more shared experiences. This is the true power of culture. Culture is the background, the set of experiences and expectations that we each carry around with us wherever we go. Culture allows us to interact with people who are different from us, while in the process we become more alike. With every successful communication effort, big or small, culture is in transaction, in constant change. Anthropologist Edward T. Hall called culture "the medium evolved by humans to survive. Nothing is free from

COMMUNICATION IN THE WORKPLACE

Communicating Well to Land the Job

Employers consider good communication skills to be the most important factor in job performance and career advancement. But what communication skills are important in getting that job or internship? Research by the consulting firm Right Management (2008) identified five factors that make the difference:

1. **Conciseness of Answers**—Don't give long, meandering answers. They tell an interviewer that you are nervous, or didn't understand the question, or worse, that you are trying to substitute quantity for quality.
2. **Structure of Answers**—A well-conceived, concise answer to a question shows that your thinking is organized, that you know your subject matter, and that you can communicate it. Try to anticipate questions before the interview and consider possible avenues of response.
3. **Logical Flow of Information**—Logical responses show that you reason critically, connect ideas, and can be a skilled persuader.
4. **Eye Contact**—Eye contact creates rapport, engagement, and trust. It tells your interviewer that you are interested in your interaction.
5. **Clarity of Speech**—Don't mumble. Speaking clearly tells your interviewer that you are giving your words conscious thought.

Employment writer Kate Wilson (2012) offered her take on the top five communication "skills [that] are especially helpful for recent grads who may not know exactly what to expect":

1. **Think of the interview as a conversation, not an interrogation**—You're less likely to be nervous in a conversation than you would be in an interrogation, and the interviewer will have a better time talking with you.
2. **Ask questions when you are giving answers**—Just as in conversation with friends, interact by both answering and asking questions.
3. **Connect with the interviewer on a personal level**—If you discover a personal connection, a favorite sports team, a hobby, the same college, or travel to an interesting place, for example, elaborate. Making that connection could help you stand out.
4. **Use the interviewer's name**—Doing this signals that you are paying attention and that you care enough to be personal.
5. **Directly answer questions, but don't be afraid to digress**—Expand on your answers as needed to show imagination and critical thought.

The guide at **www.oup-arc.com** offers a much more detailed look at communicating successfully in interviews.

cultural influences. It is the keystone in civilization's arch and is the medium through which all of life's events must flow. We are culture" (1976, p. 14). As you might imagine, then, something as big and important as culture will have many different definitions. This text employs a definition that speaks specifically to the role of communication in culture's influence on meaning making:

culture The world made meaningful, socially constructed and maintained through communication.

> **Culture** is the world made meaningful; it is socially constructed and maintained through communication. It limits as well as liberates us; it differentiates as well as unites us. It defines our realities and thereby shapes the ways we think, feel, and act. (Baran, 2014, p. 14)

Our discussion so far should make it clear that culture is learned, negotiated, transacted, constructed, and maintained through communication. But how does culture limit *and* liberate, differentiate *and* unite? Cultural assumptions can indeed limit people's ability to express themselves. A male boss who speaks forcefully and dominates his workplace is perceived as a natural leader, a man among men. A female boss is less likely to employ force and dominance in her management style because doing so may subject her to a much different evaluation by her colleagues (Sandberg and Grant, 2015). But culture also liberates us, as it offers us a wealth of information in all our interactions, making communication easier and more effective and efficient. We know quite a bit about the people and settings in which we find ourselves because of our cultural experiences and the assumptions we make from them. They free us to make meaning more deeply, more quickly,

These women may be part of their campus's Greek culture, but they also are part of the larger American culture.

more mutually. Of course, as you'll see in Chapter 9, when these efficiencies become prejudices, they are noise, interfering with communication.

Culture differentiates *because* it defines. You communicate within your country's **dominant culture** (sometimes referred to as the **mainstream culture**): the collective cultural experience held and shared by the large majority of people. But you simultaneously belong to several **bounded cultures** (sometimes called **co-cultures**): these are your cultural identities existing within (bounded by) the larger culture. Maybe you identify with and take pride in your Latino/a or African-American heritage. Or being a country boy or a city girl sets you apart from the group. Or you stand out because you are a *Star Trek* fan or a member of a sorority.

Americans pride themselves in their ability to move between different bounded cultures (sorority member and Trekkie) and also between bounded cultures and the dominant culture (all Americans rooting for the United States in the Olympics). As different as individual Americans may be, they are still united (in this example) by their national culture. If you're American and have traveled overseas, you probably had little problem identifying other Americans around you.

dominant culture (mainstream culture) The collective cultural experience held and shared by the large majority of people.

bounded culture (co-culture) Cultural identities existing within the larger culture.

Communication and Perception

But how did those other travelers communicate to you that they were indeed American? Most likely they weren't shouting "USA . . . USA" as they went about their sightseeing. Nonetheless, they communicated their *American-ness*. This is the question of *intentionality*, expressed as, "Is it possible to not communicate?" The answer, which is no, rests on **perception**, being aware of and creating meaning from the world around us.

One way to understand the connection between intentionality and perception is to look at the work of researchers who came to be known as the Palo

perception Being aware of and making meaning from the world around us.

What is each of these instructors communicating to you? Which one is teaching Business 101? Twentieth-Century Lit?

Alto Group. In the 1960s, they offered an early challenge to the source-dominated view of communication (Watzlawick, Beavin, and Jackson, 1967). Communication does not happen when a source sends a message, they argued (as we've already seen in this chapter); it happens when a receiver draws meaning from interaction with the source. For example, on the first day of class you may meet two new professors, one of whom wears a suit while the other wears old jeans. Without a word being uttered, quite a bit of communication has occurred. The Palo Alto scholars emphasize that because every human behavior is potentially communicative (culture shapes the ways we think, feel, and act), *it is impossible to not communicate*. You've drawn meaning from those instructors' style choices, just as you can easily draw meaning from your boyfriend's or girlfriend's refusal to "communicate" with you. Unanswered texts accompanied by the silent treatment when in person may be the absence of talk, but they most certainly aren't the absence of communication.

Perception involves *selection, organization,* and *interpretation* as we interact with our environments. Back to our traveling Americans: they did not intentionally communicate their American-ness to you; you perceived it. But what was it about them that said "American"—that you noticed (or *selected*)? Was it that they were speaking English; that they seemed a bit loud and energetic; that they were wearing Nikes, jeans, and L.L. Bean backpacks? There were many other things—some new, some familiar, some exciting, some routine—going on around you, but you selected a relatively small number and then *organized* them into a collection that you *interpreted* as *American*.

We're incapable of processing the enormous tide of sensory stimuli that washes over us at all times. It's not that we're too lazy or not smart enough; there's just no advantage to doing so. In fact, if we ever attempted it, we'd be immobilized by information overload; we'd accomplish nothing. What's the temperature in the room where you're reading these words? Unless it interferes with what you're doing, there is no need to pay attention (to select) it for perception. But if the room does indeed become too hot or too cold to the point that you cannot focus on the immediate task of reading, that might change. In fact, it's quite likely that you were unaware of the temperature until we asked the question.

As you traveled abroad, the presence of people similar to and different from you was relevant to where you were and what you were doing. Therefore, what was distinctive about the Americans stood out; you paid attention to

ETHICAL COMMUNICATION

Effective communication grants power, letting you shape your own realities and those of the people around you. But like all power, it can be used for good or bad.

Ethics are rules of behavior or moral principles that guide human actions. There are *metaethics,* fundamental cultural values like justice, and there are *normative ethics,* generalized rules or principles of moral behavior such as "don't steal." How we apply both the big rules and the general guidelines to our everyday interactions is called *applied ethics.*

Your ethics are constituted by the moral choices you make. Keep in mind, though, that applying ethics is rarely the choice between equally good options, or even between good and bad ones. There's no moral dilemma in those instances. Applying ethics is quite often choosing between equally bad options. Communication ethicist Patrick Plaisance calls this "the art of uneasy compromise" (2014, p. 11). Do you stretch the truth on a resume to get a job? Lying is a bad option, but failing to get the job is also a bad option. Do you advertise sugared cereals to little kids? Targeting small children with commercials for unhealthy foods is a bad option, but so is getting fired for refusing your client's demand. What do you do?

Throughout this book, "Ethical Communication" boxes present ethical dilemmas that communicators regularly face. Examine these situations and weigh your choices. Because there is rarely a "right" choice, your task is not to pick one option over another; rather, it is to be able to explain why and how you would make a choice. As ethicist Plaisance counsels, "Ethics is about our *thinking process* . . . The focus is on the quality of the *deliberative process* and not on the outcome" (2014, p. 10; italics in the original). He continues, "Ethics is about getting good at asking the right questions, which, in turn, clarify the problem and enable us to explore more effectively possible solutions or acceptable compromises" (p. 37).

There are several ways to apply ethics. Do you practice the *Golden Rule,* doing unto others as you would have them do unto you? Do you look for the *Golden Mean,* or middle ground? Are you an absolutist, applying the *Categorical Imperative* so that your moral decision makes no exceptions? Or might you apply *utilitarianism* toward the goal of making the most people happy (or bringing unhappiness to the fewest people)? Do you don the *Veil of Ignorance,* blocking out any thought of what most benefits *you* as a path toward finding what is moral? Consider these questions as you read the "Ethical Communication" boxes in each chapter.

---

those differences. If you were an American traveling in the States, however, American-ness would not necessarily be relevant or interesting to you. In that case, you'd be more likely to pay attention to pieces of data you perceived as Hawaiian, Californian, or Southern, for example.

Individual bits of data tell us relatively little, so we have to organize them in some useful way in order to interpret them meaningfully. We accomplish this by developing **schemas**, mental structures built from past experiences that we use to process new information and organize new experiences; they are "active organization[s] of past reactions, or of past experiences" (Bartlett, 1932, p. 201). What makes up your American schema? Your Hawaiian, Californian, or Southern schemas? Where did those schema come from? They come from your experiences—your interactions, in the media and in the physical world—with *American, Hawaiian, Californian,* or *Southern* in the past.

An obvious and sometimes troubling form of schema is a **stereotype**, a generalization about people, places, or things. Stereotypes may or may not be accurate; as you'll read in Chapter 9's discussion of intercultural communication, they may mask as many truths about people, places, and things as they

schema A mental structure built from past experiences that we use to process new information and organize new experiences.

stereotype A generalization about people, places, or things.

illuminate. Yes, they may be useful in helping us quickly make meaning, but they may also produce ill-conceived or simply incorrect meanings. Yes, Americans traveling overseas often speak English, carry themselves with vigor, and wear Nikes, jeans, and L.L. Bean backpacks, but not all do.

Signs and Symbols

Meaning making is based on our perception and interpretation of signs and symbols. Recall your boyfriend's or girlfriend's refusal to talk to you. The distance you feel surely means something, most likely something not good. But is it a sign or a symbol?

Communication scholars differentiate between signs and symbols, sometimes in contradictory ways. For now, though, we'll take the more traditional route, defining a **sign** as something that signals the presence of something specific, more or less an objective substitute for that thing. A stop sign means stop. You may not want to stop; you may not stop when you encounter this sign at an intersection; however, you objectively know what it means. Likewise, the changing color of leaves signifies the coming of autumn and the letters *d-o-g* signify a canine mammal (at least in English).

But the word "dog" can be a symbol as well, just as your friend's silent treatment is more symbol than sign. A **symbol**, then, is a much more arbitrary indicator of something else. While the meanings attached to both signs and symbols are arbitrary (there is nothing inherently meaning "stop" in a hexagonal piece of red sheet metal; English speakers may have decided that *d-o-g* signifies a canine, but Spanish speakers prefer *p-e-r-r-o*), the meanings attached to symbols are more open to negotiation and more dependent on the context in which they are used. When you and your boyfriend or girlfriend sit silently while driving long-distance at night, that silence symbolizes something much different from the silence of unanswered texts. When your teammates tell you to *stop dogging it,* "dog" is a symbol for laziness, but when your

sign Something that signals the presence of something specific; relatively objective.

symbol Arbitrary indicator of something else; relatively subjective and abstract.

What do these signs signify?

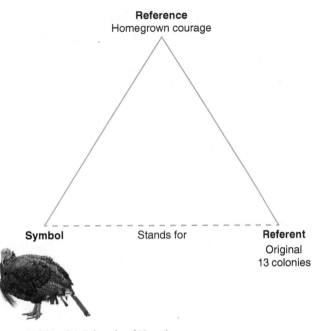

Reference
Homegrown courage

Symbol   Stands for   **Referent**
Original
13 colonies

FIGURE 1.5 Ogden and Richards's Triangle of Meaning

bosses commend you for *working like a dog,* "dog" is a symbol for hard work. As philosopher Susanne Langer wrote, symbols "are not proxy of their objects, but are vehicles for the conception of objects" (1942, p. 61). In other words, symbols are not simply substitutes for other things; they are the means by which the meaning of those things is carried, negotiated, and maintained.

In 1923, linguist C. K. Ogden and literary critic I. A. Richards offered their *triangle of meaning,* a way of understanding the relationship between an object, our sign or symbol for it, and the meaning we give it (see Figure 1.5). Although there have been many variations in the way it's represented, we still use it today. Meaning comes from the relationship between

- the referent (the object itself)
- its sign or symbol (designed to "stand in" for the referent), and
- the reference (the thoughts generated by the sign or symbol; in other words, meaning).

Keep in mind, though, that not only are signs and symbols arbitrarily assigned to their referents, but the subsequent references (meanings) are constructed and negotiated, and they vary given the context. So the triangle of meaning may show the linkage between referent, sign/symbol, and reference as pretty straightforward, but there is a great deal of individual and cultural experience that goes into forging those connections. American history offers a famous example. When the Founders determined that the Great Seal of the United States would feature the bald eagle as its centerpiece, they wanted to link the United States (referent), the eagle (symbol), and majestic bravery (reference). But Ben Franklin, in a letter to his daughter, confessed that he could not make the same connections. "The turkey is in comparison," he wrote, "a much more respectable bird, and withal a true original native of America . . . He is besides, though a little vain & silly, a bird of courage" ("The Eagle," 2012). Franklin connected the United States (referent), the turkey (symbol), and reference (home-grown courage) in a much different and personally meaningful way than did his Colonial colleagues. Nonetheless, American culture seems to have decided that it prefers the eagle to the turkey as the national symbol.

Franklin was arguing that the turkey would better symbolize (be a better stand-in for) his new nation, so he presented his version of the "facts" to his daughter. And this is one of the most important lessons of the triangle of meaning. Although communication can be **representational**—describing or conveying some objective fact or information—it is almost always **presentational**—someone's version of the facts or information. In other words, *someone* connects referent and symbol in a specific way to produce meaning. Television news offers an obvious example. There may be some observable, objective event that journalists cover, but how is the reality of that event represented? It is represented by the reporters' images and words chosen for *presentation*. Where do reporters place their cameras? Whom do they choose to interview; which interviews make it on air; and what parts of those interviews are included or edited out? These choices will produce specific meanings. This is not the work of lazy or biased reporters; this is simply the operation of the meaning triangle writ large: the connection between referent (the event), symbol (material chosen for inclusion), and reference (resulting thoughts) is different for different reporters covering the same event.

The same thing happens when you are communicating face-to-face. For example, when a classmate asks you how you did on an exam, how do you respond? You *present* your version of your performance to suggest a specific reality. Yes, you could respond representationally, for example, offering the grade itself with little inflection in your voice, "Got an 89." But more than likely you would say (present) that score somewhat shyly, concerned that your

representational communication Describing or conveying some fact or information.

presentational communication An individual person's version of facts or information.

What does each of these presentations say about attendance at this protest? Both are from the same demonstration, but the reality has been presented differently through the choices (camera angles) made by the photographer.

PERSONALLY RESPONSIBLE COMMUNICATION

What do you do with your skill as a communicator? Do you try to make the people around you comfortable when talking with them? How do you make meaning for and of yourself when you engage others and the larger culture? Do you use your role as others' looking glass to help them see a better self? How well do you interact with people who are unlike you? Do you gravitate to people who look a certain way? How would you respond to some friends' racist description of that new sophomore in the front row? What you do and say will tell them not only who you think they are, but who *you* are.

In the "Personally Responsible Communication" boxes throughout this book, you will be asked to consider just how much responsibility you carry when you communicate. Because communication is so natural and seemingly routine, it is easy to be a lazy or careless communicator. It's easy to not pay attention to the meaning we make and that others make from us. But if you truly understand this book's philosophy, you know that while communication can often be complex and its responsible use sometimes difficult, you are what you communicate.

colleague might not have done as well as you. Or, delighted by your unexpected success, you might boldly present the 89, as in "Yeah, I nailed it." If you are indeed concerned about your classmate's feelings, you might do what students typically do: you matter-of-factly present your performance as, "I did O.K." The words and actions (symbol) standing in for your grade (referent) are designed to produce a specific meaning for your friend (reference). In fact, just as there are scholars who argue that there has been no communication unless there is change in the participants, many communication experts also believe that communication is always presentational, always designed to effect new thought, to produce that change, even if the goal is as benign as getting your conversational partner to be more comfortable in your presence or to like you more (Hauser, 1986).

Communication and Identity

But why do you care what your classmate thinks about your performance on the test? Just as important, you did great, so why should you worry about protecting her feelings? You care because your identity—who you are—is transacted through communication. Regardless of who you might think you are, if you boast about your grade with little concern for your classmate's feelings, she will perceive you as not very nice, as will those who witness your behavior. Then it really doesn't matter who *you* think you are; to the world you are not nice. Like it or not, intentional or not, *you are what you communicate*. Just as important, you are always, simultaneously, all of your many identities. Sometimes one or more of these identities are more visible to you and those around you.

There are several different ways to examine the relationship between communication and identity, each highlighting a different aspect of that connection. We'll look at two, each of which adds something a little different to our understanding of that relationship: symbolic interaction and frame analysis.

THUMBNAIL THEORY

Symbolic Interaction

We develop our sense of self through interaction. We look to *significant others* to see how they behave in various roles, and then we use these social cues to guide our own behavior. How successful we are is determined by how well others see us doing. The *Looking Glass Self* is expressed as "I am what I think that you think I am."

Symbolic Interaction and the Looking Glass

Sociologist George Herbert Mead offered what has become known as **symbolic interaction** as a way to understand how people's sense of self develops from their ongoing, interlinked conversations in and with a culture. His book *Mind, Self, and Society* (1934) explains that meaning (mind) and identity (self) arise in the context of culture (society). "Through a social process," wrote philosopher Charles Morris as he explained Mead's thinking, "the biologic individual of proper organic stuff gets a mind and a self. Through society the impulsive animal becomes a rational animal, a man [*sic*] . . . [Through] the social process of communication, the individual gains the mechanism of reflective thought . . . acquires the ability to make himself an object to himself and . . . becomes a moral individual" (1959, pp. xxv–xxvi).

Mead suggested that we look at how people learn to play baseball or other team sports. We don't go online to learn how to field a grounder deep in the hole or get a good break on a sharp line drive to right field. What actually happens is that we learn to play from other players as we play the game, that is, through interaction with one another and with the game itself. But because we don't all play the same position, we each learn our specific role within the larger team and game. We do this by observing and interacting with our team members. We accept their comments, encouragement, and criticism; and if the team plays well, we enjoy our newly negotiated role as a productive teammate. Now that this role provides us with the ability to control our behavior (play better; be a better teammate) and garner the support and affection of those around us, we internalize it and our identity becomes bound up in it. We come to value ourselves to the extent that this role is respected by others.

Of course, in real life we play on many teams, that is, we have many different roles across the many different situations in which we find ourselves. You may be a ballplayer, but you may also be a marketing major, a liberal, a boyfriend, and an atheist. In each of those different situations you *take the role of others with whom you interact*, trying to judge how they perceive you. Mead identified two important *others*:

- the *significant other*—influential people in the different situations in which you find yourself
- the *generalized other*—your sense of how others see you.

What kind of friend are you? Everyone knows what *friend* means; it is a word or symbol possessing a strong cultural meaning. But you have known people who have shown themselves to be *real* friends, especially your older sister (significant other), so you may try to act as she does (role

You don't read a book on how to be a good teammate or an ever-reliable relief pitcher; you learn from playing the game.

taking), and for this your pals often commend you on your worth as a friend (generalized other). This process of creation and maintenance of identity is known as the **Looking Glass Self**; the self is accomplished by seeing ourselves as others see us. There is a well-known quote sometimes attributed to Mead, sometimes to another early sociologist, Charles Cooley (1902), from whom Mead took the term, that neatly encompasses the spirit of the Looking Glass Self: "I am not what I think I am and I am not what you think I am; I am what I think that you think I am." This quote also suggests how complex (and complicated) communication, even a simple conversation between two friends, can be. It tells us that there are not simply two people communicating (Cooley, 1902). There are actually six "selves" involved in all interactions:

- You
- The Other
- What You think of the Other
- What the Other thinks of You
- What You think the Other thinks of You
- What the Other thinks You think of Him or Her.

Imagine buying a new car. You're in the salesroom with the salesperson. You size her up as she sizes you up. You try to figure out what she thinks about you in order to present your best case for a better price; all the while, she is wondering what you're thinking about her and her sales pitch in order to get you to pay as much as possible for the car. You can easily identify the operation of the six selves in any interaction. Try it out using the situation of asking someone out for a date or getting your parents to pay for your spring break trip with your friends.

Mead borrowed Cooley's mirror analogy in order to make his central point: we can only experience ourselves in relation to others, and we do that through communication. We communicate, Mead explained, through the mutual work we undertake in assigning meaning not only to ourselves, but to the symbols (including ourselves) that surround us. He called these symbols **social objects**, that is, any objects to which we can refer to make meaning. In this way Mead makes the final significant point of symbolic interaction: identity, as the most basic social object that makes communication possible, is not only created, defined, and maintained through interaction with the social world, it is performed in that world for others to see. Have you ever dressed up, danced, or practiced a speech in front of a mirror? If so, you were performing your identity to determine how others would make meaning of it. As William Shakespeare noted, we are all performers: "All the world's a stage, and all the men and women merely players."

Frame Analysis

Sociologist Erving Goffman uses that same theater analogy to make a similar, but subtly different point. Where Mead wanted us to know that we constitute

Looking Glass Self In symbolic interaction, the idea that the self is accomplished by seeing ourselves as others see us.

social objects In symbolic interaction, any objects to which people can refer.

THUMBNAIL THEORY

Frame Analysis

We present ourselves in various situations based on our experiences of those situations, both real-world and mass mediated. The expectations we have about them and about the actors in them are called *frames*. We frame situations in an attempt to adopt an appropriate role and enact it properly.

We see ourselves in the looking glass created by our interactions with others.

frames In frame analysis, specific sets of expectations that people use to make sense of specific social situations.

upshift In frame analysis, framing a situation as less serious, more open to personal expression.

downshift In frame analysis, framing a situation as more serious, less open to expressions of personal identity.

What is this place? What role do you play in it? What cues do you see that can help you answer these questions?

our identities through interaction with others, Goffman stresses that in our everyday lives we readily and routinely learn to *perform* those identities as presentations of our different selves (Goffman, 1959). To combine an idea we have already discussed with Goffman's ideas, we use communication, which is *presentational*, to *present* ourselves. "What talkers undertake to do is not to provide information to a recipient," he wrote, "but to present dramas to an audience. Indeed, it seems that we spend most of our time not engaged in giving information but in giving shows" (1974, p. 508).

To Goffman, the various situations or settings we find ourselves in are different scenes in a play and we, life's actors, carry on different performances to let our audiences know who we are. But how do we know which role (identity) is appropriate at a given time and situation? Just as in a play, we look for cues. Goffman calls his theory **frame analysis** because those cues alerting us to the proper role we should play are embedded in what he calls **frames**—a specific set of expectations we use to make sense of the specific social situation we may find ourselves in at the time. As a close reader, you can see that frames and schemas share many similarities. No one has to tell you as you enter a classroom for the first time in a new semester to don your student identity. No one has to give you your lines or tell you what your motivation is. You enter the room, see the rows of chairs and desks, and notice an individual standing at the front. Your classroom frame directs you to raise your hand to ask a question and not to interrupt when the professor is speaking. You know why you're there and what your professor expects of you. In fact, country boy or city girl, Trekkie or sorority member, your identity is that of student as long as you maintain that frame.

But what happens when your professor begins addressing you and your classmates informally, telling a lot of jokes? You use that cue to make meaning of the changing situation, adjusting your character, presenting a variation on your student role that might be more in line with how you see yourself. You **upshift**, you frame the situation as less serious, more open to personal expression. But one of your classmates goes a bit too far, referring to the professor by an unflattering nickname. Your instructor becomes stern. You **downshift**, framing the changing situation as more serious, less open to expressions of your personal identity.

We easily upshift and downshift because we are skilled at reading **social cues** in interactions, allowing us to fine-tune our presentations of self. How do we learn to interpret or make meaning from those cues? Mead would respond, "Through communication with the various others with whom we interact." But Goffman returns to the stage analogy to investigate the question raised by that answer: If we are actors upon a stage, interacting with many different people, identifying many different significant others, each of us framing different situations and reading social cues in individual, personally meaningful ways, why does there seem to be order to our daily lives? How can we coordinate our identities and actions with others to apparently so easily *mutually* make meaning? We are able to do this be-

Our classroom frames are built in part from media's hyper-ritualized representations. What did you come to understand about school from *Glee?*

cause we share a common set of experiences with those performing with us on the stage; we share their perceptions. We've built those perceptions growing up at home, with friends, in church or temple or mosque, in the schoolyard and when traveling, reading, listening to music, texting and friending online, and watching movies and television. Yes, we may each have our individual identities, but we read from much the same script as do the other actors sharing our bounded and dominant cultures.

We personally encounter all kinds of people and situations in our everyday lives, and the people involved in those interactions choose to present specific, certainly not all, aspects of their identities. We decode—make meaning—of those cues and they become part of our frame of the situation where that encounter took place. But we also encounter all kinds of people and situations in mass media portrayals of those people and situations. Because of the way those portrayals are constructed (no media portrayal can show every single aspect and nuance of a phenomenon, so Goffman calls them **hyper-ritualized representations** of social actions), our attention is directed to a specific, narrow set of cues. We decode those cues and they, too, become part of our frame of that situation. Return to our classroom example. Yes, your classroom frame has quite a bit of everyday, "real world" experience in its make-up, but it is also composed of a lot of mass media experience as well. Think of the hundreds of television shows, movies, and books you've read that present people much like yourself in school. What might *Pretty Little Liars, 90210, Community, Glee, Ferris Bueller's Day Off, Old School, Animal House,* and the *American Pie* movies have added to your classroom frame (or schema)? Figure 1.6 shows how our experiences with the world, both in human interaction and mass-mediated, combine to constitute the frames we use to choose which identities (and which characteristics of those identities) to perform in different situations.

social cue In frame analysis, information in an interaction, allowing the fine-tuning of presentations of self.

hyper-ritualized representations In frame analysis, media portrayals that cannot represent all the nuances of a phenomenon.

SOCIALLY RESPONSIBLE COMMUNICATION

You interact not only with your friends and family, but with layer upon layer of ever larger groups and institutions. You have different roles in each and every one. You may be a friend and a son or daughter, but you may also be an employee, a boss, a patient, a customer or client, a student, a club member, a juror, an official, a citizen, and a voter. In each of these situations you are not simply you. In fact, if there are six selves involved in any face-to-face encounter, imagine how many there are in larger settings, when the expectations placed on you multiply exponentially.

When you work in a group, what identity do you assume? Are you the devil's advocate or the tension releaser? As a boss, how do you manage cultural differences that put your employees in conflict? As a citizen,

how do you make an informed vote? How do you engage in the kind of responsible talk that builds and maintains a culture benefitting everyone?

In the chapters ahead, "Socially Responsible Communication" boxes will ask you to consider just how much responsibility you have to the larger culture around you. In a world as big and complex as ours, it's easy to hide, to take the path of least resistance. But if communication is power, why would you want to cede control to others? Why would you decline the chance to make the world *your* world? The world you inhabit is the world you create. If you work responsibly to make meaning in and of your world, if you are a thoughtful and generous communicator, you will live in a more thoughtful and generous world.

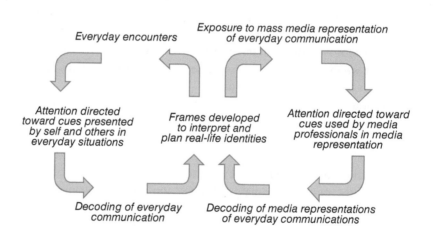

FIGURE 1.6 Frame Theory Model

What Does Communication Give You the Power to Do?

Communication is power—the power to control the making of meaning and, therefore, our own identities and realities. Even when we are talking with friends, we want to control the meaning they take from our words. Sometimes we may choose to be vague and ambiguous, but that is still our choice—we *want* the meaning to be unclear.

We use communication to meet many goals other than developing and maintaining our sense of self. We also communicate to accomplish the following:

- *Be human*—We are all social animals, as dependent on the sight and sound of others as we are on food and water. Communication is our primary means of interaction.

- *Exchange information*—We are all naïve scientists, always exploring new people, places, and things. Communication is our primary tool of discovery.

- *Build and maintain relationships*—None of us is an island; we are part of a sea of friends, family, and important others. Communication binds those ties as it defines them.

- *Have influence*—we are always persuading. From vital topics—"This is my version of me"—to those less important—"Let's go out to eat tonight"—communication is the vehicle for expressing and securing the things we want.

In all these instances we have something in mind; we want to be success-ful. We know that as people make meaning *with* us, they are making meaning *of* us. We want to control others' perceptions. We all want to be liked, and in line with this chapter's discussion of identity, others are the looking glass through which we come to see ourselves. Why wouldn't we want to shape what is reflected?

We've also learned in this chapter that the creation of meaning occurs against the backdrop of culture. And although we communicate in and with culture, much of culture's influence in shaping our meanings comes from the mass media. For example, how does a culture define attractiveness? Even if *you* do not accept your culture's view of attractiveness, if those around you do, it affects how you see yourself.

For these reasons, this text devotes space to a variety of communication skills and literacies, both face-to-face and mediated. The world contains other humans. You often have conflict with these people, many of whom come from different cultural backgrounds, making conflict resolution even more diffi-cult. Many people want to persuade you to their point of view, just as you hope to move them to yours. While you are working to make meaning of the world, producers of mass media content encourage you to accept their meanings. Social scientist Michael Crotty wrote that "meanings are constructed by human beings as they engage with the world they are interpreting. Before there were consciousnesses on earth capable of interpreting the world, the world held no meaning at all" (1998, p. 43). Becoming a better communicator gives you greater power as you engage with your world; it allows you to create a personally meaningful reality; it grants you control over the meanings that will come to define you.

Review of Learning Objectives

1.1 Illustrate how models of communication evolved from linear to transactional.

Communication was initially seen as the sending of messages from a source to a receiver. Feedback was then added to the model, as were interaction and mutual influence, resulting in the transactional perspective—communication changes communicators as they communicate.

1.2 Demonstrate how communication is an ongoing and dynamic process of creating meaning.

Communication is social—it involves people in interaction; it is a process—its parts operate interdependently and continuously; and it is dynamic—it is always changing.

1.3 Contrast the transmissional, constitutive, and ritual views of communication.

The transmissional view sees communication as the mere sending of signals from sources to receivers. The constitutive view sees communication as creating something that did not exist before. The ritual view sees communication as central to the maintenance of society and the representation of shared beliefs.

1.4 Explain the power of culture as the backdrop for creating meaning.

Communication can occur only when participants share some common experiences. Culture is the set of experiences and expectations we each carry with us wherever we go. Culture shapes the ways we think, feel, and act. As a result, culture forms the backdrop for mutually negotiating new meanings, thus creating even more shared experiences.

1.5 Describe the relationships between perception, communication, and identity.

Perception involves selection, organization, and interpretation as we interact in and with our environments. Because we cannot possibly make meaning of the flood of stimuli that surrounds us, we selectively perceive pieces of data that are personally and situationally relevant. We organize these into schemas that shape our perceptions and identities. Symbolic interaction and frame analysis demonstrate the idea that the self is constituted through interaction with others (the Looking Glass Self). We readily and routinely learn to perform our identities as presentations of our different selves by building frames for different situations.

1.6 Explain when and how communication grants power.

Communication is power—the power to control meaning making and, therefore, our own identities and realities. We communicate to be human, to exchange information, to build and maintain relationships, and to have influence.

Key Terms

communication 4
linear model 5
source 5
medium 5
receiver 5
noise 5
feedback 5
source-dominated model of communication 6
encoding 6
decoding 6
transactional model of communication 7
transmissional view of communication 7
constitutive view of communication 7
ritual view of communication 8
culture 9
dominant culture (mainstream culture) 11
bounded culture (co-culture) 11
perception 11
schema 13
stereotype 13
sign 14
symbol 14
representational communication 16
presentational communication 16
symbolic interaction 18
Looking Glass Self 19
social objects 19
frame analysis 20
frames 20
upshift 20
downshift 20
social cues 21
hyper-ritualized representations 21

Questions for Review

1. What distinguishes the linear and transactional models of communication? What are the elements of each?

2. What are the four types of noise? Give an example of each.

3. What differentiates the transmissional view of communication from the constitutive and ritual views?

4. How do you define *culture?* How does it limit and liberate, differentiate and unite, and define our realities? What are dominant and bounded cultures?

5. What are the elements involved in perception?

6. Is it possible to *not* communicate? Explain.

7. What are the elements of the meaning triangle? How do they interact to produce meaning?

8. Is communication primarily representational or presentational? Explain your answer.

9. What are *symbolic interaction* and the *Looking Glass Self?* How do they relate?

10. What are the elements of frame analysis, and how do they operate to shape our understandings of ourselves?

Questions for Discussion

1. Do you ever reflect on the question "Who am I?" Most people don't when all is well. But in times of crisis or confusion, most of us do ponder our identities. Has this ever happened to you? What were the circumstances? How did you arrive at an answer to that essential question?

2. Can you test your own experience on a sports team or club against Mead's baseball analogy? How did you learn your identity among your colleagues? How did you come to define your specific role? Who were the significant others? Why were they important to you? What did you learn from them about membership in the team or club? About yourself?

3. Have you ever committed a framing error, failing to properly read the cues? What were the circumstances? How did you salvage the situation, if you did?

Communication Research and Inquiry

For the first time, you are taking advantage of your communication professor's office hours. You hope she can answer what seems to be a simple question.

After reading the first chapter of the text, you tell her, you noticed that most of the important ideas did not seem to come from the discipline of communication. Instead, they were related to sociology, philosophy, political science, psychology, anthropology, linguistics, and literary criticism. Yes, Wilbur Schramm seemed to be a communication scholar, and James Carey, according to the text, studied communication as well as sociology, but still, many of the big concepts came from other fields. "Am I right about this?" you ask her. "Aren't I supposed to be getting an introduction to *communication?*" You prepare yourself for a condescending smile.

But your instructor surprises you. "Nice observation," she replies. "You caught something that most students miss." She explains that all social sciences borrow ideas, theories, and research methods from one another. Equally important, when you sit in an introductory communication class, you are actually getting an introduction to the social sciences, because all social sciences have the same questions at their core: How do we know our world and how it works? How do we know who we are and how to make our place in that world? How do we best use what we learn about that world and ourselves to make things better for ourselves and others? The answer to those questions, she says, is through communication.

Because communication borrows ideas, theories, and research methods from all the social sciences, there is a multitude of them. What's more, they are always evolving—some live, some die, some gain influence, others lose it. In this chapter, we will investigate the values, philosophies, and research methods that enrich not only the discipline of communication, but all the social sciences.

Learning Objectives

2.1   Define theory using analogies.

2.2   Explain the relationship between the three steps of social-scientific inquiry.

2.3   Describe the different ontologies, epistemologies, and axiologies providing philosophical support to scientific inquiry in communication.

2.4   Differentiate between traditions of communication inquiry.

2.5   Describe the benefits and drawbacks of the most common research methods employed in communication inquiry.

Theory and Scientific Inquiry

In 2012, the Kentucky Legislature challenged the inclusion of "a thorough knowledge of evolution" as part of the standardized biology testing program for the state's high school students. One critic, Senator David Givens, said, "We don't want what is a theory to be taught as a fact." But another Kentuckian, Vincent Cassone, chair of the University of Kentucky's biology department, argued for its inclusion: "The theory of evolution is the fundamental backbone of all biological research. There is more evidence for evolution than there is for the theory of gravity, than the idea that things are made up of atoms, or Einstein's theory of relativity. It is the finest scientific theory ever devised" (both in Blackford, 2012).

Defining Theory

Part of the disagreement between these two men rests on what they mean when they talk about *theory*. Senator Givens said evolution is a *theory*, not a *fact*. He is absolutely correct—a theory is not a *fact*. But it's also not a *guess*, although most of us use the word in this way in everyday conversation: "Why did the football team lose by three touchdowns?" "I'm guessing it was the refs, but that's *just a theory*." Dr. Cassone, who also would agree that a theory is not a fact—no legitimate scientist would ever make that claim—was applying a more formal, more widely accepted definition of **theory**—a unified, coherent, and organized set of explanations, concepts, and principles describing some aspect of the world. For social scientists, that aspect of the world is human social life.

theory A unified, coherent, and organized set of explanations, concepts, and principles describing some aspect of the world.

Theories provide explanations; they are the best available descriptions—a "grand synthesis"—of the sum of our knowledge of specific phenomena (Moore, 1984). Not only is a theory not a fact, good science is dedicated to demonstrating that the "best available description" is always inadequate and in need of updating. "Science," wrote renowned astrophysicist Carl Sagan, "is a self-correcting process" (in Zimmer, 2011, p. SR12). In science, every answer should produce new questions—an idea known as the **specification of ignorance** (Merton, 1967). Neuroscientist Stuart Firestein (2013) quotes Nobel laureate physicist David Gross, who argues that "the most important product of science is ignorance," and then adds that science's ability to find "truth" is "a challenge on par with finding a black cat in a dark room that may contain no cats whatsoever." Another Nobel laureate physicist, Albert Einstein, chose to liken the knowledge generated by scientific inquiry to a spotlight (see Figure 2.1). As the spotlight's circle of light increases (illuminating what we know), so does the circumference of the darkness around it (the number of things we still don't know).

But if a theory is not *fact,* how do we know it's a good theory? We consider its usefulness. How useful is the theory in explaining as accurately and thoroughly as possible what it is that needs explaining? "Questioning a theory's usefulness is wiser than questioning its truthfulness," write communication theorists Stephen Littlejohn and Karen Foss. "In matters of human life, no single theory will ever reveal the whole 'truth' or be able to address the subject of investigation totally. Theories function as guidebooks that help us understand, explain, interpret, judge, and participate in the communication happening around us" (2011, pp. 19–20). As we saw in Chapter 1, George Herbert Mead wanted an explanation for how people developed their identities in interaction with others, and Erving Goffman wondered how individuals could so seamlessly coordinate their behaviors

specification of ignorance
The idea that in science, every answer produces new questions.

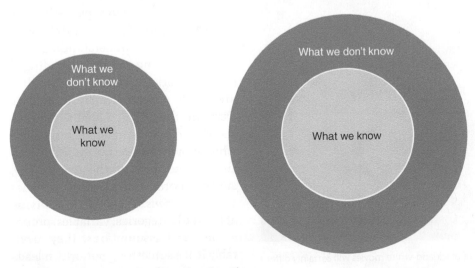

FIGURE 2.1 Every Answer Produces New Questions

and interactions in different and constantly changing settings. Both social scientists developed theories.

Another communication theorist, Em Griffin (2009, pp. 5–6), offers a valuable way of thinking about a theory's usefulness. He suggests that we think metaphorically. Think of theory as

- **A net**—Griffin quoted philosopher of science Karl Popper: "Theories are nets cast to catch what we call the 'world' . . . We endeavor to make the mesh even finer and finer" (1959, p. 59). Much as a fisherman uses a net, theory is one of communication researchers' most vital tools. They cast about the world, working to apprehend the reality that is human experience.

- **Lenses**—Theories are not mirrors; they do not reflect the world. They are camera lenses or eye glasses that shape researchers' "perception by focusing attention on some feature of communication . . . Two theorists could analyze the same communication event . . . and depending on the lenses each uses" come to different conclusions.

- **A map**—"Communication theories are maps of the way communication works . . . We need theory to guide us through unfamiliar territory." Theories, like maps, lay out the roads others have traveled, show us where we are, and offer directions about where we want to go.

Whether we imagine theories as nets, lenses, or maps, we need to keep several things in mind. Theories are *human constructions*—they are developed by people who have biases, interests, skills, and values. Theories always present someone's take on the issue at hand. People interested in intercultural communication, for example, will inevitably approach their work from a specific set of cultural assumptions. People who study conflict in families will develop a different kind of theory than will those who look at conflict in the workplace. Theories are *dynamic*—they are always changing. As the world changes, so, too, must our understanding of it. Theories shaping our understanding of communication between the genders are much different today than they were in the 1950s. Media violence theories from the days of black-and-white movies will certainly differ from those developed in the era of 3-D, single-shooter video games. Theories are *abstractions*. They reduce the issue at hand to categories, variables, propositions, and assumptions. They inevitably leave something out, which leads to the specification of ignorance and

Media violence theories from the days of black-and-white movies will certainly differ from those developed today.

the requirement that researchers use different nets of varying mesh sizes, different or sharper lenses, or more up-to-date or more detailed maps.

Scientific Inquiry

Because theories are dynamic and abstract human constructions, scholars are constantly at work refining them, making them better, or sometimes even discarding them. They do this through **scientific inquiry**: the active, systematic process of discovery, leading scholars from observation to knowledge and, eventually, to theory. That's why our "theory" of why the football team lost by three touchdowns is just a guess; it's not a theory because it is not the product of scientific inquiry. Because there are many different theories of interest to people who study communication, there are many different ways to conduct scientific inquiry (that is, many different ways to do research). But all scientific inquiry includes three steps:

- **Ask scientifically testable questions**. "How come my family keeps giving me lousy birthday presents?" is not testable. In the social sciences, testable questions are typically "How," "Why," "What if," and "Does" inquiries. "How do people know when it's their turn to talk when in conversation with others?" "Why do we tend to believe some people more than others?" "What if little kids were specifically taught to distinguish between the commercials and the television shows they watch?" "Does scaring teens about the dangers of texting while driving produce more responsible behavior than appealing to them with statistics?" These questions revolve around people, events, relationships, and other interesting phenomena in the social world. They have to do with scientific concepts, not opinions, feelings, or beliefs. They are open to investigation, using some form of systematic observation. Scientifically testable questions produce evidence and data that can be used to explain how the social world works.

- **Engage in systematic observation**. The answers to researchers' questions reside in the evidence they observe. Social scientists look for patterns, relationships, and consistencies in the social world. They engage in observation to learn why a particular phenomenon happens the way it does, or to explain something in the social world that seems new or different, or sometimes even to challenge or test the prevailing understanding that others, particularly other researchers, have of the social world. The nature of those observations—the research methods—vary dramatically for different scholars coming from different research traditions who are looking at different research questions; nonetheless, their observation is planned and systematic.

scientific inquiry The active, systematic process of discovery that leads scientists from observation to knowledge and, eventually, theory.

"How come my parents keep giving me bad gifts?" is not a scientifically testable question.

- **Develop answers**. Researchers then have to explain what they observed. This always involves definitions and descriptions based on evidence. This doesn't mean that scientists do not bring interpretation and judgment to bear on what they have observed. But it does mean that the answers they construct from their observations must be evidence-based. This is what makes science different from opinion.

Thinking logically, looking for connections, and marshaling and evaluating evidence are the hallmarks of scholarly inquiry, but they are also the products of a college education, signs of an educated critical thinker, and keys to success on the job, as you can read in the box "The Benefits of Critical Thinking."

COMMUNICATION IN THE WORKPLACE

The Benefits of Critical Thinking

"By far," explains career expert Andrea Kay, "aside from particular technical skills, what employers want most are people who can think clearly and critically, who know themselves, who have the ability to listen to others and interact respectfully" (2012). But what constitutes thinking clearly and critically on the job? Employment writer George Root (2015) says that critical thinking takes place when "employees and managers look at a situation and weigh all possible solutions before coming up with a final answer." It can be "a long process that requires input from different people within the organization," he writes, but its benefits include the following:

1. *Bringing in new ideas*—Critical thinkers reject easy assumptions, resist the temptation to see new situations as mere replays of things that have happened in the past, and rarely accept the conventional wisdom.
2. *Fostering teamwork*—Critical thinkers actively seek the knowledge, wisdom, and experience of others. As a result, more people develop a stake in a problem's solution or the efficient operation of some plan.
3. *Promoting options*—The workplace as a whole benefits from the development of a wider range of solutions or practices because critical thinkers seek and accept input from others. Critical thinking boosts innovation.

4. *Uncovering spinoffs*—Critical thinkers, because they look at problems or issues from a variety of perspectives, generate more comprehensive solutions or ideas that can be applied across a greater variety of situations.

Management consultant Chris Jones, who describes on-the-job critical thinking as "the ability to seek a deep, rigorous understanding of our challenges," argues that it tends to escape people when they need it most, so he offers seven steps for keeping it on hand (2011):

1. *Use data to drive decisions*—Replace guesswork with facts and data; challenge decisions unsupported by meaningful data.
2. *Do your homework and share it*—Citing sources for your evidence makes a stronger case and helps you explain and defend your decision.
3. *Vet your conclusions*—Talk to others because a diversity of perspectives usually ensures a better solution.
4. *Know your social media experts*—All workplaces have in-house experts as well as links to outside experts. Find them, get to know them, and engage them on social media.
5. *Reject "face value"*—Reject easy assumptions; do not accept the conventional wisdom; think outside the box.
6. *Build your skills*—Read, write, and engage others with in-depth conversations on important, complex topics.
7. *Prioritize "think time"*—Time pressure is the enemy of critical thinking. Make time for deep thought.

Three Philosophical Questions that Shape Scientific Inquiry

Social scientists approach their inquiry from many different perspectives; of course, this shapes the kind of questions they ask, the observations they undertake, and the answers they produce. These approaches differ in large part because they grow out of distinct philosophical questions about the world and how to best study it. These are questions of

- **Ontology**—What is the nature of reality; what is knowable?
- **Epistemology**—How is knowledge best created and expanded?
- **Axiology**—What is the proper role of values in research and theory building?

The ontology of chemistry and physics is simple. If something can be measured, it's real. But as we've already seen, things aren't this simple for researchers studying communication. How do they measure affection, fear, patriotism, or beauty? Communication scholars, then, consider three perspectives on the nature of reality. The *realist position* says the world is real, tangible, and measurable. It exists apart from anyone's effort to study it. If you think a tree falling in the woods makes a noise even if no one's there to hear it, you're a realist. But does the effective flow of information up and down a large corporation exist if no one is there to measure it? The *nominalist position* says that reality exists only to the extent that we humans are able to experience it through the names and labels we give to the things we find in it. For a nominalist, there is no such thing as "love"; it is not a real, tangible thing. It exists only because we've given it a name. There is a middle position, however, the *social construction position,* which says that reality is a combination of the real world "out there" and our experiences with and of it. There can be no doubt that there is something that happens between a father and his child and between two young people about to wed. We choose to call it "love," and we may even give it various names to better make meaning of it—for example, "paternal love" or "romantic love." This is where most scientific inquiry in communication operates; after all, communication is about meaning making, so it's only logical that communication researchers would be interested in how people make meaning of the world out there.

ontology Questions of the nature of reality and what is knowable.

epistemology Questions of how to best create and expand knowledge.

axiology Questions of the proper role of values in research and theory building.

The social-constructionist ontology sees a father's love for his children as real and measurable.

If you think a tree falling in the woods makes a noise even if no one's there to hear it, you subscribe to the realist ontology.

The epistemology of chemistry and physics is simple. Knowledge is best created and expanded when a lot of different scientists, all operating independently, ask similar questions, employ similar methods, and produce similar results. This community of scholars relies on the *scientific method*: they propose explanations of the phenomena of interest (hypotheses) and conduct experimental studies to test these hypotheses. Their research must be replicable; that is, researchers must provide enough information on how they did their work so they, or anyone else, can repeat the study. And again, things aren't that simple for communication researchers. Distilled water always boils at 100 degrees Celsius at sea level. No matter where the scientists may be, the water will boil at 100 degrees if they reduce the atmospheric pressure to that of sea level. But no two people are ever alike, nor are they likely to make precisely the same meaning from a communication experience. In fact, no one individual is the same from one moment to the next. So communication researchers consider two perspectives on the best way to generate and spread knowledge. The scientific method-based approach we just described is the *objectivist position*. But there is also the *subjectivist position*, which argues that the best way to generate and expand knowledge is through closing the gap between knower and known; that is, true understanding can only come from getting close to the topic of interest, from studying communication from the point of view of those who are communicating. Different communication scholars fall at different points along the continuum from objectivist to subjectivist.

The axiology of chemistry and physics is simple. Keep values out of inquiry. Many social scientists accept this standard. "Scientists, like all men and women, are opinionated, dogmatic, ideological," wrote behavioral researcher Fred Kerlinger. "That is the very reason for insisting on procedural objectivity; to get the whole business outside of ourselves" (1979, p. 264). There is a second position, however, one that realizes that it is impossible to completely keep values out of any human activity. As a result, researchers, after admitting this reality, either do their best to limit the influence of those values on their inquiry (they "bracket" them), or they embrace them as part of the work itself. It's not likely, for example, that a feminist scholar would expect us to believe that her research on the portrayal of working women on prime-time television is value-free. And there is a third axiological position, one which puts values front and center, arguing that values should drive research, which, like all good science, is intended to create change. As with epistemology, different communication scholars fall at different points along the values continuum represented by these three positions.

Sociologist Kenneth Bailey wrote, "To this day you will find within social science both those who think of themselves as scientists in the strictest sense of

> ## PERSONALLY RESPONSIBLE COMMUNICATION
>
> ## Solving Not-So-Well-Posed Problems
>
> MIT physicist Alan Lightman wrote, "Years ago, when I was a graduate student in physics, I was introduced to the concept of the 'well-posed problem': a question that can be stated with enough clarity and precision that it is guaranteed an answer. Scientists are always working on well-posed problems . . . We scientists are taught from an early stage of our apprenticeship not to waste time on questions that do not have clear and definite answers" (2011).
>
> But rarely do questions about communication—about human social life—lend themselves to these clear and definite answers. Professor Lightman recognizes this:
>
> > We cannot clearly show why the ending of a particular novel haunts us. We cannot prove under what conditions we would sacrifice our own life in order to save the life of our child. We cannot prove whether it is right or wrong to steal in order to feed our family, or even agree on a definition of "right" and "wrong." We cannot prove the meaning of our life, or whether life has any meaning at all. For these questions, we can gather evidence and
>
> debate, but, in the end, we cannot arrive at any system of analysis akin to the way in which a physicist decides how many seconds it will take a one-foot-long pendulum to make a complete swing.
>
> Although he was talking about the value of the arts and humanities, Professor Lightman could not have better expressed the challenge (or the excitement) inherent in trying to solve the not-so-well-posed problems that interest communication researchers. It may be much more difficult to measure a parent's love or to determine how a culture negotiates what is "right" and "wrong" than it is to compute the time it takes a pendulum to complete a swing. But that's no reason not to do it, and communication researchers make it their responsibility to seek knowledge in the messy world of the social sciences. What about you? What issues of human social interaction interest you? Do you ever ask yourself questions about how we create meaning? If you do, how clear and definite are the answers?

the word and those with a more subjective approach to the study of society, who see themselves more as humanists than as scientists" (1982, p. 5). Ultimately, scholars' ontological, epistemological, and axiological positions will be determined by the questions they want to answer, the nature of the observations they want to make, and the kinds of evidence they require to build the theory they think will be most useful. And still, communication researchers, like all social scientists, must confront the "messiness" of human behavior, as you can read in the box "Solving Not-So-Well-Posed Problems."

Traditions of Communication Inquiry

All communication research and the theories it produces are the products of three broad traditions of inquiry that differ in their ontology, epistemology, and axiology. They are the postpositivist, interpretive, and critical traditions.

Postpositivist Theory and Research

In the early days of communication research, social scientists wanted to be "scientific," so they looked to the traditional natural sciences for models of

Research in physics is easy because "[b]illiard balls cannot change the shape of the table, the size of the pockets, or intervene in the paths they take, or even decide whether to play the game at all" (Bandura, 2008, p. 95).

postpositivism Communication scholarship that recognizes that humans living in a social world are not as constant or predictable as the measurable elements of the physical world.

how to do research and develop theory. They saw that people studying in fields such as physics and chemistry based their work on *positivism*. Positivists believed that only quantifiable, observable, measurable phenomena were the legitimate building blocks of knowledge and theory. But there was a problem for social scientists. A gram of sulphur is always a gram of sulphur, and a hydrogen molecule always contains two atoms. But what is a gram of friendship? How many parts to a family?

So, social scientists who are committed to developing theory using quantifiable, observable, measurable phenomena practice **postpositivism**. It's as close as possible to what natural scientists do, but it recognizes that humans living in a social world are not as constant or predictable as are the measurable elements of the physical world. "Humans are not like billiard balls propelled solely by forces external to them," explains cognitive psychologist Albert Bandura. "Billiard balls cannot change the shape of the table, the size of the pockets, or intervene in the paths they take, or even decide whether to play the game at all. In contrast, humans not only think, but, individually and collectively, shape the form those external forces take and even determine whether or not they come into play. Murray Gell-Mann, the physicist Nobelist, underscored the influential role of the personal determinants when he remarked, 'Imagine how hard physics would be if particles could think'" (2008, pp. 95–96).

The theories that grow out of the postpositivist approach, much like those of positivist research in the natural sciences, seek *explanation, prediction, and control.* For example, researchers who want to explain the operation of health-oriented public service campaigns, to predict which appeals will be most effective, and to control the health-related behavior of a targeted group would rely on postpositivist theory. Researchers in this tradition believe that the world, even humans acting in a social world, exists apart from people's perceptions of it and that human behavior is predictable and patterned enough to be systematically studied. But because they believe that the social world has more variation than the physical world and that humans manage that variation by assigning meaning to it (remember Professor Bandura's billiard balls), postpositivists adopt a social-construction ontology. Like the positivists, they adopt an objectivist epistemology, arguing that knowledge is best advanced through the systematic, logical search for regularities and causal relationships employing the scientific method. And it is this reliance on the scientific method that defines postpositivism's axiology—the objectivity inherent in the use of the scientific method keeps researchers' and theorists' values out of the search for knowledge as much as humanly possible.

Interpretive Theory and Research

But many communication scholars do not want to explain, predict, and control social behavior. Their goal is to *understand* how and why that behavior occurs in the social world and how it is transacted through communication. Their **interpretive research** is the study of understanding, especially through the systematic interpretation of social actions or texts.

There are different types of interpretive research and theory. For example, some communication researchers want to understand how people in a social situation interpret their own communication behavior in that situation. Another type of interpretive work looks for hidden or deep meaning in people's interpretations of different symbol systems—for example, in media texts. An important idea running through the interpretive tradition of research and theory is that any **text**, any product of social interaction—an online video, an argument between a teen brother and sister, a Facebook wall, a blockbuster movie, or a best-selling novel—can be a source of understanding.

The ontology of interpretive theory accepts that there is no "real," measurable social reality. Instead, "people construct an image of reality based on their own preferences and prejudices and their interactions with others, and this is as true of scientists as it is of everyone else in the social world" (Schutt, 2009, p. 92). Put another way, knowledge is *local*; that is, it is specific to the interaction of the knower and the known. But because this is just as true of the researchers as it is of the texts they study, interpretivists' epistemology, how they believe knowledge is advanced, relies on the subjective interaction between the observer (the researcher or theorist) and his or her community. Naturally, then, the axiology of interpretive theory accepts, rather than disdains, the influence of the researcher's and theorist's values. Personal and professional values, according to communication theorist Katherine Miller, are a "lens through which social phenomena are observed" (2005, p. 58).

interpretive research The study of understanding, especially through the systematic interpretation of social actions or texts.

text Any product of social interaction.

Critical Theory and Research

Some communication scholars do not want explanation, prediction, and control of the social world. Nor do they seek understanding of the social world. They believe that they understand it quite well, arguing that some aspects of the social world are flawed and in need of change. Their goal is to *challenge existing ways*

Any product of social interaction, even secrets passed between teen sisters, can serve as a text worthy of inquiry.

critical theory Theory that challenges existing ways of organizing the social world and the people and institutions exercising power in it.

emancipatory knowledge The epistemology of critical research and theory; knowledge is advanced when it serves to free people and communities from the influence of the powerful.

structure In critical theory, the social world's rules, norms, and beliefs.

agency In critical theory, how humans behave and interact in the social world.

dialectic In critical theory, the ongoing struggle or debate bètween agency and structure.

of organizing the social world and the people and institutions exercising power in it. They want to gain knowledge of the social world so they can make it better. **Critical theory** is openly political, and therefore its axiology is proudly value-laden. Critical theorists study inequality and oppression. Their theories do more than observe, describe, or interpret; they criticize. Critical mass communication scholars, for example, view "media as sites of (and weapons in) struggles over social, economic, symbolic, and political power (as well as struggles over control of, and access to, the media themselves)" (Meyrowitz, 2008, p. 642). Critical interpersonal scholars would view traditional standards of conversational address between men and women in the workplace as reinforcing and maintaining patriarchy (Woods, 1988). Critical scholars argue that knowledge is advanced only when it serves to free people and communities from the influence of those more powerful than themselves. Their epistemology, then, seeks **emancipatory knowledge**. The ontology of critical theory and research, however, is a bit more complex.

For critical researchers, what is real and knowable in the social world is the product of the interaction between **structure** (the social world's rules, norms, and beliefs) and **agency** (how humans act and interact in that world). Reality, then, to critical theorists, is constantly being shaped and reshaped by the **dialectic** (the ongoing struggle or debate) between the two. When elites control the struggle, they define reality (in other words, their control of the structure defines people's realities). When people are emancipated, *they* define reality through their behaviors and interactions (agency), and furthermore, that agency can indeed change structure. For example, despite formal laws and religious and community traditions that for centuries have defined the "reality" of homosexuality as illegal, shameful, and worthy of disgust, contemporary people, through their behaviors and actions, reject those structures. Now, new structures—new realities—regarding homosexuality have been constituted. Gay marriage is legal across the United States, openly gay people are welcomed in the military, openly gay people work in virtually all professions, and it is illegal to discriminate against people based on their sexual orientation. In this instance, people's everyday interactions surrounding homosexuality challenged the structures erected by the powerful (religion, law, long-standing tradition) and, through that agency, emancipated themselves from those very structures that constrained those interactions.

Researchers and theorists interested in how routine news reporting practices delegitimize the otherwise reasonable political positions of minorities and working people, or social scientists interested in the impact of English-only school curricula on identity formation and educational performance in children whose first language is not English, would employ critical research and theory. Critical researchers believe that they confront the "big issues" of the day, as you can read in the box "Communication Inquiry Needs to Be Bigger!"

Communication Inquiry Needs to Be Bigger!

Communication researcher Dietram Scheufele (2010) recently wrote, "Communication as a discipline has come to a crossroads . . . [The] changes in how content is produced and communicated are paralleled by much more far-reaching shifts in how some cohorts in society interpret traditional notions of privacy, objectivity, and source credibility. And so far, our discipline has not done a very good job at offering answers to what have become increasingly pressing questions in various societal debates."

His argument is that communication researchers think too small. He quotes another professor who claims that social scientists "often speak in terms of 'an interesting puzzle,' a small intellectual conundrum . . . that tests the ingenuity of the solver, rather than the large, sloppy and unmanageable problems that occur in real life." We are faced, he continues, with "enough of these sloppy, unmanageable problems for our society and for us as communication scholars, ranging from mandates for a green economy, to climate change, stem cell research, and global warming. All of these issues relate to the increasingly blurring lines between science, politics, society . . . and, of course, communication. These are the same areas where most societal debates of the next 50 years will take place. And unless we as communication researchers . . . find a way to make both scholarly and public contributions to these conversations, we will increasingly be marginalized as a discipline."

Professor Scheufele's worry is less about the welfare of the discipline than it is about the well-being of the world in which it operates. We face "big, upcoming challenges" that can best be met by solid research and theory, he argues, and those who are skilled in communication inquiry have an obligation to use their skills to meet those challenges. But inquiry in and of itself is insufficient, he argues; communication researchers should undertake socially responsible inquiry, research, and theory that serve the larger good. How can this happen? Can you speculate on what communication has to do with sloppy, unmanageable problems like the green economy, climate change, stem cell research, and global warming?

Tools of Observation: Research Methods

The richness and variety of communication, its centrality to all human social and cultural interaction, and the multitude of questions this raises require that communication researchers use a variety of methods to find their answers and build their theory. Some methods are rightly associated with specific approaches to inquiry, but contemporary communication scholarship is increasingly receptive to the proposition that a method's best application is defined by the question at hand. Communication research employs **quantitative research**—inquiry relying on the collection and analysis of numerical data—and **qualitative research**—inquiry relying on the collection and analysis of symbolic data such as language and other cultural products. These data are collected using primarily three methods: experiments, surveys, and textual analysis. But don't be fooled. As with much else in this chapter, things aren't really that simple.

quantitative research Inquiry relying on the collection and analysis of numerical data.

qualitative research Inquiry relying on the collection and analysis of symbolic data such as language and other cultural products.

Experiments

experiment Research method involving the manipulation of one variable to measure its influence on another variable.

Experiments involve the manipulation of one variable (the *independent variable*) to measure its influence on another variable (the *dependent variable*). All other possible agents of influence are held constant, or controlled for. In this way, any change observed in the dependent variable is sure to be the product of the manipulation of the independent variable.

Take a classic television violence study as an example. Researchers show one group of children a violent cartoon and a second group a nonviolent cartoon. Cartoon violence is our independent variable; it is what we've manipulated. After the kids watch their cartoon, they are given 20 minutes of free play in a room filled with all kinds of toys. They are monitored through a two-way mirror, and the number of blows each child delivers to the room's inflatable clown doll is counted. Blows to the doll is our dependent variable. Experiments like this almost always employ a *control group*, participants who see no cartoon at all; they are not subjected to the experiment's manipulation of the independent variable. In the logic of the experiment, then, if those kids who saw the violent cartoon exhibited more "aggression" against the doll than those who saw the nonviolent cartoon, the cartoon violence must have "caused" that aggression. After all, kids who had seen no violence showed less aggression. And the fact that the kids who didn't see any cartoon at all showed the same nonaggression as the kids in the nonviolent cartoon condition means that it isn't cartoons that caused more blows, it was the violence in the cartoons. After all, that video violence is the only variable not common to any two groups.

But is hitting an inflatable doll really aggression? In a social-scientific experiment, researchers *operationalize* their variables; that is, they identify a behavior that, for the duration of the experiment, stands for the phenomenon of interest. Other researchers may question the particular operationalization, but they must admit that the kids who saw the violent cartoon did indeed hit the doll more times than did the kids in the other two groups. But did the violence in the cartoon "cause" the kids to deliver those blows? In the logic of the experiment, they certainly did. If all else was held constant—the kids were randomly assigned to their groups; each cartoon was exactly eight minutes long and used precisely the same characters, settings, and plot (except for the violence, of course); the playroom was identically equipped for each kid; the observer used the same definition

In this famous TV violence study by Albert Bandura, aggression, operationalized as blows to the inflatable doll, was the dependent variable.

of "hit" for all kids and was unaware of which kids had seen which cartoon or if they had seen one at all—then the only thing that could have caused the increased aggression must have been the one thing that was different.

This is **causality**—when one event precedes a second event and that second event is deemed to be a consequence of the first. And this is why experiments are the most-favored research method of postpositivists; they are the only way that causality can be demonstrated. Experiments give communication researchers other benefits in addition to the demonstration of causality. They grant researchers complete control over their inquiry; they permit precision (in our example, researchers may want to vary the kinds of cartoon violence and the age of the animated characters to refine even more precisely their definition of cartoon violence); and they are repeatable, as required by the scientific method.

But these benefits come at a price. It is difficult to generalize from a highly structured and controlled experimental setting to the larger world. Children don't view eight-minute cartoons under the watchful eye of an adult and then immediately go to 20 minutes of free play. They watch all kinds of television, as well as other media; they have different family situations, different personalities, different genetic make-ups, and different daily frustrations. Lack of generalizability is closely related to two other problems. First, in exchange for the experiment's control and precision, researchers must limit the number of variables or inputs they include in their work. Second, other experimenters may be able to replicate the procedures of the experiment, but the original experiment is still a one-time event. In our example, a replication would, at the very minimum, use different kids. The replicating researcher can't even use the same children from the original experiment because (a) they are not the same kids they were the first time around—they're older for one thing— and (b) they've already seen the cartoon, so the replication would not be a replication because maybe the increased aggression is a product of the kids' frustration at having to watch the same cartoon again.

Surveys

Surveys rely on questionnaires and interviews to solicit self-reported data from respondents. Researchers identify a population about which they want to know something, draw a sample of respondents from that group, and ask them verbal or written questions either in person, on the phone, by mail, or online. If you're of voting age, you've no doubt been surveyed. So let's use as our example a survey designed to measure the impact of a candidate's debate performance. Our researchers might be interested specifically in how voting-age women in Ohio responded. "Voting-age women in Ohio" is the *population*. But the researchers can't interview every single one of those women, so they draw a *sample,* a statistically adequate number of those people whose responses they assume will be representative of the population. That sample might be *random* (all population members have an equal likelihood of appearing in it)—or it may not be. Researchers sometimes draw *nonrandom,* or *stratified, samples* to ensure

causality When one event precedes a second event and that second event is deemed to be a consequence of the first.

survey Research method relying on questionnaires and interviews to solicit self-reported data from respondents.

the inclusion of particular categories of people. In our example they may want to make sure that single moms are sufficiently represented, as they typically refuse to take the time to answer surveys. Once these quantitative data are collected, the researchers will subject them to analysis, determine what the sample's members thought of the candidate's performance in the debate, and then argue that that's how the population, voting-age women in Ohio, reacted.

Survey research offers scholars a number of advantages. Their findings can be confidently generalized to a large population. Surveys can be conducted over time; for example, to get an even clearer picture of attitudes about the debate performance, our researchers might survey this population at the start of the campaign, the day before the debate, the day after the debate, and the morning of the election. Researchers can investigate the influence of a large number of variables. In our experimental example, the likely variables beyond watching cartoon violence, at best, could have been the children's age and gender. In our survey, the variables could have ranged from rental or ownership of home, level of education, marital status, number of children living at home, political party affiliation, likelihood of voting, household income, and on and on. This gives the product of survey researchers' inquiry greater breadth. Yes, the population of interest may have been voting-age women in Ohio, but the researchers can now comment on Democratic, married, voting-age women in Ohio who own their own homes, have some college education, no longer have children living at home, earn more than $50,000 a year, and are likely to vote. Surveys also offer greater breadth when considering the communication under examination. In our experiment, the communication variable was cartoon violence, either the presence of cartoon violence, no cartoon violence, or no cartoon at all. The survey, on the other hand, could have investigated the speaker's appearance, expertise, forcefulness, credibility, level of detail provided, quality of argument on housing, quality of argument on the economy, quality of argument on women's reproductive rights, quality of argument on education, and on and on.

But these benefits come at a cost. Surveys cannot demonstrate causality. If our Ohio women of voting age loved the candidate's performance and that candidate did indeed prevail in the election, the survey data do not tell us if the positive debate performance caused those women to vote for him or her. Survey researchers also cede some control over their inquiry. For example, some other event might occur that is as or more powerful in shaping respondents' responses than the debate itself. Maybe the morning after the debate the local paper revealed that the candidate has a long drunk-driving record. Finally, survey data are self-report data, and people often are the worst reporters of their personal data. From our example, age and gender may be easy answers to provide, but what about household income, political party affiliation, and likelihood of voting? Now imagine a different survey, perhaps one examining verbal spousal abuse in homes suffering from

Surveys permit the investigation of a large number of variables.

long-term parental unemployment. How accurate and trustworthy do you think this work's self-reported data would be?

Textual Analysis

Many communication scholars engage in **textual analysis**, the deep reading of an individual message or group of messages. Those texts, as we've already seen, can be any product of human social interaction, and the goal of the analysis is description and interpretation of the text. Researchers who engage in textual analysis usually do so from a specific point of view, so their work is subjective, although as we've read, some interpretive scholars attempt to bracket, or set aside, their personal experiences when undertaking these analyses. Nonetheless, this subjective orientation is this method's strength. It acknowledges that meaning making is local; it occurs between the reader and the text. But this is also its weakness. It lacks objectivity; different readers may make different meanings from the same text. Textual analysis also lacks generalizability. This is intentional—meaning is made between text and "reader," so there is no intention to generalize. "But," ask the method's critics, "Now what? That's your reading, and it kind of makes sense, but now what?" The interpretive researcher's response would be something along the lines of, "Now nothing. I have offered a deeper understanding of this text, its creator, and (possibly) the time and context of its delivery. That's valuable in and of itself. Feel free to find other analyses or even do your own." One example of textual analysis might be a rhetorician's analysis of a retiring religious leader's final sermon. What themes dominated? Was there a call to action or a plea for social justice? Did the sermon's narrative revolve around the life of the congregation, or the pastor's personal experiences with the faithful?

textual analysis The deep reading of an individual message or group of messages.

Mixing Methods and Traditions

Another example of textual analysis might be the work of researchers interested in how employees in a large organization ask for time off for important family matters. They might collect two months' worth of e-mail between workers, their supervisors, and the human resources office and analyze the nature of the appeals for time off that they contained. Their reading might suggest to them that there are six strategies or approaches that workers usually take, for example, asking only for what they know they can have and couching their requests in terms of organizational interests. So they compute the proportion of the total number of appeals represented by each of those six themes to determine which are most and least used. But when they notice that men tend to employ certain strategies more often than do women, they create a typology of strategy by gender. They also see that newer employees differ from company veterans in the kinds of appeals they usually make, so they expand their model to include type of appeal, gender, and years on the job. But all of this new data is quantitative: six types of appeal, two genders, zero to 44 years on the job. This work is **content analysis**, quantitative textual analysis that depends not on researchers' deep reading, but on their objective categorization and accurate measurement based on their deep reading. This is

content analysis Quantitative textual analysis that relies on objective categorization and accurate measurement.

clearly textual analysis, but it is from an objective rather than subjective orientation.

Another example of textual analysis might be the work of researchers who move into a halfway house for delinquent teens and become part of the institution's daily routine. They observe, record, and make notes on every conversation the residents have with their teachers in order to understand the nature of student-teacher interaction during class, as well as in the general daily life of the facility. These conversations are text and the researchers' transcriptions and observations are qualitative data, so this work is in the interpretive tradition. But this method represents another kind of interpretive research, **ethnography**—the study of human social interaction from the inside, in this case, by a *participant observer*. But someone working from the critical tradition might also use content analysis and ethnography. Why should employees, when approaching their bosses, be forced to strategize to get time off to tend to family? Shouldn't family be more important than work? If they have earned time off, why do they have to provide an explanation at all? Doesn't the making and shaping of requests reinforce the power disparity between employees and bosses? And why does a country as rich as ours warehouse its troubled children? Quite possibly, if these kids were more fully integrated into the life of regular school they might be better and more traditionally socialized. Who benefits from these "special" schools?

ethnography The study of human social interaction from the inside.

There is definitely a relationship between theory and research traditions—postpositive, interpretive, and critical—and the methods *typically* associated with each. But that's the point—*typically* associated. Critical scholars use experiments. The experimental study of the effects of cartoon violence is clearly designed to give voice to the less powerful (parents and kids) in their interaction with the more powerful (the media industry). Content analysis—part quantitative, part qualitative—is often used by people working in the interpretive tradition. As a result, social science scholars often mix, match, and blend their approaches as they do their work. Communication researchers William Benoit and R. Lance Holbert explain, "Understanding communication is enhanced when research is not conducted in isolation . . . [R]esearch which systematically investigates an aspect of communication with a series of related studies conducted across contexts or with multiple methods is particularly valuable in our efforts to understand communication" (2008, p. 615).

For example, one of the most famous and groundbreaking pieces of textual analysis is Janice Radway's study of romance novels (1991). Her reading revealed that the characters and plots in these books are drawn from patriarchal myths that support the ideology that the male-dominated social order is natural and just. Men are strong and aggressive; women are

Romance novels—reinforcement of patriarchal myths or readers' declaration of independence?

ETHICAL COMMUNICATION

Where Do You Draw the Line?

You are a communication researcher. You work to understand communication and human behavior because you believe that the more knowledge people have about communication, the better they can make personally useful meaning. That seems to be a noble goal. You could advise companies on the best way to inform employees about a new benefits package, or you could consult with the health department on a designated driver campaign, or you could help a school system distinguish between threatening and harmless student tweets.

But what if a tobacco company wants you to use your communication research skills to help it improve the promotional campaign for its new fruit-scented cigarette? They'd like you to conduct some interviews with young adults, survey college students in response to the company's YouTube commercials (which do not seem to be clicking), and offer a deep reading of those commercials. The pay is more than you'd make just about anywhere else; these are tough times to get a job; and smoking is legal for people over 18, so why not? But what if your best friend had lost a parent to a smoking-related disease? What if you had lost your mother, a smoker, to lung cancer? Would your personal connection to tobacco-related loss influence your decision? Should it? Why or why not?

These are not imaginary situations. Communication researchers are asked to confront issues such as this all the time, and they have to make a decision—how do they use their communication inquiry skills? In these scenarios, how would you? Would you take the job? Why or why not?

---

weak, passive, and dependent. But Radway then began meeting regularly with groups of women who also read these novels, asking them in person and through a questionnaire what they thought was happening inside those pages. Undertaking a statistical analysis of their responses and meeting with them in groups, she discovered that many of her respondents used the novels to construct personally important interpretations that rejected that patriarchal ideology. Reading the romance novel, Radway discovered, was their "declaration of independence" (1991, p. 11). Was her work quantitative or qualitative? Was it textual analysis or survey? Was it interpretive or critical? The answers to those questions are not as important as the fact that hers is very good communication inquiry; it has advanced our knowledge of meaning making.

As we've seen, different researchers adopt different methodological approaches, and sometimes even mix and match them, given their preferred ontology, epistemology, and axiology. But all communication researchers should approach their work with a commitment to right and wrong. But that distinction is not always clear cut, as you can read in the box "Where Do You Draw the Line?"

Review of Learning Objectives

2.1 Define theory using analogies.

A theory is a unified, coherent, and organized set of explanations, concepts, and principles describing some aspect of the world. It is a grand synthesis of the sum of our knowledge of a given phenomenon. Theories are nets designed to capture the world; lenses that focus attention on some aspect of the world; and maps that show the roads traveled, where knowledge currently exists, and where social scientists should go in their search for knowledge.

2.2 Explain the relationship between the three steps of social-scientific inquiry.

Communication inquiry involves asking scientifically testable questions, engaging in systematic observation, and developing answers. The nature of the questions determines the method of observation, which shapes the character of the resulting answers.

2.3 Describe the different ontologies, epistemologies, and axiologies providing philosophical support to scientific inquiry in communication.

Communication researchers conduct their work against the backdrop of three important philosophical questions of research and theory building. Ontological questions deal with the nature of reality—that is, what is knowable and measurable? Epistemological questions revolve around the issue of the best way to create and expand knowledge. Axiological questions examine the proper role of human values in research and theory building.

2.4 Differentiate between traditions of communication inquiry.

Communication research and theory are products of three broad traditions of inquiry differing in their ontology, epistemology, and axiology. They are the postpositivist tradition, which seeks explanation, prediction, and control; the interpretive tradition, which seeks understanding; and the critical tradition, which seeks emancipatory knowledge, that is, knowledge of the social world that will free people from the influence of those more powerful than themselves.

2.5 Describe the benefits and drawbacks of the most common research methods employed in communication inquiry.

Communication scholars use a variety of research methods, including experiments, surveys, and textual analysis. Experiments offer the only method for the demonstration of causality, significant researcher control over inquiry, and precision of measurement. However, the number of variables that can be investigated at one time is limited, and experiments are one-time events that may not be easily generalized to the larger world.

Surveys rely on questionnaires and interviews to solicit self-reported data from a sample, the results of which can then be generalized to a larger population. In addition to the ability to confidently generalize, surveys' other advantages are that they can be conducted over time and they offer great breadth of inquiry; that is, they can include a large number of variables. Surveys, however, cannot demonstrate causality; researchers have limited control over the environment in which they are doing their work; and survey data are self-reported, which can be unreliable.

Textual analysis is the deep reading of an individual message or group of messages. This method's subjective orientation is its greatest strength but also its greatest drawback.

Key Terms

theory 28
specification of ignorance 29
scientific inquiry 31
ontology 33
epistemology 33
axiology 33
postpositivism 36
interpretive research 37
text 37
critical theory 38
emancipatory knowledge 38
structure 38
agency 38
dialectic 38
quantitative research 39
qualitative research 39
experiment 40
causality 41
survey 41
textual analysis 43
content analysis 43
ethnography 44

Questions for Review

1. Define theory. Is a theory the same as a fact? What is the specification of ignorance?

2. What three metaphors can we use to judge the usefulness of a theory?

3. What are the three steps of scientific inquiry?

4. What questions are considered by researchers' ontology, epistemology, and axiology?

5. What is postpositivist theory? What are its ontology, epistemology, and axiology?

6. What is interpretive theory? What are its ontology, epistemology, and axiology?

7. What is critical theory? What are its ontology, epistemology, and axiology?

8. Distinguish between quantitative and qualitative research.

9. What are the benefits and shortcomings of experimental, survey, and textual analysis?

10. What are content analysis and ethnography?

Questions for Discussion

1. The ontology of critical theory revolves around the dialectic between agency and structure. Can you think of a contemporary social issue (other than acceptance of gay people) where human activity (agency) has reshaped structure (rules and norms)? What was the nature of the debate? How was communication utilized in that dialectic?

2. The axiology of communication research ranges from limiting the influence of values on inquiry as much as possible to the open celebration of values in the shaping and conduct of the work. Where do *you* think values belong in the search for knowledge?

3. Which metaphor for theory do you find most convincing in explaining what communication researchers and theorists are trying to do? Explain your answer.

3

Verbal Communication

You find yourself fighting with a friend over something silly, the meaning of a word—*voting*. Your friend says you are *unpatriotic* for not voting in the presidential election. Voting is a citizen's patriotic duty, he argues. You counter that your non-vote was actually a *vote* against the outsized influence of money in American electoral politics. You are the patriotic one, you insist, because for you, *dissent* is the highest form of *patriotism*. But your friend is not convinced, even by your lofty rhetoric. "Look," he says, "You have a *duty* to register your opinion at the ballot box; you failed the first test of *citizenship*."

This disagreement is actually over the meaning of several words beyond *voting*—*unpatriotic*, *dissent*, *patriotism*, *duty*, and *citizenship*. It has become heated because you are fighting not only about their meanings, but about the sense of self that each of you has invested in those meanings. The one word you thought was in dispute—*voting*—is actually the least abstract, most concrete of all. In the context of the election, voting is the act of going to the polls and completing a ballot. But who can say what is patriotic and unpatriotic? One person's dissent is another person's disloyalty; one person's duty is another person's freedom. And what signifies citizenship? Birthplace, a piece of paper earned through a test, a set of beliefs and values, an unconditional love of country, disappointment in your country because its actions do not match its ideals? You and your friend are not fighting over words; you are fighting over what those words mean to you and about you.

As you learned in Chapter 1, you are what you communicate. When specifically considering verbal communication, your "choice of words is choice of worlds" (Penn, 1990, p. 116). In this chapter, we'll discover how that choice is open to many different possibilities, each with the potential to aid us in making meaning for ourselves and those around us.

Learning Objectives

3.1   Explain the structure of language and the functions of its different components.

3.2   Describe the role of speech communities and speech networks in creating meaning.

3.3   Identify the relationship between language and thought.

3.4   Identify the functions of language.

3.5   Explain how we use language to make meaning.

3.6   Effectively use language to protect self-identity.

The Structure of Language

Ever since you were a child, you've heard that humans are the only species on earth that uses language. As philosopher Susanne Langer explains, "Animal 'speech' never has structure. It is merely an emotional response. Apes may greet their ration of yams with a shout of 'Nga!' But they do not say 'Nga' between meals. If they could *talk about* their yams instead of just saluting them, they would be the most primitive men [sic] instead of the most anthropoid of beasts. They would have ideas, and tell each other things true and false, rational or irrational; they would make plans and invent laws, and sing their own praises, as men [sic] do" (2013, p. 109).

In other words, apes, like many animals, can signal physical needs and states (dogs wag their tails and bark when excited; some bees emit odors to regulate the population in their hives, and some fly in specific patterns to indicate direction; dolphins whistle and squeak to identify themselves to other dolphins), but only humans have **language**, a communication system made up of formal units combined in systematic ways to cooperatively make meaning. Those *formal units* are words and sounds, that is, symbols we use to represent objects, ideas, and emotions. Your puppy's tail may signal that she's happy you're home, but only humans can say they're happy, overjoyed, delighted, ecstatic, elated, and jubilant that the plans and preparations for next week's surprise graduation party, extravaganza, and soirée appear to be progressing smoothly, without a hitch, and quite seamlessly, thank you very much!

That *systematic combining* is **syntax**, the occurrence and ordering of words and sounds to convey an intended meaning. The bumblebee's figure-eight

language   A communication system made up of formal units combined in systematic ways to cooperatively make meaning.

syntax   The occurrence and ordering of words and sounds to convey an intended meaning.

flight pattern may signal, "Come this way, not that way." That's pretty impressive for a bug. But only human language allows an infinite combination of words and sounds to impart very specific information. You can tell your friends, "Come this way, not that way, because there is a very big tree across the road. It fell during the night, but in fact its roots were weakened by last month's wind storm." Try something simpler. You know the definition of the word *friend*. But what is the intended meaning of that word when it is combined with other words and sounds in these sentences?

a. Pat and I are friendly.

b. Pat and I are friends.

c. Pat is my friend.

Although bees can communicate ideas such as "come this way," they do not have language.

It's clear that Pat and you know each other, but syntactically, the personal relationship expressed in "c" is stronger than the one in "b," which is stronger than the one expressed in "a." Let's see a bee do that!

It's important to distinguish between **grammar**, the rules describing the proper construction of phrases and sentences, and syntax, because grammar actually has little to do with meaning making. Here is a grammatically terrible sentence: "He am being yesterday at the store." You can easily figure out what it means. But here is a grammatically perfect sentence offered by linguist Noam Chomsky (1957) that makes no sense because it lacks proper syntax:

grammar Rules describing the proper construction of phrases and sentences.

Colorless green ideas sleep furiously.

This sentence has adjectives, a noun and a verb, and an adverb all in the grammatically correct spots. But these words syntactically cannot co-occur; that is, *green* can't be *colorless* and *ideas* can't be *green*, nor do they *sleep, furiously* or otherwise. But who says this sentence has no meaning? We do.

We make meaning *cooperatively* in a **speech community**, people who speak the same language and who not only "interact by means of speech," but also agree on the "proper" and "improper" use of language (Bloomfield, 1933, p. 42). Dolphin A can signal Dolphin B, "Hey, it's me." But that's about it. Humans, however, can go a bit further. You know when it's proper to identify yourself by first name only, for example when starting a conversation with the person sitting next to you on a plane: "Hi, I'm Chris." You know when it's proper to use your first and last name, for example when introducing yourself to a prospective employer: "Hello, I'm Chris Morse." When a classmate offers the standard greeting, "What's up?" you know not to answer, "The opposite of down," or "My blood pressure," or "The national debt." A simple "Not much" does the job.

speech community People who speak the same language and agree on the proper and improper use of language.

We belong to several speech networks, each with its own specific language. These quidditch teammates no doubt have their own idiosyncratic expressions.

People also belong to **speech networks**, that is, people with whom they regularly interact and speak. Like members of a speech community, they know the language, the rules for its use, and how to interpret what they hear. But because members of a speech network communicate frequently (cooperatively make meaning), they build and share a specific common language, and because of that, they build and share a greater understanding of one another. If you are reading this book, it's quite likely you are a member of the American English speech community. But you likely also belong to several speech networks. For example, you and your coworkers undoubtedly have your own "language," as do you and your teammates on the intramural quidditch team; you and your circle of friends may have your own language consisting of nicknames, made-up words, specific slang expressions, and idiosyncratic greetings and farewells.

speech networks People who regularly interact and speak with one another.

Language and Thought

How does the language we hear come to represent objects, ideas, and emotions? That is, how are language and thought related? How do words and sounds become "pictures in our heads"? One way to answer this question is simply to recall our discussion of the meaning triangle from Chapter 1. People mutually make meaning because they share a common experience with the referent, its symbol, and its reference. Think how easily and naturally the picture in our head changes given a word's connotative and denotative meanings. **Denotative meaning** is a word's explicit meaning, the one that directly comes to mind when used by a specific speech community. **Connotative meaning** is a word's more implicit, usually emotionally or culturally enriched meaning. For example, the denotative meaning of these three words is the same:

denotative meaning
A word's explicit meaning when used by a specific speech community.

connotative meaning
A word's implicit, usually emotionally or evaluatively enriched meaning.

- domicile
- house
- home.

Their connotative meaning, however, could not be clearer—You don't go to your domicile for the holidays; you don't even go to your house; you go home! Each of these words—*domicile, house, home*—produces not only a different thought, but also different types of thought. How does this happen? Linguistic and communication scholars offer several explanations. Among them are the Linguistic Relativity Hypothesis, metaphor, and the ladder of abstraction.

Linguistic Relativity Hypothesis

Sometimes called the Whorf-Sapir hypothesis after the linguists who originally developed the concept, the **Linguistic Relativity Hypothesis** asserts that the language a speaker uses influences the way he or she thinks. As Iman Tohidian explained, "The grammatical and semantic categories of each language, in addition to serving as instruments for communicating a person's thoughts, mold ideas and program mental activity. Thus, people with different native languages will not have the same view of the universe" (2008, p. 67). The classic example is the word *snow*. English speakers have one word for *snow*—maybe two, if you want to count *slush*. But Eskimo Inuit speakers have several words that acknowledge many distinctions in the cold, white stuff—it's falling; it's already on the ground; it's wind-blown. People who live in the snow think and speak differently about snow than do people who deal with it less dramatically. Think of your own experience. How many words do you have for the kind of wave you find at the beach? Most of us have a few—*big*, *small*, and possibly *OMG!* But surfers think about waves much differently. So they have a few more words for *wave*, including *A-frame, ankle-snapper, bake, barrel, bazza, big mamma, blown-out, bomb, brutal, bump, cave, chubbie, epic, glossy, ground swell, massive, section, set, soup bowl, smackable, stavewave, sucky, tesani,* and *valid.*

We can also see this connection between language and worldview in different languages' use of the second-person pronoun. English speakers, no matter how well they know the other person, no matter how old or important that other person may be, refer to others as *you.* In English, *you* is *you,* as in, "Are you happy?" But many languages have different forms of *you,* depending on how well the speakers know each other and their relative status—German speakers differentiate *Du* and *Sie;* Spanish speakers have *tú* and *usted;* and French speakers use *tu* and *vous.* In each instance, the first option is used when addressing familiar people or people of the same or lower social rank or age. Why doesn't English draw these distinctions while those other languages do? What might this say about how these languages reflect their cultures' worldview of status and rank in relationships? And why do German speakers capitalize their versions of the word *you* while Spanish and French speakers do not? The answer lies in cultural differences.

Another example of the connection between words and thought exists in the gendering of nouns. In Spanish *bridge* is *el puente,* a masculine noun. In German, bridge is *die Brücke,* a feminine noun. Both words mean *bridge,* the structure that gets one across a body of water; but German

THUMBNAIL THEORY

Linguistic Relativity Hypothesis

Different languages lead to different ways of thinking. It is impossible to understand society without understanding language, as society depends on, is shaped by, and itself shapes language. The language we use influences how we think, and vice versa.

Most people have a few words for ocean waves; surfers, however, have as many as there are boards in this shop.

speakers typically attach more romantic adjectives such as *beautiful*, *elegant*, *fragile*, *pretty*, and *slender* to their descriptions of bridges, while Spanish speakers tend to speak of bridges as *big*, *dangerous*, *strong*, *sturdy*, and *towering*, that is, as masculine (Boroditsky et. al., 2003). Do Germans see beauty in bridges, while Spaniards see their bridges as mere functional, get-me-from-here-to-there structures? This is the fundamental question underlying the Linguistic Relativity Hypothesis: "*Do different languages lead to different ways of thinking?*" In other words, are speakers of a particular language "led to think, perceive, and remember the world in a way specific to that language?" (Tohidian, 2008, p. 66–67).

The answer is yes. "Language and society are so intertwined that it is impossible to understand one without the other," writes linguist Elaine Chaika, "There is no human society that does not depend on, is not shaped by, and does not itself shape language" (1989, p 2). Tohidian agrees: "This statement best defines the relationship between language, thought, and reality, for language not only shapes the way reality is perceived but reality can also shape language." But she makes clear that the relationship is *relational*, not *causal*: "Language *does influence* thought and perception of reality but language *does not govern* thought or reality" (italics added; 2009, p. 73).

There is significant scholarly evidence supporting this view. For example, Mandarin speakers think of time as vertical, and English speakers think of it horizontally. Mandarin uses *up* and *down* as time markers, as opposed to English's *last* and *next*. Where an English speaker would say *next week* and *last week*, a Chinese speaker would say *the week below* and *the week above*. Could it be that given Americans' fast-paced existence we see time as something always behind and ahead of us, while the more traditional, reflective Mandarin-speaking Chinese see time more as a tool for building up or collecting experiences (Boroditsky, 2001)? The Navaho and English languages reflect the different values that each culture places on the importance of objects' form and shape. The endings of the Navaho verb *to carry* change given the shape of the object being carried. Could it be that the language of an ancient culture, long accustomed to carrying objects by animal or human effort, places greater significance on how difficult or easy that task might be than does a more modern, industrialized culture (Carroll and Casagrande, 1958)?

Metaphor

metaphor Unstated comparisons between things or events that share some feature.

Language and perceptions of reality are clearly related, but language can also express a deeper *cultural* reality through **metaphor**, unstated comparisons between things or events that share some feature. Researchers estimate that one out of every 25 words we encounter every day is a metaphor (Gorlick, 2011), but linguists George Lakoff and Mark Johnson explain the true beauty and value of metaphor:

> Metaphor is for most people a device of the poetic imagination and the rhetorical flourish—a matter of extraordinary rather than ordinary language. Moreover, metaphor is typically viewed as characteristic of language alone, a matter of words

rather than thought or action. For this reason, most people think they can get along perfectly well without metaphor. We have found, on the contrary, that metaphor is pervasive in everyday life, not just in language but in thought and action . . . The concepts that govern our thought are not just matters of the intellect. They also govern our everyday functioning, down to the most mundane details. Our concepts structure what we perceive, how we get around in the world, and how we relate to other people. Our conceptual system thus plays a central role in defining our everyday realities. If we are right in suggesting that our conceptual system is largely metaphorical, then the way we think, what we experience, and what we do every day is very much a matter of metaphor. (1980, p. 3)

They offer the American English-language metaphor ARGUMENT IS WAR as evidence that our metaphors structure our "everyday functioning":

ARGUMENT IS WAR

Your claims are *indefensible*.

His criticisms were right on *target*.

I've never *won* an argument with him.

If you use that *strategy,* he'll *wipe you out.*

He *attacked* every weak point in my argument.

I *demolished* his argument.

You disagree? Okay, *shoot!*

He *shot down* all of my arguments.

American English speakers routinely and naturally use this language. "It is important to see that we don't just talk about arguments in terms of war," Lakoff and Johnson wrote. They continue,

We can actually win or lose arguments. We see the person we are arguing with as an opponent. We attack his positions and we defend our own. We gain and lose ground. We plan and use strategies. If we find a position indefensible, we can abandon it and take a new line of attack. Many of the things we do in arguing are partially structured by the concept of war. Though there is no physical battle, there is a verbal battle, and the structure of an argument—attack, defense, counter-attack, etc.—reflects this. It is in this sense that the ARGUMENT IS WAR metaphor is one that we live by in this culture; its structures the actions we perform in arguing. (1980, p. 3)

But Lakoff and Johnson's example makes an equally important point about the link between metaphor and reality: metaphors not only highlight similarities, they mask differences in the compared concepts. According to the **theory of metaphor**, cultural reality is expressed in a language's metaphors. "Try to imagine a culture where arguments are not viewed in terms of war, where no one wins or loses, where

THUMBNAIL THEORY

Theory of Metaphor

Cultural reality is expressed in a language's *metaphors*, unstated comparisons between things or events sharing a common feature. Our conceptual systems (the way we view the world) are central to defining our everyday realities, and they are largely metaphorical. The ways we think, what we experience, and what we do every day are thus shaped by metaphors. Metaphors not only highlight similarities between things or events, they mask differences.

Do you see argument as war or dance?

there is no sense of attacking or defending, gaining or losing ground," they continue. "Imagine a culture where an argument is viewed as a dance, the participants are seen as performers, and the goal is to perform in a balanced and aesthetically pleasing way" (1980, p. 4). Think how differently we would behave, how much better we would get along with others, if we approached conflict or disagreement as *dance* rather than *war*. You can read about another use of the *war* metaphor in the box "*War! What Is It Good For?*"

The Ladder of Abstraction

abstract language
Language signifying concepts, qualities, or ideas.

Our meaning-making ability is also enriched, but also possibly hampered, by our ability to use **abstract language**, language signifying concepts, qualities, or ideas. Imagine you want to tell your friends about the wealthy farming family you met while on vacation. How wealthy were they? They had 17,541 cows. That's a precise, or concrete, answer, but it really doesn't tell your friends much unless they are well versed in the value of cows. So, how rich were they? They were fabulously wealthy. *Fabulously wealthy* is an abstract answer; it says nothing about how or why they are wealthy. They could be wealthy corn farmers, or they could be wealthy in land but not in money, or they could be wealthy in life, loving one another and content in their home. Which was the better answer? It depends on the meaning you wanted to make.

Linguist S. I. Hayakawa (1978) developed the **ladder of abstraction** to explain how we use various levels of abstraction to make different types of meaning, and, yes, he did so using cows (see Figure 3.1).

From the bottom of the ladder moving up, language becomes more abstract. It also becomes richer in connotation and more open to interpretation

THUMBNAIL THEORY

The Ladder of Abstraction

A visual representation of using various levels of abstraction to make different types of meaning. Moving from the bottom up on the ladder, language becomes more abstract. As it does so, it becomes richer in connotation and more open to interpretation.

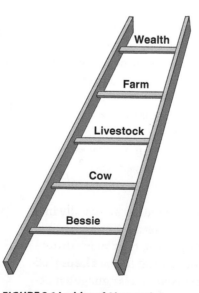

Most abstract

Wealth is extremely abstract; Bessie (and the farm) have disappeared.

A farm can be many things and may or may not include cows as assets.

If I call Bessie "livestock," I am referring to those aspects of her "cowness" that she shares with sheep, goats, etc.

If I call Bessie a "cow," I am referring to characteristics associated with all female bovines, not Bessie specifically.

That cow is ol' Bessie; the name stands for a very specific cow.

Most concrete

FIGURE 3.1 Ladder of Abstraction

War! What Is It Good For?

In a classic antiwar song from the late 1960s, the singer Edwin Starr asks, "War! What Is It good for?" The answer comes back strong: "Absolutely nothing!" But *war* as a metaphor is very useful for mobilizing.

Metaphors are valuable linguistic tools, and these implied comparisons can create deep layers of meaning. *War* means that the stakes couldn't be higher. When the United States commits itself to meeting a major challenge, it metaphorically "goes to war"—the War on Poverty, the War on Terror, the War on Drugs. The similarities are intentional: a massive, cooperative effort to defeat an enemy bent on harming the nation; no sacrifice is too big, no individual effort too small. Defeat means ruin; victory means greatness. But metaphor not only highlights similarities, it masks differences, and those differences may often be more meaningful.

In an actual war, the goal is to defeat the enemy. But who is the enemy in the War on Drugs, for example? Since the War on Drugs was declared, it has cost the United States $1 trillion, with another $51 billion added to the total every year. And yet addiction rates haven't changed, death by overdose is at an all-time high, and illegal drugs are less expensive than they've ever been. As the "war" has ground on, there have been 45 million drug-related arrests, and the United States now has the highest incarceration rate in the world, with more than 2.3 million people behind bars (Branson, 2014).

How might the situation differ if, instead of confronting America's drug problem as *war*, we considered drug abuse as *illness*, as we do alcohol abuse? President Barack Obama explained, "What we have done is instead of focusing on treatment—the same way we focused, say, with tobacco or drunk driving or other problems where we treat it as a public health problem—we've treated [drugs] exclusively as a criminal problem. I think that it's been counterproductive" (in Newman, 2015). In other words, we do not arrest alcohol abusers; we help them get treatment. Critics of the War on Drugs contend that we are locking up millions of Americans because in a war there must be an enemy, so drug users will have to do.

How can we responsibly use metaphors in shaping public opinion and policy? Is it a fair trade-off to mobilize the country toward a worthwhile goal while using imprecise, if not harmful, metaphors? Would drug abusers be more likely to seek treatment if they were understood as sick rather than as the enemy?

Who is the enemy in the *war* on drugs? What if we approached the country's drug problem as a matter of health rather than combat?

and, as a result, more likely to be misinterpreted. But what do you want to do with your words? Do you want to convey a definite physical reality? "Tom is sad" is abstract. "Tom cried uncontrollably, tears drenching his cheeks" is concrete. You'd choose the latter sentence because it makes much clearer what you want to communicate. Do you want to deceive? "My plan grants us more freedom" is abstract. "My plan grants us more freedom to deny membership in our country club to people of a different religion than ours" is concrete. You'd go with the former option because it obscures the true details of your plan. Do you want to inspire? "These new office procedures will free us to work more efficiently, more cooperatively, and more profitably" is abstract. "These new office procedures will increase our profits 1.7 percent" is concrete. Research tells us that in this instance we might want to use the abstract option, because successful charismatic leaders use "dynamic speaking skills" to motivate, make meaning, and define reality for their subordinates. They use language to "garner strong personal attraction from followers . . . articulate a compelling and evocative vision . . . and transform nature of work by making it appear more heroic, morally sound, and meaningful" (Dongil and Sosik, 2006, p. 12). *Heroic*, *morally sound*, and *meaningful* are pretty abstract.

The Functions of Language

Language is an essential part of being human; it is integral to how we behave. It is our primary means of interaction with one another. Like all communication, language is dynamic and transactional. Through talking with others we learn who they are; from how they respond to us we learn about ourselves; and from how we talk and react to one another we create, re-create, and define our relationships with them. Take this common exchange with a professor as an example. When your instructor returns your mid-semester exam, you make the proper response, "Thank you." But what have you really done? Sure, you've expressed gratitude. But you've also told her that you are a competent person because you know—and know how to use—the appropriate classroom interactional rules. You may also have increased her respect and liking for you because your warmth and courtesy stand in stark contrast to the shrugs, mumbles, and snarls she usually gets when returning tests. Language, then, serves several functions, sometimes obvious, sometimes less so, sometimes in isolation, sometimes simultaneously. Knowing the functions of language can make you a better communicator.

- Language serves an **instrumental function**. It helps you get what you want or need. Your parents certainly understand this. When asked to identify the skills that are "most important for children to get ahead in the world today," overwhelmingly—90%—responded "communication" (Goo, 2015). You, too, recognize the importance of language's instrumental function in your everyday life. For example, when you want a slice of pepperoni pizza and a root beer for lunch, you tell the server that's what you want. Your verbal order is instrumental in getting the correct meal to your table. You can read about the instrumental value of good verbal communication skills at work in the box "Speaking Well to Do Well."

- We also make use of language's **regulatory function**, to control the action of others. Comedienne Lily Tomlin explained, "We developed language because of our deep inner need to complain" (in Marche, 2012). But that's only one way we use language to control, or regulate, the behavior of others. When you want your roommates to turn off the television

instrumental function
Using language to get what is wanted or needed.

regulatory function Using language to control the behavior of others.

COMMUNICATION IN THE WORKPLACE

Speaking Well to Do Well

As business leadership coach Pramila Mathew explains, verbal skills are

the foundation upon which all deals are based. Whether it is horizontal, vertical, or lateral communication, evidence suggests that good disposure, listening, comprehension, and body language strengthen relationships and result in a healthy working climate. There exist strong group dynamics in organizations wherein the employees have open discussions and are open to feedback. (2012)

She counsels "speaking to be understood," specifically recommending the following:

1. Always be conscious of the words you speak. When possible, think for a moment before you convey your thoughts.
2. Occasionally ask for verbal acknowledgements of your words to make sure your listener has understood your point of view.

Good workplace verbal communicators, she advises, in addition to always being truthful, follow the ABCs:

Accuracy—Provide complete instructions or messages while you speak.
Brevity—Remember to KISS the message; in other words, Keep It Short and Simple.
Clarity—Work to ensure that your words are clutter-free and directional.

Another workplace trainer, Christy Eichelberger, provides seven specific rules for on-the-job talk (2010):

1. Enunciate; speak clearly.
2. Add to, but don't dominate, the conversation. Let everyone share their ideas and opinions.
3. Don't speak too quickly.
4. Always make eye contact with listeners and speakers, showing that you are interested in them and what they have to say.
5. Wait until speakers have finished what they are saying before taking your turn to talk; don't interrupt.
6. Speak calmly even when upset.
7. If you are having an informal conversation, have it in a location where it won't interfere with the work of others.

Her overall advice on good workplace verbal communication recognizes not only the instrumental function of language, but its informational and relational value as well. She writes,

The most important thing is to remain professional. Respect your coworkers and listen to their thoughts and ideas. Give everyone a chance to speak and don't take part in workplace gossip. And use [these] tips to make sure that you are successful in communicating your own thoughts and ideas and in clarifying any issues that could keep you from performing your job to the best of your ability. Being a good listener and getting your thoughts and ideas across honestly and effectively, in the best way you are able, will make you a good communicator. (2010)

so you can study, you ask them to do so. These first two functions of language are fundamental, so much so, that every one of us, beginning in kindergarten or even earlier, has been told to "use your words."

- Language has an **informative function**. We use talk to provide information for ourselves and others. We tell stories, for example, "On my summer vacation I worked at the beach and. . . ." And we ask questions, for example, "What did you do on your summer vacation?" The detail and richness of our stories—their informativeness—come in the form of language. So do the answers to our questions.

informative function Using language to provide and get information.

persuasive function Using language to change the attitudes or thinking of those around us.

lying Delivering information believed to be untrue with the intention to deceive.

• Language serves a **persuasive function**; we use it to change the attitudes, points of view, or thinking of those around us. We debate, we challenge, we cajole—and we lie. **Lying** is delivering information with the intention to deceive while believing it to be untrue, and as such it has three components: (1) the speaker offers information; (2) the speaker believes the information is not true; (3) the speaker intends to deceive or mislead. Imagine that your friends want to go to the movies but you want to go bowling. You can't physically force them to take your position, so you try to talk them into it. How far can you ethically stretch the truth when trying to persuade them? (The box "Lying" explores such questions.)

ETHICAL COMMUNICATION

Lying

Of the many things humans do that are "wrong," lying is the most common. In fact, it's an unavoidable fact of everyday life. We lie to spare our friends' feelings. We lie to escape a parking ticket. We lie to move a conversation or story along. No problem, right? After all, these are only little lies. But what about these situations, offered by ethicist Sissela Bok?

> Should physicians lie to dying patients so as to delay the fear and anxiety which the truth might bring them? Should professors exaggerate the excellence of their students on recommendations in order to give them a better chance in a tight job market? Should parents conceal from children the fact that they were adopted? (1999, p. xxviii)

So maybe these aren't exactly *little* lies, but they are *good* lies, right?

They are, if you believe that lying is permissible when there's a good reason to lie. But what's a good reason? Maybe there never is one, as the philosopher Immanuel Kant wrote in his *Metaphysics of Morals*. "The dishonor that accompanies a lie also accompanies a liar like his shadow," he argued, because "by a lie a man [*sic*] throws away and, as it were, annihilates his dignity as a man" (1797/1991, p. 225). Ethicist Tim Mazur expands on this absolutist position on lying: "People often poorly estimate the consequences of their actions or specifically undervalue or ignore the harmful consequences to society." It is impossible, he continues, "for anyone, even honorable persons, to know that a lie will bring more good than the truth; the consequences of actions are too often unpredictable" (1993).

And yet we lie and are lied to constantly. Research demonstrates "that in a given day we may be lied to anywhere from 10 to 200 times," writes professional deception detector Pamela Meyer. "In one study, strangers lied to each other three times within the first ten minutes of meeting each other. What makes this study interesting is not the volume of lies told—it's that before seeing the video of themselves lying, participants overwhelmingly reported that they had been truthful. That we underreport the number of lies we tell suggests that lying is so common, so reflexive, that we are literally unaware of the steady stream of falsehoods we utter" (2012).

How comfortable are you with Ms. Meyer's claim that you are a reflexive liar, unaware of the stream of falsehoods you utter? Maybe you're just a sensitive and competent user of the language. What do you think?

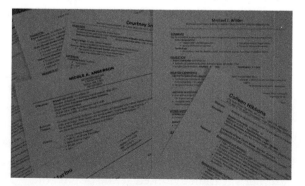

One-third of all professional resumes contain false information (Meyer, 2012).

- Language connects us to others. This is its **relational function**. We use language to establish, define, and maintain relationships. We use **small talk**, scripted and superficial conversations based on social convention, when first establishing relationships. Of course, small talk is really big talk, because it tells both you and your listener if you want to keep the relationship going after that early encounter. You can learn how to get better at small talk by reading Table 3.1, "11 Big Rules for Improving Your Small Talk."

We use language to define relationships. Are you seeing each other? Hanging out? Dating? Just dating? Hooking up? Going steady? Pinned? Engaged? Sorta engaged? When you and a friend *go out for lunch*, it's likely you each pay for your own meal. But when that lunch is during a *date*, a different set of rules and expectations is in play. We use language to maintain relationships. The things you talk about, the things that make you laugh, and the secrets you reveal keep the relationship alive.

relational function Using language to establish, define, and maintain relationships.

small talk Scripted and superficial conversations based on social convention.

Table 3.1 11 Big Rules for Improving Your Small Talk

Making a good first impression using small talk is a skill, and like all skills it can be acquired, practiced, and mastered. Here are 11 big rules for improving your small talk.

1.	*Pre-plan.* You know when you're going to be in a situation where you'll meet new people. Come up with two or three questions that might logically fit what you're doing and where you are. First day of class, fraternity or sorority rush, try-outs for a team, on-campus job fair—each brings with it at least a hundred possible small-talk possibilities. Find the ones you know you can build on when you are engaged in conversation.
2.	*Say "hello" first, smile, offer a handshake, and identify yourself.* "Hi, I'm Olga Sullivan." It's that simple.
3.	*Pay close attention to the return identification.* In other words, make sure you note and remember the name of the person you've just greeted. Then use that name.
4.	*Get the other person talking.* This is where your pre-planned questions or comments are most valuable. Make them open-ended and pertinent to the situation or location—"What do you know about this teacher?" "How's rush been going for you?" "What other sports have you tried out for?" "How many job fairs have you been to this year?"
5.	*Be nonverbally immediate.* Use eye contact and nonverbal cues to show your interest in your conversational partner. Don't look around the room when you're talking or being spoken to. Be conscious of your body language. If you appear uncomfortable, your listener will be, too.
6.	*Draw the other out.* In other words, giving feedback shows interest.
7.	*Listen more, talk less.* People who get to talk more tend to evaluate those conversations more positively (Bostrom, 1970). So let others do more of the talking, and listen to what they say.
8.	*Have something interesting to say.* You're going to have to talk, so be ready. Pay attention to current events—"What's your take on . . . ?" But be sure to avoid controversial or negative news events.
9.	*Don't be a downer.* Keep it light; accentuate the positive.
10.	*Plan your entry.* If you enter an ongoing conversation, just listen for a minute. This lets you gauge the tone of the conversation (for example, fun, professional, flirty, serious) and assess others' attitudes (you don't want to get into a dispute with someone you're just meeting). You can plan your opening comments before you become a participant.
11.	*Plan your exit.* "Always leave 'em wantin' more" works as well in small talk as it does in show business. Remember, this is an audition. You are being judged on what you say and how you say it. So pre-plan your exit line. "This has been great, but I have an 8 o'clock tomorrow." Be gracious—"It was great chatting with you." Set the stage for the next interaction—"Maybe I'll see you tomorrow in class/during rush/when the games finally start/at next month's job fair."

ritualistic function Using language to meet an important social convention or expectation.

- Language serves a **ritualistic function** when we use it to meet an important social convention or expectation. We pray or chant aloud in church, mosque, or synagogue. In some religious settings we testify. We sing *Take Me Out to the Ballgame* during the seventh-inning stretch. We salute our friends with wedding toasts and remember them in eulogies.

imaginative function Using language to bring pleasure.

- Language can bring pleasure and delight to both speaker and listener. This is its **imaginative function**. We sing songs to ourselves and for our loved ones. We whisper sweet verse to our sweethearts. We play word games and make puns with our friends in what linguist Gail Jefferson calls "the poetics of ordinary talk" (1996, p. 29). She offers this example:

Alice:	*"The speakers cost $20."*
Betty:	*"Each!"*
Alice:	*"Eatcher heart out!"*

  We're sure you can do better.

expressive function Using language to state personal feelings, thoughts, and attitudes.

- Language serves an **expressive function** when we use it to state personal feelings, thoughts, and attitudes. When your roommates refuse to turn off the television, you tell them how selfish you think they are. When your friends accept your plea to go bowling rather than to the movies, you serenade them with a few lines from the song "You Make Me So Very Happy." When your "date" tells you you're paying for your own meal, you give him or her a piece of your mind.

Language and Meaning Making

Ultimately, the function of language is to make meaning. In this section we will detail how meaning making is influenced by situational, social, and cultural factors; syntactic ambiguity; and euphemistic language. Our use of language is natural, routine, and seemingly effortless, but as we all know, the match between the meaning we intend and the meaning we ultimately make is not always precise. Rare are individuals who have never had to defend themselves with "I was only joking!" or "That's not what I meant!" or "How can you think I'd say something like that?!" There are reasons that we and the people we are talking with sometimes fail to make our intended meaning. So as we discuss how we use language to make meaning, we will also look at possible meaning-making problems.

Situational, Social, and Cultural Meaning

situational meaning Meaning made through specific forms of language that occur or are excluded in various contexts.

We make **situational meaning** through the forms of language that we include or exclude in various contexts. A joke in the classroom means something different than the same joke told at a funeral. The curse you aim at a friend during a pick-up basketball game means something much different when directed at the clerk at the dry cleaners. The more formal the situation, the more clearly we pronounce our words, the more likely we are to avoid slang, and the more likely we are to construct more elaborate sentences and phrases. It's not too difficult to see the importance of proper situational meaning making to identity: our listeners naturally make judgments about us based on the appropriateness or inappropriateness of our language use in specific situations.

Language has **social meaning** as well. This is the meaning made by our choice of word and sound alternatives when speaking with a specific group of people. For example, listeners will react quite differently to a high-level bank executive's use of sloppy grammar than they will to the same grammatical deficiency in the clerk at the dry cleaners. Bilingual speakers may choose to speak one language on some occasions and another on other occasions, depending on the location and formality of the conversational setting, how well they know the people they're talking with, and how serious the topics under discussion might be (Rubin, 1985). People in specific occupations use jargon at work but not at home. Again, the link between using socially appropriate and effective language and identity formation and maintenance is clear.

> **social meaning** Meaning made by our choice of word and sound alternatives when speaking with a specific group of people.

And inasmuch as the meaning of all symbols, including the words and sounds that make up a language, are culturally negotiated, language has **cultural meaning** as well. "The vocabulary of a language is not merely an inventory of arbitrary labels referring to objects, entities, or events," writes linguist Nancy Bonvillain, "Words also convey many kinds of cultural meanings that add to, transform, or manipulate basic senses of words" (2014, p. 58). For example, what would listeners' likely reaction be to a man who referred to his spouse as *the wife* ("I left *the wife* at home") or *the little lady* ("I'd like to introduce you to *the little lady*")? Although *the*, *wife*, *little*, and *lady* are common and seemingly innocuous words, most listeners would reject these word choices and combinations as culturally antiquated and insulting. Over the last few decades, the culture has transformed the meaning of the words this man has chosen to refer to his spouse.

> **cultural meaning** Meaning based in shared experience.

The mere *existence* of specific words also produces cultural meaning. As evidence, take the English you're using right now. English speakers note the age and sex of culturally important animals and ignore these distinctions when talking about other animals. The way we talk about horses suggests that they occupy a culturally important role. We think of them as beautiful; we groom and care for them; they are integral to several sporting activities; there are even famous literary and real horses, Flicka, Black Beauty, Silver, Shadowfax and Bill the Pony from *The Lord of the Rings*, Secretariat, and Seabiscuit, to name a few. One way in which English speakers signify horses' cultural importance, then, is through words that differentiate their sex (*mare, stallion, gelding*) age (*foal, nag*), or age and sex together (*filly, colt*). Why don't we use parallel words for squirrels?

The English language differentiates horses by gender and age. Why doesn't it do that for squirrels?

cultural presupposition
The assumption that those who share a culture share knowledge of a word's meaning.

Language makes cultural meaning in another way as well; it helps us make meaning of others and helps others make meaning of us. This is the concept of **cultural presupposition**—speakers assume that those who share their culture share their knowledge of a word's meaning (they presuppose familiarity), and as a result make judgments of those others based on their appropriate and inappropriate use of those words. Remember our boorish husband married to *the little lady*? No contemporary male should ever refer to his female partner that way; otherwise his listeners probably would not think very much of him. And people into horse racing and polo are practically required to use *filly* and *colt*, not *young female horse* and *young male horse*. And if you tell your friend that your brother plays linebacker on the school football team and he asks, "Offensive or defensive linebacker?" you can be fairly sure he is not the gridiron fan he claims to be.

Syntactic Ambiguity

Among the wonders of language are its richness and flexibility. We can say the same thing in different ways to produce the same meaning. "We'll be together forever" and "You and I, a couple 'til the end of time" have the same meaning. We can also say the same thing with slight variation to produce different shades of meaning. Recall "Pat and I are friendly" versus "Pat and I are friends" versus "Pat is my friend." These sentences are almost the same, but each has a different meaning. Ours is a grammatically, syntactically, and vocabulary-rich language. But that richness can lead to ambiguity.

Grammar, as we've seen, consists of the rules for the proper construction of phrases and sentences. But if you know the rules, you can break them to make meaning. "Ain't no way I'm pullin' an all-nighter before the exam." The grammatically horrible *ain't* and double negative don't get in the way of the meaning you hope to convey to your roommates. In fact, not only are you saying, "I'm going to bed at a reasonable time tonight," but your grammatical errors add emphasis. We sometimes call this type of construction *speaking in the vernacular,* and in this case, because your roommates share your social and cultural meaning, they'll understand.

As for vocabulary, estimates of the number of words in the English language range from 500,000 to just under a million. But no one knows for sure; for example, if you simply counted aloud from 0 to 999,999 you'd already be at one million words (Sheidlower, 2006). Then, if you add only the names of the earth's 600,000 varieties of fungus, a few words from the dictionary that have no vowel—*nth, shh, psst,* and *TV*—and for good measure *linoleum,* you'd have 1,600,005. And even though a new word is coined every 98 minutes, the typical English speaker, depending on education, knows only about 35,000 to 50,000 of the language's uncountable options and regularly uses only about a third of those (Gall, 2009). Of course, we do make vocabulary errors, either when we misuse a word, for example *aggravate* (to make worse) instead of *irritate* (to promote displeasure), or when we use a word unfamiliar to our listeners. But although they can sometimes be embarrassing, these mistakes don't often get in the way of successful meaning making, largely because we are making situational, social, and cultural meaning with our listeners; whether you use *aggravate* or *irritate*, they know what you mean. Also, speakers tend to match or converge their vocabularies; that is, they bring similar vocabularies to their conversation, further reducing the likelihood of misunderstanding.

Language is enriched by syntax as well. For example, depending on its placement and use in a sentence, *flying* can be a noun, a verb, or an adjective.

- Noun: *Flying* is fun.
- Verb: I am *flying* to Vegas tonight.
- Adjective: Watch out for *flying* debris.

But in this famous example from Noam Chomsky (1965, pp. 21–22), is *flying* an adjective or a verb?

> ### "Flying planes can be dangerous."

This sentence suffers from **syntactic ambiguity**. It can reasonably be interpreted in more than one way. Does it mean that the act of flying planes can be dangerous, or does it mean that the planes that are flying around you might hit you? Chomsky offered a simpler sentence that he argued was even more ambiguous than his flying example:

> ### "I had a book stolen."

Your friends might say, "That's horrible," because you told them, "I had a book stolen." But what if you meant you paid someone to steal a book for you, as in, "I had a book stolen"? They shouldn't feel too bad for you. Or maybe you were almost out of the store with a book under your jacket when your theft was discovered, as in, "I had a book stolen." Syntactically, the three sentences are identical, but in the first, someone stole a book from you; in the second, you arranged to have a book stolen from someone else; and in the third, you almost succeeded in stealing a book.

Naturally, we can minimize syntactic ambiguity by speaking less ambiguously, but that often stilts our language. "To fly planes can be dangerous" sounds awkward and silly. We can also add context, "I had a book stolen when I left it on the sofa in the student union." Adding context is the most obvious solution, but what if you don't want to because you just discovered the theft and the meaning you intend to convey is shock, as in "I HAD A BOOK STOLEN!"? This is the price we pay for the freedom and flexibility our language provides. But don't despair. As you'll read later in this text, we do not communicate by language alone. Contextual and nonverbal cues in the communication situation (Chapter 4) and active listening on our part and the part of our listeners (Chapter 5) greatly improve the quality of meaning making.

Euphemisms

Another way we use our language's flexibility to make meaning is through **euphemism**, the substitution of vague or less emotionally charged words for more direct options. It might be more precise, however, to say that we use

syntactic ambiguity When a sentence can reasonably be interpreted in more than one way.

euphemism The substitution of vague or less emotionally charged words for more direct options.

euphemism not so much to make meaning but to mask or soften meaning. We do this for a variety of reasons. We may hope to hide an unpleasant truth: I'm not overweight, I'm big-boned. We may want to drain our words of unpleasant emotion: My aunt didn't die, she went to a better place. We may wish to spare the feelings of another: Isn't my newborn beautiful? Yes, she's something!

Of course, the risk of miscommunication resides in the possibility that our euphemism may be our listener's literal meaning. Euphemism can also produce empty conversation, where nothing is really said and no real meaning is made. Nonetheless, most speakers easily master this art.

Language and Protecting Self-Identity: Politeness Theory

But why do we use euphemisms? Why don't we just speak directly, in a matter-of-fact way? Because we want to appear competent; we want to be liked. According to linguist Robin Lakoff, there are two language *rules of pragmatic competence:* first, be clear; and second, be polite. Ideally we try to meet both rules, but when they are in conflict, politeness prevails because it is "more important in a conversation to avoid offense than to achieve clarity . . . since in most informal conversations, actual communication of important ideas is secondary to reaffirming and strengthening relationships" (1973, pp. 297–298).

Although speakers of different languages may act according to these rules in different ways, this politeness is a universal cultural value. According to linguists Penelope Brown and Stephen Levinson's **politeness theory**, we use polite language to protect **face**, the "public self-image that every member [of a culture] wants to claim for [her or himself]" (1987, p. 161). All people have a basic need to feel appreciated and be protected—needs so thoroughly intertwined with identity that Brown and Levinson call them **face-wants**—and they specify two types. *Positive face-wants* are reflected in people's desire to be approved of and appreciated, and this leads to *positive politeness* in language. For example, speakers show concern, claim common ground, or convey cooperation, as in, "It's freezing. Are you as cold as I am? Why don't we share a cab?" *Negative face-wants* are reflected in people's desire to be unimpeded in their actions or free from intrusion, and this produces *negative politeness*, in which speakers express their reluctance to impose on hearers. Therefore, the request to share a cab might sound like this: "I don't mean to be a pain, and you'd probably prefer to be alone, but it's freezing. Would it be too big a bother if we shared a cab?"

We build these strategies into our everyday language to deal with the inevitable **face-threatening acts**, interactions, or requests that might threaten listeners' face-wants (1987, p. 60). Face-threatening acts are common and normal; after all, we interact with and rely on other people all the time. Yes, we could speak in what Brown and Levinson call *bald on-record language*—that is directly, with no concern for our listeners' face. Unless we're speaking to a close friend or family member, "Wanna share a cab?" is rude, not likely to

THUMBNAIL THEORY

Politeness Theory

People use polite language to protect *face*, the public image they try to claim. Everyone has *face-wants*. People may respond to *face-threatening* acts either directly (with little concern for listeners' face) or indirectly (off-record). We protect ourselves and others from loss of face through communication strategies called *facework*.

face The public image people try to claim.

face-wants The need to feel appreciated and be protected.

face-threatening acts Interactions or requests that might threaten listeners' face-wants.

succeed, and as a result, threatening to our own face. Or we could speak *off-record*—that is, we could be indirect, vague, or ambiguous. "It's freezing" is likely to be received simply as commentary on the weather, is not likely to succeed, and again as a result, is threatening to our own face. Of course, neither is likely to be as effective as speaking with positive or negative politeness.

It isn't too hard to hear echoes of Chapter 1's discussion of symbolic interaction and the Looking Glass Self in these ideas. Our face, that is, our self-identity, is reflected back to us in how well we protect the face of the people we are talking to. As a result, we protect ourselves from loss of face through **facework**, communication strategies designed to protect face, both ours and others. Facework is closely related to an individual's culture, as you'll see in Chapter 9, but for now you can read more about facework in the box "Speaking Inclusively."

> **facework** Communication strategies designed to protect our and others' face.

Speaking Inclusively

Sexist and racist language demeans you and your listeners. It seeps into conversation in many ways. One is the use of *markers,* adding gender- or race-specific adjectives to a description, as in *female doctor* and *male nurse.* Why designate a doctor as *female* unless there is something odd or "not usual" about a female physician? Unless we are willing to mark football player Peyton Manning as a white quarterback, there is no reason to mark Robert Griffin III as a black quarterback or Mark Sanchez as a Latino quarterback.

We are all now pretty comfortable with the use of gender-neutral pronouns and avoiding *man* when referring to all people and specific professions. "When a person runs, *he* needs good shoes" easily becomes "When a person runs, *he or she* needs good shoes," or even better, we use the plural, as in, "When *people* run, *they* need good shoes." *Mankind* readily becomes *humankind; fireman* becomes *firefighter;* and *chairman* becomes *chair.*

But more subtle is our routine selection of words that carry sexist or demeaning connotations. Why are women the *opposite* sex? Regardless of your gender, has a coach or teammate ever told you to *man up?* Why, when referring to different-sex couples, do we always put males first (*men and women, he or she, I now pronounce you husband and wife*)? Why don't men give up their family names when they get married? Why do we refer to wives by their husband's complete name (*Mrs. John Smith*) but

never the reverse (*Mr. Mary Smith*)? Why are couples referred to as *John Smith and his wife,* but never *Mary Smith and her husband?* Why do men *talk* but women *chat?* Men and women both *laugh* and *yell*, but only women *giggle* and *screech.* Why do the adjectives derived from these words all have negative connotations: *chatty, screechy, giggly?*

Inclusive language protects positive face. We all want to be approved of and appreciated. But it also protects negative face, because no one wants to be a problem or a burden. Language that suggests that others are somehow less worthy, or less powerful, challenges their self-identity. Failing to consider this challenges our self-identity as well.

Who is the doctor and who is the nurse?

Review of Learning Objectives

3.1 Explain the structure of language and the functions of its different components.

Language is composed of the systematic combining of words and sounds (syntax). The rules that describe the proper construction of phrases and sentences are grammar.

3.2 Describe the role of speech communities and speech networks in creating meaning.

Speech communities interact by means of speech and agree on the proper and improper use of language. Speech networks are composed of people who regularly interact and speak with one another, and as such share a specific common language.

3.3 Identify the relationship between language and thought.

Language's connotative meanings lead to different thoughts than do its denotative meanings. The Linguistic Relativity Hypothesis explains that people who speak different languages think about the world in different ways. Metaphor shapes thinking by highlighting unstated comparison between objects and concepts while masking differences. The ladder of abstraction graphically demonstrates how language can move from concrete to abstract depending on the speaker's intention.

3.4 Identify the functions of language.

Among language's several uses are its instrumental function (it helps us get what we want or need); its regulatory function (using language to control the behavior of others); its informative function (we use talk to provide information for ourselves and others); its persuasive function (we use it to change the attitudes of those around us); its relational function (language connects us to others); its ritualistic function (we use it to meet important social convention or expectations); its imaginative function (language brings pleasure and delight); and its expressive function (we use it to state personal feelings, thoughts, and attitudes).

3.5 Explain how we use language to make meaning.

Language has situational, social, and cultural meaning. Meaning making, however, can be hindered or advanced by syntactic ambiguity and euphemisms.

3.6 Effectively use language to protect self-identity.

Speakers want to appear competent and likable, so they use language to protect face, theirs and listeners'. Positive face-wants are reflected in the desire to be approved of and appreciated. Negative face-wants are reflected in the desire to be free from intrusion. When identity is potentially challenged by face-threatening acts, speakers employ various forms of facework for protection.

Key Terms

language 50
syntax 50
grammar 51
speech community 51
speech network 52
denotative meaning 52
connotative meaning 52
Linguistic Relativity Hypothesis 53
metaphor 54
theory of metaphor 55
abstract language 56
ladder of abstraction 56
instrumental function (of language) 58
regulatory function (of language) 58
informative function (of language) 59
persuasive function (of language) 60
lying 60
relational function (of language) 61
small talk 61
ritualistic function (of language) 62
imaginative function (of language) 62
expressive function (of language) 62
situational meaning 62
social meaning 63
cultural meaning 63
cultural presupposition 64
syntactic ambiguity 65
euphemism 65
politeness theory 66
face 66
face-wants 66
face-threatening acts 66
facework 67

Questions for Review

1. What are language, syntax, and grammar?

2. Differentiate between speech communities and speech networks.

3. Differentiate between connotative and denotative meaning.

4. What is the Linguistic Relativity Hypothesis? What does it say about the link between language and thought?

5. What is metaphor? What is its role in meaning making?

6. What is the ladder of abstraction? What does it suggest about the use of concrete and abstract language?

7. What are the eight functions of language?

8. Differentiate between situational, social, and cultural meaning.

9. What are syntactic ambiguity and euphemisms? How do they affect meaning making?

10. What are the elements of politeness theory, and how do they operate in the use of language to protect identity?

Questions for Discussion

1. Do you approach arguments as *war*? Do you typically win? As in any war, even the winners suffer some loss. What do you think you lose in the process of winning your argument/war? How might your answers to these questions differ if you thought of argument as *dance?*

2. Identify one of your important speech networks. Do you and the people who share it with you have your own specific, common language? Can you list five or ten words from your common vocabulary and explain what they mean and how they came into being? How do they reflect the cultural values of your group?

3. Do you agree that speakers want to appear competent and to be liked? If not, why not? If you do, can you imagine times when being liked and appearing competent are at odds? How might this affect the use of language, especially in shaping face-wants?

Nonverbal Communication

It is Thanksgiving break and you finally have a few days off—time away from the madness of papers, exams, and presentations. This will be an especially good holiday because you'll be spending it in the country with your relatives.

When you reach your grandparents' small town, you feel an overwhelming sense of comfort. People you know are smiling and waving as they notice you drive by. As you pull up to the house, you see the big brown and orange papier mâché turkey hanging on the front door. Your grandparents have had it since you were five. As you walk into the house, you smell the stuffed turkey roasting in the oven, the apple pie cooling on the window sill, and the crackling fire in the living room. The same family pictures from forever ago line the walls and shelves, and you think, *I'm finally home.* Grandpa hears the door and is the first to greet you with his famous bear hug. He's sporting the fishing shirt you gave him for his birthday. You feel proud as you remember finding that perfect gift for him that year. All of a sudden, Grandma, wearing her apron and smiling with excitement, comes hurrying down the hall. Later in the day, you sit down to a delectable meal, preceded by a silent moment of thanks.

This scenario may sound simple. But a closer examination reveals that the communication that occurs throughout is actually quite complex. All kinds of meaning have been made through nonverbal communication, or communication without words. People in town express that they are happy to see you through their hand gestures and facial expressions. Your family's value of honoring tradition is evident in the turkey decoration on the door. Grandpa's hug tells you he loves you a lot, and Grandma's greeting and cooking are also expressions of love and caring. The silence of the dinner prayer relays gratitude and perhaps deep-rooted spirituality. So much is said without saying a word. In this chapter, we look at all the ways in which we make meaning without speaking.

Learning Objectives

4.1   Define nonverbal communication, identifying examples.

4.2   Compare and contrast verbal and nonverbal communication.

4.3   Describe the operation of nonverbal communication and coding systems.

4.4   Describe several types of nonverbal coding systems.

4.5   Explain the role of nonverbal communication in creating meaning and identity.

What Is Nonverbal Communication?

nonverbal communication
The process of relaying messages and meanings without the use of words.

Nonverbal communication occurs when we relay messages and create meaning without the use of spoken words. Estimates vary on how much we use nonverbal communication, though you may have heard the statistic that 93 percent of communication is nonverbal. This estimate comes from the groundbreaking work of Albert Mehrabian, whose research also indicated that 38 percent of communicated meaning comes from tone of voice and another 55 percent from facial expressions (1971). Not everyone agrees with Mehrabian's precise proportions, but no one disputes his central point: *most* of our communication is nonverbal. Remember in Chapter 1 when we discussed the fact that it is impossible to *not* communicate? This is largely because of nonverbal communication. When you're in class and falling asleep in the back row, your nodding off communicates something to your professor. Sleeping in class may mean that you're bored, tired, sick, or simply didn't sleep well the previous night. But one thing is sure—you're not listening, and that message is clear. Even when you think you're not saying anything, you are actually expressing quite a bit. From hairstyles to clothing, to gestures, to home décor, nonverbal communication is constant and complex. It is important to remember that "the ability to understand and use nonverbal communication . . . is a powerful tool that helps you connect with others, express what you really mean, navigate challenging situations, and build better relationships" (Segal, Smith, and Jaffe, 2012).

The differences and similarities between verbal and nonverbal communication might seem obvious, but in actuality they entail a number of characteristics we don't often consider. The most obvious difference, as we've already pointed out, is that verbal communication involves saying words, and nonverbal communication does not. Table 4.1 summarizes the comparison. Many other distinctions revolve around important components such as culture, senses, symbolism, and intentionality.

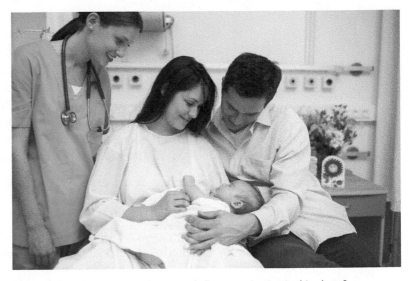

What can you conclude from the nonverbal communication in this photo?

Similarities to Verbal Communication

Looking first at similarities, both verbal and nonverbal forms of communication are *influenced by rules*. In the case of verbal communication, factors such as grammar, syntax, formal and informal language, and conventional greetings shape what we say and how we say it. Similarly, how close we stand to people when we talk with them, the style of clothing we wear, and whether we shake a person's hand are all examples of cultural rules we follow when communicating nonverbally.

Another similarity between verbal and nonverbal communication is that both are *symbolic*. Both are composed of arbitrary symbols to which we give meaning, and we, in turn, behave according to those meanings. For example, who says ♥ or <3 symbolizes love, and what's the point of saying "I love you" to someone? We give meanings to these symbols, and they evoke emotion and action in all of us.

Table 4.1 Comparing Verbal and Nonverbal Communication

	VERBAL COMMUNICATION	NONVERBAL COMMUNICATION
Similarities	Guided by rules, conventions Symbolic Influenced by culture Intentional or unintentional	
Differences	Less honest	More honest
	Involves seeing and hearing	Uses all senses
	Begins and ends	Flows continuously

Since we decide as a society on shared interpretations of these symbols, *cultural influence* is another commonality between verbal and nonverbal communication. What we do and do not verbalize are dictated in large part by the culture in which the communication occurs. American English speakers might get to a task "right away," whereas British English speakers would get to theirs "straight away." As for nonverbal communication, how and when we dress a certain way, how much eye contact we make when we talk, and what foods we eat and when we eat them are also indicative of cultural influence on communication. As intercultural communication scholar Sheila Ramsey explains:

> According to culturally prescribed codes, we use eye movement and contact to manage conversations and to regulate interactions; we follow rigid rules governing intra- and interpersonal touch, our bodies synchronously join in rhythm of others in a group, and gestures modulate our speech. We must internalize all of this in order to become and remain fully functioning and socially appropriate members of any culture. (1979, p. 111)

intentionality Whether what we communicate verbally and nonverbally is intended.

The final similarity has to do with **intentionality**, or whether what we communicate is intended; in both verbal and nonverbal communication, we communicate much that we do not intend. For one thing, we make mistakes. We may have a specific meaning or outcome in mind, but that outcome or meaning may not necessarily follow. Verbally, we may want to sound smart by using a few big words in conversation with friends, but using them incorrectly may make us sound not so smart. Nonverbally, we may want to dress in our best outfit to impress our date's parents, but all they see is someone trying just a little too hard.

Even when we have *no intention* of communicating a specific meaning—verbally or nonverbally—we may do so. Remember last chapter's discussion of sexist and racist language. Your intention might be to offer greater detail in a story about a "lady doctor," but the unintended result might be offending your listener and losing face. As for nonverbal communication, even unintended messages say something about what we are thinking. Consider a first date. You certainly do not want your date (someone you like very much) to think you are nervous. But as you sit across the dinner table, uncomfortably pausing between sentences and beginning to sweat, it becomes clear that you are. And no matter what you say (or don't say), your date is able to detect your discomfort.

Differences from Verbal Communication

The differences between verbal and nonverbal communication are just as significant. Take our dating example above; it perfectly illustrates the first difference—nonverbal communication is more honest. While you may tell your date that you are "OK," your body language offers a much more honest perspective.

How do these people simultaneously know when to clap?

A second distinction has to do with the five senses. Verbal communication involves hearing and seeing, whereas nonverbal involves all five senses—taste, touch, smell, hearing, and seeing. Of course you *see* facial expressions, and you *hear* the silence when you ask your date if you can go out again. Consider, too, the *smells* of Thanksgiving dinner that convey traditions, caring, and devotion, and the *touch* of a hug that communicates love or concern. *Tastes* and textures of food identify specific cultures and even geography; think of the cinnamon, nutmeg, and cumin in a Moroccan salad, for example.

A final difference between nonverbal and verbal communication is that nonverbal communication never stops; it continues to flow, while verbal communication begins and ends. In other words, we all stop talking at some point, but our demeanors, accessories, facial expressions, and other nonverbal indicators continue to carry meaning long after our conversations have ceased.

What do these comfort foods communicate to you?

Theory of Nonverbal Coding Systems

Our understanding of the operation of nonverbal communication is the product of research on nonverbal coding systems. One prominent example is communication scholar Judee Burgoon's work on **nonverbal coding systems** (1994), which sees nonverbal coding systems as groups or clusters of behaviors that convey meaning, for example body movements, gesticulations, and facial expressions. These clusters, or systems, share several properties:

- They are *analogic* rather than *digital*. That is, they are continuous, rather than discrete like numbers, and flow along a range or continuum. We can't classify smiles, for example, into discrete categories. Smiles, like voice volume, have gradations.

- They can be *iconic;* that is, they objectively represent the thing being represented. The symbol for "OK," for example, is the touching of the thumb and forefinger into the shape of an "O." And have you ever used your hands to outline the shape of something as you were trying to explain what you were looking for?

- Many, but not all, possess *universal meaning*. Some universally understood codes are automatic: laughing, crying, and smiling, for example. Some are less so, for example a clenched fist showing anger.

- They permit the *simultaneous transmission* of many messages. Your joy can be seen in your wide eyes, broad smile, nervous hopping, and loud

THUMBNAIL THEORY

Theory of Nonverbal Coding Systems

Nonverbal coding systems are groups or clusters of behaviors that convey meaning. These systems share several properties: They are *analogic* rather than *digital*. They can be *iconic*. Many, but not all, possess *universal meaning*. They permit the *simultaneous transmission* of many messages. They can generate or evoke an *automatic response*. And they are often *spontaneous*.

voice. In this case, your different nonverbal expressions all reinforce a single meaning. But as we saw above in our discussion of nonverbal communication's honesty, they can send different or conflicting meanings—your smile and attentive eyes say you're happy to be on the date, but your sweaty forehead and cracking voice say you're terrified to be on the date.

- They can generate or evoke an *automatic response*. What do you do when someone offers her or his hand? What do you do when someone smiles at you?

- They are often *spontaneous*. Are you a pacer? Do you twirl your hair or shift from foot to foot when nervous?

We use nonverbal coding systems to frame the verbal messages we deliver to others. **Framing** is how we structure a message by using nonverbal communication to repeat, complement, contradict, substitute for, and regulate what we say.

framing Structuring the meaning of verbal communication through the use of nonverbal cues.

Nonverbal codes can *repeat* verbal communication or vice versa. A child asks for a cookie and mom first nods her head, and then says "Yes." Her answer is the same—relayed first through nonverbal and then verbal communication. Nonverbal codes can also *complement* verbal communication. When a student goes home for the weekend and a younger sibling says, "I'm so glad you came home" while flashing a wide smile, the message is clearly being complemented through emphasis. A message can also be *contradicted*. When we ask a seemingly stressed-out friend, "What's wrong?" and she replies, "Nothing!" with an angry tone, she is verbalizing one thing, but her inflection expresses the opposite. Nonverbal codes can also *substitute for* verbal communication; for example, when we don't want to dignify someone's ridiculous question with a response, we simply roll our eyes. The last function of nonverbal coding systems is that it can *regulate* verbal communication. Such is the case when a public speaker pauses between comments or transitions, indicating to the audience that it can clap or briefly ponder the point. We all use eye contact and slight turns of our head to tell our conversational partners that it is their turn to speak.

Types of Nonverbal Coding Systems

Below we look at 11 types of nonverbal coding systems. You probably think about some of these quite often, while others might surprise you.

Proxemics

proxemics Our use of space and distance to make meaning.

Proxemics has to do with our use of *space and distance* to make meaning. Our perceptions of interpersonal space, while obviously related to our physical senses, are shaped and patterned by our cultures (Hall, 1966). Your decision of where to sit in the classroom or how close to stand to an acquaintance both have to do with proximity and what you want to communicate in making that choice. For example, you may sit in the front row to communicate that you are a diligent student. Part of your decision may have to do with **territory**, the space you consider as yours. Your territory can be either temporary or permanent.

territory The space people consider theirs.

You may routinely sit in the same seat for each class because you see it as *your* place in the room and, in turn, feel invaded when someone else sits there. You may also throw your sweater over a seat at the movies to keep others from sitting next to you.

When we think about the use of space in communication, there are four specific *distance zones* to consider: intimate distance, personal distance, social distance, and public distance. As people move from one zone to another, the degrees of intimacy change, which also determines the formality of the communication. And, depending on the culture, the interpretations of these zones and the appropriateness of language use can differ greatly. Nonetheless, in all cultures, when people communicate with one another, they use distance zones to identify the closeness and context of their relationships (Hall, 1966).

What distance zone is represented by these people?

In the United States, the range of **intimate space** is 0–18 inches and implies an extremely personal connection. The partners share total intimacy and use informal, quite personal language. Examples of intimate distance include a mother tending to her baby, two lovers talking and walking hand-in-hand in the park, or a father giving sensitive advice to his son. In each of these cases, being physically close is considered normal in American culture. But consider a different situation: think how you feel on a crowded bus, shoulder-to-shoulder with a stranger. It's usually pretty awkward; you would most definitely consider this an invasion of your intimate space. However, in India, where pushing and shoving are commonplace and culturally accepted, it's not so awkward.

Personal space implies a closer relationship and is anywhere from 18 inches to four feet in distance. Sitting with a close friend at lunch, having a casual conversation with your roommate, or reviewing business proposals with your work partner may all involve the use of personal space. Your language is informal, signifying familiarity, if not some intimacy.

The third distance zone is **social space**, four to 12 feet apart. There is little, if any, intimacy in these situations. Cocktail parties, job interviews, and wedding showers are all settings in which we would typically demonstrate social distance. In each of these cases, we are likely to be with some people with whom we are close, others who are mere acquaintances, and many we don't even know. Our talk is an appropriate mix of formal and informal language.

The final distance zone is **public space**, more than 12 feet apart. This fourth zone is the least intimate and places people into a more formal language environment. Shopping at the grocery store, attending a concert in a

intimate space 0–18 inches; distance zone that implies an extremely personal connection.

personal space 18 inches to 4 feet; distance zone that implies a close, but not intimate relationship.

social space 4 to 12 feet apart; distance zone suggesting little, if any, intimacy.

public space More than 12 feet apart; distance zone implying little intimacy and indicating a more formal language environment.

Table 4.2 The Four Distance Zones

DISTANCE ZONE	ZONE CHARACTERISTICS
Intimate distance	0 to 18 inches; informal language; total intimacy
Personal distance	18 inches to 4 feet; informal language; partial to total intimacy
Social distance	4 to 12 feet; informal and formal language; some intimacy possible
Public distance	Over 12 feet; formal language; no intimacy at all

park, or going to a flea market are all examples of settings in which we would utilize our public zones. Table 4.2 summarizes the characteristics of each zone.

Haptics

haptics Communicating through touch.

Another type of nonverbal communication is **haptics**, communicating through *touch*. Consider all the different types of physical contact we routinely enact: hugs, kisses, back slaps, handshakes, punches, massages, cheek pinches, kicks under the table, sexual intimacy, hand-holding, and tickles, for example. Certainly you can come up with several more.

Touch is an important part of human connection. Unlike our other senses, it is not localized to a specific part of our bodies. We can interact with the world literally from the top of our heads to the bottom of our feet. Touch is important, if not central, to child development, persuasion, relational development, and psychological and physical well-being. We often hear that children's emotional stability is dependent on the amount of physical bonding they experience with their caregivers. Adults also benefit from the touch of another. Scientists have linked physical bonding to emotional health and overall success. For example, Daniel Keltner, a psychologist from the University of California, Berkeley, found that basketball teams whose players had more physical contact with one another won more games. Other work has shown that eye contact and a pat on the back from the doctor can increase the survival rates of patients suffering from serious diseases (both in Williams, 2010). Researchers at Carnegie Mellon University discovered that hugs could not only reduce stress from conflict, but protect people from contracting infectious diseases. And although hugs given for a reason

Touch is an important part of human communication.

(e.g., to signal the end of a conflict) offer these benefits, the most effective hugs, it turns out, are those given "just because" (in Casner, 2015).

Keep in mind, though, that the misuse of touch can often be quite problematic. All nonverbal communication is culturally specific, and touch is especially so. It is a primary component in establishing **nonverbal immediacy**, using nonverbal cues to indicate closeness. While we all use touch to indicate different degrees of closeness, we have to consider that our nonverbal cues may be misrepresented, unintended, or simply inappropriate. Moreover, different people have different levels of tolerance for physical contact—some may consider a pat on the back harmless, while others feel threatened. As a result, there are many factors to consider in determining whether and when touch is appropriate. *Setting* is important; for example, is an arm squeeze given at work or home? *Gender* is important; for example, that heart-felt hug you gave your classmate could mean many things, especially if one of you is

nonverbal immediacy The use of nonverbal cues to indicate closeness.

PERSONALLY RESPONSIBLE COMMUNICATION

Touching in the Workplace

Any time people think of being touched in the workplace, one of the first things that comes to mind is sexual harassment. But there are ways to determine the difference between appropriate and inappropriate touching in a professional environment, and it is important to understand those distinctions before entering the workforce.

In discussing haptics, the use of touch, we referenced research studies that tie physical contact to success and self-esteem. So when is touching in the workplace inappropriate, and when is it encouraged? What if you're friends with your boss outside work and he or she gives you a congratulatory hug for meeting your quota? What if your colleague places his or her hand on your back while introducing you to a new hire? Are these behaviors appropriate or inappropriate? The answer, while perhaps not satisfying, is "it depends." It depends largely on whether the recipients share the feelings, and the context can be subjective. If a man works with his wife, for example, he may feel the status of their relationship justifies some occasional displays of affection, while she may feel it is unprofessional and uncomfortable to draw attention to their personal situation.

According to human resources consultant Amy Epstein Feldman, there are four things every employee should remember before high-fiving or hugging a coworker:

(1) *Hands off.* What seems innocent to one person may be sexual harassment to another. Keep your hands off any private areas of the body.

(2) *Know your audience.* "Any touching—even a pat on the back—before you know someone is too personal for strangers. So make sure that you really know your coworker before engaging in any physical contact, even a high five." What is the nature of your relationship with the other person?

(3) *Be sensitive to others' touching sensitivities.* "Do they lean in when you go to kiss their cheek or do they grimace and move backward? Do they initiate pats on the back or is it only one-sided?"

(4) *Remember that while touching isn't always sexual, it can be hostile.* "Poking someone in the chest while making an angry point, grabbing someone's arm or any other touching done when angry can lead to dismissal if your action is seen as physically threatening" (in Zupek, 2010).

To these we'll add a fifth. Just as it is your responsibility to remember these rules, it is also your responsibility to immediately confront any form of uncomfortable or inappropriate touching in order to avoid a potentially damaging work environment. First, express your feelings to the offending other. If things don't change, alert your superiors.

THUMBNAIL THEORY

Expectancy Violation Theory

This theory suggests that when interpersonal communication expectations are violated, we pay heightened attention to nonverbal communication in order to interpret the unexpected behavior.

female and the other male. *Relationship* is important; for example, your sarcastic tone with your friends is funny, but with your parents maybe not so funny. The consequences of miscommunication in each of these scenarios could be dramatic, but they are not always detrimental to the relationship of the communicators.

This is the contention of **Expectancy Violation Theory**, the idea that when social expectations are violated, attention to nonverbal communication is heightened, with either positive or negative effects (Burgoon and Hale, 1988). We all have expectations of other people, expectations based on social and cultural norms, our past experiences with one another, and the settings in which we find ourselves. Of course, we have expectations of verbal communication as well as nonverbal. You might not call your friends' parents by their first names unless invited to, and you would probably not break out in song at your aunt's funeral. Unlike verbal communication, however, nonverbal codes are constantly present, visible, and apparently authentic; for these reasons, we tend to make fairly quick and automatic judgments of their meaning. But whereas the violation of a verbal rule (saying something that should not be said) generally results in negative evaluations, violations of nonverbal communication expectations can sometimes lead to a favorable judgment of the violator. This is because such violations may *draw attention to something more positive* about the person; for example, "He shouldn't have worn shorts and a T-shirt to the wedding, but he did catch my eye and he is kind of cute."

Expectancy violations can also *increase your attentiveness* to the violator. Someone making abnormally long eye contact certainly gets your attention, for example, but now you might have to pay closer attention to the violator—is the staring rude or attractive? Another idea from Expectancy Violation Theory is that how we interpret violations is a function of how valuable we find the interaction, that is, its *reward valence*. To take an extreme example, a kiss on a successful second date, although possibly unexpected, will be judged much more favorably than a kiss from a stranger on the bus. But what if the violation is ambiguous? Here your *already held evaluation* of the other person becomes important. If you value the other person—for example, you envision starting a serious relationship with him or her—you will interpret the violation positively; if you do not, you will interpret it negatively.

A final haptics issue involves the impact of technology on relationships and well-being. What effect will spending more time communicating online rather than face-to-face have on the development of children? What about parents who pay more attention to their technological devices than to their kids? "Much of the concern about cellphones and instant messaging and Twitter has been focused on how children who incessantly use the technology are affected by it," explains technology writer Julie Scelfo, "But parents' use of such technology—and its effect on their offspring—is now becoming an equal source of concern to some child-development researchers" (2010, p. D1). We will have much more to say about this subject in Chapter 11, and you can read more about the use of touch in the boxes "Touching in the Workplace" and "On-the-Job Nonverbal Communication."

COMMUNICATION IN THE WORKPLACE

On-the-Job Nonverbal Communication

Career guidance writer Kori Rodley explains the importance of understanding nonverbal communication in the workplace:

> When we think of communication at work or on the job, most of us think of what we say or what is said to us. We think of the conversations we have or how our supervisor tells us what is expected. Dealing with the verbal communication can be challenging enough, and learning how to respond and behave professionally in accordance is important . . . [But] it can be just as important to pay attention to HOW things are said or the ways our coworkers stand, look, and maneuver around the workplace to understand what is truly happening (2010).

As you've read in this chapter, context is quite important. Let's look at some aspects of nonverbal communication and the particular messages they convey in a professional setting:

1. *Eye contact*—Maintaining eye contact establishes trust, but in a work setting, especially when giving a presentation, it tells others that you are confident in yourself and your words.
2. *Facial expressions*—In a work setting, smiling can have the additional benefit of contributing to a friendly atmosphere conducive to cooperation.
3. *Proxemics*—Space and distance are always important indicators of affection, hierarchy, and mood. In the workplace, where people may not know one another very well or may come from a variety of cultural backgrounds, attention to proxemics can be a career saver.
4. *Posture*—*How* you stand tells people *where* you stand; on the job, sitting or standing straight up and directly facing your colleagues says you stand with them.
5. *Vocalics*—Vocal tone and other sounds augment your spoken words. In the workplace, inappropriate tone or sounds can doom you by expressing sarcasm, impatience, and frustration.
6. *Chronemics*—Timeliness, especially in American culture, conveys respect. On the job, it conveys even more. If you are always on time—or better yet, a minute or two early—for meetings, interviews, or other work sessions, you tell those around you that you are a professional, that you value their time as well as your own, and that you expect them to meet your demands of professionalism.

The Stony Brook University Career Center offers a final hint:

> Perhaps the best thing to remember is *mirroring*—especially when it comes to your boss. Mirroring is exactly what it sounds like—a reflection of the nonverbal cues of the individual(s) you are interacting with. So if your boss makes a lot of eye contact with you, you should try to do the same. Your best bet is to be aware of how your actions "fit in" with those of everyone around you. (2011)

Chronemics

Chronemics is the use of time to communicate. If you've ever shown up to class late, or delayed calling a friend because you were angry with him or her, you can understand how time relays messages. In fact, much of our day-to-day lives revolve around the various meanings we give to time. Consider how diligently and sometimes obsessively we follow the calendar or refer to our schedules. Even our days provide us with a guide of how to interpret and utilize our time. Sunday, for example, may be football day to you, but for some it may be a day to rest after a long work week, and for others a day of celebrating religion

chronemics How we use time to communicate.

Times and dates are one way that we communicate routines and traditions.

polychronic In the use of time, multitasking.

monochronic In the use of time, focusing on one task or activity at a time.

kinesics The use of body motions in communication.

or spirituality. And then there are *time rules* we follow, depending on our culture; for example, Americans kiss romantic partners at midnight on New Year's Eve; dress up in costumes on October 31; profess affection on February 14; eat cake and ice cream on birthdays; and generally see a work day as about 9:00 a.m. to 5:00 p.m.

Different cultures use time quite differently. In Europe, employees may take two to three hours for a break in the middle of the day, and families may dedicate long periods to dining. Americans, by contrast, generally rush to tasks, as reflected in phrases such as "fast food" and "time is money." Thanks in part to media technologies, Americans tend to use time **polychronically**: they multitask. This wasn't always the case, however. Historically, Americans were long considered to be **monochronic**, focusing on one task or activity at a time. You can read more about Americans' use of time in the box "How We Spend Our Time."

Kinesics

A fourth type of nonverbal communication is **kinesics**, the use of body motions in communication. Ray Birdwhistell, one of the founders of the field of kinesics, estimated that humans can transmit through bodily movement more than 700,000 physical signals that are useful in meaning making (1970). Some of those motions include hand gestures, posture, facial expressions, leg movements, pacing, and even individual habits like hair twirling or clenching fists. Kinesics are intriguing partly because body motions make up a large percentage of body language, and of all the different types of nonverbal communication, body language is arguably the most honest.

How many times have you been told that your words are saying one thing but your body is telling a different story? Let's look at some examples that may sound familiar:

What might this student's body language be telling his professor?

→ Your roommate asks why you seem to be feeling down. You assure him you are fine, but you're not smiling and your head is down.

→ The professor calls you to her office to find out why you seem to dislike the class. You say you like the class a lot, but every day you sit in the back with your shoulders slouched and a strained look on your face.

→ You come home past curfew, and your parents want to know if you've been out partying. You say "No," but, avoiding eye contact, you stumble by them up to your room.

How We Spend Our Time

According to the Bureau of Labor Statistics' "Annual Time Use Survey" (2014), Americans spend the great majority of their time sleeping, working, and watching television. In fact, regardless of education level, watching videos on any device takes up the greatest portion of Americans' leisure time. Another recent study, this one by the Kaiser Family Foundation, shows that young people spend an average of 6½ to 7½ hours a day consuming media. Accounting for multitasking, that number increases to approximately 10 hours a day. Americans are also increasingly sleeping with their cellphones. If we include these sleeping hours as part of their media use, young people are now engaged in technology around the clock (Rideout, Foehr, and Roberts, 2010).

During our discussion of chronemics, we pointed out the many ways in which time communicates meaning. What meaning, then, do we communicate through our use of time? The United States, mostly because of advances in technology, has become an extremely fast-paced society, and a common complaint seems to be a *lack of time*. But time to do what? Is it that Americans never have enough time, *or* it is possible that they use time in ways that are not productive? In their sometimes careless use of time, do they communicate to their children that disengagement from others and from civic duty and community service is acceptable? Do Americans tell their children that these other-directed activities are not as important and constructive as working or consuming media (often in isolation)? Journalist and mother Susan Maushart explains that for American kids, "media use is not an activity like exercise, or playing Monopoly, or bickering with your brother in the backseat. It's an environment: pervasive, invisible, shrink-wrapped around pretty much everything kids do and say and think" (in Franklin, 2011). The country's teachers claim that elementary and high school students' time with media has lowered their attention spans (71%), hurt their writing skills (58%), decreased their face-to-face communication skills (59%), and dampened their critical thinking (42%; Rideout, 2012).

We need to reassess the ways we choose to spend our time and how those decisions affect others, including our children. Media time and work time need to be balanced by family time, community time, spiritual time, and reading time. More than 40% of Americans will not take a single vacation day this year, and as a nation, Americans leave unused half of all the vacation time they have rightfully earned on the job (Picchi, 2015). How do you explain this fact? How do you choose to spend your valuable time?

➡ You know your best friend's boyfriend is cheating on her. You don't want to tell her because it would be devastating, but when the two of them are around, you sit with your arms crossed and as far away from them as you can.

Body movement, then, is a highly effective form of communication, whether or not the message is intended. But as we've just seen, often the message is unintended, and people can detect the truth in spite of contradicting words. In fact, there are some who make a living as body language experts—helping law enforcement officials and others distinguish between truth and deception in people.

Nonetheless, we often intentionally use specific movements of our hands and arms to communicate. These are **gesticulations**. There are five types of gesticulations or hand/arm gestures: **emblems**, **adaptors**, **illustrators**,

gesticulation Specific movement of hands and arms to communicate.

Table 4.3 Five Types of Gesticulations

	DEFINITION	EXAMPLE
Emblems	Gestures that can be translated into words	Shaking your head "no"
Adaptors	Gestures used to fulfill a need	Pushing hair out of your face
Illustrators	Gestures that emphasize a verbal message	Using your hand to illustrate the height of a child
Affect Displays	Emotional gestures	Shaking when you are anxious
Regulators	Gestures to help the flow of speech	Raising your hand in class

affect displays, and **regulators**. Table 4.3 provides definitions and examples for each.

Vocalics

vocalics (also **paralanguage**) Sounds and rhythms other than actual words which come out of one's mouth.

Vocalics is a fifth type of nonverbal communication. Also referred to as **paralanguage**, vocalics are all the sounds and rhythms *except* for actual words that come out of our mouths (otherwise that would be verbal, not nonverbal, communication). Examples include tone, inflection, laughter, crying, articulation, pitch, coughing, shouting, whistling, and sounds made to communicate direct messages, for example when a librarian says "Shhhhh!" or when people clear their throats to get attention. The voice is able to communicate a lot of emotion; sometimes we can hear that something is wrong—or that something great has happened—just from the sound of someone's voice. And consider what vocalics do for us emotionally, mentally, and even physically. A sick child in the hospital who hears a parent's voice is comforted, and a newborn's first cry brings relief and joy to new parents.

Oculesics

oculesics The use of pupil dilation, eye movement, and eye contact in meaning making.

Oculesics is the use of pupil dilation, eye movement, and eye contact in meaning making. Although some scholars categorize oculesics as a form of facial expression, most treat it as a separate entity given the power of the eyes on their own to communicate. Years of research have demonstrated that "children and adults who avoid or are denied eye contact are more likely to suffer from depression and feelings of isolation as well as exhibit antisocial traits such as callousness" (Murphy, 2014, p. SR6). Marketers even use eye contact generated by cartoon characters on product packaging—think the Quaker Oats man, the Trix rabbit, and the Keebler elves—to create bonds of trust between brands and consumers.

The eyes are so powerful in relaying feelings that they are often referred to as "windows to the soul." In the HBO television series *Curb Your Enthusiasm*, comedian Larry David continually insists the eyes do not lie, so he stares down those he deems deceptive, violating their personal space

("The Infamous," 2010). These actions may be funny, but research suggests that Mr. David may be onto something because "only actual eye contact fully activates those parts of the brain that allow us to more acutely and accurately process another person's feelings and intentions" (Murphy, 2014, p. SR 6). Gazing and staring are associated with showing interest; increased blinking may equate to stress; squinting may be a sign of uncertainty; and looking down could create a sense of submission or guilt (perhaps the person *is* lying). As with vocalics, eye movements are directly tied to emotions. We speak about *smiling with our eyes* or notice that someone has *dark* or *sad eyes*.

Facial Expressions

Facial expressions, the use of the face's mobility in communication, are an important form of nonverbal communication. Some of the ways we make meaning from facial expressions are in our reading of smiles (expressing joy), frowns (showing sadness or dismay), crinkled foreheads (suggesting wonder or confusion), and puckered or licked lips (indicating disgust, fear, or anger). These examples represent only a few of the many dimensions of the face. Even when we attempt to hide our emotions, we use facial expressions. For instance, you may put on a "brave face" to deliver bad news. Another emotion clearly communicated through facial expressions is embarrassment. Recall from Chapter 3 our discussion of *face,* the public self-image we each hope to claim for ourselves. The concept is so named because nowhere is our momentary sense of who we are—or others' sense of who we are—more visible than in our face.

facial expressions The use of the face's mobility in communication.

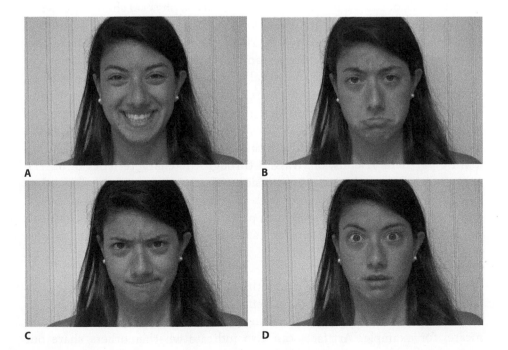

A

B

C

D

What emotion does each of these facial expressions convey?

Physical Appearance

body adornments Tattoos, piercings, and accessories.

We also communicate nonverbally through *physical appearance*. Clothing, height, weight, **body adornments** (tattoos, piercings, and accessories), skin color, ethnicity, hairstyle and color, shape, attractiveness, and hygiene are all examples of physical attributes that communicate meaning to others. Consider the following questions as you examine how physical appearance creates meaning:

→ What is likely to happen if you wear jeans to a job interview at the top law firm in the city?

→ Do we label models on the cover of fashion magazines as attractive or unattractive? Why?

→ How might a Little League team react differently to a 5-foot-tall coach versus a 6-foot-tall coach?

→ What would a patient say if a doctor with dirty hands walked into the examining room?

→ How does your grandmother feel about your piercings and tattoos?

→ Are you likely to hire an obese dietician to help you manage your health?

Physical characteristics are a major factor in day-to-day communication. Our first impressions of people are usually based on appearance. The distinctions we make between cultures are often based on how we describe its members, and many of our mainstream norms are dictated by the importance we place on physical attributes, such as what we consider attractive or unattractive. It is, of course, not uncommon that we use physical characteristics as a gauge for whether to begin a relationship (Snyder, Berscheid, and Glick, 1985). Recent research (Vernon et al., 2014) has demonstrated that facial features alone (not facial expressions) can dramatically—and quickly, in under 100 milliseconds—influence the initial impressions we make of one another. Researchers measured 65 facial features, such as eye height, nose curve, and eyebrow width, and discovered that people make near-instant judgments about others' approachability ("Do they want to harm me?") by looking at the mouth area. They judge youthfulness and attractiveness ("Are they likely romantic partners, friends, or rivals?") through the characteristics of others' eyes and eyebrows. And first impressions of others' dominance ("Can they help or harm me?") are associated with facial features such as eyebrow height and cheekbones. You can read about a particular physical appearance issue in the box "Freedom of Expression versus Professional Appearance."

Artifacts

artifacts Objects we use to identify ourselves.

Artifacts, objects that we use to identify ourselves, are also a type of nonverbal communication. Artifacts help define us and our environments and, in turn, tell others how to behave accordingly. What does a wedding ring communicate, for example? Artifacts can also indicate whether others share our

ETHICAL COMMUNICATION

Freedom of Expression versus Professional Appearance

Shortly after her graduation from college, Rachel had a hard time understanding why she could not land a job. Her resume was impressive—a 3.8 GPA, an abundance of campus and community involvement, and the completion of two internships in her chosen field, public relations. She was invited to a number of interviews with different PR firms but never got called back. She decided to turn to her communication instructor for advice.

The recent grad believed strongly in individuality and had streaks of purple and orange in her hair; piercings in her nose, lip, and eyelids; and a tattoo of a boa constrictor on her neck. The professor decided to confront the problem head on, explaining that what Rachel saw as individuality, interviewers likely perceived as unprofessionalism. Despite her strong will, Rachel took out her piercings, dyed her hair its natural brown color, and hid the tattoo beneath a blouse and chic gray suit. Two weeks later she was hired by one of the largest firms in the country.

The concepts of beauty and professional appearance are subjective and by definition stereotypes, but the dominant culture has very specific ideas, largely shaped by media, about what is physically acceptable and what is not. The reality is that, in spite of our good intentions to appreciate individuality and freedom of expression, we still deal with cultural biases relating to attractiveness and professional appearance. Better-looking people are generally considered more intelligent than others, even though there is no relationship between attractiveness and brain power. In the words of researcher Karel Kleisner and his colleagues, "a clear mental image [of] how a smart face should look does exist for both men and women . . . The 'high intelligence' faces appear to be smiling more than the 'low intelligence' faces. A similar pattern was described for the perception of trustworthiness. Perceived intelligence correlates with perceived trustworthiness and happiness" (Kleisner, Chvátalová, and Flegr, 2014, p. e81237).

Moreover, returning to our story about Rachel, other research indicates that people who attempt to violate cultural standards of attractiveness or acceptability in the workplace are treated with unfavorable bias (Hosoda, Stone-Romero, and Coats, 2006). So where is the ethical line? For Rachel, expressing herself took a backseat to getting a job; but should the biases of others have led her to compromise her individuality, a core part of her identity? Or is acquiescence to the demands of the job ethically justified because, as an employee, she represents not just herself, but also her colleagues and her firm's clients? What would you have done if you were in Rachel's Doc Martens?

---

values. If you go home for the holiday with your roommate and notice dozens of family pictures all around the house, what message is communicated about the value placed on family? When you see political bumper stickers on cars, do you judge the values of the driver based on your own political or social perspectives? Do your parents lecture you about your inability to detach from your smartphone?

Artifacts can inform us about people's jobs, interests, or hobbies. What conclusion do you come to when you see a person carrying a saxophone into a club? How do we know a person is a doctor if not for the white coat and stethoscope draped around her neck? A person wearing a backpack on campus and carrying a poster board is clearly a student.

Artifacts can also be a powerful force in allowing us to shape our own identities, as well as announce our membership in a specific culture. For instance, many young people define themselves according to objects marked

Because it isn't possible to *not* communicate, what this woman wants is impossible.

"I'm looking for something that won't say anything about me."

with popular brand names like Nike, Abercrombie & Fitch, Sony, Alex and Ani, Apple, Under Armour, and North Face, to name a few. For them it may be less about materialism and more about announcing who they are and how they fit into the culture.

Environmental Factors

Environmental factors such as temperature, weather, smells, lighting, and designs can also be a form of nonverbal communication. Have you ever noticed that many shopping malls are now designed to resemble quaint villages? The intention is to communicate security and community, making the shopping experience more inviting, which should result in more spending. Similarly, when planning a special date at your place, you might light some candles, dim the lights, and carefully choose music to set the mood.

Because environmental factors can be visually effective in communicating messages, media content often makes use of them. Film directors may use architectural differences to distinguish a European city from an American city, for example, lighting to set the scene for a romantic

Based on artifacts, it's easy to guess what this person does for a living.

encounter, or weather conditions to portray a tropical paradise or a night bound to end in disaster. News reporters broadcast from the field, foreign correspondents weigh in from various parts of the world, and embedded journalists file their stories from the war zone, not only to provide us with better context for their report, but to communicate immediacy.

Silence

A final type of nonverbal communication is *silence*. It's not a code usually considered when addressing the different types of nonverbal communication, but it is extremely powerful in relaying messages. Have you ever observed a moment of silence for a fallen soldier, or have you engaged

What does the environment tell you about this journalist's responsibilities?

in silent prayer during a religious ceremony? Have you ever given or received the "silent treatment"? People who cannot answer a question are "struck by silence." Ignoring or refusing to acknowledge the achievements or even presence of others, intentionally or otherwise, is a use of silence that can be detrimental to the self-esteem and confidence of those being shunned.

The meaning of silence, like all communication, is culture-bound. In American culture, "interpersonal silence is not well tolerated, especially between people who are not intimates. Greater familiarity leads to greater ability to refrain from speech." This, speculates linguist Nancy Bonvillain, "offers a possible explanation of Western behavior such as formulaic greetings, so-called 'small talk,' and frequent question-and-answer sequences occurring in much daily conversation." In other words, Americans use talk to *avoid silence* because, for them, silence is often read as rudeness—that is, of course, unless silence is used to reflect a difference in status between speakers. In employer/employee, teacher/student, and adult/child encounters, "individuals of higher status tend to talk more, whereas those of lower rank are expected to be silent or less talkative" (2014, p. 35).

The Role of Nonverbal Communication in Creating Meaning and Identity

Throughout this chapter we've discussed the different types of nonverbal communication and how we use each one to communicate specific messages. But the importance of kinesics, haptics, chronemics, physical appearance, artifacts, and other types of nonverbal communication rests largely in creating meaning and identity.

As with verbal communication, who we are and how we fit into the culture develop through the meanings we give to signs and symbols, and how we behave according to those meanings. The difference here, of course, is that we are applying *nonverbal* signs and symbols. For example, the amount of time we give to our loved ones reflects the value we place on relational bonds; the uniform we wear to work informs people of our professional identity; the posture and arm movements we use in delivering a wedding toast illustrate our confidence (or lack of it) as a public speaker. It is important to realize the critical role of nonverbal communication in the development of self, first by knowing what codes exist. Next, we must understand the direct and indirect meaning made from those systems. Finally, we must know how those codes affect not only the way we see ourselves but also how others perceive us.

Review of Learning Objectives

4.1 Define nonverbal communication, identifying examples.

Nonverbal communication occurs when we relay messages and create meaning without words; it is communication that is not verbalized. For example, sleeping in class communicates that you are not listening, and sweating can indicate that you are nervous.

4.2 Compare and contrast verbal and nonverbal communication.

Verbal and nonverbal communication are similar in that they are influenced by rules, and are symbolic, culture-bound, and subject to varying degrees of intentionality. Beyond the absence of spoken words in nonverbal communication, they are different in that nonverbal is more honest, involves all five senses, and never stops.

4.3 Describe the operation of nonverbal communication and coding systems.

Nonverbal communication relies on codes, clusters of behaviors that convey meaning. These codes are analogic rather than digital, and they are iconic. They possess universal meaning, permit the simultaneous transmission of many messages, can generate an automatic response, and are often spontaneous. We frame, or structure, a message using nonverbal coding systems to repeat, complement, contradict, substitute for, and regulate what we say.

4.4 Describe several types of nonverbal coding systems.

Types of nonverbal coding systems include

- Proxemics, the use of space and distance to make meaning
- Haptics, communicating through touch
- Chronemics, using time to communicate
- Kinesics, expressing meaning through body motion
- Vocalics, the sounds and rhythms, other than words, that come out of our mouths
- Oculesics, the use of pupil dilation, eye movement, and eye contact in communication
- Facial expressions, the use of the face's mobility to make meaning
- Physical appearance, including clothing choices as well as observable physical characteristics

- Artifacts, objects we use to identify ourselves
- Environmental factors, which often cue meaning
- Silence, which may be just the absence of sound, not the absence of meaning

4.5 Explain the role of nonverbal communication in creating meaning and identity.

Who we are and how we fit into the culture develop through the meanings we give to signs and symbols and how we behave according to those meanings. This is as true for nonverbal as it is for verbal communication.

Key Terms

nonverbal communication 72
intentionality 74
nonverbal coding systems 75
framing 76
proxemics 76
territory 76
intimate space 77
personal space 77
social space 77
public space 77
haptics 78
nonverbal immediacy 79
Expectancy Violation Theory 80
chronemics 81
polychronic 82
monochronic 82
kinesics 82
gesticulations 83
emblems 83
adaptors 83
illustrators 83
affect displays 84
regulators 84
vocalics/paralanguage 84
oculesics 84
facial expressions 85
body adornments 86
artifacts 86

Questions for Review

1. What are some of the similarities and differences between verbal and nonverbal communication?

2. What are the properties of nonverbal coding systems?

3. In what ways does nonverbal communication frame verbal communication?

4. What are the four distance zones in proxemics?

5. What is the relationship between haptics and expectancy violations?

6. What is the difference between polychronic and monochronic cultures?

7. What differentiates gesticulations from kinesics in general?

8. What are some framing examples of vocalics and oculesics?

9. How do facial expressions, physical appearance, artifacts, and environmental factors enhance meaning making?

10. Why is silence not necessarily the absence of meaning?

Questions for Discussion

1. Of the many types of nonverbal communication we've discussed, which is most likely to be misinterpreted? Why do you think that is the case?

2. Have you ever had your personal space violated? What were the circumstances? How did it make you feel? Was the violation intentional, and did that influence your reaction?

3. Is it fair that we attach so much importance to physical appearances? Why or why not? When is this type of meaning making harmful? When is it useful?

5

Listening

As a way to be more involved on campus, you decide to become a tour guide. During a leadership seminar early in the semester, you and the other guides are broken into small groups. The first exercise of the session requires you to form a circle and discuss the qualities required of a good campus guide. As the group chats and offers examples, you notice that Lauren, the person to your right (who is normally quite friendly), is not responding to you. In fact, she is entirely ignoring what you are saying. Once the exercise ends, you approach her and ask, "Are you angry with me?" "Of course not!" she responds, "Why do you think that?" You point out that she failed to acknowledge any of the comments that you were directing her way. Lauren laughs and then apologizes. "I'm *so* sorry. I didn't even realize you were talking to me. You were sitting to my left, and I'm deaf in that ear. Please forgive me." You are relieved, though a little embarrassed. This experience forces you to consider the difference between hearing and listening. It would have hurt your feelings if Lauren had been hearing you and not listening. But as it turned out, she simply did not hear you.

In everyday life we often worry about how to construct and deliver messages, but rarely do we consider how critical it is to *receive* those messages in an effective way. Make no mistake, though; listening is *as* important to good communication as speaking or writing. In the opening story, Lauren has a physical impediment to hearing, but she isn't a bad listener. In fact, when you expressed concern over her lack of response, she listened and responded with empathy, and she offered an explanation that made you feel better.

When we reflect on the role of listening in our lives, we often look at the negative moments associated with listening—our parents demanding that we listen to them, our friends insisting that we never listen to them, our teachers telling us that we need to be better listeners in class, and even our doctors threatening us with bad health if we don't listen to their instructions. But listening is a positive; it is the cornerstone to understanding others and understanding the world. Listening scholar Graham Bodie writes that listening is "essential to managing conversations marked by conflict and support alike, and the positive outcomes of its employment range from academic and work success to individual and relational health and well-being" (2013, p. 76). As such, practicing good listening and acknowledging its importance are central to our success as communicators. In this chapter we will focus on listening, including the types of listening, misconceptions about listening, barriers to effective listening, and advice for becoming a better, more effective listener.

Learning Objectives

5.1   Define *listening* and explain how it differs from *hearing*.

5.2   Dispel a number of misconceptions about listening.

5.3   Identify the components of effective listening.

5.4   Identify barriers to successful listening.

5.5   Outline several types of listening.

5.6   Describe steps to becoming a better listener.

What Is Listening?

Winston Churchill once said, "Courage is what it takes to stand up and speak; courage is also what it takes to sit down and listen" (in Josephson, 2011). The former British prime minister was stressing the often-neglected value of listening. Without listening, there would be no effective reception of messages; as a result, communication would suffer. And as you've already seen, listening shouldn't be confused with hearing. **Listening** is actively making meaning from the spoken messages of others; **hearing** is the physical process of receiving sounds. Hearing is physiological (the mechanical functioning of the various parts of the ear), while listening is cognitive, affective, and behavioral (Bodie, 2013). Listening is *cognitive* (mental) when we attend to, understand, receive, and interpret content. It is *affective* (emotional) when we are motivated to attend to that content. And it is *behavioral* (physical) when we give verbal and nonverbal feedback.

listening Actively making meaning from the spoken messages of others.

hearing The physical process of perceiving sounds.

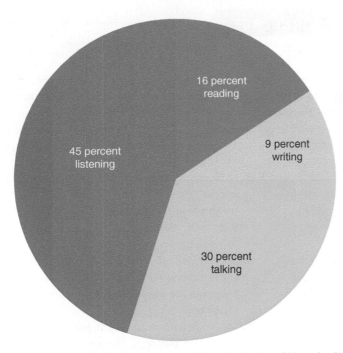

FIGURE 5.1 How Much of Our Daily Communication Time Do We Spend Listening?

As you can see from Figure 5.1, while we may devote 75 percent of a typical day to speaking and listening, we actually spend more time listening—45 percent daily—than we do speaking (Bolton, 2009). Beyond the sheer amount of time we spend at it, listening is important for many other reasons. In fact, the old joke that there's a reason humans have only one mouth but two ears isn't really that much of a joke. Listening is *crucial in building and maintaining our interpersonal relationships*. Recalling Chapter 1's discussion of symbolic interaction, you know that if this is the case, listening is *essential to our sense of self*. Psychologist Michael Nichols explains,

> Few motives in human experience are as powerful as the yearning to be understood. Being listened to means that we are taken seriously, that our ideas and feelings are recognized, and, ultimately, that what we have to say matters. The yearning to be heard is a yearning to escape our isolation and bridge the space that separates us. We reach out and try to overcome that separateness by revealing what's on our minds and in our hearts . . . If listening strengthens our relationships by cementing our connections with one another, it also fortifies our sense of self. In the presence of a receptive listener, we are able to clarify what we think and discover what we feel. Thus, in giving an account of our experiences to someone who listens, we are better able to understand ourselves. (2009, pp. 9–10)

Listening is also *central to academic and professional success*. Corporate communication consultant Bernard Ferrari makes the case this way: "Listening can well be the difference between profit and loss, between success and failure, between a long career and a short one. Listening is the only way to find

COMMUNICATION IN THE WORKPLACE

The 80/20 Rule

Listening consultant Bernard Ferrari counts among his many clients corporate powerhouses General Electric and Morgan Stanley. A firm believer in the idea that good listening means good business, he offers four benefits of listening for managers and others (2012).

- Good listeners *develop a reputation as easy to talk to.* It is among the characteristics most attributed to successful bosses. It invites openness and honesty and it generates information and ideas.
- Good listeners *ask the right questions at the right time.* This encourages others to think about their ideas and suggestions with greater depth, breadth, and clarity.
- Good listeners *sift through unnecessary information and details* in their conversations with others and get to the most important issues more quickly and efficiently.
- As a result, good listeners *move more efficiently from deliberation to decision and from decision to action.*

But how does a manager do this? Dr. Ferrari offers five rules:

1. *Apply the 80/20 rule.* Devote 80 percent of a conversation to listening and 20 percent to speaking. And use the 20 percent to ask questions rather than offering opinions and observations.
2. *Be purposeful when in conversation.* Enter and engage in conversations with a clear idea of what you want to accomplish.
3. *Focus entirely on your conversational partner.* This tells people that the conversation has importance, heightening their awareness of its value and their role in it. Naturally, this means put aside your technology!
4. *Set time and topic limits.* Your time is valuable; your conversational partner's time is valuable. You want to keep your conversations from wandering into unnecessary terrain.
5. *Challenge basic assumptions, your own and your conversational partner's.* "Become the Master of the Question," he advises, "Being the Master of the Question means using questions to reframe the conversation in order to learn more. Through careful questioning we can open up new avenues of thinking by challenging or confirming our dearest assumptions" (pp. 64–65).

out what you don't know, and marks the path to making good decisions, arriving at the best ideas. If you aspire to be better at your job, no matter what it is, listening may be the most powerful tool at your disposal" (2012, p. 2). You can read Ferrari's listening advice for successful managers in the box "Communication in the Workplace: The 80/20 Rule."

Misconceptions About Listening

Given that we spend so much of our time listening and that listening seems quite natural, we might come to the conclusion that effective listening is easy. But that's not the case. The fact that people routinely overestimate the quality of their own listening skills (Carrell and Willmington, 1996) may well be the result of several misconceptions they have about listening:

- **Misconception 1: Hearing is the same as listening.** We've already discussed the distinction between listening and hearing; nonetheless, let's take a less academic approach to this particular myth. How many people with perfectly good hearing do you know who happen to be terrible listeners? The fact that these people exist, more than anything else, tells you there is a difference.

- **Misconception 2: Listening is easy, natural, and effortless**. Again, your own experience tells you otherwise. Think of the lectures you've had to endure that were difficult to listen to (not only in school, but from parents and disapproving friends). We are not born with good listening skills; they are not a natural gift. Rather, it takes effort and practice to become a skilled listener. You can evaluate your own skill as a listener by taking the self-evaluation on page 98.

- **Misconception 3: Listening is a difficult skill to learn.** This chapter is devoted to teaching you effective listening skills, and as you read further you'll see that if you do indeed want to become a better listener, the lessons are not that difficult. This is because we typically have the basics in place. After all, we learn to listen from our earliest years, and we spend quite a bit of time engaged in the act. Because of listening's apparent ease and naturalness, we may not be the listeners we *could* be, but if we are motivated to apply good listening skills across the many communication situations in which we find ourselves, the personal, social, academic, and career rewards we receive will reinforce those skills.

- **Misconception 4: Listening is simply a matter of intelligence**. Intelligent people don't necessarily make better listeners. Have you ever had a college instructor, a holder of an advanced degree and seemingly quite intelligent, who simply would not listen to you? There is no direct link between brainpower and listening skill. Being intelligent may mean having a better vocabulary, and that might aid listening comprehension (Vineyard and Bailey, 1960), but that doesn't mean that smart people are better listeners. In fact, they may become more easily bored with a conversation, or they may "tune out" and start thinking about something other than the conversation at hand. That would render them very poor listeners.

- **Misconception 5: Read more, listen better**. A larger vocabulary may aid comprehension (you can't make meaning from a conversation filled with words you've never heard), but that doesn't mean people who read more are necessarily better listeners. Reading itself is no guarantee to understanding *or* to effective meaning making (Vineyard and Bailey, 1960). How often have you read something you didn't understand? Even the most avid readers will sometimes read passively; maybe they are reading just for fun, or perhaps they're uninterested in the material. Just as you can read passively or actively, you can listen passively or actively.

- **Misconception 6: Gender affects listening skill**. As you'll read in some detail in Chapter 9, there are differences, in general, between how males and females communicate. For now, though, understand that a feminine communication style places greater value on empathy, compassion, connection, and emotional messages, while a masculine communication style favors facts and outcomes and typically shies away from talking about (or listening to)

SELF-EVALUATION   How Good a Listener Are You?

Fill in each of the following blanks with _almost never_, _sometimes_, _often_, or _almost always_.

WHEN PEOPLE ARE TALKING TO ME, I . . .

1 _____ make them feel that I'm interested in them and in what they have to say.

2 _____ think about what I want to say while they are talking.

3 _____ acknowledge what they've said before offering my own opinion.

4 _____ jump in before they are finished speaking.

5 _____ allow them to complain without arguing with them.

6 _____ offer advice before I'm asked.

7 _____ concentrate on figuring out what they are trying to say, rather than simply responding to the words they've used.

8 _____ share similar experiences of my own rather than inviting them to elaborate on what they're saying.

9 _____ get them to tell me a lot about themselves.

10 _____ assume I know what they are going to say before they are finished talking.

11 _____ restate their message or instructions to make sure I understood them correctly.

12 _____ make judgments about who is and isn't worth listening to.

13 _____ make an effort to focus on them and understand what they are trying to say.

14 _____ tune out when someone begins to ramble on, instead of trying to get more involved in the conversation to make it more interesting.

15 _____ accept criticism without becoming defensive.

16 _____ think of listening as instinctive rather than as a communication activity that takes effort.

17 _____ make an effort to get them to say what they think and feel about things.

18 _____ pretend to listen when I'm not.

19 _____ respect what others have to say.

20 _____ find that listening to them complain annoys me.

21 _____ make use of questions to get them to say what's on their mind.

22 _____ make comments when they are talking that distract them.

23 _____ think they see me as a good listener.

24 _____ tell them I know how they feel.

25 _____ lose my temper when they get angry with me.

SCORING

For the odd-numbered statements give yourself:

4 points for each _almost always_   2 points for each _sometimes_
3 points for each _often_   1 point for each _almost never_

For the even-numbered statements, reverse the scoring, giving yourself:

1 point for each _almost always_   3 points for each _sometimes_
2 points for each _often_   4 points for each _almost never_

How good a listener are you?

If you scored:

85–96, you are an excellent listener.   49–60, you are a below-average listener.
73–84, you are an above-average listener.   25–48, you are a poor listener.
61–72, you are an average listener.

(Adapted from Nichols, 2009).

personal or emotional matters. In other words, females tend to engage in "rapport-talk" and males in "report-talk." Linguist Deborah Tannen explains that "many women, when they talk among themselves in situations that are casual, friendly, and focused on rapport, use cooperative overlapping: Listeners talk along with speakers to show participation and support" (1990, p. 208). But this doesn't mean that one gender is better at listening than the other. What it does mean is that different genders may have different ways of interpreting the words of their conversational partners, and they may ask those partners different kinds of questions as they seek different kinds of clarification.

When women gather to chat, listeners often talk along with speakers to show participation and support.

- **Misconception 7: In the communication process, speaking is more important than listening**. Communication scholar Mary Ellen Guffey (2004) identifies two related misconceptions that flow from this myth: speakers are able to command listening, and speakers are primarily responsible for communication success. The easiest way to debunk all three misconceptions is to recall that communication is *mutual* meaning making; it requires *feedback*; it is a *transaction* (Chapter 1). Speakers and listeners share equally in their meaning-making responsibilities. Your own experience makes this clear. Have you ever attended a talk by a completely, absolutely, fabulously interesting speaker who was talking about a subject that you loved . . . but you were too tired or hungry to pay attention? Or perhaps a classmate, your partner on a class project, was explaining quite expertly the requirements of the task but you just couldn't get past her infatuation with that jerk, Jordan. Or maybe your Communication instructor has prepared—and is delivering—the best lecture ever on misconceptions about listening, but all you can do is watch the clock and gaze out the window, knowing that spring break starts as soon as class ends. Listening research pioneer Ralph Nichols determined more than a half-century ago that effective listening was the "inherent" responsibility of the listener. He wrote,

> Learning for the listener is "inside" action on the part of the listener. The speaker has comparatively little to do with it. He [*sic*] cannot learn *for* the listener. "Telling" is not necessarily teaching, and "getting told" is not learning. Who is primarily at fault when we fail to understand, or perhaps even receive the message sent our way? . . . Is the conveyor to be held responsible because we are ill equipped to decode his [*sic*] message? (1955, p. 294)

- **Misconception 8: Listening is primarily a matter of understanding a speaker's words**. The same word or the same collection of words can have different meanings in different contexts, and words are never *just* words; as symbols, they are "vehicles" that carry meaning (Chapter 1).

They carry meaning through syntax, denotative and connotative meaning, metaphor, and abstraction (Chapter 3). And speakers' words are invariably accompanied by nonverbal communication that can emphasize, complement, contradict, substitute for, or otherwise frame the meaning we make from those words (Chapter 4).

The Components of Effective Listening

Partly in response to the misconception that listening is natural, routine, or otherwise effortless, listening scholar Judi Brownell used her research to demonstrate that good or effective listening is actually a process made up of several components that "although interrelated, can be approached as separate skill areas" (Brownell, 1990, p. 403). She took the first letter of each of those components—**H**earing, **U**nderstanding, **R**emembering, **I**nterpreting, **E**valuating, and **R**esponding—to create an acronym for her take on what is involved in effective listening, the **HURIER model** (Brownell, 1985; Table 5.1).

- *Hearing*—Hearing, as we've already seen, is the physiological process of receiving sound, and although we can hear but not listen, it is quite difficult to listen if we cannot hear.

- *Understanding*—You can hear a speaker, and maybe even work hard to listen to what's being said, but if you don't understand or comprehend the meaning of what's being said, your listening will not be successful. Recall two examples from Chapter 1, listening to a German speaker and to a professor who uses over-the-top technical jargon. Unless you speak German or are familiar with that jargon, no matter how hard you try, your attempts to understand will be in vain.

- *Remembering*—No doubt you've been scolded, probably as a child, because something someone said to you "went in one ear and out the other." You can hear something, maybe even *think* you listened to it, but unless you can store it in your memory for later use, your listening really hasn't been effective.

THUMBNAIL THEORY

The HURIER Model of Listening

Researcher Judi Brownell's approach to listening asserts that effective listening is a process made up of several interrelated components that can be understood and improved as separate skill areas. She identified hearing, understanding, remembering, interpreting, evaluating, and responding, and combined the first letter of each into the HURIER model.

Table 5.1 The HURIER Model of Listening

H	Hearing	Physically receiving the message
U	Understanding	Comprehending the message's meaning
R	Remembering	Recalling the message for later action
I	Interpreting	Meaning making between listener and speaker
E	Evaluating	Assessing the value of the message
R	Responding	Responding appropriately, verbally and nonverbally, to the message

(Source: Brownell, 1985)

- *Interpreting*—Here is where real meaning is made. Because meaning making is a mutual transaction, the interpreting component of effective listening involves two parties—speaker and listener—and two steps. Step 1 involves the listener assigning meaning to what's being said by the speaker, and Step 2 involves the listener communicating that assigned meaning, his or her understanding, to the speaker. Simply put, the listener must offer cues that she or he has interpreted the message as the speaker intended. Consider those times a friend has challenged you for not listening because your response was not what she or he had expected or wanted ("You never listen to me!" or "You don't understand me!" or "You weren't paying attention to what I was saying!"). Think, too, of the many times you've had to defend yourself with either "I didn't think that's what you were saying!" or "That's not what I meant!" When this happens, the best strategy is to ask questions to try to clarify where interpretation went awry. The interpreting component of listening sits at the root of **sender-receiver reciprocity**, the mutual and simultaneous exchange of feedback, typically subtly and nonverbally, that ensures the efficient transaction of meaning making. Think of it as signaling one another that you are on the same page at the same time.

- *Evaluating*—Here is where you make your own judgments about what you've heard. Was the speaker truthful? What was opinion and what was fact? What were the speaker's intentions or goals? What else do you know about the speaker, the communication context, or the topic that can help you judge what you've heard? Without evaluation, you are not an effective listener; you have not made meaning. You are merely a passive receiver of information. You can read about how to become a more active listener in the box "Being an Active Listener."

- *Responding*—You know this as giving feedback. But effective listening requires more; it requires giving *appropriate* feedback, both verbal and nonverbal, which tells your conversational partner that you are indeed listening.

sender-receiver reciprocity
Mutual and simultaneous exchange of feedback, ensuring the efficient transaction of meaning making.

Barriers to Effective Listening

Misconceptions about listening can—and often do—create barriers to effective listening. For example, if you see listening as effortless, you may not be as attentive to a speaker as you otherwise might be, failing to invest the proper amount of effort needed to maximize your understanding of the conversation. Or if you think listening is only about understanding the speaker's words, you won't find meaning in speech elements such as the tone, inflection, or possible nuance. In addition, if effective listening involves the proper operation of six interrelated components, there are likely to be a number of places where the process can be interrupted. For example, if you can't hear the message, you can't listen to it, nor can you understand, remember, interpret, evaluate, or respond to it. Among the most common barriers to effective listening are physical, psychological, physiological, and semantic noise; external distractions; and the adoption of a counterproductive listening style.

PERSONALLY RESPONSIBLE COMMUNICATION

Being an Active Listener

In a scene from the show *The Big Bang Theory*, roommates Leonard and Sheldon are having relationship problems—Leonard with his girlfriend, and Sheldon with a hyper-competitive colleague (Cendrowski, 2012). Leonard convinces Sheldon that they need to get these issues off their chests, and they decide to take five minutes each to share their problems. Sheldon goes first, and Leonard listens with intensity, responding in a compassionate and understanding manner. When it's Leonard's turn to speak, however, Sheldon, who has decided his problem is bigger, fails to listen to anything Leonard says and is quick to turn the conversation back to himself. This scenario illustrates the difference between active and passive listening. In this example, Sheldon leaves the conversation satisfied, while Leonard walks away frustrated. This is because Leonard was engaged in active listening, but Sheldon wasn't.

Being an active listener means showing the speaker you are engaged, interested, and prepared to respond. Keep in mind the following tips for becoming an active listener, and try applying them in class:

- Be *receptive*. That is, be open to new ideas and points-of-view.
- Take *selective notes*. Listen for the main points and base your notes on those points.
- *Provide feedback*. Participate in discussions and do not judge others; instead, critically assess their ideas.
- Listen for the implicit messages and nuanced language. In other words, *read between the lines for meaning*.
- *Use nonverbal communication in a respectful and sincere way*. Make eye contact, nod your head with affirmation, and on occasion offer a smile as appropriate. These cues express your involvement and will most certainly be noticed and appreciated.

As an active listener, you avoid distractions by focusing on the speaker, you judge the content more closely than you do the speaker, you request clarification if needed, and you make an attempt to connect.

Big Bang Theory's self-absorbed Sheldon has little idea about how to engage in active listening.

Physical Noise

physical noise Barrier to listening external to the message itself.

One obvious barrier to listening is noise, but as you learned in Chapter 1, noise can be physical, psychological, physiological, and semantic. **Physical noise** is a barrier to listening that is external to the message itself. It is what we traditionally think of when we hear the word "noise": for example, the sounds of construction work outside a classroom window while you are trying to follow a lecture, or a stranger chatting loudly on a cellphone while you try to talk with a friend. These barriers are out of listeners' control but can be overcome by seeking a quieter setting. Physical noise interferes with the hearing component of the HURIER model.

Psychological Noise

psychological noise Barrier to listening introduced by the listener's mindset.

Psychological noise has to do with the listener's mindset, and it creates barriers to listening in a number of ways. One is *hearing what you want to hear* rather than what is actually said. Listeners can be anxious, wanting to hear something that fulfills their needs or wants (Burley-Allen, 1995). When exactly was that term paper due? Your friends claim the professor said the last day of class, but you (having yet to start on the assignment) are sure you heard her say she was collecting them at the final exam.

Biased listening is another psychological barrier. It occurs when listeners prejudge a speaker or a topic as either old news, boring, overly complex, or unimportant. They tend to expend less energy in their listening, wondering instead when it will all be over.

Psychological noise can also take the form of *prejudices* that color listeners' meaning making. "Of course that's what he'd say, he's a liberal . . . or

Physical noise, here in the person of an intrusive cellphone user, can disrupt listening.

a conservative . . . or a Yankees fan . . ." or whatever group or class of people they hold in low regard. A student giving a talk on her Second Amendment freedom to openly carry her gun wherever she goes will have a tough time convincing an anti-gun activist to accept *her* freedom to carry when weighed against what he considers *his* freedom to walk the streets unafraid. But biased listening can occur in other ways as well.

Cultural differences can sometimes be barriers to effective listening. As you'll read in greater detail in Chapter 9, people from different cultural backgrounds, who likely have different experiences and expectations, can make very different meaning from the same conversation. People's realities of seemingly everyday concepts—freedom, family, dignity, work, faith, responsibility—can vary greatly from cultural group to cultural group.

Both prejudices and cultural differences can fuel another form of psychological noise, *errors in connotative meaning*. You recall from Chapter 3 that a word's connotative meaning is its more implicit, usually emotionally or culturally enriched, meaning. You and your friend may *love* being together, but you may have quite different meanings for the word *love*. Listening expert Madelyn Burley-Allen has identified a final form of biased listening, **green-flag words**: hot-button words that carry so much emotion that they cloud reason. She explains that "positive words as well as negative ones have an impact on our listening behavior. Whenever a word, phrase, or topic elicits an emotional response from us, there is a chance that what follows will not be listened to" (1995, p. 58). In effect, something is said that gives the listener the go-ahead (akin to the green flag in auto racing) to stop effectively listening to what follows. The rush of emotion that a patient experiences when the doctor says, "We've found a strange spot on your X-ray" may well overwhelm what follows: "But we've determined that it was a flaw in the film." "I love you, Pat" might green-flag inattention to what comes next: "But we can only be friends." Psychological noise can interfere with the understanding, remembering, interpreting, evaluating, and responding components of the HURIER model.

green-flag words Hot-button words that cloud reason.

Green-flag words can impede effective listening

Physiological Noise

physiological noise Barrier to listening introduced by listeners' physical discomfort.

Physiological noise addresses how listeners feel physically. If they are tired, sick, or in pain, this would certainly get in the way of enjoying or effectively listening to a speaker. *Fatigue* and *hunger* make it difficult for people to devote their full attention to listening, and each of us has a *time of the day* at which we have more energy than at other times. Have you ever chosen specific classes at specific times of day primarily because you tried to match the nature of the material to your peak performance time? If so, you were attempting to reduce physiological noise. This barrier can interfere with all six components of the HURIER model because the entire listening process is compromised.

Semantic Noise

semantic noise Barrier to listening introduced by linguistic influences on the message.

Semantic noise has to do with linguistic influences on the message, for example not understanding a speaker's language, dialect, or technical terminology. Recall our jargon-spouting instructor and German speaker from above. Semantic noise is a barrier to the understanding component of the HURIER model.

External Distractions

external distractions Information other than physical noise introduced into the communication situation that is not part of the message itself.

Barriers to effective listening often take the form of **external distractions**, information other than physical noise introduced into the communication situation that is not part of the message itself. One common form, *nonverbal distractions*, is speaker-based, for example when your conversational partner insists on twirling his or her hair, swaying back and forth, or speaking with an awkward verbal pacing. These distractions interfere with listeners' ability to focus on the message. Another common external distraction, *information overload*, is listener-based, for example when listeners attempt to focus on more than one message at a time. If you check out your buzzing smartphone while keeping one eye on the TV across the room while in conversation with a friend, your listening

Information overload is a common self-inflicted barrier to effective listening.

efficiency will surely suffer (but of course, you'd never do that!). These barriers are easily—and politely—overcome, in the first instance by alerting the speaker to the problem, and in the second, simply by offering your conversational partner the courtesy of your attention. External distractions are the barrier that most directly interferes with the hearing component of the HURIER model. But especially in the case of information overload, it's easy to see how listeners' lack of focus corrupts the entire listening process.

Counterproductive Listening Styles

Everyone at one time or another pretends to listen. Who among us has never been tripped up by this exchange?

> *"Are you listening to me?!"*
> *"Of course!"*
> *"Then what was the last thing I said?"*
> *"Well…"*

We all want to be liked by the people we are talking with, and we all interrupt on occasion. In addition, we are often self-conscious when listening to others, and we typically use our intellects when listening (otherwise, how could we interpret and evaluate what we are hearing?). But some people use these listening behaviors as their preferred style of listening (Burley-Allen, 1995). *Fakers* pretend to listen. They are know-it-alls who automatically write off topics or people as irrelevant or uninteresting, or they might decide they dislike or disagree with the speaker, judging that person without hearing what he or she has to say. Social convention, however, requires that they at least look like they are listening. Sometimes people pretend to listen because they want to please the speaker. Fakers work so hard at maintaining eye contact and appearing interested that they fail to listen at all. Fakers are those friends who smile and head-nod at inappropriate times in a conversation, working diligently to demonstrate that they're in the moment.

Dependent listeners want so badly to gain the appreciation of their conversational partner that they fail to meaningfully listen to what's being said. "In their urgency to elicit a favorable impression from the talker," explains Dr. Burley-Allen, "they focus on how they appear to others, rather than on the clarity and content of what they are saying" (1995, p. 61). Dependent listeners are those friends who pay such close attention to our every word that they try to finish our sentences for us, hoping to demonstrate that they are listening intently.

Interrupters interrupt, typically either because they are so focused on what *they* want to say that they cannot resist offering input or because they want to change the topic because they've become uncomfortable or threatened by what's being said. In both cases the interrupter's listening suffers because, in fact, he or she has stopped listening.

Self-conscious listeners lose listening focus because they are overly concerned about themselves and how well (or not) they are doing in the communication situation. They pay more attention to their own participation in the conversation than to the message itself. They're constantly asking themselves, "How am I doin'?" or "Do I sound smart?" or "Am I making the right impression?"

Finally, *intellectual listeners* "listen mostly with their heads, hearing only what they want to hear, blotting out larger areas of reality. Because they are mainly interested in a rational appraisal, perhaps as a result of their educational training, they tend to neglect the emotional and nonverbal aspects of the talker's behavior" (Burley-Allen, 1995, p. 63). Intellectual listeners focus primarily on the words that are spoken, rather than the meaning or intent they are designed to carry. No doubt you've come away from a conversation with a physician or perhaps a professor convinced that no matter how hard you may have tried to communicate, he or she simply wasn't listening to you.

These counterproductive listening styles influence all six components of the HURIER model to varying degrees. For example, fakers may not even hear what's being said; dependent listeners may not remember; interrupters may not understand; self-conscious listeners might have difficulty interpreting; and intellectual listeners may be so busy evaluating what they hear that they fail to do so efficiently. Appropriate responses are unlikely in all these examples. So not only do they impede meaningful listening, these barriers also raise an ethical issue as well: Is it unfair to listen poorly, or selfishly, or not at all to others who have invested time, emotion, and themselves in what they are saying? You can investigate this question more fully in the box "Ethical Communication: The Ethics of Listening."

Types of Listening

Given the importance of listening, it should be obvious that we engage in different types of listening depending on the situation. These types include informative listening, appreciative listening, relational (sometimes called empathic) listening, critical listening, and discriminative listening (Wolvin and Coakley, 1996).

informative listening
Listening, the primary goal of which is to understand the message.

appreciative listening
Listening for enjoyment or pleasure.

relational listening Lending a sympathetic ear, trying to identify with the speaker.

Informative listening takes place when our primary goal is to understand the message. We can consider ourselves successful if the meaning we take away aligns with the speaker's intention. We listen primarily to take in information. This is what we do in class or when we watch an instructional video—that is, when we want to learn something. **Appreciative listening** means listening for enjoyment or pleasure. For example, anytime we listen to music, watch a movie, check out a comedian on YouTube, or chat enjoyably with friends, we are engaging in appreciative listening. **Relational listening** is lending someone a sympathetic ear, trying to identify with him or her. Consider the times you've listened to a best friend's romantic problems or your sibling's issues with your parents. Having close relationships in our lives means we inevitably encounter relational or empathic listening; however, we don't have to be in a close relationship to engage in this type of listening. For example, a counselor will listen sympathetically to a couple's

The Ethics of Listening

Communication ethicist Michael Purdy (1995) argues that as a social behavior, listening "falls under the umbrella of ethics . . . And so we must ask, what does this mean for an ethics of listening? Basically, what is good or right behavior in listening?" He asks us "to focus on one fundamental aspect of listening ethics: How 'open' should our listening be?" (pp. 3–4)

Purdy offers three questions that might help us better understand the ethics of listening:

1. Is it ethical to not listen, for example, to a six-year-old who was just prattling on?
2. Is it ethical to listen to rumor?
3. Is it ethical to refuse to listen to controversial issues, for example to arguments about abortion that might strike closely to our deeply held values and sense of self?

What are your answers? Under what conditions would you think it proper to not listen?

Purdy then offers discussion of each question:

- **Not listening.** Would you be more likely to listen to this child if she or he were older than six? In other words, do you believe that the older the child is, the less proper it would be to not listen? By extension, is it ethical to not listen to adults who seem unintelligent or uninformed? He asks, "What are the consequences of shutting out and not even hearing the words of another person? On what ethical basis would this be justified?" (p. 9).

- **Listening to rumor:** "Do we pass on interpretations of feelings and stories that distort the original facts?" (p. 9). Does your relationship with the rumor-teller determine whether you listen? Does your relationship with the object of the rumor make a difference? If you listen and judge the rumor untrustworthy, you'd most likely not pass it on. What if you did listen and judged the rumor to be true? What if passing it on would damage another's reputation? "With rumor," writes Purdy, "it may be a matter of listening or not listening, but also of how to listen, what to listen for, and what to make of what we hear" (p. 9).

- **Listening to controversial issues:** "Controversial topics . . . include commitment to ideas or ideology. Therefore, we have to ask: Can the two sides hear each other's positions? If there is an issue that defines different moral stands/standards this [abortion] is such an issue. Here the issue concerns the ideal, and also the reality. Do people really listen to each other over issues like abortion? Or are their positions already set? What is there to listen for?" (p. 9).

Having now read a bit more about each ethical dilemma, have any of your original answers changed? If so, how and why? If not, why not?

---

marital dilemmas, or a nurse may spend time listening to the emotional pain endured by a patient facing terminal illness. We might end up on a long bus ride and have the questionable good fortune to be seated next to a passenger who tells us a sad tale of love lost. **Critical listening** happens when we need to make a decision based on the information offered us, when we want to evaluate or analyze what's being said. For example, when a doctor tells us there are a number of different treatment options for the malady that brought us to her office, we'll most likely listen with a critical ear to ensure the choice of the best possible remedy.

Discriminative listening is a part of all types of listening. We listen discriminatively when we pay close attention to more than the simple denotative

critical listening Listening for evaluation or analysis.

discriminative listening Paying close attention to more than the simple denotative meaning of speakers' words.

We engage in relational listening when we lend a sympathetic ear to another, even a stranger.

meaning of the words we hear. We listen for changes in speakers' emphasis, tone, force, and nuance; we attend to the nonverbal communication as intently as we do the verbal. Return to the example of informative listening that we offered earlier in the chapter, listening in class to your instructor. A good lecture involves a wealth of information—what's being said, what's not being said, what's emphasized, what's an aside, what's written on the board, what's reinforced with visuals—all of which add meaning to what the instructor has to offer (and all of which make a difference in what you learn). But why are you a student? Is it to *hear* everything your professors

SOCIALLY RESPONSIBLE COMMUNICATION

Questioning Our Cultural Speakers

In 2014, the United States was gripped by an Ebola panic. Yet not a single person both contracted and died from the disease while in the United States. So why were Americans so frightened?

In announcing its annual biggest-lie award, journalism fact-checker PolitiFact answered that question, writing,

> Fear of the disease stretched to every corner of America this fall, stoked by exaggerated claims from politicians and pundits. They said Ebola was easy to catch, that illegal immigrants may be carrying the virus across the southern border, that it was all part of a government or corporate conspiracy. Yet the claims—all wrong—distorted the debate about a serious public health issue. Together, they earn our Lie of the Year for 2014. (Holan and Sharockman, 2014)

PolitiFact offered several examples, among them Fox News analyst George Will's commentary,

> The problem is the original assumption, said with great certitude if not certainty, was that you need to have direct contact, meaning with bodily fluids from someone, because it's not airborne. There are doctors who are saying that in a sneeze or some cough, some of the airborne particles can be infectious.

Because Ebola is in reality transmitted through direct contact, not by inhaling airborne particles, PolitiFact rated Mr.

Will's words "False." But were they? Mr. Will did not directly say that people could contract the disease from a sneeze or cough, but that *there are some doctors who say so.* In fact, at least one prominent doctor had made this claim—US Senator Rand Paul, an ophthalmologist. Nonetheless, PolitiFact argued that Mr. Will failed in his responsibility as a speaker for presenting information in a misleading way. But what was listeners' responsibility in this instance?

Rather than simply hope that public discourse is entirely accurate or honest, we need to practice *discriminative listening.* We should not assume that everything we hear from those with national influence is necessarily true or in our best interests. This doesn't mean living life as a cynic; it does mean that listening critically to what we hear in the public forum is our duty.

Challenging our leaders and public speakers means that we need to set emotion aside and attempt to be objective in our assessments. How do you think Mr. Will's listeners reacted to his dire warning and its subsequent disproval? Perhaps some were disappointed in his apparent verbal carelessness. Others may have dismissed it as a simple mistake and defended their favored news commentator. Still others may have accepted that it was delivered with the best of intentions. But all had a responsibility as critical listeners to question his message, meanings, and motives.

say, or is it to *listen to and learn* from what they have to say? You can read about the responsibility inherent in discriminative listening in the box "Socially Responsible Communication: Questioning Our Cultural Speakers."

Becoming an Effective Listener

How do we become better, more efficient, and discriminating listeners? There are a number of steps you can take, some of which are related or overlap:

- **Search for something useful**. If you are in a listening situation, there must be something of interest—the person, the context, the topic—that put you there. Find something of personal value or interest in what you're hearing. If your listening is simply for fun, find a way to appreciate what you're hearing. If the topic is informational, see what you can learn. If you're talking with a friend, find worth in the relationship and therefor the value of listening. And if you have to make a decision about something, your listening should be automatically critical.

- **Be aware of what isn't said**. Communication is purposive (Chapter 1), so what speakers choose to *not* say is just as important as what they choose to say. Your romantic partner's response, "See you tomorrow," in reply to your "I love you" is meaningful not for what is said, but for what isn't. Politicians and advertisers often speak in platitudes and generalities, intentionally *not saying* what they mean. "Jobs are priority number one" and "You can be sure if it's Westinghouse" and "Magnavox gives you more" tell us little about how jobs will be created, what we can be sure of, and what we're being given more of.

- **Be transactive**. Offer appropriate feedback, ensuring that meaning making is reciprocal. Show interest verbally, using **backchannel cues**, noncommittal responses such as "Hmm," "Yeah," "I see," and "Interesting," and by asking clarifying questions when necessary. Also, show interest nonverbally, providing support through the use of head nods, facial expressions, and eye contact (Floyd, 2006).

  backchannel cues Noncommittal responses to conversational partners' talk.

- **Expend energy**. Discriminative listening takes effort. Listen actively and with purpose. If you know the issue or topic in advance, for example a performance review at work or a lecture by the campus career office on how to give a good interview, prepare for it by thinking about it in advance, reading up on the issue, and determining beforehand what you want to accomplish with your listening.

- **Reconcile thought speed and speech speed**. People normally speak at a rate of about 125 words per minute, but think at a much faster rate, at least 400 words a minute and much faster than that for some people (Goss, 1982). This is called **spare-brain time**, the difference between most people's rate of speech and the rate at which the brain can process language. Rather than default to boredom ("Get to the point, already!"), engage in critical and discriminative listening. Use the time to summarize for yourself what was

  spare-brain time The difference between most people's rate of speech and the rate at which the brain can process language.

said, critique the offered arguments and evidence, or determine what you might have presented or said that is better or more accurate.

- **Focus attention on central ideas**. Listen for the speaker's point; identify the central ideas as they are presented, and separate facts from opinions, evidence from conjecture, and examples from main points. When listeners focus on less relevant details, they frequently miss the overall message.

- **When possible, take meaningful notes**. Especially when engaging in informative and critical listening, take written notes. However, don't write down everything you hear—make your notes brief and focused on the key information. Not only does note taking improve listening effectiveness, it actually increases the degree of active listening that you bring to the communication encounter (Wolvin and Coakley, 1996).

mnemonics Memory devices based on patterns drawn from what's heard.

- **Use mnemonics**. There is also a mental form of note taking, **mnemonics**, memory devices based on patterns drawn from what's heard (the *m* is silent). In the case of test taking, these memory aids can improve student scores by as much as 77 percent (Miller, 1967). Of course, you are already familiar with *HURIER*. You may also be familiar with *ROY G. BIV*, the colors of the spectrum (**R**ed, **O**range, **Y**ellow, **G**reen, **B**lue, **I**ndigo, **V**iolet), *FANBOYS*, the seven English-language coordinating conjunctions (**F**or, **A**nd, **N**or, **B**ut, **O**r, **Y**et, **S**o), and *KINGS PLAY CARDS ON FAIRLY GOOD SOFT VELVET*, the categories in the classification of life (**K**ingdom, **P**hylum, **C**lass, **O**rder, **F**amily, **G**enus, **S**pecies, **V**ariety). Take advantage of spare-brain time to create mnemonics from what you're listening to. For example, your partner on your class project wants you to pick up some pens, tape, colored paper, and scissors at the bookstore, so you know to get *CAPS* (**C**olored paper, **A**dhesive tape, **P**ens, and **S**cissors).

- **Resist external distractions**. You can control information overload, so do it. Put down your phone and stop watching the clock. You may have to train yourself to do so, but it's worth it to improve your listening as well as your interpersonal relationships. However, you may not be able to control physical noise or a speaker's nonverbal tic. When faced with unwanted physical noise, either focus more intently or move the communication interaction. When confronted by a nonverbal tic, either concentrate more fully on the message or find a polite way to tell your conversational partner about the problem.

- **Hold your rebuttal**. Be patient; wait for the speaker to complete an idea, point, or argument. Not everyone builds arguments the same way, gets to the point by the same route, or presents information the way you do or you prefer. Consider how frustrating it is when the shoe's on the other foot—when you try to relay your thoughts to a listener who continually interrupts with counterpoints or emotional responses.

- **Be on the alert for green-flag or other hot-button words**. Rather than take these words as an excuse to stop listening, consider why they affect you so strongly. Listen more intently and wait until you better or more fully understand the speaker's point. When you've cleared your mind (or cooled down), you can more appropriately respond. Later, suggests Professor Nichols, when away from the listening situation, you should analyze more fully why the words carried so much emotional impact, "locating the original basis for our reaction to see if it still has a logical application to our current status" (Nichols, 1955, p. 297).

- **Keep an open mind**. Don't be judgmental. Listening expert Burley-Allen says that "quick and heated disagreement with the speaker's main points or arguments can cause a psychological deaf spot" (1995, p. 122). Keep an open mind; pay more rather than less attention; don't judge the other as a bad person. Disagreeing is far less judgmental than denigrating, and it focuses, rather than interferes with, listening.

- **Analyze nonverbal messages**. You know from Chapter 4 that 38 percent of the meaning we make comes from tone of voice and another 55 percent from facial expressions, so why not take advantage of this additional speaker-provided data and, at the same time, be a more empathic listener by being attentive and sensitive to his or her feelings as expressed in that nonverbal communication?

- **Evaluate and critique content, not delivery**. Unless you are the world's best speaker, you have little right to judge others' voices, nonverbal mannerisms, speaking personalities, or appearances. Of course you are free to do so; those external distractions do indeed represent noise introduced into the message by the speaker. But if you do, you may well deny yourself the opportunity to make the fullest meaning from what you hear. Remember, your responsibility as a listener is to resist external distractions, so listen for substance more than style.

- **Practice**. If you've ever played a musical instrument or taken a music appreciation class you know that appreciative listening can be improved with practice. So why not improve *all* types of listening by using daily communication encounters to work on those components of listening you want to improve. In fact, there is a significant amount of social scientific support for the idea that practice can indeed improve listening skill (Adler and Elmhorst, 2008).

- **Behave like a discriminative listener**. "If we would improve as listeners, we must behave like listeners," advises Professor Nichols. "Eminent psychologists tell us that one of the ways to achieve a habit is to behave as if we had that habit" (1955, p. 295). Make discriminative listening habitual.

Review of Learning Objectives

5.1 Define *listening* and explain how it differs from *hearing*.

Listening is actively making meaning from the spoken messages of others; hearing is the physical process of perceiving sounds. Hearing is physiological, while listening is cognitive, affective, and behavioral. Listening is *cognitive* (mental) when we attend to, understand, receive, and interpret content. It is *affective* (emotional) when we are motivated to attend to that content. And it is *behavioral* (physical) when we give verbal and nonverbal feedback.

5.2 Dispel a number of misconceptions about listening.

There are several misconceptions that interfere with successful listening: hearing is the same as listening; listening is easy, natural, and effortless; listening is a difficult skill to learn; listening is simply a matter of intelligence; read more, listen better; gender affects listening skill; speaking is more important than listening in the communication process; listening is primarily a matter of understanding a speaker's words.

5.3 Identify the components of effective listening.

Effective listening relies on the successful operation of six interrelated components that can be expressed in the HURIER model: hearing, understanding, remembering, interpreting, evaluating, and responding.

5.4 Identify barriers to successful listening.

Barriers to effective listening include physical noise, psychological noise (hearing what you want to hear; biased listening; prejudices; cultural differences; errors in connotative meaning; and green-flag words), physiological noise (such as hunger and other physical discomfort), and semantic noise (such as a speaker's heavy accent); external distractions (such as nonverbal distractions and information overload); and the adoption of a counterproductive listening style (fakers, dependent listeners, self-conscious listeners, and intellectual listeners).

5.5 Outline several types of listening.

There are five forms of listening. Informative listening takes place when the primary goal is to understand the message. Appreciative listening is listening for enjoyment or pleasure. Relational listening is lending someone a sympathetic ear. Critical listening is employed in the service of decision-making or analysis. And discriminative listening is paying close attention to more than the simple denotative meaning of what we hear. Discriminative listening should be part of all types of listening.

5.6 Describe steps to becoming a better listener.

There are several steps we can take to become better listeners. Search for something useful. Be aware of what isn't said. Be transactive. Expend energy. Reconcile thought speed and speech speed. Focus attention on central ideas. When possible, make meaningful notes. Use mnemonics. Resist external distractions. Hold your rebuttal. Be on the alert for hot-button words. Keep an open mind. Analyze nonverbal messages. Evaluate and critique content, not delivery. Practice. Behave like a discriminative listener.

Key Terms

listening 94

hearing 94

HURIER model 100

sender-receiver reciprocity 101

physical noise 102

psychological noise 102

green-flag words 103

physiological noise 104

semantic noise 104

external distractions 104

informative listening 106

appreciative listening 106

relational listening 106

critical listening 107

discriminative listening 107

backchannel cues 109

spare-brain time 109

mnemonics 110

Questions for Review

1. Differentiate between listening and hearing.

2. Identify three reasons that listening is important.

3. List eight misconceptions about listening.

4. What is the HURIER model of listening? Identify its six components.

5. What is physical noise? How does it impede effective listening?

6. What is psychological noise? Identify five forms of psychological noise.

7. What are physiological noise, semantic noise, and external distractions? How do they impede effective listening?

8. Identify and describe four counterproductive listening styles.

9. Identify and describe four types of listening.

10. Identify and describe the 16 tips for becoming an effective listener.

Questions for Discussion

1. Think about the best listener you know. Identify those characteristics that lead you to think of her or him in this way. How is being with her or him different from spending time with others you know? What can this good listener teach you that will help you become a better listener?

2. Team up with a classmate or friend and ask him or her to evaluate you as a listener. After listening to that assessment, summarize for that person what you heard and then ask him or her to reconcile the original evaluation with your listening performance on this exercise. Switch roles. Discuss what you've learned about yourself as a listener and as an evaluator of listening.

3. Although it's appropriate to say that speakers and listeners share equal responsibility in meaning making, can you make the case that in certain situations, for example a speech by a politician, an argument between romantic partners, and a conversation between two friends about one's breakup with a long-time partner, that one participant bears more responsibility that the other? Explain your position.

6

Relational and Conflict Communication

All you wanted to do was have some friends over to watch the game. But your roommate Eden is telling you that she doesn't want to be around Phil, one of the guys you invited.

You try to talk to her about it. "What's the issue?" you ask. After several "Nothings," she explains that she doesn't like the guy because he's an "Eeyore." "Like in the Winnie-the-Pooh books," she explains. You see the connection. Eden's right: Phil *is* kind of a downer, always whining and complaining. Something's always wrong. The sofa will be too soft; the sound on the TV will be too low; the snacks will be too fattening; the announcers will be biased; and the team needs to be playing in a tougher conference.

You ask Eden to just try; maybe if she gets to know him, you suggest, it might not be so bad. "It's just not worth it," she replies. "I don't need another 'friend,' especially one I know I won't particularly like." "Besides," she adds, "you know I'm bad at small talk."

We've all been there. We work to build, maintain, and manage our relationships. We sometimes work to end them. Sometimes it's easy; sometimes it's not. Not all our friends get along. Not everyone we meet is destined to be a close friend. Relationships are hard work, and as harsh as it may sound, we decide that some people are worth more of an effort than are others. Sometimes people fulfill specific needs for us, and that's all we want from them. Some relationships can be fun and rewarding; others can be difficult and unrewarding, resulting in conflict. Regardless, we shape them all through interpersonal communication.

In this chapter, we'll look at the very human necessity of using communication to build, maintain, manage, and even end relationships. And because the best relationships can experience their ups and downs, we'll also examine conflict—how and why it happens and how to manage it to ensure an equitable outcome for all involved.

Learning Objectives

6.1   Differentiate among several of the most important theories of interpersonal communication.

6.2   Examine conflict and analyze the elements that create it.

6.3   Identify different types of conflict.

6.4   Describe the stages of interpersonal conflict.

6.5   Compare different conflict management styles, and determine the style you use most frequently.

6.6   Know what to do—and what not to do—when in conflict.

The Value of Relationships

The value of relationships might seem obvious. We like having friends and family nearby. We may like being alone, but very few of us like being lonely.

Beyond this obvious value, there is even scientific evidence of the physiological benefits of meaningful interpersonal relationships. For example, research has linked the lack of social contact to harmful changes in people's immune systems (Cohen, 2013). Psychologist Barbara Fredrickson and her colleagues further demonstrated that "positive emotions, positive social connections, and physical health influence one another in a self-sustaining upward spiral dynamic" (Kok et. al., 2013, p. 1). She explained the connection, "In short, the more attuned to others you become, the healthier you become, and vice versa. This mutual influence also explains how a lack of positive social contact diminishes people. Your heart's capacity for friendship also obeys the biological law of 'use it or lose it.' If you don't regularly exercise your ability to connect face-to-face, you'll eventually find yourself lacking some of the basic biological capacity to do so" (Frederickson, 2013, p. SR14).

COMMUNICATION IN THE WORKPLACE

Mastering the Soft Skills

Research consistently indicates that employees with strong interpersonal skills are more likely to be considered for promotions. Those skills also benefit your organization. Management consultant Stephen Covey explains, "You cannot continuously improve interdependent systems and processes until you progressively perfect interdependent, interpersonal relationships" (in Rampur, 2010). Personnel manager Stephen Rampur adds, "Employees feel good if there is a favorable environment at the workplace. If employees have a mutual understanding with each other, there are fewer chances of any kind of workplace conflicts. It has also been observed that strong interpersonal relationships lead to motivation among employees" (2010).

Clearly, your career success—and that of the organization that employs you—depend in great part on what are commonly referred to as *soft skills*: "a composite of *interpersonal (people) skills* and *personal (career) attributes* . . . The ability to communicate effectively—to handle difficult conversations in such a manner that problems are resolved—is an interpersonal skill" (italics in original; DeKay, 2012, p. 451).

What soft skills do employers value most? Marcel Robles (2012) surveyed 90 business executives who identified more than 500 individual skills. Evaluating the frequency with which each was mentioned and how important these business leaders thought each was to their employees' success, she identified the *Top 10 Soft Skills Needed in Today's Workplace:*

1. *Communication*—Demonstrate good oral and speaking capabilities; have good writing, presenting, and listening skills.
2. *Courtesy*—Be respectful; have manners and know business etiquette; be gracious.
3. *Flexibility*—Be adaptable and willing to change; be a lifelong learner; accept new things, adjust; be teachable.
4. *Integrity*—Be honest and ethical; have high morals and personal values; do what's right.
5. *Interpersonal skills*—Be nice, personable, friendly, nurturing, empathetic, patient, sociable, and warm; have a sense of humor; have self-control.
6. *Positive attitude*—Be optimistic, enthusiastic, encouraging, happy, and confident.
7. *Professionalism*—Have a good appearance; be businesslike, well-dressed, and poised.
8. *Responsibility*—Be accountable, reliable, resourceful, self-disciplined, and conscientious; get the job done; want to do well; display common sense.
9. *Teamwork*—Get along with others; be cooperative, agreeable, supportive, helpful, and collaborative.
10. *Work ethic*—Be hardworking, loyal, self-motivated, and on time.

Perhaps more immediately obvious, maintaining good interpersonal relationships at work can help ensure career success, as you can read in the box "Mastering the Soft Skills."

We may want relationships—we may even need them to remain healthy—but what do they offer us? That is, what do they provide us on an ongoing basis (Weiss, 1974)? There are six **provisions of relationships**:

- *Attachment*—This is the emotional bond we have with others that gives us a sense of security. Physical and sexual touch, often present in close relationships, are also part of this provision.

- *Reassurance of worth*—We need to know that people see us as competent and of value. We look to people who matter, those with whom we have a good relationship, for that reassurance. We already have encountered

provisions of relationships What relationships offer or provide us.

this concept as symbolic interaction's significant others (Chapter 1) and the development and maintenance of face (Chapter 3).

- *Guidance*—Everyone, at least sometimes, needs advice and information, and who better to get it from than people we know and trust?

- *Reliable alliance*—We need to know we're not alone, that there are people we can trust to provide help when we need it. As singers from Frank Sinatra to Keith Urban have observed, "Everybody needs somebody sometime."

- *Social integration*—We want to know that there are people who share our values and interests and who enjoy our company. We want these people in our lives; we want to keep them close. We do that through relationships.

- *Opportunity to provide nurturance*—We need to be needed. As Barbra Streisand sang, "People who need people are the luckiest people in the world."

Robert Weiss used these provisions to distinguish between two types of relationships, *attachments* and *affiliations*. "**Attachments**," he wrote, "are based in the linkage of the relationship with a sense of security—one's own or another's. **Affiliations** are based in the linkage of the relationship with a sense of alliance" (1998, p. 679). Attachments tend to be characterized by exclusivity (for example, best friends, spouses, siblings); they are persistent (for example, when a breakup is threatened, one or both of the parties will work to maintain the attachment); and they provide security. Affiliations tend to be in the aggregate (for example, best friends have other friends); they are interrupted with ease (for example, your circle of friends changes when you are on campus as opposed to at home or work); and they are the product of a *satisfaction-seeking* or *defensive alliance*. That is, they tend to be more instrumental or functional in how we go about our daily lives. Both types of relationships are essential to how we live, and the quality of both relies on effective interpersonal communication (as you can read in the box "It Takes Two to Tango, but Someone Has to Lead").

The Role of Interpersonal Communication

Good or bad, rewarding or draining, our relationships depend on **interpersonal communication**, which we define as communication between people in relationships. A unit of two people communicating (as opposed to a group) is called a **dyad**. Not all dyads are examples of interpersonal relationships, however. You may chat with the person in line with you at the coffee shop, and for that moment, you are relating to that person—but you are not part of a relationship with him or her. You may also be a regular at that coffee shop and know the owner. You greet her by her first name; you ask about her kids'

attachments Relationships linking partners through a sense of security.

affiliations Relationships linking partners through a sense of alliance.

interpersonal communication Communication between people in relationships.

dyad Two people communicating interpersonally.

PERSONALLY RESPONSIBLE COMMUNICATION

It Takes Two to Tango, but Someone Has to Lead

If relationships are to succeed, both parties have to participate in maintaining them, and each person has to do his or her individual part.

Communication scholars Laura Guerrero, Peter Anderson, and Walid Afifi (2011) reviewed the research on **relational satisfaction**, the enjoyment or pleasure people derive from their relationships, and developed a list of 10 "prosocial behaviors" that "promote relational closeness, trust, and liking" (pp. 207–208). You'll easily recognize not only the role of interpersonal communication, but your personal responsibility in each:

Relational satisfaction benefits from prosocial behavior, such as taking walks, doing chores, or in this case, boating with your partner.

- *Positivity*—Making interactions enjoyable and pleasant; for example, giving your partner compliments.
- *Openness and routine talk*—Talking and listening; for example, asking questions about your partner's work or classes, self-disclosing, sharing your thoughts and feelings.
- *Assurances*—Giving your partner assurances about your commitment; for example, talking about the future.
- *Social networking*—Spending time with your partner's friends and family.
- *Task sharing*—Performing routine tasks and chores that are part of the relationship; for example, sharing household duties or planning finances with your partner.
- *Supportiveness*—Giving social support and encouragement; for example, offering comfort when needed or making sacrifices for your partner.
- *Joint activities*—Doing things and spending time with your partner; for example, taking walks, playing sports, or just hanging out together.
- *Romance and affection*—Revealing your caring feelings for your partner; for example, saying "I love you"

to a romantic partner or "You're a great pal" to a close friend.
- *Humor*—Using inside jokes and sarcasm; for example, giving a funny nickname to or laughing a lot with your partner.
- *Constructive conflict management*—Dealing with conflict constructively, working toward problem-solving and restoring harmony; for example, listening to your partner's positions, finding acceptable solutions, and attacking the problem, never your partner.

Think of your closest relationships, ones that are important to you: friends, family, or romantic relationships. How active are you in engaging in prosocial behaviors in each of these? How close a correlation is there between the relationships that bring you the most satisfaction and your commitment to prosocial relational maintenance?

health; she asks about your studies. That's an example of an interpersonal relationship. Of course, you have many different kinds of relationships, with friends and family members most obviously, but the common thread is some level of *personal closeness*. You may be standing closely behind that person in the coffee shop, but you share no personal closeness. If you wanted to get to know your fellow coffee drinker, however, you'd do so through interpersonal communication.

relational satisfaction
The enjoyment or pleasure people derive from their relationships.

This connection was initiated, maintained, and potentially could be ended through interpersonal communication.

We use interpersonal communication to

- *Engage* others; that is, we attempt to move the relationship from impersonal to more personal. You might start a conversation with your line mate with something like, "Coffee's great here. It's the best around, don't you think?"

- *Manage* the developing relationship. Based on the response—perhaps, "You seem to know your coffee," or "Yeah, I'm a java junky of sorts"—you might suggest meeting there the next day. Then as you get to know one another, the meaning you make from your communication tells you just how much and what kind of a relationship you want. Is this just a coffee-shop friend? Is this someone you might want to hang out with more regularly?

- *Disengage* from the relationship. You eventually decide that you need to separate from your coffee-drinking partner because you've learned from your conversations that all you really had in common was your need for caffeine. You decide you want to scale back the relationship; you do so through communication, both verbal and nonverbal.

Developing and Maintaining Relationships

The fact that we use communication to engage, manage, and disengage from relationships suggests that relationships develop. We've all made new friends by making more personal connections with acquaintances. But development isn't always forward—sometimes relationships move from more personal to less so. We sometimes drift away from friends and turn those closest to us into strangers. And relational development, either forward or backward, isn't always in a straight line. We all know that friendships ebb and flow and that our siblings are our best friends when they're not our worst enemies.

A number of interpersonal communication theories can help explain the various processes involved in developing and maintaining relationships. We'll look at four: Uncertainty Reduction Theory, Social Penetration Theory, Social Exchange Theory, and Relational Dialectics Theory.

Uncertainty Reduction Theory

Communication scholar Danielle Pillet-Shore explains why, when we meet new people, we want to get to know them better:

> Human nature abhors a lack of knowledge, order, and understanding about the surrounding social world. To act socially, humans must define and make sense . . . But when confronted with a "stranger"—a person one has never "met" and thus a person with whom one has no mutually established personal acquaintanceship—one is confronted with a person lacking definition . . . A stranger, then, embodies a locus of uncertainty. (2011, pp. 73–74)

You may ask, What's the big deal? It's a stranger—so what? The big deal is that we want to make sure we act properly; our identity is on the line. We want to properly frame the encounter and its actors (Chapter 1) so we can employ the proper facework (Chapter 3). So what do we do? We attempt to reduce the uncertainty in the encounter.

The theory that helps us understand how we do this is called, not surprisingly, **Uncertainty Reduction Theory**, the idea that we use communication to predict and explain the behavior of others in the initial stages of a relationship. Its creators, Charles Berger and Richard Calabrese, explain that central to Uncertainty Reduction Theory "is the assumption that when strangers meet, their primary concern is one of uncertainty reduction or increasing predictability about the behavior of both themselves and others in the interaction" (1975, p. 100). It's a "primary concern" because we don't like the feelings of doubt that arise in these situations—"The beginnings of social relationships are fraught with uncertainties" (Berger, 1988, p. 244). Those uncertainties are cognitive and behavioral. *Cognitive uncertainties* revolve around the fact that we are unsure of the other's attitudes and beliefs. *Behavioral uncertainties* revolve around the fact that we are unsure of how the other will act. In addition, behavioral uncertainty has two parts, or components. You want to *predict* what the other will do, and you want to *explain* the person's behavior.

Back to the coffee shop. You're simply not that uncomfortable in your uncertainties about the person in line with you. That's because you know how people usually behave in this setting, so you have already reduced your uncertainty to a degree. The stranger's attitudes? Likes coffee. The stranger's behaviors? Knows how to stand in line and pay. What else do you need to know? Uncertainty Reduction Theory explains that that depends on your *motivations* to reduce your uncertainty, and there are three factors that influence those motivations (Berger, 1979):

- **Incentives**—You will be more motivated if you perceive that the other will somehow be rewarding to you. Perhaps you recognize your line mate from communication class and think she or he could be a good study mate. Or maybe you find her or him physically attractive, so you begin a conversation. Many critics think that physical attractiveness has taken on too much importance in our culture as a relational incentive, as you can read in the box "Beauty Is Only Screen Deep."

- **Deviance**—You will be more motivated if the other acts in unexpected ways or violates the usual rules and norms of the situation. You're

THUMBNAIL THEORY

Uncertainty Reduction Theory

People use communication to predict and explain the behavior of others in the initial stages of a relationship. They work to reduce cognitive and behavioral uncertainties in an effort to determine how others think and to predict and explain their actions. If sufficiently motivated, people will engage in a variety of information-seeking strategies to reduce uncertainty in order to decide whether to advance a relationship.

incentive Motivation to reduce uncertainty based on likely reward.

deviance Motivation to reduce uncertainty if another acts in unexpected ways or violates expected rules and norms.

Deviance from expected norms sometimes motivates uncertainty reduction.

prospect of future interaction Motivation to reduce uncertainty based on the likelihood of future interaction.

information-seeking strategy Method of reducing uncertainty.

THUMBNAIL THEORY

Social Penetration Theory

Relationships move from initial interaction to greater stability through interpersonal communication. Relationships generally develop systematically and predictably from the non-intimate to the intimate. Self-disclosure drives this relational development, and it can include dissolution as well as progress. As such, interpersonal communication changes across four stages: orientation, exploratory affective exchange, affective exchange, and stable exchange.

intrigued by something about the stranger. Maybe it's the odd attire—sandals on a snowy day, purple-dyed hair, three ear piercings. Note, though, that deviance only goes so far in motivating uncertainty reduction. An unexpected kiss in response to your comment about the coffee might diminish, rather than increase, your motivation to reduce uncertainty. That unwanted smooch tells you all you need to know. (Think back to Chapter 4's discussion of Expectancy Violation Theory.)

- **Prospect of future interaction**—You will be more motivated if you think you will have to interact with the other (whether you want to or not) in the future. You always find yourself in line with this person, who seems to be about your age. Might as well find out what you can.

How do you do that? You engage in **information-seeking strategies**, different ways to reduce your uncertainty about the other (Berger and Kellerman, 1994). You could engage in a variety of strategies:

- *Passive strategies*—You can watch the other in a variety of social situations. You can do a **reactivity search**, in which you watch the other react to events in the environment. Or you can do a **disinhibition search**, observing the other in a particularly comfortable situation, when he or she is "letting her or his hair down." You just stand back and watch your coffee-shop stranger deal with the server and other people in line.

- *Active strategies*—You can ask other people about your stranger of interest. You talk to people in the coffee shop who seem to know this person.

- *Interactive strategies*—You engage the stranger in conversation, hoping that by asking questions you can elicit more information. You say (as suggested earlier), "Coffee's great here. It's the best around, don't you think?"

Social Penetration Theory

But what happens now? Your information-seeking is complete, so it's time for the relationship to evolve (if you want it to). According to Irwin Altman and Dalmas Taylor's **Social Penetration Theory**, relationships move from initial interaction to greater stability through interpersonal communication (1973). This theory is based on a number of assumptions:

1. *Relationships progress from non-intimate to intimate.* At the beginning of a relationship the parties keep the conversation at a superficial level; as they get to know one another better, they communicate more deeply.

2. *That progress is generally systematic and predictable.* Yes, there is ebb and flow; relational development is not a straight line from "Hello" to best friends for

Beauty Is Only Screen Deep

In 2011 philosopher and filmmaker Thomas Keith released *The Bro Code: How Contemporary Culture Creates Sexist Men,* an examination of how young heterosexual men are socialized toward certain expectations of women: What makes a woman attractive? What makes her a good relational partner? How should she be treated? He looked at "movies and music videos that glamorize womanizing, pornography that trades in the brutalization of women, comedians who make fun of sexual assault, [and] the recent groundswell in men's magazines and cable TV shows that revel in reactionary myths of American manhood." Think *Maxim* or MTV's *Spring Break,* music videos, and Internet pornography. His conclusions were harsh: young American men are socialized into a gendered, highly sexualized view of women that leads them to see women as objects.

The Bro Code is a documentary film, but there is a considerable body of scientific scholarship that supports Keith's argument, one that typically looks at media content less obviously sexualized than that in Keith's movie. For example, more than 25 years ago George Comstock (1991, p. 175) reviewed decades of research on young people's socialization and concluded that a "modest but positive association" exists between television exposure and the holding of traditional notions of gender and sex roles. Moreover, not only do media portrayals encourage young people's expectations of themselves, they can encourage expectations

of others. "Portrayals in television and other media of highly attractive persons," he wrote, "may encourage dissatisfaction [with] or lowered evaluations of the attractiveness of those of the pertinent sex in real life" (1991, p. 176).

More recently, Kistler and Lee demonstrated that college men who were exposed to sexual hip-hop music videos "expressed greater objectification of women, sexual permissiveness, stereotypical gender attitudes, and acceptance of rape" than those who were not (2010, p. 67). They discovered that this content was "likely to be used in [young men's] behavioral decisions." But their "most disturbing finding . . . is the significant effect of exposure on male participants' acceptance of rape myths. Men in the highly sexual hip-hop videos were portrayed as powerful, sexually assertive, and as having a fair degree of sexual prowess, whereas the women were portrayed as sexually available, scantily clad, and often preening over the men. This might have served as a cue to male participants . . . that women exist for the entertainment and sexual fulfillment of men" (p. 83). In 2012 Samson and Grabe studied the "sexual propensities of emerging adults," college men and women 17 to 25 years old, and their consumption of a wide variety of media (music videos, network and cable television, movies, and the Internet). Their results "point to media as a significant sexual socializing agent in shaping human psychosexual propensities" (2012, p. 293).

---

life. But deeper movement into a relationship tends to follow recognizable cultural patterns. You know when it's time to bring your sweetheart home to meet the parents; you know how big or small a gift is appropriate on your first Valentine's Day together. As Altman and Taylor explained, "People seem to possess very sensitive tuning mechanisms which enable them to program carefully their interpersonal relationships" (1973, p. 8).

3. *Relational development includes depenetration and dissolution.* Relationships grow, but they also wither or die. **Depenetration**, the deterioration of a relationship, often leads to its end, **dissolution**. The unraveling, according to Uncertainty Reduction Theory, is also systematic and predictable. Communication becomes less intimate; "I am . . ." and "I will . . ." become more common; "We are . . ." and "We will . . ." become less so.

reactivity search Watching another react to events in the environment.

disinhibition search Observing another in a particularly comfortable situation.

depenetration The deterioration of a relationship.

dissolution The ending of a relationship.

We use communication about ourselves to get others to know us, and when they do likewise, we get to know them.

4. *Self-disclosure is at the heart of relational development.* We use communication about ourselves to get others to know us, and when they reciprocate—when they do the same—we get to know them. Altman and Taylor explain, "Making [the] self accessible to another person is intrinsically gratifying," so we are happy to move even deeper into the relationship (1973, p. 50). This **self-disclosure**, the intentional revelation of information about oneself, not only shapes the relationship at the moment, it maps out or defines its future. This intentional revelation of information about ourselves is so important to us that we humans devote between 30 and 40 percent of all our talk solely to self-disclosure (Tamir and Mitchell, 2012).

self-disclosure Intentional revelation of information about oneself.

One way to think of interpersonal communication and relational development is to envision a relationship as an onion. Figure 6.1 can help. "The onion has four layers: the surface, the periphery, and the intermediate and central layers," explain communication scholars Paul Mongeau and Mary Lynn Henningsen, "As information is disclosed, the layers of the onion are peeled back, signifying the development of the relationship" (2008, p. 366). The *surface* is like the onion's skin, they explain. This is what is disclosed nonverbally, simply through observation—information like sex, age, and race. The *periphery* is akin to the onion's first one or two layers; self-disclosure here involves the kinds of routine information you'd share with just about anyone—facts like your home town, college major, or job. Peel a few more layers back from the onion's more outer rings, and you reach the *intermediate layers*; self-disclosure here is of information that is not really secret, but that is shared only occasionally—topics like your religion or your favorite childhood memory. Peel away all the layers of the onion and you reach its core, its *central layers*; self-disclosure here is marked by the private and cautious sharing of

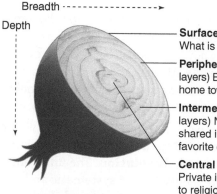

Breadth ·············· ➤

Depth

Surface (the onion's skin)
What is seen: age, sex, race

Periphery (first one or two layers) Biographical information: home town, job, major

Intermediate layers (inner layers) Not secret, but rarely shared information: religion, favorite childhood memory

Central layers (inner core) Private information: commitment to religion, brother's drug dependence

FIGURE 6.1 Social Penetration Theory's Onion Metaphor

information—you discuss your commitment to your religion or your brother's drug dependence.

This peeling away of the onion's layers—movement from impersonal to more personal communication—is guided by our culture's **norm of reciprocity**: when we reveal something about ourselves, the other person will typically respond with similar information. For example, you tell someone your name, he or she will respond in kind. You disclose your religion; you assume the person you are talking with will do the same. As a norm, reciprocity is common and expected, so when it does happen, speakers know they can continue to "peel layers"; when it does not, though, that's likely a sign that this is as far as the relationship will go.

Back to the coffee shop: You say, "Hi, I'm Pat." A response of "That's nice" will more than likely end any thoughts of further communication. But the reply "Hi, I'm Chris" says let's talk more. Of course, at later stages in the relationship, self-disclosure becomes riskier, but also more rewarding, and the onion metaphor helps us here as well.

If you cut an onion in half at its equator, it shows depth (the center core that extends from the newly exposed surface to the bottom of the onion) and breadth (the span across the surface, showing the onion's rings). Relationships, like our halved onion, have *depth*—how personal is the shared information—and *breadth*—the number of topics that can safely be discussed. As a relationship develops, as self-disclosure increases and is increasingly reciprocated, partners have more things to talk about and their communication about those things becomes deeper. It is this reciprocity-fueled depth and breadth of communication that characterize Social Penetration Theory's four stages of relational development:

- The first stage is **orientation**. This is interaction between people who do not know one another. This is the kind of relationship you might have with one of your required-course professors or with the stranger in the coffee shop. There is little sharing of personal information, and communication is based on social convention. Conversations are scripted and superficial. Here, at the surface level, small talk dominates because it serves three important communication functions. First, it is an *audition*. Good, norm-following conversation tells others that you are socially competent and aware, worthy of continued interaction. Second, it is a *mechanism for controlling self-disclosure*. Neither small-talk partner expects much self-disclosure, so each is free to reveal more personal information at his or her own speed. Finally, it's *painless and cost-free*. You haven't given up too much by providing your name and major, and if you don't move on to more personal matters, you've actually revealed very little.

- The second stage is **exploratory affective exchange**. This is the kind of relationship you might have with a student who shares a couple of classes with you or that you might have with the java-junkie stranger in those first few sit-downs at the coffee shop. Communication here is more open and comfortable, less scripted. The shared information goes beyond

norm of reciprocity The expectation that revelations about oneself will produce responses of similar information.

orientation Relational stage characterized by interaction between people who do not know one another.

exploratory affective exchange Relational stage characterized by open and comfortable communication.

the norm-approved small talk of the previous stage, but still remains at the periphery, maybe with an occasional move in the direction of the intermediate layers of the onion.

affective exchange
Relational stage characterized by much self-disclosure.

- **Affective exchange** marks the third stage. Here communication is characterized by a good deal of self-disclosure. This is where your close friends and romantic partners reside. There is increased self-disclosure, as most personal barriers have fallen. Breadth and depth of topics move freely across and between the intermediate and central layers of the onion.

stable exchange Relational stage characterized by rich, open, and free communication.

- The final stage is **stable exchange**. Communication here is rich, open, and free across all the onion's levels. You and your partner can and do talk about everything and at all levels. Often you don't have to say anything at all to communicate something important; you can finish one another's sentences.

Keep in mind, though, relationships fall apart following the same stages, but in reverse. "Once set in motion," Taylor and Altman wrote, "the exchange processes that occur in the dissolution of an interpersonal relationship are . . . systematic and proceed gradually, this time from inner (intimate) to outer (non-intimate) levels of exchange" (1987, p. 260). But why do relationships dissolve? Have you ever explained the end of a friendship, romantic or otherwise, with "I wasn't getting what I wanted out of the relationship" or "It just wasn't worth it" or "Way too high maintenance"? If so, then you know the answer, one explained by another theory of interpersonal communication and relationships, Social Exchange Theory.

THUMBNAIL THEORY

Social Exchange Theory

People evaluate relationships in a more-or-less rational manner to ensure maximum rewards and minimal costs. To assess the value of their relationships, they undertake an economics-like cost-benefit analysis.

Social Exchange Theory

Social Exchange Theory is based on a long-held assumption about human beings: "Individuals attempt to maximize their rewards and minimize their costs" (Stafford, 2008, p. 378). Social Exchange Theory, then, assumes that people evaluate their relationships in a more-or-less rational manner to ensure that this occurs; in fact, they undertake an economics-like cost-benefit analysis to assess the value of those relationships (Thibaut and Kelley, 1959). The formula looks like this:

Benefits of the Relationship − Costs of the Relationship = Value of the Relationship

It's quite likely, for example, that you have maintained relationships with many more of your high school friends than your parents did with theirs in the first few years after graduation. Let's assume that the *benefits* of those relationships to you and your parents are equal. But what about the *costs*? To stay in touch with friends today "costs" very little. You can communicate through Facebook, Twitter, Instagram, and Facetime or Skype. You always have your phone with you, and you can expect quick responses because your friends are just as attached to their phones as you. These are high-value friendships for you, but your parents did not have these technologies, so the costs of similar relationships were higher for them.

The products, or **outcomes**, of many such analyses are not as simple as the formula or this example might suggest, however. If they were, we would never question high-outcome relationships (many rewards, few costs), nor would we suffer those with low outcomes (few rewards, many costs). This is because, while we carry with us expectations of what we think we should be getting from a specific relationship, our **comparison level (CL)**, we also think about the likely outcome of other relationships, our **comparison level of alternatives (CL$_{ALT}$)**. In other words, as we interact with our environments and the people in them, we are constantly judging our current relationships against ones we've had in the past (**CL**) and against ones we think we might have in the future (**CL$_{ALT}$**).

What are the costs and benefits of keeping your high school friends?

Return to our example of high school friends. The results of your analysis revealed that these were high-outcome friendships for you; they return more than they cost. But compare those relationships to possible alternatives—for example, relationships with the people around you at school. The cost, or ease of communication, in both cases may be about equal. But as you look around, talk to people, and think about it, you may decide that building new relationships might return *even greater* reward. In addition, none of your new classmates knew the "old you," so maybe you are free to grow up a bit faster, to reinvent yourself as an adult. That's a pretty good reward as well. If the outcome of this alternative cost-benefit analysis outweighs that of maintaining your high school friendships, you'll start to drift away from those older friendships and replace them with a new set of relationships.

outcome Product of relational cost-benefit analyses.

comparison level (CL) Expectations of benefit from a specific relationship.

comparison level of alternatives (CL$_{ALT}$) Likely benefits from other relationships.

Relational Dialectics Theory

This all sounds so reasonable. We use communication to reduce uncertainty when we first meet new people; we share (or don't share) communication as we develop and manage the relationships that grow out of those encounters; and we make relatively pragmatic judgments about what we want from those relationships and the value of maintaining them. If only it were that easy.

The theories we've looked at so far were never intended to suggest that relationships were easy. Instead, as *stage theories,* they are designed to "describe how people initiate, escalate, and dissolve relationships. More specifically, these theories explain *how and why interpersonal communication changes* as relationships move from strangers or acquaintances to close friends or romantic partners, and perhaps back again" (emphasis added; Mongeau and Henningsen, 2008, p. 363). There is, however, another approach to understanding the role of communication in relationships—*dialectical theories*; they view interpersonal communication as the mechanism we use to manage the inevitable and necessary tensions that exist in all relationships.

Relational Dialectics Theory

Meaning making between relationship partners emerges from the interplay of competing discourses. Relationships have a variety of internal and external tensions in need of resolution—dialectics—that are negotiated through partners' discourse.

dialectic Tension in need of resolution.

discourse What is said and its interpretation in negotiating relational tensions.

connection-autonomy Tension between the need to remain connected and the need to be independent.

inclusion-seclusion Tension between doing things together and engaging as a couple with others.

Relational Dialectics Theory, then, "is a theory of the meaning making between relationship parties that emerges from the interplay of competing discourses" (Braithwaite and Baxter and, 2008, p. 349). If you've been in a real friendship or a serious romantic relationship, you know that they are often filled with **dialectics**, tensions between opposing forces that need resolution. **Discourses** are what we say and how we interpret what we say in negotiating relational tensions. Relational Dialectics Theory's central assumptions (Baxter and Braithwaite, 2008) are the following:

- *Meanings emerge from the struggle of different, often opposing discourses.* Relational development is not linear; it is the product of the ongoing push and pull of partners' various needs. Contradiction—differences of opinion—is inevitable (it will happen) and necessary (it must happen for growth) in relationships. "Whatever you want, dear, anything you say" gets pretty old pretty fast in most relationships.

- *The interpretation of discourses occurs both in the moment and over time.* Partners react to what is said when it is said, but they also make overall meaning of individual conversations and collections of conversations that occur at different times during the relationship. Rather than develop by stages, argues the dialectical approach, relationships are characterized by constant change based on immediate and ongoing meaning making. More than likely you'd interpret "I love you" on the second date a bit differently than you would on the fifty-second. It's even possible you might never actually hear those words, but know very well from all the conversations you've had with your partner that you are indeed loved (or not).

- *The interpretation of competing discourses constitutes social reality.* Recall our discussion of the constitutive role of communication from Chapter 1. Reality is not *reflected* in what we say; it is constituted, or *created*, by what we say. At what stage is your relationship? Where on the onion are you? Your communication with your partner and the meanings you mutually negotiate will determine the reality of your relationship. Are you going steady? Does that mean you and your partner are exclusive? *You* may say and think you are, but that doesn't make it so, because your partner may *say* "going steady" but may *interpret* it much differently than you do.

What are the dialectics that must be negotiated in most relationships? There are three primary ones, and each has an *internal* (inside the relationship) and *external* (with others outside the relationship) dimension (Baxter, 1990):

- **Connection-autonomy dialectic**—This is the struggle between the need to remain connected to the other and the need to be independent. You love your family and you want to stay in touch, but you're a grown-up now, and they need to let you be one. You love your boyfriend or girlfriend, but you also need some time to yourself. This is the most common tension in relationships precisely because how close you and your partner are defines the relationship. Played out externally, this is the **inclusion-seclusion dialectic**. Here the tension is between doing things together and engaging as a couple with others. "You know, we spend so much time together that we never see our friends anymore." "You're right, but we're so busy we never have time to ourselves." "But our friends are getting really mad at us." You and your partner must resolve the tension with your friends, and you must also resolve for yourselves how you want to respond to it.

- **Certainty-uncertainty dialectic**—This is the struggle between finding comfort and security in the relationship and needing a bit of novelty and excitement. Too much certainty makes a relationship boring; too much uncertainty makes it uncomfortable. "What do you want to do?" "I don't know. What do you want to do?" "I don't know. Wanna try something different?" "Like what?" "I don't know—maybe going to a late movie." "I don't know—you really wanna be out that late?" This tension manifests itself externally as the **conventional-unique dialectic**: you want to be the couple that everyone says is special. "There's no one in the world like you two!" But you must balance that against the values and expectations of those around you, especially those you deem important. The tension may be coming from the outside, but you and your partner have to negotiate it internally.

- **Openness-closedness dialectic**—This is the struggle between being able to say anything and the need for discretion. You may completely dislike your best friend's sister, and honesty has always been an important part of your friendship, but maybe your aversion to her is something you should keep to yourself. When dealing with the external world, this is the **revelation-concealment dialectic**: there are some things you want to share with the world; there are some things that are just for you two. When does a couple announce a pregnancy? When do "friends" announce an engagement or a breakup? Again, you may feel pressure from outside the relationship to reveal what you prefer to hold private, but it is you and your partner who must negotiate how you two, as a couple, will respond.

These tensions exist for a reason. Their negotiation not only defines the relationship, it defines the people in the relationship. It shapes their identity internally ("You are the best girlfriend/boyfriend ever!") and externally ("How can you let her treat you like that?"). These tensions are negotiated through communication. Relational Dialectics Theory calls this **praxis**—the choice of specific communication actions. Do you and your partner *deny* the tensions? Do you *segment* the tensions, for example, autonomous at work, connected at home? Do you *balance* the tensions, for example, spending meaningful time together, but not smothering one another?

Interpersonal Communication and Conflict

Even the best communicators in the best relationships can fail to balance these personal and relational needs. When this happens, there is **conflict**, "an expressed struggle between at least two interdependent parties, who perceive

certainty-uncertainty Tension between the need for comfort and security and the need for novelty and excitement.

conventional-unique Tension between being the couple others want and defining the relationship for yourselves.

openness-closedness Tension between being able to say anything and the need for discretion.

revelation-concealment Tension between meeting others' demands for information and the relational need for discretion.

praxis Choice of specific communication actions.

conflict An expressed struggle between at least two interdependent parties who perceive incompatible goals, scarce rewards, and interference from the other party.

Conflict is natural and normal, especially between friends.

incompatible goals, scarce rewards, and interference from the other party in achieving their goals" (Wilmot and Wilmot, 1978, p. 9).

Disagreement is not conflict; friends and lovers will—should—often disagree. You no doubt disagree with a lot of what your friends do and think. But those disagreements do not typically produce conflict. Conflict is a behavior; it is an *expressed* struggle of ideas, values, wants, or needs. Communication scholars Joyce Wilmot and William Wilmot explain: "Relational conflict is communicative behavior; it is impossible to have conflict without verbal or nonverbal behavior, or both. The 'expression' may be very subtle, but it must be present for the activity to be interpersonal conflict" (p. 10). They go one step further, in fact, and argue that the parties in conflict must agree that they are, indeed, in conflict. For example, you may tell a friend that you'd prefer to stay in and study rather than go work out together, and you may even be annoyed that your friend asked while you were studying. That resentment may show in your bad mood and lack of conversation, but if your friend doesn't recognize your angry nonverbal cues, you two are not in conflict.

There also has to be *interdependence* for conflict to arise. Now imagine that you and a friend are working together on a class project that's due tomorrow morning. You need your friend to contribute to complete the project well and on time. But your friend would rather go to the gym than work on it. In Wilmot and Wilmot's words, conflict will arise because "each person's choices affect the other" (p. 12).

Conflict develops when interdependent people *perceive incompatible goals,* but the "perceived" in that phrase is just as important as the "incompatible." For example, you want to take the bus to the gym but your friend wants to drive. You may perceive these preferences as incompatible, except that they are less incompatible than you might think. The *real* goal for both of you is to get there. Your friend may prefer driving because she or he doesn't have money for the bus, but you explain that once you consider the price of gas and parking, taking the bus is actually less expensive (that's something you both want). Your goals, in fact, are not incompatible; you just thought they were. Wilmot and Wilmot call this *identifying other goals* and *stressing mutually good ways* to avoid conflict. But some goals are indeed incompatible. You want to work on your class project and time is running out. Your friend, satisfied with the project as it is, wants to go to the gym to maintain a personally important exercise regime. Conflict will most likely ensue.

This issue of perception holds true for *scarcity of rewards*, too. If you had all the time in the world, you and your friend could go to the gym *and* work on your class project. But few of us live in such a beautiful world, so Wilmot and Wilmot, after reminding us that a reward is "any positively perceived physical, economic, or social consequence," explain that "rewards, or resources, may be 'real' or perceived as real by the person. And perception of scarcity, or being limited, may be apparent or real" (p. 11). People argue over money, gangs battle for turf, children compete for their parents' time—all more or less quantifiable. But what is the scarce reward involved when romantic partners quarrel over jealousy? Is "love" or "affection" quantifiable? Can it be scarce? It can if one of the partners thinks that any love or affection (real or perceived) shown to another diminishes the amount now available for him or her. After an insult, what scarce reward might be at the root of the subsequent conflict? Respect, self-esteem, and face are likely answers (Chapter 3). These are of great social consequence to any of us who like to think of ourselves as competent humans.

Conflict also requires *interference*. Hoping to force you into going to the gym, your friend hides your textbook and the materials for your class project, interfering with your goal (getting a good grade) and denying you a scarce reward (that good grade). But that's an obvious example. What is the interference that leads to the jealous lovers' quarrel or to the post-insult conflict? What goal has been thwarted? Again, maintenance of respect, self-esteem, or face is an important goal for all of us. Recall Chapter 1's discussion of the looking glass: the self is accomplished by seeing ourselves as others see us. What self is reflected in a lover suspected of straying or a friend who demeans?

Types of Conflict

Because interference can take different forms and because it is the *perceptions* of reward scarcity and goal incompatibly that produce conflict, there will be many different types of interpersonal conflict. Communication researcher Mark Cole (1996) identified five general categories of conflict:

- **Affective conflict** occurs when people acknowledge an incompatibility of emotions and feelings. This describes the conflict between jealous romantic partners. As interdependent members of a couple, each assumes an equal degree of affection from the other. But if they disagree about that level of affection, conflict can easily arise.

- **Conflict of interest** occurs when people acknowledge incompatible preferences for a course of action. Interested in benefiting the environment, you want to take the bus. Interested in getting there more quickly, your friend wants to drive.

- **Value conflict** occurs when people acknowledge differences in their deeply held feelings about the worth or importance of significant aspects of their lives. Consider married couples from different religions. Jewish-Christian couples might fight over circumcision, or Atheist-Christian couples might argue over baptizing their children. But value conflict need not always

affective conflict When people acknowledge an incompatibility of emotions and feelings.

conflict of interest When people acknowledge incompatible preferences for a course of action.

value conflict When people acknowledge differences in their deeply held feelings about the worth or importance of significant aspects of their lives.

For interfaith couples, the wedding season may be a time of interpersonal discomfort because it may involve conflict over deeply held values.

cognitive conflict When people acknowledge incompatibility in their perceptions about something of importance.

goal conflict When people acknowledge incompatibility in the individual outcomes they hold for a given plan or action.

latent conflict When there is a problem, but the differences are not so great that one or both sides want to act on them.

involve religion; value conflict revolves around disagreement over deeply held feelings about matters of significance, faith-based or otherwise. Two people of the same, different, or no religions may hold greatly differing views about gun safety and find themselves in constant conflict over one partner's volunteer work for the Brady Campaign to End Gun Violence.

- **Cognitive conflict** occurs when people acknowledge incompatibility in their perceptions about something of importance. You *know* that the class project needs more work; your friend *knows* it's fine as is. Cognitive conflict is about incongruity of cognitions—how and what people think about something—not necessarily the reality of that something. Little Jordan just *knows* that Mommy and Daddy love Little Matt more; Little Matt *knows* with just as much certainty that Mommy and Daddy love Little Jordan more.

- **Goal conflict** occurs when people acknowledge incompatibility in the individual outcomes they hold for a given plan or action. Your goal for the class project is to earn an A. That's why you've put in so much time and effort and why you're willing to pass up a trip to the gym. Your friend's goal for the project is to pass, maybe with a pretty good grade. That's why a few hours at the gym the night before the project is due seems like a reasonable plan of action.

Stages of Interpersonal Conflict

The fact that interpersonal conflict can be negotiated means that it moves through different stages. In each stage, how the parties communicate differs, as do their goals. Human rights scholar Eric Brahm (2003) identified seven conflict stages, *latent conflict, emergence, escalation, hurting/stalemate, de-escalation/ negotiation, settlement/resolution,* and *reconciliation.* We'll discuss each separately, and you can see a visual representation of these stages in Figure 6.2.

Latent conflict exists when there is an "uneasy peace" or an "unspoken truce." There is a problem between the parties, but for one reason or another, the differences are not so great that one or both sides want to act on them. The roots of the problem may have existed for some time or perhaps there may be a new conflict of goals, but sometimes open conflict doesn't take place. You may have always known that your friend put exercise before study, and there were times when that off-kilter priority bothered you quite a bit, but it was never that big a deal until it threatened to damage your performance on the class project.

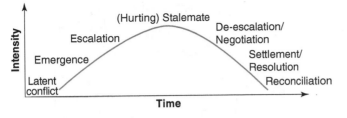

FIGURE 6.2 Stages of Interpersonal Conflict

That interference with your goals most likely would trigger the next stage, **emergence**. It may be one event or a number of smaller occurrences that move the conflict into the open, but now the conflict is overt and has to be dealt with. It is likely, now that it is in the open, that the conflict will suffer **escalation**; it will increase in intensity and in the severity of the tactics used in keeping it alive. Escalation, however, can indeed lead to a speedy settlement/resolution and even reconciliation. Now that you have convinced your friend of the importance you place on doing well on the project, he or she agrees that the gym isn't such a good idea.

Escalation can also lead to **stalemate**, when neither side can prevail but neither is willing to back down or give in. People often find it quite difficult to back down, as they have so much of their identity invested in the conflict, especially after it has escalated; backing down now becomes an even bigger challenge to their sense of self. But if and when the cost of continuing the stalemate becomes too great, when it exceeds any benefit to be derived from keeping the conflict alive, it becomes a *hurting stalemate*.

A stalemate that hurts is an invitation to begin **de-escalation and negotiation**. You're at a stalemate; you continue to argue over your friend's commitment to the project and what your friend sees as your obsessiveness over grades. You can sit there and argue, but the clock is ticking. Soon you will have no time for either the project or the gym. The cost of the stalemate is about to exceed any benefit either of you might gain from getting your way. De-escalation/negotiation is the only rational route out of this conflict. Maybe you re-evaluate your goals; maybe you seek a compromise that satisfies you both without too much loss of face.

Perhaps, as you work to resolve the conflict once and for all, you even look for a mutually beneficial **settlement/resolution**, removing the underlying causes of the conflict, possibly by redefining your individual goals so they are no longer incompatible. Now comes **reconciliation**. In its simplest form, it is making up, putting the conflict behind you. But reconciliation is more than a simple apology. You may even have to repair some relational damage. You and your friend work out a mutually beneficial solution to the work/gym conflict, maybe two hours on the project and a late night trip to the gym, followed by a stop for a frozen yogurt.

Conflict Management Styles

How we communicate throughout these stages depends in large part on our preferred individual **conflict style**, a general predisposition to deal with

emergence When conflict becomes open.

escalation An increase in the intensity of a conflict and the severity of tactics used in pursuing it.

stalemate When neither side can prevail, but neither is willing to back down or give in.

de-escalation and negotiation Reduction of conflict through communication between the parties.

settlement/resolution Removing the underlying causes of the conflict.

reconciliation Making up; putting the conflict in the past.

conflict style A general predisposition to deal with conflict in a particular manner.

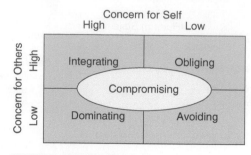

FIGURE 6.3 Conflict Styles

conflict in a particular manner. We may deal differently with different conflicts with different people in different contexts, but each of us has a more-or-less "go to" approach, one composed of the balance between our *concern for our own interests* and *our concern for the interests of the person with whom we are in conflict* (Kilmann and Thomas, 1975). There are five general conflict styles: integrating, obliging, dominating, avoiding, and compromising (Rahim and Magner, 1995). We'll take a closer look at each, and you can see how they relate to self- and other-concern in Figure 6.3.

Those who employ the **integrating style** of conflict resolution show high concern for others as well as for themselves. They favor collaboration and open and direct communication to examine the differences that may be causing the conflict and to reach a mutually acceptable solution. This is a very effective and valuable conflict style because it stresses fairness to all involved. It demonstrates empathy for others and recognition of their feelings. Naturally, this would seem to be an effective way to handle most conflicts, but it takes time and effort. After all, the conflict exists for a reason, and an integrating conflict resolution style is sometimes difficult to maintain when dealing with an unwilling conflict partner. Consider the evening before the class project was due. If you and your friend could have simply put yourself in the other's shoes and talked things out until you found a satisfactory solution, you may not have had time for the gym or your project. And if one of you was indeed willing to take the time and energy to work things out, there is no guarantee that the other would have been on board with the effort.

The **obliging style** suggests little concern for self-interest and greater concern for the interests of others. People who employ this style try to minimize differences and emphasize common ground in an attempt to meet the needs of others. This is a useful strategy when maintaining the relationship with the other is more important than coming to a self-satisfactory resolution to the conflict. But the downside is that it might produce a false or temporary solution to the problem. You can only give in to (oblige) your friend so often before you finally tire of being the one to constantly make the accommodation.

Those who see conflict as a win-lose or zero-sum process typically demonstrate the **dominating style** of interpersonal conflict resolution. It comes from a higher regard for one's own interests than those of the other. This style often relies on force, loud and forceful verbal language, and domineering or

integrating style Conflict resolution style showing high concern for others as well as for one's self.

obliging style Conflict resolution style showing little concern for self-interest and greater concern for the interests of others.

dominating style Conflict resolution style showing a higher regard for one's own interests than those of the other.

aggressive nonverbal communication. This style may produce an occasional "victory," but usually at the expense of the relationship. And because the outcome is a "win" for one side and a "loss" for the other, there is no real resolution to the conflict, and it may well appear again. Your friend may have bullied you into setting aside your schoolwork and going to the gym, but it's not likely you had a good time once there; it's equally unlikely you will ever partner on a project with him or her again.

The **avoiding style** is associated with low concern for the self and low concern for the other as well. You might know this as "passing the buck," or "agreeing to disagree." Obviously, it minimizes the immediate discomfort of the conflict, but it does nothing to move you to a resolution. The problem (and therefore the conflict) persists. But it does have its advantages, particularly if the conflict is over something unimportant. *Bowling or the movies? Who cares? We'll do what you want to do.* Every one of us has had some version of this conversation with someone whom we value.

Finally, the **compromising style** involves moderate concern for self-interest as well as moderate concern for the interests of the other. It is characterized by give-and-take, the sharing of information and ideas, and the mutually acceptable giving up of something by both sides. Most of us have an almost automatic positive reaction to compromising. After all, who could find fault with negotiating a mutually satisfactory resolution to a conflict? You could. You and your friend decide to split the evening between working on your class project and going to the gym. But now you have only half the time you'd originally intended to give to your project, far too little in your mind to produce the kind of work that will guarantee you the A you value.

The dominating style of conflict resolution demonstrates a higher regard for one's own interests than those of another.

avoiding style Conflict resolution style showing low concern for the self and for another.

compromising style Conflict resolution style showing moderate concern for self-interest and for the interests of another.

Resolving Conflict: What to Do and What Not to Do

Regardless of how we choose to enact our preferred conflict style, there are a number of communication practices that we should undertake when in conflict, as well as many we should avoid.

What to Do

Communication scholars Judith Martin and Thomas Nakayama offer seven suggestions for dealing with conflict. As you read them, keep in mind these two warnings. First, there are no easy answers to dealing with conflict; and second, although there are times when self-restraint is the best strategy, there are also times when "it may be appropriate to assert ourselves and not be afraid of strong emotion" (2010, p. 450).

1. *Stay centered and do not polarize.* Rid yourself of either-or thinking and do not assume that the other's motives are simple, or even worse, wrong or selfish. Be open to perspectives closer to the center of your differing perspectives. Here is where self-restraint becomes important. You can get angry, but you must move past that emotion and not act out those feelings. You may be mightily frustrated with your friend's lack of commitment to your class project, but rather than lash out, might there not be a solution closer to the center of the study/gym divide? Why not suggest breaking up work on the project with periodic 15-minute sessions on the basketball court just outside the library?

2. *Maintain contact.* Yes, it makes sense to occasionally walk away from the conflict—what we often refer to as "taking a time out" or "going to a neutral corner." But it is important to maintain communication; it makes no sense to shut the other out, as this ensures no movement toward a resolution. Remember this chapter's lesson on dialectics. **Dialogue**, the full, honest, meaningful exchange of information and feelings, is essential to meaning making in conflict situations because it is the only way to balance competing perceptions of reward scarcity and goal incompatibility. You and your friend can storm out of the study room, but you will have no partner to help you complete the project, and your friend will have no companion for the workout.

3. *Recognize the existence of different conflict management styles.* Martin and Nakayama tell us that the combination of different styles in a given conflict situation can lead to a "dance" that may not serve the cause of resolution very well. Two avoiders may coexist, but their relationship might suffer from long-standing latent conflict, only to be triggered by some later event. A dominator and an obligor may come to a quick resolution of their conflict, but at what cost to the interests of the obligor and the relationship between the two?

4. This is why the parties in conflict should *identify their preferred conflict management styles.* We've already seen that we often apply different styles in different conflict situations, but being aware of our preferred style helps us make better sense of how we are making meaning of the conflict. We can ask ourselves questions like, "Why am I so willing to compromise on this issue? Is that what I really want to do?" or "Why am I fighting so hard to get my way? Is this really that important to me?" You and your friend can much more easily resolve your conflict over the class project if you are aware of each other's conflict resolution styles because you will be less likely to question the other's motives.

5. *Be creative and expand your style repertoire.* If your preferred style isn't working, try something else. For too long you avoided conflict with your friend, and now, the night before the project is due, you might want to try compromising.

dialogue Full, honest, meaningful exchange of information and feelings.

6. *Recognize the importance of the context of the conflict.* You've read throughout this text that meaning is always made in context. Conflict, then, happens for many reasons, often reasons that have little to do with the immediate interaction between the participants. Maybe it's really not about the gym. Perhaps your friend feels that the warm, affectionate part of your relationship is disappearing under the stress of schoolwork.

7. *Be willing to forgive.* "Teaching forgiveness between estranged individuals is as old as recorded history; it is present in every culture and is part of the human condition . . . Forgiveness is also a basic human instinct that has also served humans well . . . At a very fundamental level, forgiveness ensures that we get along with both family and close friends and helps establish and maintain cooperative relationships with nonrelatives; and overall, forgiveness is the best strategy for human beings in the long term—it can deliver freedom from fear and freedom to resume normal, peaceful relations. In fact, it is in our self-interest to forgive" (Martin and Nakayama, 2010, pp. 455–456).

The final stage of conflict is its best: reconciliation.

What Not to Do

Conflict can often be an opportunity to build a better relationship than existed before. But if managed poorly, conflict can also be destructive. None of us would dispute the value of forgiveness, but most of us at one time or another have felt that something someone said or did to us was indeed unforgivable. Relationship expert John Gottman calls the things we should never say or do when in conflict—the unforgivable—the "Four Horsemen of the Apocalypse" (1993), after the Bible story warning of Conquest, War, Famine, and Death. For Gottman, *criticism, contempt, defensiveness,* and *stonewalling* signal the coming of the end of a relationship.

Criticism, complaints about the other, isn't always a bad thing. They can often be the trigger that moves latent conflict into the open and toward resolution. But criticism should never be about the personality, characteristics, morals, or motives of the other. There is a world of difference between "I don't think you're working as hard on this project as you should be" and "What's your problem? You know we have to get this done for tomorrow, but you just don't care." Conflict-enflaming criticism often takes the form of generalizations about the other person: *You always . . . You never . . . That's just like you . . . Why are you always so . . . You're the kind of person who . . .* Make criticism a critique of the specific issue at the root of the conflict, not about the person.

criticism Complaints about another.

Contempt, an attack on the self-worth of another, often takes the form of insults. "What's your problem? You know we have to get this done for tomorrow,

contempt An attack on the self-worth of another.

ETHICAL COMMUNICATION

Sugar-Coated Hostility

As you've read, most conflict is over *perceived* incompatible goals, *perceived* scarcity of rewards, and *perceived* interference. So why do people resort to intentional miscommunication if clearer expression might help balance those perceptions? *Passive aggressiveness* is deliberate miscommunication meant to hide expressions of anger, distrust, or disagreement without acknowledging the underlying feelings at the root of the problem. It is sugar-coated hostility. It's an abuse of communication; it's not the truth; it's unethical. To help us recognize when hidden hostility is being directed our way, psychologist Signe Whitson (2012) identified 10 phrases often employed by passive-aggressive conflict partners:

1. *"I'm not mad."* Rather than admit the problem (remember, conflict must be expressed), passive-aggressive people would rather stay angry.
2. *"Fine." "Whatever."* Withdrawal from conflict is a primary passive-aggressive strategy. These words shut down open, honest communication.
3. *"I'm coming!"* This is verbal agreement but behavioral resistance.
4. *"I didn't know you meant now."* Passive-aggressive people use delay and procrastination to frustrate their conflict partner.
5. *"You just want everything to be perfect."* Passive-aggressive people, when forced to comply with a

given request, will intentionally carry it out in a poor or inefficient manner. When confronted, they will defend their work and counter-accuse others of being rigid and unreasonable.

6. *"I thought you knew."* Passive-aggressive people choose to express their anger by failing to share or offer information when it might otherwise prevent a problem. They claim ignorance, defend their inaction, and covertly take pleasure in the trouble and pain of other people.
7. *"Sure, I'd be happy to."* This is another case of verbal agreement but behavioral resistance. An angry friend might say he'll turn in your assignment for you but mysteriously loses it on the way to class.
8. *"You've done so well for someone with your education level."* This technique is known as the backhanded compliment, what Whitson calls the "ultimate socially acceptable means by which the passive aggressive person insults you to your core."
9. *"I was only joking."* This is passive-aggressive people's tactic of openly expressing hostility but hiding behind social convention.
10. *"Why are you getting so upset?"* Passive-aggressive people are often so committed to their deceit that they become quite adept at maintaining their cool and feigning surprise when their target finally has had enough.

---

but you just don't care" is bad enough, but "What's your problem? You know we have to get this done for tomorrow. Are you lazy or just stupid?" is even worse. Contempt, either verbal (name calling, sarcasm, mocking, hostile humor) or nonverbal (eye rolling, snickering, sneering, making faces) demeans the other. Contempt is the most corrosive of the horsemen because it communicates disrespect. It is even more damaging when displayed in front of others not involved in the conflict. Contempt can also be communicated through **passive aggressiveness**, a deliberate and masked way of expressing disrespect, as you can see in the box "Sugar-Coated Hostility."

Defensiveness, or denying responsibility for one's behaviors, frequently manifests itself as

- playing the victim—"Why do you always pick on me?"
- playing dumb—"Me? What are you talking about?"

passive aggressiveness
A deliberate and masked way of expressing disrespect.

defensiveness Denying responsibility for one's behaviors.

- making excuses—"It's not my fault."
- counter-complaining—"You do it, too."
- "yes-butting"—"Yes, you're right, but no way that's a problem."

Defensiveness devalues the feelings of the other as illegitimate and tells him or her that he or she is not worthy of your interest or attention.

Stonewalling is withdrawing from the dialogue to avoid conflict. Stonewalling isn't taking a time out to let things cool down. It is terminating communication. It is the stony silence, the one-syllable yes/no/grunt response, the change of subject, the turning your back, and the silent treatment. All are disrespectful, suggesting disapproval, smugness, and disregard.

stonewalling Withdrawing from dialogue to avoid conflict.

Review of Learning Objectives

6.1 Differentiate among several of the most important theories of interpersonal communication.

Uncertainty Reduction Theory suggests that we use communication to predict and explain the behavior of others in the initial stages of a relationship. Social Penetration Theory posits that relationships move from initial interaction to greater stability through interpersonal communication. Social Exchange Theory says that people evaluate relationships in a more-or-less rational manner to ensure maximum rewards and minimal costs. Relational Dialectics Theory, rather than arguing that relationships move through stages, contends that meaning making between relationship partners emerges from the interplay of competing discourses.

6.2 Examine conflict and analyze the elements that create it.

Conflict is an expressed struggle between at least two interdependent parties. Its elements include not only interdependence, but the perception of incompatible goals, scarce rewards, and interference from another party in achieving those goals.

6.3 Identify different types of conflict.

There are several types of conflict. Affective conflict occurs when people acknowledge an incompatibility of emotions and feelings. Conflict of interest occurs when people acknowledge incompatible preferences for a course of action. Value conflict occurs when people acknowledge differences in their deeply held feelings about the worth or importance of significant aspects of their lives. Cognitive conflict occurs when people acknowledge incompatibility in their perceptions about something of importance. Goal conflict occurs when people acknowledge incompatibility in the individual outcomes they hold for a given plan or action.

6.4 Describe the stages of interpersonal conflict.

There are seven stages of conflict. Latent conflict exists when there is a problem, but the differences are not so great that one or both sides wants to act on them. Emergence may be triggered by one event or a number of smaller occurrences that move the conflict into the open. Once in the open, conflict will suffer escalation, an increase in the intensity of a conflict and in the severity of tactics used in pursuing it. Escalation can lead to stalemate, when neither side can prevail but neither is willing to back down or give in. But if and when the cost of continuing the stalemate becomes too great, it becomes a hurting stalemate, an invitation to begin de-escalation and negotiation. This may lead to settlement/resolution, removing the underlying causes of the conflict, possibly producing reconciliation.

6.5 Compare different conflict management styles, and determine the style you use most frequently.

Conflict style is a person's general predisposition to deal with conflict in a particular manner. It is a function of the balance between concern for one's own interests and concern for the interests of the other. The integrating style of conflict resolution shows high concern for others as well as for one's self. The obliging style suggests little concern for self-interest and greater concern for the interests of others. The dominating style comes from a higher regard for one's own interests than those

of the other. The avoiding style is associated with low concern for the self and low concern for the other as well. The compromising style involves moderate concern for self-interest and for the interests of the other.

6.6 Know what to do—and what not to do—when in conflict.

There are several conflict "dos and don'ts." Among the things we should do are stay centered (and do not polarize), maintain contact, recognize the existence of different conflict styles, identify our preferred conflict styles, be creative and expand our style repertoire, recognize the importance of the context of the conflict, and be willing to forgive. Among the things not to do are engage in criticism, show contempt, become defensive, and stonewall.

Key Terms

Questions for Review

1. What are the six provisions of relationships?

2. What two kinds of uncertainty do people attempt to reduce upon initial encounters?

3. What are Social Penetration Theory's four assumptions?

4. What are self-disclosure and the norm of reciprocity? How do they relate?

5. According to Social Penetration Theory, what are the four stages of relational development?

6. What are Social Exchange Theory's two comparison levels? How do they operate?

7. What are the four major relational dialectics? Describe each and name its external parallel.

8. Define conflict and the five forms of conflict.

9. What are the stages of interpersonal conflict? Describe each.

10. Name and describe the four conflict management styles.

Questions for Discussion

1. Do you stay in close touch with one or more of your high school friends? What are the costs and benefits of doing so? How do the costs and benefits of those relationships compare with those of your college relationships? Use Social Exchange Theory to explain why you maintain the friendships you do.

2. Have you ever been attracted to a stranger and, as a result, attempted to negotiate a relationship? If so, explain the development of that relationship using Social Penetration Theory's stages. Where on the onion did the relationship eventually settle? Why?

3. What is your preferred conflict management style? What does it say about you as a person? Do you ever vary your approach to conflict resolution? If so, how, and under what conditions?

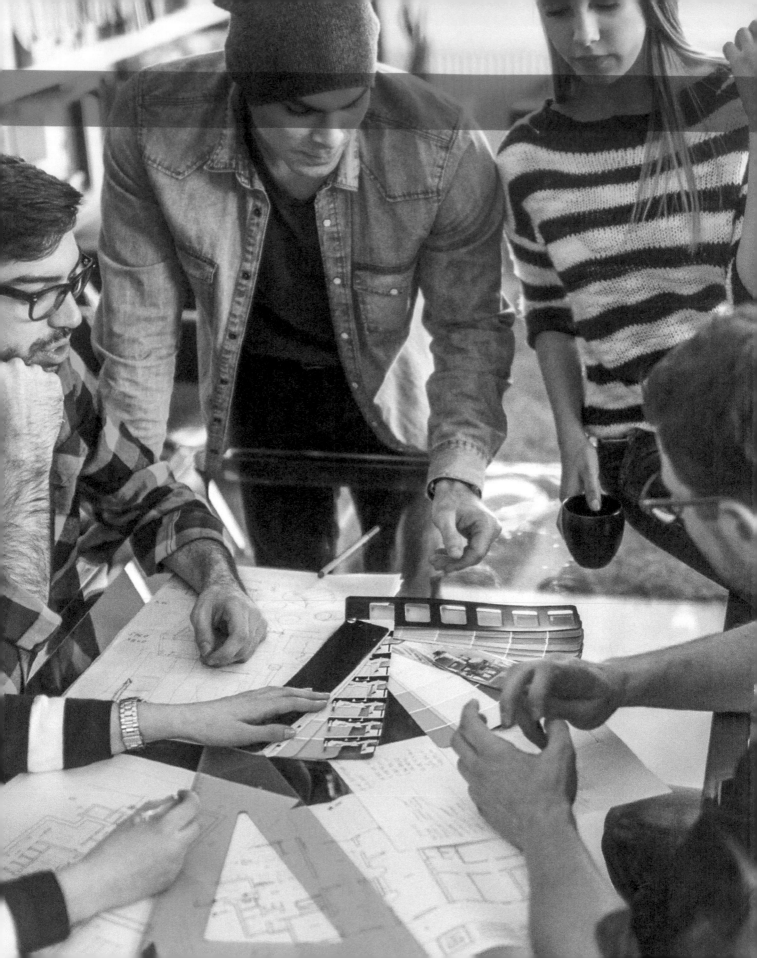

7

Communicating in Small Groups

The semester is coming to a quick close, and your big group presentation, which counts as much as the final exam, is scheduled for next week. You're not really sure how it's going to go. You dislike working in groups for many reasons, and all of your concerns have come to fruition with this particular project. Two of the members are students you barely know, and the other two are people you don't like and with whom you have little in common. Because the class is Introduction to Communication, you feel especially pressured to perform well; throughout the semester you've studied topics like interpersonal communication and, especially pertinent, group dynamics. Not delivering a good presentation might be indicative of your inability to grasp the course's concepts. And sad to say, all the issues you studied regarding group conflict and breakdown are exemplified in your experience working with this assigned team.

In the first few weeks of meetings, two students failed to show up on a number of occasions, claiming their classes conflicted with the meeting times (even though they said nothing when the five of you together constructed the schedule). One student insisted on being the group's "leader" despite the others' desire to have equal input in how things got done. Another member did absolutely no research and relied on everyone else to meet required deadlines. And each participant had different ideas about how to approach the project and what to include as part of the presentation. It was a disaster waiting to happen, and you found yourself constantly thinking, "Why couldn't the professor simply have assigned independent projects?"

Working in groups demands specific communication skills. Without these skills, it can be extremely difficult to effectively negotiate schedules, deadlines, problem-solving, rules, responsibilities, and outcomes. According to communication theorists Stephen Littlejohn and Karen Foss, we often ask, "Is it better to do things yourself or to work with a group?" The answer, they tell us, "depends on how well the group works together, how focused it is, and how much creative and critical thinking the group allows. How well does the group weigh information, how effectively does the group create options, and how critically does it evaluate ideas?" (2011, p. 264). We will examine the many characteristics of group communication in this chapter, hoping to answer at least some of these questions.

Learning Objectives

7.1 Describe the various types of groups.

7.2 Explain the dynamics of group structure, recognizing the stages of group development.

7.3 Discuss types of group cohesion and the factors that cause group breakdown.

7.4 Describe different styles of leadership and forms of power.

7.5 Identify ways to improve your group communication skills.

Types of Groups

small groups Collections of 3 to 15 people with a common purpose.

You may dislike working on group projects, but keep in mind these important points. First, working in **small groups**, collections of three to 15 people with a common purpose, is a fact of life. You were born into a group, and as you began to make friends, you willingly became a member of many more. Second, groups are not only essential to helping you make your way in the world, they can be fun and rewarding. It's pretty difficult to cover all 10 positions on your softball team without some assistance, and more than likely you'd lose every tug-of-war at every picnic you ever attend if you had to pull the rope by yourself. In fact, you might never even get to a picnic without the benefit of some organizational structure, or group work. You can read about two very successful and important groups in the box "Forming a Group."

primary groups Groups offering members affection and belonging.

Groups are classified depending on both their structure and purpose. Two broad categories are *primary groups* and *task-oriented groups*. **Primary groups** offer their members affection and a sense of belonging. Members transact routines, traditions, and personal communication with full knowledge that these will affect future interactions. Members of primary groups are bound by close, intimate communication and are connected through history and emotion. These groups are "primary" because they are central to our basic needs, and they are the first groups to which we belong. Examples include families and groups of friends.

Task-oriented groups are just that, groups convened and constructed to serve a purpose. They can be long-term, formal organizations or they can be short-term, ad hoc operations, for example the group you're working with on the Communication class project. Here is a more detailed description of the different types of task-oriented groups. Keep in mind that these groups can be structured either formally or informally:

They come in different shapes and sizes, but families are a primary group because their members are connected by intimacy.

→ **Participant-driven groups**: Participants in these groups attempt to overcome obstacles or achieve goals by drawing on the emotional support provided by other members. Examples include Alcoholics Anonymous, family counseling groups, cancer survivor groups, grief support groups, and homecoming committees.

→ **Information-presentation groups:** These groups are organized specifically to provide information and awareness on topics of interest to people. Examples include health awareness groups, job centers, and Chamber of Commerce groups.

→ **Decision-making groups:** The ultimate goal of these groups is to come to consensus on a given issue or number of issues. The decisions often result in documents outlining procedural changes. Examples include boards of directors, evaluation committees, judicial and military review boards, juries, judging panels, and school committees.

→ **Skill-building groups:** Building skills among members or sometimes among non-members is the primary goal of these groups. Examples include public speaking workshops, leadership-building groups, writing workshops, choral groups, and youth and intramural sports teams.

task-oriented groups Groups convened and constructed to serve a purpose.

Dynamics of Group Structure

Regardless of its type, the **dynamics** of every group—how the group structures itself to achieve its goals—are driven by four common elements: *norms, roles, ranks,* and *controls* (DeFleur, D'Antonio, and DeFleur, 1984). **Norms** are the rules that govern the behavior of group members. They can be unspoken and understood, or they can be formal and written down. For example,

dynamics How a group structures itself to achieve its goal.

norms Rules that govern a group.

Forming a Group

In 1980, a mother devastated by the death of her 13-year-old daughter at the hands of a drunk driver decided to take action. With no real resources or connections, Sue LeBrun-Green assembled a small group of equally concerned mothers. They built what would become one of the most significant service organizations in US history, Mothers Against Drunk Driving (MADD). During its more than 30 years in operation, the group has challenged reluctant politicians and battled liquor lobbies, helping reduce fatal alcohol-related traffic accidents. As a result, more than 300,000 lives have been saved, and in 2011, for the first time, the annual number of US drunk driving fatalities fell below 10,000 ("Drunk Driving," 2012).

In 1968, another mother, Peggy Charren, founded ACT (Action for Children's Television), which "aimed to ensure quality and diversity in television programming for children and adolescents and to eliminate commercial abuses directed at children" ("Action," 2015). What started as a small group of individuals grew into thousands of members, and its efforts eventually led to the *Children's Television Act of 1990*, federal legislation designed to increase educational and informational programming for kids. Although the organization dissolved in 1992, as it determined that it had met its goals, Charren and a group of her associates continue to lobby on behalf of children and their right to quality television content.

People like LeBrun-Green and Charren are a testament to the importance and power of group communication. In both cases, these pioneers began with a simple passion, a small number of participants, and the will to invoke change in what they viewed as a broken system—and they succeeded. We have a social responsibility to *organize* if we have expectations of a better society. One way to do that is to form groups with people who share our concerns and our desire to make a difference.

The power of groups is extraordinary. They teach us about leadership, relationships, and the importance of interdependence. They teach us about ourselves. They unite voices and can serve as critically influential forces, bringing about change for future generations.

---

players on a basketball team understand that missing practice means a game on the bench and that an untucked shirt at practice means laps. They also know that the rule book stipulates that the ball must be advanced only by pass or dribble and that there are two halves to a game.

roles Specific tasks and responsibilities of group members.

Roles are the specific tasks and responsibilities of each member. In a rock band, for example, one member plays the electric guitar, another the drums, one plays the keyboard, a fourth member plays the bass guitar, and one person is the lead singer. If all members perform their roles as expected, the group functions effectively.

ranks Hierarchal structure of the group.

Ranks are represented by the hierarchal structure of the group; for instance, a typical community group consists of a president, vice president, secretary, treasurer, membership chair, fundraising coordinator, and the general membership. In other words, some members simply have more important roles, and more authority, than others.

controls Rewards, punishments, or behavioral consequences for group members.

Finally, **controls** speak to the rewards and punishments, or behavioral consequences, that group members face. A violinist might be moved up to first chair in a chamber ensemble for superior performance or demoted to third chair for careless playing, and a hockey player could get sent to the penalty box for high-sticking or roughing. Every group, no matter how formal or informal, operates according to these four dynamics.

Let's consider an elementary school classroom, since most of us have experienced membership in this group. Some of the typical norms (rules) include *raise your hand before speaking, don't shove your classmates on the playground, line up in an orderly fashion,* and *be respectful to your teacher and peers.* Even before we got to school, at a very young age, we understood that rules like this existed because of our socialization in primary groups. **Socialization** is how, through our early interaction with family, friends, and other influential people, we learn to be members of a group.

An elementary class is a group structured by roles, rules, ranks, and controls.

socialization How we learn to be members of a group through our early interaction with primary groups.

Our elementary school classroom also provides a good example of group roles. The pupils know they are there to learn, while the teachers are there to instruct on subjects like arithmetic, reading, writing, and finger painting. Perhaps there is a student-teacher or teacher's assistant, whose job it is to help the teacher with a number of tasks like cleaning up the room, helping individual students, or reading stories while the teacher corrects papers. Everyone in the class has specific responsibilities, which are made clear through participation in the group.

The ranks, or hierarchal structure, are also evident in the classroom. The person with the highest rank is the teacher, followed by the teacher's assistant, and then the students, who have the least authority. Of course, if you consider the administrative staff, you might see the superintendent as sitting at the top of the group, followed by the principal, the assistant principal, the teacher, and so on. Just like norms, we are all aware of ranks and roles at very young ages. Even infants intuitively know their parents to be caregivers as they experience being nurtured through diaper changings, feedings, and physical affection.

Controls are also something children learn and understand well. Punishments and rewards are a critical part of socializing children toward proper values, ethics, and morals because it is through the use of controls that they develop a sense of right and wrong within a specific cultural context. For example, in the early grades of school, children are reprimanded through "time outs," having recess taken away, visiting the principal's office, and doing extra homework. They are rewarded with silver stars, leadership roles, and various certificates of achievement.

The dynamics of group structure are found in all types of groups. And while all groups possess these characteristics, they may differ in the formality of their structure, which in turn determines the rigidity and formality of the four structural dynamics.

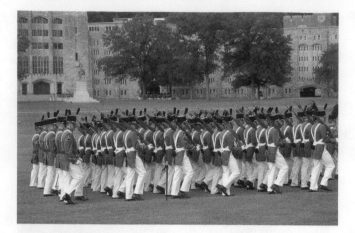

Why is a military unit considered a formal group?

informal group communication Less rigid, more relaxed, often spontaneous group communication.

formal group communication Structured group communication heavily coded with specific rules.

THUMBNAIL THEORY

Structuration Theory

The way we routinely communicate in and about the groups we belong to shapes those groups and guides people's behaviors in them. Our interactions not only use the group's established structures but also reproduce or reinforce those structures. Every time we engage in a group practice, we are helping produce and reproduce the institutions that undergird it, but the seeds of change are also present in those interactions.

Informal and Formal Communication in Groups

Depending on the group, different patterns of communication between members may be informal or formal. In **informal group communication**, the language is less rigid, more relaxed, often spontaneous, and less bound by specific rules, for example, the way a group of friends or a family interacts. In **formal group communication**, the language is quite rigid, extremely structured, and heavily bound by very specific rules, for example the communication patterns in an army unit or a jury. In a circle of friends, members feel free to say what they want and are relaxed doing so. But jury members must communicate and operate within the guidelines of strict language and rules—a sequestered jury cannot have contact with anyone outside the group until a judgment on the case is reached; they must select a foreman; they must understand language codes such as "reasonable doubt," "circumstantial evidence," and "burden of proof."

There are many different group structures in a given culture, and while the communication that characterizes them is more formal for some than others, they all fall somewhere along a spectrum of informal to formal communication, as in Figure 7.1. As you can see, while a class of students may not employ as formal a communication structure as an army unit, it certainly operates more formally than does a senior-citizen coffee club. Where on that spectrum would you put a little league team? A study group? A sales team? A hip-hop performance group? In coming to your conclusions, did you consider the formality of language and the rigidity and formality of rules, ranks, roles, and controls?

INFORMAL - - - -[senior-citizen - - - -[class - - - -[army - - - FORMAL
                 coffee club]   room]   unit]

FIGURE 7.1 Spectrum of Group Formality

Structuration Theory

Sociologist Anthony Giddens (1976) wanted to explain how, through the way we routinely communicate in social systems, we produce and reproduce groups. He called his idea **structuration theory** and highlighted two concepts important to understanding its basic premise—the way we communicate in the groups we belong to shapes the rules of those groups, which ultimately shape the way we behave in those groups:

1. Structures are the rules and resources produced from people's interactions "involved in the production and reproduction of social systems"

(Giddens, 2003, p. 455). Those social systems could be an educational institution, a high-tech workplace, an intramural sports team, or a class group project. *Rules,* whether "official" or learned through our interactions in those settings, guide our behavior. *Resources* are elements extant in the social system, for example relationships, friendships, or specialized knowledge, available for our use.

2. There is a *duality of structure*, that is, all our interactions in those settings use established structures and at the same time reproduce or reinforce those structures. "In a real sense, every time we engage in a practice, we are helping to produce and reproduce the institutions that undergird it" (Poole and McPhee, 2005, p. 178).

Giddens is a social philosopher interested in power and how it operates. He argued, therefore, that "the inherent relation between production and reproduction involved in the idea of the duality of structure carries with it the implication that the seeds of change are present in every moment of the constitution of social systems across time and space" (2003, p. 455). In other words, by accepting structures as they are, we are bound or constrained by them; but if we challenge those structures, we can contribute to beneficial change.

Here's a simple example. If every time your campus club had an election the winning candidate for president was a male and the winning candidate for secretary was a female, you and your group members would, knowingly or not, be reinforcing the sexism that "undergirds" your group. But you could use the group's structure to make change. You could use its rules, for example its nomination and election processes, to put people of both genders into office. You could use its resources, for example, your influence and friendship with other members, to ensure that that happened. In doing so, you'd be challenging and eventually altering those structures that constrained who could lead your group and in what capacity. "Talk is action," write Daniel Modaff and Sue DeWine. "If structure is truly produced through interaction, then communication is more than just a precursor to action; it is action" (2002, p. 107). You can read about how interaction within a group, both formal and informal, shapes the working of the group and its members' behaviors in the box "You Make the Rules."

The Five Stages of Group Development

You've likely endured an experience similar to the one in the chapter's opening vignette. Through that group exercise you became aware, either consciously or subconsciously, of the developmental process common to most task-oriented groups. According to psychologist Bruce Tuckman, this process consists of five stages: *forming, storming, norming, performing,* and *adjourning* (Tuckman and Jensen, 1977).

The **forming** stage of group development occurs when members initially convene, meeting each other for the first time. Some refer to it as the introductory stage because it involves first impressions, self-consciousness, predictions of productivity, and a mental mapping of how the different personalities will influence designated roles. Group members engage in polite small talk,

forming Stage when members initially convene.

PERSONALLY RESPONSIBLE COMMUNICATION

You Make the Rules

In a study titled "The Policy Exists but You Can't Really Use It," communication scholars Erika Kirby and Kathleen Krone (2002) examined the case of a large company that offered its employees family leave benefits. They argued that when benefits rules are vague, *"the work group is where they are most likely interpreted . . . work groups let us know if we actually have flexible work hours and places"* (p. 53, italics in original). What they discovered is that despite institutional policies (formal rules), it was communication within groups of colleagues (resources) that reinforced a "work first/family second" reality (informal rules) for the employees. "The crew will reward or punish you," (p. 64) and "[t]he bosses have never made me feel guilty. I have had other people at work make me feel guilty" (p. 65) are indicative of how group members would use communication to influence the structures within which they operated. The researchers noted that "[w]omen who utilized the policies felt resentment from coworkers, and even the men were cognizant of needing to balance 'use' versus 'abuse' so as not to be seen (and treated) as a less committed worker," and they concluded that group structures both enabled—in the form of formal rules—and constrained—in the form of the "unwritten" rules produced by members' use of resources—the people who structured them (p. 69).

Structuration theory argues that individual people, as they engage others in groups, are free to act. As a result, they bear the responsibility for transforming those groups' structures through "acts of resistance" (Hoffman and Cowan, 2010, p. 220). In other words, your group will not change to meet your needs and expectations unless you challenge the structures that constrain you. If you are male and in a club, would you be content if your club's leadership was always in men's hands? If not, what would you do about it? If you are female, would you stay in a group that insisted on seeing you only through your gender? Would you attempt to change things? How? Finally, when on the job, would you enact communication behaviors that ensured maximum freedom for all your colleagues, even if you might not personally benefit?

disclosing little to others because they lack familiarity. Members are concerned with issues of inclusion as they negotiate their compatibility with one another, and there is anxiety over the potential for communication breakdown because of the number of potentially disruptive factors, such as varying personality dynamics and the likely number of antagonistic opinions (members invariably offer more opinions than raise questions; Bales, 1970). This, obviously, is a much different scenario than communicating one to one.

You may remember from Chapter 6 the multiple complexities of dyadic communication, or communication between two people. But now consider what occurs in a group. If miscommunication is inevitable between two people, just imagine how adding four, six, or eight people might increase the likelihood of breakdown. Remember, too, the Looking Glass Self from Chapter 1. When we discussed the perceptions we have of others and ourselves as we engage in interpersonal interactions, some of the factors at play were *how we see ourselves, how the other person sees us, what we want the other person to see,* and *what the other person wants us to see.* Now consider how much more complex communication becomes in group situations where everyone is attempting to manage the many perceptions of themselves and others. The complexity increases exponentially, often causing *group breakdown,* which we'll address later in the chapter. This is one reason that people often dislike working in groups. It requires juggling multiple personalities and opinions. This realization begins during the group's formation but it is magnified in the storming stage.

In the **storming** stage of group development, members experience conflict. They are acquainted with one another at this point and are more comfortable disclosing points of view and ideas. As they discuss appropriate paths toward task completion and group accomplishment, they contend with and must resolve differences. This often leads to arguments, miscommunication, and a deviation from the goal at hand. Disagreement is arguably the most prevalent characteristic of the storming stage, as individual members fear a loss of identity in a sea of conflicting perspectives. Still, resolution of these issues must occur if the group is to transition into the norming stage.

The **norming** stage is characterized by group members' willingness to work together toward a common goal. They put their previous differences behind them as they come to an agreement on how to best complete the task before them. Productivity accelerates, and members understand and appreciate each other's contributions. Most of all, they see themselves as part of a larger entity and not simply a collection of individuals with personal opinions. They help each other and clearly recognize that they are bound by a common cause.

Once a group gets beyond the storming and norming stages, it can get on with the task of achieving its goals—or performing.

Once this normalcy comes to the group, conflict dissolves, and members are collectively operating at the highest level of efficiency. The group begins to reach and complete its goals. This is the **performing** stage of group development. Procedural and relational obstacles are no longer an issue since meeting the objective is the utmost priority. Members evaluate and assess their performance as a collective unit and even learn something about who they are as they reflect on their identities within the group. It is in this stage that members can confidently report success in achieving their goals.

In the **adjourning** stage, members depart from one another *and* the task. This detachment is not necessarily because the goal is complete and the group is successful. Adjournment may be the result of the failure of the group, as members are simply unable to finish the task. Whether the goal has been achieved or not, it is critical to assess the experience during this stage if members are to learn from their time together and apply that knowledge to subsequent group membership.

storming Stage when members experience conflict.

norming Stage when members begin working together toward a common goal.

performing Stage when the group begins to reach and complete its goals.

adjourning Stage when members depart from one another and the task.

When a group raises funds for a cause, its members experience assignment-based cohesion.

group cohesion The willingness to participate in and perform required activities.

Group Cohesion and Breakdown

Group cohesion binds members together as they accept their membership and their duties. It is a function of mutual interest as members see that their goals can be best met within the group (Lewin, 1948). Margaret DeFleur and her colleagues identified four types of group cohesion (2014):

- *Sentiment-based cohesion* relies on the relational closeness of the group's members. Examples of sentiment-based groups include family and friendship circles. Members of these groups are bound by the feelings of affection they have for one another.

- *Reward-based cohesion* is built on the idea that members are in some way rewarded for the successful completion of the task. For example, participants in a successful weight-loss group are rewarded with slimmer, healthier bodies, and the best National Football League team is rewarded with a Super Bowl victory.

- *Assignment-based cohesion* is goal-oriented. Group members, for example those in a fundraising club, work together toward achieving a specific goal, in this case hoping to raise enough money to satisfy their cause. Another example might be a town's board of education, whose assignment it is to determine an appropriate school curriculum.

- Finally, *dependency-based cohesion,* which is more common in large organizations and companies than in small groups, links groups to each other by way of separate tasks. In other words, a bicycle manufacturer has one group making the handlebars, another working on the tires, and still another group putting together the frames, but they are all linked by the common goal of manufacturing completed bicycles.

Despite the presence of cohesion, groups can sometimes experience total breakdown. For example, while the members of a family may love each other very much, the emergence of an alcohol problem in one of its members can create dysfunction, pulling the family apart. Or one of the group members from the chapter-opening example simply refuses to meet deadlines or contribute in any meaningful way in a fit of spite over having been denied the role of project leader. **Group breakdown** occurs when conflict emerges among members, causing deterioration or dissolution. A number of factors can contribute to group breakdown. Among the more common are *normative confusion*, *rank ineffectiveness*, and *groupthink* (Sundstrom, DeMeuse, and Futrell, 2009).

group breakdown Deterioration or dissolution of a group as a result of conflict.

Normative confusion occurs when the group's rules and expectations have not been clearly defined or established. Think about your experiences with group conflict. Have you been part of a group project in which one of the members seemed confused about when the group was meeting, how often it was meeting, or for how long? Not knowing and, ultimately, not conforming

normative confusion When group rules and expectations are not clearly defined or established.

to the group's agreed-upon rules can result in disintegration. At the very least, it puts a bigger burden on those following the initial, agreed-upon agenda.

Another common cause of group breakdown is **rank ineffectiveness**, or a failure of leadership; that is, the leader(s) of the group are viewed as ineffective. Later in the chapter we will discuss different leadership styles and their impact on groups. We all know what it's like to work in a group where the leader is self-appointed, too bossy, unable to motivate the team, or too lax in her or his approach to problem-solving. Perhaps the leader just annoys us. When someone is supposed to lead but is unable to do so, the result is often an unproductive group.

A third possible reason for group breakdown is **groupthink**. This phenomenon results when voices within a group are suppressed because of pressure—real or imagined—from others, resulting in a lack of thoughtful examination of the problem or task at hand. Psychologist Irving Janis placed the blame for groupthink squarely at the feet of group cohesion, arguing that it provides high group satisfaction but low productivity (1989). He defined groupthink as "a mode of thinking that people engage in when they are deeply involved in a cohesive in-group, when the members' strivings for unanimity override their motivation to realistically appraise the alternative courses of action" (in Schwartz and Wald, 2003, p. A15). Engaging the critical listening skills of individual members and asking them to express their reservations, as well as encouraging discourse and accepting disagreement, can mitigate the problem of groupthink and allow all voices to be heard and all opinions to be considered. Sometimes the "loudest" voice does not represent the most effective idea, and it is the job of the group's leader to ensure that everyone participates in the ongoing conversation. In fact, Janis suggests that the leader refrain from expressing an opinion until well into the group's deliberations.

If you've worked on group projects in school, you are all too aware of the numerous complaints students have regarding group dynamics. You can find some of the more common dissatisfactions in Table 7.1. How might you resolve some of these issues? What are some other problems you've experienced that aren't represented there? As you can see, more than one of those concerns has to do with bad leadership.

Systems Theory

Group membership carries certain responsibilities, as you can read in the box "Our Responsibility to the Group." One theory that helps us understand why is **systems theory**, the idea that groups operate as systems, that is, as "sets of interacting components that together form something more than the sum of the parts" (Littlejohn and Foss, 2011, p. 50). Three assumptions (Ackoff, 1981, pp. 15–16) are central to the idea of groups as systems:

1. Each member has an effect on the functioning of the whole.
2. Each member is affected by at least one other member in the group.
3. All possible subgroups of members also have the first two properties.

In other words, all members of the group (the system) are constrained by their dependence on others, and the group will operate according to this interdependence. Consider a family. Each member has a different role of great importance to the family dynamic; however, the family group as a whole is a much stronger entity than

rank ineffectiveness Group members question the legitimacy of messages transmitted by those in positions of authority.

groupthink When voices in a group are suppressed by pressure from others.

THUMBNAIL THEORY

Systems Theory

Groups operate as systems, in which all parts (members) are interdependent. Change in one part produces change in another. Systems are goal-oriented, and as such, work to sustain and monitor themselves. They do so through feedback loops, in which the parts communicate with each other and are mutually changed by that communication.

Table 7.1 Common Student Complaints About Working in Groups

1.	There are slackers in the group who want to be "carried" by everyone else.
2.	The student who wanted to be the leader is not very organized.
3.	The leader is bossy and disrespectful to the other students.
4.	We can't seem to coordinate our schedules to accommodate group time and research.
5.	I know the group selection was random, but we all have conflicting personalities and don't get along.
6.	The group is too big or too small for the amount of research/work assigned.
7.	Some members are too shy and while they contribute in work, they do not contribute to the discussion.
8.	Members take disagreements about the work personally.
9.	One student is aggressive and often ambushes the opinions of others.
10.	A few students are friends and always make the others feel like outsiders.
11.	The leader thinks she/he is always right about every point and doesn't listen to others.
12.	Half of us are commuters, making scheduling and meeting too difficult.
13.	Some members can't get past their general I-hate-working-in-groups attitude.
14.	Some of the students are poor speakers and will bring us down in the presentation.

any one individual member. If one person disappoints or fails the others, the entire family feels the effects. A divorce, for example, will alter not only each family member's individual role, but the way the family operates as a system.

Another important concept of systems theory is that systems are *goal-oriented*: they exist to serve some purpose (here it's easy to see why systems theory and group communication make a good fit). As such, they sustain (keep themselves going) and regulate themselves to achieve their intended outcome. How do they do this? Through communication, naturally.

In a system, this communication is called a *feedback loop*. The parts (members) interact with one another, and as one part changes in response to that communication, so too does the other, resulting in change by the first part. The feedback is "looped" back and forth, producing ongoing change that moves the system (the group) in the direction of success. Systems also monitor their environments; that is, members constantly judge the product of their work, sensing when the system is in need of change. Children of divorce notice that the house is much messier than it was before the parents separated, and you and your group-mates receive an e-mail from the instructor alerting you to a missed deadline for your bibliography. This external information becomes part of the group's interactions, and the system (hopefully) changes accordingly.

Leadership and Power

Every group has a member or a few members who either assume or are appointed to a leadership role. But before we discuss styles of leadership and

Our Responsibility to the Group

Interdependence—how we and others rely on and are influenced by one another—is essential to group success. We thus have an ethical responsibility to do our part in ensuring that our groups meet their goals. For example, on a school project, your contributions should be as significant as those of your peers if you expect a good grade. In family, helping with younger siblings makes it possible for parents to focus on goals that serve a greater system purpose, such as facilitating a failing grandparent's home life. Professionally, we have a responsibility to heighten our expectations of ourselves in our work groups; we should take pride in what we've accomplished and in the satisfaction of setting high standards for others. In all of these examples, a system must be sustained and controlled to achieve its goals and to avoid group breakdown. It is critical that individuals operating within those systems understand and fulfill their roles in the group's sustenance and success. This is the ethical choice that we automatically and implicitly make when becoming part of group.

You're in college now, and the system that was your family when you were a high school student has had to change. How have your roles and responsibilities within this new family system been altered? How has change in your role affected other members of that original system? Have feedback loops been strengthened or weakened? How closely do you monitor the working of your family system now that your place in it has changed?

---

forms of power, it's important to define *leadership* itself. **Leadership** is when "an individual influences group members to achieve a common goal" (Nort-house, 2007, p. 3). Sounds pretty basic, right? But we all know that effective leadership is much more complex, as those in authority don't simply "influence" others; they also motivate, challenge, enable, and inspire. Leaders must understand the group's dynamics and, based on that awareness, determine the best paths for reaching those common goals. Good leaders also make sure that everyone, before embarking on the task at hand, is clear about the agreed-upon norms, ranks, roles, and controls. Finally, it is critical that good leaders adopt a leadership style conducive to the personalities and structure of the group.

leadership When an individual influences group members to achieve a common goal.

Styles of Leadership

The three most common leadership styles are *authoritarian*, *democratic*, and *laissez-faire* (Lewin, Lippitt, and White, 1939).

Authoritarian leaders often do not accept input from members of the group and maintain complete control of such things as decision-making and rules. Some may see this leader as more of a dictator than a leader. One-way communication is characteristic of this leadership style, which can often be problematic for those who wish to have a say in the process. Still, some people flourish under authoritarian leaders, especially those subordinates who are more passive, less focused, and need high levels of guidance. Have you ever experienced a leader who takes full control of the group whether the other members like it or not? How did that work out for you?

authoritarian leader Does not accept input from members and maintains complete control of the group.

A **democratic leader** encourages full and equal participation among individuals in the group. This leader will solicit opinions, advice, and ideas from members

democratic leader Encourages full and equal participation among group members.

What type of leadership does the president of the United States employ? Would President Eisenhower have employed the same leadership style as supreme commander of the armed forces in World War II that he did as president?

and is typically the most appreciated type of leader. This is a person who believes the best outcome will arise from a multitude of voices, and while this leader has the final say in matters, she or he does not make a decision without consideration of all members. As a result, group participants come to feel worthy and valued. Can you think of a situation where democratic leadership may have some drawbacks? What about in a case where group members cannot reach consensus in a timely fashion?

Finally, **laissez-faire leaders** (from the French, meaning *to let people do as they choose*) are hands-off leaders. They provide little to no guidance to group members and expect everyone else to make the decisions. Under this style of leadership, the rules and roles are often badly defined or perhaps never made clear during the group's formation. Group members tend to be unmotivated under laissez-faire leaders, which often results in breakdown and even dissolution. Have you ever been in a group where the leader did not lead, but instead delegated leadership responsibilities to other members? Are there situations where this style of leadership might be effective?

After identifying these most prevalent leadership types, Lewin concluded that authoritarian-led groups were less creative, more rigid, and more dysfunctional than democratically run groups, which produced the best results. Groups with laissez-faire leadership were more unproductive and less efficient than those with the other leadership styles (Lewin, Lippitt, and White, 1939).

laissez-faire leader Provides little guidance and expects group members to make decisions.

Forms of Power

power The ability, capacity, or authority to move others to act as desired.

What is it that drives strong leadership? Typically, it's the **power** inherent in the position—the ability, capacity, or authority to move others to act as desired. Psychologists John French and Bertram Raven (1959) identified several forms of power that explain why people in subordinate positions follow their leaders. Among them are these seven: *coercive*, *reward*, *referent*, *legitimate*, *expert*, *informational*, and *connectional* power.

Leaders who possess *coercive power* have the authority to inflict punishment. A courtroom judge, for example, can hand down a sentence, or a drill sergeant can reprimand subordinates with physical exercise. This is the most negatively perceived type of power because it can so easily be abused or wrongly or unethically administered.

Reward power is the opposite of coercive power. Leaders who exhibit reward power are in a position to "pay" members for compliance or achievement. A sales manager may provide her team bonuses based on the number of new accounts. A professor gives good grades for well-written papers, and a father can allow his kids extra computer time or a later bedtime for good behavior. As you can imagine, this can be a very motivating type of power and is

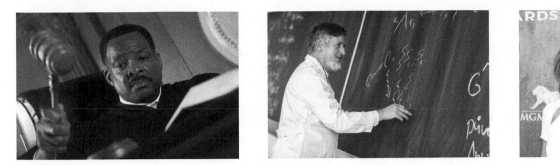

What types of power does each of these individuals possess?

certainly more positive than coercive power. However, reward power can also have its drawbacks. A reward that is deserved but never comes can create resentment or anger toward the leader. Return to our sales manager; perhaps the team brought in a record number of new accounts but the manager then decides that her subordinates should have done even better to earn their bonuses.

The third type is *legitimate power*. Leaders who possess legitimate power do so primarily because of their status. Politicians such as state senators, governors, or congressional representatives all have considerable power because of their positions in the government. This is evident through their ability to make hugely impactful decisions, propose legislation, and initiate action that can affect thousands of citizens and organizations. People who hold legitimate power often have considerable influence over a number of social, professional, and personal groups. Politicians who take friends to dinner may be offered complimentary bottles of wine or the best table in the restaurant simply because of their powerful status. And legitimate power can be abused. Political sex scandals are a regular occurrence. These typically involve power disparities between influential men and female subordinates, for example the alleged misdeeds of presidential candidate Herman Cain (accused several times of sexual harassment of employees), accusations of rape of a hotel maid against the former head of the International Monetary Fund, Dominique Strauss-Kahn, and multiple charges of sexual assault against influential comedian and actor Bill Cosby.

Referent power is based on admiration and liking. Accomplished athletes like LeBron James, Peyton Manning, and Danica Patrick possess referent power, as do celebrities such as Samuel L. Jackson, Jennifer Lopez, and Brad Pitt, who have a commanding presence on a movie set. Referent power, for example, is evident in one-time teammate Troy Brown's evaluation of quarterback Tom Brady's leadership: "It doesn't matter whether he's right or wrong. People listen to him. He gives you a look that makes you know if you do what he tells you, it'll be fine" (JockBio, 2012). Consider, too, the groups you've worked with in school. It's probably safe to say you were more responsive to the leaders you liked than those you didn't.

Attractiveness is an important factor in determining how much one is liked. We humans are hard-wired—genetically predisposed—to respond more favorably to those we consider attractive as opposed to those we do not. "Good-looking men and women are generally regarded to be more talented, kind, honest, and intelligent than their less attractive counterparts," writes psychologist Ray Williams, "Meritocracies are supposed to champion intelligence, qualifications, and experience. But physical and social attraction deliver substantial benefits in all social interaction—making a person more persuasive, able to secure the co-operation of colleagues, attract customers, and sell products" (2012). It's easy, then, to see why teenagers in friendship groups model themselves after the peers they deem most attractive and cool, primarily because they, too, want to command the same levels of respect and admiration from others. As you might conclude, however, a major drawback to referent power is that it can be awarded on a superficial basis, rendering the person in power unworthy of admiration. Just think of all the teen movies featuring high school "mean girls" and clueless jocks.

Expert power is based on the amount of knowledge or expertise a person has in a given area. Doctors know medicine, and math professors know algebra and geometry. People who want to overcome an addiction will likely choose a support group led by a doctor because doctors are *experts*, and they trust that a doctor will use his or her power to benefit the group. When we have a big math exam and struggle with some of the concepts, we sign up for the study group led by our professor who uses her knowledge to clarify the things we don't understand. It all adds up, right? However, sometimes even expert power can have its negative qualities. For example, a doctor so enthralled with his own expertise that he doesn't listen to his patients can misdiagnose an illness. A math professor who is an expert in her field may have difficulty leading the study group because she cannot comprehend members' lack of math competency. Expert power requires that knowledge be used in an appropriate and moral fashion; otherwise, expertise-based leadership can produce neglectful or hurtful situations for group members who depend on that expertise.

Those who have access to information that others lack possess *informational power*. For example, people who work with classified material, like those in government, or individuals who have access to private records, like adoption agencies or health industries, can exert influence over those in need of that information. Their power resides in their ability to control the availability and accuracy of information. Even on a more personal level, informational power is always present. Have you ever withheld the time and place of a group gathering to exclude a troublesome member? A club treasurer may present a pessimistic accounting of upcoming costs to thwart members' ambitious and expensive plans for an end-of-semester blowout. As you can see in these two examples, the exercise of informational power is fraught with ethical implications. Who decides on the propriety of withholding information? It's quite likely that the holder of the information and those who might otherwise benefit from it have differing answers to this question.

Finally, there is *connectional power*, authority "earned" by virtue of whom the leader knows and the support from members that he or she gains as a result. Discussions of leadership sometimes exclude connectional power because it is not something that resides in leaders themselves, but is attributed to them. Members attribute certain skills or characteristics to leaders based on their assumptions of the other people those leaders are thought to know. For example, have you ever had a professor who constantly reminded you of "the time I taught at Harvard" or the teammate who is quick to inform the group that "famous athlete So-and-So is my neighbor"? Again, these examples suggest that connectional power may be a relatively weak form of authority for group leaders, and those who exercise it too frequently may rightfully have their leadership questioned.

Group success, especially the success of goal-oriented as opposed to primary groups, depends in large part on how well leaders negotiate their power in ways beneficial to the entire group. There is no single best exercise of power; different people, different types of groups, and different situations encountered by those people and groups will ultimately determine the most effective form of leadership and exercise of power.

Improving Your Group Communication Skills

Many students cringe at the thought of group projects and presentations. It's often disconcerting to have to rely on others in your quest for a decent grade. For a student who desperately needs a good grade in order to pass the class or one who hopes to maintain her 3.9 GPA, putting their fate in someone else's hands is a threatening prospect. Students who are more socially challenged often struggle in group situations, as do those who have issues with delegating tasks because they want total control. Learning how to improve your group communication skills can make the difference between a successful group experience and the worst time of your college—or professional—career. You can learn a bit more about how to make your group tasks work—a common reality of the contemporary workplace—in the box "12 Cs for Successful Teamwork."

Like it or not, you will face group assignments throughout your personal and professional lives, so the best way to deal with them is to, first, accept them; second, embrace them; and third, be better prepared to shape them into positive experiences. Let's look at some of the ways you can do just that.

1. Understand the *dynamics and components* of group communication, which hopefully you've accomplished in your reading of this chapter. You should share your knowledge with those who do not know as much about group communication as you. Exercise your expert power!

2. As the group forms, *encourage each member to vocalize his or her feelings* about the project. Ask a lot of questions about what members feel to be their strengths and weaknesses, what areas they would prefer to explore, and what they see as their roles and responsibilities in the group. This makes everyone feel that they have an equal say in the establishment of group norms and tasks.

3. Allow all members to develop a *sense of ownership* in the goal. Discuss how the task at hand impacts them and reward any achievements or strides made by each individual.

COMMUNICATION IN THE WORKPLACE

12 Cs for Successful Teamwork

"People tend to think that teams are the democratic—and the efficient—way to get things done" writes organizational psychologist and team expert J. Richard Hackman. "I have no question that when you have a team, the possibility exists that it will generate magic, producing something extraordinary, a collective creation of previously unimagined quality or beauty. But don't count on it. Research consistently shows that teams underperform, despite all the extra resources they have" (in Coutu, 2009).

From reading this chapter, and no doubt from having quite a bit of experience working with teams yourself, you know that Professor Hackman is on to something. But teamwork can be very successful, and it is a fact of the contemporary American workplace. As such, human resources counselor Susan Heathfield (2013) suggests 12 Cs for ensuring the success of working in groups:

1. *Clear expectations*—Have leaders clearly communicated expectations for the team's performance and outcomes? When those expectations are met, are they acknowledged or rewarded?
2. *Context*—Do team members understand where their work fits within the context of the larger organization's goals, principles, vision, and values?
3. *Commitment*—Do team members *want to* participate in the team?

4. *Competence*—Do team members think that the other members have the necessary knowledge, skills, and capability to meet the group's goals?
5. *Charter*—Has the team clearly defined and communicated its goals, desired outcomes, timelines, and methods?
6. *Control*—Do team members have sufficient freedom and power to feel ownership in their tasks? Do team members clearly understand their boundaries? Is there effective leadership?
7. *Collaboration*—Do group members understand team and group processes? Are they interpersonally working together effectively?
8. *Communication*—Do team members communicate clearly and honestly with each other?
9. *Creative innovation*—Is the larger organization really interested in change? Does it value creative thinking, new ideas, and unique solutions?
10. *Consequences*—Do all team members feel responsible and accountable for the group's achievements? Does the organization offer rewards or recognition when teams are successful?
11. *Coordination*—Do cross-function and multi-department teams work together effectively?
12. *Cultural change*—Does the larger organization appreciate that the more it can change its work climate to support teams, the more it will benefit from the work of those groups?

4. Keep in mind that while authoritarian and laissez-faire leadership may have some benefits (depending on the type of group), always assume that *democratic approaches* are the best way to negotiate issues in the group.

5. Constantly work toward *building cohesion*. What are the commonalities among group members? Determine the factors that bind group members and reference those similarities during moments of conflict or disagreement.

6. *Encourage preparedness* from members. Once a meeting schedule is established, everyone should be clear about group expectations—what each member should bring to the meetings, the protocol at meetings, and who will run the meetings.

7. Offer continual reminders that *everyone benefits from a successful outcome*. This will serve to help individuals remain motivated as they work toward completing the task.

8. Suggest regular, *open dialogue* about how the group can continue to improve without alienating or insulting any one member. Speak *collectively* rather than individually—for example, "We're getting behind" rather than "Alex, you're holding us back."

9. Engage in *trust-building* exercises to enhance group cohesion and encourage honesty among members. Some groups do this by asking members to disclose information about themselves as a means of showing willingness to share with other members.

Disclosure creates trust in group members because it shows a willingness to share feelings with others.

10. Make members *aware of the interdependent nature of the project*. Reflect on the success of the assignment should everyone give 100% versus the possible scenarios if any one member does not. Explaining that the project is a *unified effort* can help individual members understand that success is dependent on their individual, specific contributions.

11. Engage in *good listening*. This is arguably the most important path toward building a productive group. Contributing with ideas, research, and strategies is certainly significant, but the ability to truly hear what others have to say not only shows open-mindedness but a level of respect that is rewarded by the appreciation of others. Build referent power!

12. *Avoid group breakdown*. This should be relatively easy to achieve if the group engages in some of the practices listed here, such as maintaining open dialogue and good listening, building trust and cohesion, and bringing democratic approaches to group issues.

Review of Learning Objectives

7.1 Describe the various types of groups.

The two broad categories of groups are primary groups (offering members affection and a sense of belonging) and task-oriented groups (designed to serve a purpose). Task-oriented groups can be further categorized as participant-driven (uses other members' emotional support to overcome obstacles or achieve goals), information-presentation (organized to provide information and awareness), decision-making (convened to come to consensus on an issue or issues), and skill-building groups (goal is to build skills among members or sometimes non-members).

7.2 Explain the dynamics of group structure, recognizing the stages of group development.

Group dynamics are driven by four elements. *Norms* are the rules that govern the behavior of group members. *Roles* are their specific tasks and responsibilities. *Ranks* are the hierarchal structure of the group. *Controls* are the rewards and punishments for group members. Depending on the group, different patterns of communication between members may be informal or formal.

There are five stages of group development. In the *forming stage*, members initially convene, meeting each other for the first time. In the *storming stage*, members experience conflict. In the *norming stage*, members find cohesion. In the *performing stage*, members collectively operate at a high level of efficiency. In the *adjourning stage*, members depart from one another and the task.

7.3 Discuss types of group cohesion and the factors that cause group breakdown.

There are four types of group cohesion. *Sentiment-based cohesion* is built on the relational closeness of the group's members. *Reward-based cohesion* relies on the idea that members are rewarded for the successful completion of the task. *Assignment-based cohesion* is achieved when group members work together toward achieving a specific goal. *Dependency-based cohesion*, more common in large organizations, links groups to each other by way of separate tasks.

Group breakdown occurs when conflict emerges, causing deterioration or dissolution. It can occur from *normative confusion*, when the group's rules and expectations have not been clearly defined or established. *Rank ineffectiveness*, when those in positions of power appear to lack legitimacy, is another cause. *Groupthink*, when some group members suppress other members' voices, can also cause breakdown.

7.4 Describe different styles of leadership and forms of power.

There are three common leadership styles. *Authoritarian leaders* do not accept input from members of the group, and maintain complete control. *Democratic leaders* encourage full and equal participation from group members. *Laissez-faire leaders* are hands-off leaders. Democratic leadership is considered the most effective.

Leadership depends on the exercise of various forms of power. *Coercive power* is the authority to inflict punishment. *Reward power* comes from the ability to reward members for compliance or achievement. *Legitimate power* resides in leaders' status. Referent power is based on admiration and liking. *Expert power* resides in the amount of knowledge or expertise possessed by a leader. *Informational power* comes from having access to information that others do not possess. *Connectional power* is authority earned by virtue of whom the leader is assumed to know.

7.5 Identify ways to improve your group communication skills.

You can improve your group communication skills in a number of ways, including the following:

- Understand the dynamics and components of group communication.
- Encourage members to vocalize their feelings.
- Allow all members to develop a sense of ownership in the goal.
- Assume that democratic approaches are the best way to negotiate group issues.
- Constantly work toward building cohesion.
- Encourage preparedness from members.
- Offer continual reminders that everyone benefits from a successful outcome.
- Suggest regular, open dialogue, and speak collectively rather than individually.
- Engage in trust-building exercises.
- Make members aware of the interdependent nature of the project.
- Engage in good listening.

Key Terms

small groups 144
primary groups 144
task-oriented groups 145
participant-driven groups 145
information-presentation groups 145
decision-making groups 145
skill-building groups 145
dynamics 145
norms 145
roles 146
ranks 146
controls 146
socialization 147
informal group communication 148
formal group communication 148
structuration theory 148
forming 149
storming 151
norming 151
performing 151
adjourning 151
group cohesion 152
group breakdown 152
normative confusion 152
rank ineffectiveness 153
groupthink 153
systems theory 153
leadership 155
authoritarian leader 155
democratic leader 155
laissez-faire leader 156
power 156

Questions for Review

1. What is the difference between primary and task-oriented groups?

2. What are the four types of task-oriented groups? What does each hope to accomplish?

3. What are the four elements of group structure? Define each.

4. Distinguish between informal and formal group communication.

5. What are the five stages of group development, and what happens in each?

6. What are the four types of group cohesion? Describe each.

7. What is group breakdown, and what are its three possible causes?

8. Name and describe the three most common forms of leadership.

9. Name and describe the seven forms of power.

10. Describe the basic assumptions behind structuration theory and systems theory.

Questions for Discussion

1. What are the best and worst group experiences you have ever had? Can you explain the success and failure of each in terms of group cohesion and leadership styles?

2. Have you ever held a leadership position in a group? What was it? What was your leadership style? How successful a leader do you think you were, and can you reflect on why you performed as you did?

3. Your Communication class is a group. As what kind of group would you classify your class? How would you describe its norms, and how did they come to be? How many different roles can you identify among your class members? Have ranks or a hierarchy become apparent? What controls exist, and who ensures their enforcement? How did this group structure come to be? Can you explain it in terms of structuration or systems theory?

8

Organizational Communication

You graduated from college four months ago and just landed a marketing position at a prestigious company. As you reflect on your job search and the day-to-day demands of your new career, you realize it's a completely different world from the one you experienced as an undergraduate. For one thing, getting hired was no easy task. You applied to dozens of job openings. You revised and rewrote your resume and cover letter a hundred times as you began to better recognize the expectations of the corporate world.

When you were finally called to interview for your current position, you were excited, but your momentum had been thrown off by those months of rejection. Still, you researched the company, and in the interview remembered all the important interactional rules you learned in Communication class—make eye contact, answer and ask questions, engage in good listening, be interpersonally immediate. Despite some small nervousness, you got the job. Next stop, human resources. You were briefed on sexual harassment, ethics in the workplace, salary structure, and benefits.

In your ongoing efforts to dissect the inner workings of your company and your place in it, you realize the value of having studied organizational communication. You understand that much of your success is contingent on the relational aspects of the job—that is, communicating effectively with your colleagues. Even more concepts from your Communication class are now applicable, such as building morale, managing workplace conflict, choosing an appropriate leadership style, and assessing group dynamics. While you never could have been fully prepared for what the corporate world had in store, you are certainly better equipped than recent graduates without those skills.

As this vignette illustrates, entering the workforce calls into focus quite a number of different communication skills. This is because organizations (companies, nonprofits, corporations, governmental agencies, and the like) exist as their own structures, separate systems composed of specific rules, hierarchies, languages, and tasks. They employ specific groups of people with particular skills, all contributing to a clear outcome or objective. Like other groups, organizations are influenced by outside factors, such as politics, the environment, society, and the economy, to mention only a few. In this chapter, we examine how communication, both formal and informal, allows organizations to meet their intended goals, especially through well-structured bureaucracy, effective leadership, and productive organizational culture.

Learning Objectives

8.1 Describe the foundations of organizational communication.

8.2 Explain the ways messages can move within an organization.

8.3 Examine the roles, rules, ranks, and responses in the organizational system.

8.4 Give examples of the operation and value of bureaucracy in organizations.

8.5 Differentiate various positive and negative organizational communication traits.

8.6 Describe how people are socialized into an organization's culture within its climate.

Defining Organizational Communication

organization A structured social collectivity that has overall and individual goals, coordinates the activity of its members, and is embedded within an environment of other organizations.

organizational communication Any communication, verbal or nonverbal, that occurs within an organization.

Organizations involve members and relationships between those members. As such, communication scholar Katherine Miller defines an **organization** as a "social collectivity [having] organizational and individual goals, coordinating activity, organizational structure, and the embedding of the organization within an environment of other organizations" (2012, p. 11). Communication scholars study *organizational communication* as a way to understand the relational dynamics of those who operate within them. These relationships may include superiors and subordinates, colleagues, team members, human resources personnel and employees, and even intimate workplace relationships. Regardless of the relationship, the organization plays a huge role in shaping the dynamics of—and therefore, the meaning made from—those interpersonal exchanges. Therefore, **organizational communication** is any communication, verbal or nonverbal, that occurs among members of the same organization.

"The foundation of any complex organization," researchers Terrance Albrecht and Betsy Bach tell us, "is the communication process occurring between people. Interaction among members—and the relationships they form—are the primary way in which people move from a disorganized state of individuals to an organized, coordinated group of relatively interdependent organization members, capable of collectively accomplishing tasks, adapting to environments, and reaching mutually rewarding goals" (1997, p. 3). There are a number of ways in which those sharing an organizational environment communicate:

- Electronically (e-mails, texts, messaging, social networking sites, PowerPoint slides)
- Verbally (presentations, meetings, luncheons, face-to-face negotiations, interviews, informal conversations)
- Nonverbally (dress codes, work ethic, levels of productivity)

Regardless of the platform, the messages flowing within an organization are quite distinct in both type and movement. In the following section we consider organizational messages—what they are, how they work, and the directions in which they flow.

Types and Movement of Organizational Messages

Messages flowing within organizations can move in various directions—upward, downward, or horizontally. The direction of this movement is significant because it helps establish the existence of a **hierarchal structure**, levels of power within the organization. Figure 8.1 shows a typical hierarchical structure.

hierarchal structure Levels of power within an organization.

The way employees deal with specific types of messages can differ dramatically, and so can the consequences. For example, imagine you are part of a sales team and are sending an e-mail to your colleagues regarding company protocol. How might the structure and wording of your message differ from one sent to your manager about the same issue? You would likely be more guarded in a message to your superior, trying to make sure nothing could be misinterpreted or could reflect badly on you or

Organizational communication exists throughout the workplace and includes specific kinds of messages.

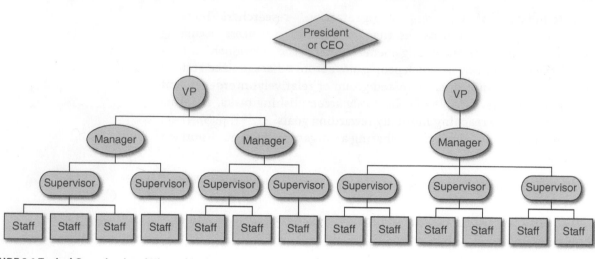

FIGURE 8.1 Typical Organizational Hierarchical Structure

your colleagues. Perhaps the wording would be more formal with your manager than it might be with your colleagues, and you would most likely have spent more time writing the e-mail.

Upward Messages

upward message Messages that flow from lower to higher ranked employees.

A message from a subordinate to a superior or boss is an **upward message** because it is sent from someone in a lower ranked position to someone in a higher ranked position. A request for a raise in pay, a letter of resignation, various reports, request for funding, or monthly updates on product sales are indicative of upward messages.

Some organizations have formal procedures for that upward flow, such as specific e-mail, phone, and paper-based suggestion systems, or periodic performance assessments. Not all do, however. "Despite the value of upward communication networks, a common and valid complaint among employees is that there are not appropriate vehicles available to carry messages from subordinate to superior," explains organizational communication researcher Alan Zaremba. "Upward communication networks are rarities and are often not authentic when they do exist. This is due more to human nature than to ignorance of the value of these networks. People, no matter who they are and no matter how confident they might be, are reluctant to solicit rejection" (2003, p. 133).

Take this example. You supply your boss with a detailed assessment of your team's progress over the last six months. You and your colleagues did a

Upward communication is sometimes fraught with danger.

ETHICAL COMMUNICATION

Could You Blow the Whistle?

You're five years into a successful career with a big company when you learn that it is illegally dumping toxic waste into streams. These streams are deep in the woods but eventually flow into your city's water supply. What do you do? If you alert your superiors and they ignore you for months, what then? What if your managers, and even some of your colleagues, seem to be distancing themselves from you, and you start to hear whispers of snitch and informer? What if your family is depending on you for a steady income?

Whistleblowers are people who reveal improper organizational activities that superiors wish to conceal. Whistleblowers can report internally—that is, they can alert the organization's leaders to the problem—or they can report externally. The federal government, through its Office of the Whistleblower Protection Program, offers protection to whistleblowing employees. Federal law, through the Securities and Exchange Commission's Office of the Whistleblower, also protects private-sector financial workers who report their organizations' illegal activities. The military, too, protects whistleblowers who report abuse to Congress under the Military Whistleblower Protection Act, and the IRS maintains a Whistleblower Office to protect those who alert it to tax fraud. Private organizations such as the National Whistleblowers Center help whistleblowers defend themselves against retaliation. And a number of major media outlets participate in SecureDrop, an online whistleblower submission system open to the public that allows whistleblowers to anonymously send information and documents to journalists while protecting their identity.

Despite these protections, and the esteem they seem to imply for the act of whistleblowing, many people never consider coming forward, either internally or externally. Doing so could mean losing their job and their friendships inside and outside the organization. "Everyone I know who has been a whistleblower has sacrificed their career," said Tom Doyle, founder of Catholic Whistleblowers (in Forliti, 2013).

Back to you—could you blow the whistle? Revisit this ethical dilemma after you read this chapter's section on organizational culture. Ask yourself if your response might change had you been part of an organizational culture that promoted trust and membership. How might you contribute to creating such a culture?

---

good job, meeting expectations. But there were some personnel problems, especially the issue of absence among two key members. You effectively handled this tricky personnel issue and still met the output targets the organization set for you. But what meaning does your manager make from your account? That you had a personnel problem and would quite likely have *exceeded* expectations if you had not allowed this interference. In this case, your honest and detailed accounting of your team's work has not benefited you.

And what happens if the message you send upward is about serious problems in the way the organization operates—and that message is unwelcome? Even worse, what happens if that message expresses or even suggests disagreement with the way your superiors are doing their work? You may decide to say nothing or else equivocate. Communication researcher Ryan Bisel and his colleagues call this outcome the **hierarchical mum effect**. This self-imposed "suppression of dissent produces a barrier to organizational

hierarchical mum effect Self-imposed suppression of dissent in upward messages.

learning and adaptation" (Bisel, Messersmith, and Kelley, 2012, p. 128). You can read about some of the challenges created by unwanted upward messages in the box "Could You Blow the Whistle?"

Downward Messages

downward message Messages that flow from higher to lower ranked employees.

A **downward message** moves from boss to subordinate, higher rank to lower rank—for example, a notice of termination, procedural or policy changes, notification of new hires, and changes in operations.

Despite communicators' best efforts, messages can be distorted, or misinterpreted, as they move up or down the hierarchy. Downward messages tend to suffer more **serial distortion**: they are altered and reshaped as they move through various stopping points between the original source and the intended receiver. One obvious reason for distortion as information passes from the big boss through lower levels is the amount of encoding and decoding involved. Think of the game of telephone, when you whisper a secret to a friend, who passes it on to the next person, who likewise passes it on, and so on. By the time the information makes its way back to you, it most surely has been altered. But there are four other factors that impede meaning making as messages flow downward: adding, leveling, sharpening, and assimilating.

serial distortion Alteration of messages as they move through stopping points between the original source and the intended receiver.

Adding occurs when intermediaries add to the original message, changing its meaning either in fact (less likely) or in tone (more likely). A vice president may ask your manager to congratulate you on your successful first year with the company, but when your manager adds that you can expect "big things" to come your way (raise? promotion? company car? corner office?), she has unwisely altered the VP's message.

Leveling is the opposite of adding; it is when intermediaries shorten the original message. Original messages get leveled for a number of reasons; for example, some people simply write or speak less voluminously than do others. But messages can also be shortened because of more problematic reasons. There may be strained relations between people along the downward line of communication, or people may omit information or details that reflect poorly on themselves or even on those above them.

Sharpening is when intermediaries reduce a message to its most sensational or thematic core. "Until the holiday rush brings the expected boost in business, two employees will be laid off, one from sales and one from customer service" becomes "There will be layoffs!!"

Assimilation happens when intermediaries reshape messages to be more palatable to intended recipients. Few people, even bosses, like to deliver bad news. "If the IT people do not improve their performance, the whole unit will be replaced and their duties outsourced to an independent contractor" becomes "Come on, people, we need to do better. The VP is losing patience, and you know how she can be."

Horizontal Messages

horizontal message Messages exchanged between colleagues of similar rank.

A **horizontal message** is one exchanged between colleagues, usually those who share the same rank or position. As you read earlier in the text, communication can fall anywhere on a spectrum from formal to informal, depending on the context. Informal communication in the workplace is most likely to occur in the horizontal passing of information among coworkers, which is not without its benefits. In fact, research demonstrates that "workers are more productive if they have more social interaction. So a bank's call center introduced a shared 15-minute coffee break, and a pharmaceutical company replaced coffee makers used by a few marketing workers with a larger café area. The result? Increased sales and less turnover" (Lohr, 2014, p. A1). The two common forms of this less structured, yet quite valuable form of organizational communication are *grapevine* and *water cooler communication*.

Grapevine communication refers to messages and rumors that make their way around an organization; in the end, these may bear little resemblance to the original message. If frequent encoding and decoding distorts more formal messages as they flow down the hierarchy, imagine the kinds of distortion that happen in the grapevine. Grapevine communication entails no formality and is most likely to occur when an organization or company is facing some difficulty, for example an impending layoff, declines in profit due to recession, or a reorganization. The grapevine can take any one or all these forms (Davis, 1953):

Water cooler and grapevine conversations are two informal methods of employee communication.

grapevine Informal chain of communication that spreads through an organization, often leading to message distortion.

- *Single strand*—One person passes information on to another, who then informs a third, and so on in a single, linear flow of information.

- *Gossip*—One person tells many others.

- *Probability*—People randomly inform others.

- *Cluster*—Of those people who have been informed, one tells others. Of those others, one tells others, and on and on.

Keith Davis, a pioneer researcher of informal organizational communication, explains that the grapevine "cannot be abolished, rubbed out, hidden under a basket, chopped down, tied up, or stopped. If [it is] suppressed in one place, it will pop up in another . . . It is as hard to kill as the mythical glass snake which, when struck, broke itself into fragments and grew a new snake out of each piece" (1972, p. 263). How should an organization deal with this form of communication, which, by definition, is unauthorized? Davis says, accept it, understand how it operates, and when appropriate, make sure to use it to complement the formal network.

Another form of informal organizational communication is **water cooler communication**, when employees engage in conversation (not necessarily

water cooler communication Informal chat within an organization.

work-related) while on breaks or during pauses in the workday. These talks may include *outward information* (what's going on outside working hours but is related in some way to the organization), for example, which employees are dating other employees, or *inward information* (what's occurring inside the workday), such as treatment of employees by management or inequities in pay and designated responsibilities. Much as they have with the grapevine, contemporary organizations have come to embrace the water cooler, understanding that these informal channels

- Give stressed workers an opportunity to vent their feelings.
- Create a climate of free-flowing feedback, which can benefit the organization.
- Build company morale.
- Encourage a more closely knit, interpersonal work community.
- Are essential to maintaining the organizational "system" as a whole.

PERSONALLY RESPONSIBLE COMMUNICATION

Status Update: I've Just Been Fired

Which of these situations will get you fired?

(1) You're a waitress, and you post Facebook photos of local policemen with the caption "Those stupid cops better hope I'm not their server."

(2) You're a teacher who takes to Facebook to criticize her students, complaining that "it would be easier to be at home than have to go through this."

(3) You're a reporter for a newspaper, and you comment on your town's murder rate, Tweeting, "What?!?! No overnight homicides? You're slacking, Tucson."

(4) You work for a transportation company, and you post online, "At OnBoard you will receive no health insurance, sick days, vacation days or one single benefit. You will ride around on unsafe buses, without the benefit of a PA system, or sometimes even a seat."

(5) You work at a nonprofit organization, and you and some of your colleagues complain on Facebook about another coworker's intention to go to management about your work performance.

These are all real incidents: numbers 1 through 3 got people fired; 4 and 5 didn't (all from Gordon, 2013, and Ballman, 2013). The difference lies in what the National Labor Relations Act considers *concerted activity*—that is, employees' freedom to act together to try to improve pay and working conditions or to fix job-related problems. Situations 1 through 3—insulting police officers, complaining about your students, and joking about murder—have little to do with working conditions or on-the-job problems. But situations 4 and 5 clearly are about organizational activities and work conditions. Concerted activity occurs "when: (1) union or union-free employees get together to discuss wages, hours, or other working conditions; (2) one or more employees threaten or suggest group action; or (3) one or more employees voice concerns—on a safety or comparable topic—that impact or concern a larger group of fellow employees" (Temple and Stuhldreher, 2013).

So how far can you go in your social media commentary, especially when frustrated about something or someone at work? Remember the principle that should guide *all* your Internet communication: *never post or tweet anything you wouldn't say to your mother or to your boss's face*. The principle of concerted activity may give you legal protection in some instances, but what you post and tweet says much about you and your organization. Why risk not only your job but loss of face?

New communication technologies, especially social networking sites, greatly expand the reach—and therefore the impact—of grapevine and water cooler chat. This expanded impact is not always for the better, as you can read in the box "Status Update: I've Just Been Fired."

The Organization as a System

One way to look at organizational communication is through Systems Theory (Chapter 7). As you may remember, systems are "sets of interacting components that together form something more than the sum of the parts" (Littlejohn and Foss, 2011, p. 50). Central to systems theory is the idea that systems are *goal-oriented*; that is, they operate to serve some specific function. Naturally, effective communication among the system's components will determine how well the system fulfills its goal.

Of course, not all systems are the same. One type is a **closed system**: its components communicate solely with one another; it will continue to fulfill its goal as long as its components function as designed. Think of the heating system in your house. The temperature of a room triggers a response from the thermostat, which triggers the furnace to turn on or off, heating or cooling the room—and then the process repeats. This endless series of **feedback loops** constitutes a circular communication process in which messages travel back and forth, achieving ongoing mutual adjustment (and in this case, keeping you comfortable). Of course, your home heating system is very simple compared with a big organization's system of interactions.

Organizations are **open systems**; their components interact continuously, not only with one another, but also with the environment outside the system. For example, a vitamin company might employ scientists, sales representatives, marketing professionals, lobbyists, and health specialists, among others. The people in these different roles perform specific functions, but they all share the *overall* goal of producing a healthy, successful product and creating profit for the organization. In addition to communicating internally, the people in these roles have external interactions. The scientists must read and react to the research findings of outside scientists. The sales representatives have to contend with competitors who work to undercut them on price, and the marketing professionals have to contend with government rules about allowable health claims. By definition, the lobbyists exist to interact with the outside environment, and the health specialists must conduct research on real people to continue to improve and adapt the company's products. Each of these interactions can change the functioning of everyone else in the system.

closed system A system whose components communicate solely with one another.

feedback loop Circular communication process in which messages travel back and forth across a system, making possible ongoing mutual adjustment.

open system A system whose components continuously interact not only with one another, but with the environment outside the system.

The thermostat in your home's heating system communicates solely with other elements of that system, rendering that system closed. Elements in an open system such as an organization, however, are routinely buffeted by a host of outside influences.

Mountains of paperwork may come to mind when we think of bureaucracy, but organizations, while they might be able to manage with smaller piles of paper, could not function without bureaucracy.

policy Statement that provides a blueprint of how an organization operates, its goals, and expected outcomes.

protocol Detailed methods used in achieving goals and outcomes.

bureaucracy The norms, ranks, roles, and controls of an organization.

THUMBNAIL THEORY

Weber's Theory of Bureaucracy

Bureaucracy is not only positive but necessary to a functioning system. A bureaucracy functions through *authority*, *specialization*, and *rules*. Bureaucracies in and of themselves do not obstruct productivity, but communication breakdown does.

To ensure that their open system continues to operate as intended in the face of these external realities, organizations establish predetermined guidelines, often referred to as *policies* and *protocols*. **Policies** are statements that provide a blueprint of how the organization operates, its goals, and its expected outcomes. **Protocols** are the detailed methods used in achieving those outcomes. For example, it might be a company's *policy* to perform an annual assessment of each department. How it proceeds in making that happen, for example appointing a special assessment committee or possibly creating evaluation forms, would occur through specific *protocols*. Like any other system, the rules that govern an organization and the effectiveness with which they are communicated are critical to its operational success.

How this is routinely accomplished might surprise you. One factor often thought to inhibit communication success in the workplace, making protocols and policies much harder to follow than would otherwise be the case, is *bureaucracy*. When we typically think of bureaucracy, we envision the loss of productivity because of mountains of "red tape," tons of paperwork, and the hierarchical attitudes of those in leadership positions who act insensitively toward their employees. But **bureaucracy** is nothing more than the roles, rules, ranks, and controls that make up the organization. The negative view of bureaucracy persists despite the important benefits it offers any complex system; after all, complicated organizations need leadership and guidelines. In fact, the larger an organization, the more complex its structure, creating many more channels of communication, and consequently, more opportunity for breakdown, therefore requiring even more bureaucracy. (If you've noticed that this sounds familiar to Chapter 7's discussion of the elements of group dynamics—*norms, roles, ranks,* and *controls*—it is because in both cases these are the means by which all groups can best meet their goals. Of course, larger groups—organizations—are more dependent on rules than are smaller, more flexible groups, as we will discuss.)

So how do organizations as systems communicate effectively to maximize productivity and avoid all of the so-called bureaucratic obstacles that hinder the process? Max Weber's **Theory of Bureaucracy** (1946) attempts to answer this question. Weber determined that bureaucracy serves to ensure a well-functioning system through three basic principles: *authority* (hierarchy, that is ownership and leadership), *specialization* (a fixed division of labor and specification of roles), and *rules* (guidelines that govern performance and the centralization of decision-making). Sociologist W. Richard Scott (1981) added two additional principles: *equal treatment of all employees* (the idea that technical qualifications, not favoritism or other non-work factors, are the main criteria of evaluation), and *employment as career* (the idea that employees have a sense of security and are protected against arbitrary dismissal).

This view of how organizations should operate clearly presents bureaucracy as not only positive, but necessary to a functioning system. As such, bureaucracies in and of themselves do not obstruct productivity, but rather it is the people who operate within them who occasionally do so. As sociologist Charles Perrow (1986) explained, organizational failures are not necessarily the fault of bureaucracy; after all, everything—roles, rules, ranks, and controls—should be clearly laid out. When breakdowns do occur it is because

- *Organizations are open systems,* subject to buffeting from outside and often hostile environments, and it is impossible to eliminate those outside influences. Let's use a much-maligned bureaucracy, the Internal Revenue Service, better known as the IRS. Over the last 20 years, because of anti-IRS sentiment among some in Congress (and little public affection to counter that sentiment), its budget has been repeatedly cut and its workforce reduced by 25 percent.

- Organizations, especially larger ones, sometimes *have trouble adapting to the non-routine or non-typical occurrences or tasks* that those outside influences create. During that same period, the number of individual tax returns that the IRS must annually process has increased by more than 25 percent, to well over 230 million. As a result, the number of audits that it conducts has been cut in half, its ability to prevent tax fraud has been diminished, and the waiting time for phone help has increased from 15 minutes a few years ago to more than an hour today.

- And as you might imagine in a system as complex as an organization, no matter how well-crafted the policies and protocols put in place to ensure that the components interact with maximum efficiency, they are put into practice by humans, and *humans are fallible.* Communication breakdown—and system disruption—is likely. Like the people they must deal with under these circumstances, IRS employees become frustrated and angry, sometimes with those they are helping, sometimes with the organization itself. Admitting that she would never dream of recommending IRS employment to anyone, one long-time employee said, "Morale is horrible. People are looking for a way to get out of the government" (in Packer, 2013, p. 21).

Positive and Negative Organizational Communication Traits

In fact, communication breakdown is more than likely; it's inevitable, as organizations are made up of humans with different personalities, communication styles, and character traits. **Communication traits**, the ways in which we behave as part of an organization, create meaning for those around us, and others react according to those meanings. Some of those traits are positive because the effects they have on others produce beneficial outcomes. The opposite

communication traits Traits exhibited by members of an organization, such as assertiveness, secrecy, superiority, motivation, empowerment, supportiveness, and intimidation.

Table 8.1 Workplace Communication Traits

POSITIVE	NEGATIVE
Empowerment	Intimidation
Assertiveness	Aggressiveness
Supportiveness	Secrecy
Motivation	Superiority

work identity An individual's persona (as presented or perceived) in the workplace.

empowerment Granting authority to another based on trust and confidence.

intimidation Belittling others to make them feel powerless.

holds true for negative traits; they can be toxic in the work environment. In either case, it is through their various traits that members establish a **work identity**—how they want to be perceived by their colleagues. The workplace communication traits most commonly addressed by organizational communication scholars are *supportiveness, motivation, empowerment, assertiveness, aggressiveness, superiority, secrecy,* and *intimidation.* Table 8.1 shows the positive and negative counterparts of workplace communication traits.

Empowerment involves giving people authority. In doing so, we express confidence and trust in them. Conversely, when we engage in **intimidation** of colleagues, we belittle them, making them feel small and powerless. It doesn't take much to recognize the value difference in the workplace between these two communication traits. A positive outcome is much more likely to result when an individual feels empowered rather than intimidated. Think about a salesperson who meets regularly with the regional sales manager. Which of the following approaches will result in more sales, and which manager would you rather have?

Manager #1: *"You've got this! You're a great salesperson. Go out there and show them your stuff!"*

Manager #2: *"You really need to make this sale. Kelly's doing at least 20% more business than you. What's wrong with you? You know there will be consequences if you don't perform."*

assertiveness Confidently presenting ideas and contributing to organizational conversation and growth.

aggressiveness Speaking one's mind without a professional filter.

Assertiveness is a second positive communication trait. People who confidently assert themselves in the workplace offer ideas and contribute to organizational conversation and growth. They respectfully speak their minds. **Aggressiveness** is a different matter altogether. Colleagues who act aggressively speak their minds, but without a professional filter, and act cruelly toward others. They are not afraid to hurt people to get what they want and are more likely to show hostility through verbal attacks, offensive language, or unprofessional behaviors. Consider the case of colleagues Meg and Cindy:

Meg and Cindy worked together on a business presentation they were expected to deliver to their superiors. They both knew that only one of them would eventually be promoted. The two weeks of preparation became a nightmare for Meg. She did all the research and came up with most of the ideas. Still, she recognized this was a "team" project and felt she needed to treat it as such. Cindy, on the other hand, refused to do her part, telling Meg her ideas were ridiculous and would never fly with the "higher ups." Besides, Cindy wasn't about to work with "someone not as talented" as she thought herself to be. When the bosses LOVED the ideas from the presentation, Cindy was happy to take the lion's share of credit. In fact, she spread the rumor that Meg did nothing on the project. Clearly, Meg was the assertive member and Cindy the aggressive one. Let's hope the bosses were onto Cindy.

Supportiveness is among the most productive communication traits in the workplace. Supportive people provide encouragement, empathy, understanding, and help to those around them, even when it may not be part of their job description. **Secrecy**, on the other hand, is seclusion and concealment that causes others to suspect a hidden agenda. The secrecy of a superior is especially corrosive. Supervisors who keep to themselves, who isolate themselves from their workers, create the perception that they are unapproachable and foster an atmosphere of doubt and distrust. Employees of secretive superiors fear being shut out of conversations about important or difficult issues such as layoffs, firings, wage decreases, and benefit changes. You can imagine how toxic this uncertainty can be to communication effectiveness in an organizational system.

> **supportiveness** Providing others with encouragement, empathy, understanding, and help.

> **secrecy** Seclusion and concealment that causes others to wonder about a hidden agenda.

The fourth positive communication trait is **motivation**: drive, visible interest, and incentive to produce. This positive work identity is highly contagious, creating motivation in others through example. Motivated employees see everyone as a potential success story because they believe in the power of good attitudes and common goals. **Superiority** runs counter to motivation. Members of an organization who see themselves as superior to others imply that they rank higher, are more respected, and perform better. Even if that's true in an individual case, superiority represents a company atmosphere that is divisive, leaving workers unmotivated and bitter.

> **motivation** Drive, visible interest, and the incentive to produce.

> **superiority** Higher rank, more respect, and better performance as a means of putting oneself above others.

These positive and negative traits say something about the individuals who possess them. If you're positive and inspired, your colleagues will be too. As such, these communication traits become vehicles through which we pattern and deliver messages, and ultimately determine how we are perceived as professionals. Employees who demonstrate positive traits are much more likely to get promoted, gravitate into leadership roles, and extract more productivity from their workers and colleagues. Employees who demonstrate negative traits are detrimental to the success of the organization because they foster an environment of low morale and low productivity. You can read about how to deal with colleagues whose negative communication traits inevitably produce workplace conflict in the box "Dealing with On-the-Job Conflict."

Organizational Climate and Culture

Organizations, as systems, are only as effective as their individual parts, and those parts—the organization's people—operate not only within the organization's bureaucracy, but within its climate and culture. Organizational climate and culture are closely related, and both are forces that arise naturally from and shape the life of the organization.

COMMUNICATION IN THE WORKPLACE

Dealing with On-the-Job Conflict

On-the-job conflict makes going to work miserable, increases your level of stress, and hampers your performance. Organizations cannot function smoothly when employees feel this way. But keep in mind that conflict can be an opportunity for constructive change.

Human resources consultant Susan Lankton-Rivas (2008) explains that workplace conflict comes in many forms. Examples include interpersonal differences with a colleague, frustration over superiors' or subordinates' unwillingness to listen to your ideas or instructions, and annoyance with colleagues who do not carry their share of the work. She offers eight strategies for overcoming on-the-job conflict and turning it to your advantage:

1. *Approach conflict with an open mind*—Workplace conflict is not about winning; it's about dealing with people with differing points of view. Find a mutually satisfactory solution.
2. *Consider what might have caused the conflict*—Is the problem about differing work or communication styles? Is it a difference of opinion? Is it about rank and power? Think about what you might have contributed to the problem.
3. *Be respectful of differences*—Today's workplaces are more diverse than ever; you'll spend your entire career interacting with colleagues of different ages, cultures, and backgrounds. You want respect, so respect others.
4. *Ask your coworker what you might have done to upset him or her*—Communicate your willingness to talk the problem out and solve the matter together.
5. *Listen carefully*—Don't jump to conclusions. Acknowledge others' feelings, listen, and then paraphrase what you heard. Fully understand the issue before responding.
6. *Carefully consider the type of language you use*—Use "I" rather than "you" statements. Rather than "*You don't understand me,*" try "Maybe *I'm* not being clear." Communicate blamelessly; for example, rather than "*You seem to have a problem with me,*" try "There seems to be some tension."
7. *If conflict continues, get some help*—Ask someone you respect (and who is not involved) for advice on handling the problem.
8. *Be sure the problem is resolved*—Feeling better about the situation is not enough. Make sure your coworker feels that the issue has been resolved satisfactorily. Don't be afraid to discuss how you might avoid future conflict.

---

organizational climate The meaning employees attach to the policies, practices, and procedures they experience, and the behaviors they observe being rewarded, supported, and expected.

Organizational climate is the "social information process that concerns the meaning employees attach to the policies, practices, and procedures they experience and the behaviors they observe being rewarded, supported, and expected" (Schneider, Ehrhart, and Macey, 2013, p. 381). Essentially, the climate is the product of employees' interactions with the functioning of the organization.

For example, leadership is central to organizational climate, as leaders' style and effectiveness shape members' day-to-day behaviors and expectations. The organization's structure also influences its climate, as it is a visible expression of how it values its members and their expertise. Are there, for example, cross-departmental or cross-interest teams? Is the organization rigidly hierarchal, or streamlined and democratic? Other factors also shape climate. Does the organization have set standards of accountability; do its members take responsibility for their performance and behavior? Are performance and competencies rewarded fairly and tangibly? Is there a well-expressed statement of the organization's vision and strategies? These formal factors—these policies, practices, and procedures—constitute the climate in which people perform their duties, facilitating or impeding the organization's success. Climate tends to be communicated down and then throughout the organization, whereas an organization's culture tends to permeate all levels of the system.

Organizational culture is the pattern of shared basic assumptions or inferences that members learn from the organization's stories, myths, traditions, and everyday experiences and observed behaviors. If members believe that these assumptions and inferences are useful and contribute to the organization's success, they see them as valid and pass them on to new members as the best way to think, feel, and act. As such, the organization's culture sets its norms, values, and beliefs. Eric Eisenberg and his colleagues are even more specific, defining organizational culture as "the language of the workplace, the performance of managers and employees, the formal and informal practices that mark an organization's character (such as rites and rituals), and the display of meaningful artifacts like architecture, interior design, posters, and furniture. Moreover, the cultural approach [to understanding organizations] foregrounds the human desire to see organizational life as an opportunity to do something meaningful" (Eisenberg, Goodall, and Trethewey, 2010, p. 103).

> **organizational culture**
> Pattern of shared basic assumptions or inferences that members learn from an organization's stories, myths, traditions, everyday experiences, and observed behaviors.

As in any culture, a person new to the environment must adapt through *socialization,* learning behaviors from others (as discussed in Chapter 7), and *assimilation,* becoming fully integrated into that culture. In an organizational setting, socialization typically takes three forms. Naturally, the first thing new employees must learn is information about the job they have been hired to do, and they need to understand exactly what is expected of them in undertaking that task. This is *task socialization. Workgroup socialization* happens as newcomers learn the specifics of the particular group of people with whom they'll be working, their goals, rules (formal and informal), and values. But those newcomers belong not only to their work group, they are also part of a larger organizational culture, so they also experience *organizational socialization,* learning the organization's values, goals, customs, rules, preferred leadership and communication styles, and politics. One way that organizations display their values is through their commitment to corporate social responsibility, as you can read in the box "Doing Well by Doing Good."

> **organizational assimilation**
> Process by which individuals become integrated into the culture of an organization.

Organizational assimilation is "the process by which individuals become integrated into the culture of an organization" (Jablin, 2001, p. 755), and it occurs in three communication stages:

Eyeglass manufacturer FGX International uses artifacts to express the values of the people behind those Foster Grants.

SOCIALLY RESPONSIBLE COMMUNICATION

Doing Well by Doing Good

Corporate social responsibility (CSR) is the integration of business operations and organizational values. More specifically, it is operating an organization "in a manner that accounts for the social and environmental impact created by the business. CSR means a commitment to developing policies that integrate responsible practices into daily business operations" (As You Sow, 2013).

Companies of all sizes practice CSR because of its wide range of benefits. These include attracting better clients, saving money, and generating social good will (Thorpe, 2013). In addition, CSR activities may increase profit. Research has shown that practicing CSR changes consumer behavior toward those companies for the better (Mohr and Webb, 2005); it enhances customers' respect for the brands, leading to increased purchasing intent (Lai, Yang, and Pai, 2010). CSR can even create a "halo effect," in which consumers are more sympathetic toward an organization in cases of product-related harm or controversy (Klein and Dawar, 2004). "The vast majority of consumers around the world say that when companies engage in corporate social responsibility (CSR), they have a more positive image of the company (95%), are more likely to trust the company (94%), and would be more loyal to the company (93%)," explains public relations firm Cone Communications (2013).

Then there is the benefit of an improved organizational culture. Business writer Devin Thorpe interviewed several companies about their CSR programs and discovered that "51 of 59 believe that they have happier employees and 45 of the 59 believe they end up with better employees, either as a result of being able to attract better talent or that the CSR programs help to develop better employees." One of his interviewees added that CSR "lifts morale and builds capability among the team, [and] it also clears people's minds, allowing them to make better decisions" (2013).

And finally, a growing number of socially responsibly investors will not deal with a company unless it has a CSR program in place. In fact, 73 percent of investment managers say that socially responsible investment indicators are now common (As You Sow, 2013).

Doing well by doing good, then, has obvious organizational benefits. Organizations including As You Sow and CSRWire help companies develop, maintain, and report CSR activities. Their membership includes, among thousands of others, General Electric, McDonald's, Safeway, Whole Foods, Apple, Dell, HP, Best Buy, Coca-Cola, PepsiCo, Nestlé Waters, Starbucks, Target, Gap, Home Depot, Walt Disney, and DuPont.

anticipatory socialization stage Learning about work through a lifetime of communication.

organizational entry and assimilation stage Moving from being an organizational outsider to organizational insider.

disengagement and exit stage Movement from one part of an organization to another, or leaving altogether.

1. People learn about work through communicating with their world. They have lives before they join their new organization, and they are socialized about work by talking with family and friends, seeing work represented in the mass media, and even in other jobs of their own. These socializing experiences make up the **anticipatory socialization stage**.

2. The **organizational entry and assimilation stage** begins on newcomers' first day with the organization and continues until they are no longer outsiders but are in fact integrated insiders. Mistakes are often forgiven early in this stage, and work roles are negotiated among newcomers, their colleagues, and their superiors.

3. Eventually, people leave the organization, either through movement from one part of the organization to another or by leaving altogether. This is the **disengagement and exit stage**. As in the dissolution process of an interpersonal relationship (Chapter 6), departing employees disengage from the relationships they have built with colleagues and superiors

as they withdraw from their work and the organization itself. They talk with them less frequently and less personally.

Strong Organizational Cultures

Organizations that effect this socialization and assimilation with skill tend to be **strong cultures**; they "experience long-term business success. Strong cultures result in greater employee satisfaction, increased productivity, greater customer satisfaction, and customer trust. Strong cultures also possess a system of formal and informal rules that indicate how employees as well as the organization as a whole are to behave. Thus, a strong corporate culture enables workers to feel as if they are making positive contributions to the organization. This, in turn, results in a more productive worker" (Avtgis, Rancer, and Madlock, 2010, p. 61). Organizational experts Terrence Deal and Allan Kennedy (1982) identified six interrelated communication-based elements that help build strong organizational cultures:

strong culture An organization that effectively socializes and assimilates its members.

1. *History:* This is an organization's shared narrative of its past. It establishes the foundation for its culture. Its long-standing traditions keep people anchored to the organization's core values.

2. *Values and beliefs:* An organization's identity is expressed by its shared beliefs—what we consider important, what we stand for.

3. *Rituals and ceremonies:* Rituals (for example, casual Fridays) and ceremonies (for example, award recognition lunches) recognize and celebrate organizational values. These are the everyday practices that bring people together.

4. *Stories:* A constant theme of this text is that you are what you communicate. The same holds true for organizations. Their stories reveal and celebrate their values and recognize the actions of employees who best personify those values in action. From these organizational tales, employees come to learn what is expected of them and understand what the organization stands for.

5. *Heroic figures:* These are the employees and managers who are the most respected, best regarded, and most highly rewarded for their embodiment of the organization's values. They include, for example, the employee of the month, whose picture is in the lobby; the top salesperson, who has a reserved parking spot near the door; and the manager who received a $10,000 bonus for her innovation of the call center reporting system. They serve as role models, and their success marks the organization's aspirational ideal.

6. *The cultural network:* We know this as the grapevine and water cooler talk. Deal and Kennedy identify several different members of the cultural network. *Storytellers* interpret what they see going on around them, and from that create stories that embody the organization's values. *Gossipers* put their own take on daily events and provide entertainment. *Whisperers* are conduits to power. The higher-ups listen to them, and their

The reserved parking spot is a sign that its holder is an organizational hero.

colleagues know they can use them to informally and safely get a message to the top (possibly softening the hierarchical mum effect). *Spies,* on the other hand, provide their own information to the bosses, letting them know what's really going on. *Priests and priestesses* are the guardians of the organization's cultural values. They are much respected by all levels of the hierarchy and know the organization's history. Their colleagues know they will use the organization's historical responses, values, and beliefs to make sense of any situation.

Dealing with Diversity in an Organizational Culture

Like any culture, an organizational culture is made up of diverse groups. Consider how many different types of people there are in any one company: women, men, bosses, employees, people of different races, different religions, different ethnicities, people who specialize in specific areas, educated professionals, IT people, lesbians, uneducated laborers, managers, young people, middle-aged people, the elderly, single mothers, Republicans, people who like their job and people who don't, physically fit people, unhealthy people, the marketing team, people of different height and hair color, environmentally conscious people, Democrats—and the list goes on. These are bounded cultures (Chapter 1) within the larger organizational culture.

Once you gain membership in an organization, just as you would as part of any other culture, you must learn the language of that organization, get to know its members, understand the interpersonal dynamic of those members, and know how each person fits into the culture as a whole. At your college or university, for instance, you need to know the language, which includes concepts like tenure, assessment, curricula, transcripts, recruitment, commencement, and adjuncts. You are also aware of the many roles that exist—the bursar, professors, admission counselors, academic advisers, students, and resource librarians. And finally, you have to understand how those different groups interact on campus.

Even though you may be interacting with all these people in terms of their roles or duties, you are also interacting with them as individual human beings. For example, in the admissions department, how many employees are female, black, Muslim, or gay? Learning the organization's language, getting to know its members, understanding their interpersonal dynamics, and knowing how each individual fits into the system as whole will help you better navigate company policies and protocols. Perhaps more important, it will help you understand how to effectively communicate with each member of the many bounded cultures that your organization houses. Back to your school—do you communicate the same way with your peers as you do with your professor? Do you treat the janitorial staff with the same level of respect as you do the university vice presidents? Do you act the same way toward students who share your ethnic or racial heritage as you do toward those who do not?

This suggests the importance of effective *intercultural communication,* "interaction between people whose cultural perceptions and symbol systems differ enough to influence the communication event" (Samovar et al., 2013, p. 8). We will examine intercultural communication in great detail in Chapter 9, but here we want to stress that organizations—and the people in them—that embrace diversity and the communication

Organizations are becoming increasingly diverse, echoing the culture as a whole.

challenges and benefits it brings are better prepared to negotiate a work culture increasingly influenced by **globalization**. As organizations spread their reach overseas, those that can rely on a diverse, pluralistic employee base well versed in intercultural communication benefit in the following ways:

globalization The process in which organizations extend their business to different parts of the world, becoming more globally integrated.

1. Miscommunication is less likely because the organization's values encourage its members to acclimate to a diverse communication culture. A multicultural workplace encourages one-on-one interactions, allowing members to better understand each other's communication practices.

2. Discrimination, racism, and harassment are not tolerated in a diverse work environment. And because there is a direct correlation between harassment and loss of workplace productivity, an organization that encourages diversity is much less likely to foster a climate of harassment, and therefore, more likely to have more productive employees.

3. All employees feel full membership, fostering an open, outspoken organizational culture rich in ideas and creativity. For instance, a European hired by an American company may have different views on employee motivation than do his or her US colleagues because Europeans typically believe in a more relaxed work environment. As a result, this one-time outsider might provide new strategies for getting the most out of the company's workers by suggesting longer breaks, midday massages, or other rest techniques.

4. An organization that encourages diversity *inward* will also be more effective *outward.* Consider an American employee who travels abroad to conduct business in China. Understanding and appreciating Chinese business customs and language is likely to result in strong business relationships, and is much more likely to occur if that American employee is already comfortable operating in a multicultural work environment.

Review of Learning Objectives

8.1. Describe the foundations of organizational communication.

An organization is a social collectivity with organizational and individual goals. As such, organizational communication is any communication that occurs electronically, verbally, or nonverbally between or among members of an organization.

8.2. Explain the ways messages can move within an organization.

An organization's messages move in an upward, downward, or horizontal direction. Upward messages tend to be more formal and are open to distortion. Formal, downward messages are also typically subject to serial distortion in the form of adding, leveling, sharpening, and assimilation. Horizontal messages, typically informal, are an important part of an organization's functioning and take the form of the grapevine or water cooler communication.

8.3. Examine the roles, rules, ranks, and responses in the organizational system.

Organizations are systems, composed of interdependent parts that work toward a common goal. The system is guided by individual roles and responsibilities embodied in its policies and protocols. As a complex system, organizations require bureaucracy, which functions through authority, specialization, the centralization of decision-making, equal treatment of all employees, and a sense of employment as career.

8.4. Give examples of the operation and value of bureaucracy in organizations.

Complex systems rely on bureaucracy for efficient operation, but when they do not function as intended, the fault does not necessarily rest with bureaucracy itself. Because they are open systems, they are subject to outside environments; they sometimes have trouble adapting to non-routine or non-typical occurrences, or to tasks that those outside influences create; and their policies and protocols, no matter how well crafted, are put into practice by fallible humans.

8.5. Differentiate various positive and negative organizational communication traits.

Because organizations are made up of many different people, there tend to be many different personalities, communication styles, and character traits. Among the beneficial organizational communication traits are empowerment, assertiveness, supportiveness, and motivation. Among the negative communication traits are intimidation, aggression, secrecy, and superiority.

8.6. Describe how people are socialized into an organization's culture within its climate.

Organizational newcomers first undergo task socialization, learning information about the job and understanding what is expected of them. Workgroup socialization is the learning of the specifics of the particular group of people with whom they'll be working. Organizational socialization is learning the organization's values, goals, customs, rules, preferred leadership and communication styles, and politics.

Organizational assimilation, the process by which individuals become integrated into the culture of an organization, occurs in three communication stages. The anticipatory socialization stage occurs as people learn about work through communicating with their world. The organizational entry and assimilation stage begins on their first day with the organization and continues until they are no longer outsiders. Mistakes are often forgiven early in this stage, and work roles are negotiated among newcomers, their colleagues, and their superiors. Eventually they leave the organization. This is the disengagement and exit stage.

Key Terms

Questions for Review

1. Define *organization* and *organizational communication*.

2. What are upward messages, downward messages, and horizontal messages? How might each suffer distortion?

3. What is serial distortion? What are the five ways it can occur?

4. What is the grapevine? Water cooler communication? What is their value to an organization?

5. What are the five basic principles of the Theory of Bureaucracy (Weber's original three and the two added by Scott)?

6. What is the value of bureaucracy to complex organizations?

7. What are the four positive and four negative organizational communication traits? Describe each.

8. Differentiate between organizational climate and organizational culture.

9. What are the three forms of socialization into an organizational culture? What elements are necessary for a strong organizational culture?

10. Organizational assimilation occurs in three stages. Name and describe each.

Questions for Discussion

1. Do you typically think of bureaucracy in negative terms? Describe a time when bureaucracy got in the way of something important you wanted to do at school. Now imagine your college or university without its bureaucracy. Would that make your functioning in that organization easier? More difficult? Explain your answer.

2. Have you ever had a boss or colleague who demonstrated some or all of the negative communication traits detailed in this chapter? What were the circumstances? How did this situation limit your productivity, if it did? How did you deal with that person?

3. Have you ever been part of an organization with an active grapevine? What were the circumstances? How well did that grapevine work? What was the most important piece of information you learned from the grapevine, and how did it influence your work situation?

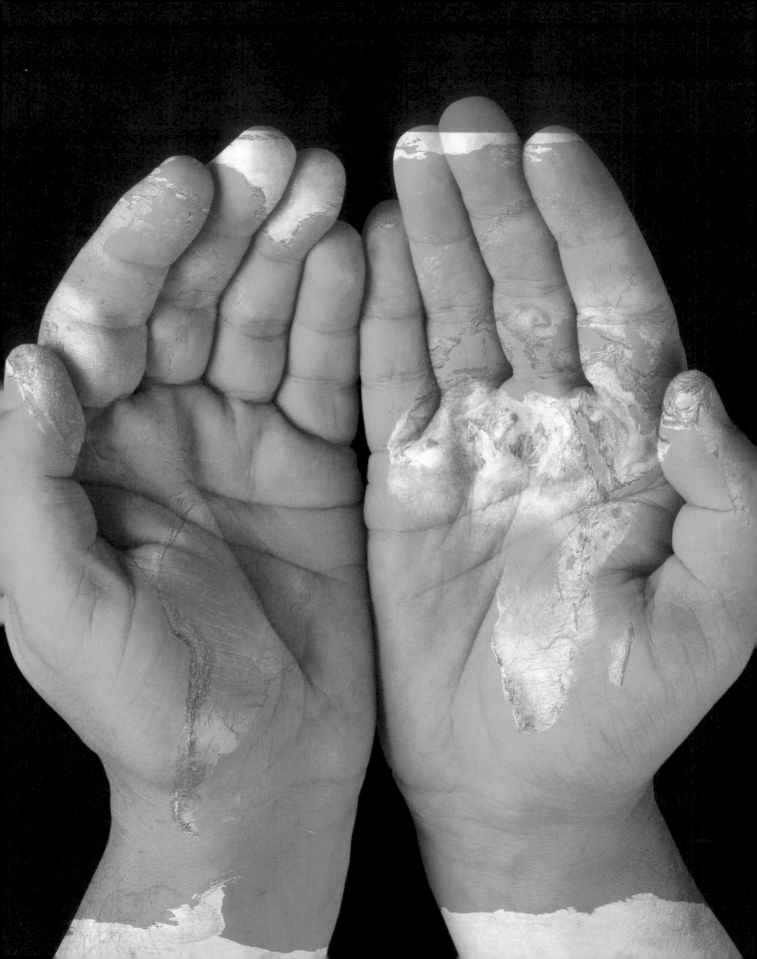

Intercultural Communication

Alternative vacation? You'd never heard of it. But many of your friends and classmates were taking the plunge, so why not you? Your campus was encouraging students to travel to a United Nations–run school for underserved children in South Africa. The goal: to help the kids with their English while teaching them good hygiene and health practices.

You figured it was time to take a risk and do something culturally challenging, so you signed up. On your way to Cape Town, you were concerned about your safety as well as your ability to communicate. You had also heard that the food is barely edible, that there is a huge chance of contracting a disease, and that South Africans don't like visitors very much. But after traveling halfway around the globe, you arrive at the school and are greeted by five happy toddlers. Dressed in beautiful colors, they gather around you, intrigued by your presence. You are overwhelmed by the warmth of their welcome. This is not what you thought it would be.

By the time you board your flight to return home, you have been mesmerized by everything you've discovered. You also feel silly about the misconceptions you'd had about South Africa and the people who live there. You are already missing the children and craving *braai*, South African barbecue. The experience was eye-opening, educational, even miraculous.

The biggest lesson from this opening story is that communicating with people from another culture is not as threatening as it might seem. As we will see in this chapter, attempting to understand one another despite our differences not only helps disabuse us of stereotypes and inaccurate generalizations, it makes us better people—more compassionate, more cultured, more human.

Learning Objectives

9.1   Describe the elements of intercultural communication.

9.2   Identify the obstacles to and accelerators of intercultural communication.

9.3   Describe how various cultural values affect communication.

9.4   Explain attitudes toward diversity and the problem with tolerance.

What Is Intercultural Communication?

In Chapter 1 we looked at the purpose of culture. We learned that culture serves many functions—for example, defining us, liberating and limiting us, uniting and sometimes separating us. We also discovered that many different cultures (called *bounded* or *co-cultures*) make up our larger, dominant culture. These social communities distinguish us by gender, age, sexual orientation, ethnicity, activities, clothing, and personal preferences, among other things. This chapter focuses on how movement between those cultures affects communication. **Intercultural communication** "involves interaction between people whose cultural perceptions and symbol systems differ enough to influence the communication event" (Samovar et al., 2013, p. 8).

The construction, delivery, and interpretation of messages will naturally vary when we address people outside our own bounded cultures. Think about how your communication changes when addressing your peers (people sharing your student culture) versus your professors (with whom you share your larger college or university culture). You quite naturally move from informal language to more formal language. A more obvious example would be your ability to communicate clearly when studying abroad or even when traveling to other parts of the country. Different languages and dialects can, at times, make effective communication a challenge. Look at the various dialects represented by New Yorkers, Southerners, Bostonians, and Canadians. Even nonverbal communication can vary depending on the culture. In the United States, for example, eye contact is a sign of respect, while Asian cultures view prolonged eye contact as offensive. Bulgarians interpret head nodding as meaning "no," not "yes"—quite the opposite of most other cultures. In this chapter we look at intercultural communication as a critical area of study for both global unity

intercultural communication Interaction between people whose cultural perceptions and symbol systems differ enough to influence the communication event.

and as a means for better meaning making in our own country. The United States is indeed becoming more pluralistic: by 2020 the United States will be a **majority-minority country**; that is, there will be no single racial or ethnic majority among its people (Wazwaz, 2015).

The key to successful intercultural communication is understanding how people from other places and backgrounds interact in their own cultures, using their own sets of symbols and interpretations to express traditions, beliefs, values, roles, and rules. The first step in this process of understanding is to recognize the *obstacles* and *accelerators* associated with doing so.

The United States is becoming increasingly more diverse, making intercultural communication competence increasingly more important.

Obstacles to Intercultural Communication

majority-minority country When there is no single racial or ethnic majority among a country's population.

Intercultural theorists study obstacles and accelerators that develop when people communicate between or across cultures. That is, they are interested in what hinders intercultural communication and what fosters it. We will begin by addressing six obstacles to effective intercultural communication: stereotyping, labeling, prejudice, discrimination, chauvinism, and ethnocentrism.

Examples of stereotypes include statements like *Black people make the best athletes, Asian students are particularly good at math and science, gay men are great at interior design*, and *women are emotionally weaker than men*. Stereotyping, as we saw in Chapter 1, happens when we broadly characterize people or groups, often inaccurately. Stereotyping is a clear hindrance to effective intercultural communication for four reasons. Stereotypes

1. Serve as filters, and often what's filtered out is the truth.
2. Assume that culture-specific characteristics apply to each member of a group, even when they do not.
3. Are often exaggerated and oversimplified.
4. Are often difficult to change once formed.

Stereotypes begin to form early in childhood. In fact, ample scholarly evidence suggests that children who have more exposure to diverse groups hold fewer stereotypes throughout their lives (Meshel and McGlynn, 2004). Researchers have also demonstrated that positive interaction among children of different cultural groups can counteract false or negative stereotypes (Stephan, 1999). Exposure to and participation in other cultures, therefore, are key to bettering intercultural communication skills. You can learn more about how to avoid stereotyping in the box "Stereotyping versus Generalizing."

SOCIALLY RESPONSIBLE COMMUNICATION

Stereotyping versus Generalizing

Stereotyping forces people into categories or attributes characteristics to them that may not apply. This categorization, though, is part of how the human brain operates. "While this storage system [categorization] assists with organization and use of the stored information," explains researcher Adam Oliner, "it can have the unwanted side effect of associating characteristics with subjects for whom the association may be inaccurate. This generalization, specifically as it applies to humans, is known as stereotyping." In fact, he adds, stereotyping is one of our brain's more complex functions because it involves "the task of storing and retrieving information about other people in order to interact with them or predict their behavior" (2000).

The original categorization might be automatic, but what happens next is not. "Implicit cognitive effects are often reduced by focusing [people's] attention on their judgment task [to] provide a basis for evaluating [others] . . . aimed at reducing such unintended discrimination" (Greenwald and Banaji, 1995, p. 4). In other words, while quick categorization may be evolutionarily hard-wired, stereotyping is a controllable cognitive process. Stereotyping might be a natural side effect of our ingrained cognitive categorizing, but the attitudes and behaviors that it sometimes produces—racism, prejudice, and discrimination—are not. So the question becomes, if we are prone to this categorization process, how do we ensure that what follows is not damaging to ourselves and others? We certainly have a social responsibility to do so.

Perhaps the answer lies in our ability to distinguish between *stereotyping* and *generalizing*—the first is *negative* and the second *natural*. If we accept Olin's premise that categorizing is natural, one way to avoid stereotyping is to recognize that we cannot help our initial flow of thought, but we can control our subsequent thoughts and behaviors. It is morally acceptable to make cultural generalizations. How else do we make educated guesses about others in an attempt to understand them? For example, to say that all Americans are violent is a stereotype. But to say that there tends to be more violence portrayed in American media than in other countries' media is an educated characterization.

While cognitive categorizing may be an unconscious act, how we translate those categories into behaviors is quite deliberate. It requires that we think about people as individuals, not as categories (what Greenwald and Banaji called *focusing our attention on the judgment task*). We can then condition ourselves to automatically separate generalizations from stereotypes.

---

labeling Describing individuals using names we believe categorize them.

A second obstacle to effective intercultural communication is **labeling**, or using names to categorize individuals and groups. We all remember labels from high school like *nerd*, *dumb jock*, *loser*, *rich girl*, and *social outcast*. The problem with labeling is that it often becomes a self-fulfilling prophesy; that is, something happens or becomes real because we have made it so with our words. If we label someone a *social outcast*, for example, we will not interact with him or her (denying ourselves a potential friend). The label in fact turns that person into a social outcast, which is not only unfair but hurtful.

prejudice Negative attitude toward a group based on little or no experience.

discrimination Overtly excluding, avoiding, or distancing oneself from another group.

Prejudice and discrimination are two other obstacles to successful intercultural communication, and the two concepts are often confused. **Prejudice** is "a negative attitude toward a cultural group based on little or no experience," while **discrimination** "is the overt actions one takes to exclude, avoid, or distance oneself from other groups" (Martin and Nakayama, 2001, p. 44). Prejudice is an attitude; discrimination is a behavior. Prejudice often grows out of the stereotypes we hold. For example, Julie's story begins with prejudice born of stereotyping and ends with discrimination:

In the film *Mean Girls,* the stereotypical roles of high school students are played out, and we see the labeling process that develops as a result.

> Julie graduated from college with a degree in journalism. She applied for a job as a local news reporter for a radio station. The station's news department was composed of an all-male staff, which Julie saw as strange but not uncommon in the broadcasting business. Still, she was confident in her writing, investigative reporting, and presentation skills, and was subsequently offered a chance to interview. What she didn't know was that the news director believed female news reporters were more emotional than their male counterparts (a stereotype). The news director had agreed to interview Julie despite the fact that he thought she probably couldn't handle the job because she was a female (a prejudice). Julie's interview turned out to be the best among the several potential candidates. She was clearly the most qualified and ready to take on the challenges of a demanding newsroom. Unfortunately, she did not get the job (discrimination) because of the news director's prejudice.

Chauvinism is a fifth obstacle to effective intercultural communication. Simply put, this is when people believe themselves to be superior to others. Americans often attribute chauvinism to men, but anyone can be chauvinistic. A female executive, for instance, can look down on her male and female subordinates, or older teenagers can act superior toward their younger peers simply because they view age as hierarchal. In any case, while chauvinism is not limited to men, the term is typically attributed to males who express feelings of gender superiority.

chauvinism Believing oneself to be superior to others.

A final obstacle to successful intercultural communication is **ethnocentrism**, a form of cultural exclusion. *Ethno* indicates ethnicity, race, or culture, and *centrism* refers to being at the center of something. Ethnocentrism, then, is the belief that one's own culture lies at the center of everything; it is a superior culture, better than any other culture. Ethnocentric bias is an obvious hindrance when relating to those from a culture that is not the "superior" one. In the United States, the media and political discourse often reflect ethnocentric bias by using phrases such as "the greatest country on earth" or "the world's greatest democracy." Many of the persuasive techniques and symbols used in US news and advertising imply that if you disagree, you are somehow less of a person. But different cultures and individuals might view these ideals and values quite differently.

ethnocentrism Belief that one's own culture is the best.

The "Naturalness" of Prejudice: Two Theories of Culture and Identity

in-group Those with whom one identifies.

out-group A group seen as other than one's own.

THUMBNAIL THEORY

Social Identity Theory

People do not have a single self, but rather several selves that correspond to their different group memberships. Group membership, in and of itself, creates a self-identification that will favor the in-group at the expense of the out-group.

We see these impediments to successful intercultural communication all around us, and rare are human beings who do not occasionally feel a preference for people in their **in-group**, those with whom they identify, over people in an **out-group**, a group other than their own. Two closely related theories that consider the relationship between identity and culture help explain this "natural" prejudice.

Social Identity Theory

The first is **social identity theory**, the idea that a person does not have one self, but rather several selves that correspond to her or his different group memberships. Originally developed by social psychologists Henri Tajfel and John Turner (1979), it argues that group membership, in and of itself, creates a self-identification that will favor the in-group at the expense of the out-group. The researchers were able to demonstrate in a series of experiments that the mere act of categorizing oneself as a member of a group—no matter how meaningless, even by the flip of a coin (Are you a Heads or a Tails?)—was sufficient to produce in-group favoritism and out-group disfavor. Why? Once people recognize that they have membership in a given group, they work to increase their self-esteem by positively differentiating their in-group from some other out-group; for example, "I'm an American; Americans are the best! Foreigners are not American; they must be inferior. Therefore, as an American, I am superior to foreigners." Echoing symbolic interaction (Chapter 1), social identity theory argues that people find *positive distinctiveness* in a collective significant other, in this case, their in-group. They define their sense of identity in terms of "we" rather than "I."

Matthew Hornsey explains the process:

> Human interaction ranges on a spectrum from being purely interpersonal on the one hand to purely intergroup on the other. A purely interpersonal interaction (which Tajfel and Turner believed to be rare) involves people relating entirely as individuals, with no awareness of social categories. A purely intergroup interaction is one in which people relate entirely as representatives of their groups, and where one's idiosyncratic, individualizing qualities are overwhelmed by the salience of one's group memberships. [Social identity theory argues] that sliding from the interpersonal to the intergroup end of the spectrum results in shifts in how people see themselves and each other. (2008, p. 206)

We rarely interact with others without at least some recognition of their membership in some other social category, for example, gender, race, profession, or nationality. Comedian Stephen Colbert lampoons those who would argue otherwise when he says, "I don't see race. Am I white? People tell me I am, but am I?" So the question now becomes what motivates a shift from the interpersonal to the intergroup end of the spectrum in our interactions with others; that is, when does group membership become salient in making out-group judgments? Certainly the communication context and nature of the interaction are important, but the constant element in this shift is the value or significance in constructing their identities that people give to their in-group membership. If your identity is very heavily wrapped up in your group membership, then the other's group membership becomes important in your interaction. For example, if you're a white supremacist and your entire identity is defined by the color of your skin, the race of the person with whom you're speaking is always an issue. If you're a reasonable human being, it's not. Let's return to Mr. Colbert's "I don't see race" assertion. Of course he does; we all do. We all see race, gender, nationality, status, and a host of other identifiers of group membership. But these only become important in our judgment of others to the extent that those memberships are important to our judgment of ourselves.

Identity Negotiation Theory

Communication scholar Stella Ting-Toomey (2005) offers a second explanation for our tendency to favor people like ourselves and disfavor others: **identity negotiation theory**, the idea that our identities are the product of negotiating *our* self-identification with *others'* self-identifica-

Comedian Stephen Colbert claims, with great irony, that he does not see race.

tion. That is, when we interact with others we, to varying degrees, assert, challenge, and possibly modify our assumptions about our own and their identities. Ting-Toomey says that this process begins in childhood, as we work to establish first our *personal identities* and then our *cultural identities*. We learn from our family interactions who we are, but then we undertake the wider task of developing just what that means. What does it mean to be a male or female? What does it mean to be Asian, Irish, a Mid-Westerner, an Atlanta Hawks fan? Through social interaction with and outside the family, we learn about and build attachments to larger cultural groups; after all, just as social identity theory suggests, it makes us feel better to belong to groups that we value. And again, just as social identity theory tells us, our commitment to that group-based identity is a function of how important membership in that group is to us. "Identity, thus, is constructed in communication in various cultural settings," write theorists Stephen Littlejohn and Karen Foss. "When you communicate within a familiar cultural group, you will experience more security, inclusion, predictability, connection, and consistency; but when you interact across cultures, you may experience the opposite—vulnerability, differentiation, unpredictability, autonomy, and change—leading to a lack of stability and even the possibility of transformation" (2011, p. 105).

THUMBNAIL THEORY

Identity Negotiation Theory

Our identities are the product of negotiating our self-identification with others' self-identification. When we interact with others we, to varying degrees, assert, challenge, and possibly modify our assumptions about our own and others' identities.

There is an important intercultural communication lesson in these two theories. Yes, in-group favoritism is natural and normal; and yes, it is easier to interact with those with whom we are familiar. Membership in these comfortable groups boosts our self-esteem. But it is only by stepping out of our "comfort zone" that we can transform who we are and negotiate an identity that is truly ours, one constructed with a richness of experiences and interactions. As Littlejohn and Foss explain, too much unquestioned and unchallenged cultural identity can "lead to ethnocentrism; too little can lead to confusion. Too little change leads to stagnation; too much change will lead to chaos" (2011, p. 105).

Accelerators of Intercultural Communication

cultural transformer Someone who shifts effortlessly among and between multiple cultural mindsets and cultural identities.

How do we become what Ting-Toomey (1999) calls a **cultural transformer**, someone who can shift effortlessly among and between multiple cultural mindsets and cultural identities? The route to finding that balance is effective intercultural communication. Just as there are factors that hinder successful intercultural communication, there are those that enhance it, including cultural relativism, understanding others' cultural values, cultural pluralism, and cultural participation.

cultural relativism Belief that people vary in behaviors, feelings, traditions, and values depending on their culture.

Relativism in general asserts that things like morals, values, and meanings are related to specific contexts, and no perspective or standpoint is more uniquely privileged over any other (Howson, 2009). **Cultural relativism**, then, is the belief that people vary in their behaviors, feelings, traditions, and values depending on the cultures in which they live; and the fact that their beliefs are different from those of others doesn't make them any less or more valued. Once you recognize this as a communicator, you become more *culturally inclusive*, recognizing and respecting the differences of others as you experience diversity in cultures.

cultural values A culture's gauges for determining right from wrong.

A second accelerator of intercultural communication is an *understanding of cultural values,* what they are, and their relevance to any given culture. **Cultural values** are gauges for determining right from wrong; that is, they are behavioral guidelines. Cultural values are deeply rooted in all people, making them extremely influential in shaping how members of a given culture behave. In American culture we value things like freedom, efficiency, time, and materialism. When our freedoms are infringed upon or coworkers slack off on the job, we consider these to be violations of our values. But not all countries share our values or our interpretation of how those values should be expressed. Americans, for instance, typically do not revere their elderly people as much as Africans do theirs. Americans value individuality and freedom, but Chinese culture sees social harmony as much more important than any one individual's need. Regardless of the culture, the values people adopt are acquired in similar ways—through school, media, government, friends, family, and social structures—in other words, through interaction with that culture (Chapter 1). These values are first and foremost established to sustain the operation and success of the culture itself, but they can also be a source of misunderstanding for those who have not shared those same interactions.

Another accelerator of successful intercultural communication is **cultural pluralism**, when people maintain the practices and identities of their bounded-culture affiliations within the larger culture. For example, a family who moves to the United States from India might maintain their Indian traditions by wearing saris (Indian dresses), cooking foods like pakoras (fried vegetables and meats) and naan (a type of Indian bread), or following their native religion, which might be Hinduism or Sikhism.

cultural pluralism Maintaining the practices and identities of one's bounded culture within the larger culture.

Cultural pluralism, naturally, raises questions of the value and place of **assimilation**, when a person identifies with or integrates into another culture. For example, because they desire inclusion, children brought to live in the United States from another country often want to fit in with their new environment. They might do so by abandoning their homeland traditions and adopting the typical American kid's way of life. By the time they reach their teenage years, they might identify more as American than they do with their birthplace. It is difficult to characterize assimilation as an obstacle or accelerator simply because, depending on the circumstance, it can be either. Some people may feel it is a positive development that the children in our example establish a sense of inclusion and belonging, since they must adapt to another culture. Others make the counter-argument and mourn the loss of connection the children once had with their original traditions and beliefs. After all, doesn't its diversity make America great?

assimilation Identification with or integration into a different culture.

Nonetheless, the contemporary view is in favor of pluralism, and proponents of cultural pluralism sometimes use two metaphors, one old and one new, to make their case. For more than a century now, especially at the height of Asian and European immigration to the United States in the early years of the last century, Americans spoke proudly of their country as a **melting pot**; all the immigrants' values, beliefs, music, food, celebrations—all the things that made their cultures unique—would "melt together" and mix with the existing American culture, forming an even better, harmonious whole. But might not everyone lose a little when what was special and good about those now-melted elements is lost? How would you feel if there was no soccer, hockey, lacrosse, Italian food, Afro-Caribbean music, yoga, martial arts, Costa Rican coffee, hummus, or salsa dancing? Maybe a salad might be a better metaphor, argue pluralism's proponents. America's strength is not that it is a giant melting pot, but that it is a great big wonderfully tasty salad. In this salad America's bounded cultures are thrown together and mixed up like the ingredients of a salad, each maintaining its own distinct flavor and contributing to the taste of the salad as a whole. The individual richness of each ingredient (culture) is valued for itself and for what it contributes to the whole. And when we want to enjoy that salad, we can combine several ingredients into a big mouthful of American culture, or we can pick out some Chinese dim sum here or maybe some Irish line dancing there.

melting pot Metaphorical image in which all cultures blend together into one harmonious whole.

Some people who come from other cultures may choose to assimilate by adopting their new culture's traditions, while others may want to maintain their original cultural identity.

cultural participation Involving oneself in another culture.

The fourth accelerator is *cultural participation*. Any time people learn another language or students study abroad, they are engaging in **cultural participation**—the act of involving themselves in another culture. Sampling ethnic cuisine like Thai food is one way to participate in a different culture, and trying your hand at Egyptian basket weaving or Brazilian dance fighting are others. Any time we open ourselves up to one of these new experiences, we are engaging a different bounded or co-culture. In doing so, we chart unfamiliar territory and gain appreciation for other people's way of life. Also, when we

PERSONALLY RESPONSIBLE COMMUNICATION

Cultural Participation

Cultural participation can be a fun intercultural communication accelerator. It's as easy as becoming an active member of a group outside your personal comfort zone. At most colleges and universities there are several organizations for specialized cultures. For example, the University of California–Berkeley has a club called Active Minds that is involved in removing the stigma surrounding mental illness. The University of Connecticut has the African Students' Association for anyone interested in African culture. Florida State has the Aikido Club, which teaches students about Japanese martial arts. And Northwestern University has the Ballroom, Latin, and Swing Team, encouraging students to experience intercultural dance. The goal of these and other organizations like them, of course, is to cater to an increasingly pluralistic student body while promoting the value of difference.

Regardless of how you choose to participate, acquainting yourself with other cultures helps humanize those with whom you are unfamiliar and who don't fit the stereotypes imposed on you by your own culture. It is the responsibility of every person, especially those who live in a pluralistic country like ours, to embrace, participate in, and celebrate the differences that make us whole.

What Would You Say?

Whatever your personal level of intercultural communication competence, you know that prejudice and disrespect are all too common. In a single month in 2015, for example, media reported a school nurse shouting racial slurs at an 11-year-old student, a professor writing to the *New York Times* calling African Americans lazy, and a high school excluding special needs students from its yearbook. You might take satisfaction in the fact that you know better. But is that enough? What would you have done if you were directly affected?

An ethical communicator understands that when we stand up for the rights of one, we stand up for the rights of all. Martin Niemöller, a man who spent seven years in World War II Nazi concentration camps, articulated this fundamental human truth: "First they came for the Socialists and I did not speak out. Because I was not a Socialist. Then they came for the Trade Unionists and I did not speak out. Because I was not a Trade Unionist. Then they came for the Jews and I did not speak out. Because I was not a Jew. Then they came for me—and there was no one left to speak for me" (US Holocaust Memorial Museum, 2012).

It is the ethical responsibility of every person in a culture to stand up for others in that culture, to ensure that no one is debased or isolated simply because of who they are. Actress and activist Anne Hathaway faced this situation. She grew up wanting to become a nun, but she left the Catholic Church because of its position on homosexuality. She explained, "There are people who've said that I'm being brave for being openly supportive of gay marriage, adoption . . . [W]ith all due respect, I humbly dissent. I'm not being brave. I'm being a decent human being" (One Equal World, 2015).

So, imagine that you and a friend are out and she sees two guys holding hands. She turns to you and says, "You know I'm not a homophobe, but . . ." What would you say? Would you even wait to hear what follows "but"? How might Ms. Hathaway respond? Why would—or should—your response be any different?

participate in other cultures we may begin to see their commonalities or come to value even more their differences. If you're willing, this participation is actually quite easy, as you can read in the box "Cultural Participation."

The last and perhaps most important accelerator of effective intercultural communication is *avoiding the obstacles* already addressed in this chapter—stereotyping, labeling, prejudice, discrimination, chauvinism, and ethnocentrism. But what do you do when you see others engaging in these destructive practices? What is your obligation as a true cultural transformer? The box "What Would You Say?" can help you consider these questions. And while we must certainly avoid these obstacles in our everyday lives, they can be especially detrimental in the modern workplace, as you can read in the box "Improving On-the-Job Intercultural Communication."

How Cultural Values Shape Communication

Many factors—geographic, political, economic, educational, historical, and technological—shape a culture's character. But how does that culture influence the way people interact? It should come as no surprise that our cultural experiences shape who we are and how we see the world. But keep in mind that people from different cultures may have different values. What do different cultures hold dear, and how do those values shape communication?

Dutch organizational communication researcher Geert Hofstede, after surveying more than 100,000 people from 50 countries, attempted to answer this question, offering his "value dimensions" as an answer (1983). He originally identified four dimensions along which cultures could be differentiated—*collectivism versus individualism*, *power distance*, *uncertainty avoidance*, and *masculinity versus femininity*. Hofstede explained that these dimensions "relate to very fundamental problems which face any human society, but to which different societies have found different answers. They are used to explain (1) different ways of structuring organizations, (2) different motivations of people within organizations, and (3) different issues people and organizations face within society" (p. 46). Naturally, these differences have implications for how people communicate in the various contexts in which they find themselves. Anthropologist Edward Hall added a fifth dimension, one even more closely tied to how people communicate. You may remember Hall as the theorist from Chapter 1 who told us that culture is "the medium evolved by humans to survive. Nothing is free from cultural influences. It is the keystone in civilization's arch and is the medium through which all of life's events must flow" (1976, p. 14). In differentiating *high-context* and *low-context* cultures, he hoped to stress that "one of the functions of culture is to provide a highly selective screen between man [*sic*] and the outside world. In its many forms, culture therefore designates what we pay attention to and what we ignore" (1976, p. 85).

Before you read on, though, remember that these dimensions represent ranges or continua that identify how given cultures, in general, typically view their worlds. No culture sits at any extreme, and no individual member of a given culture necessarily exhibits all (or even any) of the characteristics associated with his or her culture; after all, to think that way would be stereotyping.

individualistic versus collective cultures Measure of a culture's commitment to the individual versus the group.

The first dimension is **individualistic versus collective cultures**. "As members of individualistic cultures are socialized into their culture, they learn the major values of their culture (e.g., independence, achievement) and acquire preferred ways for how members of the culture are expected to view themselves (e.g., as unique persons). Members of collectivistic cultures learn different major values (e.g., harmony, solidarity) and acquire different preferred ways to conceive of themselves (e.g., as interconnected with others)" (Gudykunst et al., 1996, pp. 512–513). As a result, people in individualist cultures tend to value the goals, needs, and rights of the individual. Those in collectivist cultures value the goals, responsibilities, and obligations of the group.

In individualistic cultures such as the United States, Great Britain, and Australia, the strong individual—one who is independent and stands apart from "the herd"—is valued. But in collective cultures such as China, Japan, and many Latin American countries, the needs of the many outweigh the needs of the few. In individualistic cultures, the individual is the most important entity

COMMUNICATION IN THE WORKPLACE

Improving On-the-Job Intercultural Communication

The contemporary workplace is diverse and often includes colleagues from many other nations. The Bureau of Labor Statistics, for example, reports that there are 25 million foreign-born people in the US labor force, accounting for 16.1 percent of the total workforce (2013). And there's also a pretty good chance that someone born outside the United States will be your boss. About 20 percent of the CEOs of America's 500 biggest corporations are foreign-born (Bluestein, 2015).

Romana Stratton, business executive and management trainer, explains what this means for your career: "The modern environment we live and work in is increasingly complex. The exponential growth of technology has resulted, amongst other things, in the evolution of language and how we communicate. We now find ourselves communicating with people from different cultures increasingly both in our work and personal surroundings. As a consequence, successful intercultural communication is rapidly becoming an important challenge to master to ensure effective communication—particularly in the workplace" (2012).

She offers eight rules for improving intercultural communication in the workplace:

1. *Discourage the pack mentality*—Make sure that any behaviors that shut out specific colleagues are never tolerated.

2. *Use humor*—Well-judged humor has its place on the job; it improves morale and builds unity. But in a multicultural workplace, remember that what one speaker finds funny may well offend colleagues from a different culture.

3. *Celebrate cultural differences*—Cultural differences can enrich the workplace, in terms of morale and on-the-job productivity. After all, people with differing experiences may offer different approaches to workplace issues and problems.

4. *Discourage any sign of racial prejudice*—Intolerance, prejudice, or divisiveness should never be tolerated on the job.

5. *Stay in touch*—Managers or team leaders must always stay connected to the people working for them. This ensures that should an issue arise, they can respond quickly.

6. *Walk a mile in another person's shoes*—Empathize and find common ground to improve interpersonal communication.

7. *Communicate well*—Always make sure the message has been correctly received.

8. *Give it time*—Working in an intercultural environment is not always as easy as you'd like. But organizations can benefit from differences in perspective, so be patient. Use the inevitable problems to learn how to do things differently and better.

---

in any social setting; uniqueness and maintenance of individual self are rewarded. As a result, communication tends to be open, forceful, and direct, with more attention paid to what "I" want to say rather than to what "you" may want to hear. Hofstede's research indicated that Western democracies tended toward individualism. In collective cultures, emphasis is placed on structure and collaboration, always with consideration of how everyone within the group is affected by the behaviors of any one member. People remain steadfast and true to their groups (family, friends, or work, for example) and operate to protect the best interests of the collective many. Communication, then, serves more of a bonding, rather than information-sharing, function. *How* you say something is often more important than *what* it is you say. Hofstede argues that a majority of the people on earth live in collectivist cultures.

Loss of face exists in all cultures because all people have a need for dignity and respect.

power distance How people of a given culture manage status and hierarchy.

Individualistic and collective cultures also have different ideas about *face*. You may remember from Chapter 3 that face is the public self-image that all members of a culture want to claim for themselves. Face, as your *public* identity "is how *others* see you. [It] is acquired, maintained, and lost through social interactions" (Samovar et al., 2013, p. 208). And as you might imagine, because they differ in their expectations of how their members should interact, individualistic and collectivist cultures will deal with face differently. When people lose face in individualistic cultures, when they embarrass themselves, for example, they alone suffer the consequences. Why not? Their face (public identity) is built through their own, individual effort, independent of much reliance on others. Face was theirs to build; it's theirs to lose. In collectivist cultures, however, when people lose face, it brings insult and dishonor to the entire group. Again, why not? Identity in collectivist cultures is not individually constructed; it is built and maintained through membership in the group. A member of a family who embarrasses him- or herself, for example, shames his or her family and is more likely to be disowned by the family than is a person who does the same in an individualistic culture.

The second cultural value dimension is **power distance**. Running along a continuum from high to low, power distance refers to how people in a given culture deal with matters of status and hierarchy. As Hofstede and his colleagues explain, all cultures must negotiate "the fact that people are unequal" (Hofstede, Hofstede, and Minkov, 2010, p. 55). How do high and low power-distance cultures do this? "Individuals from high power distance cultures accept power as part of society. As such, superiors consider their subordinates to be different from themselves and vice versa [and] that power and authority are facts of life" (Gudykunst, 2001, p. 41). Countries like Mexico, India, Saudi Arabia, and the Philippines are high power-distance cultures because of the importance they place on hierarchy—people are expected to know their place and the communication norms that apply, especially with others of different rank. But low power-distance cultures find inequality troubling. They "are guided by laws, norms, and everyday behaviors that make power distinctions as minimal as possible" (Brislin, 2000, p. 288). Low power-distance countries include the United States, Israel, Ireland, Canada, and Sweden because people there are expected to interact in an equitable way despite rank, role, or position. Consider a typical classroom at your school. Low power-distance cultures encourage a great deal of discourse among students and between students and faculty. But at universities in high power-distance cultures, professors rule supremely; they are the only authority, and there is much less exchange of ideas and opinions.

Hofstede's third value dimension is **uncertainty avoidance**, "the extent to which the members of a culture feel threatened by ambiguous or unknown situations" (Hofstede et al., 2010, p. 191). People in high uncertainty-avoidance cultures are uncomfortable with unpredictability and ambiguity; their communication evidences consensus, resistance to change, and rejection of the new or deviant. And naturally, something doesn't have to be very different to be deviant. Communication is quite rules-based, following well-established conventions. Greece, Japan, Belgium, and Peru are typical of high uncertainty-avoidance cultures. Those in low uncertainty-avoidance cultures accept, maybe even relish, life's uncertainty. They are more tolerant of the new and different, and are more willing to take risks. These traits show up in their everyday communication. There is more openness and freedom of expression, less reliance on interactional rules. For example, consider the many different ways American students greet one another, the wealth of expressions they use to simply say, "Hi." The United States, Sweden, Great Britain, and Jamaica are low uncertainty-avoidance cultures.

The fourth cultural dimension is **masculinity/femininity**. Masculine cultures have clearly defined sex roles and exhibit and encourage "male" characteristics such as assertiveness, competitiveness, wealth, hierarchy, and ambition. Naturally, these values show up in communication; there is much more "me" and "I" talk, more open expression of material comfort, and greater amounts of conversational challenge. Feminine cultures tend to be more nurturing, empathetic, and compassionate. These values, too, appear in everyday talk. "We" and "you" appear more often, as do terms of affection and interest. These distinct cultural contexts also differ in their expectations of men and women. Men are clearly dominant in masculine cultures. It's almost a cliché now, but in the United States and other masculine cultures, an assertive male boss is *tough* and *demanding*, while an assertive female boss is *nagging*, *overbearing*, and *trying to be too much like a man*. But in feminine cultures, there is more flexibility of gender roles. In fact, what makes these cultures feminine is that "both men and women are supposed to be modest, tender, and concerned with the quality of life" (Hofstede et al., 2010, p. 140). In Hofstede's analysis, the Scandinavian countries are the most feminine, while Japan, Austria, Italy, and the United States are masculine.

One final dimension meriting our attention is Hall's distinction between **high- and low-context cultures**. *High* and *low* pertain to the amount of meaning derived from the communication context or environment, rather than from the spoken communication itself. People in high-context cultures require less detailed explanation than those in low-context cultures. They make meaning implicitly from a given setting or situation and, unlike those in low-context cultures, don't need to rely on detailed verbal information to get

uncertainty avoidance A culture's comfort with difference and ambiguity.

masculinity/femininity Measure of a culture's commitment to gender roles and the characteristics that accompany them.

high- and low-context cultures Measure of the degree of communication-shaping information present in communication settings.

THUMBNAIL THEORY

Hall's Differentiation of High- and Low-Context Cultures

High and *low* pertain to the amount of meaning inherent (existing in) the communication context or environment. People in high-context cultures require less detailed explanation than those in low-context cultures because the context (for example, participants, occasion, or communication goals) provides cues for meaning making. In low-context cultures, meaning resides in the explicit code or message, that is, the message itself.

the message. Think of the way you behave at a funeral (a very high-context communication setting). The cues—grieving family, somber conversation, and dark attire—make it clear how you are to behave and how free, or not, you are to communicate as you wish. Now think of lunch at the student union (a very low-context communication setting). The cues, by contrast, tell you very little about how to act, leaving you free to be individual, idiosyncratic, and expressive in your communication.

In high-context cultures, then, much of the meaning resides in the context of the communication—who's speaking, what is the occasion, what's happening nonverbally—not the words themselves. In fact, in very high-context cultures such as Japan, Korea, and China, speakers know to *ignore* the words (the *explicit code*, in Hall's terms) and pay attention to the *understood* meaning. Young people in Japan even have an expression, *kuuki yomenai*, to describe people who are bad at "reading the atmosphere," as it's literally translated. In high-context cultures you never want someone to text that you're *KY* (Meyer, 2014). In low-context cultures, primarily North American, Western European, and Scandinavian nations, on the other hand, meaning resides in the explicit code or message. Plain, direct, to-the-point communication is valued. Americans supposedly "say what they mean and mean what they say."

Attitudes Toward Diversity and the Problem with Tolerance

Hofstede's Dimensions of Cultural Differentiation

Cultures can be differentiated along four dimensions: collectivism versus individualism, power distance, uncertainty avoidance, and masculinity versus femininity. These dimensions explain cultural differences in how groups and organizations are structured, what motivates people to behave as they do, and the kinds of issues people routinely encounter. These differences have implications for how people communicate.

One of the motivations for Hofstede's research was the question, "What happens when people from different cultural backgrounds interact; what problems arise from their different orientations, expectations, and modes of communication?" His goal, and that of those who study intercultural communication, is to reduce errors, or in the vocabulary of this text, to improve meaning making between all people. This is an essential task if we intend to be moral, ethical, and evolved inhabitants of a multicultural world. We can more effectively engage in intercultural communication if we observe the following:

1. *Recognize that we are all, to some degree, prejudiced and have a natural preference for in-group favoritism.* Social identity theory and identity-negotiation theory explain our natural tendency to find comfort in our own in-groups. And as you read in the social responsibility box, we all have a natural tendency to cognitively store and categorize data. When we encounter new experiences, we call up those categorizations in order to make sense of the experience in front of us. But in doing so, we can also call up prejudices we've developed over time.

   We see this tendency played out in an early scene from the 2004 Academy Award–winning film *Crash,* when two young African-American men are engaged in a conversation about racial stereotyping. One of the

men is complaining about a waitress whom he believes refused to
serve them because they're black
(even though the waitress herself
is African-American). He also
points out a white couple walking
to their car who, it appears to
him, are suspicious and fearful of
him and his friend because of
their race. The man claims that
each of these three people is engaging in racial stereotyping. The
irony of the scene is that as the
two men finish their conversation, they pull out guns and steal
the white couple's vehicle. The
entire film specifically addresses
gender, race, and class prejudice.

In the award-winning movie *Crash*, we see accusations of racial prejudice, as well as
the ironies that sometimes accompany stereotyping.

But it also illustrates the ethical test we face when our preconceived
ideas—our prejudices—are occasionally accurate. Only when we make an
effort to understand that those preconceptions are based on both biased
and unbiased information can we step back and reframe those positions
in a way that sifts out our prejudices and allows objectivity to define our
interactions with individuals who are different from us.

2. *See all people as human first.* While our physical characteristics, beliefs,
   and preferences may differ, at our core we all need the same things—
   physical and emotional interaction with others, mental and physical
   health, happiness, a sense of belonging, self-esteem, and dignity. But
   each of us is also flawed. We experience anger and we make mistakes.
   When we see all people as human *first,* we understand that characteristics like skin color, race, sexual orientation, and ethnicity are superficial,
   having little to do with a person's basic values, needs, and overall humanness. When we humanize people, we equate them with ourselves, and
   this should be the basis from which we experience others and approach
   diversity. Think about how many times you've had doubts about another
   student based on nothing more than an initial, superficial impression.
   But once you came to know him or her, became friends, or at least came
   to see that individual as someone who bore little resemblance to your
   original assumptions, the more you saw her or him as human and not
   threatening. Fear of the unknown is mitigated by familiarity and
   open-mindedness.

3. *Understand that each person has a different set of experiences.* **Role-taking** is
   our ability to put ourselves in the position of others in order to better understand them. The act of role-taking tells others that we know that just
   as our experiences shape what we believe and how we feel, so do theirs,

role-taking Ability to put
oneself in the position of
others to better understand
them.

and their experiences may well, in fact most certainly will, differ from our own. When American college student Maggie met her Chinese roommate Xiang for the first time, for example, she thought they would never get along. Besides the obvious cultural differences, Xiang was painfully shy and Maggie was extremely outgoing. They eventually became best friends as Maggie learned more and more about her roommate's life. Xiang was the seventh of nine children, and her home life in China was so chaotic that she was rarely able to be heard among the many voices of her siblings. As a result, she grew up to be a passive young adult who simply needed someone like Maggie to help her find her voice. Although an only child who "ruled the roost," Maggie was able to put herself in Xiang's shoes in order to better grasp the circumstances that led to Xiang's shyness.

assumptions Sets of information automatically interpreted as factual.

intercultural communication competence Degree of successful meaning making with communicators from different backgrounds.

4. *Avoid making assumptions about others.* **Assumptions** are sets of information that we automatically interpret as factual without evidence. Consider and challenge your own assumptions; take the time to examine individual circumstances. One person at a time, we can disabuse ourselves of damaging assumptions.

5. *Increase your self-knowledge.* In order to truly understand others, you must first know *yourself*. The more you know yourself, the better you relate to others. When you truly understand what defines you, you come to realize that the things that really matter are common to everyone. You are better able to separate the superficial definitions of you from the meaningful ones, and you can more easily do the same with others.

6. *Understand that developing effective intercultural communication competence is an ongoing process.* **Intercultural communication competence** is the degree to which we can successfully make meaning with communicators from different backgrounds. It is a process. Not all of us are good at it, and although we can get better, it requires two kinds of thinking. The first is *holistic*: an intuitive, gut-level knowledge of what is and should be. We've already seen that because of stereotyping, assumptions, and other gut-level ways of knowing, something else is necessary. The second way of thinking we need to invoke is *analytical*: conscious reflection on what is and what should be. These are the ideas of intercultural communication scholar William Howell (1982), who identified four levels of intercultural communication competence:

THUMBNAIL THEORY

Howell's Levels of Intercultural Communication Competence

The acquisition of intercultural communication spans four levels: unconscious incompetence, conscious incompetence, conscious competence, and unconscious competence. True competence occurs when a person's holistic and analytical understanding of intercultural communication are in synch.

- *Unconscious incompetence*—This is the "I'm just being me" approach. This works great when you are with people like yourself, when you don't have to think about differences. But it may not be the best approach in intercultural communication settings when differences do matter. "You just being you" is likely to produce communication errors and hurt feelings.

- *Conscious incompetence*—In an intercultural communication interaction you may understand that things aren't going very well, but you don't understand why. You're conscious of your failings. At least that's a start.

- *Conscious competence*—That's what this chapter is all about, becoming aware of what it takes to be an effective intercultural communicator, consciously avoiding the impediments and applying the accelerators. But, as Howell would argue, even though this may be a necessary step toward true competence, it's not the ultimate goal.

- *Unconscious competence*—You're "in the zone"; effective intercultural communication is happening without any thought. Your holistics and analytics are in synch.

What assumptions do you make about this group of people? Why?

7. *Assume mutual respect when encountering those who may be different from you.* In the US judicial system, a person is innocent until proven guilty. In other words, until evidence to the contrary is presented, the judgment of a person begins from the premise of innocence. This is analogous to the concept of *assumed mutual respect* in intercultural encounters. When we meet someone for the first time, we should automatically begin the dialogue from a position of respect unless the other person presents us with some indication that she or he is undeserving of that respect. Imagine how different the world would be if those with religious or political differences possessed this attitude. Perhaps we'd see less conflict and a willingness to communicate about the compatibility of our ideas and values rather than the differences.

8. *Have a problem with tolerance.* Many well-meaning observers still consider tolerance a positive attitude when communicating interculturally. But imagine if a classmate asked you if you liked him, and you responded, "Well, I tolerate you." Better yet, what if someone said that about you? It's demeaning and insulting. The idea of promoting tolerance toward others, as opposed to respect or interaction, is unfortunate. Mohammed Mahallati, presidential scholar in Islamic studies at Oberlin College, explains, "Difference is a blessing, not a challenge. We define ourselves by knowing other people. We know our world by learning about difference. What is the word we often use? Tolerance. Is that a positive notion? Not really. 'For the time being, I will tolerate you?' I'm against the concept. It means difference is a threat. Difference is a blessing and you don't tolerate a blessing. You embrace it" (in Koerth-Baker, 2011). The best way to succeed as an intercultural communicator is not to tolerate diversity but to respect and celebrate it.

Review of Learning Objectives

9.1 Describe the elements of intercultural communication.

Intercultural communication involves interaction between people whose cultural perceptions and symbol systems differ. It is an essential form of meaning making in increasingly pluralistic cultures. The key to successful intercultural communication is understanding how people from other places and backgrounds interact in their own cultures.

9.2 Identify the obstacles to and accelerators of intercultural communication.

Obstacles to intercultural communication include *stereotyping* (applying characteristics to people or groups that may or may not apply); *labeling* (describing individuals using names we believe categorize them); *prejudice* (a negative attitude toward a group based on little or no experience); *discrimination* (overtly excluding, avoiding, or distancing oneself from another group); *chauvinism* (believing yourself to be superior to others); and *ethnocentrism* (the belief that your own culture is superior to all others). Accelerators include *cultural relativism* (the belief that people vary in their behaviors, feelings, traditions, and values depending on their individual cultures); understanding others' *cultural values; cultural pluralism* (maintaining the practices and identities of a bounded culture within the larger culture); *cultural participation* (involving yourself in another culture); and *avoiding the obstacles to intercultural communication*.

9.3 Describe how various cultural values affect communication.

A number of relational and communication dimensions distinguish one culture from another. Among them are *individualism versus collectivism* (a culture's commitment to the individual versus the group); *high versus low power distance* (its recognition of and comfort with hierarchy); *high versus low uncertainty avoidance* (its willingness to tolerate ambiguity); *masculinity versus femininity* (its commitment to gender roles and the characteristics associated with different genders); and *high versus low context* (a measure of the degree of communication-shaping information present in interactional settings that goes beyond the words themselves).

9.4 Explain attitudes toward diversity and the problem with tolerance.

Tolerance implies putting up with difference. Successful intercultural communicators do not simply tolerate cultural diversity; instead, they celebrate it. This behavior includes (1) recognizing that, to some degree, we are all prejudiced and naturally have a favorable in-group bias; (2) seeing all people as humans first; (3) understanding that everyone has different sets of experiences; (4) avoiding making assumptions about others; (5) increasing self-knowledge; (6) understanding that developing effective intercultural competence is an ongoing process; and (7) practicing mutual respect when encountering others who may be different.

Key Terms

intercultural communication 188
majority-minority country 189
labeling 190
prejudice 190
discrimination 190
chauvinism 191
ethnocentrism 191
in-group 192
out-group 192
social identity theory 192
identity negotiation theory 193
cultural transformer 194
cultural relativism 194
cultural values 194
cultural pluralism 195
assimilation 195
melting pot 195
cultural participation 196
individualistic versus collective cultures 198
power distance 200
uncertainty avoidance 201
masculinity/femininity 201
high- and low-context cultures 201
role-taking 203
assumptions 204
intercultural communication competence 204

Questions for Review

1. What are six obstacles to effective intercultural communication?

2. Differentiate between stereotyping, prejudice, and discrimination.

3. What are five accelerators of effective intercultural communication?

4. What is assimilation and how does it relate to the melting pot and salad metaphors?

5. Explain social identity theory and identity negotiation theory. How are they similar, and how do they differ?

6. What are Hofstede's four value dimensions of culture?

7. What does Hall's notion of high- and low-context cultures tell us about how communication is transacted in those different settings?

8. What are Howell's four levels of intercultural competence?

9. Name and define the two types of thinking required for developing intercultural communication competence.

10. What's wrong with tolerance?

Questions for Discussion

1. Are you troubled by the fact that the United States will soon become a majority-minority country? If you are, why? If you aren't, why not? What does your answer say about your commitment to diversity and effective intercultural communication?

2. What's the problem with chauvinism? Shouldn't we all be proud of our national culture and our individual bounded or co-cultures? Can any good come of chauvinism? If you say yes, explain your response. Same thing if you say "no."

3. The Martin Niemöller quote in the Ethical Communication box is very famous, but maybe it's outlived its usefulness. After all, nothing like the Nazi roundup of those who were different could ever happen again. Or could it? What is Niemöller's real message, and how does it apply to how we live our lives today?

Mass Communication

Spring break is around the corner, and you can't wait to relax by the beach with friends. You are ready to leave behind the chaos of school and work. But then your friend suggests that you really escape by going without your phones, your laptops, TV, and other media technology. The thought scares you. How will you ever survive a week without texting, without your music, without checking your favorite websites and watching your favorite shows? Nonetheless, you accept the challenge. If your friend is willing to leave media behind, so can you. Besides, how nice would it be to have no intrusions for a whole week?

When you arrive at the shore, you instinctively reach for your smartphone to post a photo of yourself on vacation, but there's no phone. OK, you think, I can do this. As the hours pass, you become a bit anxious. By day two, you develop a mild headache. It could be from lack of sleep, but as you think more and more about your loss of contact with the outside world, the ache becomes worse. By days three and four, you're growing moody and snapping at your friends. By day five, you are mildly depressed, stressed, experiencing stomachaches, and looking forward to returning home to your mediated life. This one-week vacation seems like a month.

Once you get back to campus, your nerves start to calm down, and miraculously, the headache subsides as you turn on your phone and crash in front of the TV. Is it possible you were feeling the effects of *media withdrawal*? You've never really bought into the idea. But as you think about it, you realize the physical and emotional symptoms seem surprisingly similar to those that accompany drug and alcohol withdrawal.

The impact of media is massive, and yet we often underestimate its magnitude and take for granted the influence that media have over our daily lives. In this chapter, we move away from various forms of interpersonal communication to focus on mass communication and the pervasive role it plays in our culture.

Learning Objectives

10.1   Describe the differences between interpersonal and mass communication.

10.2   Discuss the relationship between culture, communication, and mass media.

10.3   Identify the characteristics of media consumers.

10.4   Identify the characteristics of media industries.

10.5   Describe several theories associated with mass communication.

What Is Mass Communication?

How can you possibly understand the impact of media if you've never experienced life without it? We are so immersed in our mediated culture that we can't imagine how to exist outside it, and because of its *assumed* presence, we don't give it much thought. Media theorist Marshall McLuhan would often pose the question, "Does a fish know it's wet?" The answer, of course, is no . . . not until it's dry. He was making the point that we can't truly appreciate how enveloped we are by media because our mediated culture has evolved into a natural state of being. Just as a fish doesn't know it's wet because it knows no other reality, we are often unaware of media's impact on us and the world around us. As our opening vignette suggests, we are "fish out of water" when stripped of our ubiquitous technologies and our ability to engage in mass communication.

Up to this point, we have largely focused on interpersonal communication, which is between people in relationships. **Mass communication** occurs between mass media and their audiences. Mass media include television, radio and music, Internet, video games, newspapers, magazines, books, cellphones, and movies, as well as the industries that support these platforms, like advertising and public relations. In Chapter 1 we examined communication by considering components such as the sender (encoder), message, receiver (decoder), feedback, noise, and fields of experience. The same components are part of mass communication, where the sender is a particular medium. If that medium is television, for example, the receivers are the viewers, and the messages are programs and commercials. Just as with interpersonal communication, the complexity of the process becomes much more

mass communication
Communication occurring between mass media and their audiences.

apparent when we assess the meanings, interpretations, and effects of those messages.

Why Study Mass Communication?

So why is mass communication such an important area of study? One obvious reason is simply the amount of time it occupies in our lives—an amount we often underestimate. Adult Americans spend 12 hours each day engaged with media (eMarketer, 2014). Deducting 8 sleeping hours from the 24-hour day leaves a mere 4 hours for all other activities. This means that Americans spend more time engaging with media, especially television, than with anything (or anyone) else.

Another reason to study mass communication is to consider the effects of all that media consumption. Let's start with cellphone use. Recent research has linked it to attention-span deficits and to disengagement from friends and family (Merlo, Stone, and Bibbey, 2013). In addition, sexting (sending sexually explicit messages or images via cellphone) has become an issue, and so has texting while driving. Those who text and drive are 23 percent more likely to have an accident than are those who don't, and one-fourth—1.3 million crashes a year—involve texting drivers (Texting and Driving Safety, 2015). Growing Internet use has presented its own issues, such as Internet addiction, cyberbullying, children's access to inappropriate material, and loss of privacy. We will discuss social media use in depth in Chapter 12. Traditional media like television, video games, and music serve as catalysts for ongoing concern over issues such as violence, sexualized content, childhood obesity, cheapening of democratic discourse, and stereotyping of gender and race.

Regardless of the **medium** (the vehicle conveying the message; *media* is its plural), media content affects—negatively and positively—both individuals and the culture in which they live. And both low-quality and high-quality media content influence us in a multitude of ways. Studying mass communication gives us insight about all of those effects. As media theorist James Potter explains, "We need to develop an appreciation for the wide range of effects that show up in the full spectrum of the population. Many of these effects are [too] subtle to observe at any given time, but this does not make them unimportant. To the contrary, many of the most influential effects on each of us are those that occur during our everyday lives and sneak in 'under the radar' so that we are unaware of how they are changing our habits and the way we think until someone points it out" (2012, p. 12).

Finally, arguably the biggest reason for studying mass communication, like any area of communication, has to do with the way we relate to one another. The meaning we make from media messages often determines our values, beliefs, and behaviors—including how we conduct ourselves in the

"I'm not sure Dad, but I think I wet the bed."

How would the little guy know?

medium(media, pl.) Vehicle conveying a message.

Does *Hawaii Five-O*'s Steve McGarrett, played by Alex O'Loughlin, represent attractiveness in our culture? Why or why not?

relationships we maintain. For example, how does Internet messaging affect the way you communicate with family members or the expectations you have of friends? How do certain news networks shape your political views? Or how do you know what's considered attractive? Media messages influence ideas of attractiveness. Consider celebrities who consistently appear on magazines' lists of the "most beautiful people," actors like Alex O'Loughlin, Eva Mendes, Bradley Cooper, and Mila Kunis. We may look for partners who fit those ideas, and we may even expect ourselves to fit those standards. Later we will examine the link between media, communication, and culture, but first, we will consider the differences between interpersonal communication and mass communication.

Interpersonal Communication versus Mass Communication

When we mentioned cellphones as a medium, you probably wondered how they could be considered a *mass* medium. After all, phones have traditionally been used as a way to engage in interpersonal conversation. But today's smartphones can channel a vast array of digital content. While you may occasionally use your phone to address one or a few people at a time, cellphone technology has blurred the distinctions between interpersonal and mass communication. Making calls ranks only fifth in the ways people spend time using their smartphones (Walsh, 2012). Consider all the other functions that device serves. You can watch a television program or movie; you can stream music, play video games by yourself or with distant competitors; and you can access the Internet. This **convergence** (the erosion of traditional distinctions among media) renders the smartphone a technology of mass communication, making it a bit more difficult to think of interpersonal and mass communication as *completely* different.

convergence Erosion of traditional distinctions among media.

Another reason that cellphones can be classified as a mass medium is that they allow us to create our own mediated messages such as websites and blogs (potentially reaching millions of people), altering our role in the mass communication process from passive consumers to active content producers. Over a decade ago, technology writer Dan Gilmor (2004) summed up this change when he wrote that the world is now populated by the "people formerly known as the audience." We are no longer mere recipients of media content; we are

Table 10.1 The Differences and Similarities between Interpersonal and Mass Communication

INTERPERSONAL COMMUNICATION	MASS COMMUNICATION
1. Communication involves two or a few people	**1.** Communication can involve millions of people
2. Involves immediate, direct feedback	**2.** Involves delayed, inferential feedback
3. Messages are flexible and alterable	**3.** Once delivered, messages cannot be changed
4. Communication is personally relevant	**4.** Communication is often formulaic

also creators. Tens of millions of people around the globe maintain blogs, and 100 hours of video are uploaded to YouTube alone every minute (Smith, 2015). And every time you make an addition to your Facebook page you become a media content creator. Although this empowerment of the people formerly known as the audience further complicates our ability to easily draw distinctions between interpersonal and mass communication, there are still specific characteristics that *traditionally* separate the two, as you can see in Table 10.1.

The first, most obvious difference is the number of people involved in the communication process. Interpersonal communication involves two or a few people, while mass communication can involve millions of communicators. Having a conversation with your best friend means that for each of you, there is an audience of *only* one person. On the other hand, when a television network like NBC broadcasts *Sunday Night Football,* it can command an audience of nearly 30 million people in the United States alone. This dramatic difference in the number of message recipients produces other distinctions between the two forms of communication.

A second distinction has to do with feedback. How do we know that *Sunday Night Football* has such a large following? The number "nearly 30 million" was taken from audience measurement company Nielsen, which provides ratings to the broadcast industry. It reflects the number of people who were tuned in (on a variety of platforms) to the game on a specific time and date. One week after the football game aired, Nielsen was able to provide its calculation. This rating serves as *feedback* to the network regarding the "popularity" of the program. Because the information was provided a full week after the program aired, the feedback is at best *indirect,* and because it represents only the sets tuned in and not whether people actually liked the broadcast (or even if they watched at all) it is **inferential feedback**. What's the feedback for a movie? Box office. Magazines and newspapers? Circulation. Advertising? Sales. All are delivered well after the original message has been created, and all are inferential. Have you ever gone to a movie you didn't like? Read a newspaper or magazine story with which you seriously disagreed? Bought a product because it was on sale, not because you liked its commercial? In each of these cases, your feedback has told the original sender little about what you thought of the message. This type of feedback differs markedly from the direct and immediate feedback of interpersonal communication, such as in a conversation with your

inferential feedback
Indirect, often delayed feedback.

Broadcasts of professional football are habitually among television's highest rated programs, but we don't know how popular a given game is right away—we must wait for the ratings to reveal the size of the TV audience.

formulaic When media messages hew closely to proven formulas.

best friend. If you ask a question or make a comment, you get an instant response; you don't have to wait a week or longer. Even the fastest television ratings, the overnights, are delivered many hours after the original message.

A third difference between interpersonal and mass communication is the nature of the message, something also influenced by the size of the audience. Let's say you're conversing with your friend and you make an inappropriate comment. Judging from your friend's face and vocal tone, you realize you committed an indiscretion. In an effort to make amends, you quickly apologize and rephrase your comments. All is fine because your interpersonally communicated message is immediately alterable. Unfortunately, this is not possible with a mass-communicated message such as a television program. Once the content is packaged and aired, there is no altering of the message. Any offensive, inappropriate, or confusing content cannot be changed or deleted because the material has been edited into a final product.

And this leads to the final distinction between mass communication and interpersonal communication—the flexibility of the messages. During conversations with friends, we often engage in highly experimental communication; we exchange ideas, thoughts, and opinions; we joke, tease, and play word games. We value the unique, unpredictable, and personal nature of the conversations that we and our friends tailor specifically for one another. Media messages are not flexible and rarely experimental. In fact, because the message has to appeal to a mass audience, the content is quite **formulaic**, meaning that content producers stick primarily with proven formulas in determining what will make a successful show. As producer John Landgraf (who had 53 different projects in development with the national TV networks from 1999 to 2003 but only one that lasted on air for more than one season) explained, "I always got the same dumb note from the networks. 'Can you make the character more likable?' Not make them more exciting, more compelling, more interesting, no, it was always make them more likable" (in Carr, 2013, p. B1).

But return for a moment to convergence. Is the Internet micro-blogging technology Twitter interpersonal or mass communication? There is no production expense, no advertisers expecting a mass audience, nor are there network executives demanding that you make yourself more likable. Twitter users can be as bold and imaginative as they want in fewer than 140 characters; participants can react to content in real time, and they can share their material with one person or a million people. Again, more on this in Chapter 12.

The similarities between interpersonal and mass communication are just as significant as their differences. First, both are *symbolic*. The messages from each are constructed from symbols, and those symbols provide meaning. We make a very different meaning from the American flag in a car commercial than we do from the American flag at an uncle's funeral, but we make meaning nonetheless. Second, the messages we receive from both are *ambiguous*. They can be interpreted in many ways depending on the receivers' fields of experiences. For instance, politically conservative viewers might interpret information from the liberal *Rachel Maddow Show* much differently than those who are politically progressive, just as you might be less accepting of the arguments of a stranger who does not share your political views than you would be of those from a family member who agrees with you politically.

Another similarity is that both take place in specific and deliberate *content environments*. For instance, when we go to the theater to see a movie or to our favorite restaurant to dine with friends, we have definite expectations of what kind of communication will occur in these settings, and we interpret it in those contexts (Chapter 1). But this commonality is being challenged by the way we use new technologies, specifically, in our multitasking. Younger, more media-savvy people are rarely without cellphones or other handheld devices, so their interpersonal content environments often clash with their media content environments. You would be very annoyed if your friend kept chatting throughout the movie, but do you feel the same when that friend continues to play *Farmville* when you are having a conversation? Consider the frustration of parents who watch their kids text at the dinner table or the professor who lectures to a classroom of students checking their Facebook accounts on their laptops. It's becoming increasingly complicated trying to distinguish mass communication from interpersonal communication because of the way we now routinely use and prioritize media. But it is important that we do so, and that's why we will now look at the link between culture, communication, and mass media, and discuss the impact of media on contemporary culture.

A conversation between friends can weather all kinds of risks, but conversations in television shows and movies, like those among the characters on *Sex in the City*, are often formulaic and safe.

Culture, Communication, and Mass Media

If we accept the notion that we live in a media-heavy culture and use those media to communicate, then we must also accept the fact that mass media, communication, and culture are inextricably linked. In other words, they don't simply coexist; they exist as a single, inseparable

Politically conservative viewers might interpret information from *The Rachel Maddow Show* much differently than those who are politically liberal.

entity. To fully grasp the true influence of media, we must first understand its power in the culture. One way to do this is to consider mass media as cultural storytellers who shape our ideas, feelings, and thoughts through the messages they send, ultimately shaping and defining our realities (Gerbner, 2010). Ask yourself what it means to be a contemporary college student. Does it mean behaving and thinking like one? And how does a college student behave and think? Equally important, how much of your idea about what it means to be a college student is influenced by culture—and therefore by media?

Consider Kayla's profile:

Kayla Hansen is a 20-year-old woman born and raised in New Jersey. She attends Rutgers and is majoring in Child Psychology. She has three roommates who, like her, are all on the track team and receive scholarships. Every Friday and Saturday night they enjoy going to Chili's. They enjoy listening to Taylor Swift when they're just hanging out, and they also love watching television together, especially *The Real Housewives of Atlantic City*. They constantly compete over who has the most Alex and Ani bracelets, and as athletes, they swear by Nike products—it's the only gear they wear. By their own admission, Kayla and her friends are more occupied with boys than they are with studying, community service, or their internships. They are never without their iPhones and send dozens of text messages each day. Their Facebook pages are flooded with pictures of the four of them, even though they each have over a thousand other Facebook friends. When she graduates, Kayla wants to eventually become a school counselor so she can help young kids negotiate what she calls "the very superficial and high-stress culture" in which they live.

You probably can relate to Kayla's life as a college student or know people who can. However, Kayla wasn't born wearing Nike sneakers, watching reality television, and liking Taylor Swift. Mass media helped shape her culture, which influenced her choices in becoming who she is. Media tell us stories about ourselves and we, in turn, act out roles within those stories (recall Goffman's frame analysis from Chapter 1). Clearly, Kayla's story is an American tale, written in part by an American media structure. That structure presented Kayla with a series of narratives from which she made meaning, and then she applied those meanings in her ongoing efforts to self-identify.

Often, however, we contest cultural rules, and we can make individually meaningful choices. For instance, Kayla's friend from home prefers handmade jewelry over trendy Alex and Ani bracelets and she boycotts a popular product because of its manufacturer's unethical practices. When we contest the culture, we, not the media industries, determine our own stories. But we are never really free from media's influence. You know the Alex and Ani bracelet wearer is judged differently than the do-it-yourselfer; and what's with that hippie girl, boycotting this and boycotting that? You can read about the common practice of assuming that only *other* people are influenced by media in the box "The Third-Person Effect."

Another factor influencing the nature of our mediated culture is money. With very few exceptions, our media system is composed of profit-making industries; they operate as businesses. As a result, their real customers, the people whom they must ultimately satisfy, are their advertisers, not their audiences. What is NBC's goal in airing *Sunday Night Football*? That is, what does it hope to produce that it can sell to make a profit? Viewers. We are the product sold to advertisers. Many critics feel that this actuality cheapens culture, as narratives that can deliver a more saleable product will predominate. A simple test of this idea is to compare the variety and depth of themes that find their way into movies and novels (where the audience pays and, as such, is the real customer) with those typically found in prime-time television (where

---

The Third-Person Effect

Have you ever thought that violent video game or television content can have negative effects on others, but not on you? Or that other people fall for those slick commercials, but not you? You're just too smart for that. We all, at one time or another, have felt immune to media's influence, just as we have often thought that others surely must be affected. This is the *third-person effect*—the idea that others are affected by media messages but we are not. In fact, so powerful is the third-person effect that we even extend it to our children, but with a twist: *our* children are unaffected by harmful content and benefit greatly from good or educational content but *their* children suffer the effects of bad content and reap none of the benefits of the good (Meirick et al., 2009).

One problem with thinking that we (and our families) are unaffected by media is that both positive and negative effects go equally unobserved. When we think of "effects," we usually focus on violence, sexual content, and commercialism rather than considering the pleasure we derived from a meaningful song or a well-written novel. Despite what many may believe, the point of studying media effects isn't to learn that seeing a character shot on *Strike Force* will make people run out and shoot someone. Actually, the effects that are of most concern to social scientists are the subtle ones, for instance, how we view the world as a result of our repeated exposure to crime and violence in entertainment and news programming. Does this material desensitize us to real-world violence? Are we more stressed and suspicious of others in our everyday lives as a result of constant exposure to dark messages and themes? And can a piece of content have both positive and negative effects? Whatever the impact, it is often subtle, and we are all affected in different ways.

We have a responsibility as individuals to recognize the many ways in which we are influenced by media; otherwise, we grant them too much power over our behaviors, emotions, and values. Recognizing media influence empowers us to better deconstruct the messages presented to us and then reassemble them in a way that better serves our own individual meaning making. In the next chapter we look more closely at how to do this in a critical and productive manner.

advertisers pay and, as such, are the real customers). You can conduct the same test by comparing pay-cable and streaming-service television programs like *Homeland*, *House of Cards*, *Girls*, and *Game of Thrones* (where the audience is the customer) with even the best of commercial television (advertiser-supported programming).

This complaint about the influence of profit is particularly important to critics of news media. What happens, they ask, when in the pursuit of profit, news organizations take a sensational approach to their programming rather than focusing on hard news that might serve a more democratic function? Murders, car crashes, factory fires, and missing babies dominate the news, but only when there is no celebrity divorce or royal wedding available for reporting. As the media "have become increasingly more dependent on advertising revenues for support," writes media critic Robert McChesney, "it has become an anti-democratic force in society" (1997, p. 23). "Privately owned news media seek profit and they will cut corners to get it," explains sociologist Michael Schudson, "They will seek to reduce costs even at the risk of limiting the quality of journalism. They may reduce the size of the editorial staff or close an overseas bureau. They may be reluctant to assign a reporter to an investigation that will take weeks or months to yield a story" (2011, p. 119). What

Which is likely to get more news coverage and why: Al Gore's climate change awareness campaign or the Duchess of Cambridge's pregnancy?

happens to a culture when its people know more about celebrities in drug rehab than they do about issues surrounding education, employment, and the economy? Money, say these critics, is the driving force in propelling media industries toward a very specific, self-serving agenda.

There is, however, an alternative view. Media companies in search of profit (that is, in search of an audience that it can sell) must offer content that will attract those audiences. That's why, despite their seeming overreliance on formulaic content—the many crime scene investigation (CSI) programs, reality TV shows, and singing and dancing contests—there is often some very good content. Commercial media's defenders may say there is nothing formulaic about certain shows (*Breaking Bad*, for example), and moreover, they argue, people get the news and journalism they want. That's why partisan cable news networks like MSNBC and Fox are more popular than more objective CNN and why local TV news is dominated by crime stories. There is also this paradox of American journalism: "If commercial news organizations fail to make profits, they will go out of business or they will limp along at a level that prevents them from investing in news gathering" (Schudson, 2011, pp. 118–119).

Characteristics of Media Consumers

There are three easily identifiable characteristics of today's media consumers: (1) they are *platform agnostic*, (2) they are *media multitaskers*, and (3) they are susceptible to *media addiction*. As **platform agnostics**, media consumers are neutral about the medium through which they access their content. If for example, you want the latest Katy Perry or Bruno Mars song for your smartphone, it may not matter to you if you pirate the tune from an illegal download site, buy it from iTunes or YouTube, rip it from a CD, or have it streamed to your laptop by Pandora or Spotify, as long as you get the song. You have no loyalty to the platform, only to the song itself. Likewise, if you are interested in getting your hands on the latest book in the *Fifty Shades of Grey* series, you don't care whether it comes from online Amazon or bricks-and-mortar Barnes & Noble, and you may choose to read it on an e-reader, or a tablet, or a laptop, or a smartphone, or even on paper pages. As a platform agnostic, you place more importance on the content than on the technology through which it is delivered. Platform agnostics present a challenge for media businesses who, like other businesses, want repeat customers loyal to their specific methods of delivery.

Contemporary media consumers are also **media multitaskers**. They rarely use one medium at a time. For example, a third of America's Twitter users tweet about the television shows they are watching at the time, and 44 percent of tablet owners and 38 percent of smartphone owners are on social networking sites while watching television (Bannon, 2012). It's not uncommon, in fact, for multitaskers to use several different media *simultaneously*. Think about when you're writing a paper for class. You do it on your computer, and during the writing process you regularly minimize your document

platform agnostic Neutrality in choice of content-delivery technology.

media multitasking Using more than one medium simultaneously.

to check Facebook, e-mail, and Twitter accounts, all while listening to music and watching *Dancing with the Stars* on television. It's also quite likely that you're texting on your cell, too.

Unlike platform agnosticism, the possible negative consequences of multitasking fall more to the consumer than to the media industries. It certainly poses a dilemma for advertisers who struggle to get their marketing campaigns noticed by a cognitively fragmented audience, but the adverse effects on the multitaskers appear much more serious. Reduced attention spans, **aliteracy** (a decrease in thoughtful reading), and a reprogramming of memory and focus functions are just a few of the problems they face. Media multitasking is nothing if not an activity of distraction. Research shows that when an activity (like homework) is coupled with another activity (like Internet surfing), task performance decreases (Foehr, 2006). Other research indicates that distractions affect how we process information, changing the memory system and rendering information less useful later on. Additionally, when young people are forced to use only one medium at a time, they often find it mentally difficult, exacerbating all of these potential concerns (Richtel, 2010). Think about how you would feel if, while writing a paper, you were unable to engage with any other media. You may feel anxious and somewhat agitated, which brings us to our next point.

aliteracy Loss of thoughtful reading.

media addiction Over-attachment to media.

Media addiction, over-attachment to media, is a characteristic of many media consumers. Some psychologists believe that media, especially social media, can develop into an addiction, while others believe the word "addiction" is used much too casually when connected to media use. Still, the fact remains that young people have a difficult time in the absence of their media technologies (Clayton, Leshner, and Almond, 2015). For the Media Generation, access is about connection, and the way young people stay connected to the world is though social media. For years, researchers have studied addiction to more traditional media like television and video games, but much of today's inquiry focuses on the Internet and cellphones. In a study conducted at the University of Maryland, students were asked to go 24 hours unplugged, that is, without media. Most could not do it. According to education writer Jenna Johnson, "It's very easy to confuse these students with crack addicts who went cold turkey, smokers not given the comfort of a patch while quitting, and alcoholics forced to

Laptop open, television on, listening to music, no doubt a smartphone nearby. Media multitasking defines Generation M.

dry up" (2010). Students reported being anxious, miserable, and feeling frantic in their cravings of media. "I clearly am addicted and the dependency is sickening" confessed one student, "I feel like most people these days are in a similar situation, for between having a Blackberry, a laptop, a television, and an iPod, people have become unable to shed their media skin" (Moeller, 2010).

How much like these students are you? Do you ever reflect on the amount of media you consume and how dependent on the media you may or may not be? There's much more to be said about media-fueled distraction and addiction in Chapter 12, but for now we'll step back from our own media use and look at some characteristics of the media industries that we interact with and how that engagement influences our culture.

Characteristics of Media Industries

Media industries, old and new, are being shaped and reshaped by several forces that not only affect their economic structures, but the nature of mass communication itself. They include concentration of ownership, hyper-commercialism, fragmentation, globalization, and convergence.

Concentration of ownership, the ownership of many different media companies by an increasingly small number of conglomerates, has dramatically reduced the diversity of media sources available to consumers. Thirty years ago, 50 companies owned 90 percent of the media content consumed by Americans; today the number is six—Comcast, News Corp, Disney, Viacom, Time Warner, and CBS (Bart, 2014). With a mere six conglomerates having such dominant power over the creation and dissemination of content, we are left with fewer sources to which we can turn, fewer options for entertainment and news, and therefore a depleted number of perspectives.

concentration of ownership Ownership of many different media companies by an increasingly small number of conglomerates.

Because these six giant companies own almost all of the country's most prominent media outlets, including television and radio stations, newspapers, film studios, cable companies, and magazines, the values and perspectives of the parent company naturally filter down to its numerous subsidiaries. "One need not be a devotee of conspiracy theories," writes media law expert Charles Tillinghast, "to understand that journalists, like other human beings, can judge where their interests lie, and what risks are and are not prudent, given the desire to continue to eat and feed the family" (2000, p. 145). Imagine you are a reporter for ABC's *Good Morning America* (owned by Disney) and you are tasked with providing viewers with a "sneak peek" at a new Disney theme park. Now imagine you do not like the place. How likely are you to give the park a negative review, knowing that "Mickey Mouse" signs your paycheck (Jackson, 2013)? Now, a bit more significantly, you are still a reporter for ABC, but on the hard news side. How deeply do you dig into allegations of lax safety inspections at Disney's theme parks brought to you by a whistleblower? What do you do? You want to do your job as well as you can, but you need a paycheck. This is only one of the many ethical issues facing modern journalists. You can read about another in the box "The Role of the Photojournalist."

◢ ETHICAL COMMUNICATION

The Role of the Photojournalist

In 2012, *New York Post* photographer R. Umar Abbasi was in the city's subway when a homeless man fatally pushed another man, Ki-Suck Han, onto the tracks in front of an oncoming train. The photographer captured a horrific, now-famous picture of the man "about to die," which became the *Post's* front-page image. The photo's publication fueled a national debate about the media in America. *New York Times* media critic David Carr wrote, "The *Post* cover treatment neatly embodies everything that people hate and suspect about the news media business: not only are journalists bystanders, moral and ethical eunuchs who don't intervene when danger or evil presents itself, but perhaps they secretly root for its culmination" (2012).

In 1993, South African photographer Kevin Carter traveled to southern Sudan to report on a devastating famine. He took a haunting photo of a starving Sudanese baby girl, weakened and crouched over, and a vulture lurking in the background. Carter soon came under severe global criticism for failing to help the girl. The *St. Petersburg Times,* for example, editorialized, "The man adjusting his lens to take just the right frame of her suffering might just as well be a predator, another vulture on the scene" (in Ricchiardi, 1999). But was the photojournalist truly a vulture, or was he using his talent to inform the world of a severe humanitarian crisis?

In both instances, media published disturbing photos that raised important questions about the responsibility of the professionals who took them. The *Times* condemned the publication of the *Post's* subway

A powerful but controversial media image.

image but published Carter's vulture photo, suggesting that one image was unethical and the other was newsworthy and valuable. But are they that ethically different?

Most good journalists would argue that they are. As soon as a journalist embeds him- or herself in a story, that event becomes a constructed story, a fiction. In the case of Carter, the plight of the Sudanese people was an already unfolding story; he was doing his job by reporting on it. Abbasi, on the other hand, took part in a story by failing to assist. Had he helped Han, there would have been no story. Had Carter helped the Sudanese child, the story would have been the same—the starvation in southern Sudan would have persisted, but the image that brought much attention to the issue would not have been published. What do you think?

Critics contend that this narrowing of views limits the diversity of voices, in contradiction to what Americans have long considered essential to their ability to govern themselves. Democracy is predicated on the idea that people, in order to ensure a free society, need a wide range of information on which to base their judgments. That information is supposed to come not only from *a multitude of tongues,* but from *a variety of antagonistic voices.* If we do not receive a wide range of relevant, objective information about matters big and small—unemployment, gun safety, gay rights, women's issues, war and peace, the economy, the cost of college, anything that touches how we live our lives—how are we supposed to make good decisions or vote intelligently on these issues?

The second force reshaping mass communication is **hyper-commercialism**, the increasing amount of commercial content appearing in the media. It appears most obviously simply as more advertising, but also as the mixing of commercial and non-commercial content. Research suggests that the average American is exposed to as many as 5,000 commercial messages a day, up from about 500 a day in the 1970s (Johnson, 2009). And your own viewing tells you that from 20 to 25 percent of a prime-time television hour is devoted to commercials, and you no doubt have seen more than a few of the Internet's more than 5 trillion annual ads, up from 200 billion in 1997 (Lunden, 2012). Amidst this **clutter**, or commercial overload, advertisers must find new ways to grab our attention. One way is to make sure we can't ignore their messages, fast-forward through them, or change the channel. Among their strategies are product placement, brand entertainment, ambient advertising, and synergy.

Product placement occurs when ads are placed in and become part of media content. For example, if you've seen the movie *The Avengers,* you've seen paid-for placements, that is, commercials, for ABC, Acura, aussieBum, Black Sabbath, Bose, CNN, Colantotte, C-SPAN, Dr. Pepper, Farmers Insurance, Harley-Davidson, Jansport, LG, MAC Cosmetics, MSNBC, NASA, NY1, Oracle, Plantronics, Rimowa, and Southwest Airlines, among others. Today, there are very few feature films that do not include product placements. Big blockbusters are particularly welcoming to product placement since they are extremely expensive to make, and their producers look to advertisers to supplement production costs. And it's not just movies; it's all commercial media. Globally, advertisers spend just under $11 billion a year on placements in TV, film, online and mobile content, video games, and music, with the United States, Brazil, and Mexico accounting for three-quarters of that amount (PQ Media, 2015). "We have come to an intersection of media and content where marketing is content and content is marketing," explains Angela Courtin, marketing chief at Relativity Media, a movie studio that actively encourages the blending of advertising and content (in Downey, 2015).

Like product placement, **brand entertainment** is a fusion of entertainment and content; however, brand entertainment occurs when content is consciously developed around a specific brand. Director Ridley Scott's movie *The Polar Bears* was created by Coke as a way to capitalize on the popularity of its well-known holiday television commercials. *Battleship*, *G. I. Joe*, *Stretch Armstrong*, and the many installments of *Transformers* are movies based on Hasbro toys. The *Pirates of the Caribbean* movies and *Mr. Toad's Wild Ride* are based on amusements at Disneyland.

Ambient advertising, placing ads in natural or otherwise nontraditional settings, is yet another strategy to make sure we can't miss the message. Logos imprinted on beach sand, stairs

hyper-commercialism The increasing amount of commercial content appearing in the media.

clutter Commercial overload.

product placement When ads are placed in and become part of media content.

brand entertainment When content is developed around brands.

ambient advertising Ads in otherwise nontraditional settings.

Is *The Fast and the Furious* a movie or a very long commercial?

in public buildings made to look like stacks of newly released books, and brand logos temporarily tattooed onto real people's foreheads are all examples of ambient advertising.

synergy Promotion of a single media product across multiple real-world and media platforms.

Synergy occurs when a number of different companies team up to sell one product across a number of real-world and media channels. Let's say Disney releases a children's film. The movie plays in theaters; its characters appear in Disney's programming on the Disney-owned ABC television network and Disney-owned cable channels; Disney-owned book and magazine companies publish movie-based stories; and the actors are interviewed at courtside during Disney-owned ESPN's broadcasts of college basketball. At the same time, McDonald's markets character-based toy figures in its happy meals; JC Penney sells clothes and bedding covered with the film's images; Toys "R" Us supplies the games, accessories, and toys based on the movie; and Welch's markets fruit snacks in the shape of the characters. While there is only one product, the original film, many companies take part in its promotion, marketing, and selling.

audience fragmentation Splintering of media audiences into increasingly smaller units.

Audience fragmentation is a third force reshaping media. It occurs as audiences become more segmented (less "mass") and media content is increasingly specialized to reach those fragments. For example, before television, radio commanded a national audience. When television came along, radio was forced to become more localized, so radio content had to be specialized in order to reach different audiences in a thousand different towns and cities. Today we have radio formats like talk, country, classic rock, and dozens of others. Cable did the same thing to television, offering hundreds of channels compared to the three or four stations offered by over-the-air television in the pre-cable days. As the content became more specialized, giving viewers many more choices, the audience fragmented among those choices. Networks like ABC, NBC, and CBS were now sharing audience with HBO and Showtime. And today, these outlets are sharing audience with streaming services like Netflix and Amazon Prime, who themselves are sharing audience with YouTube, making the audiences for each smaller and more specialized.

globalization Increasing worldwide operation of media companies.

A fourth reality characteristic of contemporary media is **globalization**. When media companies operate globally, the world becomes a smaller place—at least in terms of communication. As newer technologies render national borders invisible, media companies and individuals alike can communicate just as easily with people in faraway China as they can with those next door. For example, virtually every US film and video production company, including HBO and the Discovery Networks, maintains operations in Asia (Frater, 2014). The American situation comedy *Friends* is the world's most popular television show for helping people learn English (Hofs, 2012), and in 2014 *Transformers: Age of Extinction* was the number one movie in Russia, China, Columbia, and South Africa. *Godzilla* was number one in Egypt. *The Lego Movie* was the box office winner in the United Kingdom, and *Maleficent* was the most-seen movie in Brazil and Mexico (Sedghi, 2014).

cultural imperialism Influencing other countries through non-local mass media.

Many critics, here and abroad, worry that countries with the most powerful media structures become **culturally imperialistic**, "invading" and influencing other countries through mass media. What impact, they ask, do Western media have on the traditions and values of other cultures? As global mass communication becomes easier, is it possible that the messages and meanings created by Western media will shape the perceptions of other nations? Other nations do indeed think so; they worry about globalization's impact. For example, American hip-hop music is outlawed on Jamaica's broadcasting system; in Iran, where all Western music is banned from radio and television, a person can be arrested for uploading music videos based on Western tunes like Pharrell's *Happy*. Communist China and democratic South Korea both limit the number of American movies that can appear on their theater screens, and there is an official movement afoot in Russia to prohibit the use of American words such as *bar*, *restaurant*, *sale*, *performance*, and *trader*, punishable by fines and loss of jobs (Pomerantsev, 2013).

These young Iranians were jailed for their YouTube *Happy* dance.

The final force reshaping the media industries and therefore mass communication is *convergence*. As you saw earlier in the chapter, this erosion of distinction between media is a dramatic development in how we interact with media and their content. Technologies continue to merge, making data and communication access more efficient. But what does this do to existing technologies whose functions migrate to newer, converged technologies? Most obviously, they must find new business models. More music is being sold now than at any time in history, yet the traditional recording companies, late to accept legal downloading, have seen their profits dwindle over the last decade. More people read the news than ever before, but because they do so online, on smartphones, and on tablets, traditional newspapers are losing money at a record pace. The same is true for the traditional magazine and book industries. But what may be bad for the big record labels may be good for music fans, as there is more music available for less cost. What may be bad for newspapers may be good for news readers, as there is more news from more sources at lower cost. What may be bad for the magazine and book industries may be good for readers, as there are more magazines and books published every year than ever before. But how much good music will be made when artists cannot earn a living from the new music environment? How much good journalism will be undertaken if everyone reads the news online for free and our traditional sources of tough, hard-hitting journalism—newspapers and magazines—go out of business? And what does a "good book" mean when anyone with a laptop can become a novelist by self-publishing on the Internet?

Convergence is a remarkable advance for mass communication but a frightening advance for the mass media industries. In fact, all the traditional media industries are undergoing *disruptive transition*; that is, their long-standing business models are under constant attack from digital alternatives as they attempt to transform how they operate. For those hoping for careers in the media, though, this might actually be a good thing, as you can read in the box "Finding a Career in the Media."

COMMUNICATION IN THE WORKPLACE

Finding a Career in the Media

There's little doubt that the media industries are undergoing massive change, and you've probably heard that media jobs are disappearing. That's partly true. But *every* industry employs mass communication professionals. Beyond the obvious examples of advertising and public relations, every good-size corporation and nonprofit has its media producers—its writers, photographers, videographers, Web masters, and social media managers. And then there's the Internet itself. Employment in American Internet businesses has increased 54 percent since 2009, overtaking broadcast and cable television, magazines, and radio as top employers of media professionals (Johnson, 2012).

What, then, is the best way to find a mass communication career? Industry professionals suggest these practices:

1. **Know your options**—The possibilities are nearly limitless. There are millions of mass communication jobs that are not part of a newspaper or radio or television station.
2. **Think globally**—Companies increasingly communicate across borders. Be interculturally aware to make yourself more attractive to organizations, and be willing to travel or relocate.
3. **Develop a specialty**—A specialty gives you direction and makes you more attractive to potential employers.
4. **Work on your writing**—Solid writing skills will give you an advantage over other job seekers.
5. **Network**—As in any industry, networking makes finding work in the media far easier. Join media-oriented student and professional organizations, and take internships in media companies. Learn as much as you can and make contacts.
6. **Stand out**—Know what's going on in the world of mass communication. Read trade journals like *Broadcasting & Cable, Editor & Publisher, Advertising Age,* and *Variety*. Being in the know will show your potential employer that you are committed to your field.
7. **Remember the basics**—The old rules apply when searching for a job in the media. Keep your resume simple, highlighting your most impressive skills and accomplishments. Dress well for your interview, stay positive, ask questions about the company, and send a thank-you note immediately afterward.

THUMBNAIL THEORY

Cultivation Theory

Media have long-term, gradual but significant effects because their stories form mainstream society's widely shared conceptions of reality. We live in terms of the stories we tell, and media tell them all through news, drama, and advertising to almost everybody most of the time.

Theories of Mass Communication

Given the importance of mass communication and its many forms, you shouldn't be surprised that there are quite a few well-developed theories regarding the meaning-making relationship between mass media and their audiences. We'll address four theories that have had important and ongoing influence on our current thinking about the relationship between people and the media: cultivation theory, social cognitive theory, critical cultural theory, and social responsibility theory.

Cultivation theory is sometimes referred to as *cultivation analysis* or the *cultivation hypothesis*. Initially developed by George Gerbner in the 1970s, it originally dealt specifically with television effects, although its explanation of how we come to understand our world has been extended to other media. Here, though, we'll stay with Dr. Gerbner's original thinking. Cultivation theorists argue that television has long-term effects that are gradual but significant, for example, an increased belief that the world is a cruel place. They say viewers who watch a significant amount of television develop the **Mean World Syndrome**; that is, they begin to view the world as a much more dangerous place than it really is. Because television shows violence and crime in much higher levels than exist in the actual world, heavy viewers cultivate a reality that is far different from that of light viewers. As Gerbner explained, "The repetitive pattern of television's mass-produced messages and images forms the mainstream of the common symbolic environment that cultivates the most widely shared conceptions of reality. We live in terms of the stories we tell—stories about what things exist, stories about how things work, and stories about what to do—and television tells them all through news, drama, and advertising to almost everybody most of the time" (Gerbner et al., 1978, p. 178).

Like any theory, cultivation analysis comes with some criticisms. Some feel the theory doesn't take into account the social aspects of television viewing, like the consumer's socioeconomic background, ethnicity, developmental stages, gender, family attitudes, race, and viewing contexts. For instance, families that consume television critically by discussing the content they watch may significantly reduce the cultivation effect among their members.

Social cognitive theory was created by psychologist Albert Bandura in the early 1960s at a time of widespread concern about the effects of televised violence. Bandura's theory suggests that people learn behaviors, or **model** them, simply by observing them. This behavior can manifest itself through either *imitation* or *identification*. **Imitation** occurs when the observed behavior is directly replicated. For example, if a teenage girl watches her favorite *Gossip Girl* character buy a specific Coach bag and she, in turn, buys the same product, she has imitated what she has seen. **Identification** is copying the observed behavior to a degree but not replicating it. So instead of buying the same Coach bag, the girl might buy a pair of UGGs—copying the character's brand-name purchasing behavior, if not the exact purchase.

Bandura's most famous social cognitive theory experiment is his 1965 "Bobo doll" study (see chapter 2.) He showed nursery school children a short film in which a character was either rewarded for aggression or punished for those same behaviors. After viewing, each child was given a "free play" period in a room full of toys of all kinds, including an inflatable punching doll. Children who saw the filmed aggression rewarded showed more aggressive activity during the play period, and those who saw it punished displayed less. Social cognitive theory concludes that not only can children learn simply by observation, but when they see a forbidden behavior rewarded or even unpunished, there is a greater likelihood that the learned behavior will be enacted. By the same token, if they see a behavior punished, they are less likely to enact it (although they have still learned it and later, if there is sufficient incentive, they can indeed enact what they learned observationally). Some criticisms of social cognitive theory include the argument that not everyone who sees something in the media models what they've seen and that it may overestimate the power of mass media and underestimate that of individuals' own meaning-making abilities.

Mean World Syndrome The more media people consume, the meaner they think the world to be.

THUMBNAIL THEORY

Social Cognitive Theory

People learn, or model, behaviors by observing them. Modeling can occur as imitation, when observed behaviors are directly replicated, or through identification, when behaviors are copied to a degree but not replicated.

modeling Learning through observation.

imitation Direct replication of observed behavior.

identification Copying of observed behavior, but in a more general manner.

THUMBNAIL THEORY

Critical Cultural Theory

Our social world is the product of the interaction between structure and agency, and although media industries tend to support structure and would seem to have the advantage in the mass communication process, audiences have power in agency, that is, their beliefs, values and behaviors.

Neo-Marxism Elites maintain influence over society by control of the superstructure.

Another theory with significant contemporary influence is **critical cultural theory,** based in **Neo-Marxist theory**. While traditional Marxism argued that elites control the public through their ownership of the *base,* or the means of production (if you want a job, you do what you're told), Neo-Marxism says that in contemporary society elites exert their influence not through ownership of the farms and factories, but by their control of the *superstructure,* or the culture—institutions like the schools, religion, and media. "Media provide the elite with a convenient, subtle, yet highly effective means of promoting worldviews favorable to their interests," explain Stanley Baran and Dennis Davis. Critical cultural theory sees the media as "a public arena in which cultural battles are fought and a dominant, or hegemonic [imposed from above], culture is forged and promoted. Elites dominate these struggles because they start with important advantages. Opposition is marginalized, and the status quo is presented as the only logical, rational way of structuring society. Values favored by elites are subtly woven into and promoted by the narratives of popular programs" (Baran and Davis, 2015, p. 23).

Consider the war in Iraq and the global financial crisis of 2008. In both instances the media failed to do their jobs, first, by failing to question the government's motives and evidence before entering the war ("Never before has a nation had 100 percent confidence about its intelligence with 0 percent information," wrote senior CIA analyst Melvin Goodman, 2013), and second, in not properly investigating the unethical practices of major financial institutions on Wall Street before the big crash ("The watchdogs barked, but often off in the distance, and then went on their way," said press critic Greg Mitchell, 2009, p. 16). Neither government officials nor bankers felt the true backlash of these devastating events.

More recently, the most-reported news story in 2014 on the three commercial TV networks (ABC, CBS, and NBC) was the weather. The Winter Olympics and North Korean anger over the movie *The Interview* were also in the top 20. Although 2014 saw a historic mid-term election in which Republicans took control of both houses of Congress, and despite the fact that it was a year of record income inequality and swelling ranks of the poor, "Politics was practically purged from the nightly news agenda in 2014. Never have midterm elections been treated with such disdain. And never have federal domestic policy debates made such little news. Not a single White House nor Capitol Hill correspondent qualified for the Top 20 ranking of reporters. The economy logged record lows [of coverage] too" (ADT Research, 2015). Who benefits, ask Neo-Marxist theorists, when important electoral and economic news is absent from people's media diets?

These scholars can explain how and why the media industries failed the public in these instances, but critical cultural theory suggests what the public can do to make sure those failures do not happen again. As you read in Chapter 2, critical cultural theorists claim that the reality of our social world is the product of the interaction between *structure* (the social world's rules, norms, and beliefs) and *agency* (how we act and interact in that world). They believe that media industries support structure; after all, media shape our beliefs and

Media Conduct

The assumptions of social responsibility theory are based on **libertarian thought**; that is, people cannot effectively govern themselves without access to professionally and responsibly created and disseminated information.

Do you feel the media generally meet the standards of social responsibility? Do they provide us with the news and entertainment content we need in order to make reasonable, effective, even humane decisions? A recent national survey of American adults demonstrated that only 40 percent—an all-time low—had a great deal or fair amount of trust in the mass media, compared with 53 percent in 1997 (McCarthy, 2014). Further, 18- to 34-year-olds are likely to describe the news media with terms like *garbage, lies, one-sided, propaganda, repetitive,* and *boring,* and they indicate that being informed about the news is not important (Poindexter, 2012). Do you agree? Why or why not? If so, what will you do about it?

---

values and guide us toward specific behaviors. In other words, they structure our daily lives. But we have agency. We have our beliefs and values; we engage in those behaviors. Yes, argue critical cultural theorists, there is a *dialectic,* an ongoing struggle or debate, a tug-of-war between the media and the public as each works to make meaning. But if we simply accept that the media have more advantages in the mass communication process than do their audiences, media will have no incentive to provide us with better information and entertainment. But if we believe that structure is only as powerful as we allow it to be and that we set the standards through our media-use expectations and choices, our agency becomes our power. We, however, have to be aware that we have that power, and that's the lesson of Chapter 11, Media Literacy. For now, though, we need to keep in mind that in the American political and economic system, media industries have a responsibility to the public; that is why we grant them the protection of the First Amendment. You can read more about their obligations in the box "Media Conduct."

Earlier, in our discussion of personally responsible communication, we focused on the need for audiences to think critically about media's impact. Here we turn to the responsibilities of the media industries to their audiences. **Social responsibility theory** argues that media industries and professionals must serve the public if they are to be free of government control. It is a **normative theory**, which means that it sets standards (norms) to guide media conduct that are based on society's *ideal* values, and it is against those standards that the public should judge the media's performance. For American media, social responsibility theory identifies eight basic assumptions regarding the operation of media outlets and the performance of media professionals. Denis McQuail (1987) outlined these basic principles:

- Media have obligations to society that they must fulfill.
- They should meet them by setting high or professional standards of informativeness, truth, accuracy, objectivity, and balance.

libertarian thought
A self-governing people require access to responsibly created and disseminated information.

THUMBNAIL THEORY

Social Responsibility Theory

In exchange for the great deal of freedom they enjoy, media industries must meet certain standards of socially responsible operation, not the least of which is to put service above profit.

normative theory
Setting standards to guide media conduct based on society's ideal values.

- Because they accept this duty, media should be self-regulating within the framework of law and established institutions.
- Media should avoid whatever might lead to crime, violence, or civil disorder or give offense to minority groups.
- The media should reflect the diversity of their society, giving access to various points of view and to rights of reply.
- The people have a right to expect high standards of performance, and if not met, official intervention can be justified to secure the public good.
- Media professionals should be accountable to society as well as to the financial bottom line.

Review of Learning Objectives

10.1 Describe the differences between interpersonal and mass communication.

Interpersonal communication involves two or a few people, while mass communication can involve millions of communicators. In interpersonal communication, feedback is direct and immediate; in mass communication, it is inferential and delayed. The message in interpersonal communication is immediately alterable; in mass communication, once sent, it is unalterable. Messages in interpersonal communication are flexible; in mass communication they tend to be formulaic.

10.2 Discuss the relationship between culture, communication, and mass media.

Our personal sense of self and our understanding of our world and others in it are developed and influenced by a culture whose meanings are shaped to a large degree by mass media. Media tell us stories about ourselves and we, in turn, act out the roles we play in those stories. But we can contest the cultural meanings; we can make individually meaningful choices. But we are never really free from media's influence, as we share the culture with others who are making meaning from media just as we do.

10.3 Identify the characteristics of media consumers.

Contemporary media consumers are platform agnostic, media multitaskers, and are susceptible to media addiction.

10.4 Identify the characteristics of media industries.

American media industries are overwhelming for-profit businesses, and that reality affects their content. The nature and operation of these industries are currently being shaped and reshaped by several forces, including concentration of ownership, hyper-commercialism, audience fragmentation, globalization, and convergence.

10.5 Describe several theories associated with mass communication.

Given the vastness and complexity of mass communication, it is obvious that there are hundreds of theories that attempt to help us understand that process. Four that hold great contemporary interest are cultivation theory, explaining how media realities become people's realities; social cognitive theory, explaining how people learn to model or copy what they see in the media; critical cultural theory, which attempts to explain how media industries dominate meaning making; and social responsibility theory, establishing standards for the operation of our media system against which its performance can be judged.

Key Terms

mass communication 210
medium 211
convergence 212
inferential feedback 213
formualic 214
platform agnostic 219
media multitaskers 219
aliteracy 220
media addiction 220
concentration of ownership 221
hyper-commercialism 223
clutter 223
product placement 223
brand entertainment 223
ambient advertising 223
synergy 224
audience fragmentation 224
globalization 224
culturally imperialistic 224
cultivation theory 226
Mean World Syndrome 227
social cognitive theory 227
model 227
imitation 227
identification 227
critical cultural theory 228
Neo-Marxist theory 228
libertarian thought 229
social responsibility theory 229
normative theory 229

Questions for Review

1. What are the distinctions between interpersonal and mass communication? What are their similarities?

2. What are platform agnosticism and media multitasking?

3. What is concentration, and what are its likely effects on media content?

4. What is hyper-commercialism and what are its likely effects on media content?

5. What are product placement, brand entertainment, ambient advertising, and synergy?

6. What is audience fragmentation, and what are its likely effects on media content?

7. What is globalization and what are its likely effects on media content?

8. What is convergence and what are its likely effects on media content?

9. What are the basic arguments of cultivation theory, social cognitive theory, critical cultural theory, and social responsibility theory?

10. How are libertarian thought and social responsibility theory related?

Questions for Discussion

1. While it is impossible to deny that audiences are the product produced and sold in the commercial media business, there is disagreement about the relative influence of advertisers and those audiences. Yes, advertisers buy audiences, so their interests would seem to be most important to media companies; but if audiences weren't served by those companies, there would be nothing to sell to advertisers. When a television network is trying to decide what to air or a magazine what stories to run, whose interests do you think they consider first? Defend your answer.

2. Answer these questions:

   a. *Do you believe that most people are just looking out for themselves?*

   b. *Do you think that you can't be too careful in dealing with people?*

   c. *Do you think that most people would take advantage of you if they got the chance?*

   These questions form the basis of cultivation theory's argument that the more television you watch, the more mean you think the world to be (the Mean World Syndrome). Does this relationship hold for you? If not, why not? If yes, can you explain that outcome in terms of cultivation theory?

3. Are you generally satisfied with the media's performance, or are you generally unhappy? Why do you respond as you do? Can you draw distinctions between the different media industries, for example, maybe you think the movie and video game industries are just great, but newspapers and popular music continue to fail you? Defend your answers using the principles of social responsibility theory.

Media Literacy

On the first day of media literacy class, your professor explains that throughout the semester, you will carefully examine television shows, music lyrics, films, advertisements, and websites. This will be easy and fun, you think. The professor devotes the first three lectures to Disney films, movies you grew up watching and loving. She talks about the racial stereotyping in *Aladdin*, the gender stereotyping in *Beauty and the Beast*, and the historical inaccuracies in *Pocahontas*. Suddenly, you find yourself a bit put off. How could anyone criticize the hit movies of an iconic, kid-friendly company like Disney—the "Happiest Place on Earth?"

But as the semester rolls on, you begin to realize not only how much media you consume, but how passively you do, without a lot of critical thought. During a break, you return home to find your parents working at their computers and your nine-year-old sister watching a Beyoncé video, emulating the star. What would have been no big deal to you a semester ago now has you a little annoyed and eager to talk about it with the family. You watch with your sister for a few minutes, explaining how the lighting, sound, camera movements, and editing make what the singer is doing seem particularly glamorous and exciting. You further explain that this is a grown woman, not a little kid. Then you turn the video off and sit down with your sister *and* parents. For an hour you discuss the meaning of the lyrics, and the effects and overall social implications of videos like this on the behaviors and attitudes of young girls. Your parents are stunned.

The point of media literacy, the subject of this chapter, is to promote conscious and critical consumption of the media content we see and hear daily. As we learned in the last chapter, media have a pervasive influence on our culture. American adults, on average, consume 12 hours and 14 minutes of media a day, including watching television, browsing the Internet, and using mobile devices like smartphones and tablets (eMarketer, 2014). There is little question that people in our culture, especially millennials (those born after 1980), define themselves and their generation by their technologies (Taylor and Keeter, 2010).

With so much of our individual identities and our culture's values shaped by media narratives, it is important that we create a basis for evaluating those messages. We need to be media-literate consumers. Media educator Len Masterman explains, "In contemporary societies the media are self-evidently important creators and mediators of social knowledge. An understanding of the ways in which the media represent reality, the techniques they employ, and the ideologies embedded within their representations ought to be an entitlement of all citizens and future citizens in a democratic society" (2013, p. x).

Learning Objectives

11.1   Identify the assumptions and elements of media literacy.

11.2   Identify the skills necessary to practice media literacy.

11.3   Describe the importance of media literacy in identity formation.

11.4   Explain the cultural impact and importance of media literacy.

What Is Media Literacy?

Remember your high school English classes? You likely studied a number of novels and were asked to discuss what you read. You considered each novel's cultural relevance, the quality of the writing, the robustness of character development and narrative description, and of course, themes. In fact, for more than a century we have viewed reading, interpreting, and critically analyzing literary texts as an essential skill for an educated person. But in today's media culture, young people are spending more time not with novels but with other **media texts**—that is, content that comes from an ever-growing array of communication technologies such as the Internet, television, radio, video games, and smartphones and tablets. These have become the texts of choice for millennials and the following generation. As with literary texts, learning to critically and responsibly assess this new mediated content is key to the enhancement of our culture and ourselves. **Media literacy** is the ability to read, interpret, critically assess, and productively use media texts. The term is often used interchangeably with *media education*, which involves incorporating media analysis

media texts Content originating from communication technologies.

media literacy The ability to read, interpret, critically assess, and productively use media texts.

skills into learning environments such as school curricula or parenting. Our concern in this chapter, however, is strictly media literacy.

The idea of promoting media literacy is gaining momentum in light of our heavy media consumption habits. (The growth of the field has also created job opportunities, as you can read in the box "Careers in Media Literacy") There has been a particular focus on children's media literacy, as children represent an especially vulnerable media audience. Organizations such as the American Psychological Association and the American Academy of Pediatrics have developed guidelines outlining the ethical implications of marketing to children, arguing that they "lack the cognitive capacity to recognize advertising's persuasive intent"(Kunkel, 2004). Children are not as capable as adults in distinguishing fantasy from reality, nor can they always tell commercial from non-commercial content.

Young people are immersed in media, making media literacy critical to understanding our culture.

COMMUNICATION IN THE WORKPLACE

Careers in Media Literacy

Because the foundation of media literacy is critical thinking, it has obvious career value. Media literacy pioneer Art Silverblatt explains, "Many companies now place a value on employees who have the ability to interpret and construct messages using the different 'languages' of media, such as film and television, audio, and the Internet" (2010). But the majority of careers specifically in media literacy are in the field of education. Silverblatt lists three educational environments where the demand for media literacy professionals is predicted to grow:

1. **Elementary and secondary teaching**—All 50 states list media literacy among their desired academic outcomes.
2. **College and university teaching**—Hundreds of American institutions of higher education teach either

selected classes or full curricula in media literacy. Media literacy programs are increasingly appearing in departments beyond Communication, Mass Communication, and Media Studies, such as Education.

3. **Educational consulting**—Enterprising and entrepreneurial students can develop consulting careers in media literacy. Dr. Silverblatt provides these suggestions of ways to consult:
   - Conduct professional development workshops for teachers.
   - Develop classroom materials for teachers.
   - Introduce media literacy to groups not reached through the conventional school system, such as parents. Many parents' groups hire speakers to conduct programs they consider vital to successful parenting, including how to contend with media messages.

Consider, too, the importance of media literacy in identity formation and in the process of meaning making, which we will discuss in more detail later in the chapter. For example, researchers from a variety of social sciences have demonstrated a significant correlation between media, negative body image, and eating disorders. Media messages tell females in particular that they must be thin and beautiful to achieve social acceptability. The following statistics speak to the power of these messages: 80 percent of American girls have been on diets by age 10; one-third of American boys and the majority of girls between 6 and 8 years old wish their bodies were thinner; and almost 1.3 million adolescent American girls have anorexia—a rate that rose 119 percent between 1999 and 2006 alone (Pai and Schryver, 2015).

If culture shapes our perceptions of ourselves, and we live in a heavily mass-mediated culture, it's clear that media contribute to the identities and meanings we create. Being media literate means asking the right questions about the content to which we are exposed. This questioning, in turn, encourages healthier attitudes about who we are, our roles and responsibilities in society, and our importance in the lives of those close to us.

Media Literacy Scholarship

The systematic study of media literacy is a relatively new addition to communication scholarship. "Almost all the writing about media literacy was published in the last three decades," explains media scholar James Potter (2010, p. 675). In reviewing that body of work, Professor Potter was able "to identify four common themes where there is general agreement across the writings about media literacy" (p. 681):

1. "The mass media have the potential to exert a wide range of potentially negative effects on individuals . . . [T]he media also offer a range of potentially positive effects." You read much about media effects in the previous chapter.

2. "The purpose of media literacy is to help people protect themselves from the potentially negative effects. The purpose of becoming more media literate is to gain greater control over influences in one's life, particularly the constant influence from mass media." For example, media literacy programs demonstrating the sexual objectification of women in the media can produce significant effects on cognitive, attitudinal, and behavioral responses to advertising. Such programs help women shield themselves against these potentially harmful representations (Reichert et. al., 2007).

3. "Media literacy must be developed. No one is born media literate." There are numerous curricula for people of all ages, designed to build those skills (for example, Christ, 2006). This chapter will introduce you to the approach taken by one US-based media literacy professional group, the National Association for Media Literacy Education.

4. "Media literacy is multi-dimensional. The media constantly influence people in many ways—cognitively, attitudinally, emotionally, physiologically, behaviorally—both directly as individuals as well as indirectly

through other people, institutions, and culture. Therefore, increasing one's media literacy requires development along [these] several different dimensions." For example, in an extensive review of the literature on **media literacy interventions**—efforts to build specific media literacy skills—Se Hoon Jeong and his colleagues (2012) showed that these activities produced positive effects on media knowledge, criticism, perceived realism, media influence, beliefs about behavior, attitudes, self-efficacy, and actual behavior.

Professor Jeong's research team, after examining scores of media literacy efforts, could confidently argue that media literacy interventions are "an effective approach for reducing potentially harmful effects of media messages. Intervention effects were found across divergent topics for diverse audiences, for a broad range of media-related (e.g., knowledge) and behavior-related (e.g., attitudes and behaviors) outcomes. . . . Intervention effects did not vary according to target age, the setting, audience involvement, and the topic, suggesting that interventions can be equally effective across a broad spectrum of settings (e.g., school, community, or lab), age groups, levels of audience involvement, and topics (e.g., alcohol, violence, and sex)" (Jeong, Cho, and Hwang, 2012, p. 464). Here we will look a bit deeper at three types of media literacy efforts.

PARENTAL MEDIATION. We'll start with kids and advertising. Moniek Buijzen and Patti Valkenburg (2005) showed that parental mediation could help elementary school children better deal with the flood of advertising that washes over them. They found that parents are able to reduce their children's level of materialism and the frequency with which they demand the products they see advertised by engaging in *active mediation*; that is, while watching with their children deliberately offering commentary and judgments about TV commercials and actively explaining the ads' techniques and selling intent. In addition, parents who engaged in *concept-oriented communication* with their kids were able not only to reduce their levels of materialism and demand for advertised products, but could also reduce the amount of parent-child conflict that often results from kids' demands for what they see on TV. Concept-oriented communication is simply actively discussing consumer matters with children, even away from the TV, helping them become more critical consumers. Both techniques were more effective in improving children's responses to advertising than was restricting their viewing. If these intervention techniques sound familiar, recall how you handled the opening scenario, when you went home to find your sister engrossed in a Beyoncé video.

Research such as this has contributed to **parental mediation theory**, which stresses taking an active role in managing and regulating children's interactions with media. Parental mediation theory argues that quality interpersonal communication between parents and children about media-related issues is a requisite part of what we now consider to be good parenting. This interaction can take a number of forms. Active mediation is talking with

media literacy interventions Attempts to build specific media literacy skills.

THUMBNAIL THEORY

Parental Mediation Theory

Parental mediation theory stresses the importance of parents taking an active role in managing and regulating their children's interactions with media. It involves *active mediation*—talking with children about media content; *restrictive mediation*—setting rules and limits on children's media use; and *co-viewing*—engaging in media consumption with children. A fourth form of parental mediation is Internet-specific: *participatory learning* involves parents actively engaging in Internet use with their children.

ETHICAL COMMUNICATION

Advertising to Children

One of the most controversial issues in media ethics is marketing to children. Children's brains are still developing, so they do not possess the same critical-thinking capacities as adults. Is it fair for them to be targets of sophisticated and powerful marketing? Those who oppose the practice argue that it is inherently unethical because of children's inability to distinguish fact from fiction. Some liken it to sending children into a commercial war zone without armor (Kunkel et al., 2004).

In the United States, children watch an average of 16,000 television commercials a year (A. C. Nielsen, 2015), and marketers spend approximately $17 billion annually in child-targeted advertising (Campaign for a Commercial-Free Childhood, 2015). By contrast, countries such as Australia, Canada, Great Britain, Sweden, and most other industrialized nations not only prohibit or seriously restrict advertising to children, but they also require media literacy education in schools. Media literacy cannot change the pace at which children's brains develop, but it can mitigate some of the adverse effects accompanying *womb-to-tomb marketing*, or lifelong exposure to advertisements. "It is a parent's worst nightmare," writes parenting expert K. J. Dell'Antonia. "Disney has almost certainly already colonized your 3-year-old's brain. McDonald's has planted a flag in there, too, along with My Little Pony and Pepsi and even Toyota. Preschoolers recognize brand names and symbols, and they are increasingly willing and able to make judgments about products and people based on associations with those brands" (2010). Social science has not only demonstrated children's familiarity with product branding, but it has also discovered a strong link between that familiarity and childhood obesity (McClure, 2012).

Do you think advertising to children is ethical?

Do you think advertising to children is ethical? Before you answer, imagine that you have two children, ages four and six. Now imagine that a big ad agency has offered you the chance to design online video games that reward children for finding hidden characters from a sugar cereal called Fluffy Yummies. The reward (which you will make easily attainable) is a two-minute video featuring the singing Fluffy Yummy band. Do you take the job? Why or why not?

children about media content, as we just saw in the Buijzen and Valkenburg research. *Restrictive mediation*, as the name suggests, is setting rules and limits on children's media use, for example controlling how much screen time they might have in a given day, or limiting which programs they can watch or which websites they can visit. *Co-viewing* is when parents engage in media consumption with their children, for example watching television, reading a magazine, or going to the movies together. There is also an Internet-specific form of parental mediation, *participatory learning*. It acknowledges that while the Net can indeed be a risky place for children, parents, by engaging in Internet use and other activities such as searching for information, gaming, and social networking, can strengthened their relationship with their kids while teaching them better Internet habits, boosting their creativity, and even enriching their cognitive development (Clark, 2011). You can read about ethical questions surrounding aiming commercials at kids in the box "Advertising to Children."

BODY-IMAGE INTERVENTION. But remember, media literacy isn't just for kids. Janelle Coughlin and Cynthia Kalodner attempted a media literacy intervention with college-age girls who were at high risk for eating disorders. They developed a media literacy program called ARMED (**A**cknowledging and **R**ejecting the **M**edia's influence on **E**ating and body image **D**isturbance), which uses videos and discussion to "explain and define the thin body ideal and provide a history of the thinning standards of beauty . . . to provide a useful

Media play a big role in the development of every individual's self-image.

model for understanding the process by which the media leads to disturbances in eating behaviors . . . to inform participants about the techniques used by the media to create ideal images, and to arm women with cognitive strategies for challenging the messages they receive from the media by focusing on the unreality of media images" (2006, pp. 38–39). Their research showed that eight weeks after the 90-minute intervention, "college women at high-risk for eating disorders reported significant reductions in body dissatisfaction, drive for thinness, feelings of ineffectiveness, and internalization of societal standards of beauty" when compared to those high-risk women who had not participated in the ARMED session (p. 40).

REFLECTION ON MEDIA CONTENT. Media literacy interventions can increase media's beneficial effects as well as limit its unwanted ones. A team of psychologists led by Tom Farsides encouraged adolescents to reflect on the personal meaning of what they were watching when exposed to prosocial (positive and inspirational) media characters. The researchers found that after engaging in this practice, adolescents showed higher levels of empathy and a greater inclination toward altruism (willingness to help others). "People are free to enjoy basking in the warm glow resulting from identifying with the heroism and saintliness regularly enacted by characters in the media," they wrote, "but that pleasant time in front of the screen could [also] lead to prosocial effects through encouragement to reflect on what's being watched rather than simply escaping into the content" (Farsides, Pettman, and Tourle, 2013, p. 6).

Using scenes from the 1989 movie *Dead Poets Society* (in which the teacher, played by Robin Williams, not only preaches empathy but practices it), the researchers demonstrated evidence of what they called the *Don Quixote Effect*— the "cognitive and emotional assumption of idealism"; in other words, reflection on media content can close the gap between identifying with fictional characters and emulating them in real life (p. 6). And just to prove that it wasn't only teenagers who could benefit from this simple intervention, they produced the same results with adults studying to become physicians in

In Miguel de Cervantes' famous novel *Don Quixote*, the idealistic title character inspires his sidekick, Sancho Panza. Similarly, media literacy interventions can encourage what's known as the Don Quixote Effect, the power of prosocial media content to foster empathy and idealism.

medical school after encouraging them to reflect on the values portrayed by fictional doctors in a medically themed TV show (*E.R.*) and movie (*Patch Adams*). Those who took the time to personally reflect on the characters' behaviors reported that they saw them "as role models that should, could, and would be personally emulated."

How were the participants in these two studies encouraged to reflect on what they had seen? In other words, what was the media literacy intervention? For adolescents, it was what the authors called a *reflection workbook*, a short publication that accompanied the screening that asked a series of questions about what the teens had just seen. For the medical students, the intervention was simply asking them to reflect.

Some Core Concepts of Media Literacy

Creating a foundation for becoming media literate requires knowledge of some key concepts. These concepts, which may seem obvious when you read them, typically go unacknowledged—or at least remain out of our consciousness—when we consume media texts:

- Media messages are manufactured.
- Commercial media are businesses.
- All media content expresses value messages; that is, it reflects or expresses the values of the content producer.

Media *messages are manufactured* by people whose values and priorities may or may not reflect yours. Additionally, editing content or writing scripts requires content producers to make decisions about what should or should not be included in a given narrative. Depending on the images and words they choose for a particular piece of content, the producers' version of the story can change dramatically. Evidence of this can be found in **agenda-setting theory**, the idea that media may not always tell us *what to think*, but they certainly tell us *what to think about*. For example, in television news the very presence or absence of a story dictates whether the story is important according to the news organization airing it. In fact, news is only news if news people tell us it's news. The amount of time dedicated to a story also makes a statement about the content producer's judgment of its value as a newsworthy piece. But these decisions may not be the ones you would have made, nor do they necessarily represent what's important to you. And what's more, they contain biases and perspectives that are embedded in the manufacture of the message. Recall what you read in Chapter 1—all communication is presentational; it is always someone's version of the facts or information. This is as true for mass communication as it is for interpersonal communication.

As content producers decide which stories are "important," their primary consideration is money. *Commercial media are businesses* and therefore their first priority is turning a profit, *not* informing or entertaining their audiences. This is, in and of itself, not a bad thing. We all have been moved by a great movie, delighted by a wonderful song, entranced by a funny television show, informed by a well-crafted news report. But it is important to remember that these outcomes are the byproduct of media companies' drive for profit. It is not their goal.

So whose values are presented in media? Simple—what we see is primarily the product of the media owners' and content producers' values. And whether or not we agree with any given message, it's clear that all *media contain value messages*. Consider the contents of fashion magazines like *Vogue, Elle,* and *Cosmopolitan*. First, each carries far more advertising than editorial content, suggesting that profit is their central concern. Second, look at the types of articles promoted on the covers—*10 Sexy Ways to Please Your Man, Make-up Tips That Will Make Your Friends Jealous, The Latest "Must Haves" in Your Wardrobe, The Ultimate 2-Week Diet: Lose 10 Pounds in 14 Days*. All of these articles relay someone's notions of what it means to be a woman. Apparently, women are consumed by pleasing men, how they dress and look, and being skinny. Is this really how women in our culture feel, and more to the point, how they should be presented? These themes extend to teen magazines as well, so it's no wonder that we have a self-esteem crisis among young women in our culture (Vandenbosch and Eggermont, 2012). Where are the articles on careers, culture, education, and health? Where are the essays on being happy with ourselves, aging gracefully, finding joy in consuming less? If they exist at all, they're exceedingly difficult to find.

Look at this magazine's cover lines. Whose values do they represent?

Media Literacy Questions

The National Association for Media Literacy Education (NAMLE) outlines several core principles of media literacy (Table 11.1; 2007a), and in doing so, suggests a number of key questions that we should ask when we analyze media messages. Asking these questions of media's texts—the television shows we watch, the music we listen to, the advertising that surrounds us—is a convenient way to begin engaging content, moving from passive consumption to proactive, critical consumption. NAMLE's key questions involve *audience and authorship*, *messages and meanings*, and *representations and realities* (2007b).

Let's use the popular video game *Call of Duty: Advanced Warfare* to address some of the concepts in Table 11.1. Looking first at the questions associated with **audience and authorship**, we learn that *Call of Duty: Advanced Warfare* is a first-person shooter video game, created and published by Activision. The platforms for which it was designed, that is, the different devices on which gamers can play *Advanced Warfare*, include laptop and desktop computers and dedicated

audience and authorship
Questions about authorship, purpose, economics, impact, and response.

Table 11.1 Core Principles of Media Literacy

KEY QUESTIONS TO ASK WHEN ANALYZING MEDIA MESSAGES		
Audience and Authorship	Authorship	Who made this message?
	Purpose	Why was this made? Who is the target audience (and how do you know)?
	Economics	Who paid for this?
	Impact	Who might benefit from this message? Who might be harmed by it? Why might this message matter to me?
	Response	What kinds of actions might I take in response to this message?
Messages and Meanings	Content	What is this about (and what makes you think that)? What ideas, values, information, and/or points of view are overt? Implied? What is left out of this message that might be important to know?
	Techniques	What techniques are used? Why were those techniques used? How do they communicate the message?
	Interpretations	How might different people understand this message differently? What is my interpretation of this and what do I learn about myself from my reaction or interpretation?
Representations and Reality	Content	When was this made? Where or how was it shared with the public?
	Credibility	Is this fact, opinion, or something else? How credible is this (and what makes you think that)? What are the sources of the information, ideas or assertions?

(Source: The National Association for Media Literacy Education [NAMLE], 2007b).

consoles like the various Sony PlaySta-
tions and X-Boxes. The game's huge
popularity and economic success have
allowed the *Call of Duty* series to become
its own franchise, much like the Harry
Potter books and movies. While there
are many versions of the game, this particular edition, *Advanced Warfare*, was
assigned an "M" rating by the ESRB, the
Entertainment Software Ratings Board.
Asking questions about *audience*, we
might learn that while the "M" rating
(Mature: 17 and older) indicates a more
mature target audience for *Advanced
Warfare*, young teens also make up a
large proportion of the game's players.

We recognize the use of digital technology to deliver realistic images of war, but how critical are we of the messages they convey and the motives of their creators?

Questions regarding *impact* and *response* are also essential because they force us
to be accountable in our assessment of the material. For example, we know that
the primary goal of Activision is not necessarily to entertain young kids or to
teach them important life lessons. It's to make money. That's not a bad thing, but
it is important in shaping our response to the game. So, how should we respond?
We might recognize that the content may be harmful to kids under a certain age,
and we might then proactively attempt to prevent or limit their exposure. We
might also decide that we have a responsibility to tell other people what we think,
especially those whose decisions affect younger audiences.

Analyzing **messages and meanings**—questions about content, techniques, and interpretations—we would recognize the use of sophisticated digital technology to deliver realistic images of war, including death, suffering,
blood and gore, and vulgar language. But we might also see that there are obvious absences—we never see the consequence of players' aggression or the points
of view of those not representing the "good guys." While players are given a simulated opportunity to kill people, they never face the consequences of real death
and therefore may become desensitized to the actual act, both from the perspective of the shooter and the victim. There may be as many interpretations of
this content as there are players, but you may come to the conclusion that the
folks at Activision—by the choices they made of what to include and what to
exclude—encourage some meanings and discourage others.

messages and meanings
Questions about content,
techniques, and
interpretations.

Finally, looking at **representations and reality** can be useful in assessing
the context and credibility of the video game. For example, the adult language is
not necessarily limited to the game itself. Because this is an online game, it is
possible for players to communicate with each other in different locations
around the world. This means that young kids can be exposed to the language of
adult players. We may see teenagers playing in the context of their safe, at-home
console boxes, but in actuality they may be involved in a violent, simulated,
global warzone. But the ESRB protects kids from this, right? After all, it assigns
the ratings. Asking questions about *credibility*, you would learn that the ESRB is

**representations and
reality** Questions about
content and credibility.

a part of the video game industry itself. This means that the ESRB answers to the video game companies, not to consumers. In other words, ratings may have less to do with protecting underage users than with deflecting criticism and keeping more stringent regulation at bay (Bushman and Cantor, 2003).

But, you protest, it's only play—you are not affected by violent video games. Actually, play is essential to youngsters' emotional and psychological development, but that's not the point. The point isn't even the effects of violent video games (although there is a wealth of scientific evidence of their impact, for example, Anderson et al., 2010). The point is that issues like this represent only a small portion of what can be revealed by asking the right questions about this and other media narratives. They force accountability in our media selections. We have a tendency to rationalize our individual media choices, asking, "What's *bad* about it?" Media-literate people, however, raise the more appropriate, meaningful question, "What's *good* about it?"

It is the responsibility of all of us to be critical of the messages we consume; otherwise, rather than creating our own meanings from these messages, we allow content producers to construct them for us. This approach to media literacy also tells us that questioning only *content* is not enough. We must also evaluate what we consume by considering not just the material itself but where it comes from, who creates the messages, the motives of the creators, and the platforms over which the messages are distributed.

What Does It Mean to Be Media Literate?

Now that you understand some of the key media literacy concepts and why media literacy is important, we can address the many elements that constitute being media literate.

Characteristics of Media-Literate People

Media scholar Art Silverblatt identified seven elements necessary for true media literacy (2008, pp. 4–5):

1. **Media-literate people develop critical thinking skills enabling them to make independent choices about which media content to select and how to interpret the information they receive through the media.** Our ability to question the content to which we are exposed, rather than passively absorbing it, means we ultimately make better choices for ourselves, and in the case of parents, for our children. Doing this means being able to interpret the messages we get through television, radio, film, Internet, smartphones, and advertising. Because these messages are prevalent in our lives and culture, the ability to question and sift out material that does not match our individual values makes us smarter consumers. Just as important, because most media content is **polysemic**, legitimately open to different interpretations (Hall, 1980), when we do

polysemic Legitimately open to different interpretations.

choose to consume a given piece of content, we should make sure we are applying the interpretation that best meets *our* needs. Sometime the meaning we make may be the one the producer encourages; in this case we make the intended or **preferred reading**. But we can also make our own meaning from media content by creating a personally meaningful interpretation that differs in some important ways from the one the producer intended. This is our **negotiated reading**. For example, you watch a humorous online weight-loss commercial featuring two women talking badly about themselves because they can't fit into last year's jeans. The producer wants you to not only laugh, but feel bad about your own weight. That's the intended or preferred meaning. You can create your own negotiated meaning by enjoying the humor—after all, it was funny—but read the spot as commentary on the pressures faced by today's women.

2. **Media-literate people understand the process of mass communication.** You'll notice that the Mass Communication chapter of this textbook (Chapter 10) precedes the Media Literacy chapter, and for good reason. In order to be media literate, it is important that you first understand how media industries work, the impact and priorities of those industries, and the relationship between audiences and the mass media. Now that you've read about the effects of mass media and the cultural role they play, you have a much more coherent understanding of the importance of media literacy.

3. **Media-literate people are aware of the impact of the media on both the individual (micro-level) and society (macro-level).** Media have effects. Otherwise, why would advertisers spend billions of dollars a year using the media to influence people? Why would the First Amendment of the US Constitution grant the media constitutional protection if media did not matter? Those effects can happen on an individual or a societal level. For example, we've seen a lot of criminal profiling in news, especially of people who make headlines by opening fire on crowds of people, as in the tragic shootings at Virginia Tech and in Aurora, Colorado; Columbine, Colorado; Newtown, Connecticut; and Charlestown, South Carolina. It seems media influence is always among the considerations in our attempts to explain why someone would shoot unarmed innocent people.

Let's return to our video game example, *Call of Duty: Advanced Warfare.* We've already established its adult themes, including war and killing. Retired US Army officer Lt. Col. David Grossman has been outspoken on the connection between video game violence and aggressive behavior. He believes that when we put violent games in the hands of our children, we are in effect teaching them to kill (Grossman, 2009). He argues that the US military trains soldiers to become desensitized to killing using a training program that employs violent games—and it works. In fact, ever since *Doom* introduced the **single-shooter game** (in which players wield weapons and view the killing from their

preferred reading The producer-intended meaning of a piece of media content.

negotiated reading Audience members' personally meaningful interpretation of a piece of media content.

single-shooter game Video game in which players wield weapons and view the killing from their personal point of view.

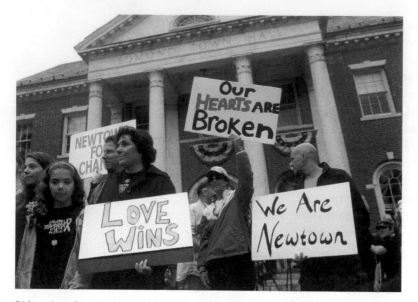

Did media influence play a role in the tragic events at Sandy Hook Elementary School in Newtown, Connecticut?

micro-level effects Media effects at the individual level.

macro-level effects Media effects at the cultural level.

personal point of view), games have become a primary teaching tool for military personnel likely to face warfare (Mead, 2013). So how do we as a culture rationalize the idea that these games have no impact on cognitively undeveloped kids when they appear to have an effect on adult soldiers? The idea that a teenager is going to run out and kill people after playing *Call of Duty: Advanced Warfare* is absurd and is not the point. Desensitizing kids to the idea of killing and torture, however, is. And understanding the role of these games in the life of any child and the overall cultural implications is critical.

Here we see the distinction between understanding media influences as individual (**micro-level**) and cultural (**macro-level**) **effects**. Yes, you (the micro level) may not run out and shoot someone after playing a violent video game, but you live in a world (the macro level) that is possibly more accepting of violence as a means of problem-solving and less troubled by the incidents of mass murder that happen all too frequently. The awareness of media effects speaks less to the idea that content *causes* people to commit crimes and more to the notion that we cannot simply rationalize our consumption choices away using the third-person effect (the idea that others are affected but I'm not; see Chapter 10). The truth is that all individuals are in some way influenced by media messages, and those effects are perpetuated in the culture. What is your answer to this question: Whom would you vote for, the candidate who wants to get tough on crime, or the one who wants to pay elementary schoolteachers more and reduce class size? How do you think most Americans would answer? Why do so many people think the world is a mean and dangerous place? For this reason, media-literate people consider not just the impact of media on individuals, but also on the culture as a whole.

4. **Media-literate people develop their own strategies for analyzing and discussing media messages.** Media-literate individuals know it's not enough to say "That stinks," or "Loved it," when evaluating media. For example, a common media literacy exercise is to come up with personally meaningful strategies for distinguishing good media messages (those which enhance our consuming experience) from poor media messages (those which lower our standards for consuming content). The struggle is to reconcile our subjectivity toward the content with the ability to

Which program would you point to as objectively better, *Modern Family* or *Rich Kids of Beverly Hills*? Why?

objectively identify and judge its quality. This is not an undoable task. Take two popular recent television programs, *Modern Family* and *Rich Kids of Beverly Hills*. What criteria might you include in your evaluation? Quality of writing? Character development? Amount of humor? Cultural relevance? Production values? Add more criteria if you'd like. For each of the programs, give a score of 1 to 10 (1 being lowest, 10 being highest) based on your criteria. How does *Modern Family* score? *Rich Kids?* Which scored higher? Do you watch either of these programs? If you watch both, which do you prefer, and does your preference match your scoring? If you watch only one, is it the higher scorer, and if it isn't, why do you watch it? There is no right and wrong in this little exercise, just an opportunity to examine for yourself why you make the content decisions you do—a hallmark of a media-literate person.

5. **Media-literate individuals have an awareness of media content as "text" that provides insight into our contemporary culture and ourselves.** If media reflect our culture, the question becomes, "Do we like what we see?" Mass media are our cultural storytellers, and the stories they tell "help define our realities, shaping the way we think, feel, and act" (Baran, 2014, p. 14). When media construct narratives, those narratives say something about the culture in which they are created, disseminated, and consumed. Television shows *Glee*, *Grey's Anatomy*, *Scandal*, and *Modern Family*, which represent gay relationships as indistinguishable from other loving unions, say something about our culture's comfort with all kinds of families. News organizations that engage in racial stereotyping or partisan reporting represent a culture that is racist and politically unaware. When sensational headlines and reality television gain more

attention than stories about poverty, schools, or the environment, it says something about what we think is important. Just as media practitioners have a duty to act responsibly in their construction of media messages, so, too, do media consumers have a responsibility to be thoughtful in their choice of messages.

6. **Media-literate individuals promote the cultivation of enhanced enjoyment, understanding, and appreciation of media content.** The point of media literacy is not that all media are bad. In fact, just the opposite is true. The ability to appreciate and enjoy media content and media technologies is a separate issue from using them productively and appropriately. People who are media literate have a respect for media; otherwise, they wouldn't invest so much time thinking and talking about them. Remember the earlier discussion about high school literature? Your teachers made you study those works because the more you understood them, the more you could enjoy them and others like them. Clearly, people who know more about popular music find more enjoyment in listening. People who know more about the movies love the movies more. Greater enjoyment flows from the ability to make meaning making personal, and media literacy aids personal meaning making.

7. **Media communicators have a responsibility to produce effective and responsible media messages.** When we typically think of media communicators we tend to think of news anchors, film producers, songwriters, Web designers, and television executives. And yes, they are in fact media communicators, all of whom have a responsibility to provide content of value to an audience. But in the age of the Internet, we are all content producers. As you might remember from Chapter 10, we are the "people formerly known as the audience." For example, Internet research company Technocrati typically tracks more than 100 million active blogs worldwide. Fifty-four percent of American Internet users have uploaded original photos or videos (Duggan, 2013), and speaking specifically of news, 37 percent "have contributed to the creation of news, commented about it, or disseminated it via postings on social media sites" (Purcell, Rainie, Mitchell, Rosensteil, and Olmstead, 2010).

You and your peers use the Internet in a very democratic fashion, creating your own blogs, websites, and social network profiles. You have a lot to say, and potentially millions of people who have access to your messages will read, hear, or see them. CyberJournalist.net has created a *Blogger's Code of Ethics* outlining how we, as Internet users, should conduct ourselves as online content creators. They include the following:

- **Be honest and fair**—Never engage in plagiarism; distinguish factual information from fictional information; never publish information you know is inaccurate; and provide sources whenever feasible.

- **Minimize harm**—Show compassion and sensitivity for those who may be adversely affected by your information; recognize that gathering and disseminating information may cause harm to others; show good taste by not pandering to lurid curiosity; and recognize that only an overriding public need can justify intrusion into anyone's privacy.

- **Be accountable**—Admit mistakes and correct them promptly; disclose conflicts of interest, political affiliations, activities, and agendas; deny favored treatment to advertisers and special interest groups; maintain high standards; and expose unethical practices of other bloggers.

What are your responsibilities in creating a Facebook page?

The Skill of Being Media Literate

Media literacy is a skill. No one is born with it and we can get better at it through practice. Here are some basic skills typical of media-literate people:

1. **Paying close attention to media messages and being able to separate valued content from noise.** Consider television news. Many veteran journalists claim that actual journalism is becoming extinct as major cable news networks align themselves with specific political parties and, because of their profitability, **soft news** stories (sensational stories that have little real connection to people's everyday lives) are given more attention than **hard news** stories (stories that aid people in making intelligent decisions about their everyday lives). Media-literate consumers know how to sift out the propaganda and focus on information that serves a more democratic function because they take many factors into account, such as credibility, accountability, and motives. The result is they are better able to make value judgments about their world and themselves.

2. **Setting high standards when it comes to media content and expecting media producers to live up to those standards.** Earlier in the chapter we examined *Modern Family* and *Rich Kids of Beverly Hills* using a pre-constructed set of criteria. In the end, we were able to establish some very obvious quality differences between these two programs. Media-literate individuals expect television networks to provide quality content rather than deliver programs that are designed to do little more than make money, regardless of quality. If this is what we demand, this is what we will get. Equally important, when we expect more of media producers, we make a statement about who we are as an audience, our judgments, and our values.

3. **Having the ability to always ask questions even when the source is seemingly credible.** Judgments of what's credible are often quite subjective. Is something "credible" only if it concurs with your opinions or values? Is it "credible" only if it aligns with your political or religious

soft news Sensational stories that have little real connection to people's everyday lives.

hard news Stories that aid people in making intelligent decisions about their everyday lives.

beliefs? We live in a society where people are increasingly distrustful of media. In fact, as you read in the previous chapter, distrust in the media is at a record high, with 60 percent of Americans reporting not very much trust or none at all (McCarthy, 2014). So how do we know whom to trust? Sometimes the most seemingly credible sources need to be questioned. These questions of authenticity and credibility are particularly compelling when considering the Internet. Imagine yourself a graduate student in chemistry and basing part of your thesis on a website constructed by a 15-year-old boy—embarrassing, to say the least. A media-literate person would not have made that mistake because consideration of authorship would have been a factor in judging the site's credibility.

4. **Being knowledgeable about the terms (or language) of media industries so messages can be both deconstructed and constructed effectively and accurately.** One of the goals of media literacy is to educate people about the language of media, that is, the terms and concepts needed to fully understand how media operate and how their content is consumed. In addition, media literacy encourages understanding production values (editing, lighting, cinematography, script writing) so consumers can not only identify what

---

PERSONALLY RESPONSIBLE COMMUNICATION

Being a Proactive Media Consumer

So you don't like reality TV, sensationalist news, and the overwhelming images of sex and violence in the media. Well, what are you going to do about it? Media literacy asks that we become *active* consumers, but it also recognizes that we have a personal responsibility to be *proactive* consumers as well. Voicing your opinion with your family members, friends, and peers is certainly a start, but you can be even more active in your media literacy.

Being media literate runs along a continuum from passive to proactive consumers, with active consumers falling in the middle. Passive consumers probably don't know much about media literacy and possess none of the skills required to meaningfully read, interpret, and assess content. Active consumers have some understanding of the importance of media literacy and even use some critical thinking skills when consuming media content. Proactive consumers, on the other hand, are extremely media literate individuals who not only want to affect how their family and friends are influenced by media but also want to make a difference in the culture.

Passive ┄┄┄> Active ┄┄┄> Proactive
consumers   consumers   consumers

Figure 11.1 Continuum from Passive to Proactive Consumers

Imagine that your little sister is reading and watching her favorite magazine website, a site featuring a lot of sexual references and advice. We can illustrate your possible responses on a continuum (Figure 11.1). You could do absolutely nothing, which makes you a passive consumer (and a poor sibling). You could also turn off the computer and have a conversation with her about what's going on in the articles and videos and why the site may not be suitable for her. In this case, you're an active consumer. Or you could turn off the computer, have a conversation with your sister, and then work with her to create a blog aimed at kids her age designed to address the issues behind material like the website that originally caught your attention. Now you're truly a proactive consumer. If you choose the third option, you will have raised awareness not just in your family, but for all the readers of your new family blog.

goes into making a message, but can also create and influence messages themselves. You can see how to become much more active in your media literacy in the box entitled, "Personally Responsible Communication: Being a Proactive Media Consumer."

Media Literacy and Meaning Making

Throughout this chapter, we have reiterated that the point of media literacy is to be critical consumers of media. Being *critical* of content requires us to make meaning from that content. For example, to determine whether a news story is objective or nonpartisan, we first must determine the implicit and explicit message of the story. We must also be aware of how the approaches to creating the story contributed to its intended meaning. Was the coverage of a recent political campaign slanted? What meaning do we derive from sensational stories prioritized over economic, political, or civic headlines? Why are certain models selected to appear in the magazine and television ads we see? Think about how you construct your social networking profiles. You probably make specific content choices to create specific meanings, and professional content creators do the same—quite likely with more skill and resources.

Media-literate people are better able to discern the meanings built into media texts because they do not passively absorb the content. They consume it in a critical fashion, asking questions that reach beyond the information provided, looking at motives, interpretations, and credibility. The result is a deeper, more critical understanding. Media-literate people construct meanings from media messages, which helps them behave in more culturally productive ways, for example, choosing political candidates based on their policies and understanding of important issues affecting the country, or rejecting representations of people and values that do not serve personally important needs. These behaviors tell others *who we are*, *what we believe*, and *what is our role in the culture*.

All of these celebrities—Angelina Jolie, Gisele Bündchen, Salma Hayek, and Beyoncé—look very different, so what exactly is it that makes them "beautiful"?

Media Literacy and Identity

As we discussed in earlier chapters, identity is constructed through interaction with many others—parents, friends, social circles, colleagues, and media, to name a few. Media literacy, of course, deals primarily with *media's* contributions to identity formation. For instance, how do we come to know what's attractive or handsome in our culture? And then, how do we apply those definitions to ourselves?

Media ideals of beauty include women like Angelina Jolie, Gisele Bündchen, Salma Hayek, and Beyoncé. All of these celebrities look very different, so what exactly is it that makes them "beautiful"? Surely the answer cannot be as simple as "media tell us what to think, and therefore we think it." But media do set the agenda for us, greatly affecting not only our perceptions of the culture but our perceptions of ourselves in the culture. Media-literate individuals may agree these women are "beautiful," but they also recognize the many factors that contribute to media beauty (digitization, lighting, professional make-up design). As physically attractive as these women may be, they represent standards of physical perfection that are largely unattainable for most women. Those who fail to look critically at these media constructions of identity are less likely to form their own identities based on *real* rather than *ideal* values. Instead, they let someone else dictate who they are, what they believe, and their roles in society. Although always evolving, much of our identity and sense of self are formed during childhood and adolescence. The identity issues that arise from media influence are particularly disconcerting when it comes to the messages aimed specifically at young people, as you can read in the box "Socially Responsible Communication: Countering the Kinderculture."

SOCIALLY RESPONSIBLE COMMUNICATION

Countering the Kinderculture

First introduced by psychologist Shirley Steinberg, the term *kinderculture* describes a world of adultified and commodified children, a culture in which corporations construct our childhood. It encompasses the idea that our modern media constantly present children with messages that disregard childhood altogether. "The result is a consumer public of little girls, for example, who wear chastity rings and hip-clinging jogging pants with 'Kiss My Booty' in glitter on the backside. With one voice, adults tell kids to stay clean, avoid sex and drugs, go to Disneyland, and make vows of celibacy . . . with another voice, the corporate side markets booty clothing, faux bling, and sexualized images of twelve-year-olds" (2011, p. 1). In other words, children receive contradictory messages about whether to act like kids or like adults.

As a culture, are we rendering childhood obsolete? Whatever your feelings on the matter, it is hard to ignore the impact of media on the personalities, behaviors, and identities of children.

Providing children the tools they need to negotiate their identities and values against the onslaught of media messages means a nation of physically, mentally, and emotionally stronger kids. Type-2 diabetes, eating disorders, depression, and anxiety have all been scientifically linked to the kinderculture. Should a teenage girl look like a Victoria's Secret model, or should she eat Doritos and drink Coke? Should children be watching *Dora the Explorer*, or should they be playing violent video games? As parents, educators, and adult siblings, we have a responsibility to recognize the importance of giving our children every advantage in making decisions about their own well-being. As a society, we need to more closely assess our children's behaviors and attitudes and react accordingly. A good starting point is advocating media literacy in the school curricula, recognizing that doing so would help kids to become better critical thinkers, would encourage their active citizenship in our democracy, and would encourage them to make better sense of their world, of who they are now, and of who they hope to become.

Media Literacy and Democracy

In introducing this chapter, our intent was to discuss the cultural importance of media literacy. What could be more culturally relevant than addressing the sustenance of our democracy and our role as citizens? When we contemplate the notion of citizenship, we typically think of being active members of our communities, or we measure our contributions to the political process. But the way we come to understand these processes, as well as to benefit from them, is to rely on our media to provide us with the information necessary to voice our opinions, contribute to the cultural discourse, or cast a vote. Therefore, knowledge of issues and trust in those who disseminate information are critical to the functioning of our democracy. Media literacy teaches us to be critical consumers, to reject those messages that do not benefit our democratic process, and to disregard those whose opinions are merely politically or economically motivated. It encourages us to question *everything* we consume and empowers us to extract what we need in order to contribute meaningfully to the culture. There is no separating democracy and citizenship from media literacy. The fundamental principles of democracy and media literacy are closely aligned—both are constructed around the idea that people have a right to form their own identities, values, and judgments based on their skilled reading of honest and accurate information.

Review of Learning Objectives

11.1 Identify the assumptions and elements of media literacy.

Media literacy is the ability to read, interpret, critically assess, and productively use media texts. Scholarship on media literacy suggests that media have the potential to exert a wide range of negative and positive effects on individuals; its goal is to help people protect themselves from potentially negative effects; it must be developed; and it is multidimensional. Media literacy requires that we ask questions of audience and authorship, messages and meanings, and representations and realities when we interact with media texts. Media-literate individuals know that media messages are manufactured, commercial media are businesses, and all media messages reflect and influence values. As such, there are seven elements necessary for true media literacy: critical thinking skills enabling people to make independent choices about which media content to select and how to interpret the information they receive; an understanding of the process of mass communication; an awareness of the impact of the media on both individuals and society; the development of strategies for analyzing and discussing media messages; an awareness of media content as "text" that provides insight into contemporary culture and ourselves; the cultivation of enhanced enjoyment, understanding, and appreciation of media content; and a responsibility to produce effective and responsible media messages.

11.2 Identify the skills necessary to practice media literacy.

The skills necessary for media literacy are paying close attention to media messages and being able to separate valued content from noise; setting high standards when it comes to media content and expecting media producers to live up to those standards; possessing the ability to ask questions even when the source is seemingly credible; being knowledgeable about the terms (or language) of media industries so messages can be both deconstructed and constructed effectively and accurately.

11.3 Describe the importance of media literacy in identity formation.

We develop our identities—*who we are, what we believe*, and *our role in the culture*—through interaction with our environment and the people in it. In our heavily mass-mediated world, that interaction is increasingly with the media. Media literacy gives us control over meaning making when we engage the media.

11.4 Explain the cultural impact and importance of media literacy.

We make meaning of the world in which we live through interaction with that world and the people in it. In our heavily mass-mediated world, that interaction is increasingly with the media. Our realities of beauty, fairness, childhood, war, our political and business leaders—in fact, of just about every aspect of our culture—are influenced by the meanings we make from media content. Media literacy gives us control over meaning making when we engage the media.

Key Terms

media texts 236
media literacy 236
media literacy interventions 239
parental mediation theory 239
agenda-setting theory 242
audience and authorship 244
messages and meanings 245
representations and reality 245
polysemic 246
preferred reading 247
negotiated reading 247
single-shooter game 247
micro-level effects 248
macro-level effects 248
soft news 251
hard news 251

Questions for Review

1. What are the three assumptions of the communication discipline's systematic study of media literacy?

2. What is parental mediation theory? What are active and restrictive mediation, co-viewing, and participatory learning?

3. In analyzing media texts, what questions should you ask about representations and reality?

4. In analyzing media texts, what questions should you ask about the audience and authorship?

5. What are the seven elements of media literacy?

6. What are some examples of micro-level and macro-level media effects?

7. What skills are involved in media literacy?

8. What is the difference between being an active and a proactive consumer of media messages?

9. What does *kinderculture* mean, and what does it have to do with media literacy?

10. What is the link between media literacy, citizenship, and democracy?

Questions for Discussion

1. Discuss the ways in which media messages influence you and your peers. Give examples.

2. Discuss ways you could be a more proactive consumer of media content. If you do not generally approach media in this manner, why not? If you do, what do you gain from being proactive?

3. How media literate do you believe you are? What about your friends? Do you think you are more media literate than they are? Explain your answers.

12

Social Media and Communication Technologies

You just don't understand it. You have a great resume, a lot of community service, and a ton of leadership experience on campus. As you explain to your Communication instructor, "My GPA is pretty good, and after being in your class, I think my speaking and interpersonal skills are much improved." "So what's the problem?" she asks with a smile, trying to calm you down. You tell her, "I keep getting interviews and even call-backs for second meetings, but for some reason I never get an offer." She thinks a moment and says, "Let's see your letter and any other writing you've been asked to show." You hand your instructor your cover letter and the essay an interviewer asked you to prepare. "These look fine," she says, "actually really fine. I see why you get interviews." "But why aren't I getting job offers?" you wonder aloud.

She hands you her laptop and says, "Show me your Facebook page." "Really?" "Yes, really," she says. "There's nothing there that could hurt me," you tell her. "I know to keep all my 'college-life stuff' private." "Do your friends keep that stuff to themselves? Do you know who they share your comments and photos with? Do you know who their friends are? Are you tagged in any of their photos? And how hard do you think it is for people who really wanted to dig out the real Facebook-you to find everything they need? Remember," she continues, "Facebook encourages sharing; that's its business plan; that's why it makes sharing so seamless and easy. And recall, too, what I told you when we discussed mass communication in class: if you aren't paying for the medium, you're being sold."

Your instructor in this story knows what she's talking about. Eighty percent of American employers say they Google prospective employees (Joyce, 2014), and more than half have rejected candidates because of material they found online (Grasz, 2014). There are companies selling data-digging services to employers, promising to reconstruct people's "true" identities from all the bits of themselves they willingly left in cyberspace. Those outfits don't even have to work very hard, as 11 percent of social network users say they have posted material they later regretted (Madden, 2012)—and those are just the ones who admit it.

double-edged sword The same technology can be used for good or bad.

What your instructor is telling you is that modern communication technology is a **double-edged sword**: it has both favorable and unfavorable consequences. The very tools that let you stay in touch with friends and express yourself in new ways can also open you up to unwanted evaluation by acquaintances and strangers. There is no inherent good or bad in our new personal communication technologies—the Internet, smartphones and tablets, and social networking sites like Facebook and Twitter. Good and bad reside in the use we make of them, and that is the theme of this chapter.

Learning Objectives

12.1   Identify the warning signs of Internet addiction, depression, and distraction.

12.2   Explain why and how people use social networking sites for identity construction and maintenance and for relational communication.

12.3   Describe potential relationships between social media and social isolation, popularity, and self-disclosure.

12.4   Present an informed opinion in the debate over face-to-face communication versus computer-mediated communication.

The Promise and Peril of New Communication Technologies

computer-mediated communication People interacting via digital technology.

Writing in 2005, communication theorist Charles Berger attempted to summarize the available knowledge on **computer-mediated communication** (**CMC**), humans interacting via digital technology. He wrote that there were two dominant areas of research. The first, he said, was on "the potential deleterious effects of the new technology's use. Internet addiction . . . and the role Internet use may play in inducing social isolation and loneliness . . . A second research area of interest to interpersonal communication researchers invokes face-to-face interaction as a kind of gold standard against which to compare computer-mediated communication" (2005, p. 430). Today, research is also focusing on several other issues related to how changing technology affects communication. These include cyberbullying, sexting, endless distraction, loss of interaction with the real world, cheapening of friendship, disappearance of privacy, and even disruption of brain activity. All of these are common worries surrounding our online communication.

Professor Berger was also correct in saying that the introduction of every new communication technology is invariably accompanied by predictions of doom. In his essay he mentioned television, which critics worried would turn us into mindless couch potatoes. He could also have added predictions that movies would destroy literacy, radio would kill musicianship, and comic books would breed juvenile delinquency (Davis, 1976). Even the arrival of the printing press frightened many people. In 1470 Italian Benedictine monk Filippo de Strata published his famous tract, *Polemic against Printing*, proclaiming, "This is what the printing presses do: they corrupt susceptible hearts . . . The pen," he wrote, presumably in longhand, "is a virgin; the printing press is a whore" (Pinsky, 2010, p. 15; Sabev, 2009, p. 177). Father Filippo may have thought highly of the pen, but some 1,800 years earlier, Greek philosopher Plato wasn't quite convinced about the value of *that* technology. He saw writing "as a passive, impersonal product that serves as a poor substitute for speech." Unlike speech, he argued in *Phaedrus*, "writing is inhuman, a thing, a technological product; it weakens the memory of those who rely on it; it cannot respond to new questions; and it cannot defend itself" (in Ong, 2002, pp. 274–277).

Why do we have such reactions to new media? Recall one of this text's central themes—communication gives people the power to make meaning. So every change in the way we communicate threatens somebody's meaning-making power. Those *somebodies* are usually people with a vested interest in keeping modes of communication the way they are; after all, *they're* already doing just fine. Movies, radio, comic books, and television—all more open and available to more people than the theater, the symphony, and novels—challenged the power of traditional cultural elites. Father Filippo feared the printing press specifically because it meant that many, many more books could be produced and read by many more people, weakening the power of Church and Crown to make meaning for their subjects. He was right to worry. Soon after the arrival of the printing press, Europe was transformed by the Protestant Reformation and later the Enlightenment.

We now know that writing, the printing press, and all the communication technologies that may have once been frightening are not harmful in themselves. They have opened up new worlds and new realms of consciousness for us; they have increased our knowledge, experiences, and wisdom.

But while communication technology may be *neutral*—neither good nor bad—it is *not benign*—it matters; it changes the way we communicate. "All media, from the phonetic alphabet to the computer," explains influential communication theorist Marshall McLuhan, "are extensions of man [sic] that cause deep and lasting changes in him and transform his environment" (1962, p. 13). Changes in communication technology, he argued, inevitably produce profound changes in people, culture, and society because they literally extend our senses through time and space. Television and movies let us see around

Social Media, Social Connection, and Social Power

How do you use the power of new communication technologies? Your voice is side by side on the Internet with those of the world's biggest mass communicators. Your e-mail address and Facebook page occupy the same digital real estate as the websites of the *New York Times* and *Fox News*. You can "talk" to one person or thousands, and you can electronically enlist those people to spread your message.

People are using these technologies to change the world in ways big and small. The Arab Spring, the ongoing pro-democracy movement currently reshaping life for tens of millions of people in a dozen Middle Eastern countries, was born and raised on social media and YouTube. Social networking has also been activists' primary tool in the fight to ensure that everyone's content travels the Internet at the same speed and for the same price. *Net neutrality* is the idea that Internet service providers, primarily cable companies, cannot prioritize some users over others. It became law because of "an incredibly engaged, incredibly passionate user base [given] the tools to respond," said Internet activist and Tumblr director of social impact and public policy Liba Rubenstein. "Our community is the source of our power," explained online craft site Etsy's director of public policy Althea Erickson. While contemplating the new rule, the Federal Communications Commission was inundated with four million public comments in favor of net neutrality, unleashed, in the words of *New York Times* technology writer Jonathan Weisman, by "the longest, most sustained campaign of Internet activism in history" (all quotes from Weisman, 2015, p. A1).

Another example of Internet activism is the story of 14-year-old Julia Bluhm. She began an online movement to convince *Seventeen* magazine to print at least one "real," unaltered picture of a young girl each month. Nearly 100,000 people took up Julia's cause, and the magazine responded by creating a Body Peace Treaty encouraging healthy self-image and pledging

It was social media users who convinced *Seventeen* to present unaltered images on its covers.

to never again digitally alter images of girls' bodies in its pages.

Forty-four percent of 18- to 29-year-olds "like" or promote political material on social media. Thirty-four percent use social media to encourage their friends to vote, and one-third regularly post links to political stories (Anatole, 2013). What about you? Have you used any of your digital tools for political or social action? If yes, what have you done, and how satisfied are you with its results? If not, why not?

the world, into the past, and into the future. Recordings let us hear music created by artists a century ago in distant places. The same is true of CMC. Using Internet video service Skype, we can see and hear our friends on the other side of the globe. Smartphone, tablet, or laptop in hand, we are powerful; wherever we go, we carry with us the world's accumulated knowledge and a connection to 3 billion other technology users around the world. That's pretty impressive, but it's neither good nor bad. What we do with that power is what matters. You can read how some young digital natives have challenged some fairly powerful cultural players in the box "Social Media, Social Connection, and Social Power."

A Connected World

If you were born during or after the 1980s, you are a digital native. That is, you've never lived in a world without the Internet, World Wide Web, and the other technologies they make possible. So you might not see the changes in communication they have brought about. As you read in Chapter 10, Marshall McLuhan would ask if a fish knows it's wet, and his answer is "No" because a fish is always wet. A fish can only know *wet* if it knows *dry*. Because you've always floated in an ocean of technology, you don't know what it's like *not to* live in a 24-hour-a-day, 7-days-a-week, 365-days-a-year, constantly connected environment. But unlike our fish, you can think and reflect on your "wetness" in order to become aware of it. So, let's dive into the ocean of new personal communication technologies.

Three billion people worldwide are connected to the Internet. That's 35 percent of the planet's population and a 566 percent increase since 2000. Eighty-eight percent of North Americans use the Internet, a 39 percent increase since 2000 ("Internet," 2015). There are more mobile wireless connections on the planet (7.4 billion) than there are people (7.1 billion; Timberg, 2013), and more people on earth have cellphones than have toilets (Wang, 2013). In the United States, 80 percent of adults have Internet-capable smartphones, and just over

We swim in a sea of technology.

half have tablet computers (Lunden, 2015). In 2015 alone, people downloaded 235 billion **apps** (short for *application*, a program or software connecting mobile devices to specific websites; Martin, 2015). In 2009, for the first time, the amount of non-voice data sent over cellphones exceeded that of voice data. Journalist Clive Thompson explained, "This generation doesn't make phone calls, because

app Short for *application*; program or software connecting mobile devices to specific websites.

everyone is in constant, lightweight contact in so many other ways: texting, chatting, and social network messaging" (in Vanderbilt, 2012, p. 52). In fact, making calls ranks only fifth in the amount of time we spend with those devices (02, 2012). In 2012 smartphones even surpassed traditional desktop and laptop computers as the platform of choice for sending and receiving e-mail (Walsh, 2012).

Social networking sites (SNSs) did not exist until 1995, when Classmates.com went online. Others followed: Friendster in 2002, LinkedIn and MySpace in 2003, and then, in 2004, Facebook. If Facebook was a country, its 1.4 billion users would make it the largest in the world. Seventy-two percent of online American adults are Facebook users. Since 2009 Facebook has been the most-visited website in the United States, and it accounts for 6 percent of all the time the world's Internet users spend online (Smith, 2015). Twitter, which limits messages to 140 characters, went online in 2006 and now has more than half a billion registered users. Twitter users send a total of 500 million tweets (messages) a day ("Twitter Usage," 2015).

Changes in communication technology on this scale and at this pace were certain to cause concern, some of it misplaced, but some of it quite reasonable. You can read about one set of ethical concerns in the box "Who Owns the Social Networking You?" An inconvenient truth of social-networking life is that we willingly, often enthusiastically, give up our privacy in exchange for the contact with others it affords us. Free services like Facebook, Instagram, and Twitter have to monetize somehow. So the ethical decision ultimately is ours. How much of our privacy, of ourselves, are we willing to give away to stay connected? But before you answer, read this list of potentially unethical infringements on your privacy routinely practiced by virtually all major SNSs (Shannon, 2012):

- Making users' data available to third parties for commercial, surveillance, or data mining purposes.

- Use of facial-recognition software to automatically identify people in uploaded photos.

- Collection and publication of user data by third-party applications without users' permission or awareness.

- Use of automatic "opt-in" privacy controls.

cookies Software involuntarily loaded onto computers to track online user activity.

- Use of "**cookies**" (tracking software involuntarily loaded onto users' computers) to track online user activities after they have left a social networking site.

- Use of location-based social networking for stalking or other illicit monitoring of users' physical movements.

- Sharing of user information or patterns of activity with government entities.

- Encouragement of users to adopt voluntary but imprudent, ill-informed, or unethical information-sharing practices, either with respect to sharing their own personal data or sharing data related to other people and entities.

ETHICAL COMMUNICATION

Who Owns the Social Networking You?

At the end of 2012, Instagram announced new privacy and terms-of-service rules on its company blog. The popular digital filter and photo-sharing app company, which had been acquired by Facebook a few months earlier, informed its 100 million users that (a) it could share your information with Facebook and advertisers; (b) you could appear, without your knowledge and without compensation, in an advertisement not only on Instagram and Facebook, but in the ads of anyone who paid Facebook and Instagram; (c) people who didn't use Instagram could appear in ads without their knowledge or permission if they had their photograph taken and shared on the service by someone who did use it; and (d) the company was under no obligation to tell you that you or your content were being used in an ad or in what way. Additionally, the only way to opt out was to quit the service before January 16, 2013, because after that, simply using Instagram meant you had agreed to their terms. If you quit after that date, Instagram still retained the rights to your material even though you had dropped the service.

Reaction was swift and negative. Many of the service's users claimed that Instagram and Facebook had made "a stark declaration of corporate over personal rights" (Smith, 2012).

The new policy was quickly suspended, but in late 2013, after the furor subsided, Facebook again reasserted its right to use its users' posted materials in ads (Goel, 2013). These actions raised one of social networking's most troubling ethical issues: Who owns the content we post, and because we put so much of ourselves into sites like Facebook and Instagram, who owns us?

Who owns your pics? Instagram's claim that it owned the photos you post is only one of several important privacy issues that users must negotiate in exchange for new communication technology's many benefits.

Communication scholars and legal experts see this as an ethical issue because privacy is a basic human right, and violations of our privacy are, by their very nature, unethical (Roggensack, 2010). Ethics are also in play because our culture values privacy as an essential aspect of personal freedom and liberty. Internet security expert Bruce Scheier explains, "For if we are observed in all matters, we are constantly under threat of correction, judgment, criticism, even plagiarism of our own uniqueness. . . . We lose our individuality, because everything we do is observable and recordable" (in Carr, 2010). In fact, many Americans do seem to have some qualms about their loss of privacy. Fifty-nine percent think that Facebook is the company that poses "the greatest threat to the future of privacy." Forty percent think it's Twitter (Peterson, 2014). Are these people just being paranoid, or do they have a point? Explain your answer.

How many of these routine uses of your content and personal data by SNS were you aware of? Do you find any more troublesome than others? Do any bother you enough to, if not quit social networking, at least be more judicious about what you post? But if you alter the you that you put "out there," what becomes of the real you? What factors might you consider to arrive at a fair trade-off?

Changing technology also raises workplace issues; for example, which method of Internet communication is best suited for on-the-job interactions? You can find the answer in the box "E-mail vs. Social Networking Sites."

COMMUNICATION IN THE WORKPLACE

E-mail versus Social Networking Sites

While it's true that adults of all ages use e-mail and social networking to similar degrees, you don't need research to tell you that younger adults spend more time on SNS and older adults rely more on e-mail. That research does exist (Madden, 2010), as do data demonstrating that social networking is hugely popular—the number of social networking users surpassed the number of e-mail users in 2009, and time spent on social networking sites topped time with e-mail for the first time in 2007 (Carlson and Angelova, 2010). You also know that in your personal life you are free to use whichever technology best suits your needs at any given time for any given purpose. On the job, however, there may be distinct advantages to one over the other.

Despite evidence that social networking use at work annually costs the American economy $650 billion in wasted productivity (Shore, 2012), many companies have adopted *enterprise social network programs* such as Yammer. That is, to accommodate employees' natural and necessary need to interact on the job, they set up exclusive social networking networks accessible only to the organization and its internal users. There workers can share thoughts and ideas and post photos, updates, and other material likely to be of interest to colleagues, all without leaving work. There are, however, seven definite career benefits to choosing e-mail over social networking when in the workplace, as executive recruitment expert Jonathan Bennett explains (2013):

1. **E-mail provides a level of privacy and professionalism not present on SNS**—When using e-mail to communicate with external people, you don't have to be their friend, and you can better control the information they know about you.
2. **E-mail in-boxes provide a one-stop location for tasks and a more efficient manager of one-to-one messages**—Your in-box is an electronic "go to folder," enabling more efficient management of tasks and meetings.
3. **E-mail raises fewer privacy issues**—Only your e-mail's chosen recipient gets your message (unless your message is forwarded).
4. **E-mail operates across all platforms and applications**—SNSs are proprietary; that is, Facebook only allows its users, LinkedIn its. E-mail is universal across all servers and e-mail brands.
5. **A working e-mail address is as essential a career tool as a passport or driver's license**—Every online service or product sign-up requires an e-mail address to authenticate your identity.
6. **Social networking sites do not provide a professional online space for business one-to-ones**—You wouldn't arrange an important meeting with a customer or client, for example, on an SNS.
7. **E-mail raises fewer issues of ownership of information**—Your organization legally owns the data you transmit over its e-mail servers. However, there is considerable controversy (and legal uncertainty) about who owns material posted on SNS from the workplace and even away from the job if it has a connection to work.

The Dark Side of New Communication Technologies

Parents worry that their kids are too easily distracted by technology. Teachers say students are too dependent on search engines like Google. People worry that their friends are addicted to the Internet. Most teens, when they get their first computer or smartphone, also get a lecture on limits—how, when, and for how long they can be connected. We'll look at three common concerns aimed at the new personal communication technologies: addiction, depression, and distraction.

Addiction

Americans average more than 6 hours a day on the Internet. That's 42 hours a week, essentially a full-time job. And 18- to 29-year-olds average even more (Bennett, 2015). Computer users visit an average of 40 websites a day. The average person, regardless of age, sends or receives 400 texts a month, four times the number in 2007, and two-thirds of these "average" smartphone users report **phantom-vibration syndrome**, feeling their phones vibrate when in fact they are not (Dokoupil, 2012). More than half of Americans 18 to 34 years old would rather wait in line at the DMV, get a root canal, spend a night in jail, give up an hour of sleep a night for a year, or clean the shower drains at the local gym than take down their social media profiles (Conway, 2012). These data are for average or typical users. But there are indeed those who suffer from **Internet addiction**, characterized by "spending 40 to 80 hours per week, with [individual] sessions that could last up to 20 hours. Sleep patterns are disrupted due to late night logins, and addicts generally stay up surfing until 2:00, 3:00, or 4:00 in the morning [despite] the reality of having to wake up early for work or school" (Young, 2004, p. 405).

Several countries, notably China, Taiwan, and Korea, treat Internet addiction as a genuine psychiatric problem and operate government-funded treatment facilities for addicts. Even Google, in the heart of Silicon Valley, maintains an in-house "mindfulness movement," designed to teach its employees the dangers of becoming overly dependent on their technology. In 2013, after years of debate, the American Psychiatric Association added "Internet Addiction Disorder" to its authoritative list of recognized mental illnesses, the *American Diagnostic and Statistical Manual of Mental Disorders*.

Addiction occurs because even in moderate Internet use, our brains rewire, that is, they alter physiologically. Researcher Gary Small and his colleagues studied two groups of Internet users, veterans and novices. Looking at their brains through a scanner, they found that the veteran Web users had "fundamentally altered prefrontal cortexes." They then instructed the novices to go home and return a week later after having spent five hours online during those seven days. When these participants returned, their brain scans showed changes similar to those of the long-time Internet users (Small et al., 2009). "The technology is rewiring our brains," said Nora Volkow, director of the National Institute of Drug Abuse. She compares the lure of digital stimulation not to that of drugs and alcohol; rather, the drive is more akin to that for food and sex, both essential but counterproductive in excess (in Richtel, 2010b, p. A1). And that is when addiction occurs, with excess.

phantom-vibration syndrome Feeling a phone vibration when none exists.

Internet addiction Pathological dependence on digital technology.

One sign of Internet addiction is interrupted sleep patterns.

Studying the brains of diagnosed Internet addicts, Fuchun Lin and his colleagues found evidence of disruption to the connections in nerve fibers linking the brain areas involved in emotions, decision-making, and self-control. "Overall," they wrote, "our findings indicate that IAD [Internet Addiction Disorder] has abnormal white matter integrity [extra nerve cells that speed up brain functioning] in brain regions involving emotional generation and processing, executive attention, decision making, and cognitive control . . . The results also suggest that IAD may share psychological and neural mechanisms with other types of substance addiction and impulse control disorders" (Lin et al., 2012). Yes, internet addiction exists. But there is another edge to this sword. The Gary Small research we mentioned just above also found that moderate Internet use could indeed enhance brain circuitry in older adults. You can check your own level of Internet addiction using the box "Internet Addiction Self-Diagnosis."

PERSONALLY RESPONSIBLE COMMUNICATION

Internet Addiction Self-Diagnosis

If you were reading the text closely, you might have noted that a typical college-aged student spends more than 40 hours a week online. According to Kimberly S. Young of the *Center for Online Addiction*, that is in the range of Internet addiction. So, are you addicted? Professor Young has created a self-diagnostic (2004, p. 404), and if you have ever worried that you spend too much time online, you owe it to yourself to take this test. Remember, too, that this is about *Internet addiction,* not *computer addiction.* So you must consider all the devices—computers, smartphones, tablets, or game consoles—you use to connect to the Net. Also keep in mind that most people, while quite aware of the communication technologies they rely on, are typically unaware of the real amounts of time they spend with them (Hundley and Shyles, 2010). So think hard and honestly about your Internet use before you answer.

(1) Do you feel preoccupied with the Internet (thinking about previous online activity or anticipating next online session)?

(2) Do you feel the need to use the Internet with increasing amounts of time to achieve satisfaction?

(3) Have you repeatedly made unsuccessful efforts to control, cut back, or stop Internet use?

(4) Do you feel restless, moody, depressed, or irritable when attempting to cut down or stop Internet use?

(5) Do you stay online longer than originally intended?

(6) Have you jeopardized or risked the loss of a significant relationship, job, educational or career opportunity because of the Internet?

(7) Have you lied to family members, therapists, or others to conceal the extent of involvement with the Internet?

(8) Do you use the Internet as a way of escaping from problems or of relieving feelings of helplessness, guilt, anxiety, or depression?

Dr. Young explains how to interpret your answers:

Only nonessential computer/Internet usage (i.e., non-business or nonacademic related use) should be evaluated, and addiction is present when [you] answer yes to five (or more) of the questions during a six-month period. This list offers a workable definition of Internet addiction to help us differentiate normal from compulsive Internet use, but these warning signs can often be masked by the cultural norms that encourage and reinforce its use. That is, even if a person meets all eight criteria, signs of abuse can be rationalized away as "I need this for my job" or "It's just a machine" when in reality, the Internet is causing significant problems in a user's life. (2004, p. 404)

How did you fare? Do you show signs of Internet addiction? If yes, what will you do about it? If no, how have you been able to avoid overreliance on this technology?

Depression

Because depression is often tied to addiction, it too has drawn the attention of parents and medical and psychological professionals. The American Academy of Pediatrics says that research has uncovered **Facebook depression**, "depression that develops when preteens and teens spend a great deal of time on social media sites, such as Facebook, and then begin to exhibit classic symptoms of depression. Acceptance by and contact with peers is an important element of adolescent life. The intensity of the online world is thought to be a factor that may trigger depression in some adolescents" (O'Keeffe and Clarke-Pearson, 2011, p. 802). Psychologist Sherry Turkle reports that young people, those in their teens and early twenties, tell her they become exhausted by always having to put themselves "out there," and are unable to look away for **fear of missing out**, or **FOMO**, a finding supported by research indicating that average smartphone users check their phones 221 times a day, typically beginning while still in their morning beds; and these are *average* users (Allen, 2014). This "time suck" is among the primary reasons that 61 percent of American Facebook users voluntarily take breaks from the site for periods of several weeks or more, and that of all US Internet users, 20 percent are former Facebookers who have quit the site altogether (Rainie, Smith, and Duggan, 2013).

Raghavendra Katikalapudi and a team of researchers electronically monitored in real time the Internet usage of 216 college undergraduates, 30 percent of whom showed signs of depression. They found that the depressed students were the most intense Web users; they exhibited more peer-to-peer file sharing, heavier e-mailing and online chatting, more video game play, and the tendency to quickly switch between many websites and other online resources than did the other students. The authors explained that each of these characteristics is related to depression. Quickly switching between websites may reflect *anhedonia*, an inability to experience emotions, as Web users desperately look for emotional stimulation. Heavy e-mailing and chatting may signify a relative lack of strong face-to-face relationships, as these students work to maintain contact either with distant friends or new people they met online (Katikalapudi et al., 2012).

Unlike the physiological brain research on Internet use, this work on depression is correlational, that is, while there is a demonstrable relationship between depression and this type of Internet use, no one can confidently claim that one "causes" the other (maybe already depressed people gravitate toward the Internet). Nonetheless, the link exists, and depression is a serious problem, especially for college students. In fact, the Center for Collegiate Health reports that more than 45 percent of all students who visit a campus counseling center mention depression as a problem, with 16 percent citing it as their foremost problem (2015).

Distraction

Addiction and depression are related to abnormal or excessive connection to digital technology. The issue of distraction, however, deals with our more typical, everyday use of the new communication technologies. All of us "normal"

Facebook depression
Depression that develops from overuse of social networking sites.

fear of missing out (FOMO)
Inability to disengage from social networking for fear of missing something.

users have been warned by friends and family to unplug. You know the concerns: young people "tweet and blog and text without batting an eyelash. Whenever they need the answer to a question, they simply log onto their phone and look it up on Google. They live in a state of perpetual, endless distraction, and, for many parents and educators, it's a source of real concern. Will future generations be able to finish a whole book? Will they be able to sit through an entire movie without checking their phones? Are we raising a generation of impatient brats?" (Rogers, 2011).

There is no doubt that time spent in front of a screen means less time spent interacting traditionally with the larger world and the people in it. But the real question here is how our use of technology *influences* our interaction with the larger world and the people in it when we do leave the screen. For example, research suggests that time spent with digital devices deprives people's brains of needed downtime. "Downtime lets the brain go over experiences it's had, solidify them and turn them into permanent long-term memories," explains learning researcher Loren Frank. When the brain is constantly stimulated, "you prevent this learning process" (in Richtel, 2010a, p. B1).

There is also research indicating that the speed of our digital communication technologies is conditioning us to be impatient and easily distracted in the offline world. There is evidence that constant connection reduces attention span; for example, 71 percent of the nation's teachers say their students' attention spans are reduced a lot or somewhat because of their screen time (Rideout, 2012); but you only have to look at your own behavior. Are you easily distracted in class? Do you get impatient when an e-mail or text is not acknowledged as quickly as you'd like? Which would you rather do, immerse yourself in a nice, long novel, or catch the story on video? "More and more, life is resembling the chat room," explains Dr. Elias Aboujaoude, director of the Impulse Control Disorders Clinic at Stanford University. "We're paying a price in terms of our cognitive life because of this virtual lifestyle" (in Parker-Pope, 2010, p. A13).

There is little question that changes in how we interact with the actual world are occurring. But there are those who see the change as normal, if not beneficial. One argument is that any individual loss of memory is more than compensated for by access to that repository of the world's knowledge, the Internet. We should, explains, psychologist Daniel Wegner,

THUMBNAIL THEORY

Transactive Memory

Because nobody can remember everything, people in groups can remember some things personally and then build their memory by knowing who else might know what they don't. People learn who knows something or where they can find it without learning what the information itself might be.

Accept the role of the Web as a mind-expander and wonder not at the bad but at the good it can do us. There's nothing wrong, after all, with having our minds expanded. Each time we learn *who* knows something or *where* we can find information—without learning *what* the information itself might be—we are expanding our mental reach. This is the basic idea behind so-called **transactive memory** . . . [N]obody remembers everything. Instead, each of us in a couple or group remembers some things personally—and then can remember much more by knowing who else might know what we don't. In this way, we become part of a transactive memory system. Groups of people commonly depend on one another for memory in this way—not by all knowing the same thing, but by specializing. And now we've added our computing devices to the network, depending for memory not just on people but also on a cloud of linked people and specialized information-filled devices. We have all become a great cybermind. As long as we are connected to our machines through talk and keystrokes, we can all be part of the biggest, smartest mind ever. (2012, p. SR6)

Another view is that yes, constant connection is indeed rewiring our brains, and this is as it should be. We experience the world not in a worse way, but in a *different* way. Digital learning researcher Kathy Davidson explains,

Younger generations don't just think about technology more casually, they're actually wired to respond to it in a different manner than we [non-digital natives] are, and it's up to us—and our education system—to catch up to them . . . When my students go to the Web and they're searching and they're leaving comments and they're social networking and they're Facebooking and they're texting at the same time—those are their reflexes. They are learning to process that kind of information faster. That which we experience shapes our pathways, so they're going to be far less stressed by a certain kind of multitasking that you are or than I am, or people who may not have grown up with that. (in Rogers, 2011)

In fact, there is evidence suggesting that SNS information, even strangers' Facebook status updates, are much more likely to be remembered than sentences from books and people's faces. Laura Mickes and her colleagues explained that because social networking's brief posts are "largely spontaneous and natural emanations of the human mind," they are "the sort of information that our memories are tuned to recognize . . . That which we readily generate," they said, "we also readily store" (Mickes et al., 2013).

How Computer-Mediated Communication Affects Identity and Relationships

Addiction, depression, and distraction have to do with how people use and abuse communication technologies. But what about the communication that takes place? How has it changed as a result of these technologies? Has it been altered for better or worse, or is it a new form of communication altogether? We look at two important lines of inquiry on CMC: its role in identity construction and maintenance, and its influence on interpersonal communication.

Social Network Sites and Identity Construction and Maintenance

Why do we use SNSs to interact with others, especially when distance isn't a factor? Isn't face-to-face communication more satisfying? For many it is. Half of the country's 13- to 17-year-old social media users, true digital natives, find actual human interaction their favorite way to communicate with friends; half of those because it's more fun, and a third because it makes understanding easier (Rideout, 2012, p. 11). Nonetheless, with the number of Facebook users alone approaching one-and-a-half billion, there must be something that takes people online for their interaction with others.

Psychologists Ashwini Nadkarni and Stefan Hofmann developed what they called the *dual-factor model* of Facebook (FB) use, which can also be applied to other SNS use. They explain, "FB use is primarily motivated by two basic social needs: (1) *the need to belong*, and (2) the *need for self-presentation*. The *need to belong* refers to the intrinsic drive to affiliate with others and gain social acceptance, and the *need for self-presentation* refers to the continuous process of impression management. These two motivational factors can co-exist, but can also each be the single cause for FB use" (italics in the original; 2012, p. 245). The need to belong, as you learned in Chapter 6, is important because people are highly dependent on social support from others, and exclusion can cause loss of self-esteem and emotional well-being. Self-esteem, then, serves as a *sociometer*, a monitor of acceptability by others. Because social network sites foster a sense of belonging, their use can increase self-esteem and therefore feelings of acceptability. Indeed, Gonzales and Hancock (2011) demonstrated that the simple act of updating and reading one's own profile on an SNS was sufficient to boost self-esteem. The need for self-presentation online is the same as offline. Again, as you learned earlier, this time from Chapter 1, we know ourselves through our interaction with others, and if others who are of importance to us are online, that's where we must be to present ourselves. But this raises the question, *how* do we present ourselves on social networking sites?

You control the "you" that you present to the ever-expanding social networking world. How do you use that freedom?

In the early days of the Internet, 1993, *The New Yorker* magazine published a cartoon featuring two dogs in front of a computer. The seated dog looks away from the keyboard to inform the other pup, "On the Internet, nobody knows you're a dog." Because of the Internet's anonymity, people, even canines, could be anything they wanted to be. And sometimes what they wanted to be was rude or bullying, a byproduct of their anonymous membership in the massive population of Internet users. This is *de-individuation*, when people, protected by a mask of anonymity, cease to see themselves as individuals and therefore fail to see others that way. As a result, they treat those others in ways they would never consider when face to face. Yes, there are still e-meanies and cyberbullies, but many Internet sites have responded by doing away with anonymity, requiring users to identify themselves with their real names before they allow postings or comments. "If I'm writing something, and I know my mom and my colleagues and my daughters are going to read it, I'm going to be on my best behavior," explains psychologist Dacher Keltner (in Hill, 2012, p. D5).

But the real change in Internet self-presentation has come about because of SNS. Now people on sites like Facebook announce their sex, age, location, romantic status, occupation, and social attachments. Not only do people publicly declare their identities, they add to and update them with regularity. As a result—and returning to the theme of the *New Yorker* cartoon—on SNS everybody knows you're a dog because *you've told them* you're a dog.

But if you're going to tell them you're a dog, why not tell them that you're a particularly smart and talented dog? There is little doubt that social network site users employ "screen names, profiles, and messages" as means to "foster others' impression formation about them" and that "users may select what information they want to include in a profile to highlight their most positive qualities" (Zywica and Danowski, 2008, p. 6). But how do they do this and why? Mitja Back and his colleagues tested the **idealized virtual identity hypothesis**, the tendency for creators of social network site profiles to display idealized characteristics that do not reflect their actual personalities. They learned that it doesn't happen very much. In fact, they discovered that for most people, online social networking (OSN) "may constitute an extended social context in which to express one's actual personality characteristics, thus fostering accurate interpersonal perceptions. OSNs integrate various sources of personal information that mirror those found in personal environments, private thoughts, facial images, and social behavior, all of which are known to contain valid information about personality." This led them to propose the "**extended real-life hypothesis** [which] predicts that people use OSNs to communicate their real personality" (Back et al., 2010, p. 372). But why? Why not create the identity you wish you could have? The researchers suggested two reasons that it would be difficult to do so even if you wanted to: "Creating idealized identities should be hard to accomplish because (a) OSN profiles include information about one's reputation that is difficult to control (e.g., wall posts) and (b) friends provide accountability and subtle feedback on one's Profile" (p. 372). We know this as symbolic interaction: identity is constructed and maintained through interaction with others; we peer into the Looking Glass for "accountability and subtle feedback" to know who we are.

At the time Mead developed his notion of symbolic interaction, the 1930s, people communicated primarily face to face. But today, even though our online communication is computer-mediated, it remains just as relational, just as much a social action. We still conceive of ourselves in relation to other people. We remain social objects that others observe and we continue to know ourselves through their responses to us. The difference is that on social networking sites we can direct—through our selection of information for profiles, profile and other pictures, status updates, and posts—others' attention to those symbols we most want them to use to make meaning of us. When we select our profile picture, for example, or snapshots from our birthday party or statement of our relationship status, we have knowledge of how others in our network will respond to them, so consciously or otherwise we attempt to

idealized virtual identity hypothesis Tendency for creators of social network site profiles to display idealized characteristics not reflective of their actual personalities.

extended real-life hypothesis Tendency for social networking site users to communicate their real personalities.

communicate something about ourselves that we deem meaningful. After all, we could choose any image from a near-limitless supply, and we are free to list our relationship status as anything we want. The SNS identity we construct cannot be separated from our social interactions on the SNS. In other words, we present ourselves based on who others think we are, which itself is based on the responses from others we have already received, just as Mead and symbolic interaction would have predicted.

And how do we use the SNS's power to direct others' attention to specific aspects of ourselves? Researchers Zhao, Grasmuck, and Martin argue that we use the power of selection to present not false, but *hoped-for* identities. They wrote, the "hoped-for possible selves users projected on Facebook were neither the 'true selves' commonly seen in [anonymous] MUDs or Chat Rooms, nor the 'real selves' people presented in localized face-to-face interactions. The Facebook selves appeared to be highly socially desirable identities individuals aspire to have offline but have not yet been able to embody for one reason or another" (2008, p. 1830). Speaking of self-presentation on the Internet in general (as opposed to social networking sites in particular), technology writer Navneet Alang wrote of hoped-for identity construction for people who feel they are on the outside: "Freed from the myriad ways in which our bodies are read, interacting with others through this virtual self can, despite its immateriality, still have real-world effects. The shy person's brash Twitter persona, the immigrant's perfectly hybrid avatar, the gay youth's sex-positive blog: all these marginalized identities suddenly have another place in which to explore themselves and become anew" (2012).

Obviously, then, all kinds of people make their way to an SNS for all kinds of reasons. Petter Brandtzæg identified five more-or-less distinct types of users in an in-depth analysis of the SNS activity of 2,000 people of all ages over a two-year span (2012, pp. 476–477):

- *Advanced users:* These are the people on all the time, demonstrating "frequent usage and a very diverse and broad SNS behavior." They take advantage of most or all of the SNS's capabilities.

- *Debaters:* These users are "highly active in discussions and debating" and are frequent, often the heaviest, users of SNS.

- *Socializers:* These people engage primarily in socializing with friends, family, and other people on the sites. Social interaction is of primary importance for these users. They aren't big on discussion and debating or following others' discussions.

- *Lurkers:* People in this category regularly use SNS, but do so less frequently than the other types. They social network primarily to kill time, look at photos, find information about friends, and "see if somebody has contacted me." They are passive consumers of what others have contributed to the site.

- *Sporadics:* People in this category are almost nonusers. They connect only occasionally to see if somebody has tried to get in touch with them.

The Internet and Interpersonal Communication

The real goal of the Brandtzæg research was not to identify different types of users. It was actually designed to weigh the "social costs and benefits" often attributed to social networking, leading the author to conclude that use of SNSs is associated with "social capital and might strengthen social bonds as SNSs give free and easy communication with family, friends, and acquaintances regardless of time and place . . . Examining the results [of this research] in light of the current media debate, they do not support the anxiety about 'antisocial networking' or low social involvement. SNS communication does not seem to replace intimacy or face-to-face interaction. In

Face-to-face communication has long been considered the gold standard of interpersonal communication. But that view is starting to change.

fact, SNS users are actually more likely to socially interact face-to-face and report more social capital compared to nonusers" (pp. 481–482). Social capital in this instance is the building of social connections and social networks and the resulting norms and trust that are built which enable people to act together more effectively.

But haven't we already seen that scholarly discussion of CMC tends to revolve around the assumption that face-to-face communication (FtF) is superior, the "gold standard" (Berger, 2005, p. 430)? This belief stems from two differences between these forms of interaction. First, FtF is *immediate and direct,* whereas CMC is *mediated,* or *filtered.* In FtF, communicators can see and hear one another; they can read facial expressions, gestures, voice pitch, rate of speech, that is, all the nonverbal cues that frame spoken communication (Chapter 4). Moreover, FtF communicators share a common, context-providing physical space, further facilitating effective and efficient meaning making.

CMC, however, offers little contextual information and few, if any, social cues. This is the **cues-filtered-out theory** (Kiesler, Siegel and McGuire, 1984). FtF is assumed to lead to less miscommunication than does CMC for a second immediacy-related reason, **mutual knowledge** (Krauss and Fussell, 1990). Mutual knowledge is information the communicating parties share in common *and know* they share. Communicators can establish mutual knowledge through *direct knowledge* (they have firsthand experience with one another), *category membership* (the assumptions they make about each other's knowledge based on the social categories they are assumed to belong to), and *interactional dynamics* (their reading of nonverbal reactions and direct feedback). These elements are typically present in an FtF setting, even between relative strangers. The speakers are in one another's presence, so they have at least a little direct knowledge of one another. They can see the gender, race, possibly occupation, and a host of other likely social categories that each may belong to. And as we've already seen, feedback and nonverbal communication are immediate and direct.

In CMC, especially among relative strangers, these elements are typically lacking. Catherine Cramton investigated mutual knowledge in CMC and discovered that miscommunication would occur because in the relative absence of mutual knowledge, communicators, presumably conditioned by FtF communication, falsely assumed that others understood their information (2001). This failure to appreciate the limitations of CMC, argue Justin Kruger and his colleagues, may well stem from overconfidence and egocentrism. In a series of five experiments testing e-mailers' ability to convey sarcasm, they demonstrated that

> without the benefit of paralinguistic cues such as gesture, emphasis, and intonation, it can be difficult to convey emotion and tone over electronic mail . . . [P]eople tend to believe that they can communicate over e-mail more effectively than they actually can . . . [T]his overconfidence is born of egocentrism, the inherent difficulty of detaching oneself from one's own perspective when evaluating the perspective of someone else. Because e-mail communicators "hear" a statement differently depending on whether they intend to be, say, sarcastic or funny, it can be difficult to appreciate that their electronic audience may not. (Kruger et al., 2005, p. 925)

Their findings held even when the communicators were personally acquainted.

But there is a more generous view of the availability of social and contextual cues in CMC, **social information-processing theory** (Lea and Spears, 1992), which argues that these cues do indeed exist. CMC often contains emoticons, text symbols, or pictographs, used to express emotions. Choice of technology, too, provides context. E-mail carries more gravity than text messaging. A text message suggests more intimacy than a tweet or SNS posting. And because silence and chronemics are forms of nonverbal communication, both contribute significantly to CMC meaning making. Walther and Tidwell (1995) demonstrated that differences in the time of day an e-mail message is sent, from daytime to nighttime, and response delays of as little as 24 hours (that is, silence) significantly influence the degree of liking the communicators express for senders and receivers and the perceived sense of urgency communicated by the message. Tyler and Tang (2003) examined chronemic rhythms in e-mail communication, identifying the existence of **response expectations**, senders' "expectations as to when they anticipate to receive a response to a message they sent," and **breakdown perception**, "when the sender believes that something has gone wrong, and will take further action" (p. 253). Breakdown perception occurs when senders think a pause is already too long and judge it as silence.

THUMBNAIL THEORY

Social Information Processing Theory

Face-to-face and computer-mediated communication are more-or-less equal in quality because the latter often offers a rich variety of social and contextual cues used to facilitate communication.

CMC offers emotions as a substitute for many forms of nonverbal communication. How many can you identify?

Kalman and Rafaeli (2011) investigated CMC delays and silence in terms of expectancy violation theory. As you read in Chapter 4, this is the idea that when our interpersonal expectations are violated (for example, when someone enters our intimate space), our attention to this nonverbal communication is heightened. As a result, we work to interpret the behavior—is it a welcomed sign of increased intimacy, or is it an unwanted, possibly threatening intrusion?

As you might remember, the meaning we make from the violation depends on our judgment of the person making it. Kalman and Rafaeli discovered that users of e-mail are sensitive to delays and silence, are aware of norms regarding reply time, have expectations about those norms, and actively consider the nature of the other in judging whether delay or silence is indeed a violation of those expectations. This led them to comment on "the richness of text-based CMC." They wrote that their work "contributes to the discussion of the richness of CMC, and whether CMC is a poor substitute for traditional communication channels, or whether it is an alternative to traditional communication channels the unique affordances of which make it neither superior nor inferior to traditional communication. The findings reported [in their research] support the latter assertion by adding to the accumulating evidence that text-based CMC is able to convey nonverbal cues, and that these cues interact with communicator attributes" (p. 65). Remember, too, that not all CMC is text-based, but more on that later in the chapter.

The second difference between FtF and CMC traditionally suggesting the superiority of the former is that FtF is **synchronous**, that is, people interact immediately, in real time, and can simultaneously send and receive messages. CMC, on the other hand, is **asynchronous**, there is a delay of some length, regardless of how short, between sending and receiving. Here, too, there is scholarship questioning this assumption. Kruger and his colleagues see value in the time afforded by asynchronicity, "Compared with synchronous media, asynchronous text media such as e-mail more readily allow for reflection and reconsideration of one's communication before transmission" (Kruger et al., 2005, p. 934). This argument is based in users' ability to control their CMC. Considering only text-based CMC such as e-mail, instant messaging, and texting, users can control the pace and length of communication and speed of response. In addition, as we've already seen, CMC offers the opportunity for more careful crafting of the self in communication interactions (Walther, 1996).

Much of the presumed superiority granted to FtF communication over CMC is based in **media richness theory**, which views communication media as falling along a continuum of lean to rich, based on their contribution to the quality of meaning making. FtF is traditionally considered the superior medium because its immediacy provides greater personal information-carrying capacity (you and the other can observe each other in real time and in context) and it is synchronous (providing instant feedback). You can see the importance of

response expectations Senders' expectations about the timing of anticipated response.

breakdown perception When senders believe no response is forthcoming and take action.

synchronous communication Immediate, real-time communication interaction.

asynchronous communication Delay of some length between sending and receiving.

THUMBNAIL THEORY

Media Richness Theory

Different media's contribution to meaning making falls along a continuum of lean to rich, as judged by criteria such as the presence of instant feedback, the use of multiple cues and natural language, and the medium's personal focus.

immediacy and synchronicity in the four factors that make a medium rich (Daft and Lengel, 1986):

- *Presence of instant feedback*, making possible the asking and answering of questions.
- *Use of multiple cues*, such as physical presence, words, nonverbal signs, numbers, and graphic symbols.
- *Use of natural language*, which, because of its universality, can convey meaning across a wide set of concepts and ideas.
- A *personal focus*.

The more a means of communication displays these attributes, the richer it is. Using these criteria, then, FtF is typically considered the "richest" and something like a mailed letter the "leanest," with other forms of communication in between. But let's take these elements one at a time and consider CMC in their light.

- *Instant feedback*: Where on the continuum would you place chat rooms and instant messaging? Where does texting accompanied by a web-cam fall? Where do you put Web services like Skype, Oovoo, and FaceTime that allow real-time video chats?
- *Multiple cues*: They are present in web-cam and video CMC, and even text-based CMC can be augmented with multiple cues such as photos, videos, and links to other places on the Internet. For example, imagine an FtF conversation with friends in which you want to tell them about your trip to Brazil. You may be a great interpersonal communicator, and your descriptions may be vivid. You'd no doubt do a good job. Now imagine that same conversation via an SNS or even e-mail. You can write the same descriptions, albeit without the flair and emotion you might have shown in person. You can gather carefully selected photos you've taken into a slide show (accompanied by quiet samba music) and post it to your site or provide a link to it in your e-mail. You can also include links to the nicely produced YouTube videos of your stay in Rio de Janeiro that you uploaded, as well as links to websites and other videos offering more information and insight into that South American destination.
- *Natural language*: Again, it is present in web-cam and video CMC, and assuming that you are communicating with others who speak your language, your post or e-mail text, written in your common tongue, is a natural language. But more than that, video and audio, and the Web itself, are natural languages to digital natives like you.
- *Personal focus*: Other than the inability to physically touch the other, contemporary CMC can be every bit as personally focused as FtF.

Vivian Sheer combined notions of communication control and rich media in her investigation of young people's use of CMC in building friendships, demonstrating that "media richness aided in both social and task communication . . . Use of rich features, such as webcam and [instant messaging], seemingly facilitated the increase of acquaintances, new friends, opposite-sex friends, and, thus, the total number of friends. Primarily text-based messaging, however, helped with the progression toward close-friendship more than did rich features" (2011, p. 101).

But what is a "friend" in the age of social media? What becomes of traditional understandings of friendship when the average Facebook user has 338 friends and more than half have over 200 (Smith, 2014)? Is MIT psychologist Sherry Turkle (2012) correct when she says, "We expect more from technology and less from each other?" "People can't get enough of each other," she says, "if and only if they can have each other at a distance in amounts they can control." She labels this the "Goldilocks effect—not too close, not too far, just right." As we saw earlier in this chapter, there's no doubt that there are lonely, disengaged, even

Because of technologies like Skype and Oovoo, CMC is rapidly shedding its text-based identity.

depressed people immersed in the new technologies. But communication scholars have gone quite deeply into a number of CMC issues connected to new digital friendships and relationships. We'll look at four: social isolation, how shy and popular people use social network sites for friendship, online self-disclosure, and its close cousin, relational development.

Social Isolation

Is the Goldilocks effect real? That is, do the new communication technologies distance us from one another as they connect us? You've heard the argument in many forms. We are losing our sense of community. We are increasingly socially isolated, hanging out with smaller numbers of people, and the ones we do spend time with are very much like ourselves, all because of the Internet, SNS, and smartphones. "The implications of such a trend are alarming," write Keith Hampton and his colleagues. "They indicate a decline in the availability of broad social support within social networks in the form of companionship and instrumental and emergency aid and an increased likelihood that important matters are discussed only within small, closed groups" (Hampton, Sessions, and Her, 2010, p. 131). Their analysis of more than 20 years' worth of data from the US General Social Survey (a standard core of demographic, behavioral, and attitudinal questions asked annually and overseen by the National Science Foundation) suggests that these fears of atomized, isolated Americans, while not completely unreasonable, are overblown. They found that "neither Internet nor mobile phone use is associated with having fewer core discussion confidants or having less diverse ties with whom to discuss important matters" (p. 148). In fact, they discovered that smartphone ownership and some SNS activity actually increased the number of close confidants, and Internet users

Using your own experience, can you argue that the Goldilocks effect does not exist?

were far more likely to discuss important issues with people outside their immediate families and even with those of different politics.

Psychologist John Cacioppo, author of *Loneliness* (Cacioppo and Patrick, 2008) and an expert on America's "epidemic of loneliness," recently conducted an experiment looking "for a connection between the loneliness of subjects and the relative frequency of their interactions via Facebook, chat rooms, online games, dating sites, and face-to-face contact." Journalist Stephen Marche (2012) asked him what he found. "The greater the proportion of face-to-face interactions, the less lonely you are. The greater the proportion of online interactions, the lonelier you are," explained Professor Cacioppo. So, asked Marche, doesn't this mean that Facebook and the new communication technologies actually do make people lonelier? Cacioppo, recognizing technology's double edge, answered that Facebook is merely a tool, and its effectiveness depends on how we use it. "If you use Facebook to increase face-to-face contact, it increases social capital," he said. "Facebook can be terrific, if we use it properly. It's like a car. You can drive it to pick up your friends. Or you can drive alone."

Shy and Popular Users

But what if you have few friends to pick up as you drive around? In other words, do social networking sites help people make and maintain friendships, or are they places where those who are already popular offline go to enhance their popularity and those who are less popular go to compensate for their real-world inadequacies? Researchers Jolene Zywica and James Danowski (2008) call these the *Rich Get Richer* (social enhancement) and *Poor Get Richer* (social compensation) hypotheses, respectively. Studying the Facebook use of more than 600 collegiate students, they found significant evidence to support both hypotheses. "Those more sociable (extroverted) and with higher self-esteem are more popular both offline and on Facebook—supporting the Social Enhancement hypothesis," they wrote. "At the same time, another subset of users who are less sociable (introverted), have lower self-esteem, and are less popular offline, support the Social Compensation hypotheses because they are—and strive more to look—popular on Facebook—and think that is important."

In other words, already popular people used the site to augment that popularity, and less popular people were also more popular on Facebook than offline. This is because they were willing to reveal more information about themselves and express different facets of their personalities to their online friends than they were to their offline friends. "Rather than making strategic moves to enhance popularity," wrote the authors, these shy users "may just feel more comfortable expressing their true selves online rather than offline" (p. 19).

Equally important is the *quality* of friendship experienced by users with less offline popularity. In a study of shy people's use of Facebook, Levi Baker and Debra Oswald demonstrated that for "relatively shy individuals, Facebook use was positively associated with satisfaction, importance, and closeness with Facebook friends . . . refut[ing] warnings . . . that CMC use might cause shy individuals to become even more socially withdrawn and isolated. The current data clearly demonstrate that shy individuals' use of Facebook is associated with better quality friendships" (2010, pp. 883–884).

Facebook Envy and Our Sense of Well-Being

But, staying with Professor Cacioppo's car analogy, maybe driving the car in and of itself brings with it a different set of problems, just as if we never walked anywhere any more, denying ourselves needed exercise and more immediate, tactile interaction with the world around us. Ethan Kross and his colleagues (Kross et al., 2013) examined that very issue, asking if Facebook use influences users' subjective well-being, that is, how they feel about themselves. Subjective well-being operates on two levels: how we feel about ourselves in the moment, and how satisfied we are, in general, with our own lives. "We text-messaged people five times per day for two-weeks to examine how Facebook use influences the two components of subjective well-being," they wrote, "Our results indicate that Facebook use predicts negative shifts on both of these variables over time. The more people used Facebook at one time point, the worse they felt the next time we text-messaged them; the more they used Facebook over two-weeks, the more their life satisfaction levels declined over time" (p. 1).

The researchers were able to dismiss the two likely alternative explanations for what they found, "First, interacting with other people 'directly' did not predict declines in well-being. In fact, direct social network interactions led people to feel *better* over time. This suggests that Facebook use may constitute a unique form of social network interaction that predicts impoverished well-being. Second, multiple types of evidence indicated that it was not the case that Facebook use led to declines in well-being because people are more likely to use Facebook when they feel bad—neither affect [mood] nor worry predicted Facebook use and Facebook use continued to predict significant declines in well-being when controlling for loneliness" (italics in original; p. 4).

Might that damage to our sense of well-being be due to **Facebook envy**, users resentful of others' happiness as represented on SNS? Hanna Krasnova and her colleagues tested that hypothesis and discovered that, indeed, that was the case for large numbers of Facebook users, as many as one in three. They found that "envy about '*travel and leisure,*' '*social interactions*' and '*happiness*' belong to the three most frequently mentioned causes of envy triggered by Facebook use" (italics in original; 2013, p. 7). As any SNS user knows, these are the self-selected topics that most people tend to emphasize in their online presentations; few of us post the shameful or depressing things in our lives. But does Facebook envy produce declines in users' sense of well-being? The authors themselves wrote that the major contribution of their work was its demonstration of the link between "the spread and ubiquitous presence of envy on SNS" and the undermining of "users' life satisfaction" (p. 13). And you? Are you free of Facebook envy?

Facebook envy Users envying others' happiness as represented on SNSs.

Self-Disclosure and Relational Development

Do online friendships develop in ways similar to real-world relationships? That is, what roles do self-disclosure and uncertainty reduction, both essential to relational development, play on social networking sites? If you still hold to the FtF-as-gold-standard philosophy, you might argue that they must be different and inferior processes. But the available evidence suggests you'd be wrong. Different? Somewhat. Inferior? Maybe not.

In an experiment in which college students were asked to judge the "like-ability, trust, friendliness, and interest of others" by examining their Facebook profiles, Cynthia Palmieri and her colleagues discovered that what happens online mirrors what happens offline. That is, people whose profiles offered low levels of self-disclosure produced little uncertainty reduction and thus, a less positive reaction from those who "met" them. High levels of self-disclosure produced more uncertainty reduction and, therefore, more liking (Palmieri et al., 2012). Bruce McKinney and his colleagues suggested that SNSs produce their own "disclosure norms" based on what others have disclosed, clarifying just what kinds of information and how much of it is appropriate for sharing. This, in turn, produces "a positive attitude about such information sharing" (McKinney, Kelly, and Duran, 2012, p. 116). Recall Chapter 4's discussion of the value of reciprocity in enhancing relational development, and it's not very difficult to see that with greater opportunity for thoughtful control of self-disclosure, clear norms of appropriateness about what can and cannot be disclosed, and a positive attitude toward reciprocity, friendships can be every bit as real and meaningful online as off.

Review of Learning Objectives

12.1 Identify the warning signs of Internet addiction, depression, and distraction.

Many people suffer from Internet addiction, spending 40 to 80 hours a week online. Overreliance on digital technology for connection and stimulation can also fuel depression. And while there is little debate that our interaction with digital technology is changing how we engage the world, disagreement exists over the harmfulness of this change.

12.2 Explain why and how people use social networking sites for identity construction and maintenance and for relational communication.

People are attracted to SNSs by the need to belong and the need for self-presentation. We have an intrinsic drive to affiliate with others and gain social acceptance and, as explained by symbolic interaction, a need for self-presentation to engage in impression management. And while the Internet's anonymity can allow false presentations of self, most SNS users present fairly accurate or hoped-for identities.

12.3 Describe potential relationships between social media and social isolation, popularity, and self-disclosure.

Personal communication technologies are often condemned as fostering social isolation, creating a false sense of popularity, and impeding meaningful self-disclosure. Remembering that technologies work as double-edged swords, there is some truth to these criticisms. But use of these increasingly mature technologies by increasingly savvy users may be obviating these problems, as research consistently demonstrates their potential value.

12.4 Present an informed opinion in the debate over face-to-face communication versus computer-mediated communication.

The supposed superiority of face-to-face communication is based on its immediacy and synchronicity. But contemporary forms of CMC may offer people equal levels of these two communication-enhancing factors as they are increasingly rich forms of interaction.

Key Terms

double-edged sword 260
computer-mediated communication (CMC) 260
app 263
cookies 264
phantom-vibration syndrome 267
Internet addiction 267
Facebook depression 269
fear of missing out (FOMO) 269
transactive memory 270
idealized virtual identity hypothesis 273
extended real-life hypothesis 273
cues-filtered-out theory 275
mutual knowledge 275
social information-processing theory 276
response expectations 276
breakdown perception 276
synchronous 277
asynchronous 277
media richness theory 277
Facebook envy 281

Questions for Review

1. What does it mean to say that personal communication technologies are neutral but not benign? What is the double-edged sword of these technologies?

2. What is phantom-vibration syndrome, and how does it relate to Internet addiction?

3. What are Facebook depression and fear of missing out (FOMO)?

4. What is transactive memory?

5. What two basic social needs drive our use of social networking sites?

6. What are the idealized virtual identity and the extended real-life hypotheses?

7. Differentiate between the cues-filtered-out and the social information-processing theories.

8. Explain response expectations and breakdown perception in terms of expectancy violation theory.

9. Explain media richness theory.

10. What are the Rich Get Richer and Poor Get Richer hypotheses?

Questions for Discussion

1. Have you ever been troubled by the amount of time you spend engaged with digital technologies? If not, why not? If yes, what was the immediate cause, if any, of your concern? What, if anything, did you do about it?

2. Have you ever encountered in your social networking experience an obvious case of a friend misrepresenting him- or herself? If so, what did you do about it? Was your response direct or indirect? How might symbolic interaction have predicted your response and its effectiveness?

3. Have you ever posted something online that you later regretted? What was it, and what was your regret? Do you have internal or personal rules about what you allow yourself to post or to self-disclose? How did you arrive at these rules?

Persuasion and Social Influence

No way can you pass up this offer—a free ticket plus a round-trip ride to the conference championship game. The problem, though, is that it's a Sunday-night, nationally-televised contest and you wouldn't get back to campus until noon on Monday. That means you'd have to get your Communication instructor to give you a make-up for the quiz you'll miss at 9 a.m. But that might not be too big a problem because you've done everything right to get her to think well of you. You're respectful; you sit in the front row and are always attentive; you come to class neatly dressed and groomed, always smiling. But you may already have spent any benefit these favor-building maneuvers earned you when you asked to miss a Friday class so you could leave early for your brother's wedding—and when you had to convince her to give you an extra day for your term paper first draft because your printer broke—and when you tried to persuade her that your short essay on the mid-semester exam was really worth an 8 out of 10, not the 6 she "unfairly" gave you. And then there was the time you had "the flu" and missed your in-class presentation on friendship maintenance and social networking.

You're pretty good at persuasion, but this challenge may be out of even your league. You recall Abe Lincoln's commentary on persuasion, "You can fool some of the people all of the time, and all of the people some of the time, but you can't fool all of the people all of the time," especially a professor who's no doubt heard it all before—and probably all from you.

We are always persuading, even if it is at a very basic level. In this chapter, we will look at efforts to influence others through communication—instances when we consciously, actively intend to alter another's thoughts or actions.

Learning Objectives

13.1   Explain the characteristics and importance of persuasion.

13.2   Distinguish between values, attitudes, beliefs, and behaviors, and explain how those distinctions influence persuasion.

13.3   Explain balance theory and cognitive dissonance theory.

13.4   Describe the influence that source, message, and receiver characteristics have on persuadability.

13.5   Explain the workings of the elaboration likelihood model of persuasion.

13.6   Distinguish between different processes of attitude change.

THUMBNAIL THEORY

Speech Acts Theory

Whenever we speak, we hope to accomplish some goal. We use communication, however routinely or diligently, to influence.

persuasion Communication specifically intended to shape, reinforce, or change the responses of others.

What Is Persuasion?

The theory of **speech acts**, developed by linguist and philosopher John Austin (1962), argues that whenever we speak, we hope to accomplish some goal. When we speak, we have intentions. As a result, we choose how we want to express ourselves based on what we want others to think, accept, or do. In other words, we are always to some degree persuading. For example, when you greet your classmates with "What's up?" your words are less important than your intentions. If the words *what's up* were the most important part of your greeting, you'd expect answers like "Certainly not my GPA." Your intention, the reason you chose to express yourself as you did, was not even to get them to acknowledge you; it was to get them to think well of you. After all, you could have simply nodded in their direction. When you tell friends something as routine as "The sky was blue," your intention is to have them accept that the sky was one color rather than another. As you should remember from Chapter 1, the transactional view of communication assumes that communication does not occur unless change occurs in the participants. Speech acts theory wants us to understand that people try, however routinely or intentionally, to influence that change.

   Persuasion, however, is communication *specifically intended* to shape, reinforce, or change the responses of others (Miller, 1980). *Response shaping* occurs when we encounter new information, requiring some judgment or evaluation. For example, you may be looking for a new car, and Chevrolet uses a sophisticated advertising campaign to favorably shape your response to its latest-model Camaro. As another example, you meet someone named Alex on the first day of class, and you use an invitation to a Friday night concert to shape your relationship. In response shaping, the movement is from no response to some response. *Response reinforcing* occurs when communication deepens our commitment to already held attitudes or behaviors. You like big, powerful, American-made cars, and Camaro has always been your favorite. Chevy uses its ad campaign and an online video game to further cement that favor. You and Alex now have a nice friendship, so you extend a Thanksgiving invitation to deepen that bond. In response reinforcing, the movement is from one degree of response to another, typically deeper. *Response changing* occurs when communication moves our attitudes or behaviors from an existing or established position to another. You currently drive an 11-year-old Subaru, but Chevy's combination of skilled marketing, low finance rates, and a $2,000 cash rebate convince you to buy the new Camaro. You and Alex are great friends, but you want to become more. You propose on bended knee, which produces just the response you want. You are no longer just friends; you're engaged. In response changing, the movement is from one condition to another, different condition.

These examples highlight two important characteristics of persuasion. The first is intentionality. As communication scholars James Stiff and Paul Mongeau explain, "Although one can argue that all communication is by its very nature persuasive and that many activities might inadvertently affect the responses of others . . . persuasive activity [considers] behaviors that are *intended* to affect the responses of others" (italics in original; 2003, pp. 4–5). Your big brother's love affair with the Camaro may have influenced your affection for big, powerful, American-made cars, but he did not persuade you to that position. Alex may be head-over-heels for you just because you are who you are. You didn't have to employ your persuasive skills; all you did was be yourself. The second characteristic of persuasion—whether shaping, reinforcing, or changing—is that sometimes it occurs over time, but sometimes it is quite sudden; sometimes it takes repeated persuasive attempts, sometimes just one. Typically, though, change occurs over time and with exposure to repeated messages.

It is important to understand persuasive communication for two reasons. First, much of your daily communication is composed of efforts to persuade or influence others—so you might as well get good at it. Second, you are the recipient of a constant stream of persuasive communication from others, often via mass media—so you need to decide which persuasive efforts are worthy of your response and which to reject.

Specifically, persuasion is essential to *interpersonal communication and the building and maintenance of relationships*. In almost every interaction with another—a friend, a family member, a boss, a stranger—we engage in communication for the purpose of altering or

Skilled communicators can shape, reinforce, or even change your responses. What's your impression of Chevy's Camaro? Where did it come from?

modifying how they think about something (their beliefs, attitudes, values, or behaviors, which we will discuss in the next section). We want our professor to give us a make-up quiz, our friends to have lunch with us, our sister to lend us her car, our boss to let us leave work early on Friday, that stranger to support a ban on plastic shopping bags.

This last example suggests another domain where persuasion is essential, the *conduct and maintenance of our social institutions*. In a democracy, it is the people who decide. But in the process of deciding, we have to receive and create messages that help us and others do just that. In other words, we have to persuade others to our view of an important matter, just as they

COMMUNICATION IN THE WORKPLACE

Four Dos and Four Don'ts of Workplace Persuasion

Researcher and organizational leadership expert Jay Conger spent 12 years studying persuasion in the workplace. Why did he give the topic so much attention? "If there ever was a time for businesspeople to learn the fine art of persuasion, it is now," he explained. "Gone are the command-and-control days of executives managing by decree . . . Work today gets done in an environment where people don't just ask What should I do? but Why should I do it?" (1998).

Professor Conger's work led him to propose four dos and four don'ts for on-the-job persuasion:

The Four Dos

1. *Do establish your credibility*—Workplace credibility comes from expertise and good interpersonal relationships. Show sound judgment and be well informed. Demonstrate that you can be trusted to listen and to consider the interests of others.
2. *Do frame your goals in a way that identifies common ground with those you intend to persuade*—What are the shared benefits of your goal with those of the people you hope to persuade? Study their needs and desired outcomes; talk to them. If you can't find any shared advantages, adjust your position until you do.
3. *Do reinforce your positions using vivid language and compelling evidence*—Supplement the data supporting your argument with examples, stories, metaphors, and analogies to enliven your position.

4. *Do connect emotionally with your audience*—Understand the value of emotions in colleagues' decision-making. Show your own emotional commitment to your position (but don't overdo it) and develop an accurate sense of your audience's emotional state. Then adjust the tone of your persuasive message accordingly.

The Four Don'ts

1. *Don't attempt to make your case with an opening hard sell*—Don't paint a bulls-eye on your message, giving those prone to disagreement something to attack.
2. *Don't resist compromise*—Compromise is not defeat; it is essential to constructive persuasion. Show your flexibility and willingness to respond to your audience's concerns. Compromise can produce better, more lasting, shared outcomes.
3. *Don't think the secret of persuasion lies in presenting great arguments*—Logic and data are valuable when attempting to persuade others, but so, too, are your credibility, the strength of your interpersonal relationships, the ability to connect emotionally, your use of vivid language, and your skill at finding mutually beneficial outcomes.
4. *Don't assume workplace persuasion is a one-time effort*—Effective persuasion is a process, not a thing. Colleagues, even well-intentioned, rarely reach consensus on a single try.

work to persuade us to theirs. Democracy does not work unless there is a "multitude of antagonistic tongues," that is, many divergent points of view (*Associated Press v. United States*, 1945). The more skilled you are at persuasive communication, the greater the likelihood that your voice will be heard. Persuasive communication is also central to educational institutions, such as your college or university. You had to convince the school to admit you (and eventually to grant you a degree). And health and medical institutions increasingly rely on persuasive communication for greater efficiency and more productive delivery of services. Many of their influential health communication efforts are conducted online and in the traditional mass media. As you can image, there is definite career benefit in being skilled in the art of on-the-job persuasion, as you can read in the box "Four Dos and Four Don'ts of Workplace Persuasion."

The third area where persuasive communication is essential is in the *operation and maintenance of mass media institutions*. Our commercially supported mass media institutions prosper by selling audiences to advertisers. The way they do that is by exposing us to a near-constant stream of commercial messages—estimates range from 3,000 to 20,000 a day (Lamourex, 2014)—all designed to persuade us. Even on the Internet, not generally considered a commercial medium, Americans view 9.9 billion streamed video commercials a month, totaling just under four billion minutes of sound-and-motion-enriched persuasion (O'Malley, 2013). Recognizing the persuasive power of mass communication, non-commercial entities such as public broadcasting stations, charities, and other social interest groups also place their messages in the media in hopes of influencing us.

Even non-commercial public interest groups recognize the power of an effective ad campaign. Here is an example from the group Adbusters.

Values, Attitudes, Beliefs, and Behaviors

The "somethings" that persuasion is intended to shape, reinforce, or change are people's beliefs, attitudes, values, and behaviors. **Values** are people's deeply held judgments about the worth or importance of various aspects of their lives; they are "abstract goals that people consider to be important guiding principles in their lives" (Maio and Olson, 1998, p. 294). We value

value Deeply held judgment about the worth or importance of various aspects of people's lives.

phenomena such as helpfulness, trust, family, freedom, education, truth, equal rights, security, and childhood. In war, we say our enemies are less human, deserving of destruction, because they "do not share our values." Values are central to people's sense of self, and therefore shape their beliefs and attitudes.

Beliefs and attitudes are closely related, as you can see in Milton Rokeach's classic definition of an **attitude**, a "relatively enduring organization of beliefs around an object or situation predisposing one to respond in some preferential manner" (1968, p. 112). Attitudes, then, are *enduring;* they are more than passing thoughts such as, "Yeah, that's a cool car" or "I like the saxophone." As Stiff and Mongeau explain, attitudes "are formed over a long period of time and are frequently reinforced. As such, they are relatively stable and are difficult to change." They are "cluster[s] or combination[s] of several related cognitive elements. These cognitive elements are defined as beliefs that cluster around a central attitude object, and the entire cluster of beliefs is the attitude about the object" (2003, p. 12).

A **belief** is a proposition about something, "faith that something is real or is true" (Potter, 2012, p. 41). According to Rokeach, there are three types of beliefs: descriptive, prescriptive, and evaluative. *Descriptive beliefs* are objective assertions that can be proven or disproven. *Prescriptive beliefs* are subjective assertions of goodness versus badness or correctness versus incorrectness. They cannot be proven or disproven. Finally, *evaluative beliefs* are subjective assertions of affect or judgment (liking versus disliking). They, too, cannot be proven or disproven. Let's use smoking cigarettes as our attitude object (the concept around which our beliefs might cluster). *Scientific evidence convincingly demonstrates that smoking cigarettes is harmful to one's health.* This is a descriptive belief—it can be proven to be the case. *It's wrong (bad or incorrect) that cigarettes are so readily available.* This prescriptive belief cannot be proven or disproven, because while it may be perfectly true to you, someone else might think differently. *I can't stand the fact that cigarettes are still legal* is an evaluative belief. This is your personal, or subjective, position—many people applaud the fact that cigarettes are legal—and your subjective position can neither be proven nor disproven. These different—and different types of—beliefs about smoking (and quite likely many more) cluster together to form your attitude toward smoking.

Attitudes are not only relatively stable clusters of beliefs, they are *predispositions to respond;* that is, they are likely to lead to some outcome, oftentimes a **behavior**—a concrete, observable action. Given the cluster of beliefs you have surrounding smoking and the resulting anti-smoking attitude you hold (all based on the high value that you place on health), you would most likely refuse your friend's offer of a cigarette, or you might write a letter to the editor of your school's paper to protest its acceptance of tobacco ads.

There are three important facts to keep in mind, though, about the connection between attitudes and behaviors:

- First, sometimes those attitude-produced responses are not visible. Yes, you might refuse the offer of a smoke, a quite visible response, but you might also come to think less of your friend because she is a smoker or

---

attitude A relatively enduring organization of beliefs around an object or situation predisposing one to respond in a preferential manner.

belief A proposition about something; faith that something is real or is true.

behavior Concrete, observable action.

because she doesn't know how you really feel about smoking. That response, though real, would not be visible.

- Second, although there quite often is a link between attitude and behavior, sometimes the two are not in synch. You may have an anti-smoking attitude, but perhaps you hope to develop a deeper relationship with your tobacco-offering friend. If your attraction to your friend is stronger than your objection to smoking, your acceptance of her offer may well belie your attitude toward smoking.

- Finally, behaviors can alter attitudes. If you accept the offer of a cigarette and are smoking with your friend, you need to balance your attitude and behavior. Now that you are behaving in a certain way, you adjust your attitudes and beliefs, and possibly even your values.

Balance Theory

One common explanation for why attitudes and behaviors sometimes don't match is balance theory, and the most widely accepted explanation for how behaviors can change attitudes is dissonance theory. Psychologist Fritz Heider developed **balance theory** in 1946. His basic argument is that people want to be cognitively balanced; that is, they want the things and people in their lives to be in harmony. Balance theory is sometimes called *P-O-X theory* because it involves attitudes and behaviors in situations that involve three elements:

- P—the person
- O—another person
- X—the attitude object.

Our view of the relationship between these three elements will be either balanced or imbalanced, and we don't like imbalance. Balance theory, then, argues that because we prefer balanced over unbalanced states, we are motivated to change either our attitudes or our behaviors to create balance. Figure 13.1 shows the relationship between the three elements in our smoking example.

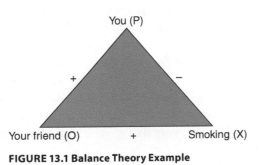

FIGURE 13.1 Balance Theory Example

You have a positive attitude toward your friend, so there is a + between P and O. Your friend has a positive attitude toward smoking, so there's a + between O and X. But you have a negative attitude toward smoking, meaning there's a – between P and X. This relationship is out of balance (two positives multiplied by a negative produce a negative). How do you fix it? You could change your attitude toward your friend; that way, a negative multiplied by a negative multiplied by a positive equals a positive, and you have balance. Or you could change your attitude toward smoking, producing the same result (multiplying three positives produces a positive). And now, not only are you no longer attitudinally predisposed against smoking, you're predisposed to behaviorally respond to the offer of a cigarette; you answer "Yes" and smoke the cigarette. But if you did that, you'd probably hate yourself. That's where dissonance theory enters the picture.

Dissonance Theory

cognitive consistency
Tendency to maintain, or to return to, a state of attitudinal balance.

THUMBNAIL THEORY

Dissonance Theory

Information that is inconsistent with a person's already held attitudes and beliefs creates a psychological discomfort (a dissonance) that must be relieved. If people know various things that are not psychologically consistent with one another, they will try to make them more consistent. They do this through the selective processes of exposure, retention, and perception.

Like Heider, psychologist Leon Festinger believed that people seek **cognitive consistency**, the tendency to maintain, or to return to, a state of attitudinal balance. His **dissonance theory**, then, argues that information that is inconsistent with a person's already held attitudes and beliefs will create a psychological discomfort (a dissonance) that must be relieved (Festinger, 1957). "If a person knows various things that are not psychologically consistent with one another," Festinger wrote, "he [*sic*] will, in a variety of ways, try to make them more consistent" (1962, p. 93).

In a classic test of dissonance theory, Festinger and Merrill Carlsmith (1959) set up a study in which they asked participants to perform a boring task (placing small wooden spools into trays and then taking them out of those same trays for 30 minutes). Those participants were then asked to convince the next participant that the task was quite exciting and interesting. The researchers paid the original participants either $1 or $20 to lie about the task ($20 in 1959 would be about $150 today). When later asked if they had enjoyed the experience, which group of paid participants do you think found it most satisfying? Wouldn't you expect it to be those earning $20? But this wasn't the case, and dissonance theory explains why. The task was boring and unpleasant, so lying about it to the next participant was worth that high pay. Those who were paid $20 admitted to Festinger and Carlsmith that they were liars. Bad job/big pay produces no dissonance. But because those who had received only $1 did feel dissonance, they reported that the job was indeed fun and exciting; they didn't want to think of themselves as liars, so in their minds they hadn't lied when they told the next participant that the job was fun. Bad job/low pay produces dissonance, but fun job/low pay produces no dissonance. Think of it this way: if someone paid you $25,000 dollars to eat a worm, you'd willingly admit that it tasted bad; after all, you are now $25,000 richer. But if you ate the worm for $10, you very likely would tell others (and yourself) that it wasn't that bad.

This experiment demonstrated two ways to reduce dissonance. First, people can alter their attitudes toward the dissonant behavior. This is what the $1 condition did: "Yes, it *was* a fun task; I didn't lie" (or in our earlier example, "I wanted to try smoking anyway"). Second, people can alter the attitudes themselves. This is what the $20 condition did: "Maybe it was a lousy job, but the pay was good, and after all, it was for science" (or in our smoking example, "Maybe smoking isn't that bad for me, and it is kind of fun to have a smoke with a friend"). Festinger called these strategies *changing the cognitive element related to the behavior* and *changing the cognitive element or elements related to the attitude*, respectively. In the first instance, there is an adjustment in the attitude-behavior connection (I don't like lying; therefore, I didn't lie); in the second, the values that cluster around the attitude are adjusted (I believe lying is wrong, but I also believe that $20 is a lot of money and I do value wealth). But these efforts to reach cognitive consistency take a lot of mental work, so why not just avoid the dissonance altogether? That's why Festinger identified a third way to avoid or reduce dissonance, one that is of particular interest to the field of communication—people can engage in various communication practices that can protect them from dissonance in the first place.

The Selective Processes

Why would communication researchers (and advertisers and politicians) find it so interesting that people utilize different communicative strategies to deal with dissonance? Because "this tendency toward equilibrium determines ... the kind of persuasive communication to which the individual may be receptive" (Rosnow and Robinson, 1967, p. 299). These strategies, collectively known as the **selective processes**, are selective exposure, selective retention, and selective perception. Naturally, they are interrelated; we have to expose ourselves to a message before we can remember or perceive it, and our perception of something we've read, heard, or seen is closely tied to how we remember it.

Selective exposure (sometimes selective attention) is our tendency to expose ourselves to or attend to messages that are consistent with the values, beliefs, and attitudes we already hold. We also tend to avoid messages that are inconsistent with those values, beliefs, and attitudes. What better way to avoid dissonance than to make sure it doesn't occur? Cable news networks MSNBC (politically and socially liberal) and Fox News (politically and socially conservative) were designed specifically to take advantage of this phenomenon. Consider, too, the effectiveness of persuasive health messages embedded in entertainment content. Smokers, for example, may well walk away from friends who are demanding they stop, and they may fast-forward through anti-smoking public service announcements on television, but they can't avoid those messages if they are an essential part of an episode of their favorite program. This is the same logic behind the many product placements (Chapter 10) in all media that we now see. Advertisers know that we selectively attend to only certain commercials, so they make their products part of the movie, book, or video game we're enjoying. Selective exposure also operates in interpersonal communication settings as well. Just as smokers might walk away from friends who are criticizing their smoking, they are just as likely to avoid communication with those friends altogether and associate with other smokers; they don't need the hassle, or as we would say, they don't need the dissonance.

selective processes Cognitive and behavioral strategies for dealing with dissonant information.

selective exposure Tendency to expose ourselves to or attend to messages that are consistent with already held values, beliefs, and attitudes.

selective retention
Tendency to most accurately remember information that is consistent with already held values, beliefs, and attitudes.

selective perception Tendency to interpret messages in ways that are consistent with already held values, beliefs.

Selective retention is our tendency to most accurately remember information that is consistent with the values, beliefs, and attitudes we already hold. Why hang on to memories that are likely to create dissonance? Selective retention has long been of interest to researchers in political communication (e.g., Surlin and Gordon, 1976) and marketing (e.g., Elias, Malden, and Deas, 2009). As you might expect, we tend to remember best and longest the political ads and speeches of the candidates we favor and the commercial messages associated with the products we buy. If you're an iPhone person, you no doubt remember many more ads for that smartphone than you do for the Droid. And think about your high school days. If you liked those four years, you probably have forgotten the many bad days and indignities they housed in favor of the good times, especially as time passes; if you didn't like high school, you'll no doubt remember the bad times more often and more clearly.

Selective perception is our tendency to interpret messages, to make meaning from them, in ways that are consistent with the values, beliefs, and attitudes we already hold. One of the most famous studies of selective perception had to do with a particularly violent college football game between Dartmouth and Princeton, one in which there were many injuries and even more penalties for unsportsmanlike conduct. When researchers Albert Hastorf and Hadley Cantrill showed a film of the game to students from both schools, 90 percent of the Princeton students thought the other side started the dirty play and a majority of Dartmouth students thought Princeton was the dirty team. These results led the researchers to conclude that "there is no such 'thing' as a 'game' existing 'out there' in its own right which people merely 'observe.' The 'game' 'exists' for a person and is experienced by him [sic] only in so far as certain happenings have significances in terms of his purpose" (1954, p. 133). Was that a strike or a ball? Was that a three-point shot or was her foot on the line? Is your candidate a flip-flopper or has his position evolved? Was the president's speech a masterful recitation of all that is good and great about our country, or was it just so much empty rhetoric? Another classic selective-perception study involved something much more important than an Ivy League football game; it had to do with how we perceive race. You can read about it in the box "Would the Razor Switch Hands Today?"

What Factors Infuence Persuasion?

What balance theory, cognitive dissonance theory, and the selective processes make clear is that those who hope to persuade others have a fairly tough task. They have to create messages that can move people to change their values, beliefs, attitudes, or behaviors while allowing those people to remain cognitively balanced, all the while making sure that they do not create so much dissonance that those messages fail to make it past the selective processes intact. Naturally, then, quite a bit of scientific attention has been paid to the factors

Would the Razor Switch Hands Today?

First, a one-question quiz. Among America's White and African-American population, which group has the highest incidence of illegal drug use? We'll give you the answer in a little bit.

For now, we will look at one of the most famous scientific demonstrations of selective perception, Gordon Allport and Leo Postman's 1945 study of rumor. The two psychologists showed people, one at a time, a drawing of an altercation aboard a train. The antagonists were a Caucasian male wielding a razor and an unarmed African-American male. After making sure that a participant had accurately understood the image, the researchers then asked that original participant to describe what he or she had seen to a person who had not seen it. These people, in turn, were asked to pass it on to the next participant, and so on, through six or seven participants. You might know this today as the game of telephone. Across multiple trials, the blade invariably moved from the hand of the White man to the hand of the Black man. In 1945 America, Allport and Postman's participants—Caucasians, African Americans, young people, older people, men and women, professionals and laborers—selectively perceived what they were hearing. Sounding remarkably like Hastorf and ·Cantrill, whose football study led them to argue "There is no such 'thing' as a 'game' existing 'out there,'" Allport and Postman concluded, "What was outer becomes inner; what was objective becomes subjective" (1945, p. 81).

But that was then; this is now, you might say. That kind of automatic prejudice is long gone for most Americans, isn't it? Now, back to the quiz. What was your response? The correct answer is there is no difference. White and

The line drawing from Allport and Postman's classic 1945 study of rumor.

Black Americans consume illegal drugs at the same rate (Lopez, 2015). But in whose hand did you put the razor (in this case, the drugs)? The US legal system invariably puts it in African-American hands. For example, African Americans represent only 13 percent of the country's illegal drug users, but they account for 36 percent of all incarcerations for illegal drug use (Common Sense for Drug Policy, 2014). If the razor wouldn't switch hands today, African Americans would represent 13 percent of all people in prison for drug-related convictions, not 36 percent.

Few of us consider ourselves prejudiced, but each of us encounters the world through our own eyes—we selectively perceive what we see and hear. How we live our lives eventually defines and redefines the norms and rules that we must live by.

that influence the effectiveness of persuasive communication. It typically falls into three categories: the characteristics of the source of the persuasive attempt, the nature of the persuasive appeal itself, and the characteristics of the target of the persuasive communication.

Source Characteristics

Of course you've noticed that the people in ads and commercials tend to be fairly attractive, but sometimes they look like ordinary folks. And you know

Similarity between source and receiver is an important factor in persuasion. That's why models in ads look like the people targeted by those commercial messages.

source credibility Receiver's perception of source's expertise and trustworthiness.

expertise Judgments of source's authoritativeness.

trustworthiness Judgments of source's character.

perceived similarity Receiver's sense of alikeness with source.

that when you read an online editorial, it usually cites credible experts you're supposed to trust. And you're aware that when advertisers target Latino consumers, they use Latino models in the ads of magazines like *Alma* and *Ser Padres*. And who among us has never tried to persuade a friend with the argument, "If I like it, you'll like it, too"? In all of these persuasive attempts, the source of the message is central to its hoped-for effectiveness. Three source characteristics that have received a great deal of scholarly attention are credibility, personal similarity, and physical attractiveness.

Source credibility, the receiver's perception of the source's expertise and trustworthiness, is positively related to successful persuasion. That is, the more credible the source, the more likely it is that the message will have its desired effect. **Expertise** involves judgments of authoritativeness, and **trustworthiness** involves judgments of character and, of course, trust (McCroskey, 1966; Hovland, Janis, and Kelley, 1953). But it's important to note that expertise and trustworthiness have less to do with the source and more to do with the receiver's *perception* of the source's expertise and trustworthiness. This is why it is against the law to represent a spokesperson in a commercial as a doctor if he or she isn't an actual physician and why any assertion of objective scientific evidence—such as "two out of three dentists agree"; "tests prove that with these videos your baby can read"—must in fact be supported by actual science. We regularly use credible sources in our everyday interpersonal communication. The topics and persuasive goals might be different, but we have all used variations of these appeals: "My aunt is a commercial angler and she says eels are much better bait than squid." "My father is a professional chef and he says boil the pasta with the lid off." "I was a Girl Scout and I'm telling you, you need to stake that tent better." You can read more about how source credibility in advertising is assessed and policed in the box "The Federal Trade Commission and Advertiser Credibility."

The degree of **perceived similarity** between would-be persuaders and their receivers also influences persuasion. This alikeness suggests a personal connection, and whether you want to think of that bond's value as bringing greater balance ("We're alike and she favors that position" means three plusses on the balance triangle) or helping to reduce dissonance ("He's like me, so I should attend to what he's saying" or "We're alike, so his views can't be too dissonant"), the value of perceived source-receiver

SOCIALLY RESPONSIBLE COMMUNICATION

The Federal Trade Commission and Advertiser Credibility

The Federal Trade Commission (FTC) is charged with making sure that advertisers' claims are truthful; in other words, the FTC's job is to ensure that advertising operates in a socially responsible manner. In judging the credibility of commercial messages, the FTC allows advertisers quite a bit of leeway. You probably realize that elves don't bake Keebler cookies, that polar bears don't drink Coca-Cola, and that Coors beer isn't as cold as the Rockies. These are examples of *puffery,* obvious exaggerations designed to attract our attention. Keebler, Coke, and Coors aren't trying to deceive us; they're simply puffing up their products. But the FTC does target advertising that is *designed to mislead* or that makes seemingly credible but unfounded scientific claims.

For example, the FTC clashed with POM Wonderful over the juice-makers' assertions that the drink is "heart therapy" and "the antioxidant superpower," that it "saves prostates," and that it can help people "cheat death." All of these claims may well be true, but they are unsupported. The POM Wonderful ads are intentionally deceptive, according to the FTC, because in the absence of "competent and reliable scientific evidence," consumers have no capacity to judge their credibility (Goldstein, 2013, p. 24).

The FTC collectively fined four weight-loss companies—Sensa Products, L'Occitane, HCG Diet Direct, and LeanSpa—$34 million for promising that their products would help consumers get lean and fit by simply sprinkling a powder on their food, applying a cream, or putting drops of liquid on their tongue. None of these assertions were supported by scientific evidence, although as explained in its commercials, Sensa Products' owner was indeed a doctor who had appeared on *Oprah,* CNN, and numerous other media outlets (Wyatt, 2014, p. B1).

Most professionals in the advertising industry welcome the FTC's actions against misleading advertising because they understand the importance of source credibility. They know that the more we believe that advertising lacks credibility, the more difficult it will be for them to persuade us toward their positions, products, and services. In fact, industry organizations such as the American Association of Advertising Agencies maintain codes of practice that expressly forbid false advertising for this very reason.

How credible do you find most advertising? Should commercial messages for different kinds of products be held to different standards of truthfulness? For example, should different rules apply to ads that make health or medical claims, as opposed to those attempting to sell us products like cars and beer? How good a job do you think the ad industry does in maintaining source credibility? Does it need the government's help?

similarity is clear. That's why we see just as many everyday-looking people in ads, especially ads for everyday or must-have products such as soaps, cleaners, mid-priced cars, and health insurance. And that's why, as mentioned earlier, Latino and Hispanic faces fill the commercials of Latino- and Hispanic-oriented media.

Perceived similarity is actually a combination of *membership similarity* and *attitudinal similarity* (Simons et al., 1970). Persuaders attempt to build **membership similarity** by referencing common demographics, group and organizational memberships, and experiences. We are all familiar with mass-mediated and personal appeals that begin with membership markers such as "Commuting students like us . . . ," "I'm in the National Rifle Association and . . . ," and "We've all had that (fill in the blank) feeling." In fact, merely sharing the same

membership similarity
Source-receiver similarity built on common demographics, group and organizational memberships, and experiences.

or a similar name with a persuader leads to an increased likelihood of attitude change because persuadees more easily relate the presented information to themselves, more thoughtfully examine it, and remember it to a greater degree than if that information was presented by someone with a dissimilar name (Howard and Kerin, 2011).

attitudinal similarity
Source-receiver similarity built on common values, beliefs, or attitudes.

Persuaders express opinions that sit well with their targets' existing values and beliefs to build **attitudinal similarity**. Again, none of us is a stranger to persuasive pitches such as "We all love a good movie, so why don't we . . ." and "We are the greatest nation in the world, so there's no reason we can't . . ." It's important to remember that perceived similarity is most effective when the membership and attitudinal similarities have something to do with the issue at hand, especially as it is linked to judgments of trustworthiness (Simons et al., 1970). For example, "We all love a good movie, so why don't we get a Netflix subscription" and "We are the greatest nation in the world, so there's no reason we can't give adequate healthcare to returning veterans" might be effective approaches. But "We all love a good movie, so why don't we protest cuts to Medicare" and "We are the greatest nation in the world, so there's no reason we can't all have chocolate ice cream for Passover" might not work as well.

social reinforcement
Welcoming of influence because we find the company of physically attractive people socially rewarding.

There is considerable scientific evidence that receivers' judgments of persuaders' physical attractiveness—both in the media and in interpersonal communication—shape their views of persuaders' credibility, trustworthiness, expertise, and liking. It's only logical, then, that sources' perceived physical attractiveness influences the effectiveness of their persuasive communication for the better (Chaiken, 1986; Patzer, 1983). There is even evidence that this relationship is biological, that is, hard-wired as a natural part of the brain's chemical functioning (Theodoridou et al., 2009). There are three other explanations for this attractiveness/persuasiveness link (Stiff and Mongeau, 2003). One is **social reinforcement**—we find the company of

Which of these two men would you trust to watch your books while you run out to put money in the parking meter? Why?

physically attractive people socially rewarding, so we welcome their influence. A second explanation is based in **heuristics**, simple decision-making rules that substitute for more careful analysis of persuasive messages. Stated simply, we usually agree with people we like; we like attractive people; Pat is attractive. Good enough; no need to expend mental energy; I agree with Pat's message. A final explanation is another heuristic, the **halo effect**, the idea that what is beautiful must be good.

Message Characteristics

If the nature of the persuader influences a message's power to influence, certainly message characteristics must do so as well. Most basically, a badly constructed persuasive attempt will likely fail, no matter how trustworthy or lovely its deliverer. Among other message characteristics that have received scholarly attention are the use of rational arguments, the use of evidence, one- versus two-sided appeals, the use of fear, and employing explicit and explicit appeals.

Although it is almost impossible to separate rational and emotional appeals—my very rational, data-heavy presentation on sexually transmitted infections (STI) may be the scariest thing you've ever heard—we are talking here about the use of rational arguments as a central component of a persuasive attempt. **Rational arguments** contain three elements (Toulmin, 1964). The first is *the claim*, what I want you to do or believe, that is, my conclusion. The second is *data*, my evidence, typically from an external source. Finally, the *warrant* is my argument linking the claim and the data. A typical rational argument, then, might look like this: *If you are sexually active you should have regular checkups for STIs* (claim). *The Centers for Disease Control say that half of the 19 million new STI cases every year are among college-age people* (data). *These diseases can be physically and psychologically devastating; they are very common among college students like you; you should get checked out at the Health Center where testing is free* (warrant).

Rational arguments, however, even very well-crafted and presented ones, are not always as effective as a persuader might hope. That's because they are only as good as receivers' willingness and ability to process the logic of the argument. Evidence, even good, authoritative evidence, suffers from the same limitation. In addition, evidence must pass through the selective processes—*I don't accept what the Centers for Disease Control say about anything. They just want to scare us so they can stay in business. And anyway, I'm careful in my physical relationships.* Nonetheless, if the receiver is motivated to and capable of analyzing the evidence, rational arguments can "produce general persuasive effects that appear surprisingly stable" (Reinard, 1988, p. 46). Evidence also has the additional benefit of increasing perceptions of the credibility of the persuader.

A specific case of rational arguments, one- versus two-sided appeals—has also been of interest to communication researchers. **Message sidedness** is how hard a persuasive appeal works to recognize and refute differing opinions or viewpoints. **One-sided messages** present only the persuader's position, for example: *A college student like you should get regular checkups for STIs.* **Two-sided messages** bring up and address opposing arguments, for example: *Yes,*

heuristics Simple decision-making rules that substitute for more careful analysis of persuasive messages.

halo effect Idea that what is beautiful must be good.

rational argument Persuasive appeal containing a claim, data, and a warrant.

message sidedness Degree to which a persuasive appeal works to recognize and refute differing opinions or viewpoints.

one-sided message Presenting only the persuader's position.

two-sided message Bringing up and addressing opposing arguments.

the test usually takes time and money, and although you can take precautions, no method of prevention is 100 percent safe. Nonetheless, the campus health center offers fast, reliable, free, walk-in testing. So there's no reason that a college student like you shouldn't get regular checkups for STIs. The long-standing view of sidedness has been that one-sided messages are more effective with less educated receivers and with people already predisposed to favor an argument. Two-sided messages work better with better-educated receivers and with those who have attitudes opposing those held by the persuader (Hovland et al., 1949). These assumptions about sidedness have received a lot of scientific debate and refinement, but contemporary thinking is that two-sided messages that refute, rather than simply acknowledge, opposing positions tend to be most persuasive because they not only confront and attempt to reduce receivers' dissonance, they also boost judgments of the persuader's credibility (Allen, 1991).

An example of a non-rational persuasive appeal that has received a great deal of research attention is the use of fear appeals. And it's easy to understand why, especially if you think about the example of persuasion we have been using throughout this section of the chapter, STIs. **Fear appeals**, persuasive messages that attempt to motivate action or change attitudes through the use of a relevant threat to the receiver, are a staple of health and safety campaigns. We're all familiar with appeals such as "Don't text and drive" and "This is your brain on drugs." We've also all seen anti-smoking public service announcements featuring people suffering from gruesome diseases and anti-drunk driving spots offering close-ups of crumpled cars and blood-stained roads. But just how effective are they? Might they not backfire because they create so much dissonance? Actually, "the stronger the fear aroused by a fear appeal, the more persuasive it is" (Witte and Allen, 2000, p. 601). Keep in mind, though, that fear is in the eye of the beholder; that is, what is important is not the fear encoded into the message, but the fear felt by its recipient.

fear appeal Persuasive message that attempts to gain influence through the use of a relevant threat to the receiver.

The evidence surrounding our final message characteristic, the effectiveness of explicitly stating the argument versus leaving recipients free to come to their own conclusions, is relatively straightforward. Both making explicit statements of a message's conclusion and explicitly stating evidence in the message produce persuasive appeals that are more effective than simply letting receivers "fill in the blanks" (Stiff and Mongeau, 2003, p. 143).

Receiver Characteristics

Obviously, it takes more than an attractive, trustworthy source and a well-crafted message to persuade us. Remember one of this text's

It's not how much fear the persuader includes in the message, it's the fear the receiver feels that shapes the response to persuasive efforts.

central themes—we make meaning together in a reciprocal transaction. So, if the source and message are important factors in a persuasive effort, the receiver must hold just as crucial a role. In fact, we've already seen the power of receivers' personal meaning making in balance theory and dissonance theory. Two receiver characteristics that have attracted much attention are gender differences and involvement. Early research findings that women were more easily persuaded than men are now rejected as artifacts of cultural bias, as most were conducted before the women's rights movement and typically involved issues that were not generally of great interest to women of the time. As persuasion researcher Alice Eagly explained,

> The historical period during which research was conducted is a major determinant of the likelihood of obtaining findings demonstrating that women are more influenceable than men. Thus, a pronounced difference in the distribution of findings is revealed by comparing studies published before 1970 with those published in the 1970s . . . In persuasion research, there is an established tradition of using messages presenting social, economic, or political issues . . . The relevance of these choices to persuasibility sex differences stems from findings that men are more knowledgeable and interested in political and economic areas than are women. (1978, pp. 95–96)

involvement Motivation to process persuasive communication because it is relevant to some personal value, outcome, or impression.

There is actually little difference between men and women in susceptibility to persuasion. Both genders are equally susceptible to persuasive communication if they have little knowledge of or are uninterested in the topic at hand.

And this raises our second receiver characteristic, **involvement**, motivation to process persuasive communication because it is relevant to some personal value, outcome, or impression (Johnson and Eagly, 1989). Distinguishing values, outcomes, and impressions is important because different types of involvement can have different kinds of influence. Involvement borne of values (*value-relevant involvement*) tends to limit or reduce attitude change. As we've already seen, values are tightly tied to identity, so persuasive appeals that touch on a person's values are unlikely to produce attitude change, although if based on those values, they can indeed produce reinforcement. The most well-crafted arguments in favor of a woman's right to control her reproductive choices will fall on deaf ears of people who value their religion's prohibitions on birth control and abortion. Involvement that is the product of a desire to produce or achieve a desired outcome (*outcome-relevant involvement*) naturally leads to more attention to and scrutiny of

She was losing him... **and she didn't know why**

LISTERINE ANTISEPTIC STOPS BAD BREATH
4 times better than any tooth paste

Early persuasion research demonstrating that women were more persuadable than men was conducted at a very different time in US history.

a persuasive message. Someone trying to make a decision between competing job offers will pay very close attention to the pros and cons of each potential employer's recruitment pitch. But this is where the quality of the arguments and evidence become important. The receiver's involvement with the message makes strong, quality persuasive efforts more effective and weak appeals less so. Finally, involvement that comes from receivers' desires to control the impressions others have of them (*impression-relevant involvement*), particularly in terms of the social consequences of expressing a particular opinion, can either enhance or inhibit persuasion. People who are highly concerned about how the acceptance (or rejection) of a given argument will affect a would-be persuader's judgment of them will "employ their attitudes as a means of advancing interpersonally oriented goals" (Levin, Nichols, and Johnson, 2000, p. 166). In other words, if it is to their social advantage to agree, they will; if it isn't, they may well not. For example, imagine that all your friends are walking 10 miles to raise funds for the Special Olympics. You want to show them that you are energetic and have a social conscience, so why not? You are easily convinced to join them.

THUMBNAIL THEORY

Elaboration Likelihood Model

When presented with a persuasive message, people will sometimes put a lot of effort into their cognition, and sometimes not. For social reasons, people are motivated to hold correct attitudes, but the amount and nature of cognitive effort that they are willing to apply is dependent on a number of individual and situational factors. Motivation and the ability to scrutinize a message lead to enduring attitude change. Less motivated processing leads to less-enduring attitude change.

cognitive miser The idea that people rely on the simplest analysis possible when confronting information.

The Elaboration Likelihood Model of Persuasion

As you've read, decades of scientific inquiry have made it clear that the effectiveness of any persuasive communication effort depends on quite a few factors. Who is the source? Is that source trustworthy, credible, expert, or attractive? What's the nature of the message? How is it structured? What are its appeals? What about the targets of those persuasive communication efforts? Are they interested in the issue, motivated to process its logic and evidence, capable of doing so?

Social psychologists Richard Petty and John Cacioppo (1986) developed a model of persuasion they called the **elaboration likelihood model** (**ELM**) that attempted to account for all these different factors. ELM (Figure 13.2) is based on two well-demonstrated assumptions about how people deal with persuasive communication. The first is that people tend to be **cognitive misers** (Taylor, 1981); that is, when we are confronted with a persuasive message, we will rely on the simplest analysis possible. We've already seen that these routine meaning-making strategies are called heuristics. Heuristics are not necessarily a bad thing; in fact, they are quite natural and useful. As Richard Miller and his colleagues explained, it would be "irrational to scrutinize the plethora of counterattitudinal messages received daily. To the extent that one possesses only a limited amount of information-processing time and capacity, such scrutiny would disengage the thought processes from the exigencies of daily life" (Miller, Brickman, and Bolen, 1975, p. 623). In other words, these mental shortcuts make everyday life possible. The second important assumption of ELM is that, for various reasons, people are motivated to hold "correct" attitudes. Balance theory and dissonance theory offer clues as to

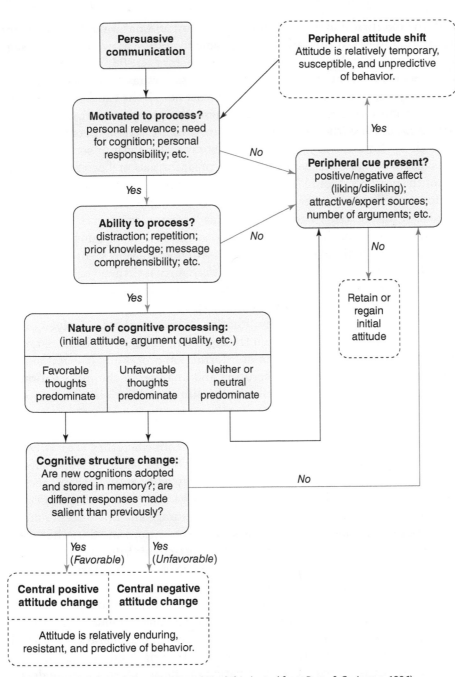

FIGURE 13.2 The Elaboration Likelihood Model (adapted from Petty & Cacioppo, 1986)

why this is the case, but Petty and Cacioppo suggest this explanation: "Incorrect attitudes are generally maladaptive and can have deleterious behavioral, affective, and cognitive consequences. If a person believes that certain objects, people, or issues are 'good' when they are in fact 'bad,' a number of incorrect behavioral decisions and subsequent disappointments may follow" (1986, p. 127). But remember, we're cognitive misers, so the researchers add, "People want to hold correct attitudes, [but] the amount and nature of issue-relevant elaboration in which they are willing or able to engage to evaluate a message [will] vary with individual and situational factors" (1986, p. 128). In other words, we're not always willing or able to process persuasive messages in a way that will get us to that correct attitude, at least not all the time. Often we take an easier, more automatic route to get there, the **peripheral route** of information processing (the right side of Figure 13.2). Engaging persuasive messages along this route depends less on elaboration (analysis or scrutiny) of the message than it does on cues unrelated to the information. Look at the middle box of the peripheral route. These are all heuristic cues with which we're familiar, for example liking (affect), attractiveness, and expertness. If those cues are present (if the source is liked or perceived as attractive or expert), there will be attitude change (the "yes" arrow leading to the first box). But because it is based not on deep thought and analysis, it will not be a very securely held new attitude. If those cues are not present (or the source is disliked or perceived as unattractive or non-expert), there will be no attitude change (the "no" arrow leading to the peripheral route's bottom box).

But, of course, there are many situations when people are involved in the message and actively work through the argument or issue. In these instances people will use the **central route** of information processing (the left side of Figure 13.2), bringing as much scrutiny and analysis to the information as possible. They engage in "issue-relevant thinking," and the "elaboration likelihood" is high. When do we undertake this mental heavy lifting? Look at the first two boxes of the elaborated route, just below "persuasive communication." People will indeed work through an argument when they are motivated by its relevance, have a need for cognition, or hold a sense of responsibility regarding the topic. If they are motivated, they will continue their message scrutiny if they are able. Here is where message and receiver characteristics mix. Does the quality of the message itself encourage and allow deeper analysis; is the receiver able to give the message full attention; and does the receiver's prior knowledge of the topic permit or short-circuit fuller analysis?

ELM sees the likelihood that people will engage in scrutiny or analysis of a persuasive effort as running along a continuum from no thought about the message to "complete elaboration of every argument, and complete integration of the elaborations into the person's attitude schemas" (Petty and Cacioppo, 1986, p. 8). This flow from elaboration to peripheral processing is represented by the arrows that lead from the left to right side of the model. At any time that the receiver loses motivation or the ability to continue deeper analysis, processing becomes more automatic, less reflective, and more likely to rely on heuristics. And even if the receiver works though a persuasive appeal but comes to no feeling either way or there is no real attitude change, the persuasive power of the peripheral cues will increase in strength. Finally, ELM argues that attitudes that are produced through elaboration will be more deeply held, more enduring, and more likely to predict the recipient's subsequent behavior. Those developed through the peripheral route will be less deeply held, less enduring, and less predictive of behavior.

peripheral route Easier, more automatic route of information processing; relies on heuristics.

central route In information processing, employing as much scrutiny and analysis as possible.

Let's return to our example of a campus effort to persuade students to visit the health center for STI testing. You hear the Dean of Students make her pitch. But you are not sexually active. You have little motivation to scrutinize her argument; as a result, your processing moves to the peripheral route. She seems professional, clearly knows what she's talking about, so yeah, you may not make a visit, but you'll keep her words in mind just in case a friend asks. But consider if you are sexually active. Now your motivation to process is heightened, and in fact, you have a friend who has suffered a serious STI, adding ability to process to your motivation. You will likely pay close attention to her appeal and take it to heart. If you had already intended to get a checkup, that intention will be reinforced, and the likelihood that you will get to the health center is greatly increased. If you hadn't before thought about going, you will think that it is, indeed, a good idea and you will plan to do so.

Processes of Attitude Change

Sometimes it may be difficult to bring about attitude change; sometimes it may be relatively easy. Sometimes attitude change is the product of thoughtful analysis of competing arguments; sometimes it may come about quickly, with little real mental effort. But attitude change does occur, and this raises a question initially investigated more than a half a century ago by Herbert Kelman, regarding "the nature of changes (if any) that are brought about by a particular communication or type of communication. It is not enough to know that there has been some measurable change in attitude; usually we would also want to know what kind of change it is. Is it a superficial change, on a verbal level, which disappears after a short lapse of time? Or is it a more lasting change in attitude and belief, which manifests itself in a wide range of situations and which is integrated into the person's value system?" (1958, p. 51). He identified three forms of attitude change—compliance, identification, and internalization—although one really isn't attitude change at all. **Compliance** occurs when a person accepts influence in order to gain a favorable reaction from the persuader but does not actually change the original attitude. People comply with others' persuasive communication, not because they have been convinced by the message, but because they expect "to gain specific rewards or approval and avoid specific punishments or disapproval by conforming. Thus the satisfaction derived from compliance is due to the *social effect* of accepting influence" (italics in original; p. 53). For example, your friends want you to blow off an optional study session in favor of a visit to the gym. Why not go? You know the material, you need the exercise, and besides, the professor won't miss you among the crowd of students who will show up. But you run into your instructor on the way to your workout, and she suggests that you should indeed attend the study session because you can never be too prepared. You ultimately attend the session because she is your professor, the very person who will evaluate your exam and assign you a grade for the course. Compliance, then, because it is *yielding* to the argument, not accepting its merits, produces no attitude change (you still would really rather be with your friends), and

compliance When people accept influence in order to gain a favorable reaction from the persuader but do not change their original attitudes.

any resulting behavioral change will be short-lived (you will attend this study session, and this one alone, only because you saw your professor on the way to the gym), as it is based on peripheral route or heuristic analysis.

Identification occurs when people accept influence because they want "to establish or maintain a satisfying self-defining relationship to another person or a group" (p. 53). Your friends want you to blow off the optional study session in favor of a visit to the gym. You know you shouldn't go. Even though you know the material pretty well, you can never know it too well. But you go to the gym. After all, these are your friends, you like them, and you will be with them for the rest of your college career. Unlike compliance, identification does produce attitude change—think balance theory and dissonance reduction. "The individual actually believes in the responses," Kelman explains, "but their specific content is more or less irrelevant" (p. 53). In other words, it isn't the persuasive message that produces change; it is the combination of specific source characteristics (trustworthiness, membership and attitudinal similarity, and social reinforcement) and receiver characteristics (outcome and impression involvement). Identification can be the product of heuristic or peripheral-route message scrutiny (they're my friends; all for one and one for all!) or more serious consideration of an appeal's arguments.

Finally, **internalization** occurs when people accept the persuader's influence because the resulting behavior and the ideas on which it is based are "intrinsically rewarding. He [sic] adopts the induced behavior because it is congruent with his value system . . . may consider it useful for the solution of a problem, or find it congenial to his needs" (p. 53). Your friends want you to blow off the optional study session in favor of a visit to the gym. You know you shouldn't go. Even though you know the material pretty well, you can never know it too well. So you weigh the different arguments of both your friends and your teacher. Ultimately, you determine that hers is more convincing, especially because a higher grade in Communication will offset that shaky performance in Statistics. Scrutiny of the persuasive efforts has moved you to internalize your professor's position and reject that of your friends. You may even start to show up at help sessions like this more often in the future.

Kelman's ideas on the processes of attitude change have the additional value of focusing our attention on power, which he defined as "the extent to which the influencing agent is perceived as instrumental to the achievement of the subject's goals" (p. 54). We saw in Chapter 1 how effective communication bestows power, and in our efforts to persuade others, we surely want our message to carry as much power as possible. Otherwise, why try to persuade in the first place? Compliance relies on the exercise of hierarchical power; that is, it has less to do with the quality of the communication and everything to do with who holds the more powerful position. Why do you comply with your professor's demand that you turn off your phone? But remember, there is no persuasion here, just the imposition of rank. Identification relies on the power of attractiveness in its broadest sense, what we already know as source characteristics such as judgments of expertness, trustworthiness, affinity, and yes, physical attractiveness. These characteristics are all carried in our communication of ourselves and our values

identification When people accept influence because they want to establish or maintain a satisfying self-defining relationship to another person or a group.

internalization When people accept influence because the resulting behavior or attitudes are intrinsically rewarding.

with others. Internalization, true attitude change, is based on the power of our message, how convincingly we communicate the tie between our claim, data, and warrant. Each of these forms of influence brings with it specific ethical considerations. For example, the exercise of power to gain compliance, on its face, seems less proper than marshaling the power of a well-crafted argument to gain internalization of a position. But parents often "pull rank" on their children to get them to comply with requests that are good for them, for example getting an inoculation, and friends often make very logical, well-crafted appeals to get others to do what is not really in their best interests, for example, skipping the optional study group to go to the gym. The ethics of persuasion, then, are not as clear-cut as they may seem. You can read one approach for determining the ethics of persuasion in the box, "The TARES Test."

ETHICAL COMMUNICATION

The TARES Test

Persuasion, by its very nature, brings with it important ethical concerns. Who are we to try to change another person's values, beliefs, attitudes, or behaviors? Most of us apply some simple standards—call them moral rules—when attempting to persuade someone. First, is the person reasonably aware that we are trying to persuade him or her? Second, are we using coercion or power to persuade? Finally, what is the desired outcome of our persuasive appeal?

Clearly, then, there is such a thing as ethical persuasion, "a communication activity that unites people . . . [while it] permits maximum individual choice" (Anderson, 1978, p. 3). It is an attempt "to effect a desired voluntary change in the attitudes and/or actions of [another]" (p. 7). Communication ethicists James Jaksa and Michael Pritchard explain that voluntary change in the receiver "distinguishes persuasion from indoctrination and coercion, which do not allow significant choice. But it also suggests that ethically acceptable modes of persuasion do not rely on deceptive manipulative tactics . . . [Ethical persuasion] show[s] respect for individuals as capable of making significant choices . . . [T]hose capable of rational choice are respected only if manipulative and deceptive tactics are avoided" (1994, pp. 76–77). Furthermore, deception in persuasion is fundamentally unethical because, according to ethicist Austin Fagothey, humans are social beings, "and the gift of speech is perhaps the chief means by which . . . [our] social life is carried on. Like all other gifts,

speech may be used or abused. Thus truthfulness is good and lying is wrong . . . [To deceive] is *morally wrong* because it is an abuse of the natural ability of communication, because it is contrary to [our] social nature, which requires mutual trust . . . and because it debases the dignity of the human person, whose mind is made for truth" (italics in original; 1976, pp. 241–242).

Communication ethicists Sherry Baker and David Martinson combined these ideals of personal freedom and human dignity to produce their TARES Test (2001). Its name is an acronym for the five principles it lays out for ethical persuasion:

- *Truthfulness* (of the message)
- *Authenticity* (of the persuader)
- *Respect* (for the persuadee)
- *Equity* (of the persuasive appeal)
- *Social responsibility* (for the common good).

Baker and Martinson present the TARES Test as a set of moral obligations we have to those we are attempting to influence. What do you think? Is this too high a standard to maintain in everyday interactions with the people around us? Can you think of situations when its individual elements might conflict, such as truthfulness and respect? Can you imagine a situation when violation of the TARES principles might actually be ethical? If yes, explain your answer.

Review of Learning Objectives

13.1 Explain the characteristics and importance of persuasion.

Persuasion is the use of communication to shape, reinforce, or change the values, beliefs, attitudes, or behaviors of another person. Persuasion is essential to interpersonal communication and the building and maintenance of relationships, the conduct and maintenance of our social institutions, and the operation and maintenance of mass media institutions.

13.2 Distinguish between values, attitudes, beliefs, and behaviors, and explain how those distinctions influence persuasion.

Values are people's deeply held judgments about the worth or importance of various aspects of their lives; *attitudes* are the relatively enduring organization of beliefs around an object or situation predisposing one to respond in some preferential manner; *beliefs* are propositions about something; and *behaviors* are concrete, observable actions. Influence occurs with varying ease with each, given the importance of each to the individual.

13.3 Explain balance theory and cognitive dissonance theory.

Balance theory argues that people want to be cognitively balanced; they want the things and people in their lives to be in harmony. Because we prefer balanced over unbalanced states, we are motivated to change either our attitudes or our behaviors to create balance. Dissonance theory argues that information that is inconsistent with a person's already held attitudes and beliefs creates a psychological discomfort that must be relieved. This can happen in a variety of ways, especially through selective exposure, retention, and perception.

13.4 Describe the influence that source, message, and receiver characteristics have on persuadability.

Persuasion can be enhanced or diminished depending on a number of factors present in the communication situation. Among the more important source characteristics are source credibility (expertise and trustworthiness), personal similarity, and physical attractiveness. Among important message characteristics are rational versus emotional appeals, message sidedness, and fear appeals. Involvement and gender are important receiver characteristics.

13.5 Explain the workings of the elaboration likelihood model of persuasion.

ELM is based on the assumption that people tend to be cognitive misers and that, for various reasons, they are motivated to hold "correct" attitudes. As a result, the amount and nature of cognitive effort they are willing or able to exert in order to evaluate messages will vary with individuals and situational factors. People often take the more automatic route to attitude formation, the *peripheral route*, because it is easier—it depends less on elaboration (analysis or scrutiny) of the message as it does on cues unrelated to the information. But there are situations when people are involved in the message and are motivated and able to actively work through the argument or issue. In these instances people will use the *central route* to process information.

13.6 Distinguish between different processes of attitude change.

There are three processes of attitude change. *Compliance* is acceptance of influence in order to gain a favorable reaction from a persuader, but there is no change in original attitudes. This, in fact, is not attitude change. *Identification* is acceptance of influence in order to establish or maintain a satisfying self-defining relationship to another person or a group. *Internalization* is acceptance of influence because the resulting behaviors or attitudes are intrinsically rewarding, congruent with existing value systems, useful for the solution of a problem, or useful to one's needs.

Key Terms

speech acts theory 286
persuasion 286
value 289
attitude 290
belief 290
behavior 290
balance theory 291
cognitive consistency 292
dissonance theory 292
selective processes 293
selective exposure 293
selective retention 294
selective perception 294
source credibility 296
expertise 296
trustworthiness 296
perceived similarity 296
membership similarity 297
attitudinal similarity 298
social reinforcement 298
heuristics 299
halo effect 299
rational arguments 299
message sidedness 299
one-sided messages 299
two-sided messages 299
fear appeal 300
involvement 301
elaboration likelihood model (ELM) 302
cognitive miser 302
peripheral route 304
central route 304
compliance 305
identification 306
internalization 306

Questions for Review

1. What is speech acts theory? What does it say about communication and persuasion?

2. What are persuasion, response shaping, response reinforcing, and response changing?

3. What are values, attitudes, beliefs, and behaviors?

4. What are balance theory and cognitive dissonance theory? How are they related?

5. What are the three selective processes? How do they operate?

6. What source characteristics influence persuasion? How?

7. What message characteristics influence persuasion? How?

8. What receiver characteristics influence persuasion? How?

9. Explain the elaboration likelihood model of information processing.

10. What are the three processes of attitude change? How do they differ?

Questions for Discussion

1. How susceptible are you to persuasion? Explain your answer in terms of some of this chapter's important concepts. For example, are there aspects of your personality and identity (receiver characteristics) that make you more or less susceptible? Do you have a low tolerance for imbalance or dissonance? What cognitive strengths do you bring to dealing with efforts to persuade you?

2. Are you typically a central or peripheral processor of persuasive communication? What factors in a message or message situation might move you from central to peripheral processing, or from peripheral to central processing? Have you ever surprised yourself at the amount (a great deal or very little) of scrutiny that you've brought to some piece of persuasive communication? What were the circumstances?

3. Have you ever engaged in coercion? What were the circumstances? Did you get the outcome you wanted? Were you OK with what you did and its results? Can you explain your coercion so that it is consistent with the TARES Test?

Health Communication

"A 61 on the mid-semester exam?" your instructor begins. "From you, a good student. How did this ever happen?"

You came to the instructor's office at his request; he obviously is concerned and wants to help, but what you have to say sounds so silly. You can hardly bring yourself to talk about it. "There's stuff going on. I'm having a little health thing."

"What kind of health thing?"

"I have wind turbine syndrome. There's this big, new wind turbine near my place and it's making me sick. The noise and the flickering shadows from the blades are making me lose sleep and give me headaches, nausea, dizziness, sometimes ringing in my ears, and just before the test, I suffered memory loss."

"How do you know that's what you have?" he asks.

"When the symptoms first started I looked them up online, and that's when I found that a lot of people are getting it."

Your professor then offers his diagnosis. You are not suffering from a *communicable* disease; you are suffering from a *communicated* disease, he tells you, an imaginary disease you think you caught because people are talking about it. Scientists all around the world have studied complaints of wind turbine syndrome—a term, he tells you, that was coined in 2006 by a pediatrician who happened to be an anti-wind activist. Those big turbines annoy some people, but they don't make anyone sick (Valentine, 2015). His suggested remedy: more media literacy and less time online.

In this chapter, we focus on the use of interpersonal and mediated communication to influence our individual decisions related to health. We will look at provider-client communication; the many interpersonal contexts in which health is discussed; how to improve use of the Internet and other digital communication technologies for finding, storing, and sharing health information; and health campaigns designed to promote good health and increase awareness of disease.

Learning Objectives

14.1   Identify the barriers to successful provider-client communication and evaluate possible remedies.

14.2   Describe the importance of family, friends, and support groups as agents of health communication.

14.3   Explain how the hospital culture itself can impede good health communication and evaluate possible remedies.

14.4   Judge the contribution of entertainment media to good and harmful health communication.

14.5   Judge the benefits and drawbacks of the Internet and social network sites as sources of health communication.

14.6   Describe the elements of an effective health communication campaign.

Communication and a Long and Healthy Life

Assuming that you are not suffering from wind turbine syndrome and have been able to retain what you have read so far in this text, the importance of the link between communication and good health should be obvious. You make meaning of yourself, your world, and your place in the world through communication, and health is a major part of your sense of self and your willingness and ability to interact with the world. You may think of health and sickness as physical experiences, but they shape your social world as well. Does your health or physical condition limit what activities are available to you and thus also limit your social circle? How are your relationships shaped by an illness, long-term or short-term, yours or a family member's? How well or poorly does your health allow you to perform in school or work, and what life opportunities does this ability open or close? If you smoke, what does that cost you in money, mobility, and friends? There is also a very practical reason for better understanding the relationship between communication and health—it will help you and those around you live longer, healthier lives.

For example, even though the United States spends more on healthcare than any other nation in the world—more than $3.2 trillion a year (Munro,

2015)—Americans die sooner and experience higher rates of disease and injury than people living in any other high-income country (Rugani, 2013). This poor performance holds across all ages and socioeconomic groups and even for non-smokers. That's a pretty bad report card for a country that spends so much on health, leading to calls "for a comprehensive outreach campaign to alert the American public about the U.S. health disadvantage and to stimulate a national discussion about its implications" (Rugani, 2013). Such an outreach campaign and national discussion, naturally, involve communication.

Many local and national efforts focus on improving the quality of doctor-patient communication.

Not only are Americans sicker and dying younger than their foreign counterparts, the United States also has a higher rate of **amenable mortality**—deaths that could potentially have been prevented by timely access to appropriate healthcare—than many other wealthy nations like France, Germany, and Great Britain (Buchanan, Fairfield, and Yourish, 2014). Researchers argue that unhealthy behaviors can be modified through effective interpersonal communication and larger, mass-mediated public health efforts (Colditz, Wolin, and Gehlert, 2012).

amenable mortality Deaths that could potentially have been prevented by timely access to appropriate healthcare.

Effective interpersonal communication—between healthcare providers and their clients and among healthcare professionals themselves—is also important in preserving well-being. Many adults have trouble following healthcare providers' routine medical advice, usually because it is not presented in terms that most people understand. When providers' instructions include too much scientific jargon and too many complex medical phrases, patients are more likely to skip necessary medical tests or improperly use their medications. In fact, the National Institutes of Health report that more than half the American population has deficient **health literacy**—the ability to obtain, process, and understand basic health information and services needed to make appropriate health decisions (Koren, 2015). These deficiencies drive up healthcare costs and damage patients' well-being. Communication problems among healthcare professionals can also produce problems for them and patients alike. There is evidence that "communication breakdowns" between medical staff members when patients are "handed off" (passed on from one professional to the next) are the single largest cause of medical error. "In almost all serious avoidable episodes of patient harm, communication failures play a central role," explains physician Michael Leonard. "By teaching caregivers new models of 'structured communication' we can make sure that we are all in the same movie" (in Landro, 2006, p. D1).

health literacy Ability to obtain, process, and understand basic health information and services needed to make appropriate health decisions.

And then there are effects related to the Internet and social networking sites; both have become primary sources of healthcare information, not all of which is reliable (Hamblin, 2014). Seventy-two percent of patients go online for health information, 20 percent while sitting in a physician's waiting room.

"There's an app for that" is an increasingly common response to many personal health questions.

They report feeling more confident and better prepared to talk with the doctor in their upcoming session (Koren, 2015).

The involvement of technology in good health runs even deeper than that. For example, smartphone apps that track or manage users' health, exercise, diet, and weight regimes are quite common. There's an iPhone app for diabetics that receives data every five minutes from a glucose monitor implanted in the owner's body. It analyzes that information and transmits instructions to pumps, also implanted in the user's body, that dispense insulin (to lower blood sugar) or glucagon (to raise it) as necessary ("There's an App," 2014). Another app, the iTBra, monitors shifts in the wearer's body temperature that might indicate the presence of a growing breast cancer tumor, analyzes the data, and sends the results to the user's smartphone (Davies, 2015).

But recall our discussion of technology's double-edged sword from Chapter 12: technology's benefits may have corresponding drawbacks. For example, technology writer J. D. Sartain (2014) warns, "As companies collect vast amounts of user-generated data [from e-implants], there will be multiple opportunities to monetize that data by, say, targeting shoe advertisements for a fanatic runner or backpacks for a devoted hiker. [Insurance companies] and pharmaceutical firms will be keenly interested in this data, too." A second problem is that while many Internet users may now be more knowledgeable about their health and healthcare options, they are also more likely to find misinformation (as our opening vignette suggests). "Dr. Internet is always very dangerous," explains science journalist Charles Seife, "You can get great information out there, but at the same time, fringe ideas—things that are believed by only a couple dozen or a couple hundred people—are there on the Internet and they can sometimes be just as prominent as the stuff in the mainstream" (in Scribner, 2014). Healthcare experts, for example, point to Internet misinformation linking children's inoculations to autism as a, if not the, prime driver of the re-emergence of measles, once judged eradicated in the United States, as thousands of parents declined to have their children given protective shots (Bruni, 2015). A third potential issue is that while the Internet may produce better-informed patients and potentially improve the face-to-face interaction between people and their healthcare professionals, it can also cause problems, as traditional notions of power and meaning making in those crucial relationships are challenged.

Recognizing the poor state of Americans' health and well-being and the many advantages and challenges posed by communication to that state of affairs, the US Department of Health and Human Services (2010) proposed a 10-year program for improved health promotion and disease prevention called *Healthy People 2020*. Central to this ambitious plan to set and monitor national health objectives is a series of 13 health communication objectives. You can read them in

Table 14.1 *Healthy People 2020* **Communication Objectives**

Objective 1	Improve the health literacy of the population.
Objective 2	Increase the proportion of persons who report that their healthcare providers have satisfactory communication skills.
Objective 3	Increase the proportion of persons who report that their healthcare providers always involved them in decisions about their healthcare as much as they wanted.
Objective 4	Increase the proportion of patients whose doctor recommends personalized health information resources to help them manage their health.
Objective 5	Increase the proportion of persons who use electronic personal health management tools.
Objective 6	Increase individuals' access to the Internet.
Objective 7	Increase the proportion of adults who report having friends or family members with whom they talk about their health.
Objective 8	Increase the proportion of quality health-related websites.
Objective 9	Increase the proportion of online health information seekers who report easily accessing health information.
Objective 10	Increase the proportion of medical practices that use electronic health records.
Objective 11	Increase the proportion of meaningful users of health information technology.
Objective 12	Increase the proportion of crisis and emergency risk messages intended to protect the public's health that demonstrate the use of best practices.
Objective 13	Increase social marketing in health promotion and disease prevention.

(Source: US Department of Health and Human Services, 2010).

Table 14.1, and when you do, you'll see that taken together, they are a call for (a) improved provider-client communication; (b) improved communication between friends, family, and others involved in the many social, organizational, and cultural contexts in which health is discussed; (c) improved use of the Internet and other digital communication technologies for finding, storing, and sharing health information; and (d) improved performance of health campaigns designed to promote good health and increase awareness of disease. These, then, are the four broad areas that will shape this chapter's discussion of **health communication**—the study and use of interpersonal and mediated communication to inform and influence individual decisions that enhance health.

health communication
Study and use of interpersonal and mediated communication to inform and influence individual decisions that enhance health.

Health Communication in Provider-Client Settings

The *Healthy People 2020* initiative specified that achieving its objectives will require better listening by healthcare providers, better and more understandable explanations, greater demonstration of respect for clients, spending more time with them, and more involvement and interaction (Table 14.1). Why identify these specific communication issues for improvement? Because these are the aspects of provider-patient interaction that most people find wanting. Consider this scenario:

You arrive 15 minutes early for your annual visit to the doctor. Your appointment time arrives. You wait another 30 minutes. A nurse finally calls your name and takes you to an examination room. He tells you, "Someone will be right with you." You wait another 15 minutes and a technician enters the room to take your blood pressure, temperature, and other vitals. You're told, "The doctor will be right in." You wait another 15 minutes. The doctor arrives, obviously in a hurry, grunts, hums, and makes a variety of other sounds as she reviews your medical history file and the data the technician just collected. She tells you to take a deep breath; listens to your lungs through her stethoscope; asks if there are any particular concerns you might have; and says all seems well and she'll see you next time.

How closely does this match your experience? How satisfied are you typically with your interactions with your healthcare providers? Now imagine that the reason for your visit is not routine; you're sick or hurt or have a serious illness. The pressure on your doctor to get as much good information from you as possible is matched only by your need to provide it; the doctor's need to understand what you are experiencing is matched only by your need to understand what she is telling you. Good meaning making is essential; miscommunication is damaging. It is no surprise, then, that as Jock Hoffman, a medical risk manager, explains, "effective and safe health care rides on the rails of effective communication" (2012). How valuable is good interpersonal provider-client communication? A review of the scientific literature conducted by Stanford University's Center for Compassion and Altruism Research and Education (Dean and Doty, 2014) revealed that warm, interpersonal interaction between healthcare providers and their patients holds significant healing power. For example:

- When physicians are good communicators, patients are twice as likely to heed their advice.

- When anesthesiologists encourage surgical patients during the immediate postoperative period, they heal faster, are discharged from the hospital sooner, and require 50 percent fewer narcotics.

- Patients who experience warm interpersonal care are more likely to divulge important information to their healthcare providers, making diagnosis more accurate.

- Emergency room patients who have warm interpersonal interaction with their healthcare providers are less likely to return to the emergency room for the same medical issue.

But why do provider-patient failures to communicate occur more often than they should? One reason is that for all their fine medical and technical education, *lessons in interpersonal communication are not a major part of healthcare providers' training.* This deficiency exists despite evidence that such instruction can improve interpersonal communication competence (Kaufman, Laidlaw, and Macleod, 2000) and the recognition that better communication between providers and patients can increase **patient activation**, that is, their involvement in their own health improvement and adherence to recommended treatments (Alexander et al., 2012). Even something as simple as providers maintaining eye contact can lead patients to better health outcomes, greater adherence to medical advice, and an improved likelihood to seek treatment for later problems (Murphy, 2014).

patient activation Involvement in one's own health improvement and adherence to recommended treatments.

A second reason for miscommunication is that medical professionals are trained in the *technical jargon* of their profession; their patients are not. This highly specific, highly context-based language is a necessity for precise meaning making between professionals. Doctors, nurses, surgeons, and anesthesiologists have to be talking the same language when dealing with life-altering or life-threatening situations. "A little bit of a squooshie feeling in the patient's tummy," probably will not produce a meaningful or useful response from those involved in someone's care. Providers' use of highly technical jargon is reinforced through interaction with other healthcare professionals and becomes their natural language. But it is not the public's natural language. (Quick: What's a myocardial infarction? You don't want one—it's a heart attack.) "The specialized language of the medical profession is inappropriate for dialogue with the average person," explains health literacy expert Rima Rudd. She suggests that patients should insist that their providers speak in everyday terms, ask questions if they don't understand something, and seek out healthcare facilities with patient libraries and librarians who can offer assistance (in Landro, 2003, p. D2). You can test your own knowledge of medical language using Table 14.2.

In recognition of this problem, most states' Medicaid offices prepare their healthcare material at between a fourth- and sixth-grade reading level. Many healthcare professionals now use drawings, multimedia presentations, and diagrams to clarify/illustrate providers' verbal messages. Others employ

Table 14.2 Test Your Knowledge of Medical Terms

Medical writer Laura Landro prepared a short list of common medical terms that she thought were unnecessarily complex (2010, p. D1). She divided them into two groups, *Not as Scary as They Sound* and *Even Scarier Than They Sound*. For how many did you know the meaning?

NOT AS SCARY AS THEY SOUND

Bronchodilator—drug to help people breathe easier
Cutaneous—related to the skin
Dyspepsia—indigestion
Petechiae—skin rash
Viral shedding—coughing or sneezing

EVEN SCARIER THAN THEY SOUND

Contraindication—when a drug or procedure may be dangerous
Encephalopathy—brain dysfunction
Recrudescence—a relapse into illness
Teratogenic—something that can hurt an unborn baby
Anaphylaxis—sudden and severe allergic reaction

specialized software that scans documents looking for difficult-to-understand words and phrases and replaces them with everyday English. There are also several online resources available that provide help with "translation." The Medical Library Association has several free, downloadable online brochures called *Medspeak in Plain Language*. There are *Medspeaks* for breast cancer, diabetes, eye disease, heart disease, HIV-AIDS, and stroke. Some are available in Spanish. The federal government offers a medical term tutorial and a translator at its National Library of Medicine website. Finally, the National Patient Safety Foundation (2015), explaining that "studies show that people who understand health instructions make fewer mistakes when they take their medicine or prepare for a medical procedure," instructs patients to always ask these three questions of their healthcare providers until they are satisfied that they understand the answer:

1. What is my main problem?
2. What do I need to do?
3. Why is it important for me to do this?

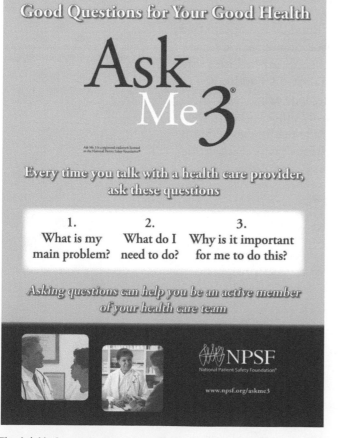

The Ask Me 3 program is one way of helping clients cut through health-care providers' jargon.

The third and fourth reasons that provider-client communication is often problematic are closely related. The *power distance* (Chapter 9) between providers and clients, especially between doctors and their patients, produces a *reluctance on the part of clients to speak up.* Not only are physicians much respected in our culture for their level of education, skill, and devotion to helping, but when we are ill or otherwise in need, that elevated status is magnified because we are, indeed, reliant on their power. Consider points from two letters to the editor sent to the *Wall Street Journal* in a discussion of doctor-patient trust. The first, from a physician, explains why the power distance necessarily exists: "The patient trusts the doctor to possess knowledge of the patient's illness and to apply this knowledge in the patient's particular best interests," wrote Dr. John Bettinger. "The essence of this trust lies in the fact that the patient cannot hope to achieve the same knowledge through a cram study on the Internet or elsewhere." The second, from 78-year-old Dwain Hanson, describes what many believe to be the product of that distance: "Doctors are harried dictators who are too busy or frustrated to engage in democratic dialogue of 60 to 180 seconds" ("Seeking," 2004, p. A17).

In fact, the "magisterial physician" stereotype is alive and well in American culture, producing either a *machine-and-mechanics relationship* or a *child-parent relationship*. In **machine-and-mechanics** interactions, physicians are experts who diagnose and fix the problem. In these interactions it is easy for doctors to forget about the human element because the patients before them are broken, in need of repair, and passive. "We focus on the body as a machine, and here are the things we do to fix it," explains emergency room doctor Lynn Sweeney, "We become so focused on the process we forget about the human element that's so integral to it" (in Freyer, 2012, p. A1). In **child-parent** interactions, the doctor is dominant and all-knowing, and the patient is submissive and reliant (duPré, 2005). Both situations are counterproductive. Doctors do not get the information they need for proper diagnosis and treatment, and patients do not get the full benefit of the doctors' expertise, do not understand the information they do receive, and do not ask for clarification or additional information.

The great power of a doctor's words is evident in the **nocebo effect**, in which patients experience a treatment effect based solely on a provider's words. For example, when doctors preface an injection with words like *sting*, *burn*, *hurt*, *bad*, or *pain*, patients will feel greater discomfort than when more benign or neutral words are used (Stromberg, 2012). Researchers Paul Enck and Winfried Häuser offer this example:

> A team of American anesthesiologists studied women about to give birth who were given an injection of local anesthetic before being administered an epidural. For some women, the injection was prefaced by the statement, "We are going to give you a local anesthetic that will numb the area so that you will be comfortable during the procedure." For others, the statement was, "You are going to feel a big bee sting; this is the worst part of the procedure." The perceived pain was significantly greater after the latter statement, which emphasized the downside of the injection. (2012, p. SR4)

This, however, creates a dilemma. Healthcare providers must be honest with their clients about all possible outcomes of treatment, but if mentioning a negative side effect increases the likelihood that it will occur, what should they do? "Better communication is the answer," write researchers Enck and Häuser, "When talking with patients, doctors and nurses often say things with unintended negative suggestions, like 'it's just going to bleed a bit' or 'you must avoid lifting heavy objects—you don't want to end up paralyzed.' We recommend more extensive training in communication for doctors and nurses to help them use the power of their words appropriately. As the great cardiologist Bernard Lown once said, 'Words are the most powerful tool a doctor possesses, but words, like a two-edged sword, can maim as well as heal'" (2012, p. SR4).

There is a growing sense that traditional levels of provider-client power distance are waning, especially in the era of the Internet and social networking. Healthcare consumers are increasingly empowered. Patients frequently see themselves not only as consumers, but as partners. They are supported in this shift by several national and local efforts. For example, although the free,

machine-and-mechanics relationship In provider-client interactions, physicians are experts who diagnose and fix the problem.

child-parent relationship In provider-client interactions, the doctor is dominant, all-knowing; the patient is submissive and reliant.

nocebo effect Experiencing a treatment effect based solely on a provider's words.

downloadable iPhone app *Touch Surgery* is designed to improve physicians' surgical skills, many doctors make it available to their patients in order to inform them about what is to take place and to calm any apprehensions. As *Touch Surgery* developer Jean Nehme explained, "We've found that it really improves patient comprehension and reduces anxiety." Science writer Zach Sokol added, "So even if *Touch Surgery* is arguably one of the most sobering games imaginable, it sure beats having a surgeon drone on about just how, exactly, he'll be inserting that scalpel into your leg. The app literally shows you, the patient, what's you're about to undergo, physically, in an accurate representation, thus tranquilizing fear of the unknown" (2013). In an even more ambitious effort, the Joint Commission, a nonprofit organization that accredits and certifies more than 19,000 healthcare organizations across the country, created with Medicare and Medicaid the Speak Up program. Speak Up employs free videos and other instructional materials to remind patients to speak up because they are the "center of the healthcare team." You can read more about this effort in the box "Speak Up."

The need for meaningful provider-client communication is greatest when it is most difficult, for example when end-of-life decisions must be made, or when a child is dying. Very few doctors have the training or the time to coach patients and their families through end-of-life conversations. Moreover, end-of-life counseling is controversial, as some people see it as the medical system's way of hastening death and saving time and money. However, providers, their patients, and patients' families can, and frequently do, employ a Physician Orders for Life-Sustaining Treatment, sometimes called a *Polst*. Unlike a living will or advanced directive, a Polst spells out specific treatment instructions and becomes a formal part of a patient's medical record. Providers can also take advantage of programs like Respecting Choices, created by the Gunderson Lutheran Health System in Wisconsin, that train nurses, social workers, chaplains, and others as advance-care planning counselors to help patients and their families document end-of-life wishes.

Originally designed to train surgeons, Touch Surgery is increasingly being used by those same doctors to acquaint patients with the procedures they are about to undergo.

Well-meaning but hurtful communication with doctors only heightens people's pain. The Institute of Medicine reported that "too often, children die and their families fail to receive competent, compassionate, and consistent care that meets their physical, emotional, and spiritual needs" (2002). Doctors are justifiably reluctant to use words like *dying* and *dead,* but euphemisms like *terminal* and *critical* often confuse family members. As a result, many hospitals across the country are instituting "relational care skills" training for their staff. In both of these difficult cases, end-of-life decision-making and interaction surrounding child deaths, hospitals are also increasingly relying on onsite medical ethics teams to sit with physicians and their clients to facilitate communication.

SOCIALLY RESPONSIBLE COMMUNICATION

Speak Up

The Joint Commission is a nonprofit health organization and program-accrediting body whose mission is to "continuously improve health care for the public, in collaboration with other stakeholders, by evaluating health care organizations and inspiring them to excel in providing safe and effective care of the highest quality and value" ("Facts About," 2015). To that end, it coupled in 2002 with federal health programs Medicare and Medicaid to undertake what has become a remarkably successful example of socially responsible communication, Speak Up.

In an effort to reduce healthcare errors, this national campaign urges patients to become more active in their interactions with medical professionals by turning themselves into involved and informed members of the healthcare team. To help people do this, Speak Up offers free brochures, posters, buttons, coloring books, and videos (it has its own YouTube channel; search YouTube for "The Joint Commission") on a wide variety of patient safety topics that encourage patients to

- **S**peak up if you have questions or concerns. If you still don't understand, ask again. It's your body and you have a right to know.
- **P**ay attention to the care you get. Always make sure you're getting the right treatments and medicines by the right healthcare professionals. Don't assume anything.

- **E**ducate yourself about your illness. Learn about the medical tests you get and your treatment plan.
- **A**sk a trusted family member or friend to be your advocate (advisor or supporter).
- **K**now what medicines you take and why you take them. Medicine errors are the most common healthcare mistakes.
- **U**se a hospital, clinic, surgery center, or other type of healthcare organization that has been carefully checked out.
- **P**articipate in all decisions about your treatment. You are the center of the healthcare team.

Examples of the many active Speak Up campaigns include Help Prevent Errors in Your Care, Help Avoid Mistakes in Your Surgery, Planning Your Follow-up Care, Help Prevent Medical Test Mistakes, Know Your Rights, and Understanding Your Doctors and Other Caregivers. And while individuals can access any of the Speak Up materials, thousands of hospitals and clinics participate, knowing that better-informed patients produce better health outcomes. These providers print Speak Up materials for placement in patients' rooms; sponsor local public service announcements; include Speak Up content in patient information packets, websites, and newsletters; distribute material at wellness fairs; share it on hospitals' closed circuit television systems; and use it for staff education and orientation.

A fifth reason for poor provider-client communication is the most mundane—*time*. Although physicians actually spend more face-to-face time with their patients than they did just a few years ago, they increasingly feel that it is still insufficient. "As the practice of medicine grows more complex, physicians may be frustrated because they have too much to discuss with their patients in too little time," explained Paul B. Ginsburg, president of the Center for Studying Health System Change. In other words, there's just too much to talk about. For example, scientific advances have created a larger number of diagnostic and treatment options in need of discussion, and people are living longer with chronic illnesses that require more complex care and coordination among different caregivers (in Cassil, 2003).

Table 14.3 Four Habits Model

HABIT	SKILLS
Invest in the beginning	Create rapport quickly; elicit patient's concerns; plan the visit with the patient
Elicit the patient's perspective	Ask for patient's ideas; elicit specific requests; explore the impact on the patient's life
Demonstrate empathy	Be open to patient's emotions; make at least one empathic statement; convey empathy nonverbally; be aware of your own actions
Invest in the end	Deliver diagnostic information; provide education; involve patient in making decisions; complete the visit

Healthcare facilities are increasingly dealing with this time crunch through communication training, specifically in the "art of the interview." Among the most successful efforts is health provider Kaiser Permanente's Four Habits model (Table 14.3). It teaches four fundamental communication behaviors: (1) invest in the beginning of the visit and build rapport; (2) elicit the patient's perspective; (3) demonstrate empathy; and (4) involve patients at the end of the visit in designing a treatment plan. Physician Terry Stein, the program's creator, explained that the habits remind "clinicians of the importance to talk to patients in their own terms, not in our medical jargon. The result is the quality of diagnosis goes up, which impacts first-time right treatment, which impacts health outcomes, and also helps to deepen the trust between patient and physician" (in Greenberg, 2010).

There is a sixth reason for failures to communicate in the healthcare setting: *fear of malpractice lawsuits,* and it is not completely misplaced. Each year, one out of every 14 American doctors will be sued for malpractice. And although the large majority of those claims—80 percent—are dropped or dismissed, they are still quite costly to those physicians in money, emotional well-being, and future willingness to interact openly with patients (Daily Briefing, 2013). Nonetheless, there is evidence that good provider-client communication reduces the likelihood of legal action, while at the same time there is evidence that poor provider-client communication can increase the probability of a lawsuit (Hoffman, 2012).

If evidence indicates that better communication can reduce physicians' risk of malpractice claims, why are some still reluctant to be more open with their patients? "Many doctors really want to be open and apologize to patients, but are led to believe it can end up in financial disaster, when the truth is quite the opposite," explains Richard Boothman, a hospital risk officer (in Landro, 2007, p. D5). The truth is quite the opposite because hospitals are increasingly adopting a **disclosure-and-apology strategy** over the past's more common **defend-and-deny approach**. Many states have passed laws saying that doctors' apologies cannot be used against them in any subsequent legal action, and a growing number of hospitals have instituted policies

disclosure-and-apology strategy Requires healthcare providers to promptly disclose errors, and when appropriate, apologize to patients and families.

defend-and-deny approach When errors occur, healthcare providers remain silent or deny responsibility.

requiring doctors and nurses to promptly disclose errors, and when appropriate, to apologize to patients and families. There is a national movement, the Sorry Works Coalition (sorryworks.net) that enlists states, insurance companies, and providers in an effort to promote full disclosure and apologies as an alternative to lawsuits. Its protocol calls for an apology if an analysis of a given situation indicates that an error occurred or standard care was not provided, followed by admitting guilt, providing an explanation, indicating how the problem will be addressed and eliminated in the future, and an offer of compensation.

Recognition of the importance of good provider-client interpersonal communication found its way into the 2010 federal overhaul of the US medical system, the Affordable Care Act, often called Obamacare. Beginning in 2012, the national health plan, Medicare, began withholding payment to hospitals unless they met quality standards of medical care. But one-third of the withholdings, totaling hundreds of millions of dollars, are tied to patients' satisfaction with their providers' performance as measured on HCAHPS (Hospital Consumer Assessment of Healthcare Providers and Services). Every year, one-quarter of the 36 million people admitted to a hospital receive a questionnaire covering issues such as how well their doctors and nurses communicated and the facilities' cleanliness and quiet. "Even when the care is technically perfect," wrote medical reporter Felice Freyer, "patients can still feel disgruntled over things such as long waits, bad food, cranky staff, or anything that feels like a lack of concern—such as a simple failure to make eye contact" (2012, p. A8). Patient satisfaction scores are posted nationally at www.HospitalCompare.hhs.gov. In response, hospitals have appointed personnel with titles such as "chief experience officer" to monitor staff performance and have instituted communication-based staff-patient interaction programs such as the Cleveland Clinic's HEART—Hear the concern, Empathize, Apologize, Respond, and Thank.

Health Communication Contexts

Obviously, communication about health and well-being quite often takes place away from the individual provider-client interaction. We will look at four distinct contexts—family and friends, health and illness support groups, the hospital culture itself, and entertainment mass media.

Friends and Family

One of *Healthy People 2020's* communication objectives is increasing the number of people who have friends or family with whom they talk about their health (Table 14.1). This goal recognizes the value of significant others in maintaining good health and in times of need brought on by illness or accident. Athena duPré has identified two types of health-related communication support provided by family and, of course, friends (2005). In fact, the American

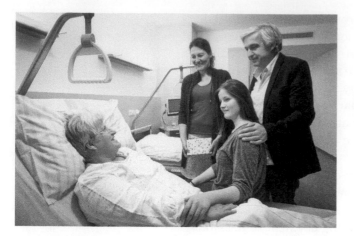

The medical profession is expanding its definition of family for the benefit of providers as well as for patients.

action-facilitating support Giving information or physically assisting someone in need.

nurturing suppor Helping others feel better about themselves and their situation.

Academy of Family Physicians (2009) defines "family" as "a group of individuals with a continuing legal, genetic and/or emotional relationship" and insists that in instances of treatment (for example, hospital stays, emergency room visits, and consultations with providers), it is patients who define their "family" and how they wish them to be involved in care, care planning, and decision-making. By this definition, friends can indeed be family.

Friends and family offer **action-facilitating support** when they give information, for example, looking up and passing on online treatment information, and when they physically assist someone in need, for example providing transportation, helping with medicines, or doing the chores. **Nurturing support** involves helping others feel better about themselves and their situation. A woman might take her wheelchair-bound brother-in-law on an outing in the park, or a friend might simply provide a soft shoulder and open ear to someone in despair. These greater levels of family and friend support not only help people through difficult health problems, but in addition,

> research has demonstrated that the presence and participation of family members and friends—as partners in care—provides cost savings, enhances the patient and family experience of care, improves management of chronic and acute illnesses, enhances continuity of care, and prevents hospital readmissions . . . The research is also clear that isolating patients at their most vulnerable times from the people who know them best places them at risk for medical error, emotional harm, inconsistencies in care, and costly unnecessary care . . . In addition, research indicates that for many older patients, hospitalization for acute or critical illness is associated with reduced cognitive function. Families and other "partners in care" are much more keenly aware of any change in cognitive function than hospital staff and therefore are a valuable resource during hospitalization. (Institute for Patient- and Family-Centered Care, 2010, p. 3)

Recognizing the demonstrated value of family and friend support, some hospitals now convene "family councils" designed to offer input on their needs; others are designing therapeutic gardens and play areas where families and friends can interact. Although private rooms have been standard for all new hospital construction since 2006 in order to reduce the spread of infection and provide a quieter environment, many hospitals have taken the idea one step further, making those rooms even more spacious and providing space for support-friendly furniture like convertible sofa beds. These activities, explains medical writer Laura Landro, are "inspired by a growing movement known as family-centered care. In addition to offering a safe and soothing environment, it calls for allowing families to be present and involved, including during invasive procedures and doctors' morning teaching rounds" (2013, p. D1). The research further demonstrates that facilitating family interaction, among other comforting room-design factors, can lead to a 30 percent reduction in patients' requests for pain medication, quicker recovery and rehabilitation, and shorter stays, all of which diminish not just costs but also the chances for accidents and infections (Kimmelman, 2014).

Support Groups

Health and illness support groups are also an important social context for health communication, and there is research indicating that participants in health-oriented groups find face-to-face support groups slightly more satisfying than groups found online (Van Uden-Kraan et

In person or online, support groups have proven themselves valuable for patients and their loved ones.

al., 2011). The advantages of face-to-face support groups are that they provide participants with an opportunity to see others like themselves in person and hear them talk, access to touching or other nonverbal support, opportunities for informal social time, and finding others to connect with socially or for extra support. The disadvantages are that participants may want more contact than the typical once-a-month or once-a-week group meeting; they may dislike the leader's leadership style; they may feel uncomfortable talking about their health with people from the same locale or community; meeting schedules may be inconvenient or difficult to meet; and the group may have one or more members who impede the work of the whole.

Even with their occasional disadvantages, support groups are valuable contexts for supportive communication. For example, a recent survey of people participating in one of WomenHeart's many hospital-based support groups across the country found that 93 percent felt that their quality of life was enhanced; 85.3 percent had improved their ability to communicate with their healthcare provider; 93 percent increased their understanding of heart disease; 85.6 percent believed that attending meetings helped them cope with challenges in maintaining their treatment/medication regimen; 86.2 percent believed that attending meetings helped them better communicate and explain their heart disease with family members, friends, and coworkers; and 85 percent reported improved treatment compliance and adherence (WomenHeart, 2012). In addition, there is evidence that the simple act of helping others in a support group benefits the helpers as much as it does the recipients of their help. It increases their sense of self-worth and value, while reducing their feelings of powerlessness, helping them "gain a sense of personal control when discussing their illness" (Wright, Sparks, and O'Hair, 2008, p. 94).

Hospital Culture

One organizational context in which quality health communication can be a matter of life or death is the hospital itself. There is considerable evidence that

adverse event Unintended injury or complication caused by healthcare management.

poor communication among hospital staff is a leading cause of avoidable surgical errors, with "communication breakdown" during hand-off (when a patient is moved from one unit to another or turned over to new staff during a shift change) the single largest source of error. In fact, "**adverse events** (AEs) in hospitals are now widely agreed to be a serious problem, annually killing more people than breast cancer or AIDS. An AE is usually defined as an unintended injury or complication . . . caused by healthcare management rather than by the patient's underlying disease process" (de Vries et al., 2008, p. 216). As a result, the approximately 440,000 people who die every year from preventable hospital error constitute the third-leading cause of death in America—behind heart disease and cancer—and account for one-sixth of all the nation's annual deaths (Allen, 2013).

There are two major aspects to the problem of poor hospital staff communication. One is embedded in the culture of the hospital itself—the deference that nurses and other staff typically pay to surgeons (the captains of the ship). The other is a product of the complexity of many routine hospital activities. "Consider the seemingly simple task of dispensing a drug at a hospital," explains physician Kevin Pho, "It's actually a complex process that requires five interdependent steps: ordering, transcribing, dispensing, delivering, and administering. A poorly designed system can lead to an error in any of those steps, with a potentially deadly outcome" (2012).

Many hospitals have instituted programs intended to change hospitals' typically hierarchical culture to the point that nurses and other staff feel comfortable speaking up. For example, "Changing the culture of the operating room is an essential aspect" of Transforming the Operating Room, a communication-improvement program instituted by VHA, an alliance of more than 2,400 not-for-profit hospitals. "Historically, the operating room is run in an isolated fashion with the surgeon at the helm, but with very little additional structure. Research has shown that this environment is no longer working and no longer is safe for patients. The Transforming the Operating Room program will help realign the power structure in the surgical suite so that physicians and hospital staff can work as an inter-dependent team" ("VHA," 2005). It calls for improvements such as safety pauses and time-outs to allow people in the operating room to speak up if they have a concern and for pre- and post-surgical briefings with all involved staffers. Another innovation adopted by many hospitals is the Preoperative Safety Briefing, developed by the Kaiser Permanente health group, in which "members of the surgical team meet briefly before every surgical procedure to identify and manage potential threats to patient safety; using a checklist adapted from the aviation industry, the team strives to enhance patient safety through better communication, teamwork, and situational awareness among health care providers. The program has virtually eliminated wrong-site surgeries, enhanced operating room staff satisfaction and perceptions of safety, and reduced nurse turnover" (DeFontes and Leonard, 2008).

Borrowing effective communication tools from other contexts has also helped reduce errors attributed to carrying out complex procedures, especially during hand-overs. Another Kaiser Permanente program, SBAR—Situation, Background, Assessment, and Recommendation—is an adaptation of the procedures used on nuclear submarines to quickly brief officers during a change of command ("SBAR," 2011). Admitting that it is "often criticized for poor communication," Great Britain's National Health Service has adopted SBAR to improve communication during hand-over.

Entertainment Mass Media

Sometimes for better, sometimes for worse, entertainment mass media can be an important source of health information. We've already seen in Chapter 10 that media can influence our views of ourselves and our realities, so it should be no surprise that they can influence how and what we think about health, ours and others. Of course, mass media cannot mirror reality because reality is simply too big. So what we see reflected is a "fun house mirror" version of reality. Some things appear bigger than they really are; some things appear smaller; and some things disappear altogether. And this is certainly the case for movie and television portrayals of health and medicine. As long ago as 1984, researchers were able to show that although the medical world is the source of a huge amount of media content, the media "reality" of health and healthcare is largely hospital-based, with technology and medical experts featured at the expense of primary care (family doctors or general practitioners). Family care, preventive care, and community health rarely appear. Doctors are always present; nurses not so much (Garland, 1984). How much has entertainment media's representation of health and medical issues changed? Think of *House*, *ER*, and *Grey's Anatomy* as you answer.

But entertainment media's contribution to health knowledge and behavior stretches far beyond perceptions of doctors and hospitals. There is a massive body of contemporary science demonstrating that entertainment media can encourage unhealthy behavior. For example:

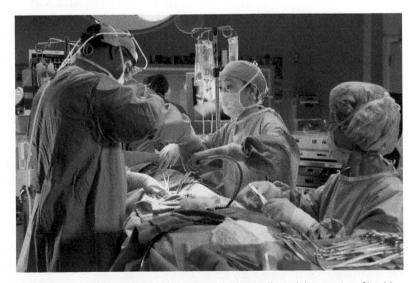

Much of what we believe we know about doctors, hospitals, and the practice of healthcare is shaped by popular mass media representations, like those in *Grey's Anatomy*.

- Studying young people 11 to 22 years old, Marina Krcmar and Kathryn Greene found "a link between exposure to violent television in the form of violent drama, realistic crime shows, and contact sports and participation in various forms of risk taking: problem drinking, drinking and driving, delinquency (vandalizing, trespassing, truancy), reckless driving, and drug use" (2000, p. 195).

- Albert C. Gunther and his colleagues found a "robust

connection" between "protobacco exposure" (seeing cigarette ads as well as media characters smoking on-screen) and adolescents' belief that their friends smoked which, in turn, increased the likelihood that they themselves would smoke (Gunther et al., 2006).

- Jerry Grenard and his team of researchers demonstrated that adolescents are susceptible to televised alcohol commercial persuasion, and their positive response to those ads influences "some youth to drink more and experience drinking-related problems later in adolescence" (Grenard, Dent, and Stacy, 2013, p. e369).

TDP (thinness depicting and promoting) media Media that feature conspicuously thin female characters.

- After reviewing scores of studies demonstrating that "exposure to **TDP (thinness depicting and promoting) media** leads to distorted body-image perceptions in school-age females and college women," Kimberly L. Bissell and Peiqin Zhou went a step further and examined the specific contribution of two types of media—entertainment and sports media—for possible associations with body-image distortion and eating disorders. They found that overall exposure to entertainment media in general was not related to eating disorders in college-age females, but those "who were exposed to 'thin-ideal' television scored fairly highly on the eating-disorder subscales [anorexia, bulimia, body dissatisfaction, drive for thinness]" (2004, p. 16). In addition, they demonstrated that the television programs these women watched most frequently featured "conspicuously thin" female characters and that those who consumed the greatest amount of this fare were "more likely to be dissatisfied with the way they looked and may even have taken dangerous steps to modify their body shape" (p. 17).

- As for little children, evidence of the negative impact of early television consumption to lifelong physical health problems is just as persuasive. Early television viewing has been linked to sedentary behavior, leading to obesity, diabetes, and poor dietary habits, not to mention mental health issues such as poor school performance, lack of imagination, and an inability to focus (Boyse, 2010).

The Hollywood, Health & Society program links television producers and health experts to bring medically accurate information to the screen. Millions of viewers learned effective exercise and weight-loss skills from *The Biggest Loser.*

There are, however, efforts to use entertainment media to promote healthy attitudes and behaviors. After conducting research showing that most people believe the medical information they see on television dramas and soap operas, the Centers for Disease Control and Prevention (CDC) developed a program called Hollywood, Health & Society. This program works to ensure the accuracy of the health information that appears on television, and it assists program producers in creating health-focused plots. As a result, meaningful AIDS awareness and prevention storylines have found their way into soap operas such as *The Bold and the Beautiful* and prime-time shows like *Law and Order: SVU*. If you were watching, you might have learned about Alzheimer's disease and post-traumatic stress disorder from *Grey's Anatomy*, autism from *Parenthood*, and weight loss and exercise from *The Biggest Loser*. Going even further, *So You Think You Can Dance* spawned a congressionally endorsed National Dance Day to promote active lifestyles.

ETHICAL COMMUNICATION

Direct-to-Consumer Prescription Drug Advertising

Direct-to-consumer prescription drug advertising (DTCA) is advertising prescription drugs to the public using popular commercial media. It is illegal in every country other than the United States and New Zealand. You know these drugs—Viagra, Cialis, Celebrex, Vioxx, Lipitor, and many others. The practice became legal in the United States in the mid-1980s and has grown to be a $5 billion-a-year business. The typical American television viewer sees as many as nine prescription drug ads a day, totaling 16 hours per year, far exceeding the amount of time spent with a primary care physician. Moreover, every dollar spent on DTCA increases sales of the advertised drug by an estimated $2.20 to $4.20 (Ventola, 2011).

Nonetheless, DTCA is quite controversial. Efforts to lift restrictions in Canada and Europe arise quite regularly, and proposals to ban, or at least more tightly regulate, the practice in the United States are also common. While even DTCA's harshest critics admit that the practice does have a few benefits, they argue that its drawbacks outweigh them. Here are the arguments typically offered by proponents and opponents, and there is research to support each contention (see Ventola, 2011):

Benefits of DTCA
- Informs, educates, and empowers patients
- Encourages patients to contact a clinician
- Promotes patient dialogue with healthcare providers
- Strengthens a patient's relationship with a clinician
- Encourages patient compliance
- Reduces underdiagnosis and undertreatment of conditions
- Removes the stigma associated with certain diseases
- Encourages product competition and lower prices.

Drawbacks of DTCA
- Does not adequately inform patients
- Overemphasizes drug benefits
- Promotes new drugs before safety profiles are fully known
- Manufactures disease and encourages drug over-utilization
- Leads to inappropriate prescribing
- Strains relationships with healthcare providers
- Wastes appointment time
- Is not rigorously regulated
- Increases costs.

However, none of these arguments (for or against) addresses the ethical issues surrounding DTCA. Among the moral questions often raised about the practice are

- Is it ethical that DTCA usually offers visual effects that emphasize benefits and very fast speech to downplay risks?
- Is it ethical to persuade people who are not in a knowledgeable position to judge the complexity of the medical issues alluded to in the ad?
- Is it ethical to manufacture disease, for example, RLS, restless leg syndrome?
- Is it ethical to "medicalize" routine aspects of ordinary life, such as the thinning hair and weight gain that come with age?
- Is it ethical to direct attention away from personal and societal solutions to health issues and toward expensive drug-based remedies in the pursuit of profit?

Where do you stand on the ethics of DTCA? Who benefits from DTCA? Who loses?

Do these efforts work? Susan Morgan and her colleagues measured the influence of organ donation storylines in four television dramas, *CSI: NY*, *Numb3ers*, *House*, and *Grey's Anatomy*, and discovered that "viewers who were not organ donors prior to exposure to the dramas were more likely to decide to donate organs if the drama explicitly encouraged donation, portrayed characters revealing how they had become donors, and discussed the merits of donating" (Morgan, Movius, and Cody, 2009, p. 135). Shelia Murphy and her colleagues showed similar effects for a lymphoma storyline on the television drama *Desperate Housewives* (Murphy e. al., 2011). They demonstrated that involvement with the show's characters improved not only knowledge of cancer, but produced healthy behavioral change as well. The influence of another aspect of entertainment media on people's health literacy, however, raises some important ethical questions. The issue is the propriety of a nearly unprecedented American commercial practice, and you can read about it in the box "Direct-to-Consumer Prescription Drug Advertising."

Health Communication and the Internet

Several *Healthy People 2020* objectives have to do with making more effective use of the Internet for health communication (Table 14.1), and there is little wonder why. Fifty-nine percent of US adults—72 percent of all Internet users—search online for health information, and as we've already seen, one-third of Americans go to the Web to diagnose medical conditions. Eight in 10 of those efforts begin at a search engine like Google, Bing, or Yahoo rather than at a health-specific site, giving rise to the concern that the Internet helps create **communicated diseases** (imagined diseases that spread because people communicate about them, like wind-turbine syndrome). Another concern is that it has become a haven for **cyberchondriacs**, people who compulsively search online for information about real or imagined symptoms of illness. "On the Internet, every headache becomes a brain tumor in four clicks or less," jokes Ron Gutman, founder of medical website HealthTap (in Heussner, 2013). But in fact, more than 40 percent of people's e-diagnoses are eventually confirmed by a clinician (only 18 percent had their e-diagnoses disconfirmed), suggesting that people are actually making good use of the technology (Fox and Duggan, 2013). Not only do they make good use of the new technology, they embrace it. Eighteen percent of Americans say they would like to insert a microchip inside their body to continually monitor their health, sending them and their doctors constant electronic updates, and more than one in five believe that technology will someday eradicate altogether the need for doctors (Simpson, 2013). For now, though, we'll look at several of the most common applications of the Internet to health communication.

communicated disease An imaginary disease that spreads because people communicate about it.

cyberchondriac Person who compulsively searches online for information about real or imagined symptoms of illness.

One obvious health communication use of the Internet is as a substitute for a visit to a health professional. More people visit "Dr. Google" every day than visit actual health professionals, and many healthcare providers are taking advantage of that fact to deliver even better care. Many hospitals, clinics, and physicians maintain blogs to help people navigate, evaluate, and interpret online health information, often in advance of a visit. HealthTap, with 10 million monthly visitors and a network of 71,000 physicians, allows its members to ask doctors questions directly from their mobile devices or the Web (Kokalitcheva, 2015). Ringadoc provides real-time Internet videoconference consultations with physicians, and the app Doctor on Demand connects users "face to face" with a physician anytime and anywhere. Physicians at the University of Texas Medical Branch read ultrasounds, X-rays, and echocardiograms of their patients, as do thousands of other doctors. But they do it for the men and women at the scientific research station in Antarctica via Internet **telemedicine**, the delivery of health services by Internet video. Numerous doctors offer—and most health plans now pay for—**e-visits**, in which physicians and patients interact virtually instead of face to face. Used primarily to eliminate office visits for routine illnesses, patients simply enter their symptoms into an online system, and doctors, typically with the patients' health records electronically accessible, use that information to send a diagnosis and, when necessary, a prescription. Evaluation of e-visits undertaken by the American Medical Association suggests that the resulting diagnoses are accurate and far less costly to render (Mehrotra et al., 2013). Not only are e-visits effective and cost-efficient, they facilitate health communication in other ways as well. Doctors can attach to their replies information such as patient-education materials, lab results, prescriptions, referrals, and links to well-vetted Web sites.

Other new technology health communication advances abound. There are literally thousands of online support groups for people and families dealing with illness. They may lack the personal touch of a face-to-face group, but they provide 24/7 availability and sometimes much-wanted anonymity. Quite often their members collaborate with scientists and drug companies in medical and public health research. The CDC not only makes hundreds of diagnostic and information videos available on YouTube, it even holds health fairs in virtual worlds like *Second Life*. The American Cancer Society maintains an office there. Several government agencies and public health groups provide safety information sites, many of them interactive. For example, the National Library of Medicine runs a Household Products Database that offers user-friendly information on the possible toxicity of thousands of household products. The Environmental Protection Agency does the same for pesticides and other environmental hazards.

Social networking is also becoming an important site for health communication. As you'll soon read, it has proven most valuable in the promotion of health campaigns, but health officials also study information shared among social networking friends in the service of promoting good health. For

telemedicine Delivery of health services by Internet video.

e-visit When a physician and patient interact virtually rather than face to face.

example, health officials have developed an app that searches for keywords in users' newsfeeds to alert them to their increased risk of catching the flu (Christakis and Fowler, 2010). If three of your friends report that they missed class and two others say they're kind of achy, you're likely to receive the message, "You have a chance of getting the flu *today*." Other researchers apply the same approach to sexually transmitted infections (STI). "Real-world social networks—in other words, a person's circle of friends and sexual partners—have already proved to be strong predictors of STI risk. It follows that sites like Facebook, which convene all of those real-world connections in one virtual setting, have huge potential in this arena." Again, the idea is that if keywords in people's posts suggest sexually risky behavior or social contact with an infected individual, they might get a message to exercise extra care. Alternatively, in states where sexual-partner notification is the law, people diagnosed with an STI can be asked for a list of sexual partners and friends whom they think might benefit from testing. Those people can then be contacted using Facebook with an alert that someone they know has been diagnosed with an STI, they might be at risk, and they should be tested (Clark-Flory, 2012). There's also an app, Hula, that allows people using their smartphones for location-based online dating (I'm here and looking for a date, are you interested?) to share time-stamped and verified STI lab results with potential partners.

Despite the impressive evidence that health professionals and people are making heavy and varied use of the Internet for health communication, there is for many users the lingering question of personal privacy. Their quite reasonable feeling is that anything on the Internet can be hacked. Nonetheless, a large majority of Americans, 72 percent, report that they trust healthcare providers with their personal data, trusting the healthcare industry even more than they do advertisers, social networking sites, the government, and even banks (GfK, 2014). Maintaining that trust, encrypted and password-protected secure message systems are now virtually universal in electronic provider/client exchanges.

Health Communication Campaigns

In 2012 Facebook founder Mark Zuckerberg, recognizing that his site's members want to present themselves as good, likable, giving individuals—people whom others would want to "friend"—offered them a simple way to indicate their status as an organ donor on their Facebook page's Timeline, under Life Event. "We believe that by simply telling people that you're an organ donor, the power of sharing and connection can play an important role," Zuckerberg explained (in Jacobs, 2012). Facebook is also at the heart of an effort to promote safe sex among high school and college students. Sheana Bull and her colleagues devised an experiment in which they sent different messages to different recipients. Those who received News Feed messages about sexual health—items about "condom negotiation," HIV testing, and healthy sexual relationships in a weekly feature called Just/Us—showed better rates of condom use. The researchers chose to use News Feed rather than information from more formal safe-sex advocates because "there is little evidence to suggest a majority of youth actively seek out and engage with organizations on Facebook. Thus, approaches like that of Just/Us to 'push' messages out through RSS feed offer one way to get messages in front of a large number of youth" (Bull et al., 2012, pp. 472–473).

Successful public health campaigns have existed long before the coming of social networking sites, and *Healthy People 2020* specifically called for even greater use of those methods and greater recognition of their best practices (Table 14.1). You are probably familiar with past national campaigns such as "This Is Your Brain on Drugs," "Milk . . . It Does a Body Good!," the anti-smoking "I Learned It by Watching You!," "Buckle Up with the Crash Test Dummies," and "Friends Don't Let Friends Drive Drunk." If conducted expertly, these campaigns can be quite effective, accounting for valuable alterations in target audiences' behavior (see Snyder, 2007).

These campaigns typically pursue one of two goals, either to raise awareness of important health issues or to change individuals' health behaviors and attitudes. In either case, effective implementation should follow some variation of these steps, as described by the CDC's (2011a) *CDCynergy* program for planning, managing, and evaluating public health communication programs:

GET CAUGHT BUZZED DRIVING AND IT COULD COST YOU $10,000.

BUZZED DRIVING IS DRUNK DRIVING.

This public service health campaign, and scores of others like it, may have saved millions of lives.

- *Review background information to define the problem* (determine what's already out there).
- *Set communication objectives* (decide what you want to accomplish).

- *Analyze and segment target audiences* (decide whom you want to reach).
- *Develop and pretest message concepts* (decide what you want to say).
- *Select communication channels* (decide where you want to say it).
- *Select, create, and pretest messages and products* (plan how you want to say it).
- *Develop promotion plan/production* (determine how you will get your message and product used).
- *Implement communication strategies and conduct process evaluation* (get it out there).
- *Conduct outcome and impact evaluation* (assess how well you did).

The CDC even offers suggestions on how to bring a successful health campaign to the workplace, as you can see in the box "Getting Health Messages to Employees." Nonetheless, even the best, most creative, most effective health campaigns inevitably fail to change the behaviors of everyone in their target group. You can read why in the box "The Health Belief Model."

PERSONALLY RESPONSIBLE COMMUNICATION

The Health Belief Model

Public health campaigns have been with us for a long time, and so has the question of why some people fail to respond to them. In the 1950s, perplexed as to why people would refuse to take advantage of free chest X-rays to screen for tuberculosis, psychologists came to the conclusion that people's beliefs about how susceptible they were to a disease, coupled with their perceptions of the benefits associated with trying to avoid it, influenced their willingness to act (Becker, 1974). The resulting Health Belief Model (Rimer and Glanz, 2005, p. 13) argued that "six main constructs influence people's decisions about whether to take action to prevent, screen for, and control illness . . . [P]eople are ready to act if they

- Believe they are susceptible to the condition (*perceived susceptibility*)
- Believe the condition has serious consequences (*perceived severity*)
- Believe taking action would reduce their susceptibility to the condition or its severity (*perceived benefits*)
- Believe costs of taking action (*perceived barriers*) are outweighed by the benefits

- Are exposed to factors that prompt action (e.g., a television ad or a reminder from one's physician to get a mammogram) (*cue to action*)
- Are confident in their ability to successfully perform an action (*self-efficacy*)."

Using the Health Belief Model, take a free program offered by your campus health service that might apply to you but that you do not use and explain why you don't take advantage of it. Some programs typically offered by campus health services include (for men) genital and testicular exams; discussions on food and vitamin supplements; programs on steroid use and its effects; (for women) annual pap smear and breast exams; contraceptive counseling; (for all) testing, treatment, and counseling for sexually transmitted infections; HIV testing and counseling; nutrition and diet counseling; blood pressure checks; and diet and weight loss programs. Now, perform the same analysis on a program that you have used. Did you learn anything from this exercise about your health literacy? If yes, what did you learn? If not, can you explain why not?

COMMUNICATION IN THE WORKPLACE

Getting Health Messages to Employees

American companies and other large organizations are increasingly bringing health campaigns to the workplace. Obviously, not only do employees who take advantage of them gain the benefit of better health, employers, too, benefit because of increased worker productivity. After all, sick employees, even if they choose to come to work, aren't productive employees.

But as the CDC cautions, "If employees are unaware of the health promotion opportunities available to them, they are unlikely to participate; and without sufficient participation, program success cannot be achieved" (2011b). Therefore, the CDC offers four strategies designed to gain greater on-the-job health campaign effectiveness:

1. **Brand the health strategy, including a logo**— Brand the campaign; give it a name (for example, "20 Days to a Healthier You" or "Walk That Tension Away"); create a logo; and use both on all materials.
2. **Define the target audience(s)**—Identify the employee group or groups to whom the campaign will be directed; tailor messages to those groups, keeping in mind demographic factors like age and nature

of their jobs; interact with employees to learn about their knowledge, attitudes, and beliefs related to health promotion; identify their needs and interests and the opportunities and barriers to access health information.

3. **Use a variety of message channels**—Use multiple communication channels to ensure that employees receive the information they need to make informed decisions. Consider e-mail, bulletin boards, newsletters, the intranet, presentations, social networking, direct communication from management, representatives of a company "wellness council," and coworkers. Pay attention to the best timing and frequency of message delivery for intended groups of employees. Be willing to pretest messages with targeted workers and make the necessary changes.
4. **Recognize and celebrate success**—Highlight employee success stories; share and celebrate them to motivate others to participate. Consider incentives—time off, company clothing, gift cards, and so on—as rewards for employees who meet their individual health behavior goals.

Review of Learning Objectives

14.1 Identify the barriers to successful provider-client communication and evaluate possible remedies.

There are six primary barriers to successful provider-client communication: providers are not trained in interpersonal communication; they rely on technical jargon; there exists a power distance between providers and their clients; clients are reluctant to speak up; providers have little time; and providers fear malpractice suits. In each instance there have been successful efforts at improvement.

14.2 Describe the importance of family, friends, and support groups as agents of health communication.

Friends and family provide action-facilitating support and nurturing support. Contemporary practices call for the patient to be the definer of "family." Face-to-face support groups offer a variety of benefits, including an opportunity to see and hear others like themselves in person, touching or other nonverbal support, opportunities for informal social time, and finding people to connect with socially or for extra support. Additionally, the simple act of helping others in a support group benefits the helpers as much as it does the recipients of their help.

14.3 Explain how the hospital culture itself impedes good health communication and evaluate possible remedies.

The complexity of even routine hospital procedures, coupled with the traditional hierarchical structure of doctor-staff interactions, can combine to create potentially dangerous communication errors. Effective communication strategies from other industries have proven successful in remedying many problems.

14.4 Judge the contribution of entertainment media to good and harmful health communication.

There is considerable scientific evidence not only that entertainment media present an unrealistic image of medicine and its practice, but also that they can encourage unhealthy activities such as aggression, smoking, drinking, body dissatisfaction, and a sedentary lifestyle. But there is also evidence that these same media are effective at encouraging good health practice.

14.5 Judge the benefits and drawbacks of the Internet and social network sites as sources of health communication.

Despite some concern that the ready availability of health information on the Internet can encourage cyberchondria and communicated diseases, many people make good use of the technology as a means of self-diagnosis, as a substitute or complement for visits to health professionals, for access to online support groups, and as a clearinghouse for a wide variety of health and safety communication. Social networking, too, has proven valuable in health information campaigns and for personal contact with at-risk individuals.

14.6 Describe the elements of an effective health communication campaign.

There are nine steps to a successful health communication campaign: review background information to define the problem; set communication objectives; analyze and segment target audiences; develop and pretest message concepts; select communication channels; select, create, and pretest messages and products; develop promotion plan/production; implement communication strategies and conduct process evaluation; and conduct outcome and impact evaluation.

Key Terms

amenable mortality 313
health literacy 313
health communication 315
patient activation 317
machine-and-mechanic relationship 319
child-parent relationship 319
nocebo effect 319
disclosure-and-apology strategy 322
defend-and-deny approach 322
action-facilitating support 324
nurturing support 324
adverse events 326

TDP (thinness depicting and promoting) media 328
communicated disease 330
cyberchondriac 330
telemedicine 331
e-visit 331

Questions for Review

1. What are communicated diseases and cyberchondria?

2. What are health literacy and health communication?

3. What are the six reasons for poor provider-client communication?

4. Distinguish between the machine-and-mechanics and the child-parent provider-client relationship?

5. What is the nocebo effect?

6. Distinguish between the disclosure-and-apology strategy and the defend-and-deny approach? What provider-client problem is each designed to confront?

7. Distinguish between action-facilitating support and nurturing support.

8. What are some of the benefits and drawbacks of face-to-face support groups?

9. How can entertainment media promote good health?

10. What is the Health Belief Model?

Questions for Discussion

1. Have you ever gone to the Internet for health information? What was your goal? Was it for diagnosis or for some other matter? Where did you begin your search? What was your experience, that is, were you satisfied with the outcome?

2. How would you rate your own health literacy? If you give yourself high marks, what factors did you consider in making that evaluation? If you gave yourself low marks, why did you do so, and what might you do to improve your health literacy grade?

3. How well did this chapter's scenario of a typical visit to the doctor match your experience? What similarities and differences have you experienced and why do you think they exist?

15

Public Speaking: An Overview

You wake up. It's 5:00 a.m. You toss and turn but have no luck getting back to sleep. And then you remember: it's your turn to deliver an informative speech in today's public speaking class. Your stomach begins to do flips, and you know if you don't fall back to sleep, you'll be a zombie for class. But why the nerves? You've prepared thoroughly for your presentation, "The Life of Samuel Langhorne Clemens." You know your topic well, and you start to go over the speech in your head—Clemens was born in 1835 and died in 1910. His pen name was Mark Twain. He was the author of classic books like *The Adventures of Huckleberry Finn*, *Life on the Mississippi*, *The Prince and the Pauper*, and a *Connecticut Yankee in King Arthur's Court*. You're definitely ready. And yet—your head hurts, your stomach's a bit queasy, and you are exhausted from sleeping so poorly all night. You have a good, old-fashioned case of public speaking anxiety.

Class begins at 1:00 p.m. sharp and the professor calls you to the front. The room starts to spin. You think, *everyone is judging me*. As you attempt to recall all the constructive criticism provided by your instructor over the past few weeks, your mind goes blank and you struggle to breathe. And then something unexpected happens. Mark Twain walks into the room! It's your English professor dressed in a white suit, wearing a white wig and moustache, and smoking a pipe. The class loves it. Your live visual aid has arrived, and the tension and awkwardness of the pre-speech silence is broken. You begin to relax as your visual aid takes his place next to you at the podium. A deep breath, and you begin, "Thank you for joining us, Mr. Twain." The class erupts with laughter and you feel a calm come over you just before delivering a flawless speech.

Wouldn't it be nice if every speech moment happened just like in this opening story? It can, and this chapter is designed to help you become more comfortable with public presentation by stressing the idea that speaking, in all forms, is a natural part of who we are as humans.

Learning Objectives

15.1   Explain the importance of public speaking.

15.2   Identify the different types of speeches.

15.3   Identify the basics of good public speaking.

15.4   Describe the steps of speech preparation.

15.5   Identify ways to overcome public speaking anxiety.

The Importance of Public Speaking

In the opening monologue of an episode of his hit television series, *Seinfeld,* comedian Jerry Seinfeld (1993) jokes, "According to most studies, people's number-one fear is public speaking. Number two is death. *Death* is number two! Now this means to the average person, if you have to go to a funeral, you're better off in the casket than doing the eulogy." Funny, yes; but the comedian also fairly accurately identified the fear many people have of public speaking. Karen Dwyer and Marlina Davidson empirically tested the claim, surveying college students. "So, is public speaking the number one fear? The answer is 'yes,'" they concluded, "it is the most common fear, selected by students more often than other fears" (2012, p. 107). Incidentally, death was not the second most common fear; it was third, just behind financial problems and ahead of loneliness.

But why should this be the case? After all, we all talk, and usually quite publicly. Why is it different when we have to stand up and speak in front of an audience? Could it be that we simply hate being judged? Perhaps it's because we have insecurities about our speaking skills. Maybe we want to live up to the impressions others have of us and we are afraid we'll fail to do so. The answer could be *all of the above,* and then some. But speaking is as natural to most humans as eating. Still, we've never heard anyone say they were *afraid of eating,* so what's going on here? Eating is a pleasure often tied to our emotions. We all know people who claim to be "emotional eaters." Eating calms us and makes us happy. Delivering a speech, however, is unnerving for many people, offering (they think) little more than stress, judgment, and the opportunity to be embarrassed.

Rest assured, public speaking has gotten a bad rap. Like eating, there are so many more benefits than costs if we do it right—including good health. Speaking is a productive contribution to our mental well-being, helping us with memory, focus, critical thinking, and other cognitive processes. In fact, verbal communication in all forms is directly tied to our ability to make meaning *and* develop understanding about ourselves, others, and our culture. Public speaking experts Ray Ross and Diana Leonard explain, "We process information in order to think about it the same way we process information to share with others. When we speak to others (formally or informally) we help them to understand our thinking processes by providing connections between our ideas" (2012, p. 6). In other words, as we become better speakers, we also become more reflective thinkers, and as we become more reflective thinkers, we become better thinkers.

Jerry Seinfeld says people would rather die than deliver a speech.

But the advantages of being an effective speaker are not limited to cognitive improvement. Relationship development, professional success, identity formation, and the encouragement of public discourse are all products of effective talk. In Chapter 3 we addressed the role of verbal communication in identity formation and maintenance, and in Chapter 6 we looked at talk in relationships. So here we will concentrate on *professional success* and *public discourse*.

Public speaking is when a speaker addresses an audience in a more structured and formal way than in a regular conversation. Many of the formally prepared presentations we deliver happen in the workplace. In fact, communication skills (speaking, writing, and critical thinking) are among the top criteria in determining job attainment and retention. Surveys routinely demonstrate that the two characteristics employers want most in their new hires are good communication skills and critical thinking (a byproduct of solid communication skills; Sternberg, 2013). Specifically regarding the issue of public speaking, research by Hart Research Associates shows that 89 percent of employers want more emphasis placed on oral communication in colleges (2010). Simply put, if you can present yourself and your ideas in an intelligible and professional manner, you are more likely than those who cannot to experience continued career growth. It doesn't matter what you have in your head or heart, if you can't communicate it, it does you little good. And as you read in Chapter 12, with Internet and smartphone technology continuing to be the communication media of choice for most students, those future job-seekers inevitably place less emphasis on presenting themselves verbally. As a result, when employers find job candidates who are adept at speaking, they rush to hire them (Weins, 2012). You can read more about the importance of public speaking to career success in the box "On-the-Job Public Speaking."

public speaking Addressing an audience in a structured and formal way.

COMMUNICATION IN THE WORKPLACE

On-the-Job Public Speaking

As you've seen throughout this text, context is crucial to meaning making. So, while the principles of good public speaking remain the same regardless of the setting, different settings suggest somewhat different approaches. As speech coach Audra Bianca (2015) explains, "For example, you would prepare a different speech for a fund-raising dinner than you would for a parent-teacher conference. Over time, you learn to think on your feet, taking information from the social environment and changing your communication patterns to suit the occasion." Communication consultant Courtney Meyer (2013) adds, "Whether you need to present to a government agency or parent company, speak in the boardroom or even talk to a group of coworkers or new employees, being in the spotlight isn't easy. Effective public speaking in or out of the workplace is a skill that you should hone—for very few people does this come naturally. Of course, the good news is that public speaking is a skill that can be learned and practiced." What are some of the on-the-job skills that can be learned and practiced?

1. **Emphasize the point**. Make sure to state the concern or issue that has put you in front of your listeners and why they need to listen.
2. **Tell your listeners how they benefit.** Your time is valuable. Their time is valuable. So explain how they'll benefit from listening to you.

3. **Identify with your audience**. This is one public speaking rule—in fact one communication-in-general rule—that never varies. Let your listeners know that you understand them, their needs, and interests as soon as you start talking. Communication is a transaction.
4. **Summarize how you developed the solution or information you are offering.** This gives your listeners a story to follow and will keep them from dismissing you or interrupting.
5. **Pass out an outline of your proposal or report.** Your listeners can make notes or questions directly next to your points and take the outline away from the talk.
6. **Anticipate criticism**. If you were in your audience, what questions, objections, and critiques would you offer? Address these issues throughout your talk. Have an answer prepared for every criticism you can think of, and, if questioned, offer your responses calmly and confidently.

Over the course of our lives we typically spend 90,117 hours at work (Manger and McPhee, 2015); as a result, much of our communication happens in a professional environment. It only makes sense, then, that improving our on-the-job public speaking skills will produce a more successful and fulfilling career.

---

public discourse Societal sharing of ideas through conversation.

Encouraging **public discourse**, societal sharing of ideas through conversation, is also an important reason to develop good speaking skills. As we've discussed in previous chapters, communicating our ideas is critical to democracy. The efficiency and accuracy with which messages are delivered helps determine the competency of the response, for example, in voting on civic issues or in managing crises like natural disasters and health epidemics. Consider the types of professionals who speak publicly on a regular basis and as a result mold public opinion—politicians, celebrities, marketers, teachers, public relations professionals, news anchors, and local officials, to name a few. These people must possess some level of public speaking skill if they are to be successful at eliciting their desired

Political Satire in Contemporary Culture

Several polls conducted over the last few years (e.g., Kelley, 2014) have revealed that viewers who get their news primarily from satire programs like *The Daily Show* are more informed about current events and issues than viewers who watch more traditional news programs. We can debate whether this is a positive development, but given the role that these political satire programs now seem to serve, the question becomes whether such satirists feel a sense of social responsibility to the audience that supports them.

Most of what personalities such as Jon Stewart say pokes fun at those in power, including big-time media personalities. Ironically, despite, or maybe because of, this satirical approach to highlighting chaos and corruption, he and those like him (John Oliver and Larry Wilmore, for example) have become among the most trusted journalists in America (Meyers, 2015). Yet in numerous interviews, Stewart has made it clear that he's a comedian and does not claim to be or want to be a journalist (for example, in Moyers, 2007).

Cultural researcher Amber Day, author of *Satire and Dissent: Intervention in Contemporary Political Debate*, commented on the issue of social responsibility, "While I don't think they [performers like Stewart] have an *automatic* responsibility as political satirists, I do think they have become popular because they do such

As a public speaker, does political satirist Jon Stewart have a social responsibility to his viewers?

a good job of pointing to the flaws of mainstream news and political discussion. In drawing our attention to the sensationalism, manipulativeness, and dishonesty of much of our political debate, they frequently provide more context and analysis of the issues than the outlets they critique" (2015). What do *you* think? Do respected public figures automatically have a social responsibility when constructing and delivering their messages, regardless of the format or genre through which they speak? And, although Jon Stewart says he's *only* a comedian, how do you think he would answer this question?

public reaction. Certainly, you could name a few speakers who have been particularly influential in your life. Think of the many individuals, past and present, who have had tremendous impact through their presentational abilities—Winston Churchill, Gloria Steinem, Walter Cronkite, Shirley Chisholm, Martin Luther King, Jr., and even Jon Stewart, to name a few. These speakers and the many others who have informed us, persuaded us, guided us, motivated us, and entertained us, even if we have never heard them speak (or even if we have never even heard of them!) have enriched our lives. Consider what Martin Luther King, Jr., achieved in the 1960s, not only for the Civil Rights Movement, but for all Americans, informing us of cultural, legal, social, and economic inequality and

Dr. Martin Luther King used words to change the world.

informative speech Speech designed to convey knowledge and understanding.

persuasive speech Speech designed to persuade an audience to a new opinion *or* reinforce an existing opinion.

persuading us to take action. For nearly two decades, comedian Jon Stewart entertained us on Comedy Central, but he also informed an entire generation of young adults about political issues affecting their country and very often persuaded them into action (Day, 2011). You can read more about the value of speakers like Mr. Stewart in the box "Political Satire in Contemporary Culture." Good speakers can deliver many types of speeches and styles effectively.

Types of Speeches

Public speaking experts typically differentiate four varieties of speeches: informative, persuasive, special occasion, and small group speeches. **Informative speeches** are speeches designed to transmit knowledge and understanding. Speeches about objects, events, concepts, or processes are all considered informative. Here are a few sample topics for each:

- *Objects:* The human heart, the US Congress, the space shuttle, the Swiss Alps
- *Events:* Mardi Gras, the Great Depression, the presidential election, the Super Bowl
- *Concepts:* Honesty, civil rights, trust, education, politics, philosophy
- *Processes:* How to administer CPR, how to make chicken parmesan, writing a business letter, how to prepare a speech

Because informative speeches are designed to relay knowledge, it is important that sources used in the speech are credible and current. Part of being a good informative speaker is being accountable for what you present and making sure the facts and data are comprehensible to your audience.

Another type of speech is the persuasive speech. The goal of a **persuasive speech** is either to move the audience toward your opinion on a specific subject *or* to reinforce existing opinions. Like informative speeches, they require research and the presentation of material based on credible findings. Unlike the informative speech however, the persuasive presentation is not necessarily neutral or objective, and often contains statements of opinion backed by outside sources. Here are some examples of persuasive topics:

- The existence of global warming
- Be an organ donor
- The dangers of smoking

- The importance of a mandatory finance class in high school
- Vote for Brynn McNamee
- Eat gluten free for a healthier lifestyle

Persuasive speeches require an understanding of all sides of the issue.

Strategically, persuasive speeches are much like debates. In order to argue your side of the issue, you need to fully understand the presumed points of the opposition. Even though the audience typically doesn't verbally counter or challenge your arguments (as each side does in a debate), there are certainly some audience members who will mentally disagree with your position; that is, they will be thinking about all the counterpoints they would make if they could. When preparing a persuasive speech, you must consider these counterarguments in order to successfully address (and hopefully deflate) the concerns of those who do not share your opinions.

A very important component of persuasion is *ethics* (Chapter 13 offers a detailed discussion of ethics and persuasion). In our current political climate of accusations, name-calling, and high-stakes campaigning, we often see candidates resort to lying about the facts or, at the very least, engaging in puffery (slight exaggerations) to win votes. We tend to see the same tactics in partisan news reporting and most certainly in advertising (Jay, 2010). It's often extremely difficult not only to separate fact from fiction but also to determine ethical from unethical commentary.

Two other kinds of speeches are **small group** (presenting for only a few people, for example at a business meeting or before a church group) and **special occasion** (presenting at an event like a roast, wedding, or funeral). As you can imagine, very few people find themselves speaking before an audience of hundreds, but most of us will at some point experience delivering a speech before a small group or at a special event. There can also be crossover in the type of speech, for example, a small group speech can also be persuasive, like a sales talk or **elevator pitch** (a short, speech, typically prepared in advance rather than on the spot, delivered in the presumed time span of an elevator ride, or 30 seconds to 2 minutes).

A special occasion speech such as a eulogy can also be informative, for instance if the speaker presents a biographical perspective of the deceased. And consider speeches given by political candidates. Naturally, politicians wish to persuade people to vote for them, but in doing so they also need to be informative about their policies, positions, and plans. Whatever the platform, style, or genre of speech, most effective speakers share a number of skills and characteristics.

small group speech Speech delivered before a few people.

special occasion speech Speech at an event like a roast, wedding, or funeral.

elevator pitch A short, often fully prepared speech delivered in the presumed time span of an elevator ride.

A Crash Course in Public Speaking

There are 20 basic rules that should receive the lion's share of your attention as you work to master public speaking, so we want to highlight these points for you in this "crash course" section. It is important to note that these basic rules assume that you have thoroughly researched your topic and have written a thoughtful speech. These rules should be more than sufficient to get you up on your feet and delivering quite competent public speeches:

1. *Know your audience*: Doing **audience analysis** as you begin to prepare your speech is a key part of a successful presentation. Basic knowledge of your listeners' demographics and characteristics will help you better understand their needs and also allow you to tailor your speech accordingly. In fact, knowing the general attitudes of the audience "will enable you to choose a topic that affects your audience's position without alienating them" (Verderber and Verderber, 2008, p. 284).

2. *Watch your posture*: Standing up straight with your shoulders pulled back instead of hunching over is a way to present yourself as someone in command. People in command of their bodies come across as more confident, more serious, and more credible. Slouching can signify fear and uncertainty, while standing erect tells an audience that you courageously preside over your message. Think about it symbolically: the higher up you are, the more powerful you appear.

3. *Make eye contact*: In Chapter 4 we discussed oculesics, the study of eye behaviors in communication. As you might remember, an important part of this research centers on making eye contact. Eye contact ignites interest and even a heightened level of attraction between communicators. So, when delivering a speech, the best strategy for nonverbally connecting with the people in your audience is simply to look at them. One way to understand the impact of eye contact is to imagine that you are a speaker gazing out into the audience and what you see is people sitting there, heads down and staring at their shoe tops. Wouldn't you interpret this as a sign that they are uninterested in what you have to say? Or simply not listening? Wouldn't you find this feeling of disconnection uncomfortable? When you make eye contact with your audience, you are offering them membership in the process.

4. *Maintain a good appearance*: Looking professional while giving a speech is common sense. Consider other situations in which you hope for positive feedback—a job interview, a business presentation, or maybe

A wedding toast is a special occasion speech.

audience analysis In preparation for a speech, gathering information about audience characteristics.

In your opinion, which speaker has more credibility?

appearing before a judge in traffic court. In each of these instances you would dress professionally because the judgments of the others you meet in these settings are important to you. The same is true in the delivery of a speech. The more "put together" you appear, the more attention and credibility you will command from those around you.

5. *Avoid mall speak*: Every generation has its own particular language. Many members of today's generation of high school and college students engage in **mall speak**; their talk is embedded with far too many "likes" and "you knows" as well as more traditional verbal or **vocal fillers** like "ums" and "uhs." And while unique speech patterns may be considered identity markers for each new generation, speech-making requires a more pluralistic language representative of a diverse audience. In fact, many people feel this so-called generational talk debases the intelligence of a speaker, and whether you agree or not, the bottom line is that some of those critics could be members of your next audience.

6. *Believe in your topic*: Perhaps the most important factor in motivating and exciting an audience has to do with the level of passion you invest in your topics. When presenters are passionate about their speeches, they are naturally more enthusiastic in their delivery and, consequently, come off as more knowledgeable about the information they are relaying. If you truly believe in what you're saying, you don't have to work so hard emotionally; therefore, the energy you would otherwise use to find that enthusiasm could be better employed focusing on delivery technique. If *you* believe in your topic, the audience is more likely to do so as well.

mall speak Embedding speech with nontraditional fillers such as "like" and "you know."

vocal filler Unnecessary transition words/sounds like *um, uh, ah.*

residual message In a speech, the larger point to be remembered.

7. *Don't barrage the audience with facts and statistics*: We've all heard the expression "death by detail," and it easily applies to speech giving. Too many statistics and numbers in a speech can detract from the **residual message**—the larger point you want everyone to remember long after the speech is over. If audience members are forced to focus on a giant mass of details, not only will they feel overwhelmed and perhaps become bored, they may also miss your larger point. For example, if you're giving a speech on Halloween safety in your town you might say, "There were 2,456 trick-or-treaters this past year here in Springfield and each child received an average of 122 pieces of candy. Therefore, the number of candy pieces totaled 299,632, of which 12% were questionable and had to be checked for safety reasons." WOW! That's a lot of data for the audience to remember! You would have been just as effective saying, "Nearly 40,000 pieces of candy this year were examined for possible tampering." You'll also notice the actual number was rounded up. Twelve percent of 299,632 is about 35,956, but nobody is likely to remember such a specific number, so you're much better off with "nearly 40,000." Statistics can often highlight a serious problem, serving as important evidence in support of a call for a solution, but if overused, they can also bombard and exhaust the audience into a state of indifference.

8. *Speak ethically*: Later in the chapter we look at the ethics of public speaking. Speaking ethically isn't only about not plagiarizing (stealing someone else's work); it's also about making an honest effort to refrain from offending people and from engaging in *ethnocentric bias*—acting like your culture, ethnicity, or values are better than everyone else's (Chapter 9). Speaking ethically and speaking with integrity are closely aligned, so an audience is likely to judge a speaker's character as directly linked to not only what's being said, but also to the overall standards of authenticity, credibility, and sensitivity that the presenter sets for him or herself.

9. *Begin and end powerfully*: The introduction and conclusion of any speech are its most important parts. The introduction is the audience's *first impression* of the speaker, the speaker's skills, and the nature of the speech. When meeting others for the first time, we tend to engage in **rapid impression formation,** making immediate judgments that shape the remainder of the encounter, as you read in Chapter 6. The same is true when an audience meets a speaker, so it is critical that the beginning of any speech be particularly strong at grabbing listeners' attention. The conclusion must also be strong because it contains the speaker's final comments, which tend to be the most-remembered ideas. The closing often reinforces the residual message, and if done well, will have the audience thinking about the speech long after it is over.

rapid impression formation Making immediate judgments of others after initial encounters.

10. *Practice, don't rehearse*: What's the difference? Someone who *rehearses* performs the speech so many times it begins to sound mechanical, as if

it's being *read* rather than *delivered*. Think about actors. They rehearse their lines, and in doing so, memorize them. Great speakers, on the other hand, practice their speeches, acquainting themselves with the material without necessarily reciting it verbatim. *Practicing* requires speakers to review their speech a few times, and then put it aside before returning to it later. Rehearsing can result in being too prepared, risking the very real possibility that the speech becomes so familiar to the speaker that the monotony and lack of emotional involvement he or she feels is transferred to the audience.

11. *Articulate, enunciate, and use proper pronunciations*: **Articulation** refers to adjustments of speech organs (jaw, tongue, and so on) to allow for the proper pronunciation of sounds, while **pronunciation** is "the act of expressing the sounds and accents of words so that they conform to accepted standards" (Ross and Leonard, 2012, p. 256). **Enunciation** is pronouncing words clearly. In order to correctly pronounce and enunciate words we need to articulate, that is, move our vocal apparatus in such a way that it allows us to utter the sounds we wish to make. There are many reasons that public speakers' quality of articulation, enunciation, and pronunciation are important, but arguably the two biggest include wanting to be fully understood by the audience and wanting to sound intelligent. In being aware of pronunciations, we also must consider **dialects**—variations in a language's vocabulary, grammar, and pronunciation. Individual audience members may not share the speaker's dialect; for example, a Bostonian delivering a speech to Southerners may confuse her listeners when informing them about the best place to "pahk" their "cahrs." According to public speaking expert Stephen Lucas, in situations like this, "The dialect may cause listeners to make negative judgments about the speaker's personality, intelligence, and competence. This is why professional speakers have been known to invest large amounts of time (and money) to master the General American dialect used by most television broadcasters" (2015, p. 247). No one dialect is inherently better or worse than another; however, in some circumstances, adjusting to a dialect common to your listeners might enhance the effectiveness of your speech.

12. *Always have water on hand*: This is an obvious point that requires little explanation. We've all experienced dry mouth, "frog in the throat," chronic coughing, or sore throats when speaking. Having a water bottle next to you throughout the speech and being able to take an occasional sip in the event that you are victimized by one of these afflictions allows you to deliver your presentation without having to stop for a long period of time or struggle uncomfortably throughout.

13. *Don't worry about nervousness*: Later in the chapter we will deal with public speaking anxiety. For now, though, keep in mind three basic tips: (1) everyone gets nervous, even professional speakers; (2) much, if not most, of your nervousness goes undetected by the audience; and (3) nervousness

articulation Adjustments of speech organs to allow for the proper pronunciation of sounds.

pronunciation Expressing the sounds and accents of words to accepted standards.

enunciation Pronouncing words clearly.

dialect Variations in a language's vocabulary, grammar, and pronunciation.

Never be afraid to use your hands. Even the most polished speakers—for example, Facebook Chief Operating Officer Sheryl Sandberg—let their hands do the talking.

is a good thing because it is an indication that you care about delivering a quality speech, and you can turn those nerves into positive energy.

14. *Don't be afraid to use your hands*: Most people talk with their hands in everyday conversations. It's natural. When you use your hands and arms during speeches you are, in fact, providing nonverbal emphasis to verbal statements. You are nonverbally communicating to the audience that you are emphatic about your points, and at the same time welcoming your listeners into your speech. Also, think in terms of *open arms* rather than *closed arms*. The first is inviting (like asking for a big hug), while the second shuts people out as if you're protecting yourself from a threatening audience. In other words, your gestures should be inviting and open.

15. *Avoid distracting body language*: Some body language can be distracting to an audience. Habits such as hair twirling, pacing, rocking, swaying, fist clenching, leaning, leg shaking, or foot tapping can prove fatal to a speech if the audience is focused on what your body is doing instead of what your words are saying. Taking control of your body enables you to employ more productive movements, which will, in turn, enhance your speech.

16. *Try to use notecards or outlines rather than scripted speeches*: There are circumstances when **scripted speeches**, word-for-word manuscripts, are appropriate, for example when the presentation is particularly lengthy. Examples would include the president's State of the Union Address or a television anchor's news broadcast. In these cases, a fully prepared speech may be required. However, as you practice becoming a solid public speaker, it is important that you gain the ability to work from notecards and outlines, that is, from a minimal text. In doing so, you become better at transitions (moving smoothly from one thought to another); you remain more aware of what you're saying; you sound less mechanical; and you don't risk losing your place amidst all the words, sentences, and paragraphs of an entire manuscript. People who develop their speech-giving skills using fewer notes tend to be better at **extemporaneous** (lightly prepared) and **impromptu** ("off-the-cuff") speeches, and they are also better able to continue their speeches in the event of technological malfunctions or other interruptions. Yes, it happens!

scripted speech Speech read word-for-word from a manuscript.

extemporaneous speech Lightly prepared speech.

impromptu speech Off-the-cuff speech.

17. *Practice using visual aids*: In a world of visual learners and tech-savvy students, it's tough to resist the urge to incorporate media into speeches. Presentation programs like Power-Point and Prezi are popular with novice public speakers looking to make an impression. Still, many students incorrectly use these aids, and the result is often a presentation that consists of little more than a speaker reading slides, bombarding the audience with too much visual information, or performing a choppy speech as she or he negotiates the technology. If you do opt to use these technologies, it's important to practice with them *before* the speech. This will ensure a smoother flow of thought as you tran-

Proper use of visual aids is critical to delivering a successful speech.

sition from one slide to the next. It is also critical that only the main points, as opposed to every statistic, quote, or piece of data, be included on the slides. You should simplify your visual aids to maintain audience concentration and to keep yourself from reading the slides rather than delivering a presentation. In sum, be judicious! Corporate trainer Steven Smith warns, "Power-Point slides with just bullet points seem to me as crutches for the speaker . . . I know that a speaker can connect with his or her audience better with stories, whiteboard drawings, and experiential exercises. That connection requires joining the energy of the participants and spontaneity on my part. My presentation plan must change to fit the energy in the room . . . The technology gets in the way of the connection between the leader and the participants" (2010).

18. *Learn proper breathing techniques*: **Diaphragmatic breathing** is simply abdominal breathing—deep breaths that allow the stomach muscles to expand. This type of breathing should occur while standing up straight to allow for clear air passages from your lungs to your head. Engaging in diaphragmatic breathing will be an essential part of your success as a speaker for the following reasons: (1) it relaxes the body, making you less nervous as you deliver the speech; (2) it allows you to project your sounds further and present a stronger voice; (3) it helps to develop lung capacity, which can prove especially beneficial when delivering lengthy and/or energetic sentences; and (4) deep breaths mean more oxygen to the brain, allowing you to more clearly focus on what you're about to say.

diaphragmatic breathing
Abdominal breathing allowing the stomach muscles to expand.

19. *Emulate speakers you respect*: Most of us can point to someone we consider a great speaker. We can also identify the characteristics in that individual bringing us to that judgment. The old adage "Imitation is the sincerest form of flattery" is a good rule to remember when thinking about public speaking. We all learn certain lessons from copying the approach of others; for example, a young girl may learn to be a good parent from watching her mother, father, or grandparents. There's nothing wrong and everything right with emulating the skills of those you admire, as long as you work

PERSONALLY RESPONSIBLE COMMUNICATION

Public Speaking Self-Assessment

Now that your speech has been delivered, you're feeling a sense of relief and even pride. You think to yourself, it's time to "back burner" the whole experience and move on to other things. Unfortunately (or fortunately, depending on how you look at it), there is still one more step in the process: *self-assessment*. You engaged in a *pre*-self-assessment before delivering the speech when you asked yourself questions like

- How will I deal with my nervousness?
- What's the best approach for me to take on topic?
- Am I aware of my strengths and weaknesses going into the presentation?

Now, with the speech finally delivered, you must complete a *post*-self-assessment by asking questions such as these:

- Did I get my point across?
- Was the audience interested?

- What seemed to be the most effective aspects of my speech?
- Were my goals met? How were my inflection, volume, and eye contact?
- How were my transitions?
- What were the best and worst parts of my speech?

Your self-assessment requires that you ask yourself a series of questions with the intent of becoming a better speaker, continually improving your skills. This step is a critical part of delivering a presentation because it involves taking responsibility for your speech and the messages you relay to your audience. Being accountable for what and how you communicate to others, by definition, makes you a better speaker because it is a responsible choice. Self-assessment or self-critique allows us to evaluate our values, consider our motives, be honest with ourselves, and perhaps take constructive criticism from others. In fact, self-assessment is often viewed as integral to self-improvement—and we all have a personal responsibility to put our best foot forward.

simultaneously to craft your own personal style. Find people you respect as speakers and adopt some of their techniques. Believe it or not, it's an excellent way to discover your own identity as a speaker.

20. *Instill confidence by knowing that you are a great speaker*: This is another piece of common wisdom that many students fail to understand. Believing you are a good speaker will yield much better results than convincing yourself you are not. The more confidence you have in yourself, the better you perform. One way to ensure your own confidence is to routinely evaluate your performances in an effort to continually improve your speech skills. The box entitled "Public Speaking Self-Assessment" can help you do just that.

Identifying the Steps of Speech Preparation

Now that you have taken a crash course in public speaking and have a broad knowledge of this valuable skill, you are ready to begin the process of writing and delivering your own speech. Where do you begin? First, you need to identify the type of speech you intend to deliver—informative, persuasive, special occasion, or something else. Then you need to decide on a topic. This is sometimes a grueling experience for many students because they often simply don't know where to look or how to find inspiration in a specific topic. The first suggestion is that you engage in **brainstorming**, generating ideas for your speech topic through the free association of words and ideas. You can do this simply by **self-inquiry**, asking questions of yourself in search of a possible topic, for example

- What are my hobbies?
- What people inspire me?
- What things interest me?
- Are there concepts I've always wanted to explore?
- Where have I traveled?

Ask questions of any and all of your areas of interest that might spark an idea. Engaging in this sort of *mental inventory* will ignite your imagination as you navigate the sea of potential topics. Another type of mental inventory is called **clustering**, making lists according to themes and word association and seeing what topics jump out at you.

Also consider utilizing Internet sites such as Google, Yahoo, AOL, and other search engines to expose yourself to possible topics you might otherwise not have considered. Keep in mind, however, that while the Internet is a valuable tool in determining your speech topic, you must be *very* careful in choosing which web sources you use in the researching and writing of your speech. Recall our Internet ethics discussion in Chapter 10 and make sure, if you intend to cite a website or blog, you consider questions of authorship, sponsorship, credibility, and timeliness of source. **Plagiarism** (stealing someone else's material) is another important ethical issue when searching for topics and supporting information, and you can read more about it in the box entitled, "Plagiarism and Public Speaking."

Once you've determined your speech type and topic, you can begin researching the idea and constructing an outline. Every thorough speech begins with an **outline**—a brief, well-organized construction of main points and subtopics for the speech. The outline is your guide, allowing you to systematically identify the movement and chronology of your speech, that is, what will be discussed and in what order. Your outline begins with a *general purpose* (the overall goal of the speech), your introduction, body (main points to be addressed), and conclusion. Figure 15.1 provides an example of a broad working outline for a persuasive speech.

A speech outline can be detailed or broad, depending on the *use* the presenter hopes to make of it. Some speakers use a broader outline for the purpose of organizing their thoughts and research (as in Figure 15.1), while others use a more extensive **speaking outline** containing a slew of additional subtopics and details (like quotes, full sentences, and statistics) for

brainstorming Generating ideas for speech topics through free association of words and ideas.

self-inquiry Asking questions of yourself in search of a possible topic.

clustering Generating ideas for speech topics by making lists of items from areas of interest in your life.

plagiarism Stealing someone else's material.

outline A brief, well-organized construction of main points and subtopics of a speech.

speaking outline Speech outline for use during the delivery of a speech.

ETHICAL COMMUNICATION

Plagiarism and Public Speaking

Plagiarism is the attempt to claim as your own someone else's words, images, or ideas. It is among the most serious ethical issues in public speaking. When you think about what public speaking is, the relaying of messages and ideas to an audience that will be influenced by those messages, it is, at the very least, dishonest to suggest you are credible or worthy of that influence when you steal from someone else. Additionally, in our high-tech world of easy information access, fact-checking, and search engines, the likelihood of being exposed as a plagiarizer has increased considerably, so it's critical as you develop your skill as a speaker that you understand the various types of plagiarism and what's at stake should you plagiarize.

Stephen Lucas discusses three major forms of plagiarism: global, patchwork, and incremental (2015, pp. 37–38). *Global plagiarism* is when a speaker steals a speech in its entirety, claiming it as his or her own. *Patchwork plagiarism* means the speaker has plagiarized from more than one source, possibly multiple sources, puts the material together as if it is unique, and attempts to credit it as her or his own. When speakers borrow from others for specific, even relatively brief parts of their speeches and fail to give credit to those from whom they borrowed the ideas, they are engaging in *incremental plagiarism*.

A speaker who steals language from others often experiences a loss of pride, dignity, and is likely to face embarrassment. For students, the consequences of plagiarism may involve receiving a failing grade for the course or being expelled from school. It's also important to look beyond the classroom to what plagiarism does to the culture as a whole. Violation of intellectual property rights and copyright infringement are only two of the important issues that can stem from plagiarism, not only hurting the plagiarist, but also undermining the values we all share. In a society that prides itself on innovation and the pursuit of knowledge, sending and receiving that knowledge under false pretense has serious consequences for everyone.

Now, imagine this scenario. You have procrastinated on preparing your three-minute persuasive speech and it's due tomorrow. Furthermore, you need at least a B on the speech to pass the class. Your friend had this very assignment three semesters ago and offers you his speech with the condition that if you get caught, he had nothing to do with it. What do you do? After all, it's still *you* giving the speech! Again, what do you do? Defend your answer.

use during the delivery of the speech. Whether or not speakers use speaking outlines, note cards, or the script of an entire speech ultimately depends on what they find most comfortable and most effective. Most public speaking instructors and coaches discourage the use of the entire manuscript primarily because they don't want to encourage a reliance on the full speech. Regardless of the preferred format, speakers should always incorporate directly on the speech pages *delivery cues* (notes to self) such as *slow down*, *articulate this sentence*, *get louder here*, and so on. Students should also make the font size large enough and be sure to spell difficult words phonetically (the way they're pronounced, for example *prō-nown-sd*) to avoid tripping up. Another useful tip is to use highlighting markers to emphasize places in the speech that require a change in tone or inflection. One thing is certain, thorough preparation and review of notes serves a speaker well in looking smart and negating nervousness.

General Purpose: To persuade an audience of students to take a public speaking class.

Specific Purpose: Public speaking is considered a "soft skill" required for success in both the personal and professional areas of our lives. Our ability to effectively communicate with those around us helps develop not only our own identities, but also the identities of those we affect. Given the importance of speaking in our everyday lives, it is important that we all possess the basic skills needed to become effective speakers. Taking a public speaking class is the first step to making that a reality.

I. Introduction
    A. Begin with Jerry Seinfeld eulogy quote
    B. Talk about the successful, well-known people who had instruction in public speaking

II. Body
    A. The qualities of a good speaker
    B. The importance of public speaking
    C. The personal benefits to becoming a good speaker
    D. The professional benefits to becoming a good speaker

III. Conclusion
    A. Tell success story of someone we all know and respect
    B. Invite students to learn about public speaking through various information sources and by registering for a public speaking class before graduating
    C. End with public speaking quote by Winston Churchill.

FIGURE 15.1 Sample Speech Outline (for a Persuasive Speech). Here is a sample of what a basic speech outline should look like. Naturally, its content will vary given the type of speech and its goal. See if you can craft similar outlines for an informative, special occasion, and small group speech. How might they differ? Be similar?

Overcoming Public Speaking Anxiety

Public speaking anxiety, the fear of public speaking, is usually the most difficult obstacle to overcome for aspiring speakers as they work to master this skill. Sometimes people refer to public speaking anxiety as *communication apprehension, speech phobia,* or *stage fright,* and these terms are often used interchangeably. It's important to note, however, that scholars in the field often make distinctions between these conditions. For the purpose of this discussion, we will refer to *public speaking anxiety* as "a situation-specific social anxiety that arises from the real or anticipated enactment of an oral presentation" (Bodie, 2010, p. 72). Regardless of how experts define certain speech anxiety conditions, those afflicted define it the same way—they hate it. As we mentioned at the chapter's outset, there are many reasons that people dread the idea of delivering presentations—they feel they're being judged; they're afraid of saying something stupid; or perhaps they are self-conscious about a speech defect like a lisp, stutter, or stammer (vocal spasms that create involuntary pausing and repetition of syllables and sounds). Whatever the case, we *all* feel nervous when we're about to address a crowd, and this nervousness can manifest itself in three distinct ways: (1) *physiologically* (for example, increased heart rate, sweating, and dry mouth), (2) *cognitively* (for example, self- doubt, feeling unprepared, and forgetting), and (3) *behaviorally* (for example, long,

public speaking anxiety
Fear of public speaking.

unnatural pausing, twirling hair, and leg shifting). The first trick to avoiding these problems and reducing nervousness is to understand that when it comes to public speaking, most people are in the same situation. Second is to recognize that much of a speaker's nervousness goes undetected by the audience. Finally, it's important to note that most audience members don't judge as much as they empathize; they relate to what the speaker is experiencing, and as a result feel sympathetic. Keeping these ideas in mind can often provide enough comfort to get you through a speech without too many anxiety-induced problems. However, if this isn't enough to calm those nerves, here are a few tips that may provide additional comfort:

1. *Be prepared*—The best way to ensure you won't look ridiculous because you said the wrong thing is to not say the wrong thing! Make sure you have researched your topic well and have practiced the speech ahead of time. This involves allowing yourself plenty of preparation time in advance of delivering the speech. There is a strong correlation between procrastination and public speaking anxiety. In anticipation of the stress they think they'll feel come presentation time, students will often delay preparing or practicing their speech, leaving themselves with little time to sufficiently complete the task, resulting in low performance evaluations and reinforcing the apprehension they felt in the first place (Behnke and Sawyer, 1999). So, one way to avoid anxiety is to be prepared.

2. *Engage in vocal warm-ups*—There is always an uncomfortable pause before a speaker begins. Sometimes cracking a joke just before you start or engaging a few audience members in conversation (unrelated to your speech) is enough to loosen up those nerves and transition confidently into the presentation. In a classroom setting, another device is referring to the speaker before you: "Mike's speech certainly covered a number of important issues, and I hope mine will provide some insight on yet another set of concerns . . ." There are many different ways to "warm up" as you prepare to deliver the speech, which will relax both you and your audience and won't be counted as a graded part of your speech. It will also warm up your vocal cords before the speech actually begins.

3. *Know perfection is unattainable*—That's right—nobody is perfect, not even your public speaking professor. Even the world's best speakers make mistakes, trip over words, and have to negotiate nervousness. Go easy on yourself when it comes to expectations of perfection. In fact, there is something to be said for appearing *real* or *natural*. To achieve this, imperfection can sometimes be an asset. For example, when a speaker makes a mistake and then uses humor to recover, some audience members may notice the mistake, but not nearly as much as they'll notice the speaker's ability to identify or relate to his or her own humanness.

4. *Convert that nervous energy*—Nervousness is a good thing. In addition to keeping speakers on their toes, nervous energy means there's a lot of reserve oomph that can be converted into *positive* energy. For example, if you're

Remember, your audience wants you to succeed.

nervous and fidgety, walk around while delivering the speech. "Work the room." Use your hands and arms to nonverbally emphasize your words. If your body is physically occupied, that's less energy devoted to nervousness.

5. *Determine your self-fulfilling prophecy*—If you imagine your speech going badly, it will. On the other hand, if you imagine yourself an excellent speaker about to embark on an extraordinary performance, you will instead make *that* your reality. The more positively we feel about ourselves and our abilities, the better we perform for others. Research has shown that how we view ourselves as speakers directly impacts our communication competencies (Ellis, 1995).

6. *Engage in visualization*—This may well be the oldest trick for overcoming public speaking anxiety. Whether it's visualizing audience members in their underwear (that old cliché) or visualizing a situation where you are an empowered leader whose words will most assuredly gain you the admiration and respect of those who receive you, visualization can be a powerful tool in combating your apprehension.

Even if you find that your anxiety cannot be *completely* eradicated, it can certainly be well managed. The most important thing to remember is that you are not alone! Many of history's most notable speakers have had to deal with nervousness, and some have had to overcome severe obstacles to defeat their

Table 15.1 Top 10 Ways to Conquer Your Fear of Public Speaking

In response to an institutional mandate to improve students' level of public speaking, the Oral Communication Program at Stanford University created its Top 10 ways to overcome public speaking anxiety:

1.	Identify what scares you about public speaking so you better conquer your fears.
2.	Breathe deeply for relaxation.
3.	Engage in physical activity before delivering your speech to warm up and calm your body.
4.	Employ plenty of practice.
5.	Visualize your success! If you can imagine it, you can make it happen.
6.	Get plenty of sleep and do not skip breakfast. A speaker needs energy!
7.	Visit the speech location ahead of time. What benefits and distractions might the venue hold?
8.	Play the "Worst Scenario Game" to minimize anxiety: "What's the worst thing that could happen to me because of delivering this speech?"
9.	Give yourself a break! Take the pressure off yourself; everyone makes mistakes.
10.	Accept constructive criticism from those willing to provide it.

(Source: Hume Center for Speaking and Writing, 2015)

public speaking anxiety—people like Winston Churchill, Sir Isaac Newton, Aristotle, and of course, King George VI, the subject of the popular award-winning movie *The King's Speech*. You see, you're in good company! You can find additional hints to overcoming public speaking anxiety in Table 15.1, and you can gauge for yourself just how much you do indeed suffer this natural but completely unnecessary affliction by taking the Personal Report of Public Speaking Anxiety in Figure 15.2.

Directions: Below are 34 statements that people sometimes make about themselves. Please indicate whether or not you believe each statement applies to you by marking whether you

Strongly Disagree = 1; Disagree = 2; Are Neutral = 3; Agree = 4; Strongly Agree = 5.

_____1. While preparing for giving a speech, I feel tense and nervous.

_____2. I feel tense when I see the words "speech" and "public speech" on a course outline when studying.

_____3. My thoughts become confused and jumbled when I am giving a speech.

_____4. Right after giving a speech I feel that I have had a pleasant experience.

_____5. I get anxious when I think about an upcoming speech.

_____6. I have no fear of giving a speech.

_____7. Although I am nervous just before starting a speech, I soon settle down after starting and feel calm and comfortable.

_____8. I look forward to giving a speech.

_____9. When the instructor announces a speaking assignment in class, I can feel myself getting tense.

_____10. My hands tremble when I am giving a speech.

_____11. I feel relaxed while giving a speech.

_____12. I enjoy preparing for a speech.

_____13. I am in constant fear of forgetting what I prepared to say.

_____14. I get anxious if someone asks me something about my topic that I don't know.

_____15. I face the prospect of giving a speech with confidence.

_____16. I feel that I am in complete possession of myself while giving a speech.

_____17. My mind is clear when giving a speech.

_____18. I do not dread giving a speech.

_____19. I perspire just before starting a speech.

_____20. My heart beats very fast just as I start a speech.

_____21. I experience considerable anxiety while sitting in the room just before my speech starts.

_____22. Certain parts of my body feel very tense and rigid while giving a speech.

_____23. Realizing that only a little time remains in a speech makes me very tense and anxious.

_____24. While giving a speech, I know I can control my feelings of tension and stress.

_____25. I breathe faster just before starting a speech.

_____26. I feel comfortable and relaxed in the hour or so just before giving a speech.

_____27. I do poorer on speeches because I am anxious.

_____28. I feel anxious when the teacher announces the date of a speaking assignment.

_____29. When I make a mistake while giving a speech, I find it hard to concentrate on the parts that follow.

_____30. During an important speech I experience a feeling of helplessness building up inside me.

_____31. I have trouble falling asleep the night before a speech.

_____32. My heart beats very fast while I present a speech.

_____33. I feel anxious while waiting to give my speech.

_____34. While giving a speech, I get so nervous I forget facts I really know.

Scoring: To determine your score, complete the following steps:

- **Step 1.** Add scores for items 1, 2, 3, 5, 9, 10, 13, 14, 19, 20, 21, 22, 23, 25, 27, 28, 29, 30, 31, 32, 33, and 34.
- **Step 2.** Add the scores for items 4, 6, 7, 8, 11, 12, 15, 16, 17, 18, 24, and 26.
- **Step 3.** Do the following math:

Take the number 72, subtract from it the total from Step 2. Then add to that number the total from Step 1. If your PRPSA score is above 131, you suffer from high public speaking anxiety. If it is between 98 and 131, you have a moderate case. If it is below 98, you have no or low public speaking anxiety.

(Note: Your score should be between 34 and 170. If it isn't, you've made a mistake in computing the score. Try again!)

FIGURE 15.2 The Personal Report of Public Speaking Anxiety. Communication scholar James McCroskey (1970) developed what has become the most widely used public speaking anxiety self-measure, the Personal Report of Public Speaking Anxiety (PRPSA). You can compute your own score by answering its 34 questions and undertaking the simple math at its conclusion.

Review of Learning Objectives

15.1 Explain the importance of public speaking.

The advantages of being an effective speaker are improved cognition, better relationship development, greater professional success, more meaningful identity formation, and the encouragement of public discourse.

15.2 Identify the different types of speeches.

There are four major varieties of speeches: informative, persuasive, small group, and special occasion speeches. Each makes special demands on the speaker.

15.3 Identify the basics of good public speaking.

The 20 basic rules of public speaking are:

1. Know your audience.
2. Watch your posture.
3. Make eye contact.
4. Maintain a good appearance.
5. Avoid mall speak.

6. Believe in your topic.
7. Don't barrage the audience with facts and statistics.
8. Speak ethically.
9. Begin and end powerfully.
10. Practice, don't rehearse.
11. Articulate, enunciate, and use proper pronunciations.
12. Always have water on hand.
13. Don't worry about nervousness.
14. Don't be afraid to use your hands.
15. Avoid distracting body language.
16. Try to use notecards or outlines rather than scripted speeches.
17. Practice using visual aids.
18. Learn proper breathing techniques.
19. Emulate speakers you respect.
20. Know you are a great speaker.

15.4 Describe the steps of speech preparation.

First, identify the type of speech to be delivered and use brainstorming, clustering, and/or the Internet to identify and settle on a topic. Second, construct an outline and then a speaking outline. Third, incorporate delivery cues directly onto the outline. Finally, thoroughly prepare and review the speech before delivery.

15.5 Identify ways to overcome public speaking anxiety.

Public speaking anxiety is the fear of public speaking. As common as it may be, it can be overcome by being prepared, engaging in vocal warm-ups, knowing that perfection is unattainable, converting nervous energy into positive energy, determining a positive self-fulfilling prophesy, and engaging in visualization.

Key Terms

Questions for Review

1. What is the difference between public speaking and public discourse?
2. What are the four major types of public speeches? Can you differentiate between them?
3. What is audience analysis? Why is it important in public speaking?

4. What is mall speak? What is its likely effect on a speech?

5. What is a speech's residual message?

6. Differentiate between articulation, pronunciation, enunciation, and dialect.

7. What is diaphragmatic breathing?

8. What are brainstorming, clustering, and self-inquiry?

9. Differentiate between scripted, extemporaneous, and impromptu speeches.

10. What is speech anxiety? What are some of its causes?

Questions for Discussion

1. Have you ever had to deliver a public speech? What was the occasion? What preparations did you make for the speech? How closely did your experience and preparation match the suggestions from this chapter?

2. Have you ever had a case of public speaking anxiety? What was the situation? How severe was it, and how did you deal with it? Did you intuitively adopt any of the remedies discussed in this chapter? Apparently you survived the experience, so looking back, how bad could it have been?

3. Who is hurt by plagiarism? Certainly the person whose words and thoughts have been stolen, but can you make the case that the plagiarizer is also damaged (beyond the likely punishment if caught)?

Glossary

abstract language Language signifying concepts, qualities, or ideas.

action-facilitating support Giving information or physically assisting someone in need.

adaptors Gestures used to fulfill a need.

adjourning Stage when members depart from one another and the task.

adverse event Unintended injury or complication caused by healthcare management.

affect displays Emotional gestures.

affective conflict When people acknowledge an incompatibility of emotions and feelings.

affective exchange Relational stage characterized by much self-disclosure.

affiliations Relationships linking partners through a sense of alliance.

agency In critical theory, how humans behave and interact in the social world.

agenda-setting theory Idea that media may not always tell us what to think, but they certainly tell us what to think about.

aggressiveness Speaking one's mind without a professional filter.

aliteracy Loss of thoughtful reading.

ambient advertising Ads in otherwise nontraditional settings.

amenable mortality Deaths that could potentially have been prevented by timely access to appropriate healthcare.

anticipatory socialization stage Learning about work through a lifetime of communication.

app Short for *application*; program or software connecting mobile devices to specific websites.

appreciative listening Listening for enjoyment or pleasure.

articulation Adjustments of speech organs to allow for the proper pronunciation of sounds.

artifacts Objects we use to identify ourselves.

assertiveness Confidently presenting ideas and contributing to organizational conversation and growth.

assignment-based cohesion Groups bound by a specific task.

assimilation Identification with or integration into a different culture.

assumptions Sets of information automatically interpreted as factual.

asynchronous communication Delay of some length between sending and receiving.

attachments Relationships linking partners through a sense of security.

attitude A relatively enduring organization of beliefs around an object or situation predisposing one to respond in a preferential manner.

attitudinal similarity Source-receiver similarity built on common values, beliefs, or attitudes.

audience analysis In preparation for a speech, gathering information about audience characteristics.

audience and authorship Questions about authorship, purpose, economics, impact, and response.

audience fragmentation Splintering of media audiences into increasingly smaller units.

authoritarian leader Does not accept input from members and maintains complete control of the group.

avoiding style Conflict resolution style showing low concern for the self and for another.

axiology Questions of the proper role of values in research and theory building.

backchannel cues Noncommittal responses to conversational partners' talk.

behavior Concrete, observable action.

belief A proposition about something; faith that something is real or is true.

body adornments Tattoos, piercings, and accessories.

bounded culture (co-culture) Cultural identities existing within the larger culture.

brainstorming Generating ideas for speech topics through free association of words and ideas.

brand entertainment When content is developed around brands.

breakdown perception When senders believe no response is forthcoming and take action.

bureaucracy The norms, ranks, roles, and controls of an organization.

causality When one event precedes a second event and that second event is deemed to be a consequence of the first.

central route In information processing, employing as much scrutiny and analysis as possible.

certainty-uncertainty Tension between the need for comfort and security and the need for novelty and excitement.

chauvinism Believing oneself to be superior to others.

child-parent relationship In provider-client interactions, the doctor is dominant, all-knowing; the patient is submissive and reliant.

chronemics How we use time to communicate.

closed system A system whose components communicate solely with one another.

clustering Generating ideas for speech topics by making lists of items from areas of interest in your life.

clutter Commercial overload.

cognitive conflict When people acknowledge incompatibility in their perceptions about something of importance.

cognitive consistency Tendency to maintain, or to return to, a state of attitudinal balance.

cognitive miser The idea that people rely on the simplest analysis possible when confronting information.

communicated disease An imaginary disease that spreads because people communicate about it.

communication The process of mutual creation of meaning.

communication traits Traits exhibited by members of an organization, such as assertiveness, secrecy, superiority, motivation, empowerment, supportiveness, and intimidation.

comparison level (CL) Expectations of benefit from a specific relationship.

comparison level of alternatives (CL$_{ALT}$) Likely benefits from other relationships.

compliance When people accept influence in order to gain a favorable reaction from the persuader but do not change their original attitudes.

compromising style Conflict resolution style showing moderate concern for self-interest and for the interests of another.

computer-mediated communication People interacting via digital technology.

concentration of ownership Ownership of many different media companies by an increasingly small number of conglomerates.

conflict An expressed struggle between at least two interdependent parties who perceive incompatible goals, scarce rewards, and interference from the other party.

conflict of interest When people acknowledge incompatible preferences for a course of action.

conflict style A general predisposition to deal with conflict in a particular manner.

connection-autonomy Tension between the need to remain connected and the need to be independent.

connotative meaning A word's implicit, usually emotionally or evaluatively enriched meaning.

constitutive view The perspective that communication creates something that did not previously exist.

contempt An attack on the self-worth of another.

content analysis Quantitative textual analysis that relies on objective categorization and accurate measurement.

controls Rewards, punishments, or behavioral consequences for group members.

conventional-unique Tension between being the couple others want and defining the relationship for yourselves.

convergence Erosion of traditional distinctions among media.

cookies Software involuntarily loaded onto computers to track online user activity.

critical listening Listening for evaluation or analysis.

critical theory Theory that challenges existing ways of organizing the social world and the people and institutions exercising power in it.

criticism Complaints about another.

cultural imperialism Influencing other countries through non-local mass media.

cultural meaning Meaning based in shared experience.

cultural participation Involving oneself in another culture.

cultural pluralism Maintaining the practices and identities of one's bounded culture within the larger culture.

cultural presupposition The assumption that those who share a culture share knowledge of a word's meaning.

cultural relativism Belief that people vary in behaviors, feelings, traditions, and values depending on their culture.

cultural transformer Someone who shifts effortlessly among and between multiple cultural mindsets and cultural identities.

cultural values A culture's gauges for determining right from wrong.

culture The world made meaningful, socially constructed and maintained through communication.

cyberchondriac Person who compulsively searches online for information about real or imagined symptoms of illness.

decoding Interpreting signs and symbols.

de-escalation and negotiation Reduction of conflict through communication between the parties.

defend-and-deny approach When errors occur, healthcare providers remain silent or deny responsibility.

defensiveness Denying responsibility for one's behaviors.

democratic leader Encourages full and equal participation among group members.

denotative meaning A word's explicit meaning when used by a specific speech community.

dependency-based cohesion Groups bound to each other by way of separate, related tasks.

depenetration The deterioration of a relationship.

deviance Motivation to reduce uncertainty if another acts in unexpected ways or violates expected rules and norms.

dialect Variations in a language's vocabulary, grammar, and pronunciation.

dialectic In critical theory, the ongoing struggle or debate between agency and structure.

dialectic Tension in need of resolution.

dialogue Full, honest, meaningful exchange of information and feelings.

diaphragmatic breathing Abdominal breathing allowing the stomach muscles to expand.

disclosure-and-apology strategy Requires healthcare providers to promptly disclose errors, and when appropriate, apologize to patients and families.

discourse What is said and its interpretation in negotiating relational tensions.

discrimination Overtly excluding, avoiding, or distancing oneself from another.

discriminative listening Paying close attention to more than the simple denotative meaning of speakers' words.

disengagement and exit stage Movement from one part of an organization to another, or leaving altogether.

disinhibition search Observing another in a particularly comfortable situation.

dissolution The ending of a relationship.

dominant culture (mainstream culture) The collective cultural experience held and shared by the large majority of people.

dominating style Conflict resolution style showing a higher regard for one's own interests than those of the other.

double-edged sword The same technology can be used for good or bad.

downshift In frame analysis, framing a situation as more serious, less open to expressions of personal identity.

downward message Messages that flow from higher to lower ranked employees.

dyad Two people communicating interpersonally.

dynamics How a group structures itself to achieve its goals.

elevator pitch A short, often fully prepared speech delivered in the presumed time span of an elevator ride.

emancipatory knowledge The epistemology of critical research and theory; knowledge is advanced when it serves to free people and communities from the influence of the powerful.

emblems Gestures that can be translated into word.

emergence When conflict becomes open.

empowerment Granting authority to another based on trust and confidence.

encoding Transforming a message into an understandable sign and symbol system.

enunciation Pronouncing words clearly.

epistemology Questions of how to best create and expand knowledge.

escalation An increase in the intensity of a conflict and the severity of tactics used in pursuing it.

ethnocentrism Belief that one's own culture is the best.

ethnography The study of human social interaction from the inside.

euphemism The substitution of vague or less emotionally charged words for more direct options.

e-visit When a physician and patient interact virtually rather than face to face.

experiment Research method involving the manipulation of one variable to measure its influence on another variable.

expertise Judgments of source's authoritativeness.

exploratory affective exchange Relational stage characterized by open and comfortable communication.

expressive function Using language to state personal feelings, thoughts, and attitudes.

extemporaneous speech Lightly prepared speech.

extended real-life hypothesis Tendency for social networking site users to communicate their real personalities.

external distractions Information other than physical noise introduced into the communication situation that is not part of the message itself.

face The public image people try to claim.

Facebook depression Depression that develops from overuse of social networking sites.

Facebook envy Users envying others' happiness as represented on SNSs.

face-threatening acts Interactions or requests that might threaten listeners' face-wants.

face-wants The need to feel appreciated and be protected.

facework Communication strategies designed to protect our and others' face.

facial expressions The use of the face's mobility in communication.

fear appeal Persuasive message that attempts to gain influence through the use of a relevant threat to the receiver.

fear of missing out (FOMO) Inability to disengage from social networking for fear of missing something .

feedback Response to a message.

feedback loop Circular communication process in which messages travel back and forth across a system, making possible ongoing mutual adjustment.

formal group communication Structured group communication heavily coded with specific rules.

forming Stage when members initially convene.

formulaic When media messages hew closely to proven formulas.

frames In frame analysis, specific sets of expectations that people use to make sense of specific social situations.

framing Structuring the meaning of verbal communication through the use of nonverbal cues.

gesticulation Specific movement of hands and arms to communicate.

globalization Increasing worldwide operation of media companies.

globalization The process in which organizations extend their business to different parts of the world, becoming more globally integrated.

goal conflict When people acknowledge incompatibility in the individual outcomes they hold for a given plan or action.

grammar Rules describing the proper construction of phrases and sentences.

grapevine Informal chain of communication that spreads through an organization, often leading to message distortion.

green-flag words Hot-button words that cloud reason.

group breakdown Deterioration or dissolution of a group as a result of conflict.

group cohesion The willingness to participate in and perform required activities.

groupthink When voices in a group are suppressed by pressure from others.

halo effect Idea that what is beautiful must be good.

haptics Communicating through touch.

hard news Stories that aid people in making intelligent decisions about their everyday lives.

health communication Study and use of interpersonal and mediated communication to inform and influence individual decisions that enhance health.

health literacy Ability to obtain, process, and understand basic health information and services needed to make appropriate health decisions.

hearing The physical process of perceiving sounds.

heuristics Simple decision-making rules that substitute for more careful analysis of persuasive messages.

hierarchal structure Levels of power within an organization.

hierarchical mum effect Self-imposed suppression of dissent in upward messages.

high- and low-context cultures Measure of the degree of communication-shaping information present in communication settings.

horizontal message Messages exchanged between colleagues of similar rank.

hyper-commercialism The increasing amount of commercial content appearing in the media.

hyper-ritualized representations In frame analysis, media portrayals that cannot represent all the nuances of a phenomenon.

idealized virtual identity hypothesis Tendency for creators of social network site profiles to display idealized characteristics not reflective of their actual personalities.

identification Copying of observed behavior, but in a more general manner.

identification When people accept influence because they want to establish or maintain a satisfying self-defining relationship to another person or a group.

illustrators Gestures emphasizing the verbal message.

imaginative function Using language to bring pleasure.

imitation Direct replication of observed behavior.

impromptu speech Off-the-cuff speech.

incentive Motivation to reduce uncertainty based on likely reward.

inclusion-seclusion Tension between doing things together and engaging as a couple with others.

individualistic versus collective cultures Measure of a culture's commitment to the individual versus the group.

inferential feedback Indirect, often delayed feedback.

informal group communication Less rigid, more relaxed, often spontaneous group communication.

information-seeking strategy Method of reducing uncertainty.

informative function Using language to provide and get information.

informative listening Listening, the primary goal of which is to understand the message.

informative speech Speech designed to convey knowledge and understanding.

in-group Those with whom one identifies.

instrumental function Using language to get what is wanted or needed.

integrating style Conflict resolution style showing high concern for others as well as for one's self.

intentionality Whether what we communicate verbally and nonverbally is intended.

intercultural communication Interaction between people whose cultural perceptions and symbol systems differ enough to influence the communication event.

intercultural communication competence Degree of successful meaning making with communicators from different backgrounds.

internalization When people accept influence because the resulting behavior or attitudes are intrinsically rewarding.

Internet addiction Pathological dependence on digital technology.

interpersonal communication Communication between people in relationships.

interpretive research The study of understanding, especially through the systematic interpretation of social actions or texts.

intimate space 0–18 inches; distance zone that implies an extremely personal connection.

intimidation Belittling others to make them feel powerless.

involvement Motivation to process persuasive communication because it is relevant to some personal value, outcome, or impression.

kinesics The use of body motions in communication.

labeling Describing individuals using names we believe categorize them.

laissez-faire leader Provides little guidance and expects group members to make decisions.

language A communication system made up of formal units combined in systematic ways to cooperatively make meaning.

latent conflict When there is a problem, but the differences are not so great that one or both sides wants to act on them.

leadership When an individual influences group members to achieve a common goal.

libertarian thought A self-governing people require access to responsibly created and disseminated information.

linear model A representation of communication as a linear process, with messages traveling from a source, through a medium, to a receiver.

listening Actively making meaning from the spoken messages of others.

Looking Glass Self In symbolic interaction, the idea that the self is accomplished by seeing ourselves as others see us.

lying Delivering information believed to be untrue with the intention to deceive.

machine-and-mechanics relationship In provider-client interactions, physicians are experts who diagnose and fix the problem.

macro-level effects Media effects at the cultural level.

majority-minority country When there is no single racial or ethnic majority among a country's population.

mall speak Embedding speech with nontraditional fillers such as "like" and "you know."

masculinity/femininity Measure of a culture's commitment to gender roles and the characteristics that accompany them.

mass communication Communication occurring between mass media and their audiences.

Mean World Syndrome The more media people consume, the meaner they think the world to be.

media addiction Over-attachment to media.

media literacy The ability to read, interpret, critically assess, and productively use media texts.

media literacy interventions Attempts to build specific media literacy skills.

media multitasking Using more than one medium simultaneously.

media texts Content originating from communication technologies.

medium (media, pl.) Vehicle conveying a message.

medium In a linear communication model, the carrier of a message.

melting pot Metaphorical image in which all cultures blend together into one harmonious whole.

membership similarity Source-receiver similarity built on common demographics, group and organizational memberships, and experiences.

message sidedness Degree to which a persuasive appeal works to recognize and refute differing opinions or viewpoints.

messages and meanings Questions about content, techniques, and interpretations.

metaphor Unstated comparisons between things or events that share some feature.

micro-level effects Media effects at the individual level.

mnemonics Memory devices based on patterns drawn from what's heard.

modeling Learning through observation.

monochronic In the use of time, focusing on one task or activity at a time.

motivation Drive, visible interest, and the incentive to produce.

mutual knowledge Information communicators share and know they share.

negotiated reading Audience members' personally meaningful interpretation of a piece of media content.

Neo-Marxism Elites maintain influence over society by control of the superstructure.

nocebo effect Experiencing a treatment effect based solely on a provider's words.

noise Anything that interferes with the process of communication.

nonverbal code systems Groups or clusters of behaviors that convey meaning.

nonverbal communication The process of relaying messages and meanings without the use of words.

nonverbal immediacy The use of nonverbal cues to indicate closeness.

norm of reciprocity The expectation that revelations about oneself will produce responses of similar information.

normative confusion When group rules and expectations are not clearly defined or established.

norming Stage when members begin working together toward a common goal.

norms Rules that govern a group.

nurturing support Helping others feel better about themselves and their situation.

obliging style Conflict resolution style showing little concern for self-interest and greater concern for the interests of others.

oculesics The use of pupil dilation, eye movement, and eye contact in meaning making.

one-sided message Presenting only the persuader's position.

ontology Questions of the nature of reality and what is knowable.

open system A system whose components continuously interact not only with one another, but with the environment outside the system.

openness-closedness Tension between being able to say anything and the need for discretion.

organization A structured social collectivity that has overall and individual goals, coordinates the activity of its members, and is embedded within an environment of other organizations.

organizational assimilation Process by which individuals become integrated into the culture of an organization.

organizational climate The meaning employees attach to the policies, practices, and procedures they experience, and the behaviors they observe being rewarded, supported, and expected.

organizational communication Any communication, verbal or nonverbal, that occurs within an organization.

organizational culture Pattern of shared basic assumptions or inferences that members learn from an organization's stories, myths, traditions, everyday experiences, and observed behaviors.

organizational entry and assimilation stage Moving from being an organizational outsider to organizational insider.

orientation Relational stage characterized by interaction between people who do not know one another.

outcome Product of relational cost-benefit analyses.

out-group A group seen as other than one's own.

outline A brief, well-organized construction of main points and subtopics of a speech.

parental mediation theory Theory stressing importance of parents actively managing and regulating children's media use.

passive aggressiveness A deliberate and masked way of expressing disrespect.

patient activation Involvement in one's own health improvement and adherence to recommended treatments.

perceived similarity Receiver's sense of alikeness with source.

perception Being aware of and making meaning from the world around us.

performing Stage when the group begins to reach and complete its goals.

peripheral route Easier, more automatic route of information processing; relies on heuristics.

personal space 18 inches to 4 feet; distance zone that implies a close, but not intimate relationship.

persuasion Communication specifically intended to shape, reinforce, or change the responses of others.

persuasive function Using language to change the attitudes or thinking of those around us.

persuasive speech Speech designed to persuade an audience to a new opinion *or* reinforce an existing opinion.

phantom-vibration syndrome Feeling a phone vibration when none exists.

physical noise Barrier to listening external to the message itself.

physiological noise Barrier to listening introduced by listeners' physical discomfort.

plagiarism Stealing someone else's material.

platform agnostic Neutrality in choice of content-delivery technology.

policy Statement that provides a blueprint of how an organization operates, its goals, and expected outcomes.

polychronic In the use of time, multitasking.

polysemic Legitimately open to different interpretations.

postpositivism Communication scholarship that recognizes that humans living in a social world are not as constant or predictable as the measurable elements of the physical world.

power The ability, capacity, or authority to move others to act as desired.

power distance How people of a given culture manage status and hierarchy.

praxis Choice of specific communication actions.

preferred reading The producer-intended meaning of a piece of media content.

prejudice Negative attitude toward a group based on little or no experience.

presentational communication An individual person's version of facts or information.

primary groups Groups offering members affection and belonging.

product placement When ads are placed in and become part of media content.

pronunciation Expressing the sounds and accents of words to accepted standards.

prospect of future interaction Motivation to reduce uncertainty based on the likelihood of future interaction.

protocol Detailed methods used in achieving goals and outcomes.

provisions of relationships What relationships offer or provide us.

proxemics Our use of space and distance to make meaning.

psychological noise Barrier to listening introduced by the listener's mindset.

public discourse Societal sharing of ideas through conversation.

public space More than 12 feet apart; distance zone implying little intimacy and indicating a more formal language environment.

public speaking Addressing an audience in a structured and formal way.

public speaking anxiety Fear of public speaking.

qualitative research Inquiry relying on the collection and analysis of symbolic data such as language and other cultural products.

quantitative research Inquiry relying on the collection and analysis of numerical data.

rank ineffectiveness Group members question the legitimacy of messages transmitted by those in positions of authority.

ranks Hierarchal structure of the group.

rapid impression formation Making immediate judgments of others after initial encounters.

rational argument Persuasive appeal containing a claim, data, and a warrant.

reactivity search Watching another react to events in the environment.

receiver In a linear communication model, the recipient of a message.

reconciliation Making up; putting the conflict in the past.

regulators Gestures to help the flow of speech.

regulatory function Using language to control the behavior of others.

relational function Using language to establish, define, and maintain relationships.

relational listening Lending a sympathetic ear, trying to identify with the speaker.

relational satisfaction The enjoyment or pleasure people derive from their relationships.

representational communication Describing or conveying some fact or information.

representations and reality Questions about content and credibility.

residual message In a speech, the larger point to be remembered.

response expectations Senders' expectations about the timing of anticipated response.

revelation-concealment Tension between meeting others' demands for information and the relational need for discretion.

reward-based cohesion Groups bound by anticipation of reward for successful completion of the task.

ritual view The perspective that communication is directed not toward the extension of messages in space but toward the maintenance of society in time and the representation of shared beliefs.

ritualistic function Using language to meet an important social convention or expectation.

roles Specific tasks and responsibilities of group members.

role-taking Ability to put oneself in the position of others to better understand them.

schema A mental structure built from past experiences that we use to process new information and organize new experiences.

scientific inquiry The active, systematic process of discovery that leads scientists from observation to knowledge and, eventually, theory.

scripted speech Speech read word-for-word from a manuscript.

secrecy Seclusion and concealment that causes others to wonder about a hidden agenda.

selective exposure Tendency to expose ourselves to or attend to messages that are consistent with already held values, beliefs, and attitudes.

selective perception Tendency to interpret messages in ways that are consistent with already held values, beliefs.

selective processes Cognitive and behavioral strategies for dealing with dissonant information.

selective retention Tendency to most accurately remember information that is consistent with already held values, beliefs, and attitudes.

self-disclosure Intentional revelation of information about oneself.

self-inquiry Asking questions of yourself in search of a possible topic.

semantic noise Barrier to listening introduced by linguistic influences on the message.

sender-receiver reciprocity Mutual and simultaneous exchange of feedback, ensuring the efficient transaction of meaning making.

sentiment-based cohesion Groups bound by relational closeness.

serial distortion Alteration of messages as they move through stopping points between the original source and the intended receiver.

settlement/resolution Removing the underlying causes of the conflict.

sign Something that signals the presence of something specific; relatively objective.

single-shooter game Video game in which players wield weapons and view the killing from their personal point of view.

situational meaning Meaning made through specific forms of language that occur or are excluded in various contexts.

small group speech Speech delivered before a few people.

small groups Collections of 3 to 15 people with a common purpose.

small talk Scripted and superficial conversations based on social convention.

social cue In frame analysis, information in an interaction, allowing the fine-tuning of presentations of self.

social meaning Meaning made by our choice of word and sound alternatives when speaking with a specific group of people.

social objects In symbolic interaction, any objects to which people can refer.

social reinforcement Welcoming of influence because we find the company of physically attractive people socially rewarding.

social space 4 to 12 feet apart; distance zone suggesting little, if any, intimacy.

socialization How we learn to be members of a group through our early interaction with primary groups.

soft news Sensational stories that have little real connection to people's everyday lives.

source In a linear communication model, the originator of a message.

source credibility Receiver's perception of source's expertise and trustworthiness.

source-dominated model A representation of communication efforts as primarily within a source's control.

spare-brain time The difference between most people's rate of speech and the rate at which the brain can process language.

speaking outline Speech outline for use during the delivery of a speech.

special occasion speech Speech at an event like a roast, wedding, or funeral.

specification of ignorance The idea that in science, every answer produces new questions.

speech community People who speak the same language and agree on the proper and improper use of language.

speech networks People who regularly interact and speak with one another.

stable exchange Relational stage characterized by rich, open, and free communication.

stalemate When neither side can prevail, but neither is willing to back down or give in.

stereotype A generalization about people, places, or things.

stonewalling Withdrawing from dialogue to avoid conflict.

storming Stage when members experience conflict.

strong culture An organization that effectively socializes and assimilates its members.

structure In critical theory, the social world's rules, norms, and beliefs.

superiority Higher rank, more respect, and better performance as a means of putting oneself above others.

supportiveness Providing others with encouragement, empathy, understanding, and help.

survey Research method relying on questionnaires and interviews to solicit self-reported data from respondents.

symbol Arbitrary indicator of something else; relatively subjective and abstract.

synchronous communication Immediate, real-time communication interaction.

synergy Promotion of a single media product across multiple real-world and media platforms.

syntactic ambiguity When a sentence can reasonably be interpreted in more than one way.

syntax The occurrence and ordering of words and sounds to convey an intended meaning.

task-oriented groups Groups convened and constructed to serve a purpose.

TDP (thinness depicting and promoting) media Media that feature conspicuously thin female characters.

telemedicine Delivery of health services by Internet video.

territory The space people consider theirs.

text Any product of social interaction.

textual analysis The deep reading of an individual message or group of messages.

theory A unified, coherent, and organized set of explanations, concepts, and principles describing some aspect of the world.

transactional model A representation of the elements of communication as interdependent and the process of communication as ongoing and dynamic.

transmissional view The perspective that communication is the process of sending and receiving information from one communicator to another.

trustworthiness Judgments of source's character.

two-sided message Bringing up and addressing opposing arguments.

uncertainty avoidance A culture's comfort with difference and ambiguity.

upshift In frame analysis, framing a situation as less serious, more open to personal expression.

upward message Messages that flow from lower to higher ranked employees.

value Deeply held judgment about the worth or importance of various aspects of people's lives.

value conflict When people acknowledge differences in their deeply held feelings about the worth or importance of significant aspects of their lives.

vocal filler Unnecessary transition words/sounds like *um, uh, ah*.

vocalics (also **paralanguage**) Sounds and rhythms other than actual words which come out of one's mouth.

water cooler communication Informal chat within an organization.

work identity An individual's persona (as presented or perceived) in the workplace.

References

Chapter 1

Baran, S. J. (2014). *Introduction to Mass Communication: Media Literacy and Culture*. New York: McGraw-Hill.

Barnlund, D. C. (1962). "Toward a Meaning-Centered Philosophy of Communication." *Journal of Communication*, 12: 197–211.

Bartlett, F. C. (1932). *Remembering: A Study in Experimental and Social Psychology*. Cambridge: Cambridge University Press.

Bergen, B. K. (2012). "Where Does Language Come From?" *Salon*, October 20. (http://www.salon.com/2012/10/20/where_does_language_come_from/).

Carey, J. (1989). *Communication as Culture: Essays on Media and Society*. Winchester, MA: Unwin Hyman.

Cooley, C. H. (1902). *Human Nature and the Social Order*. New York: Scribner's.

Craig, R. T. (1999). "Communication Theory as a Field." *Communication Theory*, 9: 119–161.

Crotty, M. (1998). *The Foundations of Social Research: Meaning and Perspective in the Research Process*. Thousand Oaks, CA: Sage.

"The Eagle, Ben Franklin, and the Wild Turkey." (2012). *The Great Seal*. (http://www.greatseal.com/symbols/turkey.html).

Enten, H. (2014). "The Politics of the Washington Redskins Name Controversy." *Fivethirtyeight*, June 20. (http://fivethirtyeight.com/datalab/the-politics-of-the-washington-redskins-name-controversy/).

Goffman, E. (1974). *Frame Analysis: An Essay on the Organization of Experience*. New York: Harper & Row.

Goffman, E. (1959). *The Presentation of Self in Everyday Life*. Garden City, NY: Doubleday.

Hall, E. T. (1976). *Beyond Culture*. New York: Doubleday.

Hauser, G. A. (1986). *Introduction to Rhetorical Theory*. New York: Harper & Row.

Langer, S. K. (1942). *Philosophy in a New Key*. Cambridge, MA: Harvard University Press.

Lasswell, H. D. (1948). "The Structure and Function of Communication in Society." In L. Bryson, ed., *The Communication of Ideas*. New York: Harper.

Mead, G. H. (1934). *Mind, Self, and Society*. Chicago: University of Chicago Press.

Morris, C. W. (1959). "Introduction." In G. H. Mead, ed., *Mind, Self, and Society*. Chicago: University of Chicago Press.

Ogden, C. K., and I. A. Richards. (1923). *The Meaning of Meaning*. London: Kegan, Paul, Trench, Trubner.

Pearce, C. G., R. Figgins, and S. P. Golen. (1984). *Principles of Business Communication: Theory, Application, and Technology*. New York: John Wiley & Sons.

Plaisance, P. L. (2014). *Media Ethics: Key Principles for Responsible Practice*. Los Angeles: Sage.

Right Management. (2002). "Top Five Communication Skills Essential to Career Success." *Right View*. (http://www.ohio.edu/hr/outplacement/upload/5_communication_skills.pdf).

Sandberg, S., and A. Grant. (2015). "Speaking While Female." *New York Times*, January 11, p. SR3.

Schramm, W. (1954). *The Process and Effects of Mass Communication*. Urbana: University of Illinois Press.

Sternberg, R. J. (2013). "Giving Employers What They Don't Really Want." *Chronicle of Higher Education*, June 17. (http://chronicle.com/article/Giving-Employers-What-They/139877).

Watzlawick, P., J. H. Beavin, and D. D. Jackson. (1967). *Pragmatics of Human Communication*. New York: Norton.

Whetton, D. A., and K. S. Cameron. (2005). *Developing Management Skills*. Upper Saddle River, NJ: Prentice-Hall.

Wilson, K. (2012). "Reviewing Key Communication Skills for Better Job Interviews." *San Francisco Examiner*, November 10. (http://www.examiner.com/article/reviewing-key-communication-skills-for-better-job-interviews).

Chapter 2

Bailey, K. D. (1982). *Methods of Social Research*. New York: Free Press.

Bandura, A. (2008). "The Reconstrual of 'Free Will' from the Agentic Perspective of Social Cognitive Theory." In J. Baer, J. C. Kaufman, and R. F. Baumeister, eds., *Are We Free? Psychology and Free Will*. Oxford: Oxford University Press.

Benoit, W. L., and R. L. Holbert. (2008). "Empirical Intersections in Communication Research: Replication, Multiple Quantitative Methods, and Bridging the Quantitative-Qualitative Divide." *Journal of Communication,* 58: 615–628.

Blackford, L. B. (2012). "GOP Lawmakers Question Standards for Teaching Evolution in Kentucky." *Kentucky .com*, August 14. (http://www.kentucky.com/2012/08/ 14/2298914/gop-lawmakers-question-standards .html).

Firestein, S. (2013). "The Pursuit of Ignorance." *TED Talks,* September 24. (http://www.youtube.com/ watch?v=nq0_zGzSc8g).

Griffin, E. (2009). *A First Look at Communication Theory.* New York: McGraw-Hill.

Jones, C. (2011). "7 Steps: Critical Thinking in the Workplace." *Talent Culture.com,* April 4. (http://www .talentculture.com/leadership/7-steps-critical-thinking-in-the-workplace/).

Kay, A. (2012). "Learn to Think if You Want to Get Hired." *USA Today,* June 8. (http://usatoday30.usatoday.com/ money/jobcenter/workplace/kay/story/2012–06–09/ learn-to-think-listen-interact/55467614/1).

Kerlinger, F. N. (1979). *Behavioral Research: A Conceptual Approach.* New York: Holt, Rinehart & Winston.

Lightman, A. (2011). "Does God Exist?" *Salon,* October 2. (http://www.salon.com/2011/10/02/how_science_ and_faith_coexist/).

Littlejohn, S. W., and K. A. Foss. (2011). *Theories of Human Communication.* Long Grove, IL: Waveland Press.

Merton, R. K. (1967). *On Theoretical Sociology.* New York: Free Press.

Meyrowitz, J. (2008). "Power, Pleasure, Patterns: Intersecting Narratives of Media Influence." *Journal of Communication,* 58: 641–663.

Moore, J. A. (1984). "Science as a Way of Knowing—Evolutionary Biology." *American Zoologist,* 24: 467–534.

Popper, K. (1959). *The Logic of Scientific Discovery.* London: Hutchinson.

Radway, J. (1991). *Reading the Romance: Women, Patriarchy, and Popular Literature.* Chapel Hill: University of North Carolina Press.

Root, G. N. (2015). "What Are the Benefits of Critical Thinking in the Workplace?" *Houston Chronicle.* (http:// smallbusiness.chron.com/benefits-critical-thinking-workplace-11638.html).

Scheufele, D. A. (2010). "The Future of Communication: Theory and Methodology?" *AEJMC Hot Topics,* July 7. (http://www.aejmc.org/topics/archives/424).

Schutt, R. K. (2009). *Investigating the Social World,* 6th ed. Thousand Oaks, CA: Sage.

Woods, N. (1988). "Talking Shop: Sex and Status as Determinants of Floor Appointments in a Work Setting."

In J. Coates and D. Cameron, eds., *Women in their Speech Communities.* London: Longman.

Zimmer, C. (2011). "It's Science, But Not Necessarily Right." *New York Times,* June 16, p. SR12.

Chapter 3

Bloomfield, L. (1933). *Language.* New York: Holt, Rinehart & Winston.

Bok, S. (1999). *Lying: Moral Choice in Public and Private Life.* New York: Vintage Books.

Bonvillain, N. (2014). *Language, Culture, and Communication.* Boston: Prentice-Hall.

Boroditsky, L. (2001). "Does Language Shape Thought? Mandarin and English Speakers' Conceptions of Time." *Cognitive Psychology, 43:* 1–22.

Boroditsky, L., L. Schmidt, and W. Phillips. (2003). "Sex, Syntax, and Semantics." In D. Gentner and S. Goldin-Meadow, eds., *Language in Mind: Advances in the Study of Language and Cognition.* Cambridge, UK: Cambridge University Press.

Bostrom, R. (1970). "Patterns of Communicative Interactions in Small Groups." *Speech Monographs, 3:* 257–263.

Branson, R. (2014). "The War on Drugs Has Failed, So Let's Shut It Down." *Huffington Post,* June 3. (http://www .huffingtonpost.com/richard-branson/the-war-on-drugs-has-fail_1_b_5439312.html).

Brown, P., and S. Levinson. (1987). *Politeness: Some Universals in Language Usage.* New York: Cambridge University Press.

Carroll, J. B., and J. B. Casagrande. (1958). "The Function of Language Classifications in Behavior." In E. E. Maccoby, T. M. Newcombe, and E. L. Hartley, eds., *Readings in Social Psychology.* New York: Holt, Rinehart & Winston.

Chaika, E. (1989). *Language the Social Mirror.* New York: Newbury House Publishers.

Chomsky, N. (1957). *Syntactic Structures.* The Hague: Mouton.

Chomsky, N. (1965). *Aspects of the Theory of Syntax.* Cambridge, MA: MIT Press.

Dongil, J., and J. J. Sosik. (2006). "Who Are the Spellbinders? Identifying Personal Attributes of Charismatic Leaders." *Journal of Leadership and Organizational Studies,* 12: 12–27.

Eichelberger, C. (2010). "Good Communication Skills in the Workplace." *Getting Hired.com,* June 23. (http: //community.gettinghired.com/blogs/articles/ archive/2010/06/23/good-communication-skills-in-the-workplace.aspx).

Gall, G. (2009). "The Words in the Mental Cupboard." *BBC News Magazine,* April 28. (http://news.bbc.co.uk/ 2/hi/uk_news/magazine/8013859.stm).

Goo, S. (2015). "The Skills Americans Say Kids Need to Succeed in Life." *Pew Research Center,* February 19. (http://www.pewresearch.org/fact-tank/2015/02/19/skills-for-success/).

Gorlick, A. (2011). "Is Crime a Virus or a Beast? When Describing Crime, Stanford Study Shows the Word You Pick Can Frame the Debate on How to Fight It." *Stanford Report,* February 23. (http://news.stanford.edu/news/2011/february/metaphors-crime-study-022311.html).

Hayakawa, S. I. (1978). *Language in Thought and Action.* Orlando, FL: Harcourt Brace Jovanovich.

Jefferson, G. (1996). "On the Poetics of Ordinary Talk." *Text and Performance Quarterly,* 16: 1–61.

Kant, I. (1797/1991). *The Metaphysics of Morals.* Cambridge, UK: Cambridge University Press.

Lakoff, G., and M. Johnson. (1980). *Metaphors We Live By.* Chicago: University of Chicago Press.

Lakoff, R. (1973). "The Logic of Politeness; or, Minding Your P's and Q's." In *Papers from the Ninth Regional Meeting of the Chicago Linguistic Society.* Chicago: Chicago Linguistic Society.

Langer, S. K. (2013). "Language and Thought." In P. Eschholz, A. Rosa, and V. Clark, eds., *Language Awareness: Readings for College Writers.* Boston: Bedford/St. Martin's.

Marche, S. (2012). "The Golden Age for Writers . . . Is Right Now." *Esquire,* December. (http://www.esquire.com/features/thousand-words-on-culture/writing-careers-1212?src=rss).

Mathew, P. (2012). "Perfecting Workplace Communication Skills: Verbal Communication." *MMM Training Solutions.* (http://www.mmmts.com/pdf/article/Perfecting%20Workplace-Communication-Skills-Verbal-Communication.pdf).

Mazur, T. C. (1993). "Lying." *Issues in Ethics,* 6: Fall. (http://www.scu.edu/ethics/publications/iie/v6n1/lying.html).

Meyer, P. (2012). "How to Spot a Liar." *Huffington Post,* November 9. (http://www.huffingtonpost.com/pamela-meyer/how-to-spot-a-liar_b_2094610.html).

Newman, T. (2015). "It's 'Counterproductive' to Treat Drug Use as a Criminal Problem, Obama Says." *Alternet,* January 23. (http://www.alternet.org/drugs/obama-treating-drug-use-criminal-problem-counterproductive?akid=12715.131137.vJuCtD&rd=1&src=newsletter1030769&t=19).

Penn, C. R. (1990). "A Choice of Words Is a Choice of Worlds." *Vital Speeches of the Day,* December 1: 116.

Rubin, J. "The Special Relation of Guarani and Spanish in Paraguay." In N. Wolfson and J. Manes, eds., *Language of Inequality.* The Hague: Mouton.

Sheidlower, J. (2006). "Word Count." *Slate,* April, 10. (http://www.slate.com/articles/life/the_good_word/2006/04/word_count.html).

Tohidian, I. (2008). "Examining Linguistic Relativity Hypothesis as One of the Main Views on the Relationship between Language and Thought." *Journal of Psycholinguist Research,* 38: 65–74.

Chapter 4

"American Time Use Survey Summary." (2014). *Bureau of Labor Statistics,* June 18. (http://www.bls.gov/news.release/atus.nr0.htm).

Birdwhistell, R. Y. (1952). *Introduction to Kinesics.* Louisville: University of Kentucky Press.

Bonvillain, N. (2014). *Language, Culture, and Communication.* Boston: Prentice-Hall.

Burgoon, J. K. (1994). "Nonverbal Signals." In M. L. Knapp and G. R. Miller, eds., *Handbook of Interpersonal Communication.* Thousand Oaks, CA: Sage.

Burgoon, J. K., and J. L. Hale. (1988). "Nonverbal Expectancy Violations: Model Elaboration and Application to Immediacy Behaviors." *Communication Monographs,* 55: 58–79.

Casner, S. (2015). "Can Hugs Make You Healthier?" *Salon,* January 31. (http://www.salon.com/2015/01/31/can_hugs_make_you_healthier/).

Franklin, R. (2011). "Connectivity Conundrum." *New Republic,* January 26. (http://www.tnr.com/article/the-read/82164/children-technology-ipod-computer-dependent).

Hall, E. T. (1966). *The Hidden Dimension.* New York: Anchor.

Hosoda, M., E. F. Stone-Romero, and G. Coats. (2006). "The Effects of Physical Attractiveness on Job-Related Outcomes: A Meta-Analysis of Experimental Studies." *Personnel Psychology,* 56: 431–462.

Kleisner, K., V. Chvátalová, and J. Flegr. (2014). "Perceived Intelligence Is Associated with Measured Intelligence in Men but Not Women." *PLoS One,* 9: e81237.

Mehrabian, A. (1971). *Silent Messages.* Belmont, CA: Wadsworth.

Murphy, K. (2014). "Psst. Look Over Here." *New York Times,* May 18, pp. SR 6–7.

Picchi, A. (2015). "The United States of No Vacation." *CBS News,* January 6. (http://www.cbsnews.com/news/the-united-states-of-no-vacation/).

Ramsey, L. (1979). "Nonverbal Behavior: An Intercultural Perspective." In M. Asante, E. Newmark, and C. Blake, eds., *Handbook of Intercultural Communication.* Beverly Hills, CA: Sage.

Rideout, V. (2012). "Children, Teens, and Entertainment Media: The View from the Classroom." *Common Sense Media,* Fall. (http://www.commonsensemedia.org/sites/default/files/research/view-from-the-classroom-final-report.pdf).

Rideout, V. J., U. G. Foehr, and D. F. Roberts. (2010). *Generation M2: Media in the Lives of 8- to 18-Year-Olds.* Menlo Park, CA: Kaiser Family Foundation.

Rodley, K. (2010). "Understanding Nonverbal Communication in the Workplace." *Yahoo! Voices*, January 13. (http://voices.yahoo.com/understanding-nonverbal-communication-workplace-5250639.html?cat=31).

Scelfo, J. (2010). "The Risks of Parenting While Plugged In." *New York Times*, June 9, p. D1.

Segal, J., M. Smith, and J. Jaffe. (2012). *Nonverbal Communication: Improving Your Nonverbal Skills and Reading Body Language.* Helpguide.org, September. (http://www.helpguide.org/mental/eq6_nonverbal_communication.htm).

Snyder, M., E. Berscheid, and P. Glick. (1985). "Focusing on the Exterior and the Interior: Two Investigations of the Initiation of Personal Relationships." *Journal of Personality and Social Psychology*, 48: 1427–1439.

Stony Brook University Career Center. (2011). "Non-Verbal Communication in the Workplace." *Stony Brook University*, July 19. (http://sbcareercenter.blogspot.com/2011/07/non-verbal-communication-in-workplace.html).

The Infamous Larry David Staredown. (2010). *YouTube.* (http://www.youtube.com/watch?v=CuEnGTuqjh8).

Vernon, R. J. W., C. A. M. Sutherland, A. W. Young, and T. Hartley. (2014). "Modeling First Impressions from Highly Variable Facial Images." *Proceedings of the National Academy of Sciences of the United States of America,* 10.1073/pnas.1409860111: 1–9.

Williams, R. B. (2010). "Why Have We Lost the Need for Physical Touch?" *Scott.net*, October 1. (http://www.sott.net/article/215911-Why-Have-We-Lost-the-Need-for-Physical-Touch).

Zupek, R. (2010). "Physical Contact at Work: What Are the Boundaries?" *CNNLiving*, February 8. (http://www.cnn.com/2010/LIVING/worklife/02/08/cb.getting.physical.at.work/index.html).

Chapter 5

Adler, R., and J. Elmhorst. (2008). *Communicating at Work.* New York: McGraw-Hill.

Bodie, G. B. (2013). "Issues in the Measurement of Listening." *Communication Research Reports,* 30: 76–84.

Bolton, E. B. (2009). "IFAS Leadership Development: Listening to Learn." *Florida Cooperative Extension Service,* January. (http://edis.ifas.ufl.edu/he748).

Brownell, J. (1986). "A Model for Listening Instruction: Management Applications." *ABCA Bulletin,* 48: 39–44.

Brownell, J. (1990). "Perceptions of Effective Listeners: A Management Study." *Journal of Business Communication,* 27: 401–415.

Burley-Allen, M. (1995). *Listening: The Forgotten Skill.* New York: John Wiley & Sons.

Carrell, L. J., and S. C. Willmington. (1996). "A Comparison of Self-Report and Performance Data in Assessing Speaking and Listening Competence." *Communication Reports,* 9: 185–191.

Cendrowski, M. (2012). *The Big Bang Theory: The Extract Obliteration. CBS Television,* Season 6, Episode 6.

Ferrari, B. T. (2012). *Power Listening.* New York: Penguin.

Floyd, K. (2006). *Communicating Affection: Interpersonal Behavior and Social Context.* Cambridge: Cambridge University Press.

Goss, B. (1982). *Processing Information.* Belmont, CA: Wadsworth.

Guffey, M. E. (2004). *Essentials of Business Communication.* Toronto: Nelson Education.

Holan, A. D., and A. Sharokman. (2014). "2014 Lie of the Year: Exaggerations about Ebola." *PolitiFact.Com*, December 15. (http://www.politifact.com/truth-o-meter/article/2014/dec/15/2014-lie-year-exaggerations-about-ebola/).

Josephson, M. (2011). "QUOTE: Courage Is What It Takes to Stand Up and Speak; Courage Is Also What It Takes to Sit Down and Listen—Winston Churchill." *What Will Matter*, November 29. (http://whatwillmatter.com/2011/11/quote-courage-is-what-it-takes-to-stand-up-and-speak-courage-is-also-what-it-takes-to-sit-down-and-listen-winston-churchill/).

Miller, G. R. (1967). "An Evaluation of the Effectiveness of Mnemonic Devices as Aids to Study." *ERIC.* (http://eric.ed.gov/?id=ED011088).

Neel, J. (2010). "How Many People Die from Flu Each Year. Depends on How You Slice the Data." *PBS.org,* August 26. (http://www.npr.org/blogs/health/2010/08/26/129456941/annual-flu-death-average-fluctuates-depending-on-how-you-slice-it).

Nichols, M. P. (2009). *The Lost Art of Listening.* New York: Guilford Press.

Nichols, R. G. (1955). "Ten Components of Effective Listening." *Education,* 75: 292–302.

Purdy, M. W. (1995). "Ethics in Listening. What's to Say?" Paper submitted to the Annual Convention of the Speech Communication Association, San Antonio, TX.

Tannen, D. (1990). *You Just Don't Understand: Women and Men in Conversation.* New York: HarperCollins.

Vineyard, E. E., and R. B. Bailey. (1960). "Interrelationships of Reading Ability, Listening Skill, Intelligence, and Scholastic Achievement." *Journal of Developmental Reading,* 3: 174–178.

Wolvin, A., and C. G. Coakley. (1996). *Listening.* Madison, WI: Brown and Benchmark.

Chapter 6

Altman, I., and D. A. Taylor. (1973). *Social Penetration: The Development of Interpersonal Relationships*. New York: Holt, Rinehart, and Winston.

Baxter, L. A. (1990). "Dialectical Contradictions in Relationship Development." *Journal of Social and Personal Relationships*, 7: 69–88.

Berger, C. R. (1979). "Beyond Initial Interaction: Uncertainty, Understanding, and the Development of Interpersonal Relationships." In H. Giles and R. St. Clair, eds., *Language and Social Psychology*. Oxford: Blackwell.

Berger, C. R. (1988). "Uncertainty and Information Exchange in Developing Relationships." In S. Duck, ed., *Handbook of Personal Relationships*. New York: Wiley.

Berger, C. R., and R. J. Calabrese. (1975). "Some Explorations in Initial Interaction and Beyond: Toward a Developmental Theory of Interpersonal Communication." *Human Communication Research*, 1: 99–112.

Berger, C. R., and K. Kellerman. (1994). "Acquiring Social Information." In J. A. Daly and J. M. Weimann, eds., *Strategic Interpersonal Communication*. Hillsdale, NJ: Erlbaum.

Brahm, E. (2003). "Conflict Stages." *Beyond Intractability*, September. (http://www.beyondintractability.org/bi-essay/conflict-stages).

Braithwaite, D. O., and L. A. Baxter. (2008). "Relational Dialectics Theory." In L. A. Baxter and D. O. Braithwaite, eds., *Engaging Theories in Interpersonal Communication*. Los Angeles: Sage.

Cohen, D. (2013). "Why Does Being Lonely Make You Ill?" *BBC News*, February 22. (http://www.bbc.co.uk/news/health-21517864).

Cole, M. (1996). *Interpersonal Conflict Communication in Japanese Cultural Contexts*. Unpublished Dissertation, Arizona State University, Tempe.

Comstock, G. (1991). *Television and the American Child*. San Diego: Academic.

Cutrona, C. E. (2004). "A Psychological Perspective: Marriage and the Social Provisions of Relationships." *Journal of Marriage and Family*, 66: 992–999.

DeKay, S. H. (2012). "Interpersonal Communication in the Workplace: A Largely Unexplored Region." *Business Communication Quarterly*, 75: 449–452.

Frederickson, B. L. (2013). "Your Phone vs. Your Heart." *New York Times*, March 24, p. SR14.

Gottman, J. M. (1993). "A Theory of Marital Dissolution and Stability." *Journal of Family Psychology*, 7: 57–75.

Guerrero, L. K., P. A. Anderson, and V. A. Afifi. (2011). *Close Encounters: Communication in Relationships*. Thousand Oaks, CA: Sage.

Keith, T. (2011). *The Bro Code: How Contemporary Culture Creates Sexist Men*. Northampton, MA: Media Education Foundation.

Kilmann, R. H., and K. W. Thomas. (1975). "Interpersonal Conflict-Handling Behavior as Reflections of Jungian Personality Dimensions." *Psychological Reports*, 37: 971–980.

Kistler, M. E., and M. J. Lee. (2010). "Does Exposure to Sexual Hip-Hop Music Videos Influence the Sexual Attitudes of College Students?" *Mass Communication and Society*, 13: 67–86.

Kok, B. E., K. A. Coffey, M. A. Cohn, L. I. Catalino, T. Vacharkulksemsuk, S. B. Algoe, M. Brantley, and B. L. Frederickson. (2013). "How Positive Emotions Build Physical Health: Perceived Positive Social Connections Account for the Upward Spiral between Positive Emotions and Vagal Tone." *Psychological Science*, 24: 1123–1132.

Martin, J. N., and T. K. Nakayama. (2001). *Experiencing Intercultural Communication*. Mountain View, CA: Mayfield.

Mongeau, P. A., and M. L. M. Henningsen. (2008). "Stage Theories of Relational Development." In L. A. Baxter and D. O. Braithwaite, eds., *Engaging Theories in Interpersonal Communication*. Los Angeles: Sage.

Pillet-Shore, D. (2011). "Doing Introductions: The Work Involved in Meeting Someone New." *Communication Monographs*, 78: 73–95.

Rahim, M. A., and N. R. Magner. (1995). "Confirmatory Factor Analysis of the Styles of Handling Interpersonal Conflict: First-Order Factor Model and Its Invariance across Groups." *Journal of Applied Psychology*, 80: 122–132.

Rampur, S. (2010). "Interpersonal Relationships at Work." *Buzzle.com*, July 13. (http://www.buzzle.com/articles/interpersonal-relationships-at-work.html).

Robles, M. M. (2012). "Executive Perceptions of the Top 10 Soft Skills Needed in Today's Workplace." *Business Communication Quarterly*, 75: 453–465.

Samson, L., and M. E. Grabe. (2012). "Media Use and the Sexual Propensities of Emerging Adults." *Journal of Broadcasting and Electronic Media*, 56: 280–298.

Stafford, L. (2008). "Social Exchange Theories." In L. A. Baxter and D. O. Braithwaite, eds., *Engaging Theories in Interpersonal Communication*. Los Angeles: Sage.

Tamir, D. I., and J. P. Mitchell. (2012). "Disclosing Information about the Self is Intrinsically Rewarding." *Proceedings of the National Academy of Sciences*, 109: 8038–8043.

Taylor, D. A., and I. Altman. (1987). "Communication in Interpersonal Relationships: Social Penetration Processes." In M. Roloff and G. R. Miller, eds., *Interpersonal Processes: New Directions in Communication Research*. Newbury Park, CA: Sage.

Thibaut, J. W., and H. H. Kelley. (1959). *The Psychology of Groups*. New York: Wiley.

Weiss, R. S. (1974). "The Provisions of Social Relationships." In Z. Rubin, ed., *Doing unto Others*. Englewood Cliffs, NJ: Prentice Hall.

Weiss, R. S. (1998). "A Taxonomy of Relationships." *Journal of Social and Personal Relationships*, 15: 671–683.

Whitson, S. (2012). "Backhanded Compliments and Sugarcoated Hostility." *Psychology Today*, February 3. (http://www.psychologytoday.com/blog/passive-aggressive-diaries/201202/backhanded-compliments-and-sugarcoated-hostility).

Wilmot, J. H., and W. W. Wilmot. (1978). *Interpersonal Conflict*. Dubuque, IA: Wm. C. Brown.

Chapter 7

Ackoff, R. L. (1981). *Creating the Corporate Future*. New York: John Wiley & Sons.

"Action for Children's Television." (2015). *Harvard Graduate School of Education, Special Collections*. (http://www.gse.harvard.edu/library/collections/special/act.html).

Bales, R. F. (1970). *Personality and Interpersonal Behavior*. New York: Holt, Rinehart, and Winston.

Coutu, D. (2009). "Why Teams Don't Work." *Harvard Business Review*, May. (http://hbr.org/2009/05/why-teams-dont-work.

DeFleur, M. H., P. Kearney, T. G. Plax, and M. L. DeFleur. (2014). *Fundamentals of Human Communication*. New York: McGraw-Hill.

DeFleur, M. L., W. V. D'Antonio, and L. B. DeFleur. (1984). *Sociology: Human Society*. New York: Random House.

"Drunk Driving Fatalities Fall Below 10,000." (2012). *Mothers Against Drunk Driving*, December 10. (http://www.madd.org/blog/2012/december/drunk-driving-fatalities-fall.html).

French, J. R. P., and B. H. Raven. (1959). *The Bases of Social Power*. In D. Cartwright, ed., *Studies in Social Power*. Ann Arbor, MI: Institute for Social Research.

Giddens, A. (1976). *New Rules of Sociological Method*. New York: Basic Books.

Giddens, A. (2003). "The Time-Space Constitution of Social Systems." In P. Kristivo, ed., *Social Theory: Roots and Branches*. Los Angeles, CA: Roxbury.

Heathfield, S. (2013). "12 Tips for Team Building." *About.com*. (http://humanresources.about.com/od/involvementteams/a/twelve_tip_team.htm).

Hoffman, M. F., and R. L. Cowan. (2010). "Be Careful What You Ask For: Structuration Theory and Work/Life Accommodation." *Communication Studies*, 61: 205–223.

Janis, I. (1989). *Crucial Decisions: Leadership in Policy Making and Crisis Management*. New York: Free Press.

JockBio. (2012). "Tom Brady: What They Say." (http://www.jockbio.com/Bios/Brady_Tom/Brady_they-say.html).

Kirby, E. L., and K. J. Krone. (2002) "The Policy Exists but You Can't Really Use It." *Journal of Applied Communication Research*, 30: 50–77.

Lewin, K., R. Lippitt, and R. K. White. (1939). "Patterns of Aggressive Behavior in Experimentally Created Social Climates." *Journal of Social Psychology*, 10: 271–301.

Littlejohn, S. W., and K. A. Foss. (2011). *Theories of Human Communication*. Long Grove, IL: Waveland Press.

Modaff, D. P., and S. DeWine. (2002). *Organizational Communication: Foundations, Challenges, and Misunderstandings*. Los Angeles: Roxbury.

Northouse, G. (2007). *Leadership Theory and Practice*. Thousand Oaks, CA: Sage.

Poole, M. S., and R. D. McPhee. (2005). "Structuration Theory." In S. May and D. K. Mumby, eds., *Engaging Organizational Communication Theory and Research: Multiple Perspectives*. Thousand Oaks, CA: Sage.

Schwartz, J., and M. Wald. (2003). "Is 'Groupthink' Part of the Problem with NASA Again?" *Grand Rapids Press*, March 23, p. A15.

Sundstrom, E., K. P. DeMeuse, and D. Futrell. (1990). "Work Teams: Applications and Effectiveness." *American Psychologist*, 45: 120–133.

Tuckman, B. W., and M. A. C. Jensen. (1977). "Stages of Small-Group Development Revisited." *Groups and Organization Studies*, 2: 419–427.

Williams, R. B. (2012). "'I'm Successful Because I'm Beautiful': How We Discriminate in Favor of Attractive People." *Psychology Today*, August 18. (http://www.psychologytoday.com/blog/wired-success/201208/im-successful-because-im-beautiful-how-we-discriminate-in-favor-attractive).

Chapter 8

Albrecht, T. L., and B. W. Bach. (1997). *Communication in Complex Organizations: A Relational Approach*. New York: Harcourt Brace.

As You Sow. (2013). "What Is SCR?" *Asyousow.org*. (http://www.asyousow.org/csr/).

Avtgis, T. A., A. S. Rancer, and P. E. Madlock. (2010). *Organizational Communication*. Dubuke, IA: Kendall Hunt.

Ballman, D. (2013). "Facebook Posts and Tweets That Can Get You Fired." *AOL.com*, May 24. (http://jobs.aol.com/articles/2013/05/24/facebook-twitter-get-employees-fired/).

Bisel, R. S., A. S. Messersmith, and K. M. Kelley. (2012). "Supervisor-Subordinate Communication: Hierarchical Mum Effect Meets Organizational Learning." *Journal of Business Communication*, 49: 128–147.

Cone Communications. (2013). *2013 Cone Communications/Echo Global CSR Study. Conecomm.com*. (http://www.conecomm.com/global-csr-study).

Davis, K. (1953). "Management Communication and the Grapevine." *Harvard Business Review,* September–October: 43–49.

Davis, K. (1972). *Human Behavior at Work: Human Relations and Organizational Behavior.* New York: McGraw-Hill.

Deal, T. E., and A. A. Kennedy. (1982). *Corporate Cultures: The Rites and Rituals of Corporate Life.* Reading, MA: Addison-Wesley.

Eisenberg, E. M., H. L. Goodall, and A. Trethewey. (2010). *Organizational Communication.* Boston: Bedford/St. Martins.

Forliti, A. (2013). "Minn. Church Whistleblower Says She Has No Regrets about Speaking Out, But 'Didn't Do Enough.'" *Minnesota Star Tribune,* October 22. (http://www.startribune.com/local/minneapolis/228794371.html).

Gordon, C. (2013). "Chili's Waitress Fired over Facebook Post Insulting 'Stupid Cops.'" *AOL.com,* May 16. (http://jobs.aol.com/articles/2013/05/16/chilis-waitress-fired-facebook-post/).

Jablin, F. M. (2001). "Organizational Entry, Assimilation, and Disengagement/Exit." In F. M. Jablin and L. L. Putnam, eds., *The New Handbook of Organizational Communication: Advances in Theory, Research, and Methods.* Newbury Park, CA: Sage.

Klein, J., and N. Dawar. (2004). "Corporate Social Responsibility and Consumers' Attributions and Brand Evaluations in a Product Harm Case." *International Journal of Research in Marketing,* 21: 203–217.

Lai, C. S., C. J. Yang, and D. C. Pai. (2010). "The Effects of Corporate Social Responsibility on Brand Performance: The Mediating Effect of Industrial Brand Equity and Corporate Reputation." *Journal of Business Ethics,* 95: 457–469.

Lankton-Rivas, S. (2008). Overcoming Conflict in the Workplace." *Boston Globe,* May 14. (http://www.boston.com/jobs/news/articles/2008/05/14/overcoming_conflict_in_the_workplace/).

Littlejohn, S. W., and K. A. Foss. (2011). *Theories of Human Communication.* Long Grove, IL: Waveland Press.

Lohr, S. (2014). "Unblinking Eyes Track Employees." *New York Times,* June 22, p. A1.

Miller, K. (2012). *Organizational Communication.* Boston: Wadsworth.

Mohr, L. A., and D. J. Webb. (2005). "The Effects of Corporate Social Responsibility and Price on Consumer Responses." *Journal of Consumer Affairs,* 39: 121–147.

Packer, G. (2013). "Business as Usual." *New Yorker,* October 28, pp. 21–22

Perrow, C. (1986). *Complex Organizations: A Critical Essay.* New York: Random House.

Ritman, A. (2013). "World Wide Web Inventor Calls for Protection of Whistleblowers." *Hollywood Reporter,* October 22. (http://www.hollywoodreporter.com/news/world-wide-web-inventor-calls-650314).

Samovar, L. A., R. E. Porter, E. R. McDaniel, and C. S. Roy. (2013). *Communication between Cultures.* Boston: Cengage.

Schneider, B., M. G. Ehrhart, and W. H. Macey. (2013). "Organizational Climate and Culture." *Annual Review of Psychology,* 64: 361–88.

Scott, W. R. (1981). *Organizations: Rational, Natural, and Open Systems.* Englewood Cliffs, NJ: Prentice Hall.

Temple, M., and P. J. Studldreher. (2013). "Work, Gripes and Facebook Posts—How Far Do Labor Laws Go to Protect Employees?" *Forbes.com,* August 22. (http://www.forbes.com/sites/theemploymentbeat/2013/08/22/work-gripes-and-facebook-posts-how-far-do-labor-laws-go-to-protect-employees/).

Thorpe, D. (2013). "Why CSR? The Benefits of Corporate Social Responsibility Will Move You to Act." *Forbes,* May 18. (http://www.forbes.com/sites/devinthorpe/2013/05/18/why-csr-the-benefits-of-corporate-social-responsibility-will-move-you-to-act/).

Weber, M. (1946). *From Max Weber: Essays in Sociology.* New York: Oxford University Press.

Zaremba, A. J. (2003). *Organizational Communication: Foundations for Business and Management.* Mason, OH: Thomson.

Chapter 9

American Civil Liberties Union. (2005). "Racial Profiling: Definition." *ACLU.org,* November 23. (http://www.aclu.org/racial-justice/racial-profiling-definition).

Amato, J. (2013). "Being Black in New York Is No Stroll in the Park." *Crooks and Liars,* March 25. (http://crooksandliars.com/john-amato/being-black-new-york-isnt-stroll-park).

Bluestein, A. (2015). "The Most Entrepreneurial Group in America Wasn't Born in America." *Inc.,* February, pp. 44–50, 100–101.

Brislin, R. (2000). *Understanding Culture's Consequences on Behavior.* Fort Worth, TX: Harcourt.

Bureau of Labor Statistics. (2013). "Labor Force Characteristics of Foreign-Born Workers Summary." *U.S. Government,* May 23. (http://www.bls.gov/news.release/forbrn.nr0.htm).

Greenwald, A. G., and M. R. Banaji. (1995). "Implicit Social Cognition: Attitudes, Self-Esteem, and Stereotypes." *Psychological Review,* 102: 4–27.

Gudykunst, W. B. (2001). *Asian American Ethnicity and Communication.* Thousand Oaks, CA: Sage.

Gudykunst, W. B., Y. Matsumoto, S. Ting-Toomey, T. Nishida, K. Kim, and S. Heyman. (1996). "The Influence of Cultural Individualism-Collectivism, Self Construals, and Individual Values on Communication Styles across Cultures." *Human Communication Research, 22*: 510–543.

Hall, E. T. (1976). *Beyond Culture*. New York: Doubleday.

Hofstede, G. (1983). "National Cultures in Four Dimensions: A Research-Based Theory of Cultural Differences among Nations." *International Studies of Management and Organization, 13*: 46–74.

Hofstede, G., G. J. Hofstede, and M. Minkov. (2010). *Cultures and Organizations: Software of the Mind*. New York: McGraw-Hill.

Hornsey, M. J. (2008). "Social Identity Theory and Self-categorization Theory: A Historical Review." *Social and Personality Psychology Compass, 2*: 204–222.

Howell, W. S. (1982). *The Empathic Communicator*. Belmont, CA: Wadsworth.

Howson, A. (2009). "Cultural Relativism." *EBSCO Publishing.* (http://www.ebscohost.com/uploads/imported/thisTopic-dbTopic-1247.pdf).

Koerth-Baker, M. (2011). "Islamic Scholar: Difference Is a Blessing." *Boing-Boing*, April 5. (http://boingboing.net/2011/04/05/islamic-scholar-diff.html).

Littlejohn, S. W., and K. A. Foss. (2011). *Theories of Human Communication*. Long Grove, IL: Waveland Press.

Martin, J. N., and T. K. Nakayama. (2001). *Experiencing Intercultural Communication*. Mountain View, CA: Mayfield.

Meshel, D. S., and R. P. McGlynn. (2004). "Intergenerational Contact, Attitudes, and Stereotypes of Adolescents and Older People." *Educational Gerontology, 30*: 457–479.

Meyer, E. (2014). "Looking Another Culture in the Eye." *New York Times*, September 14, p. BU8.

Oliner, A. J. (2000). "The Cognitive Roots of Stereotyping." *Massachusetts Institute of Technology*, October 19. (http://adam.oliner.net/comp/stereotyping.html#use).

One Equal World. (2015). "Anne Hathaway." *OneEqual World.com.* (http://www.oneequalworld.com/profiles/anne-hathaway/).

Samovar, L. A., R. E. Porter, E. R. McDaniel, and C. S. Roy. (2013). *Communication between Cultures*. Boston: Cengage.

Stephan, W. (1999). *Reducing Prejudice and Stereotyping in Schools*. New York: Teachers College Press.

Stratton, R. (2012). "How to Improve Intercultural Communication in the Workplace." *Extreme Business.com*, February 5. (http://extremebusiness.com.au/how-to-impove-intercultural-communication-in-the-workplace).

Tajfel, H., and J. C. Turner. (1979). "An Intergrative Theory of Intergroup Conflict." In W. G. Austin and S. Worchel, eds., *The Social Psychology of Intergroup Relations*. Monterey, CA: Brooks/Cole.

Ting-Toomey, S. (1999). *Communicating across Cultures*. New York: The Guilford Press.

Ting-Toomey, S. (2005). "Identity Negotiation Theory: Crossing Cultural Boundaries." In W. B. Gudykunst, ed., *Theorizing about Intercultural Communication*. Thousand Oaks, CA: Sage.

Toobin, J. (2013). "Rights and Wrongs." *New Yorker*, May 27, pp. 36–43.

US Holocaust Memorial Museum. (2012). "Martin Niemoller: First They Came for the Socialists . . ." *USHMM.org*, May 11. (http://www.ushmm.org/wlc/en/article.php?ModuleId=100073920).

Wazwaz, N. (2015). "It's Official: The U.S. is Becoming a Minority-Majority Nation." *U.S. News and World Report*, July 6. (http://www.usnews.com/news/articles/2015/07/06/its-official-the-us-is-becoming-a-minority-majority-nation).

Wong, E. (2013). "A Chinese Virtue Is Now the Law." *New York Times*, July 3, p. A4.

Chapter 10

ADT Research. (2015). "Top 20 Stories of 2014." *The Tyndall Report*, January. (http://tyndallreport.com/library/YearinReview2014.pdf).

Bandura, A. (1965). "Influence of Models' Reinforcement Contingencies on the Acquisition of Imitative Responses." *Journal of Personality and Social Psychology, 1*: 589–595.

Bannon, D. (2012). State of the Social Media Report 2012. *Nielsen.com.* (http://blog.nielsen.com/nielsenwire/social/2012/).

Baran, S. J., and D. K. Davis. (2015). *Mass Communication Theory: Foundations, Ferment, and Future*. Boston: Cengage.

Bart, P. (2014). "Anti-Amazon Rebels Remind Us Bigger Isn't Always Better." *Variety*, August 19, p. 28.

Bureau of Labor Statistics. (2013). "Media and Information." *U.S. Government*, January. (http://www.bls.gov/spotlight/2013/media/).

Carr, D. (2012). "Train Wreck: The *New York Post's* Subway Cover." *New York Times*, December 5. (http://mediadecoder.blogs.nytimes.com/2012/12/05/train-wreck-the-new-york-posts-subway-cover/).

Carr, D. (2013). "Shunning the Safe, FX Indulges Its Dark Side." *New York Times*, February 4, p. B1.

Chozick, A., and C. Rohwedder. (2011). "The Ultimate Reality Show." *Wall Street Journal*, March 18. (http://online.wsj.com/article/SB10001424052748703899704576204443433487336.html).

Clayton, R. B., G. Leshner, and A. Almond. (2015). "The Extended iSelf: The Impact of iPhone Separation on Cognition, Emotion, and Physiology." *Journal of Computer-Mediated Communication, 20*: 119–135.

Downey, K. (2015). "Product Placement V2.0 is Hot Brand Strategy." *TV News Check*, January 21. (http://

www.tvnewscheck.com/article/82404/product-placement-v20-is-hot-brand-strategy).

eMarketer. (2014). "Mobile Continues to Steal Share of US Adults' Daily Time Spent with Media." *eMarketer.com*, April 22. (http://www.emarketer.com/Article/Mobile-Continues-Steal-Share-of-US-Adults-Daily-Time-Spent-with-Media/1010782).

Foehr, U. G. (2006). "Media Multitasking among American Youth: Prevalence, Predictors, and Pairings." *Kaiser Family Foundation*, December. (http://www.kff.org/entmedia/upload/7592.pdf).

Frater, P. (2014). "Asia's Television Hub." *Variety*, December 15.

Gerbner, G. (2010). "The Mean World Syndrome—Media as Storytellers (Extra Feature)." *Media Education Foundation*, February 18. (http://www.youtube.com/watch?v=ylhqasb1chI).

Gerbner, G., L. Gross, M. Jackson-Beeck, S. Jeffries-Fox, and N. Signorielli. (1978). "Cultural Indicators: Violence Profile No. 9." *Journal of Communication*, 28: 176–206.

Gilmor, D. (2004). *We the Media—Grassroots Journalism by the People, for the People*. Sebastopol, CA: O'Reilly.

Goodman, M. A. (2013). "How the Iraq War Was Sold." *Truthout*, February 9. (http://www.truth-out.org/news/item/14443-how-the-iraq-war-was-sold).

Hofs, M. (2012). "'Friends' Helps Global Television Audience Learn English." *Kaplan International*, December 3. (http://kaplaninternational.com/blog/friends-helps-learn-english-40/).

Jackson, J. (2013). "13th Annual Fear and Favor Review." *Extra!*, February, pp. 9–11.

Johnson, B. (2012). "Internet-Media Employment Fuels Digital Job Growth." *Advertising Age*, September 30. (http://adage.com/archive-date?pub=35&vol=83).

Johnson, C. A. (2009). "Cutting Through Advertising Clutter." *CBS News*, February 11. (http://www.cbsnews.com/8301–3445_162–2015684.html).

Johnson, J. (2010). "Fighting a Social Media Addiction." *Washington Post*, April. (http://voices.washingtonpost.com/campus-overload/2010/04/fighting_a_social_media_addict.html).

Lunden, I. (2012). "Analyst: Twitter Passed 500M Users in June 2012, 140M of Them in US; Jakarta 'Biggest Tweeting' City." *TechCrunch*, July 30. (http://techcrunch.com/2012/07/30/analyst-twitter-passed-500m-users-in-june-2012–140m-of-them-in-us-jakarta-biggest-tweeting-city/).

McCarthy, J. (2014). "Trust in Mass Media Returns to All-Time Low." *Gallup*, September 17. (http://www.gallup.com/poll/176042/trust-mass-media-returns-time-low.aspx).

McChesney, R. W. (1997). *Corporate Media and the Threat to Democracy*. New York: Seven Stories Press.

McQuail, D. (1987). *Mass Communication Theory: An Introduction*, 2nd ed. Beverly Hills, CA: Sage.

Meirick, P. C., J. D. Simms, E. S. Gilchrist, and S. M. Croucher. (2009). "All the Children Are above Average: Parents' Perceptions of Education and Materialism as Media Effects on Their Own and Other Children." *Mass Communication and Society*, 12: 217–237.

Mitchell, G. (2009). "Watchdogs Failed to Bark on Economy." *Editor and Publisher*, April, p. 16.

Moeller, S. D. (2010). "24 Hours: Unplugged." *International Center for Media and the Public Agenda*, April. (http://withoutmedia.wordpress.com/).

Poindexter, P. (2012). *Millennials, News, and Social Media: Is News Engagement a Thing of the Past?* New York: Peter Lang.

Pomerantsev, P. (2013). "Liberate the Language!" *London Review of Books*, January 29. (http://www.lrb.co.uk/blog/2013/01/29/peter-pomerantsev/liberate-the-language/).

Potter, W. J. (2012). *Media Effects*. Los Angeles: Sage.

PQ Media. (2015). "PQ Media: Double-Digit Surge in Product Placement Spend in 2014 Fuels Higher Global Branded Entertainment Growth as Media Integrations & Consumer Events Combo for $73.3B." *PR Web*, March 13. (http://www.prweb.com/releases/2015/02/prweb12487911.htm).

Ricchiardi, S. (1999). "Confronting the Horror." *American Journalism Review*, January/February. (http://www.ajr.org/article.asp?id=825).

Richtel, M. (2010). "Digital Devices Deprive Brain of Needed Downtime." *New York Times*, August 25, p. B1.

Schudson, M. (2011). *The Sociology of News*. New York: Norton.

Sedghi, A. (2014). "Beyond the UK and US: What Films Are Top of the Box Office for the Rest of the World?" *Guardian*, November 25. (http://www.theguardian.com/news/datablog/2014/nov/25/beyond-the-uk-and-us-what-films-is-the-rest-of-the-world-watching).

Smith, C. (2015). "By the Numbers: 60 Amazing YouTube Statistics." *Expandedramblings.com*, January 2. (http://expandedramblings.com/index.php/youtube-statistics/).

Texting and Driving Safety. (2015). "Because Texting and Driving Kills." *TextingandDrivingSafety.com*. (http://www.textinganddrivingsafety.com/texting-and-driving-stats/).

Tillinghast, C. H. (2000). *American Broadcast Regulation and the First Amendment: Another Look*. Ames: Iowa State University Press.

U.S. Ad Industry Employment. (2013). *Advertising Age Marketing Fact Pack 2014*, December 30, p. 34.

Walsh, M. (2012). "Mobile to Become Top Email Platform." *MediaPost*, May 1. (http://www.mediapost.com/publications/article/173702/mobile-to-become-top-email-platform.html#axzz2H2uFXa1S).

Chapter 11

Anderson, C. A., A. Shibuya, N. Ihori, E. L. Swing, B. J. Bushman, A. Sakamoto, H. R. Rothstein, and M. Saleem. (2010). "Violent Video Game Effects on Aggression, Empathy, and Prosocial Behavior in Eastern and Western Countries: A Meta-Analytic Review." *Psychological Review,* 136: 151–173.

Baran, S. J. (2014). *Introduction to Mass Communication: Media Literacy and Culture.* New York: McGraw-Hill.

Buijzen, M., and P. M. Valkenburg. (2005). "Parental Mediation of Undesired Advertising Effects." *Journal of Broadcasting and Electronic Media,* 49: 153–165.

Bushman, B. J., and J. Cantor. "Media Ratings for Violence and Sex: Implications for Policymakers and Parents." *American Psychologist,* 58: 130–141.

Campaign for a Commercial-Free Childhood. (2015). "Marketing to Children Overview." *Commercialfreechildhood.org.* (http://www.commercialfreechildhood.org/resource/marketing-children-overview).

Christ, W. G. (2006). *Assessing Media Education: A Resource Handbook for Educators and Administrators.* Mahwah, NJ: Erlbaum.

Clark, L. S. (2011). "Parental Mediation Theory for the Digital Age." *Communication Theory,* 21: 323–343.

Coughlin, J. W., and C. Kalodner. (2006). "Media Literacy as a Prevention Intervention for College Women at Low- or High-Risk For Eating Disorders." *Body Image,* 3: 35–43.

Dell'Antonia, K. J. (2010). "Preschoolers Know All about Brands." *Slate,* April 3. (http://www.slate.com/articles/double_x/doublex/2010/04/preschoolers_know_all_about_brands.2.html).

Duggan, M. (2013). "Photo and Video Sharing Grow Online." *Pew Internet and American Life Project,* October 28. (http://pewinternet.org/Reports/2013/Photos-and-videos.aspx).

eMarketer. (2014). "Mobile Continues to Steal Share of US Adults' Daily Time Spent with Media." *eMarketer.com,* April 22. (http://www.emarketer.com/Article/Mobile-Continues-Steal-Share-of-US-Adults-Daily-Time-Spent-with-Media/1010782).

Farsides, T., D. Pettman, and L. Tourle. (2013). "Inspiring Altruism: Reflecting on the Personal Relevance of Emotionally Evocative Prosocial Media Characters." *Journal of Applied Social Psychology,* 43: 2251–2258.

Grossman, D. (2009). *On Killing: The Psychological Cost of Learning to Kill in War and Society.* New York: Back Bay Books.

Hall, S. (1980). "Encoding and Decoding in the Television Discourse." In S. Hall, ed., *Culture, Media, Language.* London: Hutchinson.

Jeong, S., H. Cho, and Y. Hwang. (2012). "Media Literacy Interventions: A Meta-Analytic Review." *Journal of Communication,* 62: 454–472.

Kunkel, D., B. L. Wilcox, J. Cantor, E. Palmer, S. Linn, and P. Dominick. (2004). *Report of the APA Task Force on Advertising and Children.* Washington, DC: American Psychological Association.

Masterman, L. (2013). "Foreword: The Media Education Revolution." In A. Hart, ed., *Teaching the Media.* New York: Routledge.

McCarthy, J. (2014). "Trust in Mass Media Returns to All-Time Low." *Gallup,* September 17. (http://www.gallup.com/poll/176042/trust-mass-media-returns-time-low.aspx).

McClure, A. C. (2012). "Familiarity with Television Fast-Food Ads Linked to Obesity." *American Academy of Pediatrics,* April 29. (http://www.aap.org/en-us/about-the-aap/aap-press-room/pages/Familiarity-With-Television-Fast-Food-Ads-Linked-to-Obesity.aspx?nfstatus=401&nftoken=00000000-0000-0000-0000-000000000000&nfstatusdescription=ERROR%3a+No+local+token).

Mead, C. (2013). *War Play: Video Games and the Future of Armed Conflict.* New York: Houghton Mifflin Harcourt.

National Association for Media Literacy Education. (2007a). *Core Principles of Media Literacy Education in the United States.* (http://namle.net/publications/core-principles/).

National Association for Media Literacy Education. (2007b). *Key Questions to Ask When Analyzing Media Messages.* (http://namle.net/publications/core-principles/).

Pai, S., and K. Schryver. (2015). "Children, Teens, Media, and Body Image." *Common Sense Media.* (https://www.commonsensemedia.org/research/children-teens-media-and-body-image).

Potter, W. J. (2010). "The State of Media Literacy." *Journal of Broadcasting and Electronic Media,* 54: 675–696.

Purcell, K., L. Rainie, A. Mitchell, T. Rosensteil, and K. Olmstead. (2010). "Understanding the Participatory News Consumer." *Pew Internet and American Life Project.* (http://pewinternet.org/Reports/2010/Online-News.aspx).

Reichert, T., M. S. LaTour, J. J. Lambiase, and M. Adkins. (2007). "A Test of Media Literacy Effects and Sexual Objectification in Advertising." *Journal of Current Issues and Research in Advertising,* 29: 81–92.

Silverblatt, A. (2008). *Media Literacy: Keys to Interpreting Media Messages.* Westport, CT: Praeger.

Silverblatt, A. (2010). "Careers in Media Literacy." *GMLP Blogging Community,* March 11. (http://www.gmlpstl.org/careers-in-media-literacy-2010/2010/).

Steinberg, S. R. (2011) *Kinderculture: The Corporate Construction of Childhood.* Boulder, CO: Westview Press.

Taylor, P., and S. Keeter. (2010). *Millennials: Confident. Connected. Open to Change. Pew Research Center,* February. (www.pewresearch.org/millennials).

Vandenbosch, L., and S. Eggermont. (2012). "Understanding Sexual Objectification: A Comprehensive Approach toward Media Exposure and Girls' Internalization of Beauty Ideals, Self-Objectification, and Body Surveillance." *Journal of Communication, 62:* 869–887.

Chapter 12

Alang, N. (2012). "Being and Not Being Here and There." *Random House.com,* September 5. (http://www .randomhouse.ca/hazlitt/feature/being-and-not-being-here-and-there).

Allen, D. (2014). "How Many Times a Day Does the Average Person Check Their Phone? 221, Apparently." *BetaNews.com,* October 10. (http://betanews.com/ 2014/10/10/how-many-times-a-day-does-the-average-person-check-their-phone-221-apparently/).

Anatole, E. (2013). "From Social Causes to Social Change." *MediaPost,* January 11. (http://www.mediapost.com/ publications/article/190856/from-social-causes-to-social-change.html#axzz2IFrnodVs).

Back, M. D., J. M. Stopfer, S. Vazire, S. Gaddis, S. C. Schmukle, B. Egloff, and S. D. Gosling. (2010). "Facebook Profiles Reflect Actual Personality, Not Self-Idealization." *Psychological Science,* 21: 372–374.

Baker, L. R., and D. L. Oswald. (2010). "Shyness and Online Social Networking Services." *Journal of Social and Personal Relationships,* 27: 873–889.

Bennett, J. (2013). "Social Media Can't Replace Email." *Social Media Today,* February 11. (http://socialmediatoday .com/jonathan-bennett/1234041/why-social-media-will-never-replace-email).

Bennett, S. (2015). "28% of Time Spent Online Is Social Networking." *Ad Week,* January 27. (http://www .adweek.com/socialtimes/time-spent-online/613474).

Berger, C. R. (2005). "Interpersonal Communication: Theoretical Perspectives, Future Prospects." *Journal of Communication,* 55: 415–447.

Brandtzæg, P. B. (2012). "Social Networking Sites: Their Users and Social Implications—A Longitudinal Study." *Journal of Computer-Mediated Communication,* 17: 467–488.

Cacioppo, J. T., and W. Patrick. (2008). *Loneliness: Human Nature and the Need for Social Connection.* New York: W. W. Norton.

Carlson, N., and K. Angelova. (2010). "Chart of the Day: Email's Reign Is Over, Social Networking Is the New King." *Business Insider,* April 14. (http://www.businessinsider .com/chart-of-the-day-social-networking-vs-email-usage-2010-4).

Carr, N. (2010). "Other People's Privacy." *Rough Type,* January 17. (http://www.roughtype.com/archives/ 2010/01/other_peoples_p.php).

Center for Collegiate Mental Health. (2015). *2014 Annual Report.* (http://ccmh.psu.edu/wp-content/uploads/sites/ 3058/2015/02/2014_CCMH_Annual_Report.pdf).

Conway, J (2012). "National Survey Reveals Consumers Are Overwhelmed by Social Media." *Business Wire,* August 1. (http://www.businesswire.com/news/home/ 20120801005524/en/National-Survey-Reveals-Consumers-Overwhelmed-Social-Media).

Cramton, C. D. (2001). "The Mutual Knowledge Problem and Its Consequences for Dispersed Collaboration." *Organizational Science,* 12: 346–371.

Daft, R. L., and R. H. Lengel. (1986). "Organizational Information Requirements: Media Richness and Structural Design." *Management Science,* 32: 554–571.

Davis, R. E. (1976). *Response to Innovation: A Study of Popular Argument about New Mass Media.* New York: Arno.

Dokoupil, T. (2012). "Is the Web Driving Us Mad?" *Daily Beast,* July 9. (http://www.thedailybeast.com/newsweek/ 2012/07/08/is-the-internet-making-us-crazy-what-the-new-research-says.html).

Goel, V. (2013). "Facebook Reasserts Posts Can Be Used for Ads." *New York Times,* November 16, p. B1.

Gonzales, A. L., and J. T. Hancock. (2011). "Mirror, Mirror on My Facebook Wall: Effects of Exposure to Facebook on Self-Esteem." *Cyberpsychology, Behavior, and Social Networking,* 14: 79–83.

Grasz, J. (2014). "Number of Employers Passing on Applicants Due to Social Media Posts Continues to Rise, According to New CareerBuilder Survey." CareerBuilder.com, June 26. (http://www.careerbuilder .com/share/aboutus/pressreleasesdetail.aspx?sd=6% 2F26%2F2014&id=pr829&ed=12%2F31%2F2014).

Hampton, K. N., L. F. Sessions, and E. J. Her. (2010). "Core Networks, Social Isolation, and New Media: How Internet and Mobile Phone Use Is Related to Network Size and Diversity." *Information, Communication and Society,* 14: 130–155.

Hill, A. (2012). "Anti-Social Media: Why Do People Lose Their Cool Online?" *Providence Journal,* October 9, p. D5.

Hundley, H. L., and L. Leonard. (2010). "US Teenagers' Perceptions and Awareness of Digital Technology: A Focus Group Approach." *New Media Society,* 12: 417–433.

"Internet Users in the World." (2015). *Internet World Statistics,* June 30. (http://www.internetworldstats.com/ stats.htm).

Joyce, S. P. (2014). "What 80% of Employers Do Before Inviting You for an Interview." *Huffington Post,* March 1. (http://www.huffingtonpost.com/susan-p-joyce/job-search-tips_b_4834361.html).

Kalman, Y. M., and S. Rafaeli. (2011). "Online Pauses and Silence: Chronemic Expectancy Violations in Written Computer-Mediated Communication." *Communication Research,* 38: 54–69.

Katikalapudi, R., S. Chellappan, F. Montgomery, D. Wunsch, and K. Lutzen. (2012). "Associating Internet Usage with Depressive Behavior among College Students." *Technology and Society Magazine,* 31: 73–80.

Kiesler, K. W., J. Siegel, and T. W. McGuire. (1984). "Social Psychological Aspects of Computer-Mediated Communication." *American Psychologist,* 39: 1123–1134.

Krasnova, H., H. Wenninger, T. Widjaja, and P. Buxmann. (2013). "Envy on Facebook: A Hidden Threat to Users' Life Satisfaction?" Paper presented to the 11th International Conference on Wirtschaftsinformatik, Leipzig, Germany, March.

Krauss, R., and Fussell, S. (1990). "Mutual Knowledge and Communicative Effectiveness." In K. Galegher, R. Kraut, and C. Egido, eds., *Intellectual Teamwork: Social and Technological Foundations of Cooperative Work.* Hillsdale, NJ: Erlbaum.

Kross, E., P. Verduyn, E. Demiralp, J. Park, D. S. Lee, et al. (2013). "Facebook Use Predicts Declines in Subjective Well-Being in Young Adults." *PLoS ONE,* 8: e69841. doi:10.1371/journal.pone.0069841.

Kruger, J., N. Epley, J. Parker, and Z. W. Ng. (2005). "Egocentrism over E-Mail: Can We Communicate as Well as We Think?" *Journal of Personality and Social Psychology,* 89: 925–936.

Lea, M., and R. Spears. (1992). "Paralanguage and Social Perception in Computer-Mediated Communication." *Journal of Organizational Computing,* 2: 321–341.

Lin, F., Y. Zhou, Y. Du, L. Qin, Z. Zhao, J. Xu, and H. Lei. (2012) "Abnormal White Matter Integrity in Adolescents with Internet Addiction Disorder: A Tract-Based Spatial Statistics Study." *PLoS ONE,* 7: e30253.doi: 10.1371/journal.pone.0030253.

Lunden, I. (2012). "First Look: Survey Warns of Consumers Turning Off from Digital Ads." *TechCrunch,* February 24. (http://techcrunch.com/2012/02/24/first-look-survey-warns-of-consumers-turning-off -from-digital-ads/).

Lunden, I. (2015). "80% Of All Online Adults Now Own a Smartphone, Less Than 10% Use Wearables." *Tech Crunch,* January 12. (http://techcrunch.com/2015/01/12/80-of-all-online-adults-now-own-a-smartphone-less-than-10-use-wearables/).

Madden, M. (2010). "Older Adults and Social Media." *Pew Internet and American Life Project,* August 27. (http://pewinternet.org/Reports/2010/Older-Adults-and-Social-Media.aspx).

Madden, M. (2012). "Privacy Management on Social Media Sites." *Pew Internet and American Life Project,* February 24. (http://pewinternet.org/Reports/2012/Privacy-management-on-social-media-aspx).

Marche, S. (2012). "Is Facebook Making Us Lonely?" *Atlantic,* May. (http://www.theatlantic.com/magazine/archive/2012/05/is-facebook-making-us-lonely/308930/).

Martin, C. (2015). "235 Billion App Downloads this year; 99% not paid." *MediaPost,* February 25. (http://www.mediapost.com/publications/article/244470/235-billion-app-downloads-this-year-99-not-paid.html).

McKinney, B. C., L. Kelly, and R. L. Duran. (2012). "Narcissism or Openness?: College Students' Use of Facebook and Twitter." *Communication Research Reports,* 29: 108–118.

McLuhan, M. (1962). *The Gutenberg Galaxy: The Making of Typographic Man.* Toronto: University of Toronto Press.

Mickes, L., R. S. Darby, V. Hwe, D. Bajic, J. A. Warker, C. R. Harris, and N. J. S. Christenfeld. (2013). "Major Memory for Microblogs." *Memory and Cognition,* January. (http://link.springer.com/article/10.3758%2Fs13421–012–0281–6#page-1).

Nadkarni, A., and S. G. Hofmann. (2012). "Why Do People Use Facebook?" *Personality and Individual Differences,* 52: 243–249.

02. (2012). "Making Calls Has Become Fifth Most Frequent Use for a Smartphone for Newly-Networked Generation of Users." *All About You,* June 29. (http://news.02.co.uk/?press-release=making-calls-has-become-fifth-most-frequent-use-for-a-smartphone-for-newly-networked-generation-of-users).

O'Keeffe, G. S., and K. Clarke-Pearson. (2011). "Clinical Report: The Impact of Social Media on Children, Adolescents, and Families." *Pediatrics,* 127: 800–804.

Ong, W. J. (2002). *Orality and Literacy: The Technologizing of the Word.* New York: Routledge.

Palmieri, C., K. Prestano, R. Gandley, E. Overton, and Q. Zhang. (2012). "Facebook: Online Self-Disclosure and Uncertainty Reduction." *China Media Research,* 8: 48–53.

Parker-Pope, T. (2010). "An Ugly Toll of Technology: Impatience and Forgetfulness." *New York Times,* June 7, p. A13.

Peterson, T. (2014). "Consumers Becoming Less Trusting of Google, Warier of Facebook, Twitter." *Advertising Age,* January 9. (http://adage.com/article/consumer-electronics-show/consumers-trusting-google-warier-facebook-twitter/290992/).

Pinsky, R. (2010). "Start the Presses." *New York Times Book Review,* August 15, p. 15.

Purcell, K., and L. Rainie. (2014). "Technology's Impact on Workers." *Pew Research Center,* December 30. (http://www.pewinternet.org/2014/12/30/technologys-impact-on-workers/).

Rainie, L., A. Smith, and M. Duggan. (2013). "Coming and Going on Facebook." *Pew Internet and American Life Project,* February 5. (http://pewinternet.org/Reports/2013/Coming-and-going-on-facebook.aspx).

Richtel, M. (2010a). "Digital Devices Deprive Brain of Needed Downtime." *New York Times,* August 25, p. B1.

Richtel, M. (2010b). "Attached to Technology and Paying a Price." *New York Times,* June 7, p. A1.

Rideout, V. (2012). "Social Media, Social Life: How Teens View Their Digital Lives." *Common Sense Media,*

Summer. (http://www.commonsensemedia.org/sites/default/files/research/socialmediasociallife-final-061812.pdf).

Rogers, T. (2011). "Our Kids' Glorious New Age of Distraction." *Salon*, August 21. (http://www.salon.com/2011/08/21/now_you_see_it_interview/).

Roggensack, M. (2010). "Face It Facebook, You Just Don't Get It." *Human Rights First*, May 25. (http://www.humanrightsfirst.org/2010/05/25/face-it-facebook-you-just-dont-get-it/).

Sabev, O. (2009). "Rich Men, Poor Men: Ottoman Printers and Booksellers Making Fortune or Seeking Survival (Eighteenth-Nineteenth Centuries)." *Oriens*, 37: 177–190.

Shannon, V. (2012). "Social Networking and Ethics." *The Stanford Encyclopedia of Philosophy*, Winter. (http://plato.stanford.edu/archives/win2012/entries/ethics-social-networking/).

Sheer, V. C. (2011). "Teenagers' Use of MSN Features, Discussion Topics, and Online Friendship Development: The Impact of Media Richness and Communication Control." *Communication Quarterly*, 59: 82–103.

Shore, J. (2012). "Social Media Distractions Cost U.S. Economy $650 Billion." *Mashable.com*, November 2. (http://mashable.com/2012/11/02/social-media-work-productivity/).

Small, G. W., T. D. Moody, P. Siddarth, and S. Y. Bookheimer. (2009). "Your Brain on Google: Patterns of Cerebral Activation during Internet Searching." *The American Journal of Geriatric Psychiatry*, 17: 116–127.

Smith, A. (2014). "6 New Facts about Facebook." *Pew Research Center*, February 4. (http://www.pewresearch.org/fact-tank/2014/02/03/6-new-facts-about-facebook/).

Smith, C. (2015). "By the Numbers: 200+ Amazing Facebook User Statistics." *Digital Marketing Ramblings*, January 22. (http://expandedramblings.com/index.php/by-the-numbers-17-amazing-facebook-stats/).

Smith, S. (2012). "Instagram to Users: You're All Unpaid (But Cherished) Interns Now." *MediaPost*, December 19. (http://www.mediapost.com/publications/article/189660/instagram-to-users-youre-all-unpaid-but-cherish.html#axzz2IFrnodVs).

Timberg, C. (2013). "Mobile Device Connections Growing Quickly." *Washington Post*, February 25. (http://www.washingtonpost.com/business/technology/mobile-device-connections-growing-quickly/2013/02/25/ca98ea98-7f51-11e2-a350-49866afab584_story.html?wpisrc=nl_tech).

Turkle, S. (2012). "Sherry Turkle: Connected, But Alone?" *TED*, April. (http://www.ted.com/talks/sherry_urkle_alone_together.html).

"Twitter Usage Statistics." (2015). *Internet Live Stats*. (http://www.internetlivestats.com/twitter-statistics/).

Tyler, J. R., and J. C. Tang. (2003). "When Can I Expect an Email Response? A Study of Rhythms in Email Usage." Paper presented at the ECSCW 2003, September, Helsinki, Finland.

Vanderbilt, T. (2012). "The Call of the Future." *Wilson Quarterly*, Spring: 52–56.

Walsh, M. (2012). "Mobile to Become Top Email Platform." *MediaPost*, May 1. (http://www.mediapost.com/publications/article/173702/mobile-to-become-top-email-platform.html#axzz2H2uFXa1S).

Walther, J. B. (1996). "Computer-Mediated Communication: Impersonal, Interpersonal, and Hyperpersonal Interaction." *Communication Research*, 23: 3–43.

Walther, J. B., and L. C. Tidwell. (1995). "Nonverbal Cues in Computer-Mediated Communication, and the Effect of Chronemics on Relational Communication." *Journal of Organizational Computing*, 5: 355–378.

Wang, Y. (2013). "More People Have Cell Phones Than Toilets, U.N. Study Shows." *Time*, March 25. (http://newsfeed.time.com/2013/03/25/more-people-have-cell-phones-than-toilets-u-n-study-shows/).

Wegner, D. M. (2012). "Don't Fear the Cybermind." *New York Times*, August 5, p. SR6.

Weisman, J. (2015). "F.C.C. Net Neutrality Rules Clear Hurdle as Republicans Concede to Obama." *New York Times*, February 24, p. A1.

Young, K. S. (2004). "Internet Addiction: A New Clinical Phenomenon and Its Consequences." *American Behavioral Scientist*, 48: 402–415.

Zhao, S., S. Grasmuck, and J. Martin. (2008). "Identity Construction on Facebook: Digital Empowerment in Anchored Relationships." *Computers in Human Behavior*, 24: 1816–1836.

Zywica, J., and J. Danowski. (2008). "The Faces of Facebookers: Investigating Social Enhancement and Social Compensation Hypotheses; Predicting Facebook and Offline Popularity From Sociability, Self-Esteem, and Extroversion/Introversion; and Mapping the Meanings of Popularity With Semantic Networks." *Journal of Computer Mediated Communication*, 14: 1–34.

Chapter 13

Allen, M. (1991). "Meta-analysis Comparing Persuasiveness of Message Sidedness: A Prudent Note about Utilizing Research Summaries." *Western Journal of Speech Communication*, 57: 390–404.

Allport, G. W., and L. J. Postman. (1945). "The Basic Psychology of Rumor." *Transactions of the New York Academy of Sciences*, 8: 61–81.

American Civil Liberties Union. (2013). "The Journalists Guide to Criminal Justice Reform 2013." *Columbia Journalism Review*, March/April: Insert.

Andersen, K. E. (1978). *Persuasion: Theory and Practice.* Boston: Allyn & Bacon.

Associated Press v. United States. (1945). *US Supreme Court Decision*, 326, U.S. 1.

Austin, J. L. (1962). *How to Do Things with Words.* Cambridge, MA: Harvard University Press.

Baker, S., and D. L. Martinson. (2001). "The TARES Test: Five Principles for Ethical Persuasion." *Journal of Mass Media Ethics*, 16: 148–175.

Chaiken, S. (1986). "Physical Appearance and Social Influence." In C. P. Herman et al., eds., *Physical Appearance, Stigma, and Social Behavior: The Ontario Symposium.* Hillsdale, NJ: Erlbaum.

Common Sense for Drug Policy. (2014). "Race and Prison." *DrugWarFacts.org.* (http://www.drugwarfacts.org/cms/Race_and_Prison#sthash.WRkTtM10.dpbs).

Conger, J. A. (1998). "The Necessary Art of Persuasion." *Harvard Business Review*, May. (http://hbr.org/1998/05/the-necessary-art-of-persuasion/ar/1).

Eagly, A. H. (1978). "Sex Differences in Influenceability." *Psychological Bulletin*, 85: 86–116.

Elias, T., S. Malden, and T. Deas. (2009). "Viral Marketing: Industry Insiders' Insight on the Impact of Diffusion, Variation, and Selective Retention." International Communication Association Annual Convention, May.

Fagothey, A. (1976). *Right and Reason: Ethics in Theory and Practice.* St. Louis, MO: Mosby.

Festinger, L. (1957). *A Theory of Cognitive Dissonance.* Stanford, CA: Stanford University Press.

Festinger, L. (1962). "Cognitive Dissonance." *Scientific American*, 207: 93.

Festinger, L., and J. M. Carlsmith. (1959). "Cognitive Consequences of Forced Compliance." *Journal of Abnormal and Social Psychology*, 58: 203–210.

Goldstein, L. (2013). "Why the FTC's Recent Ruling against POM Matters to You." *Advertising Age*, March 11: 24.

Hastorf, A. H., and H. Cantril. (1954). "They Saw a Game: A Case Study." *Journal of Abnormal and Social Psychology*, 49: 129–134.

Heider, F. "Attitudes and Cognitive Organization." *Journal of Psychology*, 21: 107–112.

Hovland, C. I., I. L. Janis, and H. H. Kelley. (1953). *Communication and Persuasion.* New Haven, CT: Yale University Press.

Howard, D. J., and R. A. Kerin. (2011). "The Effects of Name Similarity on Message Processing and Persuasion." *Journal of Experimental Social Psychology*, 47: 63–71.

Jaksa, J. A., and M. S. Pritchard. (1994). *Communication Ethics: Methods of Analysis.* Belmont, CA: Wadsworth.

Johnson, B. T., and A. H. Eagly. (1989). "Effects of Involvement on Persuasion: A Meta-Analysis." *Psychological Bulletin*, 106: 290–314.

Kelman, H. C. (1958). "Compliance, Identification, and Internalization: Three Processes of Attitude Change." *Journal of Conflict Resolution*, 2: 51–60.

Lamourex, D. (2014). "Advertising: How Many Marketing Messages Do We See in a Day?" *Fluid Drive Media*, June 2. (http://www.fluiddrivemedia.com/advertising/marketing-messages/).

Levin, K. D., D. R. Nichols, and B. T. Johnson. (2000). "Involvement and Persuasion: Attitude Functions for the Motivated Processor." In G. R. Maio and J. M. Olson, eds., *Why We Evaluate: Functions of Attitudes.* Mahwah, NJ: Erlbaum.

Lopez, G. (2015). "Black and White Americans use Drugs at Similar Rates. One Group is Punished More for It." *Vox.com*, March 17. (http://www.vox.com/2015/3/17/8227569/war-on-drugs-racism).

Maio, G. R., and J. M. Olson. (1998). "Values as Truisms: Evidence and Implications." *Journal of Personality and Social Psychology*, 74: 294–311.

McCroskey, J. C. (1966). "Scales for the Measurement of Ethos." *Speech Monographs*, 33: 65–72.

Miller, G. R. (1980). "On Being Persuaded: Some Basic Distinctions." In M. E. Roloff and G. R. Miller, eds., *Persuasion: New Directions in Theory and Research.* Beverly Hills, CA: Sage.

Miller, R. L., P. Brickman, and D. Bolen. (1975). "Attribution versus Persuasion as a Means for Modifying Behavior." *Journal of Personality and Social Psychology*, 3: 430–41.

O'Malley, G. (2013). "Nearly 4 Billion Minutes of Video Ads Streamed in February." *MediaPost*, March 15. (http://www.mediapost.com/publications/article/195903/nearly-4-billion-minutes-of-video-ads-streamed-in.html#axzz2Nu06zptn).

Patzer, G. L. (1983). "Source Credibility as a Function of Communicator Physical Attractiveness." *Journal of Business Research*, 11: 229–241.

Petty, R. E., and J. T. Cacioppo. (1986). "The Elaboration Likelihood Model of Persuasion." In L. Berkowitz, ed., *Advances in Experimental Social Psychology*, Volume 19. New York: Academic Press.

Potter, W. J. (2012). *Media Effects.* Los Angeles: Sage.

Reinard, J. C. (1988). "The Empirical Study of the Persuasive Effects of Evidence: The Status of Fifty Years of Research." *Human Communication Research*, 15: 3–59.

Rokeach, M. (1968). *Beliefs, Attitudes, and Values.* San Francisco, CA: Jossey-Bass.

Rosnow, R. L., and E. J. Robinson. (1967). *Experiments in Persuasion.* New York: Academic.

Simons, H. W., N. N. Berkowitz, and R. J. Moyer. (1970). "Similarity, Credibility, and Attitude Change: A Review and a Theory." *Psychological Bulletin*, 73: 1–16.

Stiff, J. B., and P. A. Mongeau. (2003). *Persuasive Communication.* New York: Guilford Press.

Surlin, S. H., and T. F. Gordon. (1976). "Selective Exposure and Retention of Political Advertising." *Journal of Advertising*, 5: 32–44.

Taylor, S. E. (1981). "The Interface of Cognitive and Social Psychology." In J. H. Harvey, ed., *Cognition, Social Behavior, and the Environment.* Hillsdale, NJ: Erlbaum.

Theodoridou, A., A. C. Rowe, I. S. Penton-Voak, and P. J. Rogers. (2009). "Oxytocin and Social Perception: Oxytocin Increases Perceived Facial Trustworthiness and Attractiveness." *Hormones and Behavior,* 56: 128–132.

Toulmin, S. (1964). *The Uses of Argument.* Cambridge: Cambridge University Press.

Witte, K., and M. Allen. (2000). "A Meta-analysis of Fear Appeals: Implications for Effective Public Health Campaigns." *Health Education and Behavior,* 27: 591–615.

Wyatt, E. (2014). "Weight-Loss Companies Charged with Fraud." *New York Times,* January 7, p. B1.

Chapter 14

Alexander, J. A., L. R. Hearld, J. N. Mittler, and J. Harvey. (2012). "Patient–Physician Role Relationships and Patient Activation among Individuals with Chronic Illness." *Health Services Research,* 47: 1201–1223.

Allen, M. (2013). "How Many Die from Medical Mistakes in U.S. Hospitals?" *ProPublica,* September 19. (http://www.propublica.org/article/how-many-die-from-medical-mistakes-in-us-hospitals).

American Academy of Family Physicians. (2009). *Definition of Family. Aafp.org.* (http://www.aafp.org/online/en/home/policy/policies/f/familydefinitionof.htm111k).

Becker, M. H. (1974). "The Health Belief Model and Personal Health Behavior." *Health Education Monographs,* 2: 324–508.

Bissell, K. L., and P. Zhou. (2004). "Must-See TV or ESPN: Entertainment and Sports Media Exposure and Body-Image Distortion in College Women." *Journal of Communication,* 54: 5–21.

Boyse, K. (2010). "Television and Children." *University of Michigan Health System,* August. (http://www.med.umich.edu/yourchild/topics/tv.htm).

Bruni, F. (2015). "The Vaccine Lunacy." *New York Times,* February 1, p. SR3.

Buchanan, L., H. Fairfield, and K. Yourish. (2014). "Rating a Health Law's Success." *New York Times,* May 19. (http://www.nytimes.com/interactive/2014/05/19/health/rating-a-health-laws-success.html?_r=0).

Bull S. S., D. K. Levine, S. R. Black, S. J. Schmiege, and J. Santelli. (2012). "Social Media-Delivered Sexual Health Intervention." *American Journal of Preventative Medicine,* 43: 467–474.

Cassil, A. (2003). "Physicians: So Much to Do, So Little Time." *Center for Studying Health System Change,* May 7. (http://www.hschange.com/CONTENT/558/).

Centers for Disease Control. (2011a). "Health Communication Basics." *CDC.gov,* May 10. (http://www.cdc.gov/healthcommunication/healthbasics/whatishc.html).

Centers for Disease Control. (2011b). "Communications." *CDC.gov,* May 2. (http://www.cdc.gov/workplace-healthpromotion/planning/communications.html).

Christakis, N. A., and J. H. Fowler. (2010). "Social Network Sensors for Early Detection of Contagious Outbreaks." *PLoS ONE,* 5: e12948. doi: 10.1371/journal.pone.0012948

Clark-Flory, T. (2012). "Facebook: The Next Tool in Fighting STDs." *Salon,* April 1. (http://www.salon.com/2012/04/01/facebook_the_next_tool_in_fighting_stds/).

Colditz, G. A., K. Y. Wolin, and S. Gehlert. (2012). "Applying What We Know to Accelerate Cancer Prevention." *Science Translational Medicine,* 4: March 28. (http://stm.sciencemag.org/content/4/127/127rv4.abstract?sid=5b6f43dd-be12–486b-b43b-410680a23b34).

Daily Briefing. (2013). "Inside Malpractice Lawsuits: Why So Many Doctors Don't See Them Coming." *Advisory.com,* July 31. (https://www.advisory.com/daily-briefing/2013/07/31/inside-malpractice-lawsuits-why-so-many-doctors-dont-see-them-coming).

Davies, K. (2015). "A Doc in Your Pocket." *American Way,* January, p. 48.

de Vries, E. N., M. A. Ramrattan, S. A. Morenburg, D. J. Gouma, and M. A. Boermeester. (2008). "The Incidence and Nature of In-Hospital Adverse Events: A Systematic Review." *Quality Safety Health Care,* 17: 216–23.

Dean, L., and J. Doty. (2014). "The Healing Power of Kindness." *Huffington Post,* November 16. (http://www.huffingtonpost.com/project-compassion-stanford/the-healing-power-of-kindness_b_6136272.html).

DeFontes, J., and M. W. Leonard. (2008). "Preoperative Safety Briefing Reduces Wrong-Site Surgery and Nursing Turnover, Enhances Safety Attitude." *Agency for Healthcare Research and Quality,* December 8. (http://www.innovations.ahrq.gov/content.aspx?id=1773).

duPré, A. (2005). *Communicating about Health: Current Issues and Perspectives.* New York: McGraw-Hill.

Enck, P., and W. Häuser. (2012). "Beware the Nocebo Effect." *New York Times,* August 12, p. SR4.

"Facts about Speak Up Initiatives." (2015). *The Joint Commission,* March 2. (http://www.jointcommission.org/facts_about_speak_up_initiatives/).

Fox, S., and Duggan, M. (2013). "Health Online 2013." *Pew Internet and American Life Project,* January 15. (http://pewinternet.org/Reports/2013/Health-online.aspx).

Freyer, F. J. (2012). "Practicing Better Bedside Manners." *Providence Journal,* August 10, pp. A1, A8.

Garland, R. (1984). "Images of Health and Medical Science Conveyed by Television." *Journal of the Royal College of General Practitioners,* 34: 316–319.

GfK. (2014). "How Much Does the Public Trust You?" *Advertising Age,* April 14: 29.

Greenberg, R. (2010). "4 Habits That Revolutionize a Doctor's Visit." *Huffington Post,* September 30. (http://www.huffingtonpost.com/riva-greenberg/4-habits-that-revolutioni_b_742104.html).

Grenard, J. L., C. W. Dent, and A. W. Stacy. (2013). "Exposure to Alcohol Advertisements and Teenage Alcohol-Related Problems." *Pediatrics,* 131: e369-e379.

Gunther, A. C., D. Bolt, D. L. G. Borzekowski, J. L. Liebhart, and J. P. Dillard. (2006). "Presumed Influence on Peer Norms: How Mass Media Indirectly Affect Adolescent Smoking." *Journal of Communication,* 56: 52–68.

Heussner, K. M. (2013). "Dr. Google Is As Popular as Ever—Can Real Doctors Adapt?" *GigaOM.com,* January 17. (http://gigaom.com/2013/01/16/dr-google-is-as-ever-can-real-doctors-adapt/).

Hoffman, J. (2012). "Communication Factors in Malpractice Cases." *CRICO,* March 15. (http://www.rmf.harvard.edu/Clinician-Resources/Article/2012/Insight-Communication-Factors-in-Mal-Cases#).

Institute for Patient- and Family-Centered Care. (2010). "Changing Hospital 'Visiting' Policies and Practices: Supporting Family Presence and Participation." *Ipfcc.org,* October. (http://www.ipfcc.org/visiting.pdf).

Institute of Medicine. (2002). *When Children Die: Improving Palliative and End-of-Life Care for Children and Their Families.* (http://www.iom.edu/Reports/2002/When-Children-Die-Improving-Palliative-and-End-of-Life-Care-for-Children-and-Their-Families.aspx).

Jacobs, T. (2012). "Facebook: Saving Lives, One Kidney at a Time." *Pacific Standard,* May 16. (http://www.psmag.com/health/facebook-saving-lives-one-kidney-at-a-time-42266/).

Kaufman, D. M., T. A. Laidlaw, and H. Macleod. (2000). "Communication Skills in Medical Schools: Exposure, Confidence, and Performance." *Academic Medicine,* 75: S90-S92.

Kimmelman, M. (2014). "In Redesigned Room, Hospital Patients May Feel Better Already." *New York Times,* August 22, p. A1.

Kokalitcheva, K. (2015). "Healthtap Teams with Quest Diagnostics to Let Its Virtual Doctors Order Lab Tests." *Fortune,* June 30. (http://fortune.com/2015/06/30/healthtap-teams-with-quest-diagnostics-to-let-its-virtual-doctors-order-lab-tests/).

Koren, D. (2015). "The Waiting Room Is Prime Time for Patient Engagement." *MediaPost,* February 27. (http://www.mediapost.com/publications/article/244571/the-waiting-room-is-prime-time-for-patient-engagem.html).

Krcmar, M., and K. Greene. (2000). "Connections between Violent Television Exposure and Adolescent Risk Taking." *Mediapsychology,* 2: 195–217.

Landro, L. (2003). "Doctor's Orders Are Useless if They're Befuddling.'" *Wall Street Journal,* July 3, p. D2.

Landro, L. (2006). "Hospitals Combat Errors at the 'Hand-Off.'" *Wall Street Journal,* June 28, p. D1.

Landro, L. (2007). "Doctors Learn to Say 'I'm Sorry'; Patients' Stories of Hospital Errors Serve to Teach Staff." *Wall Street Journal,* January 24, p. D5.

Landro, L. (2013). "Children's Hospitals Make Room for Mom, Dad and Diversions." *Wall Street Journal,* January 15, p. D1.

Mehrotra, A., S. Paone, G. D. Martich, S. M. Albert, and G. J. Shevchik. (2013). "A Comparison of Care at E-visits and Physician Office Visits for Sinusitis and Urinary Tract Infection." *JAMA Internal Medicine,* 173: 72–74.

Morgan, S. E., L. Movius, and M. J. Cody. (2009). "The Power of Narratives: The Effect of Entertainment Television Organ Donation Storylines on the Attitudes, Knowledge, and Behaviors of Donors and Nondonors." *Journal of Communication,* 59: 135–151.

Munro, D. (2015). "U.S. Healthcare Spending on Track to Hit $10,000 per Person This Year." *Forbes,* January 4. (http://www.forbes.com/sites/danmunro/2015/01/04/u-s-healthcare-spending-on-track-to-hit-10000-per-person-this-year/).

Murphy, S. T., L. B. Frank, M. B. Moran, and P. Patnoe-Woodley. (2011). "Involved, Transported, or Emotional? Exploring the Determinants of Change in Knowledge, Attitudes, and Behavior in Entertainment-Education." *Journal of Communication,* 61: 407–431.

National Patient Safety Foundation. (2015). *Ask Me 3.* (http://www.npsf.org/for-healthcare-professionals/programs/ask-me-3/).

Pho, K. (2012). "How Doctors Can Reduce Medical Errors, Lawsuits." *USA Today,* January 17. (http://usatoday30.usatoday.com/news/opinion/forum/story/2012-01-17/doctors-malpractice-errors/52621714/1).

Rimer, B., and Glanz, K. (2005). "Theory at a Glance: A Guide for Health Promotion Practice." *National Cancer Institute,* Spring. (http://www.cancer.gov/cancertopics/cancerlibrary/theory.pdf).

Rugani, L. (2013). "Americans Have Worse Health Than People in Other High-Income Countries; Health Disadvantage Is Pervasive across Age and Socio-Economic Groups." *National Academies.org,* January 9. (http://www8.nationalacademies.org/onpinews/newsitem.aspx?RecordID=13497).

Sartain, J. D. (2014). "Health Apps Ready to Collect Your Vital Signs, Wellness Data." *Cio.com,* July 15. (http://www.cio.com/article/2453704/health/health-apps-ready-to-collect-your-vital-signs-wellness-data.html).

"SBAR Technique for Communication: A Situational Briefing Model." (2011). *Institute for Health Improvement,* June 30. (http://www.ihi.org/knowledge/Pages/Tools/SBARTechniqueforCommunicationASituationalBriefingModel.aspx).

"Seeking Marcus Welby." (2004). *Wall Street Journal,* March 17, p. A17.

Simson, L. (2013). "Privacy Concerns Will Be Issue as Consumers Turn to Health-Care Technology." *Advertising Age,* January 14. (http://adage.com/article/guest-columnists/privacy-issue-consumers-embrace-health-technology/239102/).

Snyder, L. B. (2007). "Health Communication Campaigns and Their Impact on Behavior." *Journal of Nutrition Education and Behavior,* 39: S32-S40.

Sokol, Z. (2013). "The Gameification of Medicine: How Video Games Are Sharpening Surgical Skills." *Motherboard,* March 2. (http://motherboard.vice.com/blog/how-video-games-are-sharpening-surgical-skills).

Stromberg, J. (2012). "What Is the Nocebo Effect?" *Smithsonian,* July 23. (http://blogs.smithsonianmag.com/science/2012/07/what-is-the-nocebo-effect/).

"There's an App for That." (2014). *The Economist,* June 21, p. 76.

US Department of Health and Human Services. (2010). *Healthy People 2020.* Washington, DC. (http://www.healthypeople.gov/2020/TopicsObjectives2020/pdfs/HP2020_brochure_with_LHI_508.pdf).

Valentine, K. (2015). "Scott Walker Wants to Spend $250,000 to Study Health Impacts of Wind Turbines." *Think Progress.org,* February 6. (http://thinkprogress.org/climate/2015/02/06/3620223/scott-walker-wind-health/).

Van Uden-Kraan, C. F., C. Drossaert, E. Taal, W. M Smit, H. J. Bernelot Moens, and M. A. Vande Larr. (2011). "Determinants of Engagement in Face-to-Face and Online Patient Support Groups." *Journal of Medical Internet Research,* 13: e106.

Ventola, C. L. (2011). "Direct-to-Consumer Pharmaceutical Advertising: Therapeutic or Toxic? *Pharmacy and Therapeutics,* 36: 669–674, 681–684.

"VHA Is Transforming the Hospital Operating Room." (2005). *VHA.com,* November 16. (https://www.vha.com/AboutVHA/PressRoom/PressReleases/Archives/Pages/051116.html).

WomenHeart. (2012). "WomenHeart National Hospital Alliance." *WomenHeart: The National Coalition for Women with Heart Disease.* (http://c.ymcdn.com/sites/www.womenheart.org/resource/resmgr/docs/hha-brochure-6-12.pdf?hhSearchTerms=benefits+and+of+and+support+and+groups).

Wright, K. B., L. Sparks, and H. Dan O'Hair. (2008). *Health Communication in the 21st Century.* Malden, MA: Blackwell.

Chapter 15

Behnke, R. R., and C. R. Sawyer. (1999). "Public Speaking Procrastination as a Correlate of Public Speaking Communication and Self-Perceived Public Speaking Competence." *Communication Research Reports,* 16: 40–47.

Bianca, A. (2015). "The Importance of Public Speaking Skills within Organizations." *Demand Media,* July 31. (http://smallbusiness.chron.com/importance-public-speaking-skills-within-organizations-12075.html).

Bodie, G. D. (2010). "A Racing Heart, Rattling Knees, and Ruminative Thoughts: Defining, Explaining, and Treating Public Speaking Anxiety." *Communication Education,* 59: 70–105.

Day, A. (2011). *Satire + Dissent: Intervention in Contemporary Political Debate.* Bloomington: Indiana University Press.

Day, A. (2015). "Personal Correspondence." March 29.

Dwyer, K. K., and M. M. Davidson. (2012). "Is Public Speaking Really More Feared Than Death?" *Communication Research Reports,* 29: 99–107.

Ellis, K. (1995). "Apprehension, Self-Perceived Competency, and Teacher Immediacy in the Laboratory-Supported Public Speaking Course: Trends and Relationships." *Communication Education,* 44: 64–78.

Hume Center for Writing and Speaking. (2015). "Top 10 Ways to Conquer Your Fear of Public Speaking." *Stanford University.* (https://undergrad.stanford.edu/tutoring-support/hume-center/resources/speaking-resources).

Jay, M. (2010). *The Virtues of Mendacity: On Lying in Politics.* Charlottesville, VA: University of Virginia Press.

Kane, R. (2015). "Blurring the Lines." *Editor and Publisher,* January 19. (http://www.editorandpublisher.com/Features/Article/Blurring-the-Lines).

Kelley, M. (2014). "Study: Watching Fox News Makes You Less Informed Than Watching No News." *Slate,* January 30. (http://www.slate.com/blogs/business_insider/2014/01/30/does_watching_fox_news_make_you_less_informed.html).

Lucas, S. E. (2015). *The Art of Public Speaking.* New York: McGraw-Hill.

Manger, W., and R. McPhee. (2015). "Working Lives Revealed: What We Put Up With Over Our Years of Clocking In." *Daily Mirror,* April 14. (http://www.mirror.co.uk/incoming/working-lives-revealed-what-put-5515289).

McCroskey, J. C. (1970). "Measures of Communication-Bound Anxiety." *Speech Monographs,* 37: 269–277.

Meyer, C. (2013). "Effective Public Speaking in the Workplace." *Menlo Partners Staffing,* July 31. (http://mpstaff.com/2013/07/effective-public-speaking-in-the-workplace/).

Meyers, J. (2015). "The 10 Most Trusted Personalities in TV News. *Newsmax,* January 16. (http://www.newsmax.com/TheWire/10-most-trusted-personalities-tv/2015/01/16/id/619016/).

Moyers, B. (2007). "Transcript: Bill Moyers Talks with Jon Stewart." *Bill Moyers Journal,* April 27. (http://www.pbs.org/moyers/journal/04272007/transcript1.html).

Ross, R. S., and D. K. Leonard. (2012). *Introduction to the Speechmaking Process.* Redding, CA: BVT Publishing.

Seinfeld, J. (1993). "The Pilot." *Seinfeld,* May 20. (http://www.google.com/#hl=en&spell=1&q=According+to+most+studies,+people%E2%80%99s+number+one+fear+is+public+speaking.+Number+two+is+death.+Now+this+means+to+the+average+person,+if+you+have+to+go+to+a+funeral,+you%E2%80%99are+better+off+in+the+casket+than+doing+the+eulogy&sa=X&ei=ttiWUP7bKonh0QHK_IHABw&ved=0CBsQBSgA&bav=on.2,0r.r_gc.r_pw.r_qf.&fp=1b5b849ef3dd5694&bpcl=37189454&biw=1600&bih=754).

Smith, S. M. (2010). "Power Point Confession." *Steven M. Smith & Associates.* (http://stevenmsmith.com/powerpoint-confession/).

Sternberg, R. J. (2013). "Giving Employers What They Don't Really Want." *Chronicle of Higher Education,* June 17. (http://chronicle.com/article/Giving-Employers-What-They/139877).

Verderber, R. F., and K. S. Verderber. (2008). *Communicate!* Belmont, CA: Thomson Wadsworth.

Weins, K. (2012). "I Won't Hire People Who Use Poor Grammar. Here's Why." *HBR Blog Network,* July 20. (http://blogs.hbr.org/cs/2012/07/i_wont_hire_people_who_use_poo.html).

Credits

CHAPTER 1

Page 2: NLshop/Shutterstock; **4:** Alena Ozerova/Shutterstock; **6:** Mary Schramm Coberly; **7:** Mary Rice/Shutterstock; **7:** Rita Kochmarjova/Shutterstock; **9:** iStock/Vikram Raghuvanshi; **9:** Brent Hofacker/Shutterstock; **11:** Susan Baran; **12:** Susan Baran; **14:** Susan Baran; **14:** Susan Baran; **15:** iStock/Chris_Elwell; **16:** CHOKCHAI POOM-ICHAIYA/Shutterstock; **16:** 1000 Words/Shutterstock; **18:** Richard Paul Kane/Shutterstock; **20:** Jacob Lund/Shutterstock; **20:** Susan Baran; **21:** BEImages/Rex USA; **22:** Davis, Dennis K. and Stanley J. Baran (1980). Mass communication and everyday life: a perspective on theory and effects. Wadsworth, a division of Cengage Learning. Printed with permission.

CHAPTER 2

Page 26: michaeljung/Shutterstock; **30:** Hulton Archive/Getty Images; **31:** Darengphoto/Shutterstock; **33:** Blend Images/Shutterstock; **34:** Petar Paunchev/Shutterstock; **36:** Susan Baran; **37:** Susan Baran; **40:** Courtesy of Albert Bandura; **42:** zimmytws/Shutterstock; **44:** Susan Baran.

CHAPTER 3

Page 48: Marc Norman/Shutterstock; **51:** Photo by Lena Helvik; **52:** AP Photo/Phelan M. Ebenhack; **53:** Susan Baran; **55:** Elizabeth Watsky Photography; **56:** Hayakawa, S. I., and Alan R. Hayakawa (1978). Language in Thought and Action. Heinie/Arts & Sciences, Cengage Learning. Printed with permission; **57:** Oleg Zabielin/Shutterstock; **60:** Susan Baran; **63:** Rita Kochmarjova/Shutterstock; **67:** wavebreakmedia/Shutterstock.

CHAPTER 4

Page 70: V. J. Matthew/Shutterstock; **73:** iStock/Wavebreak: **74:** Christian Bertrand/Shutterstock; **75:** Jaimie Duplass/Shutterstock; **77:** Diego Cervo/Shutterstock; **78:** Susan Baran; **82:** iStock/klenger; **82:** Susan Baran; **85:** Susan Baran; **88:** Barbara Smaller, The New Yorker Collection/The Cartoon Bank; **88:** Minerva Studio/Shutterstock; **89:** iStock/alfimimnill.

CHAPTER 5

Page 92: iStock/PeopleImages; **99:** Susan Baran; **102:** BEImages/Rex USA; **103:** CREATISTA/Shutterstock; **104:** ZITS ©2015 Zits Partnership, Dist. By King Features: **104:** Tetra Images/Getty Images; **108:** Monkey Business Images/Shutterstock.

CHAPTER 6

Page 114: Petrenko Andriy/Shutterstock; **119:** iStock/BirdofPrey; **120:** Peter Bernik/Shutterstock; **122:** Susan Baran; **124:** gpointstudio/Shutterstock; **127:** Susan Baran; **130:** iStock/Steve Debenport; **132:** Ischmidt/Shutterstock; **133:** Brahm, E. (2003). "Conflict Stages." Beyond Intractability, September. (http://www.beyondintractability.org/bi-essay/conflict-stages); **134:** Rahim and Magner's Model of the Styles of Handling Interpersonal Conflict (Figure) in Rahim, M. A., and N. R. Magner. (1995). "Confirmatory Factor Analysis of the Styles of Handling Interpersonal Conflict: First-Order Factor Model and Its Invariance across Groups." Journal of Applied Psychology, 80: 122–132; **135:** iStock/stocknroll; **137:** pixinoo/Shutterstock.

CHAPTER 7

Page 142: iStock/AleksandarNakic; **145:** Monkey Business Images/Shutterstock; **147:** iStock/Christopher Futcher; **148:** Photo by Kristen Franco; **151:** iStock/Diane Diederich; **152:** Monkey Business Images/Shutterstock; **156:** Gen. Dwight D. Eisenhower with Lt. Gen. Lucius B. Clay during the Potsdam Conference in Berlin, July 20, 1945. Image from the National Archives and Records

Index

Page numbers followed by *t* indicate a table. Italicized page numbers indicate a figure.